The Computer Glossary

The Computer Glossary

The Complete Illustrated Desk Reference

Fifth Edition

Alan Freedman

American Management Association

Library of Congress Cataloging-in-Publication Data

Freedman, Alan, 1942-
    The computer glossary : the complete illustrated desk reference /
Alan Freedman. -- 5th ed.
        p.   cm.
    ISBN 0-8144-5020-2 (hard). -- ISBN 0-8144-7749-6 (pbk.)
    1. Computers--Dictionaries. 2. Electronic data processing-
-Dictionaries.   I. Title.
QA76.15.F734   1991
004'.03--dc20   90-1269
                                                           CIP

Printing number.

10 9 8 7 6 5 4 3 2 1

To my Mother,
Who had the vision to send me
to *Automation School* in 1960.

ILLUSTRATIONS: Irma Lee Morrison, Eric Jon Nones & Joseph D. Russo
EDITORIAL/PRODUCTION: Irma Lee Morrison
COPY EDITING: Mary E. McCann
TYPESET BY: The Computer Language Company Inc.
PUBLISHING SOFTWARE: Ventura Publisher, Version 2.0
FONTS: Bitstream Fontware, Swiss 14 pt. & Goudy Old Style 10 pt.

How Systems Relate

The symbol on the cover of this book is the corporate logo of The Computer Language Company. It was derived from the following chart, which is used in Alan Freedman's *Computer Literacy* seminars. It depicts the interrelationship of systems within the computer industry from the manager's point of view.

The management system is the set of goals, objectives, strategies, tactics, plans and controls within an organization. The information system is the database and application programs that turn the raw data into the information required by management. The computer system is the machinery that automates the process. Understanding this relationship has helped thousands of non-technical people make sense out of this field.

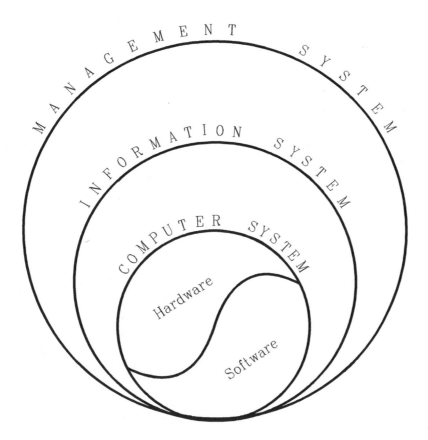

A Note From the Author

The purpose of *The Computer Glossary* is to provide a meaningful definition of every important computer term, be it a concept or a hardware or software product, old or new, for personal computers, minicomputers or mainframes. The degree of technical explanation chosen for each term is based on the term. General terms are explained for the lay person. Specific technical terms are explained with other technical terms. But, all the terms used in the definitions are defined in the book.

The Computer Glossary includes history about the major hardware vendors; the companies that truly drive this industry, as well as many historical photos of the first computers and electronic devices. The old photos are not in the book for nostalgia; they are here to remind us of the extraordinary acceleration of the technology of our era. Virtually all of this has come about in little over a hundred years; since the harnessing of electricity. It should give one pause as we race towards the newest and the fastest.

It is also the purpose of this book to make sense out of this industry in general. As impossible a task as that may be, I keep on trying with each edition. What started out over ten years ago as a 300-term compendium for my seminars is now a mini-encyclopedia for anyone interested in the high-tech world. In a sense, this book has become my life's work. And, for that, I am grateful, because I am truly interested in all the facets of this industry. I'm lucky to have had a wide variety of experience in this field, and I'm lucky to have expert professionals who are willing to help.

I hope you find reading this enjoyable. If there are terms and products you feel should be included in the next edition, please let me know. In addition, if you can add facts and perspective to any of the terms in the book, I will be happy to hear from you.

Alan Freedman

The Computer Language Company Inc.
5521 State Park Road
Point Pleasant, Pennsylvania 18950-0265
(215) 297-5999

Contents

Acknowledgements

I would like to express my appreciation and thanks to each and every one of you for your technical assistance, reviews and help with this book.

WARREN W. ANDREWS Publisher, InfoBUS Report
KAREN E. BOLLINGER Manager, Kensington Microware, Ltd.
JEFFREY S. BURNETT Vice President, The Stepstone Corporation
PETER J. CHOATE Sales Manager, Solutions/Computer Bay
DR. ELIZABETH S. COBB Research Scientist, University of Utah
GARRY DAWSON Marketing Programs Manager, Hewlett-Packard Company
EMILIO DEL BUSTO Assistant Professor, New York University
BRENDAN DIXON Support Engineer, Microsoft Corporation
THOM DREWKE President, Technical Directions, Inc.
BRUCE ECKEL President, Revolution2
MAX B. FETZER Vice President, Envirotronics, Ltd.
HAROLD C. FOLTS President, Omnicom, Inc.
LYNN S. FRANKEL Sales Representative, The William Byrd Press
ROGER FRAUMANN Director of Promotions, UNIX International
DR. GEORGE L. GERSTEIN School of Medicine, University of Pennsylvania
RICHARD W. GREENWOOD Staff Engineer (Retired), IBM Corporation
DR. PHILIP HAYES Research Computer Scientist, Carnegie Mellon University
PETER HERMSEN Systems Engineer, Apple Computer, Inc.
MARGARET A. HERRICK Principal, Margann Associates
CHARLES H. IRBY Vice President, Metaphor Corporation
STEPHEN KALLIS, JR Public Relations Manager, Digital Equipment Corp.
VERN LAUTNER Division Manager, American Management Association
MICHAEL A. LIND Director of Commercial Development, Optical Data, Inc.
KENNETH LOWRIE Systems Engineer, Novell, Inc.
ALBERT H. MEDWIN President, CGS Systems, Inc.
RICHARD P. MULDOON District Manager, UNIX System Laboratories, Inc.
HELENE OBACK-RUSSO Associate Professor, Long Island University
HOWARD J. POPOWITZ Vice President, Citicorp
C. WAYNE RATLIFF President, Ratliff Software Productions
CHRIS SEELBACH President, Probe Research, Inc.
STEPHEN SLADE Assistant Director, AI Project, Yale University
ELLEN W. SOKOL Partner, N. Dean Meyer & Associates Inc.
NADINE C. SPOTH Manager, Elxsi Corporation
JAMES R. STROH Vice President, LXD Inc.
JAMES F. SUTTER Vice President, Rockwell International
ROBERT F. WILLIAMS President, Cohasset Associates, Inc.
DR. KARL-HEINZ WINKLER Director, National Center for
Supercomputer Applications

Special Thanks

PAMELA J. BRANNAN Training Manager, Hayes Microcomputer Products, Inc.
Pamela Brannan and her competent staff helped me clarify the ultra-confusing modem and communications specifications. She continues to keep me up-to-date on this ever-changing world. Thanks Pam.

STEPHEN C. DIASCRO, JR. Senior Computer Specialist, Tandy Corporation
Steve Diascro is in the retail trade and knows well how people react to personal computers. He's been a big help on a wide variety of subjects. Thank you Steve.

JAMES J. FARRELL III Communications Manager, VLSI Technology, Inc.
I doubt if anyone understands chips better than Jim Farrell. The world of microelectronics is unbelievably complicated, and I have been very lucky to have his help. Thanks again, Jim.

STEVEN M. GIBSON President, Gibson Research Corporation
Steve Gibson knows PC hardware and software from the inside out. He helped me understand the basics and continues to help clarify this increasingly complicated world. Thank you, Steve.

MARY E. McCANN Editor, The Boston Computer Society
Mary McCann has been edting my *Straight Talk* column for years, and has helped me get to the point a lot quicker. Thanks Mary.

IRMA LEE MORRISON Vice President, The Computer Language Co. Inc.
My wife and partner, Irma Lee Morrison, has not only worked long hours on the production of this book, but she has endured more on this project than anyone else... namely, me. Trying to make sense out of the most confusing field on earth isn't always conducive to cozy evenings in front of the fireplace. I couldn't have done this without her. Thanks, Irmalee. You're terrific. I love you!

DR. JOEL N. ORR Chairman, Orr Associates, Inc.
Joel Orr's exhaustive knowledge of CAD/CAM systems and his expertise in graphics is legendary. Joel graciously gave of his time while in his office and on vacation. Thanks again, Joel.

JOSEPH D. RUSSO Designer/Illustrator
Joseph Russo provided the art direction for the book with an artistic eye that is uncanny. Only an expert can make a layout look simple. Thank you, Joseph.

GARY A. SAXER Director of Technical Services, Quarterdeck Office Systems
Gary is right on top of the PC world, especially in the areas of memory management. He helps me make sense out of the stickiest issues. Thanks Gary.

MARK J. E. SHAPIRO Systems Engineer, Apple Computer, Inc.
The Macintosh is an important part of the computer world, and Mark Shapiro has worked dilligently to keep me apprised and up-to-date on it. Thank you Mark.

VINCENT G. (SKIP) VACCARELLO President, The Saratoga Group
The staff at The Saratoga Group create the most ingenious courseware on communications. With their help, I was able to make sense out of the maddening world of IBM's SNA. Thanks Skip.

IRVING L. WIESELMAN President, Computer Printer Corporation
Irving Wieselman is an expert in the world of computer printers. His vast experience helped me wade through the rather arcane ways ink gets onto paper. Thanks, Irv.

E. R. (GENE) YOST President, Black Box Corporation
Gene Yost provided me with entre to his very competent staff of communications specialists. Pat Flanigan, Mark Bennett, Mike Ramos, Larry Clark, Randy Morse and Bill Ihrig helped me in the areas of local area networks, modems and connectivity. Thank you, Gene.

Introduction

THE COMPUTER GLOSSARY is not just a glossary...
It's a guide to Computer Literacy.

Reading *The Computer Glossary* on a regular basis will help you keep up with the terminology, concepts and perspective necessary to interact with computer professionals effectively and get the most out of computers.

If you hear a term that is not in this book, it may be the trade name of a hardware product or software package. Find out what category it falls into, and then look it up. If a term is not in the book that you feel makes an important contribution to this industry, please let me know about it.

On the next six pages are overviews for the business manager, the student and the personal computer buyer. They will provide you with an outline to work your way through *The Computer Glossary* depending on your area of interest. The terms in the outline also serve as a springboard to other terms in the book. Every computer term that is used within the definition of another term is also defined in the book.

To the Business Manager

Learning some basic concepts and a little technical jargon can go a long way in helping you deal more effectively with computer professionals.

You should understand the system development cycle, which is the series of steps that transforms information requirements into working information systems. The systems analysis & design phase must be performed slowly and carefully. The functional specifications, which are the blueprints of the information system, must make sense to you. If they don't, there's no telling what you'll wind up with.

Prototyping the new system will lead to a better definition of requirements. If prototyping is not possible, then, once you have signed off on the design, the programming must be done as quickly as possible.

Be aware of the importance of well-designed user interfaces, the advantages of database management systems (for providing future flexibility) and the many problems with standards & compatibility.

When considering a new system, you should think about all the kinds of questions that you would ideally like to be able to ask it when it is running. The computer's ability to provide answers to ad hoc questions may provide its biggest payback. Decision support tools should be integrated into the information system design from the beginning. The most important step in systems design is looking at the entire problem at the beginning, no matter how small the first phase to be implemented may be.

If you're a manager of a small business, don't be fooled. Personal computers cost only a fraction of what computers used to cost; but, people cost as much or more. Custom-developed software that requires in-depth systems analysis & design costs just as much as it used to, if not more.

Computers are invaluable for business. However, in order to ensure success with new systems, your thorough involvement with technical personnel in the design and implementation stages is crucial.

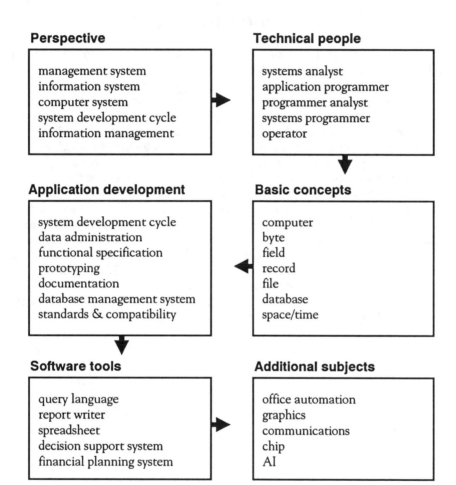

Perspective

management system
information system
computer system
system development cycle
information management

Technical people

systems analyst
application programmer
programmer analyst
systems programmer
operator

Application development

system development cycle
data administration
functional specification
prototyping
documentation
database management system
standards & compatibility

Basic concepts

computer
byte
field
record
file
database
space/time

Software tools

query language
report writer
spreadsheet
decision support system
financial planning system

Additional subjects

office automation
graphics
communications
chip
AI

To the Student

If you're planning a career in the information processing industry, you have many choices. If you're not, no matter which industry you choose to work in, a solid foundation of computer concepts will be extremely helpful in coping with it.

Within the computer industry, you can be involved at the electronics level as a computer designer or as a field service engineer. As an application programmer, you can work on solving problems in just about any field of endeavor. As a systems programmer, you can work as a technical consultant within a user organization, or you can design and develop system software for vendors. If the workings of business intrigue you, the fields of systems analysis and data administration are open to you. Sales and marketing of computer products also offer a wide variety of opportunities for people who enjoy the high-tech world.

Take some time to learn and understand the differences between the computer sciences and the information sciences. In theory, they are distinct fields; each with different objectives and disciplines. In practice, they are thoroughly intertwined, and the casual observer cannot often perceive their differences.

The flow chart on the opposite page provides a textbook-like curriculum for learning about computers. Also read the introductions *To the Business Manager* and *To the Personal Computer Buyer* on the previous and next pages.

Basics

hardware
software
data
computer
analog
digital
binary
byte
peripheral
magnetic recording
printer
monitor
modem
operating sytem
bus
space/time
chip
standards & compatibility

Programming

programming language
procedural language
non-procedural language
source language
machine language
assembly language
object-oriented programming

Application development

data administration
information system
data element
field
record
file
database
database management system
data dictionary
functional specification
systems analysis & design
system development cycle
decision support system

Office automation

office automation
word processing
electronic mail
teleconferencing

Graphics

graphics
paint program
drawing program
wireframe modeling
surface modeling
solid modeling

Communications

communications
LAN
PBX
OSI
TP monitor
front end processor
network architecture

Advanced programming

address modes
relocatable code
base/displacement
reentrant code
multitasking
multithreading

Advanced concepts

virtual memory
RISC
multiprocessing
computer architecture
pipeline processing
memory protection

To the Personal Computer Buyer

All personal computers are not equal. Before you purchase one, you must first know what you want to do with it. A particular computer may be great for graphics, but not as good for word processing, and vice versa.

The hardest thing to evaluate is the software. Each type of software package has its own set of evaluation criteria. What makes one spreadsheet better than another has nothing to do with what makes one word processing package better than another. Unless you're relying on the judgment of someone you implicitly trust, you should "test drive" programs from three different vendors before making a decision.

Choosing hardware is easier. If you plan on exchanging files of data (not just mail) with other people, compatibility is the key issue. If not, the kind of software you want to use will make the decision for you. Once the hardware brand has been selected, the right model can be chosen based upon your disk and memory requirements. Hard disk capacity determines how many different programs and how much data is available to you at all times. Memory capacity determines how many different things you can do at the same time.

Unless cost is absolutely critical, don't get a system without a hard disk. It's not worth the headaches. But, when you have a hard disk, make backup copies often!

Remember. The moment you purchase a personal computer, whether it's for home or business, you have purchased a set of standards. Make your decision carefully.

Hardware

computer
memory
magnetic disk
modem
keyboard
operating system
PC
Macintosh
Amiga
MEGA
Apple II

Software

word processing
database management system
spreadsheet
business graphics
communications program

Information basics

byte
field
record
file
database
space/time

Additional subjects

graphics
communications
chip
standards & compatibility

A

A: drive A common designation for the first floppy disk drive in DOS and OS/2. The B: drive is the second floppy disk, and C: is the primary hard disk drive.

ABC (Atanasoff-Berry Computer) The first digital calculating machine that used vacuum tubes. Started in 1939 and completed in 1942 by Iowa State Professor John Atanasoff and Clifford Berry, a graduate student, it embodied the input, memory and arithmetic unit of future computers.

Since John Mauchly, cobuilder of the ENIAC in 1946, visited Atanasoff in 1940 and corresponded with him, he was considered to be influenced by Atanasoff. In 1973, Honeywell challenged Mauchly's patents, now belonging to Sperry Univac, which had purchased Eckert and Mauchly's company years earlier, and the patents were judged invalid.

Eckert and Mauchly are considered the creators of the first electronic digital computer, but Atanasoff and Berry are acknowledged contributors.

ABC COMPUTER
(Courtesy Charles Babbage Institute, University of Minnesota)

abend (ABnormal END) Also called a *crash* or *bomb*, occurs when the computer is presented with instructions or data it can't recognize. It is the result of erroneous software logic or hardware failure.

When the abend occurs, if the program is running in a personal computer under a single-task (one program at a time) operating system, such as MS-DOS, the computer freezes up and has to be rebooted. Multitasking operating systems with memory protection will halt the offending program allowing remaining programs to continue.

If you consider what goes on inside a computer, you might wonder why it doesn't crash more often. A large mainframe's memory can contain 288 million storage cells. Within every second, millions of these cells change their state from uncharged to charged and vice versa. If one of those cells is unable to hold its charge, and that cell happens to be where operating system instructions are stored, the computer could come "crashing" to a halt. Makes you want another computer standing by just in case, doesn't it?

ABI (Application Binary Interface) A specification used in writing an application for a particular hardware platform and operating system. It details the machine language of the CPU family as well as the calls between the application and the operating system.

Ability PLUS An integrated software package for PCs from Migent, Inc., that combines word processing, database management, spreadsheet, business graphics and communications.

absolute In programming, a mathematical function that always returns a positive number. For example, ABS(25-100) yields 75, not -75.

absolute address An explicit identification of a peripheral device, of a location within the peripheral device or of a location in memory. For example, disk drive no. 2, sector no. 23 and byte no. 1,744 are absolute addresses. The computer must be given absolute addresses to reference its memory and peripherals. See *base address* and *relative address*.

absolute vector In computer graphics, a vector with end points designated in absolute coordinates. Contrast with *relative vector*.

abstract data type A user-defined data type in object-oriented programming. See *object-oriented programming*.

AC (Alternating Current) The common form of electricity from power plant to home/office. Its direction is reversed 60 times per second in the U.S.; 50 in Europe. Contrast with *DC*.

accelerator board An add-in board that replaces the existing CPU with a higher performance CPU.

acceptance test A test performed by the end user to determine if the system is working according to the specifications in the contract.

access To store data on and retrieve data from a disk or other peripheral device. See *access arm* and *access method*.

access arm A mechanical arm that moves the read/write head across the surface of a disk and is similar to a tone arm on a phonograph turntable. The access arm is directed by instructions in the operating system to move the read/write head to a specific track on the disk. The rotation of the disk positions the read/write head over the required sector.

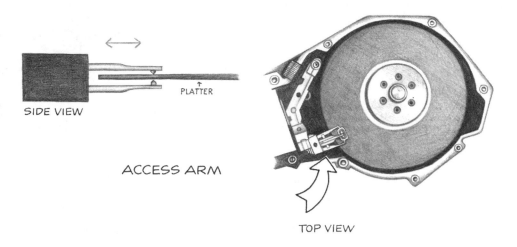

SIDE VIEW

PLATTER

ACCESS ARM

TOP VIEW

access charge A charge imposed by a communications service or telephone company for the use of its network.

access code
(1) An identification number and/or password used to gain access into a computer system.

(2) A number used as a prefix to a calling number in order to gain access to a particular telephone service.

access method A software routine that is part of the operating system or network control program which performs the storing/retrieving or transmitting/receiving of data. It is also responsible for detecting a bad transfer of data caused by hardware or network malfunction and correcting it if possible.

TAPE ACCESS METHODS
With tapes, the *sequential* access method is always used for storing data, which places the next block of data after the previous one.

DISK ACCESS METHODS
For disks, *indexed* access methods are widely used to keep track of records and files. The index is a table of contents for each file or each record within the file. The sequential method is also used when retrieval of individual records is not required. The *indexed sequential method*, or ISAM, combines both methods by providing an index that is kept in sequential order. For fastest retrieval, the *direct* access method uses a formula to convert the record's identifying field, such as account number, into a physical storage address.

COMMUNICATIONS ACCESS METHODS
Communications access methods, such as IBM's TCAM and VTAM, transfer data between a host computer and remote terminals. These routines prepare the data for transmission by placing the data into frames, or blocks, with appropriate control information. These access methods reference layers 3, 4 and 5 of the OSI model.

LAN access methods, such as CSMA/CD (Ethernet) and token passing (Token Ring), transfer data to and from connected computers on the network. These access methods reference layers 1 and 2 of the OSI model.

access time

(1) Memory *access time* is the time it takes for a character in memory to be transferred to or from the processor. Fast RAM chips have an access time of 100 nanoseconds or less.

(2) Disk *access time* is an average of the time it takes to position the read/write head over the requested track. Fast hard disks have an access time of 18 milliseconds or less. Disk access times are a common measurement for disk speed, but total performance is influenced by channel speed, interleaving design and caching.

account number A number assigned to an employee, customer, vendor or product for identification purposes. Although an account number may contain only numeric digits, it is often stored as an alphanumeric character field, since it is used for matching purposes. When stored as character data, parts of the account number can be searched independently. For example, the account number might contain a classification code, and records could be selected on this criterion.

accounting machine Refers to older office machines used to perform calculations and prepare records or ledgers, such as for billing or payroll. Punched card accounting machines were used to list and print totals.

ACF (Advanced Communications Function) Official product line name for IBM SNA programs, such as VTAM (ACF/VTAM), NCP (ACF/NCP), etc.

ACK (ACKnowledgment code) In communications, a code sent from a receiving station to a transmitting station to acknowledge that it is ready to accept data. It is also used to acknowlege the error-free receipt of transmitted data. Contrast with *NAK*, which is a negative acknowledgment.

ACM (Association for Computing Machinery) A membership organization, founded in 1947, with over 73,000 computer professionals. Its objective is to advance the arts and sciences of information processing. In addition to special awards and publications, ACM also maintains special interest groups (SIGs) in the computer field. For more information, contact ACM, 11 West 42nd Street, New York, NY 10036, (212) 869-7440.

acoustic coupler A device that connects a terminal or computer to the handset of a telephone. It contains a shaped foam bed that the handset is placed in, and it may also contain the modem.

ACOUSTIC COUPLER

ACS (Asynchronous Communications Server) A communications server that manages a pool of modems. It directs outgoing messages to the next available modem and directs incoming messages to the appropriate workstation.

active matrix LCD An LCD display technique that uses a transistor for each monochrome or each red, green and blue dot. It provides sharp contrast, speeds screen refresh and eliminates loss of cursor (submarining) on standard LCD screens.

active star A network topology that provides regeneration of signals in the central hub. Contrast with *passive star*.

ACTOR An object-oriented programming language for PCs from The Whitewater Group Inc. It runs under Microsoft Windows and has a Pascal-like syntax to ease the transition to object-oriented languages.

A/D converter (Analog to Digital Converter) A device that converts the continuously varying analog signals from instruments that monitor such conditions as movement, temperature, sound and air quality, into binary coded form for the computer. A/D converters may be contained on a single chip or can be one circuit within a chip. See *modem* and *codec*.

A/D Cycle (Application/Development Cycle) SAA-compliant software from IBM that provides a system for managing systems development. It provides a structure for storing information about all phases of an information system, including systems analysis and design, database design and programming.

Ada A Pascal-based, comprehensive programming language developed as a standard for the U.S. Department of Defense. Ada was designed as a common language for both business applications, such as inventory control, and embedded applications, such as guidance systems built into rockets.

Ada was named after Augusta Ada Byron (1815-1852), Countess of Lovelace and daughter of Lord Byron. She was a mathematician and colleague of Charles Babbage, who was developing a stored program calculator. Some of her programming notes for the machine have survived, giving her the distinction of being the first programmer in the world.

The following Ada program converts fahrenheit to centigrade:

```
with Text_IO;
procedure Convert is
  package Int_IO is new
Text_IO.Integer_IO(Integer);
  Fahrenheit : Integer;
begin
  Text_IO.Put_Line("Enter fahrenheit");
  Int_IO.Get(Fahrenheit);
  Text_IO.Put("Centigrade is ");
  Int_IO.Put((Fahrenheit-32) * 5 / 9);
  Text_IO.New_Line;
end Convert;
```

ADABAS A database management system from Software AG of North America that runs on IBM mainframes and Digital Equipment's VAX series. ADABAS is an inverted file system with relational capabilities and includes a fourth-generation language called NATURAL, which provides interactive processing and application development. An optional text module called Text Retrieval System (TRS) provides text processing capabilities, and the ADANET option provides distributed database functions.

ADAPSO (Association of Data Processing Service Organizations) A membership organization, founded in 1960, that is primarily composed of timesharing service organizations. ADAPSO is involved in improving management methods and defining standards of performance for computer services. ADAPSO is also concerned with governmental regulations as they affect the computer services field. For more information, contact ADAPSO, 1300 North 17th Street, Arlington, VA 22209, (703) 522-5055.

adapter A device that allows one system to connect to and work with another.

adaptive compression A data compression technique that dynamically adjusts the algorithm used based on the content of the data being compressed.

adaptive equalization A transmission technique that dynamically adjusts its modulation technique based on the quality of the line.

ADB (Apple Desktop Bus) A communications port for keyboards, mice, trackballs, graphics tablets and other input devices on the Macintosh. Two ADB ports are built into each SE, Mac II family and Portable computer.

ADC See A/D converter.

ADCCP (Advanced Data Communications Control Procedure) An ANSI communications protocol that is similar to the SDLC and HDLC protocols.

adder An elementary electronic circuit that adds the bits of two numbers together.

address

(1) A number of a particular memory or peripheral storage location. Like post office boxes, every byte of memory and every sector on a disk have their own unique address. After a program has been written, it is translated into machine language that references actual addresses in the computer.

(2) As a verb, to manage or work with. For example, "the computer can address 2MB of memory."

address bus An internal channel from the processor to memory across which the addresses of data (not the data) are transmitted. The number of lines, or wires, in the address bus determines the amount of memory that can be directly addressed as each line carries one bit of the address. For example, the Intel 8086/8088 processors have 20 address lines and can address up to 1,048,576 bytes. The Motorola 68020 has 32 address lines and can address over four gigabytes bytes.

Various swapping and switching techniques can be added to the hardware that allow a computer to use more memory than is directly addressable by its address bus. See EMS.

See illustration on following page.

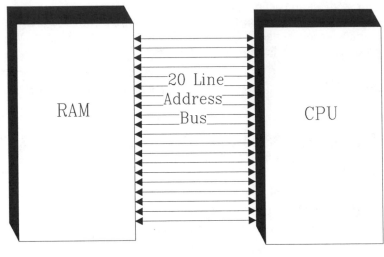

ADDRESS BUS

address mode A method by which an instruction references memory. An *indexed address* is modified by the contents of an index register before execution. An *indirect address* points to another address. Ultimately, in order to do any actual processing, the instruction must derive *real*, or *absolute addresses*, where the required data is located.

address register A high-speed circuit that holds the addresses of data to be processed or of the next instruction to be executed.

address space The total amount of memory that can be used by a program. The address space may refer to a physical memory limit or to a virtual memory limit, which includes memory and disk. For example, the Intel 80386 CPU can address 4GB of memory and 64TB of virtual memory.

address translation The transforming of one address into another. For example, assemblers and compilers translate symbolic addresses into machine addresses. Virtual memory systems translate a virtual address into a real address.

addressable cursor A cursor on a display screen that can be programmed to move to any row or column on the screen.

ADE (Application Development Environment) An IBM approach for developing applications that will run in all SAA environments. The development software is client/server based; the main functions reside in the host.

ADF (Application Development Facility) A programmer-oriented application generator from IBM that runs on IBM mainframes under the IMS database management system.

Adobe Type Manager
A font generator and utility for the Macintosh from Adobe Systems Inc. The font generator scales outline fonts into bitmapped fonts for use in non-PostScript printers. As a system utility, it generates accurate screen fonts for all point sizes from Type 1 PostScript fonts.

ADP
(1) (Automatic Data Processing) Synonymous with data processing (DP), electronic data processing (EDP) and information processing.

(2) ADP, Inc. A nationwide computer services organization that also provides international communications services.

ADP system
(Automatic Data Processing system) Same as *computer system*.

ADPCM
(Adaptive Differential PCM) A technique for digitizing speech that generates 32K bits per second. See *PCM*.

ADROIT
An authoring language for PCs from Applied Data Research, Inc., for creating computer-based training packages. It is a full-featured program that is used to create courseware that displays text and graphics and control audio and video devices.

ADRS
(A Departmental Reporting System) A report writer from IBM that runs on IBM mainframes.

AdvanceNet
A network strategy from Hewlett-Packard that incorporates OSI and SNA network architectures. In 1983, HP was the first major vendor to make a commitment to the OSI standard. AdvanceNet also supports MAP, Starlan 10, Ethernet and X.25 packet switching networks.

AFE
(Apple File Exchange) A Macintosh utility that converts data files between Mac and PC formats. It also includes a file translator between IBM's DCA format and MacWrite; however, MacLink Plus Translators can be used for additional capability.

AFIPS
(American Federation of Information Processing Societies Inc.) A membership organization, founded in 1961, with over 250,000 professionals. AFIPS serves as a national voice for the computer industry seeking to advance knowledge in the information processing sciences. For more information, contact AFIPS, 1899 Preston White Drive, Reston, VA 22091, (703) 620-8900.

AFP
(AppleTalk Filing Protocol) The client/server protocol used in AppleTalk communications networks. In order for non-Apple networks to access data in an AppleShare server, their protocols must translate into the AFT language.

AI (Artificial Intelligence) A broad range of applications that exhibit human intelligence and behavior including robots, expert systems, voice recognition, natural and foreign language processing. It also implies the ability to learn or adapt through experience.

In the future, everything we now know and think about a computer will change. By the turn of the century, you should be able to ask the average computer a question in English. Future systems will ask you what help you need and automatically call in the appropriate applications to aid you in solving your problem.

As with all new concepts in this industry, the AI buzzword will be abused to the hilt as it will refer to any and all advancements. However, the acid test of AI was defined in the 1940s by the English scientist, Alan Turing, who said, "A machine has artificial intelligence when there is no discernible difference between the conversation generated by the machine and that of an intelligent person."

Note: The term intelligence refers to processing capability; therefore, every computer is intelligent. But, artificial intelligence implies human-like intelligence. An ironic twist in terminology.

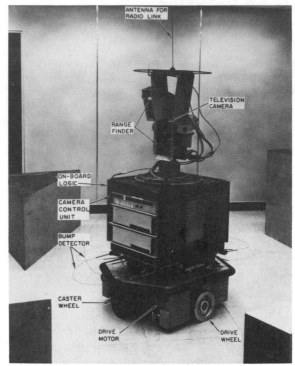

"SHAKEY" THE ROBOT

(Courtesy The Computer Museum, Boston)

Developed in 1969 by the Stanford Research Institute, Shakey was the first fully-mobile robot with artificial intelligence. Shakey is seven feet tall and was named after its shakey actions.

AIX (Advanced Interactive eXecutive) A version of the UNIX operating system from IBM that runs on 80386-based PS/2 and RT personal computers and IBM's 370 mainframe series, which includes the 9370, 4381 and 3090 series. AIX is based on AT&T's UNIX System V with Berkeley extensions.

ALC (Assembly Language Coding) A generic term for IBM mainframe assembly languages.

Aldus Persuasion A desktop presentation program for the Macintosh from Aldus Corporation. It provides the ability to create output for overheads, handouts, speaker notes and film recorders. It is known for its sophisticated transition features, such as fades, gravel, swipes and wipes.

algebraic expression One or more characters or symbols associated with algebra; for example, $A+B=C$ or A/B.

ALGOL (ALGOrithmic Language) A high-level compiler language that was developed as an international language for the expression of algorithms between people, as well as between people and machines. Introduced in the early 1960s, ALGOL achieved more acceptance in Europe than in the U.S.

algorithm A set of ordered steps for solving a problem, such as a mathematical formula or the instructions in a program.

alias
(1) An alternate name used for identification, such as for naming a field or a file.

(2) A phony signal that is created under certain conditions when digitizing voice.

aliasing In computer graphics, the stair-stepped appearance of diagonal lines. See *anti-aliasing*.

All-In-1 An office systems software from Digital that runs on its VAX series of computers. All-in-1 provides a menu to all of Digital's office systems programs, including word processing, appointment calendars and electronic mail systems.

Alpha Four A relational database management system for PCs from Alpha Software Corporation. It provides a menu-driven user interface and uses the dBASE III PLUS file format directly. It has extensive and flexible relational capabilities and has many advanced functions built into menu options allowing applications to be built without programming.

alpha test The first test of newly developed hardware or software in a laboratory setting. The next step is *beta testing* with actual users.

alphageometric See *alphamosaic*.

alphamosaic In computer graphics, a display technique for very-low-resolution images. Images are created from elementary graphics characters which, like alphabetic letters and numeric digits, are designed as part of the character set.

alphanumeric The use of alphabetic letters mixed with numbers and special characters as in name, address, city and state. All the text in this Glossary is alphanumeric.

(Courtesy The Computer Museum, Boston)

Altair 8800 A microcomputer kit introduced in late 1974 from Micro Instrumentation and Telemetry Systems. It sold for $400 and used an 8080 microprocessor. In 1975, it was packaged with Microsoft's MBASIC interpreter written by Paul Allen and Bill Gates.

Although other microprocessor kits were advertised earlier than the Altair, an estimated 10,000 Altair 8800s were sold, making it the first commercially successful microcomputer.

Alto The personal computer from Xerox Corporation that pioneered the mouse/icon environment. It was the progenitor of the Xerox Star and Apple's Lisa and Macintosh. Designed in 1973 with 128K RAM, a bit-mapped 608x808 pixel screen and a 2.5MB removable hard disk, it connected directly to an Ethernet network. By 1979, nearly 1,000 Altos were in use.

ALTO COMPUTER
(Courtesy Xerox Corporation)

ALU (Arithmetic Logic Unit) A high-speed circuit in the CPU that does the actual calculating and comparing. Numbers are transferred from memory into the ALU for calculation, the results of which are sent back into memory. Alphanumeric data is sent from memory into the ALU for comparing. The results of the comparison are tested by GOTOs. For example, `if itemA equals itemB goto update_routine`.

AM (Amplitude Modulation) In communications, a transmission technique that modulates the data signal into a fixed carrier frequency by raising and lowering the amplitude of the carrier wave. Contrast with *FM* and *phase modulation*.

Amdahl (Amdahl Corporation) A computer manufacturer founded in 1970 by Gene Amdahl, chief architect of the IBM System/360. Its purpose was to compete directly with IBM by providing a compatible mainframe with better performance. Five years later, Amdahl installed its first product, the 470/V6 computer.

Although not the first to make an IBM compatible mainframe, its advanced engineering helped it succeed where others failed. In 1984, it announced its Multiple Domain Feature, which allows a single processor to function under multiple operating environments. One CPU can provide a production environment for users while also providing a test environment for programmers.

Amdahl left the company to form Trilogy in 1979 and now heads up Andor Corporation, a manufacturer of smaller IBM compatible mainframes.

DR. GENE M. AMDAHL

(Courtesy Dr. Gene M. Amdahl)

In 1975, Dr. Amdahl is standing beside the computer he designed in 1950, the Wisconsin Integrally Synchronized Computer.

American Bell The name used by AT&T right after divestiture on January 1, 1984. They were later ordered to drop the Bell name.

Ami A word processing program for PCs from Samna Corporation that runs under Microsoft Windows. Ami Professional is a high-end version of the product that includes DTP features. Ami was designed as a Windows application and is noted for its ease of use.

Amiga A series of personal computers from Commodore Business Machines, Inc., that runs under the AmigaDOS operating system and features a window-oriented user interface called Workbench.

The Amiga 500 is geared for home use and includes built-in speech synthesis, four-voice stereo sound and color graphics with 4,096 colors. The Amiga 2000 is designed for office applications, including CAD and desktop publishing. The 2000 includes optional PC compatibility and video generation capabilities for processing NTSC video.

AMIGA 2000

AMIGAS II (Advanced Meteorological Image and Graphics Analysis System) A meteorological software package that runs on Control Data's CYBER computers. AMIGAS II can access multiple databases, analyze the data and create products in response to meteorologist/forecaster requests.

amp (AMPere) A unit of electrical current in a circuit. *Volts* measure the force or pressure behind the current. *Watts* are a total measurement of power derived from multiplying amps times volts.

amplitude The strength or volume of a signal, usually measured in decibels.

amplitude modulation See AM.

analog A representation of an object that resembles the original. Analog devices monitor conditions, such as movement, temperature and sound, and convert them into analogous electronic or mechanical patterns. For example, an analog watch represents the planet's rotation with the rotating hands on the watch face. Telephones turn voice vibrations into electrical vibrations of the same shape. Analog implies continuous operation in contrast with digital, which is broken up into numbers.

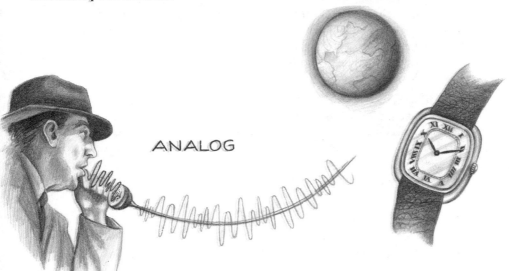

Advantages and Disadvantages
Of Analog Techniques

Traditionally, audio and video recording has been analog. Sound, which is continuously varying air vibrations, is converted into analogous electrical vibrations. Video cameras scan their viewing area a line at a time and convert the infinitely varying intensities of light into analogous electrical signals.

The ability to capture the subtle nature of the real world is the single advantage of analog techniques. However, once captured, modern electronic equipment, no matter how advanced, cannot copy analog signals perfectly. Third and fourth generations of audio and video recordings show marked deterioration.

By converting analog signals into digital, the original audio or video data can be preserved indefinitely and copied over and over again without deterioration. Once continuously varying analog signals are measured and converted into digital form, they can be stored and transmitted without loss of integrity due to the inherent accuracy of digital methods.

The key to conversion is the amount of digital data that is created from the analog signal. The shorter the time interval between samples and the more data recorded from that sample, the more the digital encoding reflects the original signal.

analog channel In communications, a channel that carries voice or video in analog form as a varying range of electrical frequencies. Contrast with *digital channel*.

analog computer A computer that accepts and processes infinitely varying signals, such as voltage fluctuations or frequencies. For example, a thermostat is the simplest analog computer. A continuously varying change in temperature causes a metal bar to bend correspondingly. Although complex analog computers are built for special purposes, most computers are *digital*. Today, digital computers can generally equal the speed of analog computers while also providing programming flexibility.

analog monitor A high-resolution video display screen that is synchronized for TV/video and/or a computer display standard. Multisync analog monitors match up with a variety of display standards. Analog monitors accept separate red, green and blue (RGB) signals for sharper contrast. If synchronized for TV, it may accept the common NTSC composite video signal. Contrast with *digital monitor*.

analysis See *systems analysis & design*.

analyst See *systems analyst*.

Analytical Engine A conceptually-sophisticated calculator designed by the British scientist, Charles Babbage (1791-1871). Started in the mid 1830s, Babbage worked on it throughout his life. Although never completed due to lack of funds and constant redesign, it represented a major advance and incorporated the basic principles of the stored program computer.

Babbage's colleague, Augusta Ada Byron, daughter of the poet Lord Byron, explained the machine's programmable concepts to the public and press. Because of her association with the machine, the Ada language was named after her.

ANALYTICAL ENGINE
(Courtesy Charles Babbage Institute, University of Minnesota)

AND, OR & NOT The fundamental operations of Boolean logic. AND is true if both inputs are true, OR is true if any input is true, and NOT is an inverter; the output is always the opposite. See *Boolean search, chip* and *gate*.

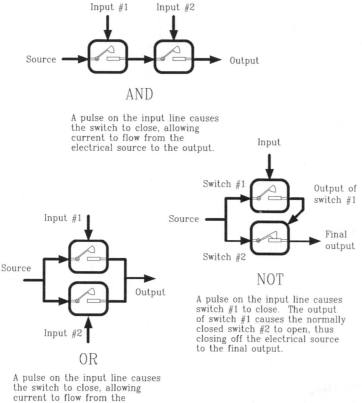

BOOLEAN LOGIC

angstrom A unit of measurement approx. 1/25 millionth of an inch. Angstroms are used to measure the elements in electronic components on a chip.

animated graphics Moving diagrams or cartoons. Often found in computer-based courseware, animated graphics take up far less disk space than video images.

anisotropic Refers to properties that vary with an external stimulus. For example, tracks on a floppy disk are not recorded exactly circular due to varying temperature and humidity.

anode In electronics, positively charged receiver of electrons that flow from the negatively charged *cathode*.

anomaly An abnormality or deviation. It is a favorite word among computer people when complex systems produce output that is unexplicable.

ANSI (American National Standards Institute) A nonprofit, privately-funded membership organization, founded in 1918, that coordinates the development of U.S. voluntary national standards in both the private and public sectors. It is the U.S. member body to the International Standards Organization (ISO) and the International Electrotechnical Commission (IEC).

Information technology standards pertain to the analysis, control and distribution of information, which includes programming languages, electronic data interchange (EDI), telecommunications and physical properties of diskettes, cartridges and magnetic tapes. For example, ANSI COBOL and ANSI C are the ANSI-endorsed versions of COBOL and C. Such languages conform to the standards (reserved words, syntax, rules) as set forth by ANSI.

For more information, contact ANSI, 1430 Broadway, New York, NY 10018.

ANSI.SYS A driver that is commonly loaded with DOS. It is used for screen control such as moving the cursor and clearing portions of the screen. It is also used as a keyboard macro processor to assign a string of commands to a function key or reassign awkwardly placed keys. Many applications have been written to use the ANSI.SYS functions.

answer only modem A modem that is capable of answering a call, but not initiating one.

anti-aliasing In computer graphics, a category of techniques that is used to smooth the jagged appearance of diagonal lines. For example, the pixels that surround the edges of the line are filled in with varying shades of gray or color in order to blend the sharp edge into the background. See *dithering*.

Antifuse A PLD technology from Actel Corporation that works the opposite of typical programmable chip methods. Instead of creating open circuits (blowing the fuse), the programming creates connections between the elements.

antivirus A program that detects and removes a virus.

ANVIL A family of CADD/CAM software products from Manufacturing and Consulting Services Inc. ANVIL-1000MD is a 2 1/2-D mechanical engineering system for 286s. ANVIL-5000pc is a mainframe package restructured for 386s that produces 3-D wireframe models with optional surface modeling and numerical control modules.

ANVIL-5000 is a 3-D mechanical engineering system for major workstations, superminis and mainframes.

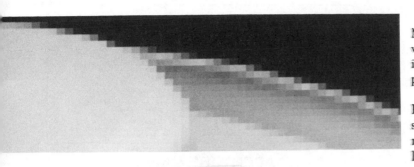

Magnified view of individual pixels.

Picture shows top right side of lid handle.

With Anti-aliasing

Without Anti-aliasing

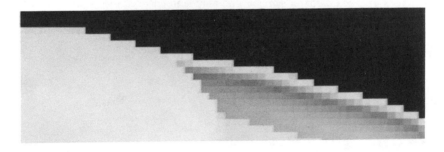

THE "UTAH TEAPOT" WITH AND WITHOUT ANTI-ALIASING

(Photos courtesy Computer Sciences Department, University of Utah)

aperture card A

punched card that holds a frame of microfilm.

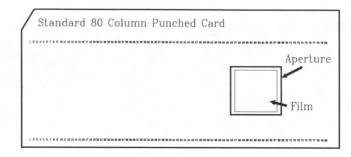

Standard 80 Column Punched Card

Aperture

Film

APERTURE CARD

API

(Application Program Interface) A language and format used by one program to communicate with another program. It may also include the commands used to interrupt the computer in order to get the attention of the other program. An API used in communications is called a *protocol.* See *interface.*

APL (A

Programming Language) A high-level, interactive scientific language noted for its brevity and matrix generation capabilities. Developed by Kenneth Iverson in the mid 1960s, it is often used to develop mathematical models. APL is used on a wide variety of computers from micro to mainframe. It is primarily an interpreted language, but compilers are also available.

PROGRAMS TALK TO EACH OTHER!

APL uses unique character symbols and may require special software or ROM chips to enable the computer to display and print them. APL is more popular in Europe than in the U.S.

The following example converts fahrenheit to centigrade:

```
[0]  CONVERT
[1]  'Enter fahrenheit
[2]  fahr ←□
[3]  cent ← 5 × (fahr-32) ÷ 9
[4]  'Centigrade is ', (₮cent)
```

Apollo (Apollo Systems Division) A manufacturer of high-performance workstations. Founded in 1980, Apollo Computer pioneered the concept of networked workstations. In 1982, it introduced its first color workstation, and in 1987, introduced its Network Computing System (NCS), which allows users to develop and run programs across networks of computers from various suppliers. Its Domain Series workstations are used in a wide range of industries including aerospace, automotive and electronics.

In early 1989, the company became the Apollo Systems Division of the Hewlett-Packard Company.

app See *application*.

app code (APPlication code) The instructions in a program that actually process data.

APPC (Advanced-Program-to-Program-Communications) See *LU 6.2*.

append To add data to the end of an existing structure. For example, in dBASE, the APPEND command starts the data entry mode and allows users to add records to the end of the file. In dBASE programming, APPEND BLANK creates a new blank record at the end of the file.

Apple (Apple Computer, Inc.) A manufacturer of personal computers and the industry's most fabled story. Founded in a garage by Steve Wozniak and Steve Jobs, and guided by Mike Markkula, Apple blazed the trails for the personal computer industry. Today, most of the original founders are not with the company, and Steve Jobs' exit is legend. For the whole story, read John Sculley's "Odyssey," published by Harper & Row.

Apple was formed on April Fool's Day in 1976. Soon after, it introduced the Apple I at the Palo Alto Homebrew Computer Club. By the end of the year, 10 retail stores were selling Apple I's.

In 1977, it introduced the Apple II, a fully-assembled personal computer with 4K of memory for $1,298. The Apple II+ was introduced with 48K in 1979.

The Apple II's open-architecture encouraged third party vendors to build plug-in hardware to enhance its capability. This, plus sound and color graphics, caused Apple IIs to become

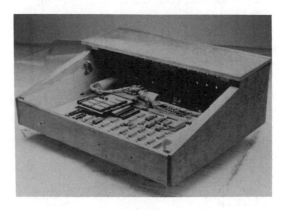

APPLE I
(Courtesy Apple Computer, Inc.)

STEVE JOBS

STEVE WOZNIAK

the most widely used computer in the home and classroom.

Apple IIs were also used in business primarily for the innovative VisiCalc software that was launched on it.

In 1983, Apple introduced the Lisa, the forerunner of the Macintosh. The Lisa was aimed at the corporate market, but was expensive and slow. It was soon dropped in favor of the Macintosh, and actually turned into a hybrid Mac for a while.

As a graphics-based machine, the Macintosh was originally successful as a low-cost desktop publishing system. Although the Mac was praised and purchased by many for its ease of use, its slow speed, small screen, closed architecture and mouse-driven user interface didn't excite corporate buyers.

Since the advent of the Mac II family in 1987, that has changed. Mac IIs offer high speed, big screens, open architecture and color, everything the previous Macs lacked. In addition, advanced software, such as HyperCard, which comes with every machine and integrates data management and multimedia, puts the Macintosh in a class by itself. Apple is once again an innovative leader and strong competitor in high-performance personal computing.

Apple II A family of personal computers from Apple Computer that has become widely used for education, business and entertainment in the home and classroom. There is a huge variety of hardware that plugs into it and software that runs on it.

Apple IIs use the 6502 microprocessor family, and run under Apple's DOS or ProDOS operating system. AppleSoft BASIC, is built into ROM in every Apple II and is always available to the user.

With a Z80 microprocessor board plugged into it, Apple IIs can run CP/M programs, such as dBASE II.

APPLE II, II+
Introduced in April 1977, the Apple II came with 4K of memory and was

APPLE IIc

(Photos on this page courtesy Apple Computer, Inc.)

designed to hook up to a TV and a cassette tape recorder. The floppy disk arrived by mid 1978. In June 1979, the Apple II+ was introduced with 48K of RAM and an improved auto-start ROM for easier startup and screen editing.

APPLE III
Yes, there was an Apple III. Introduced in September 1980, it was an enhanced model intended for business use. It was not 100% compatible with the Apple II and never caught on.

APPLE IIe, IIc
Introduced in January 1983, the Apple IIe was the next upgrade (e for enhanced). It added some needed features, such as four cursor keys instead of two, and memory was increased to 128K.

In April 1984, the IIc portable was launched with a sleek design and limited expandability.

APPLE IIGS
Introduced in September 1986, the Apple IIGS is a major upgrade. It runs most software 2.8 times as fast internally, and features enhanced color graphics and sound (the GS). The GS has improved color graphics, can generate up to 15 separate and simultaneous sounds and has built-in connectivity to an AppleTalk network.

The GS will accept most Apple II plug-in boards, but requires software written for the GS in order to activate its enhanced capabilities.

APPLE II GS

APPLE IIe

Apple key The original designation for keys on an Apple keyboard that are pressed in conjunction with another key to perform a command. A key with the outline of an Apple, a propeller, or both, is now called the *Command key*. A key with a solid Apple is the Option key.

MODEL	CPU# (Size)	CLOCK SPEED (MHz)	BUS SIZE	RAM (Bytes)	FLOPPY DISK (Bytes)	HARD DISK (Bytes)	SCREEN RES.	OS
II, II+	6502 8 bits	1.0	8 bits	48-64K	5.25" 143K	**	280x192 6 colors	DOS, ProDOS, Pascal & CP/M*
IIe, IIc	6502 8 bits	1.0	8 bits	64-128K	5.25" 143K	**	280x192 6 colors	
IIGS	65C816 16 bits	2.8	8 bits	512K-8M	5.25" 143K 3.5" 400-800K	20M	320x200 256 cols.	

APPLE II SPECIFICATIONS
* CP/M requires third party Z80 processor board
** Hard disks available from third party vendors

Apple menu A menu at the top left side of the Macintosh screen that is always available to provide access to desk accessories.

AppleShare Software from Apple Computer that turns a Macintosh into a file server. It works in conjunction with the Mac operating system and can coexist with other Macintosh applications in a non-dedicated mode.

AppleShare PC Software for PCs from Apple Computer that allows a PC workstation to reside in an AppleTalk network. It requires a LocalTalk PC Card from Apple for AT-bus workstations, or a LocalTalk Card from DayStar Communications for Micro Channel PCs.

AppleSoft BASIC The version of BASIC that comes with Apple II models. It is installed in firmware and is always available.

AppleTalk A local area networking environment from Apple Computer that is based on the OSI model and was introduced in 1985. AppleTalk is built into Macintoshes, Apple IIGS computers and LaserWriter printers. With additional hardware and software from Apple and third parties, AppleTalk protocols can be used in PCs, VAXs and UNIX workstations. AppleTalk supports Apple's twisted pair LocalTalk access method as well as Ethernet and Token Ring.

AppleWorks An integrated software package from Claris Corporation that runs on the Apple II series. Originally introduced in 1983 by Apple Computer, it combines word processing, file management, spreadsheet, business graphics and communications.

application

(1) A specific use of the computer. For example, payroll, inventory and accounts receivable are business applications.

(2) Synonymous with application program or software package. For example, word processing, spreadsheets and business graphics are applications. It often refers to the running program and the files and databases that are being worked on. Contrast with *system software*.

application developer
An individual that develops a business application and usually performs the duties of a systems analyst and application programmer.

application development language
Same as *programming language*.

application development system
A programming language and associated utility programs that allow for the creation, development and running of application programs. A database management system, including query languages and report writers, may also be part of this system.

application generator
Software that generates application programs from descriptions of the problem rather than from detailed programming. It is one or more levels higher than a high-level programming language, but still requires that the user enter mathematical, or algorithmic, expressions in order to describe complex functions. For example, a complicated pricing routine in an order entry application would take a bit of programming to enter no matter how high-level the application generator.

application layer
In communications, the interaction at the user or application program level. It is the highest layer within the protocol hierarchy. See *OSI model*.

application notes
A short list of instructions and recommendations from the vendor that are provided in addition to the normal reference manuals accompanying the product.

application package
A software package that is created for a specific purpose or industry.

application processor
The computer that is processing data. Contrast with computers that are performing control functions, such as front end processors or database machines.

application program
Any data entry, update, query or report program that processes data for the user. Contrast with *system software*.

application program interface See *API*.

application program library A collection of application programs used by an organization.

application programmer An individual who writes application programs in a user organization. Most programmers are application programmers. Contrast with *systems programmer*.

APRIL (APplication Rational Interface Logic) A logic chip from IBM that employs neural network techniques that make it capable of learning from its environment.

APT (Automatic Programmed Tools) A high-level programming language used to generate instructions for automated factory machines (numerical control machines).

arbitration A set of rules for allocating machine resources, such as memory or peripheral devices, to more than one user or program.

architecture See *computer architecture* and *network architecture*.

archive To back up data onto a disk or tape. It can imply the use of a data compression scheme to store more data than the storage medium normally holds. For example, archiving programs, such as PKZIP for the PC and Stuffit for the Macintosh, are widely used.

ARCNET A local area network from Datapoint Corporation that interconnects a wide variety of personal computers and workstations via coaxial cable, twisted pair or fiber optic cable. It uses a token passing access method at 2.5Mbps with a distributed star topology that interconnects up to 255 computers. 20Mbps versions were introduced in 1989.

Introduced in 1968, ARCNET was the first local area network technology. With adapters, it can connect to many mainframe and minicomputer networks as well.

Ardis (Advanced National Radio Data Service) A joint venture of IBM and Motorola that provides wireless data transmission in the 800MHz FM band. It covers most U.S. metropolitan areas with over 1,000 base stations.

arg See *argument*.

argument In programming, a value that is passed between programs, subroutines or functions. Arguments are independent items, or variables, that contain data or codes. When an argument is used to customize a program for a user, it is typically called a *parameter*.

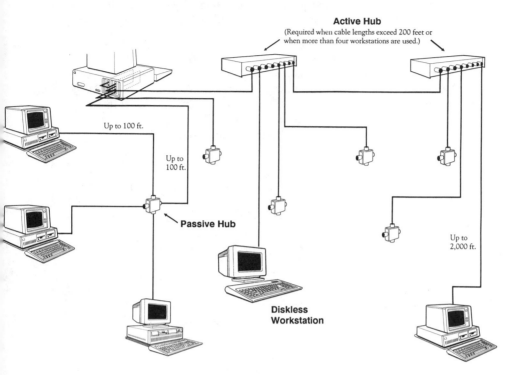

ARCNET

(Courtesy Black Box Corporation)

arithmetic expression

(1) In mathematics, one or more characters or symbols associated with arithmetic, such as 1+2=3 or 8-6.

(2) In programming, a non-text expression.

arithmetic logic unit See *ALU*.

arithmetic operators Symbols for arithmetic functions: + add, − subtract, * multiply, / divide. See *precedence*.

arithmetic overflow A result from an arithmetic calculation that exceeds the space designated to hold it.

arithmetic underflow A result from an arithmetic calculation that is too small to be expressed properly. For example, in floating point, a negative exponent can be generated that is too large (too small a number) to be stored in its allotted space.

ARQ (Automatic Repeat Request) A way of handling communications errors in which the receiving station requests retransmission if an error occurs.

array An ordered arrangement of data elements. A one dimensional array is called a *vector*, and a two-dimensional array is called a *matrix*.

Most programming languages have the ability to store and manipulate arrays in one, two or more dimensions. Multi-dimensional arrays are used extensively in scientific simulation and mathematical processing; however, an array can be as simple as a pricing table held in memory for instant access by an order entry program. See *subscript*.

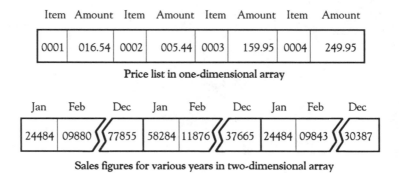

Item	Amount	Item	Amount	Item	Amount	Item	Amount
0001	016.54	0002	005.44	0003	159.95	0004	249.95

Price list in one-dimensional array

Jan	Feb	Dec	Jan	Feb	Dec	Jan	Feb	Dec
24484	09880	77855	58284	11876	37665	24484	09843	30387

Sales figures for various years in two-dimensional array

ARRAYS

array element One item in an array.

array processor A computer, or an extension to its arithmetic unit, that is capable of performing simultaneous computations on elements of an array of data in some number of dimensions. Common uses include analysis of fluid dynamics and rotation of 3-D objects, as well as data retrieval, in which elements in a database are scanned simultaneously. See *vector processor* and *math coprocessor*.

artificial intelligence See *AI*.

artificial language A language that has been predefined before it is ever used. Contrast with *natural language*.

AS (Application System) A fourth-generation language from IBM that runs on mainframes under MVS. It was originally designed for non-computer people and includes commands for planning, budgeting and graphics. However, a programmer can also produce complex applications. AS also provides a computer conferencing capability.

ascender The part of lowercase b, d, f, h, k, l, and t, that extends above the body of the letters.

ASCII (American Standard Code for Information Interchange) Pronounced "ask-ee." A binary code for data that is used in communications, most minicomputers and all personal computers.

ASCII is a 7-bit code providing 128 possible character combinations, the first 32 of which are used for printing and transmission control. Since the common storage unit is an 8-bit byte (256 combinations) and ASCII uses only 128, the extra bit is used to hold a parity bit or special symbols. For example, the PC uses the additional values for foreign language and graphics symbols. In the Macintosh, the additional values can be user-defined to enhance a font. For example, in the Macintosh version of this Glossary, the IBM PC symbols are designed into the font used for the definitions.

ASCII file A data or text file that contains characters coded in ASCII. Text files, word processing documents, batch files and source language programs are usually ASCII files. Only the first 128 characters (0-127) within the 256 combinations in a byte conform to the ASCII standard. The rest are used differently depending on the computer.

ASCII Files for Data Conversion

Data files created by BASIC programs are usually ASCII files, but files created by database programs are usually not, since they contain binary numbers and additional codes. However, the ASCII file can be used as a common denominator between incompatible formats. For example, if program A can't convert its data to the format of program B, but both programs can handle ASCII files, conversion is possible using built-in import and export functions. Dates, floating point and binary numbers may still cause conversion problems, however.

Word processing documents also have incompatible formats, but can often optionally output ASCII files that can be transferred to another system. Contrast with *binary file*.

ASCII protocol The simplest form of transmitting ASCII data and implies little or no error checking. Each character can be transmitted with a parity bit in order to provide some degree of error checking, but important data, such as numbers, and source and machine language programs, should be transmitted with a more sophisticated protocol.

ASIC (Application Specific Integrated Circuit) A chip that is designed for a specific purpose usually within a highly vertical application. It is designed by integrating standard cells from a library. ASIC design is faster than designing a chip from scratch, and design changes can be made more easily.

askSam A text-oriented database management system for PCs from askSam Systems. It holds unstructured text as well as standard data fields. The product is highly praised and noted for its text retrieval and hypertext capabilities. AskSam was introduced in 1985. In 1989, version 4.2 adds the ability to attach a graphic image to a record, which can be retrieved and displayed with the text.

STANDARD ASCII

The first 32 characters (0-31) are control codes

0	NUL	Null
1	SOH	Start of heading
2	STX	Start of text
3	ETX	End of text
4	EOT	End of transmit
5	ENQ	Enquiry
6	ACK	Acknowledge
7	BEL	Audible bell
8	BS	Backspace
9	HT	Horizontal tab
10	LF	Line feed
11	VT	Vertical tab
12	FF	Form feed
13	CR	Carriage return
14	SO	Shift out
15	SI	Shift in
16	DLE	Data link escape
17	DC1	Device control 1
18	DC2	Device control 2
19	DC3	Device control 3
20	DC4	Device control 4
21	NAK	Neg. acknowledge
22	SYN	Synchronous idle
23	ETB	End trans. block
24	CAN	Cancel
25	EM	End of medium
26	SUB	Substitution
27	ESC	Escape
28	FS	Figures shift
29	GS	Group separator
30	RS	Record separator
31	US	Unit separator
32	SP	Blank space (Space bar)

33	!	81	Q
34	"	82	R
35	#	83	S
36	$	84	T
37	%	85	U
38	&	86	V
39	'	87	W
40	(	88	X
41	)	89	Y
42	*	90	Z
43	+	91	[
44	,	92	\
45	-	93	]
46	.	94	^
47	/	95	_
48	0	96	`
49	1	97	a
50	2	98	b
51	3	99	c
52	4	100	d
53	5	101	e
54	6	102	f
55	7	103	g
56	8	104	h
57	9	105	i
58	:	106	j
59	;	107	k
60	<	108	l
61	=	109	m
62	>	110	n
63	?	111	o
64	@	112	p
65	A	113	q
66	B	114	r
67	C	115	s
68	D	116	t
69	E	117	u
70	F	118	v
71	G	119	w
72	H	120	x
73	I	121	y
74	J	122	z
75	K	123	{
76	L	124	|
77	M	125	}
78	N	126	~
79	O	127	▒
80	P		

EXTENDED ASCII

(IBM PC)

128	Ç	174	«	220	▄
129	ü	175	»	221	▌
130	é	176	░	222	▐
131	â	177	▒	223	▀
132	ä	178	▓	224	α
133	à	179	│	225	β
134	å	180	┤	226	Γ
135	ç	181	╡	227	π
136	ê	182	╢	228	Σ
137	ë	183	╖	229	σ
138	è	184	╕	230	µ
139	ï	185	╣	231	τ
140	î	186	║	232	Φ
141	ì	187	╗	233	Θ
142	Ä	188	╝	234	Ω
143	Å	189	╜	235	δ
144	É	190	╛	236	∞
145	æ	191	┐	237	φ
146	Æ	192	└	238	ε
147	ô	193	┴	239	∩
148	ö	194	┬	240	≡
149	ò	195	├	241	±
150	û	196	─	242	≥
151	ù	197	┼	243	≤
152	ÿ	198	╞	244	⌠
153	Ö	199	╟	245	⌡
154	Ü	200	╚	246	÷
155	¢	201	╔	247	≈
156	£	202	╩	248	°
157	¥	203	╦	249	•
158	₧	204	╠	250	·
159	ƒ	205	═	251	√
160	á	206	╬	252	η
161	í	207	╧	253	²
162	ó	208	╨	254	■
163	ú	209	╤	255	
164	ñ	210	╥		
165	Ñ	211	╙		
166	ª	212	╘		
167	º	213	╒		
168	¿	214	╓		
169	⌐	215	╫		
170	¬	216	╪		
171	½	217	┘		
172	¼	218	┌		
173	¡	219	█		
174		220			
175		221			

ASCII CODE

ASM

(1) (Association for Systems Managment) An international membership organization, founded in 1947, with over 10,000 administrative executives and specialists in information systems. ASM sponsors conferences in all phases of administrative systems and management and serves business, education, government and the military. For more information, contact ASM, 24587 Bagley Road, Cleveland, OH 44138, (216) 243-6900.

(2) A file extension for assembly language source programs.

ASN.1 (Abstract Syntax Notation.1) A method of describing the form of data in an OSI communication. It pertains to the Applicaiton Layer (layer 7).

aspect ratio The ratio of width to height of a frame, screen or image. When images are transferred from one system to another, the aspect ratio must be maintained in order to provide an accurate representation of the original.

assembler Software that translates assembly language into machine language. Contrast with *compiler*, which is used to translate a high-level language, such as COBOL or C, into assembly language first and then into machine language.

assembly language A programming language that is one step away from machine language. Each assembly language statement is translated into one machine instruction by the assembler. Programmers must be well versed in the computer's architecture, and, unless well documented, assembly language programs are difficult to maintain. Assembly languages are hardware dependent; there is a different language for each CPU series.

In the past, systems software (operating systems, database managers, etc.) was written in assembly language to maximize the machine's performance. Today, C is often used instead. Like assembly language, C can manipulate the bits at the machine level, but unlike assembly language, a C program can be compiled into machine language for all CPUs from micro to mainframe.

The terms assembly language and machine language are often used synonymously; however, they are not the same. For example, the assembly language statement: COMPARE A, B is translated into a machine instruction such as: COMPARE the contents of memory locations 2340-2350 with the contents of locations 4567-4577. The actual instruction generated is: 1001010101001011101010100101001.

Assembly languages are quite different between classes of computers as is evident in the example on the following page, which takes 16 lines of code for the mini and 82 lines for the micro. The example changes fahrenheit to centigrade.

assignment statement In programming, a compiler directive that places a value into a variable. For example, counter = 0 creates a variable named counter and fills it with zeros. The VARIABLE NAME = VALUE syntax is common among programming langauges.

INTEL 8086 (IBM PC)

```
cseg    segment  para public 'CODE'           shl     bx,1
        assume   cs:cseg,ds:cseg              add     bx,ax
start:                                         jmp     llp
        jmp      start1              llr:      mov     dx,offset cse
msgstr  db       'Enter farenheit '           mov     ah,9
crlf    db       13,10,'$'                    int     21h
nine    dw       9                            mov     ax,bx
five    dw       5                            ret
outstr  db       'Centigrade is $'   putval:  xor     bx,bx
start1: push     ds                           push    bx
        push     cs                           mov     bx,10
        pop      ds                  llg:     xor     dx,dx
        mov      dx,offset cseg:msgstr         div     bx
        mov      ah,9                         add     dx,'0'
        int      21h                          push    dx
sloop:                                         test    ax,ax
cent:   call     getnumb                      jne     llg
        test     ax,ax               bloop:   pop     dx
        je       exit                         test    dx,dx
        push     ax                           je      endx
        mov      dx,offset cseg:outstr        mov     ah,6
        mov      ah,9                         int     21h
        int      21h                          jmp     bloop
        pop      ax                  endx:    ret
        sub      ax,32               cseg     ends
        jns      c1                           end     start
        push     ax
        mov      dl,'-'
        mov      ah,6
        int      21h
        pop      ax
        neg      ax
c1:     mul      five
        div      nine
        call     putval
        mov      dx,offset cseg:crlf
        mov      ah,9
        int      21h                 ## HEWLETT-PACKARD HP
        jmp      sloop
exit:   pop      ds                  begin
        mov      ah,4ch              intrinsic  read,print,binary,
        int      21h                 array buffer(0:17);
getnumb:                             array string(0:3);
        xor      bx,bx               byte array b'string(*) = stri
llp:    mov      dl,0ffh             integer ftemp, ctemp, len;
        mov      ah,1                  move buffer:= "Enter fahren
        int      21h                   print (buffer,-30,%320);
        cmp      al,0dh                len:=read (string,-4);
        je       llr                   ftemp:= binary(b'string,len
        sub      al,'0'                ctemp:= (ftemp-32) * 5 / 9;
        jb       llr                   len:= ascii(ctemp,10,b'stri
        cmp      al,'9'                move buffer:= "Centigrade i
        ja       llr                   move buffer(14):= string,(-
        xor      ah,ah                 print (buffer,-32,%0);
        shl      bx,1                end
        add      ax,bx
        shl      bx,1
```

ASSEMBLY LANGUAGE

Assembly languages are quite different between mainframes, minis and micros as you can see in the exampl
It takes 16 lines of assembly language code to accept a fahrenheit number and convert it into centigrade o
3000 minicomputer, but it takes 83 lines to do it in Intel 8086 assembly language for a PC.

associative storage A technique for storing data and instantly recognizing it by its content. Using specially designed circuits, the data key is matched against all the stored keys at the same time. With this technique, there is no need to keep track of addresses.

ASSP (Application Specific Standard Part) An ASIC chip originally designed for one customer and then released to the general public.

asymetrical modem A full-duplex modem that transmits data in one direction at one speed and simultaneously in the other direction at another speed.

asynchronous

(1) Unsynchronized events, for example, the time interval between event A and B is not the same as B and C.

(2) Able to initiate a transmission at either end.

(3) In SNA, refers to independent events rather than concurrent events. For example, if one user sends mail to a party who is not available, the ability to forward the mail at a later time is considered asynchronous.

asynchronous protocol A communications protocol that controls an asynchronous transmission, for example, ASCII, TTY, Kermit and Xmodem. Contrast with *synchronous protocol*.

asynchronous transmission The transmission of data in which each character is a self-contained unit with its own start and stop bits and intervals between characters may be uneven. It is the common method of transmission between a computer and a modem, although the modem may switch to synchronous transmission to communicate with the other modem. Also called *start/stop transmission*. Contrast with *synchronous transmission*.

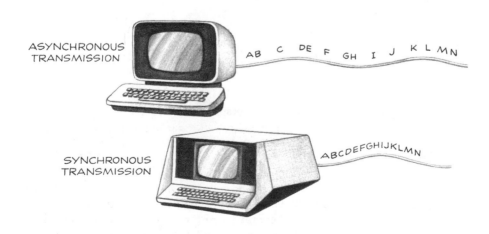

AS/400 (Application System/400) A series of minicomputers from IBM, introduced in 1988, that supersedes and advances the System/36 and System/38 series. System/36 programs run in the AS/400 in System 36 mode after they have been recompiled. System 38 programs run intact in System/38 mode. After recompilation, System/38 programs run in native AS/400 mode, which takes advantage of all system resources.

The AS/400 is designed to serve in a variety of networking configurations. It can function as a host or intermediate node to other AS/400s and System/3x machines, as a remote system to System/370-controlled networks and as a network server to PCs.

AT (Advanced Technology) IBM's first 286-based personal computer, introduced in 1984. It was the most advanced machine in the PC line and featured a new keyboard, 1.2MB floppy and 16-bit data bus. AT class machines run from three to six times as fast as XTs (8088-based PCs). See *PC*.

AT bus The 16-bit data bus used in the AT. See *PC bus*. Contrast with *Micro Channel*.

AT class A PC that uses the Intel 286 CPU and the AT bus.

IBM AT

AT command set A series of machine instructions used to activate features on an intelligent modem. Developed by Hayes Microcomputer Products, Inc., and formally called the Hayes Standard AT Command Set, it is used entirely or partially by most every modem manufacturer. AT is a mnemonic code for ATtention, which is the prefix that initiates each command to the modem. See *Hayes Smartmodem*.

AT keyboard An 84-key keyboard provided with the PC AT. It corrected the non-standard placement of the PC's return and left shift keys. See *PC keyboard* and *Enhanced keyboard*.

AT&T (American Telephone & Telegraph Company) The largest long distance communications carrier in the U.S. Once the largest corporation in America, it was relieved of its operating telephone companies on January 1, 1984, by Federal court order, AT&T has gone through a traumatic change from the world's largest monopoly to a competitive enterprise.

Its success with its PC offerings has been modest thus far. However, AT&T is a 35 billion dollar company (1988 Fortune 500) and its resources are formidable, including the famous Bell Labs where the transistor and laser were invented. In addition, AT&T has made powerful telephone-switching computers for years.

AT KEYBOARD

ATM (Automatic Teller Machine) A special-purpose banking terminal that allows users to make deposits and withdrawals. It can be a stand-alone unit or online to a central computer system. ATMs are activated by inserting a magnetic card (cash card or credit card) in the machine that contains the user's identification number.

ATM

atom In list processing languages, a single element in a list.

atomic operation An operation that cannot be divided. It cannot be broken up into parts that can be performed by different processors.

attached processor An additional CPU connected to the primary CPU in a multiprocessing environment. It operates as an extension of the primary CPU and shares the system software and peripheral devices.

attenuation Loss of signal power in a transmission.

attribute
(1) In relational database management, a field within a record.

(2) For printers and display screens, a characteristic that changes a font, for example, from normal to boldface or underlined, or from normal to reverse video.

audio The range of frequencies within human hearing (approx. 20Hz at the low to a high of 20,000Hz).

Traditional audio devices are analog, because they handle the sound waves in an analogous form. Radios maintain the audio signal as rippling waves from antenna to speaker. Sound waves are "carved" into plastic phonograph records, and audio tape records sound as magnetic waves.

Audio is processed in a computer by converting the analog signal into a digital code using various techniques, such as pulse code modulation.

audio response See *voice response*.

audiotex An voice response application that allows users to enter and retrieve information over the telephone. In response to a voice menu, users press the keys or answer questions to select their way down a path of choices. It is used for obtaining the latest financial quotes as well as for ordering products. It is also built into interactive systems that allows databases to be changed. See *VIS*.

audit An examination of systems, programming and datacenter procedures in order to determine the efficiency of computer operations.

audit software Specialized programs that perform a variety of audit functions, such as sampling databases and generating confirmation letters to customers. It can highlight exceptions to categories of data and alert the examiner to possible error. Audit software often includes a non-procedural language that lets the auditor describe the computer and data environment without detailed programming.

audit trail A record of transactions in an information system that provides verification of the activity of the system. The simplest audit trail is the transaction itself. If a person's salary is increased, the change transaction includes the date, amount of raise and name of authorizing manager.

A more elaborate audit trail can be created when the system is being verified for accuracy; for example, samples of processing results can be recorded at various stages. Item counts and hash totals are used to verify that all input has been processed through the system.

authoring program Software that allows for the development of tutorials and CBT programs.

authorization code An indentification number or password that is used to gain access to a local or remote computer system.

Authorware An authoring program from Authorware, Inc., that runs on the Macintosh. Courseware developed on the Mac can be converted to the PC.

auto answer A feature of a modem that accepts a telephone call and establishes the connection. See *auto dial*.

auto attendant A voice store and forward system that replaces the human operator and directs callers to the appropriate extensions or voice mailboxes.

auto bypass The ability to bypass a terminal or other device in a network if it fails, allowing the remaining devices to continue functioning.

auto dial A feature of a modem that opens the line and dials the telephone number of another computer to establish connection. See *auto answer*.

AutoCAD A full-featured CAD program from AutoDesk Inc., that runs on PCs, VAXs, UNIX workstations and the Macintosh. Originally developed for CP/M machines, it was one of the first major CAD programs for personal computers and became an industry standard. Many software packages import and export graphics files in DXF, AutoCAD's external file format.

autocoder IBM assembly language for 1960s-vintage 1400 and 7000 series computers.

AUTODIN (AUTOmatic DIgital Network) The worldwide communications network of the U.S. Defense Communications System.

AUTOEXEC.BAT (AUTOmatic EXECute BATch file) A Microsoft DOS file that, if present in the root directory, is executed upon startup. It contains DOS instructions that are used to initialize operating system settings, load TSRs and launch applications. The equivalent in OS/2 is *STARTUP.CMD*; however, AUTOEXEC.BAT is also executed in OS/2 when the computer is running in real mode.

automata theory An open-ended mathematical discipline within the computer sciences that concerns an abstract device called an *automaton*, which performs a specific computational or recognition function. Networks of automata are designed to mimic human behavior.

automated office See *office automation.*

automatic data processing Same as *data processing.*

automatic teller machine See *ATM.*

A VISION OF AUTOMATION
(Artist Unknown, Circa 1895)
(Courtesy Rosemont Engineering)

automation The replacement of manual operations by computerized methods. Office automation refers to the integration of clerical tasks such as typing, filing and appointment scheduling. Factory automation refers to computer-driven assembly lines and warehouses.

autostart routine Instructions built into the computer and activated when it is turned on. The routine performs diagnostic tests, such as checking the computer's memory, and then loads the operating system and passes control to it.

A/UX A version of the UNIX operating system from Apple Computer that runs on the Macintosh II series. A/UX is based on AT&T's UNIX System V with Berkeley extensions, enhancements added to UNIX at the University of California at Berkeley.

auxiliary memory
(1) A high-speed memory bank used in large mainframes and supercomputers. It is not directly addressable by the CPU, rather it functions like a disk. Data is transferred from auxiliary memory to main memory over a high-bandwidth channel.

(2) Same as *auxiliary storage*.

auxiliary storage External storage devices, such as disk and tape.

AVC (Audio Visual Connection) Multimedia software from IBM that works in conjunction with IBM's Audio Capture and Video Capture boards for the PS/2. It allows users to integrate sound and pictures into applications and includes an authoring language.

avionics Electronic instrumentation and control equipment used in airplanes and space vehicles.

awk (Aho Weinberger Kernighan) A UNIX programming utility developed in 1977 by Aho, Weinberger and Kernighan. Due to its unique pattern-matching syntax, it is often used in data retrieval and data transformation. DOS versions are also available.

back end processor Same as *database machine*.

back up To make a copy of important data.

backbone In communications, the part of a network that handles the major traffic. It may interconnect multiple locations, and smaller networks may be attached to it.

backfilling Refers to assigning EMS memory to conventional memory (below 1MB) in PCs using 8086 and 286 processors. The original motherboard chips are disabled, and the EMS chips are assigned the low memory addresses.

Backfilling lets multitasking programs, such as DESQview, run more programs concurrently in expanded memory. This has no effect on DOS applications that run in real mode.

background

(1) Non-interactive processing in the computer. See *foreground/background*.

(2) The base, or backdrop, color on screen. For example, in the PC version of this Glossary, the default colors of the text are white on a blue background. In the Macintosh version, the standard text colors are black on a white background.

background ink A highly reflective ink in optical character recognition that is used to print the parts of the form that are not going to be detected or recognized by the scanner.

background noise Any extraneous, low-level signal that has crept into a line, channel or circuit.

backing storage Any external peripheral storage, such as disk or tape. Same as *secondary storage* or *auxiliary storage*.

backlit A type of LCD screen that provides its own light source from the back of the screen. It makes the background brighter and the characters appear sharper.

backplane

(1) The reverse side of a panel or board that contains interconnecting wires.

(2) A printed circuit board, or device, containing slots, or sockets, for plugging in boards or cables.

backspace

(1) To move the screen cursor one column to the left, deleting the character that was displayed in that position. A backspace to the printer moves the print head one column to the left.

(2) To move to the previous block on a magentic tape.

backup Additional resources or duplicate copies of data for emergency purposes.

backup & recovery A combination of manual and machine procedures that can restore lost data in the event of hardware or software failure. Routine backup of files, databases and programs, and system logs that keep track of the computer's operations are all part of a backup & recovery program. See *checkpoint/restart*.

backup copy Any disk, tape or other machine readable copy of a data or program file. Making backup copies is a discipline that most personal computer users learn the hard way— after a week's work is lost.

backup disk A disk that is used to hold duplicate copies of important files. High-density floppy disks and removable disks cartridges are used for backup disks.

backup power An additional power source that can be used in the event of power failure. See *UPS*.

backup tape See *tape backup*.

Backus-Naur form Also known as Backus normal form, it was the first metalanguage to define programming languages, developed by John Backus and Peter Naur in 1959.

backward chaining In AI, a form of reasoning that starts with the conclusion and works backward. The goal is broken into many subgoals, or sub-subgoals, which can be solved more easily. Known as top-down approach. Contrast with *forward chaining*.

backward compatible Same as *downward compatible*.

bad sector A segment of disk storage that cannot be read or written due to a physical problem in the disk. Bad sectors on hard disks are marked by the operating system and bypassed. If data is recorded in a sector that becomes bad, special software, and sometimes special hardware, must be used to recover it.

BAK file (BAcKup file) In Microsoft DOS and OS/2, a commonly used file extension for backup files.

BAL

(1) (Basic Assembly Language) The assembly language for the IBM 370/3000/4000 mainframe series.

(2) (Branch And Link) An instruction used to transfer control to another part of the program.

balun (BALanced UNbalanced) A communications device that connects a balanced line to an unbalanced line, for example, a twisted wire pair to a coaxial cable. A balanced line is one in which both wires are electrically equal. In an unbalanced line, such as a coaxial cable, one line has different physical properties than the other.

BALUN

(Courtesy Black Box Corporation)

This balun connects a coaxial cable with twisted pair wires.

band

(1) A range of frequencies that is used for transmitting a signal. A band can be identified by the difference between its lower and upper limits as well as by its actual lower and upper limits, for example, "a 10 megaHertz band in the 100 to 110 megaHertz range."

(2) A contiguous group of tracks that are treated as a unit.

(3) A printing element in a band printer.

band pass filter An electronic device that prohibits all but a specific range of frequencies to pass through it.

band printer A line printer that uses a metal band, or loop, of type characters as its printing mechanism. The band spins horizontally around a set of hammers. When the desired character is in front of the selected print position, the corresponding hammer hits the paper into the ribbon and onto the character in the band.

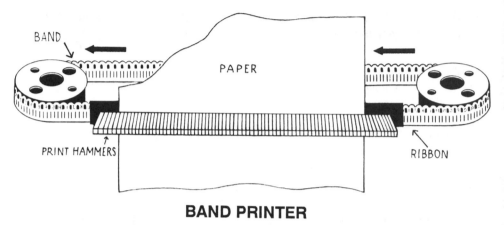

BAND

PAPER

PRINT HAMMERS

RIBBON

BAND PRINTER

bandwidth The transmission capacity of a computer or communications channel. Pure digital transmission is measured in bits or bytes per second. When digital data is converted to frequencies for transmission over carrier-based networks, bandwidth is still stated in bits or bytes per second. However, when frequencies are used as the transmission signal rather than on/off pulses, bandwidth may also be measured in cycles per second, or Hertz, the bandwidth being the difference between the lowest and highest frequencies transmitted. In this case, the frequency will be equal to or greater than the bits per second.

bank An arrangement of identical hardware components.

bank switching The engaging and disengaging of electronic circuits. Bank switching is used when the design of a system prohibits all circuits from being addressed or activated at the same time requiring that one unit be turned on while the others are turned off.

bar chart A graphical representation of information in the form of bars. See *business graphics*.

bar code A specialized code used for fast identification of items with an optical scanner. The actual coding of the bars is the width of the bar, not the height. The extended height allows tolerance for the recognition system. See *UPS* (universal product code).

BAR CODE

barrel printer Same as *drum printer*.

base

(1) A starting point or reference point.

(2) The component in a bipolar transistor that activates the switch. Same as *gate* in a MOS transistor.

(3) The multiplier in a numbering system. In a decimal system (base 10), each digit position is worth 10x the position to its right. In a binary system (base 2), each digit position is worth 2x the position to its right.

base address The location in memory where the beginning of a program is stored. The relative address from the instruction in the program is added to the base address to derive the absolute address. See *base/displacement*.

base alignment The alignment of a variety of font sizes on a baseline.

base/displacement A technique for running programs from any location in memory. The addresses in the machine language program are displacement addresses (relative to the beginning of the program). As the program is running, the hardware adds the displacement address to the base address (where the beginning of the program is currently stored) and derives the absolute address.

baseband A communications technique in which digital signals are placed onto the transmission line without change in modulation. It is usually limited to a couple of miles and does not require the complex modems used in broadband transmission. Common baseband LAN techniques are token passing ring (Token Ring) and CSMA/CD (Ethernet).

In baseband, the full bandwidth of the channel is used, and simultaneous transmission of multiple sets of data is accomplished by interleaving pulses using TDM (time division multiplexing). Contrast with *broadband* transmission, which transmits data, voice and video simultaneously by modulating each signal onto a different frequency, using FDM (frequency division multiplexing).

baseline A horizontal line to which the bottoms of lowercase characters (without descenders) are aligned. See *typeface*.

BASIC (Beginners All purpose Symbolic Instruction Code) A programming language developed by John Kemeny and Thomas Kurtz in the mid 1960s at Dartmouth College. Originally developed as an interactive timesharing language for mainframes, BASIC has become widely used on all sizes of computers, including pocket computers.

BASIC is available in both compiler and interpreter form, the latter being more popular for the casual user and first-time programmer. As an interpreter, the language is conversational and can be debugged a line at a time. BASIC can also be used as a desktop calculator.

BASIC is considered one of the easiest programming languages to learn. Simple programs can be quickly written on the fly. However, BASIC is not a structured language, such as Pascal, dBASE or C, and it's easy to write spaghetti code that's difficult to decipher later.

The following BASIC example converts fahrenheit to centigrade:

```
10 INPUT "Enter fahrenheit "; FAHR
20 PRINT "Centigrade is ", (FAHR-32) * 5 / 9
```

BASIC in ROM A BASIC interpreter stored in a read only memory chip that is available to the user at all times.

BAT file (BATch file) A Microsoft DOS or OS/2 program that is executed as if each command were interactively entered one at a time. It has a BAT extension and is created with a text editor or word processor. The BAT file is run by entering its file name at the operating system prompt. The following BAT file changes the current directory from WP to DB and loads the XYZ program. See *AUTOEXEC.BAT*.

```
C:\WP>cd \db
C:\DB>xyz
```

batch A group, or collection, of items. Batch program or batch job refers to a program that processes an entire set of data, such as a report or sort program. Batch data entry refers to typing in a group of source documents. Remote batch refers to transmitting a complete file over a network. Batch operations are also called *offline* operations. Contrast with *online, interactive* and *transaction processing*.

batch job A non-interactive program that is run in the computer, such as a listing or sort.

batch processing The processing of a group of transactions at one time. Transactions are collected and processed against the master files (master files updated) at the end of the day or some other time period. Contrast with *transaction processing*.

Batch and Transaction Processing

Information systems typically use both batch and transaction processing methods. For example, in an order processing system, transaction processing is the continuous updating of the customer and inventory files as orders are entered.

At the end of the day, batch processing programs generate picking lists for the warehouse. At the end of the week or some other period, batch programs print invoices and management reports.

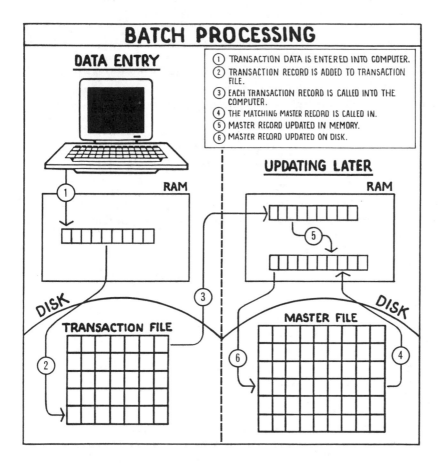

BATCH PROCESSING

DATA ENTRY

1. TRANSACTION DATA IS ENTERED INTO COMPUTER.
2. TRANSACTION RECORD IS ADDED TO TRANSACTION FILE.
3. EACH TRANSACTION RECORD IS CALLED INTO THE COMPUTER.
4. THE MATCHING MASTER RECORD IS CALLED IN.
5. MASTER RECORD UPDATED IN MEMORY.
6. MASTER RECORD UPDATED ON DISK.

UPDATING LATER

RAM

RAM

DISK

TRANSACTION FILE

MASTER FILE

DISK

batch session The transmission or updating of an entire file. Contrast with *interactive session*.

batch stream A collection of batch processing programs that are scheduled to run in the computer.

batch system See *batch processing*.

batch terminal A terminal that is set up for transmitting or receiving blocks of data, such as a card reader or printer.

batch total The sum of a particular field in a collection of items that is used as a control total to ensure that all data has been entered into the computer. For example, using account number as a batch total, all account numbers would be summed manually before entry into the computer. After entry, the total is checked with the computer's sum of the numbers. If it doesn't match, source documents are manually checked against the computer's listing.

baud rate

(1) The switching speed of a line, which is the number of changes in the electrical state of the line per second. Baud rate is equivalent to bits per second at low speeds, for example, 300 baud is the same as 300 bps. At higher speeds, the bits per second is greater than the baud rate, because one baud can be made to represent more than one bit. For example, the common V.22bis modem provides 1,200 bps at 600 baud.

(2) Commonly (and erroneously) used to specify bits per second for any modem speed, for example, 4,800 baud implies 4,800 bps.

baudot code

Pronounced "baw-doh." One of the first standards for international telegraphy developed in the late 19th century by Emile Baudot. It uses five bits to make up a character.

BBS

(Bulletin Board System) A computer system that functions as a centralized information source and message switching system for a particular interest group. Users dial up the bulletin board, review and leave messages for other users as well as communicate to other users on the system at the same time. Bulletin boards may provide access, or doors, to other application programs.

The following list of BBSs is copied with permission from Boardwatch Magazine, a monthly newsletter for the electronic BBS and online information service industry. For more information, contact Boardwatch Magazine, 5970 S. Vivian St., Littleton, CO 80127, (303) 973-6038.

ADA Information Clearinghouse	(202)694-0215
ANARC (World Radio/TV Handbook)	(913)345-1978
Applied Modeling Research (EPA Models)	(919)541-1325
Ashton-Tate Technical Support	(213)538-6196
AST Technical Services (Support)	(714)852-1872
AT&T Support (PC 6300, AT&T PC's)	(201)769-6397
Audiophile Network (High-end Audio)	(818)988-0452
Baud Town (Social BBS)	(818)893-0340
BBS Press Service (INFOMAT)	(913)478-9239
BellSouth's TUB Gateway	(404)594-3964
Best Friends (Multiline Social)	(714)832-5902
Big Peach (Automenu,Treeview Software)	(404)446-6650
Big Sky Telegraph (Rural MT Schools)	(406)683-7680
BOOK (Info 2000 Computer Books)	(215)657-6130
Boston Citinet (Boston Info)	(617)439-5699
Brown Bag Software (Support)	(408)371-7654
Buttonware (PC Software Support)	(206)454-2629
C.A.R.L. Library Service (Colorado)	(303)830-1165
Canada Remote Systems (Largest BBS)	(416)232-0442
CatHouse 206/2901 (Wildcat Software)	(805)395-0650
Cathouse II SuperSystem (TV Satellite)	(513)528-0505
Census Bureau Office Automation	(301)763-4576

Census Bureau Personnel Division ....(301)763-4574
Channel 1 (New England PC Board Sys) ....(617)354-5776
Chicago SysLink (TRS 80 Support) ....(312)622-4442
Classi Computer Fieds (Classified Ads) ....(317)359-5199
Clean Air (Health, Smoking Topics) ....(408)298-4277
Cleveland Freenet (City Info) ....(216)368-3888
COCONET (San Diego Entertainment) ....(619)456-0815
Computer Business Services (Columnist) ....(714)396-0014
Computing Canada Online (PC Newspaper) ....(416)497-5263
Crosstalk Communications (MK4/XVI) ....(404)641-1803
CTC IEEE Employment Database (Resumes) ....(508)263-3857
Dante Project (Divinia Comedia) ....(603)643-6310
DataLink RBBS System (NOAA Satellite) ....(214)394-7438
Dr. Dobbs Listing Service ....(603)882-1599
Economic Bulletin Board (Statistics) ....(202)377-0433
Eesti BBS #1 (First BBS in USSR) 7 0142 422583
ELISA II (Export License Advise) ....(202)697-3632
Employ-Net (Help Wanted Ads) ....(303)871-9504
Energy Info Admin E-Publications ....(202)586-8658
Event Horizons (Graphics Image Lib) ....(503)777-1578
EXEC-PC (Largest BBS in US, 100 lines) ....(414)789-4210
Far West (Western Canada Galacticomm) ....604)381-4430
FCC Public Access Link ....(301)725-1072
Federal Deposit Insurance Corporation ....(202)737-7264
Federal Job Information Center ....(313)226-4423
FEDLINK ALIX (Federal Libraries) ....(202)287-9656
File Cabinet (10-line PC Board Sys) ....(215)678-9854
Fishing Link (River/Lake Charts) ....(608)526-9292
Fly-Fisher's Forum ....(416)463-9090
FOG City 125/10 (Gay Community) ....(415)863-9697
Forbin Project, The (QModem SST Comm.) ....(319)233-6157
GAO Bulletin Board (Lotus, WP, dBASE) ....202)275-1050
GLIB (Gay and Lesbian Information) ....(703)578-4542
Greenpeace Environet (Ecological) ....(415)861-6503
GT PowerComm (Software) ....(713)772-2090
Hay Locator (Database Supplier/Buyer) ....(317)494-6643
Hayes Advanced Systems Support (Modem) ....(800)US-HAYES
Herpnet/Satronics (Reptile, Amphibian) ....(215)698-1905
IBM Users Group Support (Newsletter) ....(404)988-2790
Inbound/Outbound (Telephone Sales Pub.) ....(212)989-4675
Info-Source Canada (Online Pub) ....(416)574-1313
Information Resources Services ....(202)535-7661
Intel Support (Intel PC Products) ....(503)645-6275
Investor's Online Data (Market Info) ....(206)285-5359
JAG-NET (Navy Judge Advocate General) ....(202)325-0748
JDR Microdevices (Hardware Catalog) ....(408)559-0253
JOBBS (Job Listings Technical) ....(404)992-8937
Lasergems Computer Hotline ....(602)867-7258
LUMINA (Lib. Univ. of Minnesota) ....(612)626-2206
Maxi-Micro Ticker Screen (Stocks) ....(212)809-1160
MCI ONE Consultant Support (ANI Dev) ....(800-873-5548

MEDCOM BBS CLUB (Games, Chat, News) .... (800)445-4227
Micro Foundry, The (Software Support) .... (415)598-0498
Micro Message Service (News Magazines) .... (919)779-6674
Microlink B (USA Today News) .... (303)972-9600
Microrim Technical Support (R:Base) .... (206)881-8119
Monu-CAD (Designs for Tombstones) .... (607)264-3307
NANci (Naval Aviation News Magazine) .... (202)475-1973
NARDAC (Zenith Support, Federal Users)............ (804)445-1627
NASA Spacelink (Flight/Space History) .... (205)895-0028
National Agricultural Library .... (301)344-8510
National Genealogical (Family History) .... (703)528-2612
National Inst. Science Technology .... (301)948-5717
National Publishers Exchange .... (813)989-1087
NAVWESA (Naval Weapons Engineering) .... (202)433-6639
New York Macintosh Users Group .... (212)932-9513
NIST ACTS (Computer Telephone Service) .... (303)494-4775
NOAA Information Technology Exchange............ (301)770-0069
NOAA Solar (Solar Flare/Geomagnetic) .... (303)497-5000
Northrop Career Access (Employment) .... (213)938-5532
Numisnet (Coin Collecting) .... (301)498-8205
NYCENET (NYC Education Network) .... (212)769-0550
OCRWM Infolink (Radioactive Waste) .... (202)586-9359
OERI (Educational Statistics, Data) .... (800)222-4922
Old Colorado City Communications .... (719)632-2658
Online StoreDLX (PC Hardware Catalog) .... (805)656-0379
Oracle PC (South Australian TBBS) 6108 260-6222
Osprey's Nest (Birdwatching, Ecology) .... (301)989-9036
Personal Resource System (Online Pubs) .... (501)442-8777
Photo*Life (Nature Photography) .... (301)270-2638
PHYSICS Forum (Astronomical Sciences) .... (413)545-1959
PKWare (PKARC and PKZIP Utilities) .... (414)352-7176
Popular Mechanics Online....................................... (212)582-8369
ProComm Support... (314)474-8477
Public Brand Software (Shareware)......................... (317)856-2087
Publishers Information Services .... (312)342-6919
Radio Electronics (Magazine) .... (516)293-2283
Random Access Information Services .... (503)761-8100
RGB Computing (PC Sales Info. Serv.) .... (519)824-3997
Rose Media (Canadian PC Board Sys.) .... (416)733-2780
Salt Air (PCBOARD BBS Software) .... (801)261-8976
Scenix Network (USA Today, Box Office) .... (213)372-2282
Science Resources Studies (Fed Budget) .... (202)634-1764
Scooters Scientific Exchange .... (215)657-5586
SEAboard! (ARC, SEADOG, AXE Software) .... (201)473-1991
Second Ring, The (RBBS Software) .... (203)268-5315
Society for Technical Comm.................................... (202)393-3557
Software Plus (Shareware, Downloads).................... (919)577-9831
Sound Advise (20 Line PCBoard)............................ (816)436-4516
State and Local Emergency Management).............. (202)646-2887
Synergy (Turbo Basic/Turbo C/Quick C) .... (617)769-5468
Take 3 (Reviews of Movies/Video/Film) .... (602)482-1001

Talk Channel (Sexual Orientation) ....(818)506-0620
TAXACOM (Botany, FLORA ONLINE News) ....(716)896-7581
Taxonomic Reference File ....(215)972-6759
TBBS Net 104/23 (The Bread Board Sys.) ....(303)699-9248
Technotronics (LAN/PC Support) ....(212)924-6899
Telegodzilla (Home of ZModem) ....(503)621-3746
Telix Support..(416)439-8293
Texas State Law Library ....(512)463-1371
The Business (Microsoft Windows) ....(213)477-0408
The Ledge PCBoard (Textview Door) ....(818)352-3620
The LiveWire (Magazine Orders) ....(609)235-5297
The Other Ball (Adult Chat System) ....(818)358-6968
The Unique and Nifty (Graphics, etc.) ....(317)866-0725
The Well (Popular - Hourly charges) ....(415)332-6106
Thomas Business Systems (Used PC's) ....(407)395-7057
TOPS Support (TOPS LAN) ....(415)769-8874
U.S. ROBOTICS - Sit UBU Sit ....(708)982-5092
United Nations (UN Press Releases) ....(201)795-0733
US Naval Observatory (Enter @TCO) ....(202)653-1079
USA Today Distribution Service..............................(303)973-4222
USA/GDR Databank (Foreign News) ....(202)529-0140
USGS Quick Epicenter Determination....................(800)358-2663
USNO Time of Day for Clocks ....(202)653-0351
UT Library Online Catalog ....(512)471-9420
VA Property Listing (Foreclosures).........................(602)640-2371
Vacation Florida Database (Tourism) ....(407)839-0333
Vancouver ED-NET (Educational online) ....(604)734-3282
Ward and Randy's CBBS (oldest BBS) ....(312)545-8086
WeatherBank (Forcast for Any City) ....(800)827-2727
WeatherStar Pilot Briefing ....(612)296-5426
Western Digital Technical Support ....(714)756-8176
XyQuest Support (XyWrite Software) ....(508)667-5669
Ye Olde Bailey (Legal Issues) ....(713)520-1569

BCD (Binary Coded Decimal) The storage of numbers in which each decimal digit is converted into binary and is stored in a single character or byte. For example, a 12-digit number would take 12 bytes. See *numbers.*

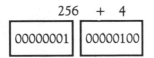

The number "260" coded in binary.

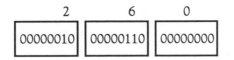

The number "260" coded in binary coded decimal.

BINARY CODED NUMBERS

BCS

(1) (The **B**oston **C**omputer **S**ociety) A nonprofit membership organization founded in 1977 by Jonathan Rotenberg. With over 28,000 members, it is the largest personal computer association in the world. Member services include user and special interest groups, a subscription to BCS publications, access to the BCS Resource Center, public-domain software, shareware and electronic services. For more information, contact The Boston Computer Society, One Center Plaza, Boston, MA 02108, (617) 367-8080.

(2) (**B**inary **C**ompatibility **S**tandard) See *ABI*.

(3) (The **B**ritish **C**omputer **S**ociety) For more information, contact BCS, 13 Mansfield St., London, England W1M 0BP.

BDOS error See *read error* and *write error*.

bead

(1) A small programming subroutine. A sequence of beads that are strung together is called a *thread*.

(2) An insulator surrounding the inner wire of a coaxial cable.

BEL See *bell character*.

bell character A control code that is used to sound an audible bell or tone in order to alert the user. In ASCII, it has a numeric value of 7.

Bell compatible A modem that is compatible with modems originally introduced by the Bell Telephone System.

Bell Labs The research and development center of the AT&T Company and one of the most renowned scientific laboratories in the world.

Bell System AT&T and the Bell Telephone Companies before divestiture. By federal court order, on January 1, 1984, AT&T divested itself of its 23 operating companies, which became seven independent regional telephone companies: Ameritech, Bell Atlantic, BellSouth, Nynex, Pacific Telesis, Southwestern Bell and US West. Bell Labs was renamed AT&T

ALEXANDER GRAHAM BELL
(Courtesy AT&T)

Bell Labs, and its Western Electric manufacturing division was renamed AT&T Technologies.

Bell 103 An AT&T standard for asynchronous 300 bps full-duplex modems using FSK modulation on dial-up lines.

Bell 113 An AT&T standard for asynchronous 300 bps full-duplex modems using FSK modulation on dial-up lines. The 113A can originate but not answer calls, while the 113D can answer but not originate.

Bell 201 An AT&T standard for synchronous 2,400 bps full-duplex modems using DPSK modulation. Bell 201B was originally designed for dial-up lines and later for leased lines. Bell 201C was designed for half-duplex operation over dial-up lines.

Bell 202 An AT&T standard for asynchronous 1,800 bps full-duplex modems using DPSK modulation over four-wire leased lines as well as 1,200 bps half-duplex operation over dial-up lines.

Bell 208 An AT&T standard for synchronous 4,800 bps modems. Bell 208A is a full-duplex modem using DPSK modulation over four-wire leased lines. Bell 208B was designed for half-duplex operation over dial-up lines.

Bell 209 An AT&T standard for synchronous 9,600 bps full-duplex modems using QAM modulation over four-wire leased lines or half-duplex operation over dial-up lines.

Bell 212 An AT&T standard for asynchronous 1,200 bps full-duplex modems using DPSK modulation on dial-up lines.benchmark A test of performance of a computer or peripheral device. The best benchmark is the actual set of application programs and data files that the organization will use. Running benchmarks on a single user computer is reasonably effective; however, obtaining meaningful results from a benchmark of a multiuser system is a complicated task. Unless the end user environment can be duplicated closely, the benchmark will be of little value. It may be more effective to find a user organization with a similar processing environment and simply monitor the operation. See *Linpack, Dhrystones, Whetstones* and *Khornerstones*.

BER (Basic Encoding Rules) One method for encoding information in the OSI environment. For example, it defines how Boolean data is coded.

Bernoulli Box A removable disk system from Iomega Corporation that connects to personal computers through a SCSI interface. Introduced in 1983, the original Bernoulli Box was an 8" floppy disk cartridge that held 10MB. Storage was later increased to 20MB. In 1987, the Bernoulli Box II provided 20MB on a 5 1/4" disk, and in 1989, storage was increased to 44MB per cartridge.

The name comes from the 18th century Swiss scientist, Daniel Bernoulli, whose principle of fluid dynamics is demonstrated in the disk mechanism. When the floppy disk is spun at high speed, it bends up and maintains a thin band of air between it and the read/write head. Unlike a hard disk in which the read/write head flies over a rigid disk, the floppy disk in the Bernoulli Box flies up to a rigid read/write head. Upon power failure, a hard disk has to retract the head to prevent a recording failure or head crash, whereas the floppy disk in the Bernoulli Box automatically bends down.

BERNOULLI BOX II

Beta The first home VCR format. Developed by Sony, it records video on 1/2" tape cassettes. Beta Hi-fi added CD-quality audio, and SuperBeta improved the visual image. Beta is now defunct, leaving VHS as the primary standard for 1/2" videotape.

beta test A test of hardware or software that is performed by users under normal operating conditions. See *alpha test*.

betaware Software in beta test that has been provided to a large number of users in advance of the formal release.

Bezier In computer graphics, a curve that is generated using a mathematical formula which assures continuity with other Bezier curves. It is mathematically simpler, but more difficult to blend than a b-spline curve. Within CAD and drawing programs, Bezier curves are typically reshaped by moving the handles that appear off of the curve.

BFT (Binary File Transmission) A standard for transmitting data between fax boards in less time than conventional modems. It does not allow transfer between fax boards and data modems.

BI bus A proprietary high-speed bus used in Digital's VAX series.

bidirectional The ability to move, transfer or transmit in both directions. For example, a bidirectional gateway allows data to be transmitted to and from a network. A bidirectional printer prints left to right and vice versa (by holding two lines of data in its buffer, it prints the next line from right to left without having to return to the left side).

BIFF (Binary Interchange File Format) A spreadsheet file format that holds data and charts, introduced with Excel Version 2.2.

bifurcate To divide into two.

Big Blue Slang for the International Business Machines Corporation that was coined because of IBM's blue covers on most of its earlier mainframes.

bill of materials A list of components that make up a system. For example, a bill of materials for a house would include the cement block, lumber, shingles, doors, windows, plumbing, electric, heating and so on. Each subassembly also contains a bill of materials; the heating system is made up of the furnace, ducts, etc. A bill of materials "implosion" links component pieces to a major assembly, while a bill of materials "explosion" breaks apart each assembly or subassembly into its component parts.

The first hierarchical databases were developed for automating bills of materials for manufacturing organizations in the early 1960s.

billion One thousand times one million. See *giga* and *nanosecond*.

binaries Executable programs in machine language.

binary Meaning two; the fundamental principle behind digital computers. All input to the computer is converted into binary numbers made up of the two digits 0 and 1 (bits). For example, when you press the "A" key on your personal computer, the keyboard generates and transmits the number 01000001 to the computer's memory as a series of pulses. The 1 bits are transmitted as high voltage; the 0 bits are transmitted as low voltage. The 1s and 0s are stored as a series of charged and uncharged memory cells in the computer.

On magnetic disk and tape, the bits are stored as positively and negatively charged spots. We see the real characters because the display screens and printers convert the binary numbers into visual characters.

The electronic circuits that process these binary numbers are themselves binary in concept. They are made up of on/off switches (transistors) that are electrically opened and closed. The current flowing through one switch turns on (or off) another switch, and so on. These switches open and close in nanoseconds and picoseconds (billionths and trillionths of a second).

A computer's capability to do work is based on its storage capacity (memory and disk) and internal transmission speed. Greater storage capacities are achieved by making the memory cell or magnetic spot smaller. Faster transmission rates are achieved by shortening the time it takes to open and close the switch and developing circuit paths that can handle the increased speeds. In order to improve the performance of a computer, we simply continue to refine the binary concept. See examples on the following page.

How Binary Numbers Work

Binary numbers are actually quite simple. They use only the digits 0 and 1 instead of 0 through 9 as in our decimal system.

In decimal, when you add 9 and 1, you get 10. But, if you break down the steps to get to 10, you find that by adding 9 and 1, what you get first is a result of 0 and a carry of 1. The carry of 1 is moved over and added to the digits in the next position on the left. In the example on the right, there are no other digits in that position, and the carry of 1 becomes part of the answer.

$$\begin{array}{r} 9 \\ +\ 1 \\ \hline 10 \end{array}$$

The following example adds 1 ten times in succession. Note that the binary method has more carries than the decimal method. In binary, 1 and 1 are 0 with a carry of 1.

Binary	Decimal
0	0
+ 1	+ 1
1	1
+ 1	+ 1
10	2
+ 1	+ 1
11	3
+ 1	+ 1
100	4
+ 1	+ 1
101	5
+ 1	+ 1
110	6
+ 1	+ 1
111	7
+ 1	+ 1
1000	8
+ 1	+ 1
1001	9
+ 1	+ 1
1010	10

128	64	32	16	8	4	2	1

Value of each position in the binary system

10,000,000	1,000,000	100,000	10,000	1,000	100	10	1

Value of each position in the decimal system

binary code A coding system made up of binary digits. See *BCD, data code* and *numbers*.

binary field A field that contains binary numbers. It may refer only to the storage of binary numbers for calculation purposes, or it may refer to a field that is capable of holding any information, including data, text, graphics images, voice and video.

binary file A program in machine language form or a file that contains binary numbers. When transmitting files to a remote computer, some protocols handle only ASCII text and cannot be used for binary files.

binary format

(1) Numbers stored in pure binary form in contrast with *BCD* form.

(2) Any information stored in a binary coded form, such as data, text, images, voice and video. See *binary file* and *binary field*.

(3) A file transfer mode that transmits any type of file without loss of data.

binary notation The use of binary numbers to represent values.

binary numbers Numbers that are stored in pure binary form. Within one byte (8 bits), the values 0 to 255 can be stored. Two contiguous bytes (16 bits) can hold values from 0 to 65,535, and three bytes, the values 0 to 16,777,215. Contrast with *BCD* (binary coded decimal) numbers in which each decimal digit takes one byte. In BCD, the maximum value in three bytes is 999.

binary search A technique for quickly locating an item of data in a sequential list. The desired key is compared to the data in the middle of the list. The half that contains the data is then compared in the middle, and so on, either until the key is located or until a small enough group is isolated to be sequentially searched.

binary synchronous See *bisync*.

binary tree A data structure in which each node contains one parent and no more than two children.

BINARY TREE

bind

(1) To assign a machine address to a logical or symbolic reference or address.

(2) To assign a type or value to a variable or parameter. See *binding time*.

(3) To link modules together. See *linkage editor*.

binding time

(1) In program compilation, the point in time when symbolic references to data are converted into physical machine addresses.

(2) In programming languages, the point in time when a variable is assigned its type (integer, string, etc.). Traditional compilers and assemblers provide early binding and assign types in the compilation phase. Object-oriented languages provide late binding and assign types at run time when the variable receives a value from the keyboard or other source.

biomechanics
The study of the anatomical principles of movement. Biomechanical applications on the computer employ stick modeling to analyze the movement of athletes as well as racing horses.

bionic
A machine that is patterned after principles found in humans or in nature, for example, robots. It also refers to artificial devices implanted into humans replacing or extending normal human functions.

BIOS
(Basic Input Output System) Software routines that contain the detailed instructions for activating the peripheral devices connected to the computer.

In the IBM PC, the BIOS resides in a read only memory (ROM) chip and accepts requests for input and output from both the operating system and the application programs.

The autostart routine in the BIOS is responsible for testing memory upon startup and preparing the computer for operation. It searches for BIOS components that are located on the plug-in boards and sets up pointers (interrupt vectors) in memory to access them. The BIOS in a compatible machine must set up the computer in precisely the same manner as does the BIOS in the IBM PC.

bipolar
A category of high-speed microelectronic circuit design, which was used to create the first transistor and the first integrated circuit. The most common variety of bipolar chip is TTL (transistor transistor logic). Emitter coupled logic (ECL) and integrated injection logic (I2L) are also part of the bipolar family. Bipolar and MOS are the two major categories of chip design.

bipolar transmission
A technique for transmitting digital data that alternates between negative and positive states.

biquinary code Meaning two-five code. A system for storing decimal digits in a four-bit binary number.

bis Second version. It means twice in Old Latin, or encore in French.

BISDN (Broadband IDSN) See ISDN.

bistable circuit Same as *flip-flop*.

bisync (BInary SYNChronous) A major category of synchronous communications protocols used extensively in mainframe networks. Bisync communications require that both sending and receiving devices are synchronized before transmission of data is started. Contrast with *asynchronous* transmission.

bisynchronous See *bisync*.

bit (BInary digiT) A single digit in a binary number (1 or 0). Within the computer, a bit is physically a memory cell (made up of transistors or one transistor and a capacitor), a magnetic spot on disk or tape or a pulse of high or low voltage travelling through a circuit. Conceptually, a bit can be thought of as a light bulb; either on or off.

Groups of bits make up storage units in the computer, called *characters*, *bytes*, or *words*, which are manipulated as a group. The most common storage unit is the byte, which is made up of eight bits and is equivalent to one alphanumeric character. See *space/time*.

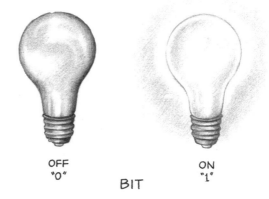

OFF
"0"

ON
"1"

BIT

bit density
The number of bits that can be stored within a given physical area.

bit flipping Same as *bit manipulation*.

bit manipulation The processing of individual bits within a byte. Processing at the bit level is typically required in low-level programming of control programs and graphics operations.

bit map
(1) In computer graphics, an area in memory that represents the video image. For monochrome screens, one bit in the bit map represents one pixel on screen.

For gray scale or color screens, several bits in the bit map represent one pixel or group of pixels on the screen.

(2) Any binary representation in which each bit or set of bits corresponds to some object or condition.

bit-mapped font
A complete set of dot patterns for each letter and digit in a particular typeface. Each font size requires an entirely different set of dot patterns. Contrast with *scalable font*.

bit-mapped graphics
The raster graphics method for generating images. Contrast with *vector graphics* and *character graphics*.

bit-oriented protocol
A communications protocol that uses individual bits within the byte as control codes, for example, IBM's SDLC. Contrast with *byte-oriented protocol*.

bit parallel
The transmission of several bits at the same time, each bit travelling over a different wire or line in the cable.

bit pattern
A specific layout of binary digits.

bit rate
The transmission speed of binary coded data. Same as *data rate*.

bit serial
The transmission of one bit after the other on a single line or wire.

bit slice processor
A logic chip that is used as an elementary building block for the computer designer. Bit slice processors usually come in 4-bit increments and are strung together to make larger processors (8 bit, 12 bit, etc.).

bit specifications
(1) Refers to the computer's internal word, or register size, which is the amount of data the processor can compute at the same time. If the clock rates are equal (16MHz, 20MHz, etc.), a 32-bit computer works twice as fast as an 16-bit computer; however, this specification measures only computational performance.

(2) Refers to the size of the computer's data bus, which is the pathway over which data is transferred between memory and the CPU and between memory and the peripheral devices. If the bus clock rates are equal, a 16-bit bus transfers data twice as fast as an 8-bit bus.

(3) Refers to the size of the address bus, which determines how much memory the processor can address directly. Each bit doubles the number, for example, 20-bits addresses 1,048,576 bytes; 24-bits addresses 16,772,216 bytes.

bit stream The transmission of binary signals.

bit stuffing Adding bits to a transmitted message in order to round out a fixed frame or to break up a pattern of data bits that could be misconstrued for control codes.

bit twiddler An individual who likes to program or work with computers. See *hacker*.

bitblt (bit BLock Transfer) In computer graphics, a hardware feature that moves a rectangular block of bits from main memory into display memory at high speed. Bitblt technology improves the performance of computers used in realtime animation and modeling on screen.

BIX (Byte Information eXchange) An online database of computer knowledge available from BYTE magazine. BIX is designed to help users fix problems and obtain information about specific hardware and software products.

Black Apple An black-colored Apple II+ that was specially made for Bell and Howell to sell with training packages. It had additional audio jacks and volume controls for mixing external audio sources.

black box Specialized hardware that converts one code into another, for example, from one communications protocol to another. A black box is a transparent solution for interconnecting incompatible hardware and/or software and should not require changes to the existing systems. Originally custom-made items, black boxes have become standard off-the-shelf products today.

Black Box Corporation An organization that specializes in data communications, computer connectivity products and LAN equipment. It offers a wide variety of hard-to-find products as well as expert services for customizing solutions to interconnection problems.

BLACK BOX

blank character A space character that takes up one byte in the computer just like a letter or digit. When you press the space bar in an ASCII computer, a character with the numeric value of 32 is created.

blank squash The removal of blanks between items of data. For example, in the expression CITY + " , " + STATE, the data is concatenated with a blank squash resulting in AUSTIN, TX rather than AUSTIN   TX.

blip A mark, line or spot on a medium, such as microfilm, that is optically sensed and used for timing or counting purposes.

block

(1) A group of disk or tape records that is stored and transferred as a single unit.

(2) A group of bits or characters that is transmitted as a unit.

(3) A group of text characters that has been marked for moving, copying, saving or other operation.

block diagram A chart that contains squares and rectangles connected with arrows to depict hardware and software components and their interconnections. For program flow charts, information system flow charts, circuit diagrams and communications networks, more elaborate graphical representations are usually used.

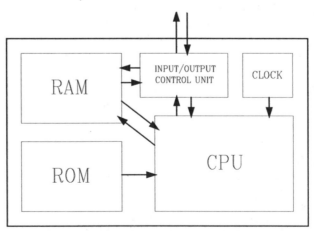

BLOCK DIAGRAM OF A COMPUTER

blocking factor The number of records in a block.

blow To write code or data into a PROM chip by blowing the fuses of the 0 bits. The 1 bits are left alone.

blow up Same as *crash*, *bomb* or *abend*.

BNC A connector used for coaxial cable. The plug looks like a cylinder with two short pins on the outer edge on opposite sides. After it is inserted, the socket is turned, causing the pins to tighten the plug within it. See *plugs & sockets*.

board Same as *printed circuit board*.

board level Electronic components that are mounted on a printed circuit board instead of in a cabinet or finished housing.

BOC (Bell Operating Company) One of the 22 telephone companies that was formerly part of AT&T and is now part of one of the seven regional Bell telephone companies.

BOF (Beginning Of File) The status of a file when it is first opened or when an instruction or command has reset the file pointer.

boilerplate Any common phrase or expression that is used over again. Boilerplate phrases are stored on disk and are copied into the document as needed.

boldface Characters that are heavier and darker on printed output and brighter than normal on a display screen.

boldface attribute A code that turns normal characters into boldface characters on a printer or display screen.

boldface font A set of type characters that are darker and heavier than normal type. In a boldface font, all the characters have been designed as bold characters. Contrast with *boldface attribute*, which converts normal characters into boldface.

bomb Same as *abend* and *crash*.

BOMP (Bill Of Materials Processor) One of the first database management systems used for bill of materials explosions in the early 1960s from IBM. A subsequent version, called *DBOMP*, was used in manufacturing organizations during the 1970s.

Boolean data Yes/no or true/false data.

Boolean expression A statement using Boolean operators that expresses a condition which is either true or false.

Boolean logic The "mathematics of logic," developed by the English mathematician George Boole in the mid 19th century. Its rules and operations govern logical functions (true/false) rather than numbers. As add, subtract, multiply and divide are the primary operations of arithmetic, AND, OR and NOT are the primary operations of Boolean logic.

To see how Boolean logic is used to create electronic circuits, you can simulate the flow of electricity through a half-adder circuit, an elementary circuit that simply adds one bit to another. There are two outputs from this, the carry bit and the result bit, and four possible combinations as is illustrated on the right.

In a digital circuit, a 1, or true, is high voltage, and a 0, or false, is low voltage. The circuit is wired together according to the following rules:

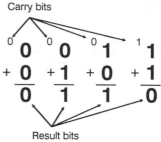

Carry bits

$$0 \quad 0 \quad 0 \quad 1$$
$$\begin{array}{r} 0 \\ + 0 \\ \hline 0 \end{array} \quad \begin{array}{r} 0 \\ + 1 \\ \hline 1 \end{array} \quad \begin{array}{r} 1 \\ + 0 \\ \hline 1 \end{array} \quad \begin{array}{r} 1 \\ + 1 \\ \hline 0 \end{array}$$

Result bits

(1) AND accepts two inputs and generates one output. It requires that both inputs be true (1) in order to produce a true output (1).

(2) OR accepts two inputs and generates one output. It only requires one input to be true (1) in order to produce a true output (1).

(3) NOT reverses the input. If a 1 comes in, a 0 goes out, and vice versa.

Trace the flow of current through the following example. The 1 is represented by the dark line, the 0 by no line. If it makes sense, try to simulate the flow of current through the examples on the following page.

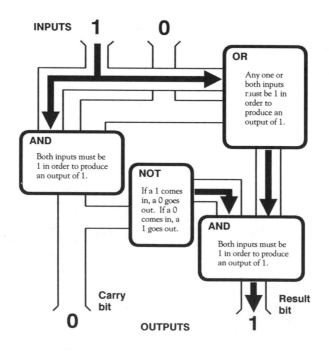

Try This!

Try simulating the flow of current through these circuits.

(a) Start with the two inputs. If the bit is a 0, draw nothing. If the bit is a 1, draw a line through the circuit path to the first OR and AND gates.

(b) Determine the output of the first AND and draw a line (or nothing) to the NOT and also to the carry bit.

(c) Determine the outputs of the OR and the NOT and draw lines (or nothing) to the second AND gate.

(d) Determine the output of the second AND and draw a line (or nothing) to the result bit.

Your outputs should be a result of 1 and a carry of 0 for the top circuit, and a result of 0 and carry of 1 for the bottom. If they're not, reread the rules and retrace your steps.

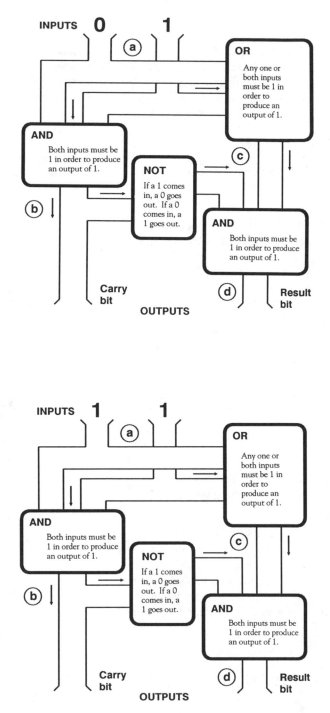

Boolean operator One of the Boolean logic operators such as AND, OR and NOT.

Boolean search A search for specific data. It implies that any condition can be searched for using the Boolean operators AND, OR and NOT. For example, the English language request: "Search for all the Spanish and French speaking employees who have MBAs, but don't work in Sales." is expressed in the dBASE command language as follows:

```
list for degree = "MBA" .and.
  (language = "Spanish" .or. language =
   "French") .and. .not. department = "Sales"
```

boot To start the computer. It comes from bootstrap, since bootstraps help you get your boots on; booting the computer helps it get its first instructions.

Personal computers have a bootstrap routine in a ROM chip that is automatically executed when the computer is turned on or reset. It searches for the operating system, loads it and then passes control over to it. The procedure for large computers often requires a sequence of button pushing and keyboard input. See *cold boot* and *warm boot*.

boot drive The disk drive that contains the operating system.

bootable disk A disk that contains the operating system and typically refers to a floppy disk. Personal computers normally look for a bootable disk in the primary floppy drive. If a hard disk system doesn't find a bootable floppy upon startup, it boots from the hard disk.

BOOTSTRAP

bootstrap See *boot.*

Borland (Borland International, Inc.) A leading microcomputer software company. Founded in 1983 by Philippe Kahn, Borland introduced its Turbo Pascal and moved the Pascal language out of the academic halls into a commercial product. Its Turbo C and Assembler have also become industry standards.

With Sidekick, introduced in 1984, Borland created the first PC desktop accessory program, which popularized the TSR, or popup, technique for DOS applications.

In 1987, it acquired Ansa Software and its highly-acclaimed Paradox database system, which continues to be improved and widely applauded.

Borland products have been translated into many foreign languages, and in fiscal 1989, foreign sales accounted for 37% of revenues.

Boston Computer Society See *BCS*.

bpi (Bits Per Inch) Used to measure the number of bits stored in a linear inch of a track on a recording surface, such as on a disk or tape.

bps (Bits Per Second) Used to measure the speed of data transfer in a communications system.

branch
(1) An instruction that directs the computer to go elsewhere in the program. Same as *goto* or *jump*.

(2) A connection between two blocks in a flowchart or two nodes in a network.

breadboard A thin plastic board full of holes used to hold components (transistors, chips, etc.) that are wired together. It is used to develop electronic prototypes or one-of-a-kind systems.

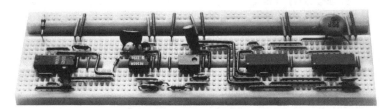

BREADBOARD

(Courtesy 3M Company)

break To temporarily or permanently stop executing, printing or transmitting.

break key A key that is pressed to stop the execution of the current program or transmission.

breakout box A device
that is connected into a
multiline cable and provides
terminal connections for
testing the signals in a
transmission. Breakout
boxes may also have a
small light for each line
that glows when a signal is
transmitted over that line.

bridge
(1) To purposefully or
inadvertently cross from
one circuit, channel or
element over to another.

BREAKOUT BOX

(2) A device that connects two
networks of the same type together. Contrast with *gateway*, which interconnects
two different types of networks. See *router* and *brouter*.

bridgeware Hardware or software that converts data or translates
programs from one format into another.

Brief A programmer's text editor for PCs from Solution Systems. It provides
such functions as automatic indentation and the ability to edit different parts of a
source program at the same time. dBrief is an add-on that customizes the
product for dBASE programmers.

British Telecom The division of the British Post Office that manages
telecommunications throughout Great Britain and Northern Ireland.

broadband A technique for transmitting large amounts of data, voice and
video over long distances. Using high frequency transmission over coaxial cable
or optical fibers, broadband transmission requires modems for connecting
terminals and computers to the network. Using the same FDM (frequency
division multiplexing) technique as in cable TV, several streams of data can be
transmitted simultaneously. Contrast with *baseband*.

broadcast To disseminate information to several recipients
simultaneously.

Brooklyn Bridge A file transfer program for PCs from Fifth Generation
Systems. One computer is designated the master, the other the slave. The user
at the master computer can manipulate the disks on the slave computer using
common DOS functions, such as COPY and DEL.

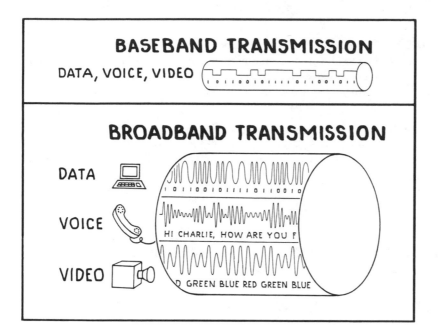

BASEBAND TRANSMISSION

DATA, VOICE, VIDEO

BROADBAND TRANSMISSION

DATA

VOICE

HI CHARLIE, HOW ARE YOU F

VIDEO

GREEN BLUE RED GREEN BLUE

brouter A communications device that performs functions of both a bridge and a router. Like a bridge, the brouter functions at the data link level (layer 2) and remains independent of higher protocols, but like a router, it manages multiple lines and routes messages accordingly.

browse

(1) To view and possibly edit a file on screen like text in a word processing document. Browse commands let the user scroll through the data horizontally by field and vertically by row or screenful.

(2) To view and edit the class hierarchy of the objects in an object-oriented programming language.

BSC (Binary Synchronous Communications) See *bisync.*

B-spline In computer graphics, a curve that is generated using a mathematical formula which assures continuity with other b-splines.

BTAM (Basic Telecommunications Access Method) An IBM communications program that is used in bisynch, non-SNA mainframe networks. Application programs must interface directly with the BTAM access method.

BTLZ (British Telecom Lempel Ziv) A data compression algorithm based on the Lempel-Ziv method that can achieve up to 4x the throughput of 2,400 and 9,600 bps modems.

BTOS The Burroughs version of the CTOS operating system. See *CTOS*.

B-tree (Balanced-tree) An organization technique for indexes. In order to keep access time to all data to a minimum, it stores the data keys in a balanced hierarchy that continually realigns itself as items are inserted and deleted. Thus, all nodes in the hierarchy always have a similar number of keys.

B+tree (Balanced+tree) A version of the B-tree indexing method that maintains a hierarchy of indexes while also linking the data sequentially. It provides both fast direct access and sequential access to data. IBM's VSAM uses this method.

bubble A bit in bubble memory or a symbol in a bubble chart.

bubble chart A chart that uses bubble-like symbols which is often used to depict data flow diagrams.

bubble memory A solid state storage technology that combines semiconductor and magnetic methods. Like disk, it holds its contents without power and is about as fast as a slow hard disk. It's used in rugged, heavy duty applications.

CONCEPTUAL PICTURE OF A
TRACK OF BUBBLE MEMORY

Conceptually, bubble memory can be thought of as a stationary disk whose bits spin instead of the disk. Bubble memory units are only a couple of square inches in size and contain a thin film magnetic recording layer. The bubbles (globular shaped bits) are electromagnetically generated in circular strings inside this layer. In order to read or write the bubbles, the strings of bubbles are made to rotate past the equivalent of a read/write head.

bubble sort A multiple-pass sorting technique that starts by sequencing the first two items, then the second with the third, then the third with the fourth and so on until the end of the set has been reached. The process is repeated until all items are in the correct sequence.

bucket Another term for a variable. It's just a place to store something.

buffer A reserved segment of memory that is used to hold data while it is being processed. In a program, buffers are created to hold some amount of data from each of the files that will be read or written. A buffer may also be a small memory bank used for special purposes.

buffer flush The transfer of data from memory to disk.

buffer pool An area of memory reserved for buffers.

bug A persistent error in software or hardware. If the bug is in software, it can corrected by changing the program. If the bug is in hardware, new circuits have to be designed. The term was coined in the 1940s when a moth was found squashed between the points of an electromechanical relay in the Mark I. Contrast with *glitch*.

bug compatible A hardware device that contains the same design flaws as the original.

bulk storage Storage that is not used for high-speed execution. May refer to auxiliary memory, tape or disk.

Bull HN (Bull HN Information Systems Inc.) A computer manufacturer that is the outgrowth of Honeywell Bull Inc., the company jointly created by Groupe Bull, Honeywell Inc., and NEC Corporation in March, 1987, from the former Honeywell Information Systems Division.

Honeywell started out in Minneapolis in 1885, when Alfred Butz began making his patented temperature controls. In 1906, Mark C. Honeywell began making water heaters in Wabash, Indiana, and later got into temperature controls. In 1927, both companies merged to become the Minneapolis Honeywell Regulator Company.

Honeywell was one of the first computer manufacturers in the U.S. In a joint venture with Ratheon, it launched the Datamatic 1000 in 1957, a monstrous, tube-driven machine. In 1959 and 1960, Honeywell introduced the Models 800 and 400, advanced second-generation computers that launched Honeywell into the computer business. In 1963, it introduced the Model 200, which was so successful at capturing IBM 1401 accounts, that IBM announced its new System/360 ahead of schedule.

In 1966, Honeywell acquired the Computer Control Company and incorporated its minicomputers into the Honeywell line. In 1970, it acquired GE's computer business and its computer division was renamed Honeywell Information Systems.

Through Honeywell's association with Bull in Europe and Bull's association with NEC in Japan, research and development was mutually explored, and product lines were jointly developed throughout the 1970s and 1980s. Honeywell offered a wide range of departmental minicomputers and mainframes to its customers throughout this time period.

In 1986, Honeywell-NEC Supercomputers, a joint venture to market NEC supercomputers in the U.S. and Canada, was formed.

As of the March 1987 merger, Honeywell Bull was a privately-held company owned 42.5% each by Bull and Honeywell and 15% by NEC. In January 1989, the company changed its name to Bull HN Information Systems to reflect a change in ownership. Bull is the majority owner with 69.4%, Honeywell, 15.6%, and NEC remaining at 15%.

bulletin board See *BBS*.

BUNCH (Burroughs, Univac, NCR, Control Data and Honeywell) The BUNCH were IBM's competitors after RCA and GE got out of the computer business.

bundled/unbundled A complete package of hardware and software for a single price. *Unbundled* systems have separate prices for each component.

bunny suit The protective clothing worn by an individual in a clean room that keeps human bacteria from infecting the chip-making process. It got its name because it makes people look like oversized rabbits.

BUNNY SUIT
(Coutesy Hewlett-Packard)

burn in To test an electronic system by running it for a specified length of time. Although an electronic component can fail at any time, weak components will generally fail within the first few hours of running. The longer the burn in period, the better the test.

burst mode An alternate method of high-speed transmission in a communications or computer channel. Burst mode implies that due to certain conditions, the system can send a burst of data at higher speed for some period of time. For example, a multiplexor channel may suspend tranmission of several streams of data and send one high-speed transmission utilizing the entire bandwidth.

burster A mechanical device that separates continuous paper forms into cut sheets. A burster can be attached to the end of a collator, which separates multipart forms into single parts.

bus A common channel, or pathway, between hardware devices either internally between components in a computer, or externally between stations in a communications network.

When bus architecture is used in a computer, the processor(s), memory banks and peripheral control units are all interconnected through the bus. The bus is divided into two channels, one to select where data is located (address bus), and the other to transfer the data (data bus). When you plug in a board into one of the expansion slots in your personal computer, you're plugging into the bus.

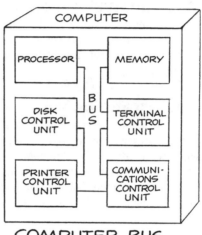

COMPUTER BUS

When bus architecture is used in a network, all terminals and computers are connected to a common channel that is made of twisted wire pairs, coaxial cable or optical fibers.

bus bridge A device that connects two similar, or dissimilar, busses together, such as two VMEbuses or a VMEbus and a Futurebus. This is not the same as a communications bridge, which connects two similar networks together.

bus extender

(1) A board that pushes a printed circuit board out of the way of surrounding boards for testing purposes. It plugs into an expansion slot, and the expansion board plugs into the bus extender.

(2) A device that extends the length of a communications channel.

(3) A device that increases the number of available expansion slots. It is an individual housing of expansion slots cabled to a board that plugs into a free slot in the original bus. It may contain its own power supply to ensure reliable operation.

bus mastering A bus design that allows add-in boards to process independently of the CPU and to be able to access the computer's memory and peripherals on their own.

bus mouse A mouse that plugs into a printed circuit board that is inserted into the computer's bus. Contrast with *serial mouse*. A bus mouse takes up one expansion slot, whereas the serial mouse takes up one serial port. The choice depends on how many devices must be connected to each type of socket.

business analyst An individual who analyzes the operations of a department or functional unit with the purpose of developing a general systems solution to the problem that may or may not require automation. The business analyst can provide valuable insights into an operation for an information systems analyst.

business graphics Numeric data represented in graphic form. While line graphs, bar charts and pie charts are the common forms of business graphics, there are many additional graphic representations available. Although some people think effectively in numbers, most people think in pictures. By transforming numerical data into graphic form, patterns of business activity can be viewed and related more quickly. Business graphics can be superimposed revealing relationships and irregularities.

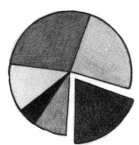

PIE CHART

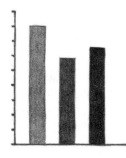

BAR CHART

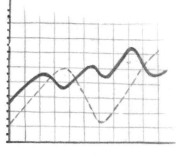

GRAPH

business information system See *information system*.

business machine Any office machine, such as a typewriter or calculator, that is used in clerical and accounting functions. The term has traditionally excluded computers and terminals.

Butterfly Switch A parallel processing topology from BBN Advanced Computers Inc., that mimics a crossbar and provides high-speed switching of data between nodes. It can also be used to create a hypercube topology.

button A physical button on a device, such as a mouse, or a simulated button on screen (icon) that is "pushed" by moving the cursor onto it and clicking the mouse.

by modem The use of a modem. Typically refers to the transmission of data over the telephone system.

bypass In communications, to go around the local telephone company for transmission of voice and data signals. Bypass is accomplished by using satellite and microwave systems, for example.

byte The common unit of computer storage from personal computers to mainframes. It is made up of eight binary digits (bits). A ninth bit may be added as a parity bit for error checking.

A byte holds the equivalent of a single character, such as the letter A, a dollar sign or decimal point. With regard to numbers, a byte can hold a single digit from 0 to 9 (decimal), two numeric digits (packed decimal) or a number from 0 to 255 (binary numbers).

Byte Specifications

The primary specifications of hardware are rated in bytes; for example, a 40-megabyte (40M or 40MB) disk holds 40 million characters of instructions and data. A one-megabyte (1M or 1MB) memory allows one million characters of instructions and data to be stored internally for processing.

With database files and word processing documents, the size of the file is slightly larger than the actual number of characters stored in it. Word processing files contain embedded codes for layout settings (margins, tabs, boldface); therefore, a 100,000-byte document implies slightly less than 100,000 characters of text (approx. 30 pages). Database files contain codes that describe the structure of the records, thus, a 100,000-byte database file holds somewhat less than 100,000 characters of data.

Unlike data and text, a 100,000-byte graphics file is not indicative of the size or nature of the image contained in it. There are various graphics standards used, and the higher the quality of the image, the more bytes are needed to represent it. A low-resolution graphics file can take as little as 8,000 bytes, while an ultra-high resolution file can take 4 million bytes, even though both images may appear on the same physical screen size.

byte addressable A computer that can address each byte of memory independently of the others. Contrast with *word addressable*.

byte-oriented protocol A communications protocol which uses control codes that are made up of full bytes. The bisynchronous protocols used by IBM and other vendors are examples. Contrast with *bit-oriented protocol*.

B5000 A family of medium to large-scale mainframes from Burroughs Corporation that was introduced in 1961 and took on many successive designations such as the B5500, B5900 and B7900. Burroughs mainframes gained a reputation early on for their advanced virtual memory capabilities. This line is now called the A Series by Unisys.

C A high-level programming language developed at Bell Labs that is able to manipulate the computer at a low level like assembly language. During the last half of the 1980s, C has become the language of choice for developing commercial software.

C can be compiled into machine languages for almost all computers. For example, UNIX is written in C and runs in a wide variety of micros, minis and mainframes.

C is programmed as a series of functions that call each other for processing. Even the body of the program is a function named "main." Functions are very flexible, allowing programmers to choose from the standard library that comes with the compiler, to use third party functions from other C suppliers, or to develop their own.

Compared to other high-level programming languages, C appears complicated. Its intricate appearance is due to its extreme flexibility.

The following C example converts fahrenheit to centigrade:

```
main() {
float fahr;
printf("Enter fahrenheit ");
scanf("%f", &fahr);
printf("\nCentigrade is %f", (fahr-32)*5/9);
}
```

C++ An object-oriented version of C created by Bjarne Stroustrup that is becoming very popular. C++ combines traditional C programming with object-oriented capability.

C: drive The common designation for the hard disk in Microsoft DOS and OS/2 operating systems.

cable A flexible metal or glass wire, or group of wires. All cables used in electronics are insulated with a material such as plastic or rubber.

cable matcher Same as *gender changer*.

cabletext A videotex service that uses coaxial cable. See *videotex*.

cache Pronounced "cash." A reserved section of memory used to improve performance. A disk cache is a reserved section of normal memory or additional memory on the disk controller board. When the disk is read, a large block of data is copied into the cache. If subsequent requests for data can be satisfied in the cache, a slower disk access is not required. If the cache is used for writing, data is queued up in memory and written to the disk in larger blocks.

Memory caches are high-speed memory banks between memory and the CPU. Blocks of instructions and data are copied into the cache and instruction execution and data updating are performed in the higher-speed memory.

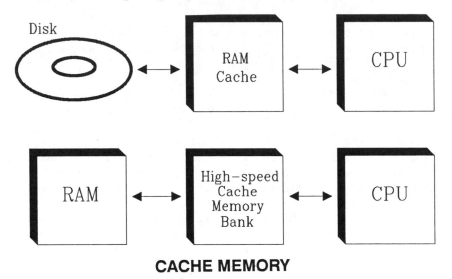

CACHE MEMORY

caching controller A disk controller with a built-in cache.

CAD (Computer-Aided Design) Using computers to design products. CAD systems are specialized workstations or high-performance personal computers that employ CAD software and input devices such as graphic tablets and scanners. CAD output is the input to computer-aided manufacturing (CAM) systems for integrating design and fabrication (CAD/CAM).

CAD software is available for generic use or for specialized uses, such as architectural, electrical and mechanical design. CAD software may also be highly specialized for creating products such as printed circuits and integrated circuits.

CAD systems are often turnkey systems which are put together by vendors that may develop or integrate software into standard or optimized hardware. Except in a few cases, CAD systems rely extensively on graphics. See *graphics, CADD,* and *CAE.*

CADAM A full-featured CAD application for mainframes from IBM, which includes 3-D capability, solid modeling and numerical control. Originally developed by Lockheed for internal use, it was distributed by IBM starting in the late 1970s . In 1989, IBM purchased the Lockheed subsidiary, CADAM, Inc.

CAD/CAM (Computer-Aided Design/Computer-Aided Manufacturing) The integration of computer-aided design with computer controlled manufacturing. It implies that the products designed in the CAD system are direct input into the CAM system. For example, after a machine part is designed in CAD, its electronic image is transferred to a numerical control programming language, which generates the instructions to control the machine that makes the part.

CADD (Computer-Aided Design and Drafting) CAD systems with additional features for drafting, such as dimensioning and text entry.

CADKEY An integrated 2-D drafting and 3-D design system for PCs from CADKEY, Inc. In addition to the ability to design machine-accurate geometric models, it offers the user a total design solution with solids creation and built-in DXF and IGES translators. Two hundred manufacturing systems link to CADKEY through its advanced CADL programming language.

CAE
(1) (Computer-Aided Engineering) Software that analyzes designs which have been created in the computer or that have been created elsewhere and entered into the computer. Different kinds of engineering analyses can be performed, such as structural analysis and electronic circuit analysis.

(2) (Common Application Environment) The software development platform that is specified by X/Open.

CAI
(1) (Computer-Assisted Instruction) An earlier term for CBT.

(2) (Computer Associates International) See *Computer Associates*.

CAL
(1) (Computer-Assisted Learning) Same as CBT.

(2) (Conversational Algebraic Langauge) A timesharing language from by the University of California.

calculator A machine that provides arithmetic capabilities. It accepts input from a keypad and displays results on a readout and/or paper tape. Unlike a computer, a calculator cannot handle alphabetic data and generally provides limited output.

call
(1) In programming, a statement that references an independent subroutine or program. The call is turned into a branch instruction by the assembler, compiler or interpreter. The routine that is called is responsible for returning to the calling program after it has finished processing.

(2) In communications, the action taken by the transmitting station to establish a connection with the receiving station in a dial-up network.

call by reference In programming, a call to a subroutine that passes addresses of the parameters used in the subroutine.

call by value In programming, a call to a subroutine that passes the actual data of the parameters used in the subroutine.

call distributor A PBX feature that routes incoming calls to the next available agent or operator.

called routine In programming, a program subroutine that performs a task and is accessed by a call or branch instruction in the program.

calling program In programming, a program that initiates a call to another program.

calling routine In programming, a program subroutine that initiates a call to another program routine.

CAM

(1) (Computer-Aided Manufacturing) An extensive category of automated manufacturing systems and techniques, including numerical control, process control, robotics and materials requirements planning (MRP).

(2) (Content Addressable Memory) Same as *associative storage*.

candela A unit of measurement of the intensity of light. An ordinary wax candle generates one candela. See *lumens*.

canned program A software package that provides a fixed solution to a problem. Canned programs for business applications should be analyzed carefully as they that usually cannot be changed very much, if at all.

canned routine A program subroutine that performs a specific processing task.

canonical synthesis The process of designing a model of a database without redundant data items. A canonical model, or schema, is independent of the hardware and software that will process the data.

capacitor An electronic component that holds a charge. Capacitors are created in varying sizes for use in electronic power supplies to the tiny cells built into dynamic RAM chips.

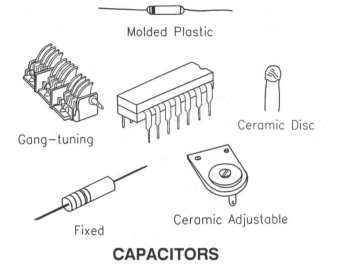

Molded Plastic

Gang–tuning

Ceramic Disc

Fixed

Ceramic Adjustable

CAPACITORS

capstan On magnetic tape drives, a motorized cylinder that traps the tape against a free-wheeling roller and moves it at a regulated speed.

CAR (Computer-Assisted Retrieval) Systems that use the computer to keep track of text documents or records stored on paper or on microform. The computer is used to derive the location of a requested item, which must be manually retrieved from a shelf, bin, or microform.

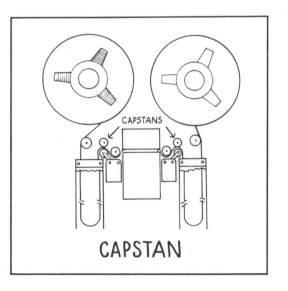

CAPSTANS

CAPSTAN

card See *printed circuit board, magnetic card, punched card* and *HyperCard*.

card cage A cabinet or metal frame that holds printed circuit cards.

card column A vertical column that is used to represent a single character of data by the combination of holes punched in it. The common IBM punched card contains 80 card columns.

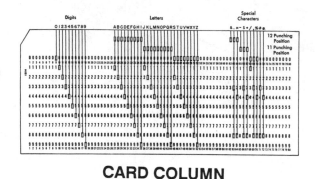

CARD COLUMN

(Courtesy IBM Corporation)

card image An exact representation of punched cards on magnetic tape or disk in which each hole in the punched card is represented by a bit in the magnetic medium.

card punch

(1) A peripheral device connected to the computer that punches holes into cards at rates of approximately 100 to 300 cards per minute.

(2) Another term for keypunch machine.

card reader

(1) A peripheral device that reads the magnetic stripes on the back of a credit card.

(2) A peripheral device that reads punched cards at approx. 500 to 2,000 cards per minute. The code is detected by light patterns streaming through the holes in the card.

cardinal number A number that states how much or how many. Contrast with *ordinal number*. If "record 43 has 7 fields," 43 is ordinal; 7 is cardinal.

caret The ^ symbol over the 6 key on a keyboard. It is used to represent a decimal point in a number as well as the control key. For example, ^Y means hold control down and press Y.

carriage The part of a printer or typewriter that controls the feeding of paper forms. In a non-Selectric typewriter, the carriage is the part that moves from side to side.

carriage return See *return key*.

carrier An alternating current that vibrates at a fixed frequency, used to establish a boundary, or envelope, in which a signal is transmitted. Carriers are commonly used in radio transmission (AM, FM, TV, microwave, satellite, etc.) in order to differentiate transmitting stations. For example, an FM station's channel number is actually its carrier frequency. The FM station merges (modulates) its audio broadcast (data signal) onto its carrier and transmits the combined signal over the airwaves. At the receiving end, the FM tuner latches onto the carrier frequency, filters out the audio signal, amplifies it and sends it to the speaker.

Carriers are used to transmit several signals simultaneously through a wire or cable. For example, several voice, data and/or video signals can travel over the same line as long as each one resides within its own carrier vibrating at a different frequency.

carrier based A transmission system that generates a fixed frequency, or carrier, to contain the data being transmitted.

carrier frequency A unique frequency that is used to "carry" data within its boundaries. The carrier frequency is measured in cycles per second, or Hertz. See *FDM*.

Carterfone decision The decree from the FCC in 1968 that permitted users to connect their own telephone equipment to the public telephone system for the first time.

cartridge A self-contained, removable storage module that contains disks, magnetic tape or memory chips. Cartridges are inserted into slots in the drive, printer or computer. See *font cartridge*.

TAPE CARTRIDGE

CAS (Communications Application Specification) A communications protocol from Intel for a combination fax and modem board that allows personal computer users to exchange data more easily with fax machines. Introduced in 1988, Intel provides both the boards and the chips.

CASE (Computer Aided Software Engineering or Computer Aided Systems Engineering) Software that is used in any and all phases of developing an information system, including analysis, design and programming. For example, data dictionaries and diagramming tools aid in the analysis and design phases, while application generators speed up the programming phase.

CASE tools provide automated methods for designing and documenting traditional structured programming techniques. The ultimate goal of CASE is to provide a language for describing the overall system that is sufficient to generate all the necessary programs.

case sensitive The distinguishing of lower case letters from upper case letters. If a language is case sensitive, "abc" will be treated differently than "ABC."

case statement In programming, a variation of the if-then-else statement that is used when several ifs are required in a row. The following example in C tests a variable called KEY1 and performs functions based on the results.

```
switch (key1)    {
   case '+':  add();  break;
   case '-':  subtract();  break;
   case '*':  multiply();  break;
   case '/':  divide();  break;
                 }
```

cash memory See *cache memory*.

cassette A self-contained, removable storage module that contains a supply reel of magnetic tape and a takeup reel.

TAPE CASSETTE

casting In programming, the conversion of one data type into another.

catalog A directory of disk files or a directory of files for a specific application. It may also refer to any map, list or directory of storage space used by the computer.

cathode In electronics, a device that emits electrons. Electrons flow from the negatively charged cathode to the positively charged *anode*.

cathode ray tube See CRT.

CATV (Community Antenna TV) The original name for cable TV, which used a single antenna at the highest location in the community. CATV also refers to the cable TV connector on a TV or VCR.

CAV (Constant Angular Velocity) A disk technique that spins the disk at a constant rate of speed. The number of bits in each track is the same, but the physical density of bits varies in each track, because the inner tracks have smaller circumferences than the outer tracks and the data transfer rate is constant. Contrast with CLV.

CB (Citizen's Band) A frequency band for radio transmission in the 27 MHz range reserved for public use without a license.

CBEMA (Computer and Business Equipment Manufacturers Association) A membership organization, founded in 1916, composed of computer vendors and business equipment manufacturers and suppliers. With over 40 members, CBEMA is concerned with the development of standards for data processing and business equipment both in the U.S. and abroad. For more information, contact CBEMA, 311 First Street, N.W., Washington, DC 20001, (202) 737-8888.

CBR (Computer-Based Reference) Reference materials accessible by computer in order to help people do their jobs quicker, for example, this Glossary on disk!

CBT (Computer-Based Training) Using the computer for training and instruction. CBT programs are called *courseware* and provide interactive training sessions for all disciplines. CBT uses graphics extensively, as well as CD ROM and videodisc.

CBT courseware is developed with authoring languages, such as Adroit, PILOT and Demo II, which allow for the creation of interactive sessions.

CBX (Computerized Branch eXchange) Same as PBX.

CCD (Charge Coupled Device) An electronic memory made of a special type of MOS transistor that can store patterns of charges in a sequential fashion. CCDs are used in TV and optical scanning devices since they can be charged by light as well as by electricity.

CCIA (Computer and Communications Industry Association) A membership organization composed of mainframe, peripheral and data communications vendors, software houses, service bureaus, leasing companies and equipment repair organizations. With over 60 members, CCIA represents interests of members in domestic and foreign trade. Working with the NIST, it keeps members advised of regulatory policy. For more information, contact CCIA, 666 11th Street, N.W., Washington, DC 20001, (202) 783-0070.

CCIS (Common Channel Interoffice Signaling) A digital communications technique that transmits voice and control signals over separate channels. The separate channels are provided by time division multiplexing the signals over the same line.

CCITT (Consultative Committee for International Telephony and Telegraphy) An international organization for communications standards. It is one of four organs of the International Telecommunications Union, founded in 1865, headquartered in Geneva and comprised of over 150 member countries.

CCP (Certificate in Computer Programming) An award for successful completion of an examination in computer programming, offered by the Institute of Certification of Computer Professionals.

CD (Compact Disc) An audio disc that contains up to 72 minutes of hi-fi stereo sound. A CD, 4 3/4" in diameter, is like a miniature phonograph record, except that only one side of the disc contains recorded material. A CD is a direct access device, and the individual selections can be played back in any sequence. Unlike phonograph records in which the disc platter contains "carved sound," the CD is recorded in digital form as a series of tiny pits that are covered with a clear, protective plastic layer. Instead of a needle vibrating in the grooves, a laser in the CD player shines light onto the pits and picks up the reflections as binary code.

Sound is converted into digital code by sampling the sound waves 44,056 times per second and converting each sample into a 16-bit number. It requires almost a million and a half bits of storage for each second of stereo hi-fi sound. The reason digital sound is so clear is that the numbers are turned into sound electronically. There's no tape hiss or needle pops and clicks to contend with. In addition, the CD can handle a wider range of volume (dynamic range), providing more realism. A soft whisper can be interrupted by a loud cannon blast. If a phonograph were pushed that far, the needle would jump out of the groove.

Other forms of CDs (CD ROM, CD ROM XA, CD-I and DVI) all stem from the audio CD. Introduced in the U.S. in 1983, sales of CDs and CD players exceeded sales of LPs and turntables in 1986.

CD audio Same as CD and DAD.

CD-I (Compact Disc-Interactive) A compact disc format that holds data, audio, still video pictures and animated graphics. CD-I provides up to 144 minutes of CD-quality stereo sound, up to 9.5 hours of AM-radio-quality stereo or up to 19 hours of single channel (monophonic) audio.

Developed by Philips and Sony, CD-I is designed for home and business use with CD-I players connected to TVs and personal computers starting in the early 1990s. CD-I discs will feature interactive games and education as well as reference works.

CD-I includes an operating system standard as well as proprietary hardware methods for compressing the data further in order to display video images. CD-I discs require a CD-I player and will not play on a CD ROM player. See *CD, CD ROM, DVI.*

CD ROM

(Compact Disc Read Only Memory) A compact disc format that is used to hold text, graphics and hi-fi stereo sound. The disc is almost the same as the music CD, but uses different tracks for data. The music CD player cannot play CD ROM discs, but CD ROM players may be able to play CD discs and have jacks for connection to an amplifier and/or

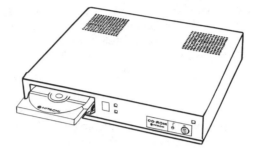

CD ROM

A CD ROM drive may look very similar to a compact disc (CD) player.

headphones. A CD ROM player is cabled to and controlled by a card that is plugged into one of the computer's expansion slots.

CD ROMs hold in excess of 600MB of data, which is equivalent to about 250,000 pages of text or 20,000 medium-resolution images. CD ROMs are becoming invaluable for large catalogs and reference works.

Audio and data reside on separate tracks and cannot be heard and viewed together. With an enhanced standard, called *CD ROM XA*, various grades of lower-fidelity audio can be heard simultaneously while viewing data. See *CD ROM XA, CDI* and *DVI.*

CD ROM Extensions

The software required to use a CD ROM player on a PC running DOS. It is made up of two software modules, (1) a driver that is specialized for the CD player by its manufacturer and, (2) a RAM resident program (MSCDEX.EXE) supplied by Microsoft, which is executed when the computer is turned on. The CD ROM Extensions usually come with the CD ROM player.

CD ROM XA

(Compact Disc Read Only Memory eXtended Architecture) An extension of the CD ROM standard that allows for the inclusion of various grades of medium to low-fidelity audio to be played concurrently while viewing data.

Announced by Philips, Sony and Microsoft in August 1988, CD ROM XA allows for data (text and pictures) to be viewed and narrated at the same time. With up to 9.5 hours of AM-broadcast-quality stereo or up to 19 hours of single channel (monophonic) audio, CD ROM XA can be also be used for language training. It also functions as a bridge between CD ROM and CD-I, since CD ROM XA discs will play on a CD-I player. CD ROM XA uses a standard CD ROM player, but requires a CD ROM XA controller card in the personal computer. See *CD-I* and *DVI*.

CDC See *Control Data*.

cdev
(Control Panel DEVice) Customizable settings in the Macintosh Control Panel that pertain to a particular program or device. Cdevs for the mouse, keyboard and startup disk, among others, come with the Mac. Others are provided with software packages and utilities.

CDP
(Certificate in Data Processing) An award for the successful completion of an examination in hardware, software, systems analysis, programming, management and accounting, offered by the Institute of Certification of Computer Professionals.

Ceefax A teletext service of the British Broadcasting Corporation.

cell
(1) An elementary unit of storage for data (bit) or power (battery).

(2) In a spreadsheet, the intersection of a row and column.

centimeter A unit of measurement that is 1/100th of a meter or approximately 4/10ths of an inch (0.39 inch).

central office A telephone switching facility that interconnects subscribers' telephone lines to each other and to intra and intercity trunk lines.

central processing unit See *CPU*.

central processor Same as *CPU*.

centralized processing Processing performed in one or more computers in a single, centralized location. It implies that all terminals throughout the organization are connected to the computers in the datacenter. Contrast with *distributed processing* and *decentralized processing*.

CENTREX PBX services provided to an organization by a local telephone company. The switching is done in the telephone company's central office rather than on the customer's premises.

Centronics interface A standard 36-pin parallel interface for connecting printers and other devices to a computer. It defines the plug, socket and signals that are used in the transmission.

This de facto standard was developed by Centronics Corporation, maker of the first commercially successful dot matrix printers. The Centronics printer was introduced in 1970, and the company was bought by Genicom Corporation in 1987.

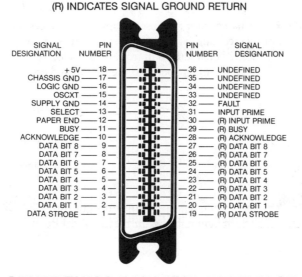

(R) INDICATES SIGNAL GROUND RETURN

SIGNAL DESIGNATION	PIN NUMBER		PIN NUMBER	SIGNAL DESIGNATION
+ 5V	18		36	UNDEFINED
CHASSIS GND	17		35	UNDEFINED
LOGIC GND	16		34	UNDEFINED
OSCXT	15		33	UNDEFINED
SUPPLY GND	14		32	FAULT
SELECT	13		31	INPUT PRIME
PAPER END	12		30	(R) INPUT PRIME
BUSY	11		29	(R) BUSY
ACKNOWLEDGE	10		28	(R) ACKNOWLEDGE
DATA BIT 8	9		27	(R) DATA BIT 8
DATA BIT 7	8		26	(R) DATA BIT 7
DATA BIT 6	7		25	(R) DATA BIT 6
DATA BIT 5	6		24	(R) DATA BIT 5
DATA BIT 4	5		23	(R) DATA BIT 4
DATA BIT 3	4		22	(R) DATA BIT 3
DATA BIT 2	3		21	(R) DATA BIT 2
DATA BIT 1	2		20	(R) DATA BIT 1
DATA STROBE	1		19	(R) DATA STROBE

CENTRONICS PARALLEL INTERFACE

(Courtesy Black Box Corporation)

CEO (Comprehensive Electronic Office) Office software from Data General Corporation that was introduced in 1981. It includes word processing, electronic mail, spreadsheets, business graphics and desktop accessories, such as a calendar and phone list.

CGA (Color/Graphics Adapter) A video display standard from IBM that provides low-resolution text and graphics. It was the first graphics standard for the IBM PC and has been superseded by EGA and VGA. CGA requires a digital RGB Color Display monitor. See PC *display modes*.

CGI (Computer Graphics Interface) A standard format for writing graphics drivers. A graphics driver is the set of instructions that activates a graphics device, such as a screen, printer or plotter. The CGI standard also includes GDI and VDI standards.

CGM (Computer Graphics Metafile) A standard format for interchanging graphics images. CGM stores images primarily in vector graphics, but also provides a raster format. Earlier GDM and VDM formats have been merged into the CGM standard.

chad A piece of paper that is punched out on a punched card, paper tape or on the borders of continuous forms. A chadded form is when the holes are cut completely through. A chadless form is when the chads are still attached to one edge of the hole.

chain printer A line printer that uses character typefaces linked together in a chain as its printing mechanism. The chain spins horizontally around a set of hammers. When the desired character is in front of the selected print position, the corresponding hammer hits the paper into the ribbon and onto the character in the chain.

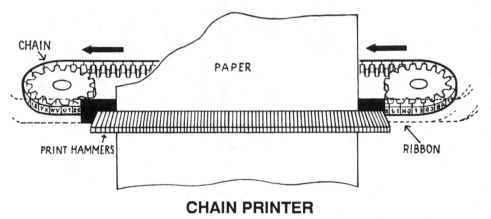

CHAIN PRINTER

chained list A group of items in which each item contains the location of the next item in sequence.

chaining The linking of items or records to form a chain. Each link in the chain points to the next item.

change file A file of transactions that is used to update a master file.

channel
(1) A high-speed metal or optical fiber pathway between the computer and the control units of the peripheral devices. Channels imply independent transmission paths in which multiple channels can transfer data concurrently with each other and with other processing. In a personal computer, the bus serves as a common, shared channel.

(2) In communications, any pathway between two computers or between a terminal and a computer. It may refer to the physical medium, such as coaxial cable, or to a specific carrier frequency (subchannel) within a larger channel or wireless medium.

channel bank A multiplexor that merges several low-speed voice or data lines into one high-speed (typically T1) line and vice versa.

channel program A set of instructions that is executed by a high-speed peripheral channel. The instruction in the program that initiates the input/output operation indicates where the channel program resides. The channel executes the channel program independently, allowing other operations to concurrently take place in the computer.

character A single alphabetic letter, numeric digit, or special symbol such as a decimal point or comma. A character is equivalent to a byte; for example, 50,000 characters take up 50,000 bytes.

character based Same as *text based*.

character cell A matrix of dots that is used to form a single character on a display screen or printer. For example, an 8x16 character cell is made up of 16 horizontal rows each containing eight dots. Character cells are displayed and printed contiguously; therefore the design of each letter, digit or special symbol within the cell must include surrounding blank space.

character code A digital code applied to data for input into the computer, primarily ASCII and EBCDIC. Same as *data code*.

character data Alphanumeric data or text. Contrast with *numeric data*.

character field A data field that holds alphanumeric characters. Contrast with *numeric field*.

character generator
(1) The circuitry that converts data characters into dot patterns for a display screen.

(2) A device which creates text characters that are superimposed onto video frames.

character graphics A set of special symbols that are strung together just like letters of the alphabet to create graphics. For example, the illustration on the following page depicts character graphics that are used to print rules and lines, bar charts and other simple pictures.

character mode Same as *text mode*.

character-oriented protocol See *byte-oriented protocol*.

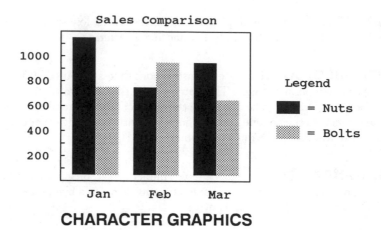

CHARACTER GRAPHICS

character printer A printer that prints one character at a time, such as a daisy wheel or dot matrix printer. See *printer*.

CHARACTER PRINTER

character recognition The ability of a machine to recognize printed text. See *OCR* and *MICR*.

character set A group of unique symbols and codes. For example, the ASCII character set contains 128 characters numbered from 0 to 127. The English character set is 26 symbols from A to Z.

character string A group of alphanumeric characters. Contrast with *numeric data*.

character terminal A display screen without graphics capability.

characteristic In logarithms and floating point, the number that indicates where the decimal point is placed.

charge coupled device See CCD.

CHARGECARD A hardware-controlled memory manager for 286 PCs from ALL Computers Inc., that turns extended memory into EMS 4.0 memory and allows unused space in the 640-1024K region to be used for drivers and TSRs. To install it, the 286 chip is removed and plugged into the CHARGECARD. The CHARGECARD is plugged back into the 286 socket.

check bits The bits that are used for error checking purposes. The bits hold a number which has been calculated from a segment of data that has been transmitted or stored. See *parity checking, check sum* and CRC.

check digit A digit that is used to ensure that account numbers are correctly entered into the computer. Check digits are added to account numbers before the numbers are actually assigned and used. Using a special formula, the check digit is calculated from the original account number and is added to and maintained as part of the number at all times, usually as the last digit of the number.

When the account number is keyed into the computer, a validation routine in the data entry program recalculates the check digit and compares it to the check digit entered. If the account number is erroneous or the digits were transposed when entered, the calculated check digit will not be equal to the check digit that was entered.

check sum A total numeric value of a block of data that is used for error checking purposes. Both numeric and alphabetic fields can be used in calculating a check sum, since the binary content of the data can be added.

Just as a check digit tests the accuracy of a single number, a check sum serves to test an entire set of data that has been transmitted or stored. Check sums can detect single bit errors and some multiple bit errors.

checkpoint/restart A method of recovering from a system failure. A checkpoint is a copy of the computer's memory that is periodically saved on disk along with the current register settings (last instruction executed, etc.). In the event of a power failure, or hardware or software failure, the last checkpoint serves as a recovery point.

When the problem has been fixed, the restart program copies the last checkpoint into memory, resets all the hardware registers and starts the computer from that point. Any transactions in memory after the last checkpoint was taken until the power failure occurred will still be lost.

child In database management, the data that is dependent on its parent. See *parent-child*.

Chinese binary An arrangment of binary digits in a vertical column on a punched card in which each punched hole represents one bit of a number.

chip An integrated circuit. Chips are approximately 1/16th to 1/2 inch square and about 1/30th of an inch thick. They hold from a few dozen to several million electronic components (transistors, resistors, etc.). The terms *chip*, *integrated circuit* and *microelectronic* are synonymous.

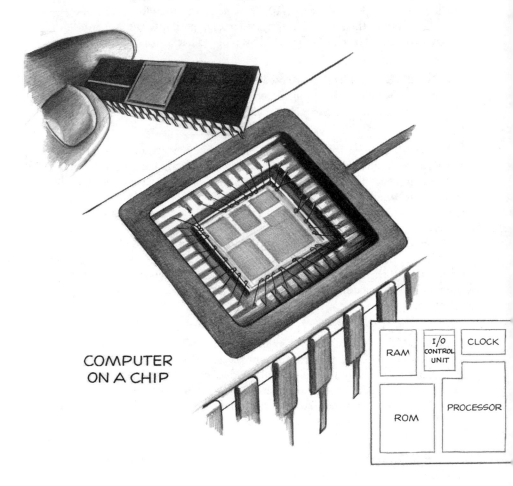

COMPUTER
ON A CHIP

| RAM | I/O CONTROL UNIT | CLOCK |
| ROM | | PROCESSOR |

Types of Chips by Function

LOGIC CHIP

A single chip can perform some or all of the functions of a processor. A microprocessor is an entire processor on a single chip. Desktop and portable computers use one or more microprocessors while larger computers may employ several types of microprocessors as well as hundreds or thousands of specialized logic chips.

MEMORY CHIP

Random access memory (RAM) chips contain from a couple of hundred thousand to several million storage cells (bits). RAM chips are the computer's internal working storage and require constant power to keep their bits charged.

Firmware chips, such as ROMs, PROMs, EPROMs, and EEPROMs are permanent memory chips that hold their content without power.

COMPUTER ON A CHIP
A single chip can contain the processor, RAM, ROM, an input/output control unit, and a timing clock. A computer on a chip is used in myriads of consumer and industrial products.

ANALOG/DIGITAL CONVERTER
A single chip can perform the conversion between analog and digital signals, for example, a codec in a telephone.

SPECIAL PURPOSE CHIP
Chips used for low-cost, consumer items, such as digital watches and calculators, may be designed from the ground up to obtain the most economical product. Chips for higher-cost products, such as video game computers, may be designed from scratch as well. Today, application specific integrated circuits (ASIC chips) can be quickly created for any special purpose.

LOGIC ARRAY AND GATE ARRAY
These types of chips contain logic gates which have not been tied together. A final set of steps applies the top metal layer onto the chip stringing the logic gates together into the pattern required by the customer. This method eliminates much of the design and fabrication time for producing a chip.

BIT SLICE PROCESSOR
Bit slice chips contain elementary electronic circuits that serve as building blocks for the computer architect. They are used to custom-build a processor for specialized purposes.

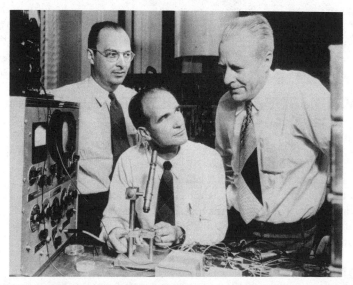

DRS. BARDEEN, SHOCKLEY & BRATTAIN (1947)
(Courtesy AT&T)

REVOLUTION

In late 1947, the semiconductor industry was born at AT&T's Bell Laboratories with the invention of the *transistor* by John Bardeen, Walter Brattain and William Schockley. The transistor, fabricated from solid materials that could change their electrical conductivity, would eventually replace all the bulky, hot, glass vacuum tubes used as electronic amplifiers in radio and television and used as on/off switches in computers. By the late 1950s, the giant first-generation computers were giving way to smaller, faster and more reliable transistorized machines.

EVOLUTION

The original transistors were discrete components; that is, each one was a separate unit soldered onto a printed circuit board to interconnect with other transistors, resistors and diodes. Since hundreds of transistors were fabricated on one round silicon wafer and cut apart only to be reconnected again, the idea of building them in the final pattern to begin with was an evolutionary one. In the late 1950s, Jack Kilby of TI and Robert Noyce of Fairchild Semiconductor created the *integrated circuit*, a set of interconnected transistors and resistors on a single chip.

Since then, the number of transistors that have been microminiaturized onto a single chip has increased exponentially, from only a handful in the early 1960s to millions by the late 1980s. Today, the space occupied by a million transistors takes up no more room than the first transistor.

**VACUUM TUBE TO TRANSISTOR
TO INTEGRATED CIRCUIT**

(Courtesy AT&T)

A byproduct of miniaturization is speed. The shorter the distance a pulse has to travel, the faster it gets there. The smaller the components making up the transistor, the faster the transistor switches. Switch times of transistors are measured in billionths and trillionths of a second (nanoseconds and picoseconds). And if that seems fast, a Josephson junction superconductor transistor has been able to switch in 50 quadrillionths of a second (femtoseconds).

LOGIC AND MEMORY

In first and second-generation computers, a computer's internal storage, or main memory, was made of such materials as tubes filled with liquid mercury, magnetic drums and magnetic cores. As integrated circuits began to flourish in the 1960s, breakthroughs in design allowed memories to also be made of semiconductor materials. Thus, logic circuits, the "brains" of the computer, and memory circuits, its internal workspace, were moving along the same path of miniaturization. By the end of the 1970s, it was possible to put a processor, working memory (RAM), permanent memory (ROM), a control unit for handling input and output and a

REVIEWING THE "PLUMBING"

(Courtesy Elxsi Corporation)

timing clock on the same chip. Within 25 years, the transistor on a chip grew into the computer on a chip. When the awesome UNIVAC I was introduced in 1951, you could literally walk into it. Who would have believed that an equivalent amount of electronics would later be built into a child's stuffed bear?

MORE EVOLUTION

Just as integrated circuits eliminated cutting apart the transistors only to be reconnected again, eventually *wafer scale integration* will eliminate cutting apart whole chips only to be reconnected again. In time, instead of adding more circuits across the surface, the circuits will be built in overlapping layers. Within the next 10 to 15 years, it is conceivable that the electronics in today's multi-million-dollar supercomputer can be built within a cube one inch square!

The Making of a Chip

Computer circuits are pathways carrying electrical pulses from one point to another. The pulses flow through on/off switches, called *transistors*, which open or close when electrically activated. The current flowing through one switch effects the opening or closing of another and so on. Small clusters of transistors form *logic gates*, which are the building blocks behind all this magic, and a specific combination of logic gates make up a circuit.

FROM LOGIC TO PLUMBING

Today, the majority of circuits being used have already been designed and reside in circuit libraries in a computer. A computer designer merely has to pick and choose ready-made modules (standard cells) from a menu. But they all had to be invented at one point, and new circuits still have to go through an elaborate process to convert logical patterns on paper into an equivalent maze of plumbing on the chip.

Today, computers help make computers. The logical design is entered into the computer and converted into transistors, diodes and resistors. Then the combination of electronic components is turned into a plumber's nightmare that is displayed for human inspection. After corrections have been made, the completed circuits are transferred to specialized machinery that create lithographic plates made out of glass, called *photomasks*. The photomasks are the actual size of the wafer and contain as many copies of the design of the chip as will fit on the wafer. The transistors are built by creating subterranean layers in the silicon, and a different photomask is created to isolate each layer to be worked on. With each layer, the same part of every transistor on every chip is constructed at the same time.

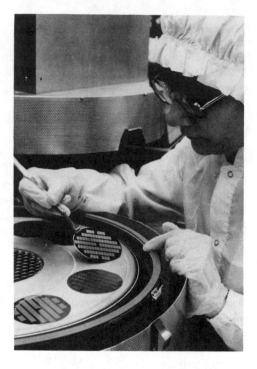

INSPECTING WAFERS
(Courtesy Hewlett-Packard Company)

CHIPS ARE JUST ROCKS
The base material of a chip is usually silicon, although materials such as sapphire and gallium arsenide are also used. Silicon is found in an unpure state in quartz rocks and is purified in a molten state. It is then chemically combined (doped) with other materials to alter its electrical properties. The result is an ingot of silicon crystal from three to five inches in diameter that is either positively charged (p-type) or negatively charged (n-type). *Wafers*, about 1/30th of an inch thick, are cut from this "crystal salami."

THE TEST FLOOR
(Courtesy VLSI Technologies, Inc.)

BUILDING THE LAYERS
Circuit building starts out by adhering a layer of

insulation (silicon dioxide) on the wafer's surface. The insulation is coated with film and exposed to light through the first photomask, thus hardening the film and insulation below it. The unhardened areas are etched away exposing the silicon base below. By shooting a gas under heat and pressure into the exposed silicon (diffusion), a sublayer with different electrical properties is created beneath the surface.

Through multiple stages of masking, etching, and diffusion, the sublayers on the chip are created. The final stage lays the top metal layer (usually aluminum), which interconnects the transistors to each other and to the outside world.

Each chip is tested on the wafer, and bad chips are marked for elimination. The chips are sliced out of the wafer, and the good ones are placed into a spiderlike package, called a *DIP* (dual in-line package). The chip is connected to the DIP with tiny wires, then sealed and tested as a completed unit. Depending on the complexity of the chip, the number of chips that make it through to the end can be less than the number that fail.

The chip-making business is an extremely precise one. Many operations are performed in a "clean room," since particles in the air could mix with the microscopic mixtures being created and easily render a chip or wafer worthless.

THE FUTURE
In order to miniaturize the elements of a transistor still further, the photomasks have to be made with x-rays or other beams which are narrower than light. Eventually, the circuit patterns will be etched directly onto the chip eliminating the entire photographic masking process.

During the 1990s, it will be commonplace to build several million transistors on a single chip. However, when wafer scale integration becomes a reality, a single wafer could hold 100 megabytes of memory, and a quantum reduction in the cost of circuitry would occur. When superconductor transistors become a reality, there will be a gigantic leap in performance. Should both technologies become production realities at the same time, watch out!

HIGH-TECH (CIRCA 1930)
(Courtesy The MIT Museum)
This "futuristic" control room simulated electrical power grids.

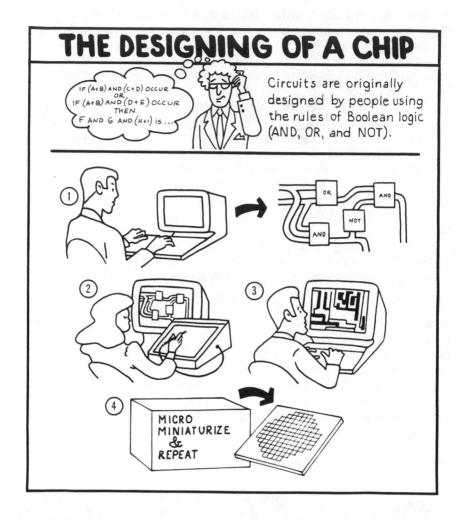

(1) All fundamental circuits are designed by people using the rules of Boolean logic. After they have been designed, they reside in disk libraries in the computer system waiting to be selected by the designer.

(2) The chip designer selects the appropriate circuits from the library and the computer generates the physical circuit paths that resemble a "plumber's nightmare."

(3) The "plumbing" is refined by a designer.

(4) The final results are further inspected to ensure that all the components are aligned properly.

(5) The "plumbing" is turned into several photomasks that will transfer the design of the elements of every transistor onto the chip.

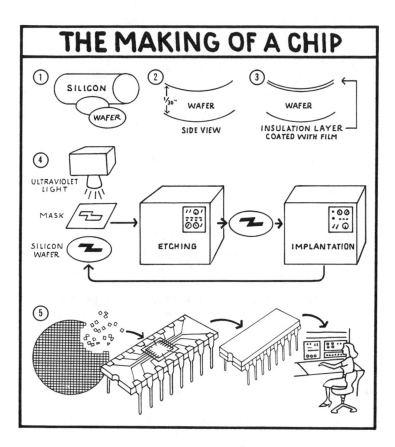

THE MAKING OF A CHIP

(1 and 2) Silicon, the raw material of chips, is refined from quartz rocks and purified. It is fabricated into salami-like ingots from three to five inches in diameter. The ingots are sliced into wafers approximately 1/30th of an inch thick.

(3) The wafer is covered with an oxide insulation layer and then coated with film.

(4) A design is transferred onto the wafer by exposing it to ultraviolet light through a mask. Wherever light strikes the film, the film is hardened along with the insulation layer beneath it. The wafer is subjected to an acid that etches out the unhardened insulation layer exposing the silicon below. The next step is an implantation process that forces chemicals into the exposed silicon under pressure, creating electrically altered elements below the surface.

Through a series of masking, etching and implantation steps, each element for every transistor is created at the same time. Millions of transistors are created together, one step at a time.

(5) The finished wafer is tested, and the bad chips are marked for disposal. The wafer is sliced into chips, and the good ones are placed into their final spider-like package. Tiny wires bond the chip to the package's "feet." Each chip is then tested individually. The number of chips that make it through to the very end can be less than the number that don't.

FORMATION OF ONE TRANSISTOR

The following steps are performed on every transistor in every chip in the wafer at the same time.

(1) The film and insulation layer are hardened after exposure to light. The dark area is the exposed, hardened part; the light area is the unexposed, unhardened part.

(2) The wafer is subjected to acid, and the acid etches out the unhardened film and insulation area exposing the silicon beneath it.

(3) Chemicals, under pressure, are implanted into the silicon creating a sublayer element that is electrically altered from the rest of the silicon.

(4) The wafer is recovered with insulation and film.

(5) The next design is transferred by photomask onto the wafer.

(6) A new hole is opened up, and chemicals are implanted to create an element within the sublayer.

(7) "The patient is sewed up once more," and another design is transferred onto the wafer.

(8) The third element is created by the same etching and implantation processes.

(9) The final stage is to tunnel through the insulation again and adhere the aluminum pathways that carry the current to and from the transistor.

Line A is the triggering line. The signal that activates the transistor comes over this line. Line B has a constant source of electricity. When a pulse comes in on line A, the middle sublayer becomes electrically conductive (the switch is closed) allowing current to travel from B to C.

FORMATION OF ONE TRANSISTOR

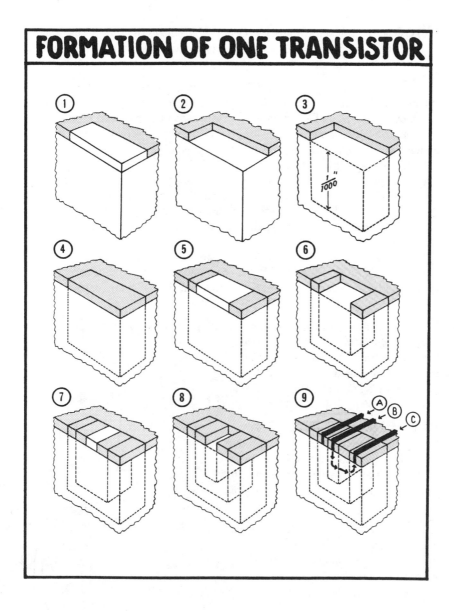

chip card See *smart card*.

chip set A group of chips designed to work together to perform a function.

CHKDSK A DOS utility that checks the status of a disk. It also reports the amount of memory currently available. See *lost cluster*.

Chooser A Macintosh desk accessory that allows the user to select a printer, file server or network communications devices, such as a network modem.

CICS (Customer Information Control System) Sometimes pronounced "kicks." A TP monitor from IBM that provides transaction processing in IBM's batch-oriented VM and MVS operating systems. A CICS session controls the transmission between many applications and the users interacting with them. It implements the upper layers (4, 5 and 6) of SNA and provides the Logical Unit (LU) necessary for SNA operation.

CICS provides device independence by letting programmers develop screen displays without having to program the specifics of the terminal that will display them. It also provides password security, transaction logging for backup and recovery and a journal of activity that can be used for analyzing session performance.

CICS is programmed by placing commands into BAL (Basic Assembly Language), COBOL, PL/I and RPG-II programs. Screen formats, terminal routing and other control information is coded in the CICS language.

CIM (Computer-Integrated Manufacturing) The integrating of office and accounting functions with automated factory systems. Point of sale, billing, machine tool scheduling and supply ordering are all part of CIM.

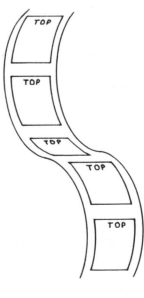

cine-oriented image A film-image orientation like that of movie film, which runs parallel to the outer edge of the medium. Contrast with *comic-strip oriented image*.

CIO (Chief Information Officer) An executive officer in charge of all the information processing departments within an organization.

CINE-ORIENTED IMAGE

ciphertext Data that has been coded (enciphered, encrypted, encoded) for security purposes.

circuit

(1) A set of electronic components that perform a particular function in an electronic system.

(2) A communications channel.

circuit analyzer

(1) A device that tests the validity of an electronic circuit.

(2) In communications, same as *data line monitor*.

circuit board Same as *printed circuit board*.

circuit breaker A protective device that opens a circuit upon sensing an overload of current. A circuit breaker is a fuse that can be reset.

circuit card Same as *printed circuit board*.

circuit switching The temporary connection of two or more communications channels. Users have full use of the circuit until the connection is terminated. Contrast with *message switching*, which stores messages and forwards them later, and contrast with *packet switching*, which breaks up a message into packets and routes each packet through the most expedient path at that moment.

CISC (Complex Instruction Set Computer) Pronounced "sisk." Computers that have large sets of instructions. CISC machines have from two to three hundred instructions, which are built into microcode. Contrast with *RISC*.

CL/1 (Connectivity Language/1) A database language from Apple Computer that allows a Macintosh to access an SQL-based database in another computer. CL/1 applications communicate with the CL/1 client program in the Mac, and the client program communicates with the CL/1 server program in the host computer.

cladding A plastic or glass sheath that is fused to and surrounds the core of an optical fiber. It keeps the light waves inside the core and adds strength to it. The cladding is covered with a protective outer jacket.

Clarion development software A family of application
development programs for PCs from Clarion Software Corporation. The primary development environment is called Professional Developer, which includes a

Pascal-like programming language, database management system, an application generator for prototyping and an optional module for dBASE compatibility.

Personal Developer is an application generator for non-programmers.

Software Distribution Kit is a customizable install and compression program for distributing software, regardless of how it was developed. The PC version of this Glossary is installed with this product.

Claris CAD A full-featured 2-D CAD program for the Macintosh from Claris Corporation that is noted for its ease of use. It provides an easy-to-learn path into CAD, while offering a majority of features found in most CAD programs.

clean room A room in which the air is highly filtered in order to keep out impurities.

clear memory To reset all RAM and hardware registers to a zero or blank condition. Rebooting the computer may or may not clear memory, but turning the computer off and on again guarantees that memory is cleared.

click To select an object by pressing the mouse button when the cursor is pointing to the required menu option or icon.

client/server In a communications network, the client is the requesting machine and the server is the supplying machine. It implies that software is specialized at each end. For example, in a network-ready database system, the user interface would reside in the workstation, and the storage and retrieval functions would reside in the server.

client/server protocol A communications protocol that provides a structure for requests between a workstation (client) and a server in a network. It refers to layer 7 in the OSI model.

clip art
A set of images used to illustrate word processing and desktop publishing documents.

CLIP ART
(Courtesy Marketing Graphics Inc.)

Clipboard A reserved segment of memory used to hold data that has been copied from a text, data or graphics document in order to insert it into another.

Clipper

(1) A dBASE compiler from Nantucket Corporation that translates programs written in the dBASE III PLUS language into executable programs. Clipper does not support all of the interactive dBASE commands, but does provide features not found in dBASE.

(2) A 32-bit RISC microprocessor from Intergraph Corporation.

clipping The cutting off of the outer edges or boundaries of a word, signal or image. See *scissoring*.

clock An internal timing device. The different varieties of clocks are:

CPU CLOCK
Uses a quartz crystal to generate a uniform electrical frequency from which digital pulses are created and used. See *clock speed*.

REALTIME CLOCK
A time-of-day clock that keeps track of regular hours, minutes and seconds and makes this data available to the programs.

TIMESHARING CLOCK
A timer set to interrupt the CPU at regular intervals in order to provide equal time to all the users of the computer.

COMMUNICATIONS CLOCK
In a synchronous communications device, the clock maintains the uniform transmission of data between the sending and receiving terminals and computers.

clock/calendar An internal time clock and month-and-year calendar that is kept continuously active with a battery backup system. Its output allows software to remind users of appointments, to determine the age of a transaction and to automatically activate tasks at specified times.

clock pulse A signal that is used to synchonize the operations of an electronic system. Clock pulses are continuous, precisely spaced changes in voltage. See *clock speed*.

clock speed The internal heartbeat and speed of a computer. The clock circuit uses the fixed vibrations generated from a quartz crystal to deliver a steady stream of pulses to the processor.
   A faster clock will speed up all processing operations provided the computer's circuits can handle the increased speed. For example, the same processor running at 20MHz is twice as fast internally as one running at 10MHz.

clone An identical copy of another device. With regard to personal computers, a clone is able to run the same software as the original machine, but does not necessarily look identical. Although clones imply 100% compatibility, that is not always the case.

closed architecture A system whose technical specifications are not made public. Contrast with *open architecture*.

closed shop An environment in which only data processing staff is allowed access to the computer. Contrast with *open shop*.

closed system A system that does not accept interconnection to foreign terminals or devices. Contrast with *open system*.

cluster

(1) A terminal control unit and its associated terminals. See *cluster controller*.

(2) A group of disk sectors that is treated as a single entity. See *lost cluster*.

(3) A group of related items.

cluster controller A control unit that manages several peripheral devices, such as terminals or disk drives.

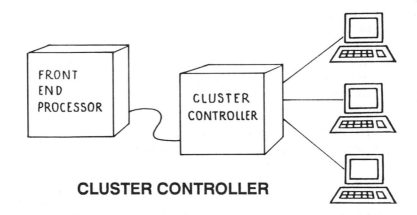

CLUSTER CONTROLLER

CLUT (Color Look Up Table) A hardware or software table that contains color mixing information (the intensity of red, green and blue) for each color in a palette or series of palettes.

CLV (Constant Linear Velocity) A disk technique that spins a disk at a varying rate of speed. By varying the speed depending on which track is being accessed, the physical density of bits in each track can be the same, thus allowing the outer tracks to hold more data than the inner tracks.

CLV mechanisms are used in CD ROM players in order to store larger amounts of data. Contrast with *CAV*. See *ZBR*.

CMI (Computer-Managed Instruction) The use of computers to organize and manage an instructional program for students. It helps create test materials, tracks the results and monitors student progress.

CMIP (Common Managment Information Protocol) Pronounced "C-mip." A protocol endorsed by OSI that defines the format for network monitoring and control information.

CMIS (Common Management Information Services) Pronounced "C-miss." A standard endorsed by OSI that defines the functions for network monitoring and control.

CMOS (Complementary Metal Oxide Semiconductor) Pronounced "C-moss." A type of integrated circuit widely used for processors and memories. CMOS uses PMOS and NMOS transistors in a complementary fashion that results in requiring less power to operate.

CMOT (CMIP Over TCP/IP) An abbreviated version of the CMIP protocol for TCP/IP networks, designed to smooth transition to OSI.

CMS

(1) (Conversational Monitor System) Software that provides interactive communications for IBM's VM operating system. It allows a user or programmer to launch an application from a terminal and interactively work with it. The CMS counterpart in MVS is called *TSO*. Contrast with *RSCS*, which provides batch communications for VM.

(2) (Call Management System) A call accounting package from AT&T for its PBXs.

CMY (Cyan, Magenta, Yellow) The color mixing system used to print colors. See *colors* and *RGB*.

CO (Central Office) A local telephone company switching station that covers a geographic area such as a town or part of a city.

co-resident A program or module that resides in memory along with other programs.

coaxial cable A high-capacity cable used in communications and video, commonly called *co-ax*. It contains an insulated solid or stranded wire that is surrounded by a solid or braided metallic shield, which is wrapped in an external cover. Teflon coating is optional for fire safety.

Although similar in appearance, there are several types of coaxial cable, each designed with a different width and impedance for a particular purpose (TV, baseband, broadband). Coax provides a much higher bandwidth than twisted wire pair.

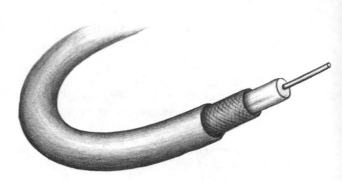

COAXIAL CABLE

COBOL (COmmon Business Oriented Language) A high-level business programming language that has been the primary business application language on mainframes and minis. It is increasingly being adapted to personal computers. COBOL is a compiled language and was one of the first high-level languages developed. Formally adopted in 1960, it stemmed from a language called *Flowmatic* in the mid 1950s.

COBOL requires more writing than other languages, but winds up more readable as a result. For example, `multiply hourly-rate by hours-worked giving gross-pay` is self-explanatory. COBOL is structured into the following divisions:

Division name	Contains
IDENTIFICATION	Program identification.
ENVIRONMENT	Types of computers used.
DATA	Buffers, constants and work areas.
PROCEDURE	The processing (program logic).

The following COBOL example converts a fahrenheit number to centigrade. To keep the example simple, it performs the operation on the operator's terminal rather than a user terminal.

```
IDENTIFICATION DIVISION.
PROGRAM-ID.   EXAMPLE.

ENVIRONMENT DIVISION.
CONFIGURATION SECTION.
SOURCE-COMPUTER.    IBM-370.
OBJECT-COMPUTER.    IBM-370.

DATA DIVISION.
WORKING-STORAGE SECTION.
77 FAHR   PICTURE 999.
77 CENT   PICTURE 999.
```

```
PROCEDURE DIVISION.
DISPLAY 'Enter fahrenheit ' UPON  CONSOLE.
ACCEPT FAHR FROM CONSOLE.
COMPUTE CENT = (FAHR- 32) * 5 / 9.
DISPLAY 'Centigrade is ' CENT UPON  CONSOLE.
GOBACK.
```

CODASYL (COnference on DAta SYstems Languages) An organization devoted to the development of computer languages. Founded in 1959, it is made up of individuals and institutions that contribute their own time and effort. COBOL is a product of CODASYL. For more information, contact CODASYL, c/o Jan Prokop, 29 Hartwell Avenue, Lexington, MA 02173, (617) 863-5100.

code

(1) A set of machine symbols that represents data or instructions. See *data code* and *machine language*.

(2) Any representation of one set of data for another. For example, a parts code is an abbreviated name of a product, product type or category. A discount code is a percentage.

(3) To write a program. See *source code* and *line of code*.

(4) To encode for security purposes. See *encryption*.

codec (COder-DECoder) An electronic circuit that converts voice into digital code (and vice versa) using techniques such as pulse code modulation and delta modulation. A codec is an A/D and D/A converter.

coder

(1) A junior, or trainee, programmer who writes simple programs or writes the code for a larger program that has been designed by someone else.

(2) A person who assigns special codes to data.

COGO (COordinate GeOmetry) A programming language used for solving civil engineering problems.

cold boot To turn the power on and boot the computer. Contrast with *warm boot*, which restarts a running computer.

collator

(1) A punched card machine that merges two decks of cards into one or more stacks.

(2) A utility program that merges records from two or more files into one file.

collector The output side of a bipolar transistor. Same as *drain* in an MOS transistor.

color cycling In computer graphics, a technique that simulates animation by continuously changing colors rather than moving the objects. Also called *color lookup table animation*.

color graphics The ability to display graphic images in colors.

color keying A technique for superimposing a video image onto another. For example, to float a car on the ocean, the car image is placed onto a color background, such as blue. The car and ocean images are scanned together. The ocean is made to appear in the resulting image wherever background (blue) exists in the car image. The ocean is cancelled wherever the car appears (no background).

color printer A printer that prints in color using dot matrix, electrophotographic, Cycolor, electrostatic, ink jet or thermal-transfer techniques. See *printer*.

colors The perception of the different wavelengths of light. It is possible to create almost all visible colors using two systems of primary colors. Transmitted colors use red, green and blue (RGB), and reflected colors use cyan (light blue), magenta (purplish-red) and yellow (CMY). Color displays use RGB and color printers use CMY.

column A vertical set of data or components. Contrast with *row*, which is a horizontal set.

COM (Computer Output Microfilm) Machines that create microfilm or microfiche directly from the computer. COM units can be stand-alone or online to the computer and receive input the same as data sent to a printer; already formatted with page headers, numbers, etc.

Using methods that take a picture of an image generated on a CRT, or by using lasers that write images directly, COM units create a film image of each page of the report. Additional graphics, such as lines and logos, may also be added.

COM file A Microsoft DOS and OS/2 machine language program ready to run that takes up less than 64K of memory. See *EXE file*.

COM1 The label assigned to serial port #1 on a PC. DOS versions up to 3.2 support COM1 and COM2, while version 3.3 supports COM1 through COM4. OS/2 supports eight COM ports.

Columns
of
text
on a
character-based
display
screen.

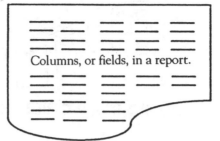

Columns, or fields, in a report.

COLUMNS OF PIXELS

Columns
of dots
in a
graphics
system.
(Raster graphics
or
dot matrix).

MAGAZINE COLUMNS

TABBED COLUMNS

EXPENSES	Planned	Actual
Rent	2,300.00	2,300.00
Electric	450.00	562.23
Gas	100.00	87.46
Water	50.00	43.23
Phone	1100.00	1457.99
Salaries	12,330.00	12,765.32
Auto	1200.00	1,371.09
Garage	225.00	225.00
Entertainment	1500.00	1,093.44
Travel	2500.00	2,788.40
Fees	6000.00	2850.00
Commissions	22,000.00	17,844.34
Advertising	5000.00	7,488.21
Miscellaneous	5000.00	2,389.20
TOTAL	59,755.00	53,265.91

NAME	STREET	BALANCE
Jones, Jennifer A.	10 West Main Ave.	0000208.49
Russo, George C.	23 East Benton St.	0000107.49
Morrison, Emil T.	1240 Parkway East	0001005.77
Fernandez, Joseph R.	39 Gate Drive	0003484.49

Columns of data
cells in a spreadsheet
or fields in a
database.

COLUMNS

comic-strip oriented mode A film image that runs the length of the film like a comic strip. Contrast with *cine-oriented image*.

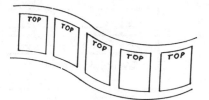

COMIC-STRIP ORIENTED IMAGE

comma delimited A record layout that separates data fields with a comma and usually surrounds character data with quotes, for example:

```
"Pat Smith","5 Main St.","New Hope","PA","18933"
"K. Jones","34 E. 88 Ave.","Syosset","NY","11724"
```

command
(1) An order given to the computer by the user. See *command-driven* and *menu-driven*.

(2) A programming language directive. Contrast with *function*.

command-driven A program that accepts commands as typed-in phrases. Command-driven programs are hard to learn, but may offer more flexibility than menu-driven programs. Once learned, command-driven programs are often faster to use, because the user can state a request succinctly. Contrast with *menu-driven*.

command interpreter Same as *command processor*.

command language A special-purpose language that accepts a limited number of commands, such as a query language, job control language (JCL) or command processor. Contrast with *programming language*, which is a general purpose language.

command processor A system program that accepts a limited number of user commands and converts them into the machine commands required by the operating system.

command shell Same as *command processor*.

COMMAND.COM A command processor for Microsoft's DOS (or OS/2 in real mode). It creates the user interface by displaying the screen prompts, accepting the typed-in commands and executing them. Other command processors, or shell programs, can be substituted for COMMAND.COM in order to provide a different user interface.

comment A descriptive statement in a source language program that is used for documentation purposes.

commercial software Software that is designed and developed for sale to the general public.

Commodore 64, 128

The Commodore 64 is a home computer introduced in 1982 by Commodore Business Machines, Inc., which includes 64K of RAM, color graphics (16 colors) and three independent tone generators. In 1986, the Commodore 128 was introduced (128-640K). It runs Commodore 64 software and, with the addition of a Z80 board, it runs CP/M software, such as WordStar and dBASE II. The 128D, introduced in 1987, added a detached keyboard and a built-in disk. Over 10 million Commodore 64s and 128s have been sold worldwide.

COMMODORE 128

common carrier A government-regulated organization that provides telecommunications services for public use, such as AT&T, the telephone companies, ITT, MCI and Western Union.

communications The electronic transfer of information from one location to another. *Data communications* refers to digital transmission, and *telecommunications* refers to all forms of transmission, including analog voice and video. In this Glossary, communications usually refers to digital transmission, excluding analog voice and video, but occasionally may encompass all forms.

The Protocol

The way communications systems "talk to" each other is defined in a set of standards called *protocols*. Protocols work in a hierarchy starting at the top with the user's program and ending at the bottom with the plugs, sockets and electrical signals. To learn about this hierarchy, see *OSI*.

Personal Computer Communications

Personal computer communications takes on several forms.

(1) Data can be transferred between two geographically distant personal computers by using modems, a telephone line and a communications program in each computer.

(2) Data can be transferred between two side-by-side computers by hooking up a null modem cable between the serial ports of both computers.

(3) Personal computers can act like a remote terminal to a minicomputer or mainframe. For example, DCA's IRMAboard plugs into a personal computer and turns it into an IBM 3278 or 3279 terminal, the common IBM mainframe terminal.

(4) Personal computers can be part of a local area network, in which databases and printers can be shared among users. If the local area network interconnects with a minicomputer or mainframe network, then personal computers can communicate with larger computers.

Minicomputer Communications

Minicomputer communications systems control as many as several hundred terminals connected to a single computer system. They support a variety of low-speed dial-up terminals and high-speed local terminals. With larger minicomputers, the communications processing is handled in separate machines, called *communications controllers*.

Since minicomputers were originally designed with communications in mind, it is usually more straightforward than with mainframes. The communications programs and operating systems are often designed as an integrated system providing a more coherent approach from the start.

Minicomputers can interconnect with a mainframe by emulating a mainframe terminal, in which case, the mainframe thinks it's talking to just another user terminal. Minicomputers can hook up directly with some local area networks, or they can interconnect with the use of a gateway, which converts the protocols.

Mainframe Communications

Mainframe systems can control several thousand remote terminals. They support a variety of low-speed dial-up terminals and high-speed local terminals.

Large mainframes use separate machines, called *communications controllers* or *front end processors*, to handle the communications processing. The controllers and front end processors take the data from the mainframes and package it for transmission over the network. They also strip the codes from the incoming messages and send pure data to the mainframes for processing.

Mainframes set the standards for communications. It's usually up to the mini and micro vendors to provide compatibility with the mainframe systems.

Analog vs Digital Communications

The most common form of long-distance communications in the world has been the telephone system, which, up until a few years ago, transmitted only voice frequencies. This transmission technique, known as *analog* communications, has been error prone, because the electronic frequencies get mixed together with unwanted, extraneous signals (noise) that invade the line for a variety of reasons.

In analog telephone networks, amplifiers are located in the line every few miles to maintain a strong signal. Their job is simply to boost the incoming signal, but they can't distinguish between a meaningful signal and noise. Thus, tiny drops of interference creeping into the line keep getting louder as the signal is boosted hundreds of times. By the time the receiving person or machine gets the signal on a noisy line, it may be impossible to decipher it.

In a *digital* network, only binary code is transmitted, in which only two distinct frequencies or two distinct voltages will ever be sent over the line. Instead of amplifiers, repeaters are used, which analyze the incoming signal and regenerate a brand new outgoing signal. Any noise that invades the line will get only as far as the next repeater and be filtered out.

That's the key to digital transmission. When only two signals (0 and 1) need to be analyzed, the data bits can be distinguished from the garble.

THE FIRST ANALOG COMMUNICATIONS (1876)
(Courtesy AT&T)
"Mr. Watson, come here. I want you."

Communications Act

The establishment of the Federal Communications Commission (FCC) in 1934, the regulatory body for interstate and foreign telecommunications. Its mission is to provide high-quality services at reasonable cost to everyone in the U.S. on a nondiscriminatory basis.

communications channel

Also called a *circuit* or *line*, it is a pathway over which data is transferred between remote devices. It may refer to the entire physical medium, such as a public or private telephone line, optical fiber, coaxial cable or twisted wire pair, or, it may refer to the specific carrier frequency transmitted within the medium, such as in a microwave or satellite channel or in a broadband local area network.

communications controller

A peripheral control unit that connects several communications lines to a computer and performs the actual transmitting and receiving as well as various message coding and decoding activities.

Communications controllers are typically nonprogrammable units designed for specific protocols and communications tasks. Contrast with *front end processor*, which can be programmed for a variety of protocols and network conditions.

communications network

(1) The communications channels that interconnect terminals and computers.

(2) The communications channels, all hardware that supports the interconnections and all software that manages the transmission.

communications program

(1) Any software that manages the transmission of data between computers and terminals.

(2) In mainframes and large minis, it is made up of access methods, network control programs and TP monitors, which reside in the computer and front end processor and collectively handle hundreds or thousands of users.

(3) A personal computer communications program manages the transmission of data to and from the computer's serial port. It includes several error checking protocols to ensure against loss of data in noisy telephone lines and also provides simple ASCII transmission for local transfers. It usually can emulate various dumb terminals for hookup to mini and mainframe networks.

communications protocol

A set of hardware and software standards for transmitting data between terminals and computers. There are many layers of protocols that may be used depending on the type of computer systems and network. See *OSI* and *OSI model*.

The Concept

Imagine two computers "talking" to each other in this simulated communications protocol:

Are you there? **Yes, I am.** Are you ready to receive? **Yes, I am.** Here comes the message—bla, bla, bla— did you get it? **Yes, I did.** Here comes the next part—bla, bla, bla— did you get it? **No, I didn't.** Here it comes again— bla, bla, bla— did you get it? **Yes, I did.** There is no more. Goodbye. **Goodbye.**

communications satellite A radio relay station in orbit 22,300 miles above the equator. It travels at the same rate of speed as the earth (geosynchronous), so that it appears stationary to us. It contains many communications channels that receive analog and digital signals from earth stations. All signals are transmitted within a carrier frequency.

The signals are amplified and transmitted back to earth, covering either a small geographical area (spot beam) or almost a third of the earth's surface. In the latter case, private data is often encrypted to prevent eavesdropping.

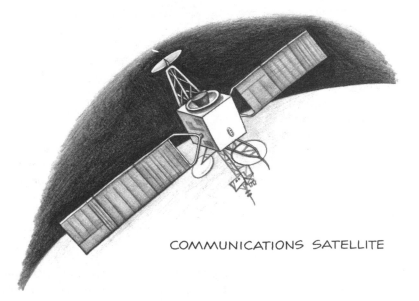

COMMUNICATIONS SATELLITE

communications server A computer in a network that manages access to external networks. It may manage a pool of modems and/or provide gateways to dissimilar networks.

compact disc See CD.

COMPACT II A high-level numerical control programming language used to generate instructions for numerical control (machine tool) devices.

compandor (COMpressor/exPANDOR) A device that improves the signal for AM radio transmission. On outgoing transmission, it raises the amplitude of weak signals and lowers the amplitude of strong signals. On incoming transmission, it restores the signal to its original form.

Compaq (Compaq Computer Corporation) A manufacturer of personal computers that was founded in 1982 by Rod Canion, Bill Murto and Jim Harris. In 1983, it shipped 53,000 COMPAQ Portables, a transportable clone of the PC, which resulted in $111 million in revenues and an American business record. The Portable's success was due to its rugged construction, its ability to run all PC software and its semi-portability (it weighed 30 pounds).

In 1984, Compaq introduced the DESKPRO family of desktop computers and achieved a computer-industry record for sales in its second year. In 1986, it was the first to offer a

COMPAQ 386

386-based machine, the COMPAQ 386, which has set an industry standard.

With revenues of over two billion in its sixth year, Compaq has become an industry leader and is internationally known for its rugged and reliable computers.

comparator A device that compares two quantities and determines their equality.

compare A fundamental capability of a computer. By comparing one set of data with another, the computer can locate, analyze, select, reorder and make decisions. After comparing, the computer can indicate whether the data were equal or which set was greater or less than the other. See *computer (The 3 C's)*.

compatibility See *standards & compatibility*.

compatibility mode A special feature of a computer and/or operating system that allows it to run programs written for a different system. Programs usually run slower in compatiblity mode.

compilation The compiling of a program. See *compiler*.

compile time The time it takes to translate a program from source language into machine language. The link editing time may also be included in the compile time.

compiler A software program that translates a high-level programming language, such as COBOL and C, into machine language. A compiler usually generates assembly language first and then translates the assembly language into machine language.

The following example compiles program statements into machine language:

Source code	Assembly Language	Machine language
IF COUNT=10	Compare A to B	Compare 3477 2883
GOTO DONE	If = go to C	If = go to 23883
ELSE	Go to D	Go to 23343
GOTO AGAIN		
ENDIF		

Actual machine code
100101010010100001010100
101010100101010010010101
10100101010001010010010

compiler language A high-level programming language that is translated into machine language before the program is executed. See *compiler*.

complement The number derived by subtracting a number from a base number. For example, the tens complement of 8 is 2. In set theory, complement refers to all the objects in one set that are not in another set.

Complements are used in digital circuits, because it's faster to subtract by adding complements than by performing true subtraction. The binary complement of a number is created by reversing all bits and adding 1. The carry from the high-order position is eliminated. The following example subtracts 5 from 8.

Decimal Subtraction	Binary Equivalent	Subtraction by Adding the complement
8	1000	1000
-5	-0101	+1011
3	0011	0011

component One element of a larger system. A hardware component can be a device as small as a transistor or as large as a disk drive as long as it is part of a larger system. Software components are routines or modules within a larger system.

composite video The video-only (no audio) portion of the standard NTSC TV signal. In composite video, the red, green and blue signals are mixed together, and the image is not as crisp as RGB (red, green and blue transmitted separately).

Some personal computers have composite video output that connects directly to a TV set

compound document A text file that contains both text and graphics. Eventually compound documents will hold voice and video.

compression See *data compression*.

compressor
(1) A device that diminishes the range between the strongest and weakest transmission signals. See *compandor*.

(2) A routine or program that compresses data. See *data compression*.

CompuServe An information utility that provides a wide variety of information and services, including bulletin boards, online conferencing, business news, sports and weather, financial transactions, electronic mail, travel and entertainment data as well as online editions of computer publications.

compute To perform mathematical operations or general computer processing. See *computer (The 3 C's)*.

compute bound Same as *process bound*.

computer A general-purpose machine that processes data according to a set of instructions that are stored internally either temporarily or permanently. The computer and all the equipment attached to it are called *hardware*. The instructions that tell it what to do are called *software*. A set of instructions that perform a particular task is called a program, or *software program*.

WHAT A COMPUTER DOES

The instructions in the program direct the computer to input, process and output as follows:

Input/Output

The computer can selectively retrieve data into its *main memory* or *RAM*, from any peripheral device (terminal, disk, tape or communications line) connected to it. After processing the data internally, the computer can send a copy of the results from its main memory out to any peripheral device. The more memory it has, the more programs and data a computer can work with at the same time.

Storage

By outputting data onto a magnetic disk or tape, the computer is able to store data permanently and retrieve it when necessary. A system's size is based on how much disk storage it has. The more disk, the more data is immediately available.

Processing
(The 3 C's®)

Once the data has been stored in the computer's memory, the computer can process it by (1) **calculating**, (2) **comparing** and (3) **copying**.

CALCULATE
The computer can perform any mathematical operation on data by adding, subtracting, multiplying and dividing one set of data with another.

COMPARE
The computer can analyze and evaluate data by matching it with sets of known data that are included in the program or called in from storage.

COPY
The computer can move data around to create any kind of report or listing in any order.

By **calculating**, **comparing** and **copying**, the computer accomplishes all forms of data processing. For example, records are sorted into a new order by **comparing** two records at a time and **copying** the record with the lower value in front of the record with the higher value.

The computer finds a specific customer out of a file of thousands of records by **comparing** the requested account number with each account number in a list until it finds a match. The dBASE query statement: SUM SALARY FOR TITLE = "NURSE" causes the computer to **compare** the title field in each record for NURSE and then add (**calculate**) the salary field into a counter for each match.

In word processing, inserting and deleting text is accomplished by **copying** characters from one place to another.

Remember The 3 C's®

If you wonder whether a computer can be used to solve a problem, identify the data on paper. If it can be calculated, compared and copied on paper, it can be processed in the computer.

(The 3 C's is a registered service mark of The Computer Language Company Inc.)

The 3 C's

CALCULATE
In the update example on the opposite page, the extended price is calculated on a group of line items in an order. A line item record is read from the disk and written into memory. The number in the quantity field is multiplied by the number in the price field, and the result is written into the extended price field. The record is then read from memory and written back on the disk. The program gets the next record and repeats the process until it reaches the end of file.

COMPARE
In the search example on the opposite page, ARIZONA records are being selected. Records are read from the disk and written into memory. The STATE field in the record is compared with the search data "AZ." If they are equal, the record is selected, in which case it is written to another disk file or it is formatted for the printer. The program then goes back and inputs the next record until the end of file is encountered.

COPY
In the sort example on the opposite page, data is input into memory and compared. If an item is out of sequence (lower when it should be higher, or vice versa), it is copied into its correct order. By copying, data can be placed into any desired sequence; for example, from low to high order (A to Z) or from high to low order (Z to A). Data can be copied into one sequence within another. For example, sales totals can be sorted into high-low order by amount within low-high order by state. The main list would be in natural alphabetic order by state, but within each state, the list would be highest sales to lowest sales.

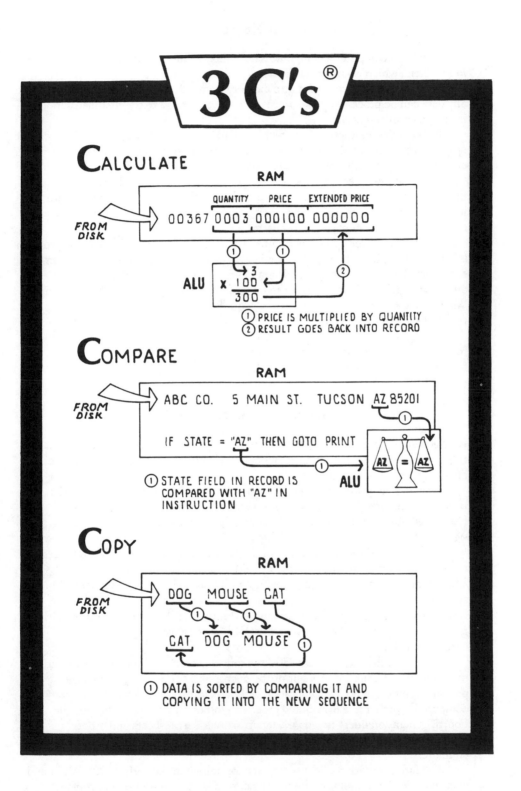

3 C's ®

CALCULATE

RAM

QUANTITY   PRICE   EXTENDED PRICE

00367 0003 000100 000000

FROM DISK

ALU

$$\begin{array}{r} 3 \\ \times\ 100 \\ \hline 300 \end{array}$$

① PRICE IS MULTIPLIED BY QUANTITY
② RESULT GOES BACK INTO RECORD

COMPARE

RAM

FROM DISK

ABC CO.   5 MAIN ST.   TUCSON AZ 85201

IF STATE = "AZ" THEN GOTO PRINT

ALU

AZ = AZ

① STATE FIELD IN RECORD IS COMPARED WITH "AZ" IN INSTRUCTION

COPY

RAM

FROM DISK

DOG   MOUSE   CAT

CAT   DOG   MOUSE

① DATA IS SORTED BY COMPARING IT AND COPYING IT INTO THE NEW SEQUENCE

The Stored Program Concept

What makes a computer a computer is its ability to call in its instructions and follow them, which is known as the *stored program concept*.

The instructions are copied into memory from a disk, tape or other source before any data can be processed. The processor is directed to go to the first instruction in the program and begin.

It copies the instruction from memory into its control unit circuit and matches it against its built-in set of instructions. If the instruction is valid, the processor carries it out. If it isn't, the computer comes to an abnormal end (abend).

The processor executes instructions sequentially until it finds a GOTO instruction that tells it to go to a different place in the program. It can execute millions of instructions per second tracing the logic of the program over and over again on each new set of data it brings in.

As computers get faster, operations can be made to overlap. While one program is waiting for input from one user, the master control program (operating system) can direct the computer to process data in another program. Large computers are designed to allow inputs and outputs to occur simultaneously with processing. While one user's data is being processed, data from the next user can be transmitted into the computer.

It can take hundreds of thousands of discrete machine steps to perform very routine tasks. Your computer could execute a million instructions to put a requested record on screen for you.

Generations of Computers

First-generation computers, starting with the UNIVAC I in 1951, used vacuum tubes as their primary switching component. Memories were made of thin tubes of liquid mercury and magnetic drums.

Second-generation systems in the late 1950s replaced vacuum tubes with transistors and used magnetic cores for memories, such as the IBM 1401 and Honeywell 800. Size was reduced dramatically and reliability was improved significantly.

Third-generation computers, beginning in the mid 1960s, introduced processors made of integrated circuits, such as the IBM 360 and CDC 6400. Third-generation also introduced operating systems and database management systems.

Online systems were widely developed throughout the third generation, although most processing was still batch oriented, in which data was keypunched onto cards or tape first.

Starting in the mid to late 1970s, the fourth generation brought us computers made entirely of chips. It brought us the microprocessor, which spawned the personal computer. Fourth generation embraces integration of small and large computers together in a distributed processing/office automation environment. Fourth-generation query languages, report writers, spreadsheets and other software packages brought the non-computer person squarely in contact with computers.

The fifth generation ought to become formalized in the early 1990s. VLSI and eventually SLSI technologies are putting current-day mainframes on everyone's desk. Voice recognition, natural and foreign language translation, fiber optics, optical disks and technologies still in the research labs are part of the fifth-generation. By the turn of the century, a computer should be able to converse somewhat intelligently with us.

Computers Come in Many Sizes

Computers can be as small as a chip or as large as a truck. The difference is in the amount of work they can perform within the same time frame. Its power is based on many factors, including its word size and the speed of its CPU, memory and peripherals. Following is a rough guide to the cost of a complete system:

Computer system type (Bits show word size)	Approximate price In 1991 U.S. $
Computer on a chip (chip only) (4, 8, 16-bit)	$2 - 75
Microprocessor (chip only) (4, 8, 16, 32-bit)	$5 - 500
Personal computer (8, 16, 32-bit)	$500 - 15,000
Supermicro (16-32 bit)	$10,000 - 25,000
Minicomputer (16, 32-bit)	$15,000 - 250,000
Supermini (32 bit)	$200,000 - 750,000
Mini-supercomputer (64-bit)	$100,000 - 750,000
Mainframe (32-bit)	$150,000 - 3,000,000
Supercomputer (64-bit)	$1,000,000 - 20,000,000

computer architecture
The design of a computer system. It sets the standard for all devices that connect to it and all the software that runs on it. Its design is based on the type of programs that will run (business, scientific, etc.) and the number of them that must be run concurrently.

The design will specify how much memory is needed and how it will be managed (memory protection, virtual memory). It specifies how concurrency is handled (interrupts, parallel processing, etc.), and how big the internal bus must be that transfers data between memory and the processor. It also specifies the word size, or number of bits processed in the registers at one time.

If a computer is designed from scratch, its native language, or instruction set, must be created, stipulating what functions the computer performs and how instructions must be written to activate them. This is the foundation of the computer. It determines how people will communicate with it forever after.

The trend toward larger and more complicated instruction sets has been recently broken with RISC computers, which perform only a handful of primary functions. The result is a leaner, faster computer, but requires more work be done by the compilers generating the software. The software has to now do what the hardware used to.

This hardware/software tradeoff is the yin/yang of the computer's architecture. In time, more system functions (operating system, database management, etc.) will be moved out of software and into hardware for improved performance. Electronic circuits are much faster when they know what to do and don't have to be told.

If fault tolerant operation is required, the computer has to be designed with this in mind from step one, as this objective influences everything.

Computers used as array processors and database machines require specialized designs in order to acquire their speed.

See *von Neumann architecture* and *RISC*.

Computer Associates (Computer Associates International, Inc.)

A leading independent software vendor with over 200 programs for micros to mainframes. Founded in 1976 by Charles Wang and three associates, its first product was CA-SORT, a utility program for IBM mainframes. The company is known in the personal computer world for SuperCalc, one of the first spreadsheets. In 1989, Computer Associates International's revenues exceeded one billion dollars with over 6,500 employees in more than 100 offices throughout the world.

computer center Same as *datacenter*.

computer designer An individual who designs the electronic structure of a computer.

computer graphics See *graphics*.

computer language A programming language, machine language or the language of the computer industry.

Computer Library An information service from Ziff Communications Company that provides a CD ROM with full-text articles and abstracts from over 100 computer magazines and periodicals. Subscribers receive a new CD ROM every month that contains articles from the preceding 12 months.

computer literacy An understanding of computers and information systems, which includes a working vocabulary about computer and information system components, the fundamental principles of computer processing and a perspective for how non-technical people can take advantage of the world of computer technology.

Computer literacy does not deal with how the computer works (digital circuits), but does imply knowledge of how the computer does its work (inputs, processes, outputs). It also includes a basic understanding of systems analysis & design, application programming, systems programming and datacenter operations.

To be computer literate in management, an individual must be able to define information requirements effectively and have an understanding of what the primary decision support tools, such as query languages, report writers, spreadsheets and financial planning systems, can accomplish. To be truly computer literate, one must understand "standards & compatibility" in this Glossary.

computer on a chip A single chip that contains the processor, RAM, ROM, clock and I/O control unit. Computers on a chip are used for myriads of applications from automobiles to toys.

computer power The effective performance of a computer. Computer power can be expressed in MIPS (millions of instructions per second), clock speed (10Mhz, 16Mhz) and in word or bus size, (8-bit, 16-bit). However, as with automobile horsepower, valves and cylinders, such specifications are only guidelines. The real power of a computer system is net throughput, which is how long it takes to get the job done.

A software package is called "powerful" when it contains a large number of features.

computer readable Same as *machine readable*.

computer science The field of computer hardware and software. It includes systems analysis & design, application and system software design and programming and datacenter operations.

Computer science does not delve into information science, the study of information and its uses. This is a failing with regard to teaching computer technology, especially in the elementary and high school grades. The emphasis is on learning a programming language or making a personal computer work with little or no study of the data and information required in a typical business.

Instead of only learning BASIC on a personal computer, which is fine for solving algorithmic problems, students should be introduced to database management systems in order to learn about transaction and master files, audit trails and the nature of an organization's information systems.

Computer Security Act A first step in improving the security and privacy of information contained in federal computer systems. Signed Jan. 8, 1988, by President Reagan, the Act:

Establishes a central authority for developing guidelines for protecting unclassified, but sensitive information stored in government computers.

Requires each agency to formulate a computer security plan, tailored to its own circumstances and based on the guidelines.

Mandates that each agency provide training for its computer employees on the threats and vulnerabilities of its computer systems.

Ensures that the National Security Agency and other defense-related government agencies not control computer security standards in civilian agencies of government.

computer services organization A an organization that offers data processing, software and/or professional computing services. It can be a service bureau that provides timesharing and batch processing services, a software house, VAR (value added reseller) or consulting firm. See *service bureau*.

computer system A system made up of the CPU, all the peripheral devices connected to it and its operating system. Computer systems fall into ranges called *microcomputers* (personal computers), *minicomputers* and *mainframes*, roughly small, medium and large. Computer systems are sized for the total user workload which is based on:

(1) The number of terminals required.
(2) The amount and nature of work that must be performed simultaneously. Interactive processing, such as questions and answers and filling in forms, is light work. Batch processing (long searches or printing an entire report) is heavy work. Computer-aided design, engineering, and scientific applications require fast mathematical processing.
(3) The amount of online disk storage necessary to hold the data. A computer system has a maximum number of peripherals that can be connected to it.

Computer System Architecture

Following are the major components of a computer system and their significance:

Component	Significance
Machine language	Compatibility with future hardware/software
Operating system	Performance and future hardware/software compatibility
Clock speed (MIPS)	Performance
Number of terminals	Number of concurrent users
Memory capacity	Performance
Online disk capacity	Amount of available information at all times
Communications	Access to inhouse and external information
Programming languages	Compatibility with future hardware
Fail-safe design	Reliability

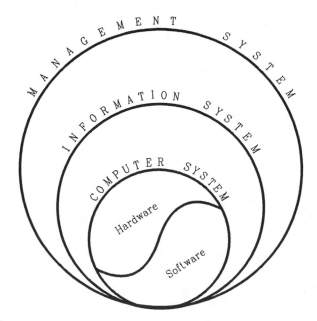

HOW SYSTEMS RELATE

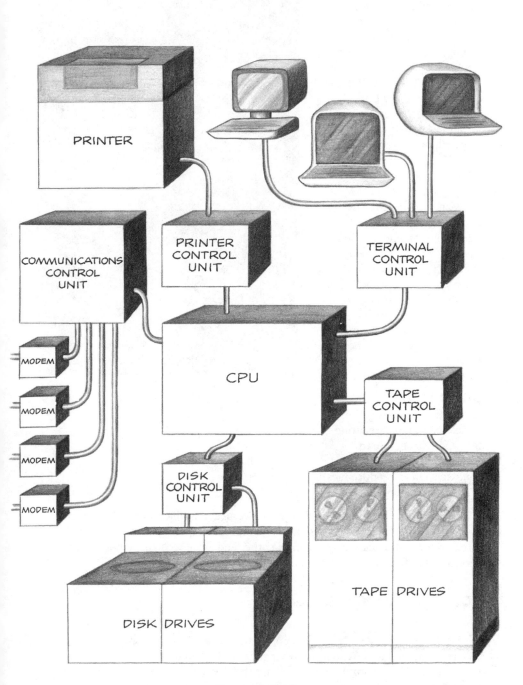

COMPUTER SYSTEM

COMSAT

(COMmunications SATellite Corporation) A private organization that launches and operates communications satellites, created by an act of Congress in 1962. In 1965, it launched the Early Bird, the first commercial satellite to retransmit signals from a geosynchronous orbit.

COMSAT provides satellite capacity to international carriers such as AT&T, MCI, RCA and others. It owns part of the International Telecommunications Satellite Corporation (INTELSAT) and is also part owner of the International Maritime Satellite Corporation (INMARSAT), which provides communications to and from ships and offshore rigs.

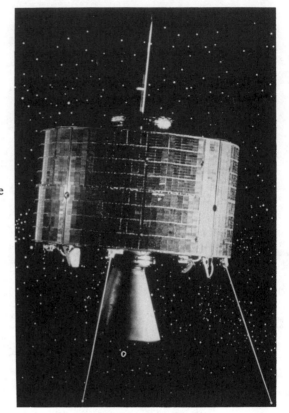

"EARLY BIRD"
(Courtesy COMSAT)

concatenate To link
various structures together. For example, concatenating files appends one file to another. In speech synthesis, units of speech called *phonemes* (k, sh, ch, etc.) are concatenated to produce meaningful sounds.

concentrator A device that joins several communications channels into
a single one. A concentrator is similar to a multiplexor, except that it does not spread the signals back out again on the other end. The receiving computer performs that function.

conceptual view See *view*.

Concurrent DOS A family of multiuser, multitasking operating
systems from Digital Research Inc., that runs on 8086 and higher PCs. Concurrent DOS environments are Microsoft DOS compatible and allow serial terminals to be used, providing an economical alternative to a local area network.

concurrent operation See *multitasking*, *multiprocessing* and *parallel
processing*.

conditional branch In programming, an instruction that directs the computer to another part of the program based on the results of a compare. In the following (simulated) assembly language example, the second line is the conditional branch.

```
COMPARE FIELDA with FIELDB
GOTO MATCHROUTINE if EQUAL.
```

conditional statement In programming, a language statement, such as an IF THEN ELSE or CASE statement, which tests a condition and branches to a subroutine based on the results of that test.

conditioning Extra cost options in a private telephone line that improve performance by reducing distortion and amplifying weak signals.

conductor A material that can carry electrical current. Contrast with *insulator*.

CONFIG.SYS A configuration file that customizes Microsoft's DOS and OS/2 to a particular hardware environment. CONFIG.SYS resides in the root directory and is examined upon startup. It is primarily used to initiate the drivers for peripheral devices that have been added to the system.

Device drivers have an .SYS extension, and the command line to add a device driver to the system is **device=drivername**. For example, to add a driver named NEWDISK.SYS, the line `device=newdisk.sys` would be added to the CONFIG.SYS file.

configuration A particular system of interrelated components, such as a computer system or communications network. To configure a system is to choose from a variety of options in order to create a customized system.

configuration file A file that contains information about a specific user, program, computer or file.

connect time The time a user at a terminal is logged-on to a computer system. See *service bureau*.

Connection Machine A family of parallel processing computers from Thinking Machines Corporation that contain from 4,096 to 65,536 processors. Connection machines can be set up as hypercubes or other topologies. They are used in applications such as signal processing, simulation and database retrieval, and require a VAX or other computer as a front end.

connector
(1) Any cable or wire that links two devices together.

(2) In database management, a link or pointer between two data structures.

(3) In flowcharting, a symbol that is used to break a sequence and resume the sequence elsewhere. It is usually a small circle with a number or other identification written in it.

console
(1) The main operator's terminal on a large computer.

(2) Any display terminal.

constant In programming, any data with fixed values within the program. Minimum and maximum amounts, dates, prices, headlines and error messages are examples of constants.

consultant An independent specialist. Consultants can act as advisors, or they can perform detailed systems analysis & design functions. They can help users formulate their information requirements and produce a generalized or detailed set of specifications from which hardware or software vendors can respond. Consultants are often used as project advisors throughout the entire system development cycle.

contact A metal strip in a switch or socket that touches a corresponding metal strip in order to make a connection that allows current to pass. Contacts are often made of precious metals to avoid corrosion.

contention The condition that arises when two devices attempt to use a single resource at the same time. *Contention resolution* is the process of resolving which device gains access first. See CSMA/CD.

context sensitive help Help screens that provide specific information about the condition or mode the program is in at the time help is sought.

contextual search A search for records or documents based upon the text contained in them as opposed to searching on key field or by file name.

context switching
(1) In a multitasking environment, to turn control over to another program under direction of the operating system. A program's context is its current state.

(2) To stop working in an application and go work in another under direction of the user.

contiguous Adjacent or touching. Contrast with *fragmentation*.

continuity check A test of a line, channel or circuit to determine if the pathway exists from beginning to end and can transmit signals.

continuous carrier In communications, a carrier frequency that is transmitted even when data is not being sent over the line.

continuous forms Paper forms that are manufactured as a series of sheets joined together with perforated edges. The forms are moved by sprockets that interlock with the holes on the left and right sides of the sheets. After printing, forms are separated manually or by a bursting machine.

control ball Same as *track ball*.

control block A segment of disk or memory that contains a group of codes used for identification and control purposes.

control break

(1) A change of data category which is used to trigger a subtotal in a report. For example, if data is subtotalled by state, a control break occurs when NJ changes to NM.

(2) The suspension of a computer operation that is sometimes accomplished by pressing the CTRL and BREAK keys simultaneously.

control character A special character that triggers some action on a display screen, printer or communications line. Control characters, such as a line feed, carriage return and escape, may or may not be printable. See *ASCII*.

control code One or more characters that are used to control a device, such as a display screen or printer. Control codes often begin with an Escape character (ASCII 27); however, this is only one example. There is an endless number of codes used to control electronic devices. The first 32 characters of the ASCII character code are used for controlling communications devices and printers (see *ASCII chart*).

Control Data (Control Data Corporation) One of the first major computer companies in the country. Founded in 1957, Bill Norris was its first president and the guiding force behind its dramatic growth. Control Data's first computer, the 1604, was introduced

WILLIAM C. NORRIS
(Courtesy Control Data)

in 1957 and delivered to the U.S. Navy Bureau of Ships. Since then, it has been heavily involved with governmental agencies.

In its first year of operation, Control Data acquired Cedar Engineering, a peripherals manufacturer, launching it into the data storage business.

In 1968, Arbitron was acquired, a computer-based audience measurement service that has contributed to the company's success ever since. Also in that year, Control Data filed an antitrust suit against IBM, which resulted in its acquisition of The Service Bureau Corporation from IBM in 1972.

Control Data has always specialized in large mainframes that have been used extensively in scientific environments and large timesharing service bureaus. Over the years, its computer series has evolved into a complete product line from workstation to supercomputer.

Control Data computers are noted for their extreme reliability and have controlled more than 300,000 hours of space flight without holding up a launch.

control field Same as *key field*.

control key Abbreviated CTRL or CTL, it is a special key on the keyboard which, like the shift key, is depressed with some other key. It is used to command the computer, and its effect is determined by the software. For example, in a word processor, Control U, might turn on underline mode.

Control Panel A routine that changes the computer's environment settings, such as keyboard and mouse sensitivity, sounds, colors and communications and printer access. It is a desk accessory in the Macintosh and a utility program in Windows.

control parallel Sames as *MIMD*.

control program Software that controls the operation of and has highest priority in a computer. Operating systems, network operating systems and network control programs are examples. Contrast with *application program*

control total Same as *hash total*.

control unit
(1) Within the processor, the circuitry that locates, analyzes and executes each instruction in the program.

(2) Within the computer, a *control unit*, or *controller*, is hardware that controls peripheral activities such as a disk or display screen. Upon signals from the CPU, it performs the physical data transfers between memory and the peripheral device.

In single chip computers, a built-in control unit accepts keyboard input and provides serial output to a display. Personal computer control units are contained on a single printed circuit board. In large computers, control units are on one or more printed circuit boards, or they may be housed in a stand-alone cabinet.

control variable In programming, a variable that keeps track of the number of iterations of a process. Its value is incremented or decremented with each iteration, and it is compared to a constant or other variable to test the end of the process or loop.

controller Same as *control unit (2)*.

controller board See *disk controller, video display board* and *control unit (2)*.

conventional memory Memory up to one megabyte in a PC. See *extended memory*.

conventional programming Using a procedural language.

conversational An interactive dialogue between the user and the computer and implies a question and answer type of session.

conversion

(1) *Data conversion* is the changing of physical media, such as from tape to disk, or the changing of data from one file or database format to another. Data conversion may also require code conversion from ASCII to EBCDIC or vice versa.

(2) *Program conversion* is the changing of the programming source language from one dialect to another, or the changing of the programs to work with a different operating system or database management system.

(3) *Computer system conversion* is the changing of the computer model and peripheral devices.

(4) *Information system conversion* requires both data conversion and either program conversion or the installation of newly purchased or created application programs.

converter

(1) A device that changes one set of codes, modes, sequences or frequencies to a different set. See *A/D converter*.

(2) A device that changes electrical currents from 60 Hz to 50 Hz, and vice versa.

cooperative processing The sharing of the workload among two or more computers such as a mainframe and a personal computer.

coordinate The intersection of two or more planes. For example, end points in 2-D vector graphics, cells in a spreadsheet and bits in memory are all identified by the intersection of a row and column.

coprocessor A secondary processor used to speed up operations by handling some of the workload of the main CPU. See *math coprocessor*.

copy To make a duplicate of the original. In digital electronics, all copies are identical.

The text in this Glossary takes up about 1.5 megabytes. During the course of writing and updating it, the text has been copied hundreds of times, causing billions of bits to be transmitted between disk and memory. Just to show that things aren't entirely perfect, a character does get garbled every once in a while. We'll have to settle for 99.9999% instead of 100%!

copy buster A program that bypasses the copy protection scheme in a software program and allows normal, unprotected copies to be made.

copy protection The resistance to unauthorized copying of software. Copy protection was never an issue with mainframes and minicomputers, since vendor support has always been vital in those environments.

In the early days of floppy-based personal computers, many copy protection methods were used. However, with each scheme introduced, a copy buster program was developed to get around it. Now that hard disks are the norm, copy protection has been abolished. In order to manage a hard disk, files must be easily copied.

core A round magnetic doughnut that represents one bit in a core storage system. A computer's main memory used to be referred to as core.

core storage A non-volatile memory that holds magnetic charges in tiny ferrite cores about a 16th of an inch in diameter. The direction of the magnetic flux determines whether it is a 1 or 0.

Developed in the late 1940s by Jay W. Forrester and Dr. An Wang, core storage was used extensively in the 1950s and 1960s. Since it holds its content without power, it is still used in specialized applications in the military and in space vehicles.

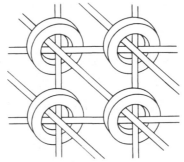

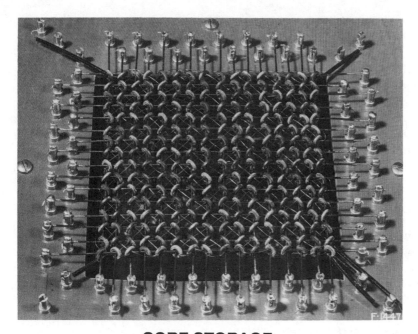

CORE STORAGE

(Courtesy The MITRE Corporation Archives)

In 1952, this core plane held 256 bits of memory for the Whirlwind I Computer. Today, a single RAM chip holds one million bits of memory.

Core System The first proposed standard for computer graphics. It was developed by the Graphics Standards Planning Committee of SIGGRAPH and was used in the late 1970s and early 1980s. The major objectives of the Core System were portability of programs from one computer system to another and the separation of modeling graphics from viewing graphics. Almost all features of the Core System were incorporated into the ANSI-endorsed GKS standard.

Corel Draw A Windows-based illustration program for 286 and higher PCs from Corel Systems Corporation. Introduced in early 1989, Corel Draw includes over 100 precision fonts and is known for its speed and ease of use. It generates its own CDR vector graphics files, but can import other popular graphics formats.

corruption The altering of data or programs due to hardware or software failure.

COS (Corporation for Open Systems) A not for profit, international research and development consortium, founded in 1986 and dedicated to assuring acceptance of an open network architecture in world markets. It is made up of some 65 information technology manufacturers and user organizations that provide development, service, and support of systems that conform to international standards, which includes OSI and ISDN.

For more information, contact Corporation for Open Systems Int'l., 1750 Old Meadow Road, Suite 400, McLean, VA 22102, (703) 883-2700.

cost/benefits analysis
A study that projects the costs and benefits of a new information system. Costs include people and machine resources for development as well as operational costs to run the system.

Tangible benefits are derived by estimating the cost savings of both human and machine resources to run the new system versus the old one. Intangible benefits, such as improved customer service and employee relations, may ultimately provide the largest payback, but are harder to quantify.

counter
(1) In programming, a variable that is used to keep track of anything that must be counted. The programming language determines the number of counters (variables) that are available to a programmer.

(2) In electronics, a circuit that counts pulses and generates an output at a specified time.

courseware
Educational software. See CBT.

covert channel
A transfer of information that violates a computer's built-in security systems. A covert storage channel refers to depositing information in a memory or storage location that can be accessed by different security clearances. A covert timing channel is the manipulation of a system resource in such a way that it can be detected by another process.

CP
(1) (Copy Protected) See copy protection.

(2) (Central Processor) See processor and CPU.

(3) See control program.

CP/M
(Control Program for Microprocessors) A single user operating system for the 8080 and Z80 microprocessors from Digital Research Inc. Created by Gary Kildall, CP/M had its heyday in the early 1980s.

CP/M was an unsophisticated program that didn't instill confidence in users, yet it was a major contributor to the personal computer revolution. Because the industry never standardized on a disk or video format for it, software developers had to support dozens of video displays and make their programs available on a myriad of disk formats. This chaos helped IBM set the standard with its PC.

Although IBM asked Kildall to provide the operating system for its new personal computer, he wouldn't agree to certain demands. IBM then went to Microsoft, which purchased an operating system from another company and turned it into DOS. Ironically, DOS was modeled after CP/M.

CPE (Customer Premises Equipment) Communications equipment that resides on the customer's premises.

CPF (Control Program Facility) The operating system for IBM's System/38 minicomputer series. CPF also includes an integrated relational database management system that is part of the overall System/38 architecture.

CPI (Characters Per Inch) Measures the density of characters on a magnetic tape or the number of printed characters.

CPM (Critical Path Method) A project management planning and control technique implemented on computers. The critical path is the series of activities and tasks in the project that have no built-in slack time. Any task in the critical path that takes longer than expected will lengthen the total time of the project.

CPS (Characters Per Second) Measures the speed of a serial printer or the speed of a data transfer between hardware devices or over a communications channel. CPS is equivalent to bytes per second.

CPU (Central Processing Unit) The computing part of the computer. Also called the *processor*, it is made up of the control unit and ALU.

A personal computer CPU is contained on a single microprocessor. A minicomputer CPU is contained on one or several printed circuit boards. A mainframe CPU is contained on many printed circuit boards.

The CPU, clock and main memory make up a computer. A complete computer system requires the addition of control units, input, output and storage devices and an operating system.

THE CPU OF THE DATAMATIC 1000

(Courtesy Honeywell Inc.)

The arithmetic logic unit (ALU) and control unit in the picture made up the CPU in Honeywell's DATAMATIC 1000 in 1957. Today, the equivalent amount of processing power is built into a single chip, and, the space of the actual circuitry takes up a quarter of a square inch and is 1/1000th of an inch thick.

The terms CPU and processor imply the use of main memory as in the sentence "data is sent to the CPU and then processed," since the data must be stored in memory in order to be processed.

CPU bound Same as *process bound*.

CPU time The amount of time it takes for the CPU to execute a set of instructions and explicitly excludes the waiting time for input and output to occur. The CPU time is always less than the total duration of time for a data processing job to be completed from start to finish.

CR (Carriage Return) The return (enter) key on a keyboard or the actual code that is generated when the key is pressed. In ASCII code, a CR has a numeric value of 13.

CRAM (Card Random Access Memory) A mass storage device, developed by NCR in the 1960s, that used removable cartridges filled with magnetic cards. In order to read or write data, a card was pulled out of the cartridge and wrapped around a rotating drum.

crash An unplanned program termination due to a hardware or software failure. See *abend* and *head crash*.

Cray Research (Cray Research, Inc.) A manufacturer of supercomputers founded in 1972 by Seymour Cray, a leading designer of large-scale computers at Control Data. In 1976, it shipped its first computer to Los Alamos National Lab. The CRAY-1 was a 75MHz, 64-bit machine with a peak speed of 160 megaflops, making it the world's fastest vector processor.

SEYMOUR CRAY
(Courtesy Cray Research, Inc.)

In 1982, Cray introduced the X-MP, a family of supercomputers that come with as much as 512MB of high-speed ECL main memory and up to 4GB of auxiliary memory, which can be used as a disk cache. Data can be transferred from auxiliary to main memory as fast as 2GB per second. The X-MP models calculate in the range of 500 megaflops.

In 1985, came the CRAY-2, a four-processor system with liquid-cooled circuits and 2GB of memory that was up to 12 times faster than the CRAY-1. In 1988, Cray introduced the eight-processor Y-MP. This 165MHz, 64-bit, 20 million dollar computer can calculate well into the gigaflop range.

In May 1989, Seymour Cray left Cray Research and founded Cray Computer Corporation.

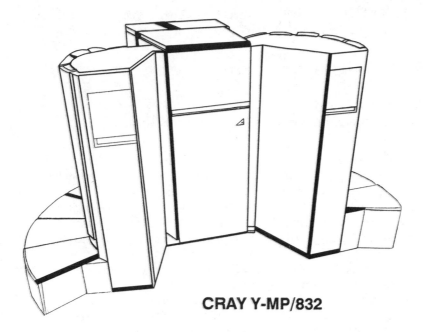

CRAY Y-MP/832

CRC (Cyclical Redundancy Checking) An error checking technique used to ensure the accuracy of transmitting digital code over a communications channel. The transmitted messages are divided into predetermined lengths which, used as dividends, are divided by a fixed divisor. The remainder of the calculation is appended onto and sent with the message. At the receiving end, the computer recalculates the remainder. If it doesn't match the transmitted remainder, an error is detected.

Cricket Presents A desktop presentation program for the Macintosh from Computer Associates. It provides the ability to create output for overheads, handouts, speaker notes and film recorders.

cross assembler An assembler that generates machine language for a foreign computer. It is used to develop programs for computers on a chip or microprocessors used in specialized applications, which are either too small or are incapable of handling the development software.

cross compiler A compiler that generates machine language for a foreign computer. See *cross assembler*.

cross tabulate To analyze and summarize data. For example, cross tabulation is used to summarize the details in a database file into totals in a spreadsheet.

crossfoot A numerical error checking technique that compares the sum of the columns with the sum of the rows.

crosshatching In computer graphics, a pattern of crossed lines.

crosstalk

In communications, an interference from an adjacent channel.

Crosstalk A family of communications programs for PCs from DCA/Crosstalk Communications. The Crosstalk products were originally developed by Microstuf, Inc., which later merged with DCA, Inc.

Crosstalk XVI, introduced in 1983, is a 16-bit version of the original Crosstalk that was developed for first-generation 8-bit CP/M personal computers. The first Crosstalk script language was introduced with this version, which has also been used by other vendors.

Crosstalk Mk.4, introduced in 1987, supports a wide variety of transmission speeds, protocols and terminals and can allow up to 15 concurrent communications sessions. It provides a user-definable menu system and a revised script language, called CASL (Crosstalk Application Script Language).

Crosstalk for Windows, introduced in 1989, is a Windows version that supports fewer terminals, but almost all the protocols. Its script language is a subset of CASL with additional commands for the Windows environment.

CRT (Cathode Ray Tube) The vacuum tube used as a display screen in a video terminal or TV. The term is often used to refer to the entire terminal.

crunch

(1) To process data. See *number crunching*.

(2) To compress data for reduced storage or transmission. See *data compression*.

cryogenics The use of materials that operate at very cold temperatures. See *superconductor*.

cryptography The conversion of data into a secret code for security purposes. Same as *encryption*.

crystal A solid material containing a uniform arrangement of molecules. See *quartz crystal*.

crystalline The solid state of a crystal. Contrast with *nematic*.

CSIC (Customer Specific Integrated Circuit) Pronounced "C-sick." Custom-developed chips from Motorola.

CSMA/CD (Carrier Sense Multiple Access/Collision Detection) A baseband communications access method that uses a collision-detection technique. When a device wants to gain access onto the network, it checks to see if the network is free. If it isn't, it waits a random amount of time before retrying. If the network is free and two devices attempt to gain access at exactly the same time, they both back off to avoid a collision and each wait a random amount of time before retrying.

CSP (Cross System Product) An application generator from IBM that runs in a variety of IBM mainframes and minicomputers. CSP/AD (application development) programs provide the interactive development part of CSP, while CSP/AE (application execution) programs are required to run an application created and generated in CSP/AD.

CSU See *DSU/CSU*.

CSV (Comma Separated Value) Same as *comma delimited*.

CTL, CTRL See *control key*.

CTOS The operating system that runs on the Intel-based Unisys B-series product line. Originally developed by Convergent Technologies (now part of Unisys), CTOS has been licensed to a number of companies, including BULL SA. It is designed for network use, and its message-based approach allows all program requests to be directed to any station in the network. Unisys' PC Emulator lets DOS applications (multiple applications in the 386) run concurrently with multiple CTOS applications.

CTOS/Open is a common specification created by the CTOS community that has been derived from existing variations of the product, including BTOS, the variation used in the Burroughs/Unisys product line.

CTS (Clear To Send) An RS-232 signal sent from the receiving station to the transmitting station that indicates it is ready to accept data. Contrast with *RTS*.

CUI (Character-based User Interface) A user interface that employs the character, or text, mode of the computer. It typically refers to typing in commands. Contrast with *GUI*.

current

(1) Present activities or the latest version or model.

(2) The flow of electrons within a wire or circuit, which is measured in amps.

(3) Current. A Windows-based PIM from IBM. It is designed for organizing appointments and contacts and allows data to be viewed in a variety of ways.

current directory The disk directory the system is presently working in. Unless otherwise specified, all commands that deal with disk files imply the current directory.

current loop A transmission system that detects the presence or absence of current as 1s and 0s rather than voltage levels.

cursor
(1) A movable symbol on a display screen that is the contact point between the user and the data. In text systems, the cursor is a blinking rectangle or underline. On graphic systems, it can take any shape (arrow, square, paintbrush, etc.) and usually changes as it is moved into different parts of the screen.

(2) A pen-like or puck-like device used with a graphics tablet. As the tablet cursor is moved across the tablet, the screen cursor moves correspondingly. See *mouse*.

cursor keys The keys that move the cursor on a display screen, which include the up, down, left and right arrow, home, end, PgUp and PgDn keys. In addition to cursor keys, a mouse or tablet cursor also moves the cursor on screen.

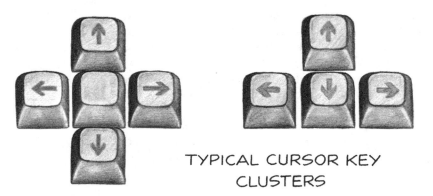

TYPICAL CURSOR KEY
CLUSTERS

customized software Software that is designed for a particular customer, in contrast with software packages that are available off-the-shelf for a particular industry, such as insurance or banking. Software packages, such as spreadsheets and database management systems, although canned, off-the-shelf packages themselves, are designed to create customized solutions to a user's problem as well.

cut & paste To move a block of text from one part of a document to another or from one file to another.

CUT mode (Control Unit Terminal mode) A mode that allows a 3270 terminal to have a single session with the mainframe. Micro to mainframe software emulates this mode to communicate with the mainframe. Contrast with *DFT mode*.

CYBER
A trade name for computers from Control Data that includes models from high-speed workstations to supercomputers.

cybernetics
The comparative study of human and machine processes in order to understand their similarities and differences. It often refers to machines that imitate human behavior. See *AI* and *robot*.

Cyberspace
An artificial reality that projects the user into a three-dimensional space generated by computer. Planned implementations by AutoDesk and others include the use of a DataGlove and a head-mounted stereoscopic display, which allow users to point to and manipulate illusory objects in their view. The term was coined by William Gibson in his novel "Neuromancer," to refer to a futuristic computer network that people use by plugging their brains into it!

cycle
(1) A single event that is repeated. For example, in a carrier frequency, one cycle is one complete wave.

(2) A set of events that is repeated. For example, in a polling system, all of the attached terminals are tested in one cycle. See *machine cycle* and *memory cycle*.

cycle stealing
A CPU design technique that periodically "grabs" machine cycles from the main processor usually by some peripheral control unit, such as a DMA (direct memory access) device. In this way, processing and peripheral operations can be performed concurrently or with some degree of overlap.

cycle time
Time interval between the start of one cycle and the start of the next cycle.

cycles per second
The number of times an event or set of events is repeated in a second. See *Hertz*.

Cycolor
A printing process from Mead Imaging (subsidiary of the Mead Corporation) that prints full tonal images like photographs. It uses a special film that is coated with light-sensitive microcapsules, called *cyliths*, that contain leuco dyes. The film is exposed to the color image that is being printed, resulting in a latent image of hard and soft cyliths. The latent image donor film is transferred onto a special Cycolor paper by being squeezed together through pressure rollers, thus releasing the dyes from the film onto the paper. The paper is then briefly heated, and the result is a full-color image that resembles a photograph.

cylinder The aggregate of all tracks that reside in the same location on every disk surface. On multiple-platter disks, the cylinder is the sum total of every track with the same track number on every surface. On a floppy disk, a cylinder comprises the top and corresponding bottom track.

When storing data, the operating system fills up an entire cylinder before moving to the next one. Thus, the access arm remains stationary until all the tracks in the cylinder have been read or written.

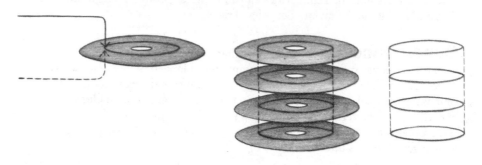

CYLINDER

C2 A minimum level of security as defined by the National Computer Security Center. See *NCSC*.

D

DA See *desk accessory* and *data administrator*.

D/A converter (Digital to Analog Converter) A device that converts digital pulses into analog signals. See *A/D converter*.

DAC See *D/A converter*.

DAD

(1) (Database Action Diagram) Documentation that describes the processing performed on data in a database.

(2) (Digital Audio Disc) Same as *CD*.

daisy chain An arrangement of devices connected in series, one after the other. Any signals transmitted to the devices go to the first device and from the first to the second and so on.

daisy wheel A print mechanism that uses a plastic or metal hub with spokes like an old-fashioned wagon wheel minus the outer rim. At the end of each spoke is the carved image of a type character.

When the required character spins around to the print hammer, the image is banged into a ribbon and onto paper. The mechanism is then moved to the next location. Daisy wheel printers print typewriter-like quality from 10 to 75 cps and have been superseded by dot matrix and laser printers.

DAISY WHEEL

damping A technique for stabilizing an electronic or mechanical device by eliminating unwanted or excessive oscillations.

Darlington circuit An amplification circuit that uses two transistors coupled together.

DASD (Direct Access Storage Device) Pronounced "dazdee." Any peripheral device that is directly addressable, such as a disk or drum.

DAT (Digital Audio Tape) A CD-quality, digital recording technology for magnetic tape. A 4mm DAT drive holds over one gigabyte of data and is used as a high-capacity backup medium for computers. See *DDS* and *D-DAT*.

data

(1) Technically, raw facts and figures, such as orders and payments, which are processed into information, such as balance due and quantity on hand. However, in common usage, both data and information are used synonymously.

The amount of data kept in the computer versus the amount of information is a tradeoff. Data can be processed into different forms of information, but it takes time to sort and sum transactions. Up-to-date information can provide instant answers.

A common misconception is that software is also data. Software programs contain instructions that are executed, or run, by the computer, not processed by the computer. Data is processed. Software is run.

(2) Any form of information whether on paper or in electronic form. In electronic form, data refers to data fields, records, files and databases, word processing documents, raster and vector graphics images and digitally-encoded voice and video.

(3) Data items in data files and databases in contrast with text, graphics, voice and video files.

(4) The plural form of datum; however, datum is rarely used.

data acquisition

(1) The automatic collection of data from sensors and readers in a factory, laboratory, medical or scientific environment.

(2) The gathering of source data for data entry into the computer.

data administration
The function within an organization that manages data. It analyzes, classifies and maintains all the data and data relationships. It coordinates the development of data models and data dictionaries, which, combined with transaction volume, are the raw materials for database design.

Database administration often falls within the jurisdiction of data administration; however, data administration functions provide the overall management of data

as an organizational resource. Database administration is the technical design
and management of the database.

Data Is Complex

The flow of data/information within a company is complex since the same data is
viewed differently as it moves from one department to the other.

For example: When a customer places an order, the order becomes a commission
for sales, a statistic for marketing, an order to keep track of in order processing,
an effect on cash flow for financial officers, picking schedules for the warehouse,
and production scheduling for manufacturing.

Users have different requirements for interrogating and updating data.
Operations people need detail, management needs summaries. Database design
must take these factors into consideration.

data administrator An individual who coordinates activities within
the data administration department. Contrast with *database administrator*.

data attribute See *attribute*.

data bank Any electronic depository of data.

data base See *database*. Database terms follow the last "data" word,
which is *data type*.

data bus An internal pathway across which data is transferred to and from
the processor. The exapansion slots in personal computers are connected to the
data bus.

data carrier
(1) A medium such as a disk or tape that can hold machine readable data.

(2) A carrier frequency into which data is modulated for transmission in a
network.

data cartridge A
removable storage module
containing magnetic tape.

Data Cell A storage device
from IBM that used strips of tape
stored in cartridges. In order to
read or write the tape, it was
selected out of the cartridge and
wrapped around a rotating drum.
The Data Cell, RCA's RACE and

DATA CARTRIDGE

NCR's CRAM were the first attempts at high-volume direct access storage in the 1960s.

data code

(1) A digital coding system applied to data for use in a computer, for example, ASCII and EBCDIC. Same as *character code*.

(2) Any coding system used to abbreviate data, for example, codes for regions, classes, products and status.

data collection The act of acquiring source documents for the data entry department. It comes under the jurisdiction of the data control or data entry department. See *data acquisition*.

data communications Same as *communications*.

data compaction See *data compression*.

data compression Further encoding of data to take up less space. For example, data stored in fixed length fields wastes a lot of space. The unused blank space can be replaced with a code stating how many blanks there are.

There are many mathematical techniques used to compress data. For example, this Glossary can be compressed 61% using PKZIP. The sparser the file, the more it compresses. Dense, machine language files can be compressed about a third. Some graphics files can be very dense, leaving little room for compaction.

data control department The function responsible for the collection of data for input into a computer's batch processing operations as well as the dissemination of the finished reports. The data entry department may be under the jursidiction of the data control department or vice versa.

data declaration Same as *data definition (1)*.

data definition

(1) In programming, the part of the program that includes the defining of data constants and data formats, such as fields, records and arrays.

(2) In file or database management systems, the process of describing the record structure to the program.

data description language See *DDL*.

data dictionary A database about data and databases. It holds the name, type, range of values, source, and authorization for access for each data element in the organization's files and databases. It also indicates which application programs use that data so that when a change in a data structure is contemplated, a list of the affected programs can be generated.

The data dictionary may be a stand-alone information system used for management and documentation purposes, or it may be an integral part of the database management system where it's used to actually control its operation. Data integrity and accuracy is better insured in the latter case.

data division The part of a COBOL program that defines the data files and record layouts.

data element The fundamental data structure in a data processing system. Any unit of data defined for processing is a data element, for example: ACCOUNT NUMBER, NAME, ADDRESS and CITY. A data element is defined by size (in characters) and type (alphanumeric, numeric only, true/false, date, etc.). A specific set of values or range of values may also be part of the definition.

Technically, a data element is a logical definition of data, whereas a field is the physical unit of storage in a record. For example, the data element ACCOUNT NUMBER, which exists only once, is stored in the ACCOUNT NUMBER field in the customer record, as well as the ACCOUNT NUMBER field in the order records.

Data element, data item, field and *variable* all describe the same unit of data and are used interchangeably.

data encryption standard See *DES*.

data entry The act of entering data into the computer, which includes optical scanning and voice recognition as well as keyboard entry.

When transactions are entered after the fact (batch data entry) and are just stacks of source documents to the data entry operator, the data entry process is error prone. Since scribbled letters or digits on the form may be entered as a best guess, it's often necessary to enter, print and review the entries manually or enter the data twice and compare the entries.

In online data entry operations, in which the operator is taking the order or information in person or over the phone, there's interaction and involvement with the transaction and less chance for error.

data entry department The part of the datacenter where the data entry terminals and operators are located.

data entry operator An individual who enters data into the computer via a keyboard or other input device, such as an optical scanner or card reader.

data entry program An application program that accepts data from the keyboard or other input device and stores it in the computer. It may be part of an application that also provides updating, querying and reporting.

The data entry program is important, because it establishes the data in the database, and it should test for all possible input errors.

Most database programs and some programming languages provide automatic validity checking functions, such as range checking and table lookups, to keep the database accurate. See *validity checking, check digit* and *intelligent database.*

data file A collection of data records. Contrast with *word processing file* and *graphics file.*

data flow

(1) In computers, the path of data from source document to data entry to processing to final reports. Data changes format and sequence (within a file) as it moves from program to program.

(2) In communications, the path taken by a message from origination to destination and includes all nodes through which the data travels.

data flow diagram A description of data and the manual and machine processing performed on the data.

data fork In the Macintosh, the part of a file that contains data. For example, in a HyperCard stack, text, graphics and HyperTalk scripts reside in the data fork, while fonts, sounds, control information and external functions reside in the resource fork.

data format Same as *file format.*

Data General (Data General Corporation) A computer manufacturer founded in 1968 by Edson de Castro. In 1969, it introduced the Nova, the first 16-bit mini with four accumulators, a leading technology at the time. During its early years, the company was successful in the scientific, academic and OEM markets. With its Comprehensive Electronic Office (CEO) software in the early 1980s, it gained entry into the commercial marketplace.

Data General's computer offerings range from the portable DG/One, the 32-bit family of ECLIPSE minis and UNIX-based systems using Motorola 88000 CPUs.

data glove See *DataGlove.*

EDSON D. de CASTRO
(Courtesy Data General Corporation)

data independence

A fundamental database management technique that allows the database to be structurally changed with minimal disruption to existing systems.

By separating the data from the processing, the detailed knowledge of every record layout is not coded into each application program. Therefore, when the record layout is updated (fields added, deleted or changed in size), the only programs that must be changed are those that use the new data.

The illustration on the right shows an application program (in machine language form) that does not use a database management system (DBMS) and thus has no data independence. Buffer space is reserved in the program for the entire record (fields A through K) regardless of how much of that data is actually processed by the program. (For an explanation of the graphical representation used in the following three illustrations, see *program*.)

The following illustration (left) shows an application program written in a language, such as Pascal or C, that uses a DBMS for its data. The program provides space for only the data it processes; in this case only fields D, G and K. As long as fields D, G and K aren't affected, this program will not have to change due to structural modifications to other parts of the record.

The following illustration (right) shows a program that uses a DBMS and is written in the DBMS's own programming language. In this case, the program provides no space for the data. The buffer space is made available (dynamically created) within the DBMS at run time. If new fields are added, the only application programs that have to be changed are those that deal with the new data. If existing data fields have been structurally changed (enlarged, shortened), then the only programs that must be changed are those that display or print the data. For example, a field that now holds a longer name may overlap an existing print column on the page.

data integrity

The process of preventing accidental erasure or adulteration in a database.

data item

A unit of data that is stored in a field. See *data element*.

data library

library The section of the datacenter that houses offline disks and tapes. Data library personnel are responsible for cataloging and maintaining the media.

DATA LIBRARY

data line

An individual circuit, or line, that carries data within a computer or communications channel.

data line monitor In communications, a test instrument that analyzes the signals and timing of a communications line. It either visually displays the patterns or stores the activity for further analysis.

data link In communications, the physical interconnection between two points (OSI layers 1 and 2). It may also refer to the modems, protocols and all required hardware and software to perform the transmission.

data link escape A communications control character which indicates that the following character is not data, but a control code.

data link protocol In communications, the transmission of a unit of data from one node to another (layer 2 in the OSI model). It is responsible for ensuring that the bits received are the same as the bits sent.

Following are the major categories of data link protocols:

ASYNCHRONOUS TRANSMISSION

Originating from mechanical teletype machines, asynchronous transmission treats each character as a unit with start and stop bits appended to it. It is the common form of transmission between the serial port of a personal computer or terminal and a modem. ASCII, or teletype, protocols provide little or no error checking and are only acceptable for text messages. Xmodem, Ymodem and Kermit are typical error checking protocols.

SYNCHRONOUS TRANSMISSION

Developed for mainframe networks using higher speeds than the early teletype terminals, synchronous transmission sends contiguous blocks of data, with both sending and receiving stations synchronized to each other. Synchronous protocols always have error checking. Examples are IBM's SDLC, Digital's DDCMP, and the international standard, HDLC.

LOCAL AREA NETWORKS
Developed for medium to high transmission speeds between stations, local area networks typically use collision detection (CSMA/CD) or token passing methods for transmitting data between nodes. Examples are IBM's Token Ring, Datapoint's ARCNET, Xerox's Ethernet and AT&T's Starlan.

data management Refers to several levels of managing data. From bottom to top, they are:

(1) The part of the operating system that manages the physical storage and retrieval of data on a disk or other device. See *access method*.

(2) Software that allows for the creation, storage, retrieval and manipulation of files interactively at a terminal or personal computer. See *file manager* and *database management system*.

(3) A function that manages data as an organizational resource. See *data administration*.

(4) The management of all data and information within an organization and includes data administration, the standards for defining data and the way in which people perceive and use it in their day-to-day tasks.

data management system See *database management system*.

data manipulation The act of processing data.

data manipulation language A language that requests data from a database management system, which is used within the application program, such as COBOL or C.

data model A description of the organization of a database.

data module A sealed, removable storage module containing magnetic disks and their associated access arms and read/write heads.

data name A name assigned to an item of data, such as a field or variable.

data network A communications network that transmits data. See *communications*.

data parallel Same as *SIMD*.

Data Physician A virus detection program for PCs from Digital Dispatch, Inc. It is designed to detect a virus and remove it, if possible.

data processing The capturing, storing, updating and retrieving of data and information. The term may refer to the entire computer industry, to only datacenter operations, or to only data processing activities, in contrast with word processing and office functions.

data processor
(1) An individual who works in data processing.

(2) A computer that is processing data, in contrast with a computer performing another task, such as controlling a network.

data projector A video machine that accepts output from a computer and projects it onto a large screen for audience viewing. See *LCD panel*.

data rate
(1) The speed of data transfer within a computer or between a peripheral device and a computer.

(2) The speed of data transmission within a communications network.

data resource management Same as *data administration*.

data set
(1) A data file or collection of interrelated data.

(2) A modem, as originally defined by AT&T.

data signal The physical data as it travels over a line or channel (pulses or vibrations of electricity or light).

data sink A device or part of the computer that receives data.

data source A device or part of the computer in which data is originated.

data stream A continuous flow of data from one place to another.

data structure The physical layout of data. Data fields, memo fields, fixed length fields, variable length fields, records, word processing documents, spreadsheets, data files, database files and indexes are all examples of data structures.

data switch A switch box
that routes one line to another.
For example, it is used to connect
multiple printers to one computer
or multiple computers to one
printer. A manual switch requires
turning a dial or pressing a button.
An automatic switch tests the lines
and provides first-come,
first-served switching.

DATA SWITCH

data system Same as *information system*.

data tablet Same as *digitizer tablet*.

data transfer The movement of data within the computer system.
Typically, data is said to be transferred within the computer, but it is
"transmitted" over a communications network. A transfer is actually a copy
function since the data is not automatically erased at the source.

data transfer rate Same as *data rate*.

data transmission The sending of data over a communications
network.

data type The kind of data being stored. Typical data types are numeric,
alphanumeric (character), dates and logical (true/false). Each programming
language allows for the creation of different data types.

   When data is assigned a type, it cannot be treated like another. For example,
alphanumeric data cannot be calculated, and the digits within numeric data
cannot be separated. Date types can only contain valid dates.

database

(1) A set of interrelated files that is created and managed by a database
management system.

(2) Any electronically-stored collection of data.

database administrator An individual who is responsible for the
physical design and management of the database and for the evaluation, selection
and implementation of the database management system.

   In smaller organizations, the database administrator and data administrator are
one in the same; however, when the two responsibilities are managed separately,
the database administrator's function is more technical.

database analyst See *data administrator* and *database administrator*.

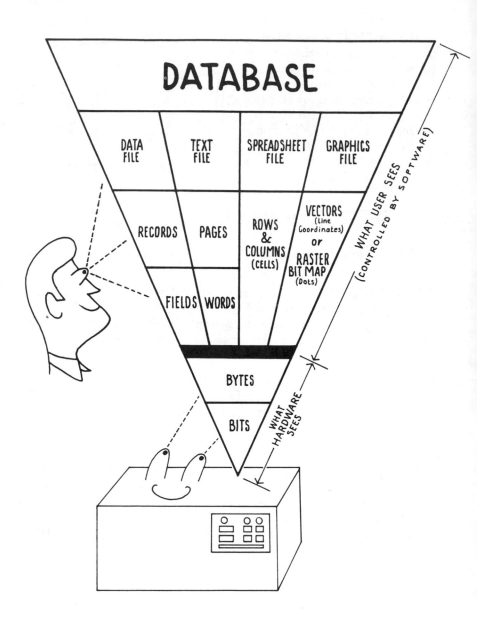

database designer See *data administrator* and *database administrator*.

database engine Same as *database manager*.

database machine A specially-designed computer for database access that is coupled to the main computer by a high-speed channel. Contrast with *database server*, which is used in a local area network. The database machine is "tightly" coupled to the main CPU, whereas the database server is "loosely" coupled in the network.

database management system
Software that controls the organization, storage, retrieval, security and integrity of data in a database. It accepts requests for data from the application program and instructs the operating system to transfer the appropriate data.

When a database management system (DBMS) is used, information systems can be changed more easily as the organization's requirements change. New categories of data can be added to the database without disruption to the existing system.

Major Features of a DBMS

DATA SECURITY AND INTEGRITY
Data security prevents unauthorized users from viewing or updating the database. Using passwords, users are allowed access to the entire database or subsets of the database, called *subschemas* (pronounced "sub-skeema"). For example, a database can contain all the data for an employee, but one group of users may be authorized to view only payroll, while others are allowed access to only work history and medical data.

The DBMS can maintain the integrity of the database by not allowing more than one user to update the same record at the same time. The DBMS can keep duplicate records out of the database; for example, no two customers with the same customer numbers (key fields) can be entered.

INTERACTIVE QUERY
Most DBMSs provide query languages and report writers that allow users to interactively interrogate the database and analyze its data. This is one of the most important features of a DBMS, as it allows users to get management information immediately.

INTERACTIVE DATA ENTRY AND UPDATING
Many DBMSs provide a way to interactively enter and edit data, allowing users to manage personal databases. However, interactive operation does not leave an audit trail of actions and does not provide the kinds of controls necessary in a multiuser organization. These controls are only available when application programs are customized for each data entry and updating function.

This is a common misconception about DBMSs for personal computers. Very comprehensive business systems can be developed in FoxBASE, Paradox and others; however, they are created by experienced programmers using the DBMS's own programming language. This is not the same as users creating personal files for their own record keeping.

DATA INDEPENDENCE
With a DBMS, the details of the organization of the data do not have to be built into every application program. The application program asks the DBMS for data by field name; for example, a coded equivalent of "give me customer name and balance due" would be sent to the DBMS. Without a DBMS, the programmer must reserve space for the full structure of the record in the program. Any change in data structure requires changes in all the applications programs.

Database Design

A business information system is made up of subjects (customers, employees, vendors, etc.) and activities (orders, payments, purchases, etc.). Database design is the process of deciding how to organize this data into record types and how the record types will relate to each other. The DBMS that is chosen is the one that can mirror the organization's data structure properly and process the transaction volume efficiently.

Organizations may use one kind of DBMS for daily transaction processing and then move the detail onto another computer that uses another DBMS better suited for random inquiries and analysis.

Overall systems design decisions are performed by data administrators and systems analysts. Detailed database design is performed by database administrators.

Hierarchical, Network and Relational Databases

Information systems are made up of related files: customers and orders, vendors and purchases, etc. A key feature of a DBMS is its ability to organize and manage these relationships.

Hierarchical databases link records together like an organization chart. A record type can be owned by only one owner. In the following example (right), orders are owned by only customer. Hierarchical structures were widely used in the first mainframe systems; however, they are often very restrictive in linking real-world structures.

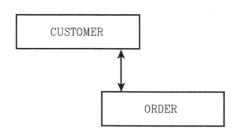

In network databases, a record type can have multiple owners. In the following example, orders are owned by both customers and products, since that's the way they relate in the business.

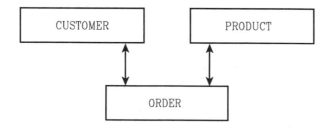

Relational databases don't link records together physically, but the design of the records must provide a common field, such as account number, to allow for matching. Quite often, the fields used for matching are indexed in order to speed up the process.

In the following example, customers, orders and products are linked by comparing data fields and/or indexes when information from more than one record type is needed. This method is more flexible for ad hoc inquiries.

CUSTOMER	ORDER	PRODUCT

Although relational database is often considered a new concept, DBMSs have traditionally provided relational capability with their hierarchical or network designs.

Intelligent Databases

All DBMSs provide some data validation; for example, they will reject invalid dates entered into date fields, alphabetic data entered into money fields. But the real processing is left up to the application programs.

Intelligent databases provide more validation; for example, table lookups will reject incorrect spelling or coding of items. There's no limit to the amount of processing that can be placed into an intelligent database as long as the process is a standardized function for that data. For example, the correct sales tax can be computed by the database and applied to all orders for the customer based on the customer's billing address.

When the validation process is left up to the individual application program, one program can allow one set of codes to be entered into a field, while another program can allow a totally different, and erroneous, set of codes. Data integrity is best served when there's one controlling source for the validation of data.

Mainframe databases have increasingly become more intelligent, and personal computer database systems are rapidly following suit. In time, all database management systems will be intelligent.

Database Machines

Database machines are specially designed computers that hold the actual databases and run only the DBMS and related software. Connected to one or more mainframes via a high-speed channel, database machines are used in large volume transaction processing environments. Database machines have a large number of DBMS functions built into the hardware and also provide special techniques for accessing the disks containing the databases, such as using multiple processors concurrently for high-speed searches.

Future Databases

The world of information is made up of data, text, pictures and voice. Many DBMSs manage text as well as data, but very few manage both with equal proficiency. Throughout the 1990s, as storage capacities continue to increase, DBMSs will begin to integrate all forms of information. Eventually, it will be common for a database to handle data, text, graphics, voice and video with the same ease as today's systems handle data. When this happens, the office of the future will have finally arrived!

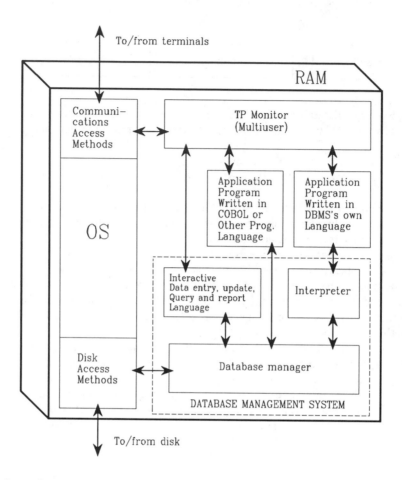

To/from terminals

RAM

Communi-
cations
Access
Methods

TP Monitor
(Multiuser)

OS

Application
Program
Written in
COBOL or
Other Prog.
Language

Application
Program
Written in
DBMS's own
Language

Interactive
Data entry, update,
Query and report
Language

Interpreter

Disk
Access
Methods

Database manager

DATABASE MANAGEMENT SYSTEM

To/from disk

database manager

(1) With personal computers, software that allows a user to manage multiple data files (same as *database management system*). Contrast with *file manager*, which works with one file at a time.

(2) Software that provides database management capability for traditional programming languages, such as COBOL, BASIC and C, but without the interactive capabilities.

(3) The part of the database management system (DBMS) that stores and retrieves the data.

database server
A computer in a local area network that is dedicated to database storage and retrieval. Contrast with *file server*, which stores many kinds of files and programs for shared use.

datacenter
The department that houses the computer systems and related equipment. The data library is part of the datacenter, and the data entry and systems programming departments may also come under its jurisdiction. A control section is usually provided that accepts work from and releases output to the different user departments.

DATACENTER

datacom (DATA COMmunications) See *communications*.

DataEase A relational database management system for PCs from DataEase International, Inc. It provides a menu-driven interface for developing applications without programming and is noted for its ease of use across the spectrum from beginners to experienced users.

DataGlove A glove from VPL Research, Inc., that is used to report the position of a user's hand and fingers to a computer. See *Cyberspace*.

DataPhone AT&T trade name for various transmission devices and services. DataPhone Digital Service is a private line digital transmission service. See *DDS*.

date math Calculations made upon dates. For example, March 30 + 5 yields April 4.

datum Singular form of data, for example, one datum. It is rarely used, and data, its plural form, is commonly used for both singular and plural.

daughter board A small printed circuit board that is attached to or plugs into a removable printed circuit board.

dazdee See *DASD*.

DB See *database* and *decibel*.

DBA See *database administrator*.

dBASE A relational database management system for PCs from Ashton-Tate Corporation. It was the first comprehensive database system for personal computers. Originally named Vulcan, dBASE was created by Wayne Ratliff to manage a company football pool. It was modeled after JPLDIS, the DBMS at Jet Propulsion Labs in L.A.

Renamed dBASE II, after George Tate and Hal Lashley formed Ashton-Tate to market it, it became a huge success within a couple of years. dBASE is the most widely used personal computer database system, and its programming language and file formats have become de facto standards.

dBASE provides a Pascal-like, interpreted programming language and fourth-generation commands for interactive use.

The following programming language example converts fahrenheit to centigrade:

```
INPUT "Enter fahrenheit  " TO FAHR
? "Centigrade is ", (FAHR - 32) * 5 / 9
```

The following fourth-generation language example opens the product file and displays green items:

```
use products
list for color ='GREEN'
```

dBASE II
Introduced in 1981, dBASE II is the original command-driven dBASE and runs on CP/M machines and PCs. dBASE II data formats and programs must be converted to run under dBASE III.

dBASE III & III PLUS
Introduced in 1984, dBASE III is a major upgrade of dBASE II that runs on PCs. It handles larger databases, includes a memo field, has more programming commands and a new menu-driven mode called the Assistant.

Introduced in 1986, dBASE III PLUS provided a number of new features, including a new Assistant menu and the ability to store queries and relational views.

dBASE IV
Introduced in 1988, dBASE IV is a major upgrade of dBASE III PLUS. It adds a query by example method for asking questions as well as an SQL language interface. Its report and forms generation screens as well as its

C. WAYNE RATLIFF
(Courtesy Ratliff Software Productions)

Assistant menus are redesigned. Many new commands and features are added to the programming language, including arrays and windows.

dBASE compiler A program that converts dBASE source language into machine language programs that can run in the computer without dBASE. See *Clipper, Force* and *Quicksilver*.

dBASE Mac A database management system from Ashton-Tate for the Macintosh that never caught on because it was incompatible with dBASE.

DB/DC (Database/Data Communications) Refers to software that performs database and data communications functions.

DBF file A dBASE data file extension. dBASE II and dBASE III files both use DBF, but are not compatible.

DBMS See *database management system*.

DBOMP (DataBase Organization and Maintenance Processor) A database management system that was derived from the earlier BOMP version developed by IBM.

DBS (Direct Broadcast Satellite) A one-way broadcast service direct from a satellite to a user's dish (antenna). DBSs are used to deliver private information and TV services.

dBXL A dBASE interpreter from WordTech Systems, Inc., that accepts the standard dBASE language and also features a menu-driven option for interactive use.

DB2 (DataBase 2) A relational database management system from IBM that runs on large mainframes. It is a full-featured and powerful database system that has become IBM's major DBMS product. DB2 uses the SQL language interface.

DB-9, DB-15, DB-25, DB-37, DB-50 A category of plugs and sockets with 9, 15, 25, 37 and 50 pins respectively. These connectors are used to hook up a wide variety of communications and computer devices. The DB refers to the physical structure of the connector and not the purpose for each of the lines.

DB-9 and DB-25 connectors are commonly used for RS-232 interfaces. DB-25 is also used on the computer end of the parallel printer cable for PCs (the printer end is a Centronics 36-pin connector).

A high-density DB-15 connector is used in the PS/2 series, which places 15 pins into the same shell as the DB-9 connector.

See illustration on the following page of a DB-25 plug and socket.

DB-25 PLUG AND SOCKET

DC

(1) (Direct Current) Electrical current that travels in one direction and used within the computer's electronic circuits. Contrast with AC.

(2) (Data Communications) An acronym for data communications; for example, a DC/DB product handles both data communications and database management.

DCA

(1) (Document Content Architecture) A set of file formats from IBM for text documents. DCA Revisable Form is a format that can be modified. DCA Final Form is a format that cannot be changed.

(2) (Distributed Communications Architecture) A network architecture from Unisys.

(3) (Digital Communications Associates, Inc.) A manufacturer of communications products, such as the IRMAboard.

DCE (Data Communications Equipment or Data Circuit-terminating Equipment) A communications device that establishes, maintains and terminates a session on a network. It may also convert signals for transmission, and is typically a modem. Contrast with *DTE*.

D-DAT A digital audio tape format for data. The tape can be divided in up to 254 partitions and provides for updating in place. D-DAT tape serves as both backup and standby storage. Contrast with *DDS*.

DDBMS (Distributed Database Management System) See *distributed database*.

DDCMP (Digital Data Communications Message Protocol) A synchronous communications protocol from Digital Equipment Corporation that is the primary data link component in its DECnet architecture.

DDE (Dynamic Data Exchange) The message protocol in Microsoft Windows that allows application programs to request and exchange data automatically. A program in one window can query a program in another window using the DDE protocol.

DDL

(1) (Data Description Language) A language used to define data and their relationships to other data. It is used to create files, databases and data dictionaries.

(2) (Document Description Language) A printer control language from Imagen that runs on the HP LaserJet series.

DDM (Distributed Data Management) Software in an IBM SNA environment that allows users to access data in remote data files within the network. DDM works with IBM's LU 6.2 session to provide peer-to-peer communications and file sharing.

DDP (Distributed Data Processing) See *distributed processing*.

DDS

(1) (Dataphone Digital Service) A private line digital service from AT&T that provides data rates from 2,400bps to 56Kbps. Private analog lines can also be connected to DDS lines.

(2) (Digital Data Service) Private line digital services from non-AT&T common carriers.

(3) (Digital Data Storage) A sequential tape format used for data backup. Data cannot be updated in place; it must be appended at the end of the existing data. Contrast with *D-DAT*.

de facto standard A format or language that is widely used and copied, but has not been officially sanctioned by a standards organization.

deadlock See *deadly embrace*.

deadly embrace A stalemate that occurs when two elements in a process are each waiting for the other to respond. In a network, it can happen if two users require the same data and the software is not sophisticated. For example, if one user is working on file A and needs file B to continue, but another user is working on file B and needs file A to continue, each one waits for the other, but both are temporarily locked out. The software must be able to deal with this.

deallocate To release a computer resource that is currently assigned to a program or user, such as memory or a peripheral device.

deblock To separate records from a block.

debug To correct a problem in hardware or software. Debugging software is finding the errors in the program logic. Debugging hardware is finding the errors in circuit design.

debugger A program that aids in debugging a program. It provides ways of stopping the program or capturing various system data at prescribed times. The debugger may be able to jump directly to the line in the source program that created the problem.

DEC (Digital Equipment Corporation) A trade name of Digital Equipment Corporation that is used in many of its products; for example, DECmate, DECnet and DECsystem. In the past, everyone referred to the company by this acronym; however, today the company encourages the use of Digital instead.

decay The reduction of strength of a signal or charge.

decentralized processing Computer systems in different locations. Although data may be transmitted between the computers periodically, it implies limited daily communications. Contrast with *distributed processing* and *centralized processing*.

decibel (dB) A unit that measures loudness or strength of a signal. People perceive loudness from a whisper of 10 dB up to about 140 dB. A noisy factory generates 90 dB and loud thunder is 110 dB. 120 dB is painful.
A decibel is a relative measurement that is derived from an initial reference level and a final observed level.

decimal Meaning 10; the universal numbering system that uses 10 digits. Computers use the binary system because it is easier to design electronic systems that can maintain two states rather than 10.

decision box A diamond-shaped symbol that is used to document a decision point in a flowchart. The decision is written in the decision box, and the results of the decision branch off from the points in the box.

decision instruction In programming, an instruction that compares one set of data with another and branches to a different part of the program depending on the results.

decision making Making choices. The proper balance of human and machine decision making is an important part of a system's design.

It is easy to think of automating tasks traditionally performed by people, but it is not that easy to analyze how decisions are made by an experienced and intuitive worker. If an improper analysis of human decision making is undertaken, the wrong decision making may be placed into the machine, which can get buried in documentation that is rarely reviewed. This is going to become much more important an issue as artificial intelligence applications proliferate.

From a programming point of view, decision making is performed two ways: (1) algorithmic - a precise set of rules and conditions that never change, or, (2) heuristic - a set of rules that may change over time (self-modify) as conditions occur. Heuristic techniques are employed in artificial intelligence systems.

decision support system (DSS) An integrated management information and planning system that provides the ability to (1) interrogate computers on an ad hoc basis, (2) analyze the information in various ways, and (3) predict the impact of decisions before they are made.

Database management systems allow users to select data and derive information for reporting and analysis purposes. Spreadsheets and modeling programs provide both analysis and "what if?" planning. However, any single application that supports a manager's decision making is not a DSS. A DSS is an integrated set of programs that share the same data and information. For example, a comprehensive DSS would even include industry data obtained from external sources that is integrated and used for historical and statistical purposes.

An integrated DSS will directly impact the management decision-making process and can change the way decisions are made within an organization. The DSS is an integral part of an information system and can be its most cost beneficial component.
See EIS.

decision table
A list of decisions and their criteria. It is designed in a matrix format that lists criteria (inputs) and the results (outputs) of all the possible combinations of these criteria. A decision table can be placed into a program to direct its processing. By changing the decision table, the program is changed accordingly.

OUTPUTS

INPUTS	APPROVE LOAN	DENY LOAN	SEE LOAN OFFICER	SEE LOAN OFFICER	
SAME JOB OVER 5 YRS	YES	NO	NO	YES	
OWNS CAR	YES	NO	YES	NO	
OWNS HOME	YES	NO	YES	NO	
IN DEBT	NO	YES	NO	NO	

DECISION TABLE

decision tree A graphical representation of all of the alternatives in a decision making process.

deck

(1) The part of a magnetic tape unit that holds and moves the reels of tape.

(2) A set of punched cards.

declaration In programming, an instruction or statement that defines data, procedures and resources to be used, but does not create an executable instruction.

DECmate A family of computer systems from Digital Equipment Corporation that are specialized for word processing. Introduced in 1981, DECmates use the PDP-8 architecture.

DECnet A communications architecture and series of related products from Digital Equipment Corporation. DECnet supports both Ethernet-style local area networks as well as wide area networks using baseband and broadband, private and/or public communications channels. It provides interconnection of PDP and VAX computers, Rainbow and VAXmate personal computers as well as PCs and Macintoshes. DECnet is built into the VAX's VMS operating system.

In DECnet philosophy, a node must be an intelligent processing machine and not simply a terminal as in other systems.

decoder Any hardware device or software program that converts a coded signal back into its orignal form.

decollator A device that separates multiple-part paper forms while removing the carbon paper.

decompress To restore compressed data back to its original size.

decrement To subtract a number from another number. Decrementing a counter means to subtract 1 or some other number from its current value.

DECstation

(1) A series of RISC-based single-user workstations from Digital Equipment Corporation, introduced in 1989, that run under ULTRIX (DECstation 3100 and 2100).

(2) A series of IBM-compatible PCs from Digital (DECstation 200 and 300), introduced in 1989.

(3) A small computer system from Digital, introduced in 1978, that was used primarily for word processing (DECstation 78).

DECsystem

(1) A series of RISC-based, 32-bit computers from Digital Equipment Corporation that run under ULTRIX. Introduced in 1989, the 5400 model is a Q-bus system; the 5800 model uses the XMI bus.

(2) A series of mainframes from Digital that were introduced from 1974 through 1980 and were the successor to the 36-bit PDP-10 computers.

DECtalk A voice synthesizing system from Digital Equipment Corporation that accepts serial ASCII text and converts it into audible speech. It is used in Touch-tone telephone response systems as well as for voice-output for visually handicapped users.

dedicated channel A computer channel or communications line that is used for one purpose.

dedicated service A service that is not shared by other users or organizations.

default A standard setting or action taken by hardware or software if the user has not specified otherwise. For example, defaults in word processing programs define the margins, tabs and page length, all of which can be changed by the user.

defragment To reorganize the disk by putting files back into a contiguous order.

degausser A device that removes unwanted magnetism from a monitor or the read/write head in a disk or tape drive.

DEL key (DELete key) A keyboard key used to delete the character under the screen cursor or some other block of data. It is often used in combination with the shift, control and alt keys to delete various text segments.

delay line A communications or electronic circuit that has a built-in delay. Acoustic delay lines were used to create the earliest computer memories. For example, the UNIVAC I used tubes of liquid mercury that would slow down the digital pulses long enough (a fraction of a second) to serve as storage.

delete To remove an item of data from a file or to remove a file from the disk. See *undelete*.

delimiter Any character or combination of characters used to separate one item or set of data from another. For example, in comma delimited records, a comma is used to separate each field of data.

Dell (Dell Computer Corporation) A manufacturer of IBM compatible PCs that was founded in 1984 by Michael Dell in Austin, Texas. Dell's first computers were sold under the PC's Limited name until 1988 when it changed to the Dell brand. Dell provides a complete line from laptops to high-end machines and sells its products directly to the end user. Dell machines are highly rated, and the company is known for its comprehensive telephone customer support.

delta modulation A technique that is used to sample voice waves and convert them into digital code. Delta modulation typically samples the wave 32,000 times per second, but generates only one bit per sample. See PCM.

DEMA (Data Entry Management Association) A professional organization devoted to the advancement of data entry management personnel. Organized in 1976, DEMA sponsors educational courses and conferences for data entry managers. For more information, contact DEMA at 101 Merritt 7 Corporate Park, Norwalk, CT 06851, (203) 846-3777.

demand paging The copying of a program page from disk into memory when required by the program.

demand processing The processing of transactions as they are entered into the computer system. Same as *transaction processing* and *realtime processing*.

Demo II A demonstration and authoring program for PCs from Peter Norton Computing, which contains its own programming language. Since an interactive session can be simulated, it allows prototyping of a user interface before writing the program. It can also be used to create CBT programs as well as sequential slide shows on screen.

demodulate To reconvert a modulated signal back into its original form by filtering the data out of the carrier frequency.

demultiplex To reconvert a transmission that contains several intermixed signals back into its original separate signals.

dense binary code A binary code that uses all possible bit patterns of the storage unit in contast with one that may have unused binary patterns.

departmental computing The processing of a department's data with its own computer system. See *distributed processing*.

dependent segment In database management, data that depends on data in a higher level for its full meaning.

dequeue Pronounced "d-q." To remove items from a queue in order to process or transmit them.

DES (Data Encryption Standard) An NIST-standard encryption technique that scrambles data into an unbreakable code for transmission over a public network. It uses a binary number as the key for encryption that offers more than 72 quadrillion combinations. The number, which can be randomly chosen for each transmission, is used as a pattern to convert the bits at both ends of the transmission.

descenders The parts of the lower case characters g, j, p, q and y that fall below the line. Sometimes these characters are displayed and printed with shortened descenders in order to fit into a smaller character cell, making them difficult to read.

descending sort The arranging of data records from high to low sequence (Z to A, 9 to 0).

descriptor A word used to identify a document in an information retrieval system that is indexed for fast searching.

deserialize To convert a serial stream of bits into parallel streams of bits.

Designer A drawing program for PCs from Micrografx, Inc., that runs under Microsoft Windows. It is a full-featured graphics design program for illustrations and CAD (64 layers) and provides almost all of the drawing tools of PostScript programs that run on the Macintosh. Designer creates its own proprietary DRW file format and also supports PIC files that are compatible with other Micrografx products.

desk accessory A Macintosh program that is always available from the Apple menu no matter what application is running.

desk checking The manual testing of the logic of a program.

DESKPRO A trade name for personal computers from Compaq.

desktop
(1) An on-screen representation of a desktop. See *Macintosh user interface.*

(2) A buzzword that is attached to almost any application traditionally performed on more expensive machines that is now run on a personal computer, such as desktop publishing and desktop presentations.

desktop accessory Software that simulates an object commonly found on a desktop, such as a calculator, notepad and calendar. For PCs, it is typically a TSR. The Macintosh counterpart is a *desk accessory*.

desktop application See *desktop accessory* and *desk accessory*.

desktop computer Same as *personal computer* or *microcomputer*.

desktop mapping Using a desktop computer to perform digital mapping functions.

desktop media The integration of desktop presentations, desktop publishing and multimedia, as coined by Apple Computer in 1989.

desktop organizer See *desktop accessory*.

desktop presentations The creation of presentation materials on a personal computer, which includes charts, graphs and other graphics-oriented information. It implies a wide variety of special effects for both text and graphics that will produce output for use as handouts, overheads and slides as well as sequences that can be viewed on screen. Advanced systems generate animation and can control multimedia devices.

desktop publishing The use of a personal computer to produce high-quality printed output that is camera ready for the printer. Desktop publishing (DTP) requires special software, a high-speed personal computer, a full-page, or two-page display monitor and a laser printer.

A laser printer is used for text and line art, but at 300 dpi, it is often used only to preview the output before it is sent to a typesetter. Typesetting systems (1,200 and 2,400 dpi) accept formatted output directly from popular systems, such as PageMaker and Ventura.

The key feature of desktop publishing is its ability to merge and manage text with graphics and display it on screen WYSIWYG style. The program can flow text around graphic objects in a variety of ways.

Text and graphics may be created in the DTP program, but very few of them have full-featured word processing and graphics capability. Usually, the creation of the work is done in word processing, CAD, drawing and paint programs and then copied into the publishing system. DTP programs accept common file formats directly.

DTP programs provide the ultimate in page layout capabilities, including a multitude of different type fonts, magazine style columns, rules and borders and page numbering in a variety of styles.

Since DTP has brought the cost of professional page makeup systems down to the personal computer level, it is often thought of as "the" way to produce inhouse newsletters and brochures. However, the professional appearance of printed material comes from graphics layout experience. Desktop publishing is no substitute for a graphics designer who knows which fonts to use and how to lay out the page in an artistic manner.

DESQview A multitasking, windowing environment from Quarterdeck Office Systems for PCs running under DOS. It allows users to keep several programs active and available at the same time, each one running in a DESQview window. The significant advantage of DESQview is that it is designed to run all DOS applications exactly as they are without modification. Even Microsoft Windows, itself a windowing environment, can be run in a DESQview window.

DESQview 386, made up of DESQview and QEMM-386 (Quarterdeck Expanded Memory Manager), manages all of the memory in the 386 as expanded memory and takes advantage of the 386's advanced modes.

DESQview also comes with a series of desktop accessories, including a calendar, notepad, calculator and communications package. Each of these accessories occupies a window, and like any DOS application running in DESQview, can be called up with a couple of keystrokes.

destructive memory Memory that loses its content when it is read, requiring that the circuitry regenerate the bits after the read operation.

detail file Same as *transaction file*.

developer's toolkit A set of software routines that are used in programming in order to link an application program to a particular operating environment (graphical user interface, operating system, database management system, etc.).

development cycle See *system development cycle*.

development system
(1) A programming language and related components. It includes the compiler, text editor, debugger, function library and any other supporting programs that enable a programmer to write a program.

(2) A computer and related software for developing applications.

development tool Any hardware or software that assists in the creation of electronic machines or software programs. See *developer's toolkit*.

device Any electronic or electromechanical machine or component from a transistor to a disk drive. Device always refers to hardware; for example, a device driver refers to software that activates the hardware.

device adapter Same as *interface adapter*.

device address See *address*.

device control character In communications, a special code that activates some function on a terminal. In ASCII, characters 17 through 20 are device control characters.

device dependent A program that is written to directly address the hardware at the machine level.

device driver See *driver*.

device independence The ability to run a program with different models of a peripheral device. It keeps the detailed instructions for activating a peripheral device within the operating system or other control program and explicitly out of the application program.

device level
(1) In circuit design, refers to working with individual transistors rather than completed circuits.

(2) Refers to communicating directly with the hardware at a machine language level.

device name A name assigned to a hardware device that represents its physical address. For example, LPT1 is a DOS device name for the parallel port.

DFT mode (Distributed Function Terminal mode) A mode that allows a 3270 terminal to have five concurrent sessions with the mainframe. Micro to mainframe software that emulates this mode can communicate with five mainframe applications simultaneously. Contrast with *CUT mode*.

DG See *Data General*.

Dhrystones A benchmark program that tests a general mix of instructions. The results of the program are expressed in Dhrystones per second, which is the number of times the program can be executed in one second. Contrast with *Whetstones*, which tests floating point operations.

DIA (Document Interchange Architecture) A standard format used in IBM's SNA networks that is used to exchange documents from dissimilar machines within an LU 6.2 session. It acts as an envelope to hold the document and does not set any standards for the content of the document, such as layout settings or graphics standards.

Diablo emulation A printer that accepts the same commands as the Diablo printer.

diacritical A mark added to a letter that changes its pronunciation, such as the French cedilla (Ç).

diagnostics

(1) Software programs that test the operational capability of hardware components, such as memory and disk drives. In personal computers, diagnostics are often permanently stored in a ROM chip and are automatically activated when the computer is started.

(2) Error messages in a programmer's source listing.

dialog box A small, on-screen window that is displayed in response to some request. It provides the options that are currently available to the user.

dial-up line A two-wire line as found in the dial-up network. Contrast with *leased line*.

dial-up network The switched telephone network that is regulated by national governments and administered in the U.S. by common carriers, such as AT&T, MCI, the Bell companies and a host of others.

diazo film In micrographics, a film used to make copies of microfilm or microfiche. It is exposed to the original film under ultraviolet light, and when developed, creates a copy with the same polarity as the original. Negative originals make negative copies, positive originals make positive copies. Diazo copies come in several colors, typically blue, blue-black and purple.

dibit Any one of four patterns obtainable from two consecutive bits: 00, 01, 10 and 11. Using phase modulation, a dibit can be modulated onto a carrier as a different shift in the phase of the wave.

DIBOL (DIgital coBOL) A version of COBOL from Digital Equipment Corporation that runs on its PDP and VAX series of computers.

dice See *die*.

dichotomizing search Same as *binary search*.

die The formal term for the square of silicon containing an integrated circuit. The popular term is chip.

dielectric An insulator, such as glass, rubber or plastic. Dielectric materials can be made to hold an electrostatic charge, but current cannot flow through them.

DIF

(1) (Data Interchange Format) A standard file format for spreadsheet and other data that are structured in row and column form. Originally developed for VisiCalc, DIF is now under the jurisdiction of Lotus Development Corporation.

(2) (Display Information Facility) A program from IBM that runs on the System/38 minicomputer. It lets users build customized programs for online access to their data.

(3) (Document Interchange Format) A file standard developed by the U.S. Navy in 1982.

Difference Engine A calculator designed in the early 1820s by the British scientist, Charles Babbage (1791-1871). The British government provided some funds for the machine, making it one of the first subsidized high-tech projects of 19th century Europe. The machine was not totally original; the concept of rods and wheels was used in earlier attempts at such devices.

DIFFERENCE ENGINE
(Courtesy Smithsonian Institution)

The Difference Engine was designed to add numbers up to six decimal places; however, it was only partially completed. In the course of building it, Babbage turned his attention to a new design, the Analytical Engine.

Differential Analyzer
An analog computational device that was built to solve differential equations at MIT by Professor Vannevar Bush during the 1930s. Less than a dozen of these machines were built, but they were known for their effectiveness in calculating ballistics tables during World War II. The machine took up an entire room and was programmed, with screwdriver and wrench, by replacing its camshaft-like gears.

DIFFERENTIAL ANALYZER

(Courtesy The MIT Museum)

Your basic hand-held programmable calculator of the 1930s.

diffusion
A semiconductor manufacturing process that infuses tiny quantities of impurities into a base material, such as silicon, to change its electrical characteristics.

digit
A single character in a numbering system. In the decimal system, the digits are 0 through 9. In binary, the digits are 0 and 1.

digital
(1) Traditionally, the use of numbers and comes from digit, or finger. Today, digital has become synonymous with computer.

(2) See *Digital Equipment*.

digital camera A video camera that records its images in digital form. Unlike traditional analog cameras that convert light intensities into infinitely variable signals, digital cameras convert light intensities into discrete numbers.

It breaks down the picture image into a fixed number of pixels (dots), tests each pixel for light intensity and converts the intensity into a number. In a color digital camera, three numbers are created, representing the amount of red, green and blue in each pixel.

digital channel A communications path that handles only digital signals. All voice and video signals have to be converted from analog to digital in order to be carried over a digital channel. Contrast with *analog channel*.

digital circuit An electronic circuit that accepts and processes binary data (on/off pulses) according to the rules of Boolean logic.

Digital Plumbing!

A digital circuit can be conceptualized as a mass of plumbing: the circuit paths are the pipes, the transistors are the valves, and the electricity is the water. Imagine opening a valve, and the water that passes through it and down a pipe will eventually reach a second valve, causing it to turn on, allowing water in another pipe to flow through the second valve, which will reach another valve, and so on.

A resistor can be viewed as a large pipe that narrows into a pipe with a smaller diameter, a capacitor as a storage tank, and a diode as a one-way valve, allowing water to flow in only one direction.

digital computer A computer that accepts and processes data that has been converted into binary numbers. All common computers are digital. Contrast with *analog computer*.

digital data Data in digital form. All data that is entered into the computer is in digital form.

Digital Equipment (Digital Equipment Corporation) A major manufacturer of computers, commonly known as DEC or Digital, was founded in 1957 by Kenneth Olson, who still heads the company. Digital pioneered the minicomputer business with its PDP computers in 1959.

Its early successes were in the scientific, process control and academic communities; however, after the VAX

KENNETH H. OLSON
(Courtesy Digital Equipment Corporation)

was announced in 1977, Digital gained a strong foothold in commercial data processing. The VAX series has evolved into a complete line of compatible computers from desktop to mainframe and uses the same VMS operating system in all of its models. The VAX machines caused Digital to achieve substantial growth throughout the 1980s.

Over the years, Digital has been widely recognized for its high-quality computer systems.

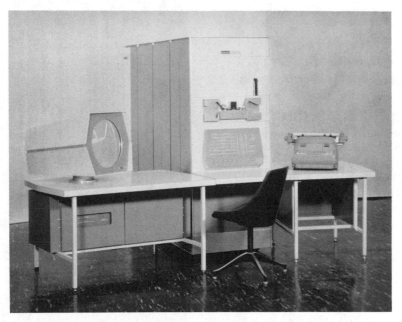

THE PDP-1, DIGITAL'S FIRST COMPUTER
(Courtesy Digital Equipment Corporation)

digital mapping The digitizing of geographic information for a geographic information system (GIS).

digital monitor A video display unit that accepts a digital, or TTL, signal from the computer. The majority of digital monitors use the same CRT technology found in a TV and must convert the digital signals to analog in order to illuminate the screen. Contrast with *analog monitor*.

digital PABX (digital Private Automatic Branch Exchange) See *digital PBX*.

Digital Paper A non-erasable, optical storage material from ICI Electronics that is used to create tapes and disks for high-capacity archival storage. The technology uses a polyester film coated with a reflective layer on top of which is adhered a dye polymer layer that is sensitive to infrared light. A laser burns pits into the film as close as half a micron apart.

Digital Paper capacities are approximately one gigabyte when used on a 5.25" disk and 600 gigabytes on a standard 2,400 foot tape reel.

digital PBX (digital Private Branch Exchange) A modern PBX that uses digital methods for switching in contrast to older PBXs that use analog methods.

digital radio The microwave transmission of digital data via line of sight transmitters.

digital recording See *magnetic tape & disk.*

digital signal processing A category of techniques that analyze signals from a wide range of sources, such as voice, weather satellites, earthquake monitors and nuclear tests. It converts the signals into digital data and analyzes it using various algorithms such as the Fast Fourier Transform.

Once a signal has been reduced to numbers, its components can be isolated and analyzed more readily than in analog form. Digital signal processing is used in such fields as biomedicine, sonar, radar, seismology and speech and data communictions.

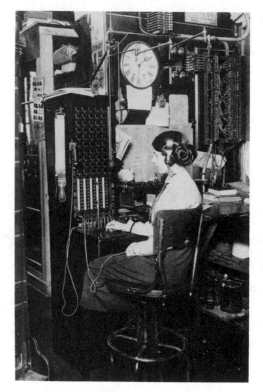

SWITCHBOARD (1915)

(Courtesy AT&T)

Hardly automatic, and by no means digital, this switchboard was sophisticated technology for its time.

digitize To convert an image or signal into digital code for input into the computer. It includes scanning an image, tracing a picture on a graphics tablet or converting camera images into the computer. 3-D objects can be digitized by a device which uses a mechanical arm that is moved on and around the object. Sound, temperature and movement are also said to be digitized when they are converted into digital code.

digitizer tablet A graphics drawing tablet that can be used for sketching new images or tracing old ones, selecting from menus or simply for moving the cursor around on the screen, all of which can be provided within a single program.

The user makes contact with the tablet with a pen-like or puck-like device called a *cursor* (mistakenly called a mouse), which is connected to the tablet by a wire. For sketching, the user draws with the tablet cursor and the screen cursor "draws" a corresponding image. When tracing an image on the tablet, a series of x-y coordinates (vector graphics) are created, either as a continuous stream of coordinates, or as end points.

Menu selection is accomplished by a tablet overlay or by a screen display. The tablet cursor selects an item by making contact with it on the overlay, or by controlling the screen cursor.

DIGITIZER TABLET

dimension One axis in an array. In programming, a dimension statement defines the array and sets up the number of elements within the dimensions.

dimensioning In CAD programs, the management and display of the measurements of an object. There are various dimensioning, or drafting,

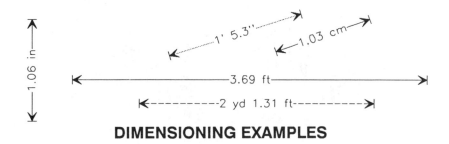

DIMENSIONING EXAMPLES

standards which determine such things as tolerances, sizes of arrowheads and orientation on the paper.

DIN connector A plug and socket used to connect a wide variety of devices. For example, the keyboard on most PCs uses a DIN connector. See *plugs & sockets*.

dingbats A group of typesetting and desktop publishing symbols from International Typeface Corporation that include fancy arrows, pointing hands, stars and circled numbers. They are formally called ITC Zapf Dingbats.

diode An electronic component that primarily acts as a one-way valve. As a discrete component or built into a chip, diodes are used for a wide variety of functions. Diodes are a key element in changing AC into DC. They are used as temperature sensors, light sensors, light emitters (LEDs).

High−Frequency   High−Current

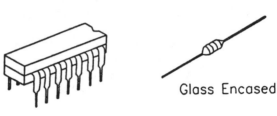

Glass Encased

DIODES

and light emitters (LEDs). In communications, they're used to remove both analog and digital signals from carriers and to modulate signals onto carriers. In digital logic, they're used as one-way valves and as switches similar to transistors.

DIP (Dual In-line Package) A housing that is commonly used to hold a chip. Tiny wires bond the chip to metal pins that wind their way down into the spider-like feet that are inserted into sockets on the printed circuit board.

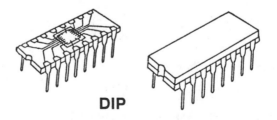

DIP

DIP switch (Dual In-line Package switch) A set of tiny toggle switches built into a housing commonly used to mount a chip on a printed circuit board. It is used to set many conditions such as assigning baud rate or port number.

Although designed for the technician, users must often set DIP switches when installing a peripheral device.

DIR (DIRectory) A CP/M and Microsoft DOS and OS/2 operating system command that lists the file names on the disk. Unless otherwise specified, DIR lists the files in the current working directory.

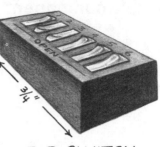

DIP SWITCH

direct access The ability to go directly to a specific storage location without having go through what's in front of it. Memories (RAMs, ROMs, PROMs) and disks are the major direct access devices.

direct access method A technique for determining the location of data on a disk by formulating the storage address from an identifying key in the record, such as account number. Using an algorithm, the account number is turned into the actual track and sector address where the data is stored. This method is faster than comparing thousands of entries in an index, however, disk space is wasted if the account numbers are not very consecutive in number.

direct memory access See DMA

direct read after write See DRAW.

directory A simulated file drawer on a disk. Programs and data for one type of application are typically kept in a separate directory, such as for word processing or spreadsheets. Directories create the illusion of separate compartments, but are actually indexes to the files which may be physically scattered over the disk.

directory management The maintenance and control of directories on a hard disk and usually refers to software that helps make it easier.

disable To turn off a function. Disabled means turned off, not broken. Contrast with *enable*.

disc An alternate spelling for disk. Compact discs and videodiscs use the disc spelling. Computer disks generally are spelled disk. Now that the two are merging, both forms will be intermixed.

discrete Any component or device that is separate and distinct and is treated as a singular unit.

discrete component An elementary electronic device that is constructed as a single unit. Before the chip, all electronic devices (transistors, resistors, diodes, etc.) were discrete. Discrete components are still used in conjunction with integrated circuits, either to augment them or because a particular type requires more electrical power than can be handled in a microminiaturized circuit.

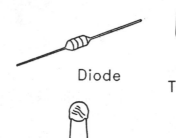

Diode

Transistor

Capacitor

Resistor

DISCRETE COMPONENTS

discretionary hyphen A user-designated place in a word for hyphenation. If the word is hyphenated, it will be split in that location rather than conforming to set rules.

dish A dish-shaped antenna that receives, or transmits and receives, signals from a satellite.

disk A direct access storage device. See *magnetic*.

disk based

(1) A computer system that uses disks as its storage medium.

(2) A program that manages its data on a disk. Contrast with *memory based*.

disk cache See *cache memory*.

disk cartridge A removable disk module that contains a single hard disk platter or a floppy disk.

disk controller The circuit that transmits and retrieves signals to the disk drive. In a personal computer, a disk controller is a printed circuit board that plugs into an expansion slot in the bus.

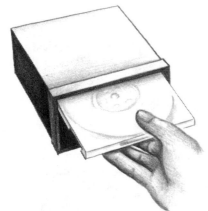

DISK CARTRIDGES

disk crash See *head crash*.

disk drive A peripheral storage device that holds, spins, reads and writes magnetic or optical disks. The disk drive may be a receptacle for disk cartridges or disk packs, or it may contain non-removable disk platters like most personal computer hard disks.

disk dump A printout of disk contents without any report formatting.

disk duplicator A device that formats and makes identical copies of floppy disks for software distribution. Disk duplicators can be simple devices with two floppy drives or elaborate automatic loading machines.

disk file Any set of instructions or data that is recorded, cataloged and treated as a single unit on a disk. Source language programs, machine language programs, spreadsheets, data files, text documents, graphics files and batch files are examples.

disk format
(1) A storage layout of a disk as determined by the physical medium and as initialized by a format program. For example, a double-density 360K floppy versus a high-density 1.2M floppy disk. See *low-level format*.

(2) A storage layout of a disk as determined by the operating system's access method. For example, a DOS format versus a Macintosh format. More specifically, a DOS 360K floppy versus a Mac 800K floppy.

(3) A type of disk, such as a 5.25" or 3.5" floppy disk.

(4) A format of a particular database, word processing or graphics file on disk.

disk management

(1) The maintenance and control of a hard disk and may refer to a variety of utilities that provide format, copy, diagnostic, directory management and defragmenting functions.

(2) The organization structure used for storing data on a disk. See *access method* and *FAT*.

disk memory Same as disk storage. In this Glossary, disks and tapes are called storage devices, not memory devices.

disk mirroring The recording of redundant data for fault tolerant operation. Data is written on two partitions of the same disk, on two separate disks within the same system or on two separate computer systems.

disk operating system See DOS.

disk pack A removable hard disk module that contains several hard disk platters mounted on a central spindle. When outside of the disk drive, it is held in a plastic container that keeps the disk platters dust free. Before insertion, the bottom of the container is removed. After insertion into the drive, the rest of the container is removed.

DISK PACKS

disk unit Same as *disk drive*.

DISKCOPY A DOS and OS/2 utility program used for making disk copies. It copies the entire disk track by track, thus it will only work with identical disk formats (a 5.25" disk can't be DISKCOPY'd to a 3.5" disk). It also formats an unformatted disk at the same time.

diskette Same as *floppy disk*.

diskless workstation A computer in a network that does not have any local disk storage. All programs and data are retrieved from the network's file server.

DISOSS (DIStributed Office Support System) A centralized document distribution and filing application from IBM that runs in an IBM mainframe under MVS. Its counterpart under VM is called PROFS.

DISOSS allows for electronic mail and the exchange of documents between a variety of IBM office devices, including Displaywriter word processors, personal computers, 8100 and 5520 computers.

dispatcher Same as *scheduler*.

dispersed intelligence Same as *distributed intelligence*.

displacement The distance from a starting point. For example, in a machine language program, the displacement is the distance an instruction is located from the beginning of the program. When the instruction is executed, the displacement is added to the *base*, which is the memory location the program starts at.

display
(1) To show text and graphics on a video or flat panel screen.

(2) A screen or monitor.

display adapter Same as *video display board*.

display attribute See *attribute*.

display board Same as *video display board*.

display card Same as *video display board*.

display cycle In computer graphics, the series of operations required to display an image.

display device See *display screen* and *video display board*.

display element
(1) In graphics, a basic graphic arts component, such as background, foreground, text or graphics image.

(2) In computer graphics, any component of an image.

display entity In computer graphics, a collection of display elements that can be manipulated as a unit.

display frame In computer graphics, a single frame in a series of animation frames.

display list In computer graphics, a collection of vectors that make up an image stored in vector graphics format. A display list processor is a graphics engine that generates graphic geometry (draws lines, circles, etc.) directly from the display list and independently of the CPU.

Display PostScript A display language from Adobe Systems, Inc., that provides a translation from elementary commands in an application program to graphics and text elements on screen. It is the screen counterpart of the PostScript printer language and is designed for inclusion in an operating system to provide a standard, device independent display language.

display screen A surface area upon which text and graphics are temporarily made to appear for display purposes. It is typically a CRT or flat panel technology.

display terminal A terminal with a display screen typically using the same CRT technology as a TV. Same as *terminal, video display unit, video display terminal, CRT, monitor* and *console*.

DisplayWrite A full-featured word processing program for PCs from IBM. It stems from the typewriter-oriented DisplayWriter word processing system first introduced in 1980.

distributed data processing See *distributed processing*.

distributed database A database that is physically stored in two or more computer systems. Although geographically dispersed, a distributed database system manages and controls the entire database as a single collection of data. If redundant data is stored in separate databases due to performance requirements, updates to one set of data will automatically update the additional sets in a timely manner. Distributed database implies that redundancy will be managed and controlled.

distributed function *Distributed function* is the distribution of processing functions throughout the organization.

distributed intelligence The placing of processing capability in terminals and other peripheral devices. Intelligent terminals handle screen layouts, data entry validation and other pre-processing steps. Intelligence placed into disk drives and other peripherals relieve the central computer from routine tasks.

distributed logic See *distributed intelligence.*

distributed processing A system of computers connected together by a communications network. The term is loosely used to refer to any computers with communications between them. However, in true distributed processing, each computer system is chosen to handle its local workload, and the network has been designed to support the system as a whole. Contrast with *centralized processing* and *decentralized processing.*

dithering In computer graphics, the creation of additional colors and shades from an existing palette. In monochrome displays, shades of grays are created by varying the density and patterns of the dots. In color displays, colors and patterns are created by mixing and varying the dots of existing colors.

Dithering is used to create a wide variety of patterns for use as backgrounds, fills and shading, as well as for creating halftones for printing. It is also used in anti-aliasing.

divestiture The breakup of AT&T, which divested itself of its telephone companies on January 1, 1984.

DL/1 (Data Language 1) The database language used in IBM's IMS database management system.

DLC
(1) (Data Link Control) See *data link* and *OSI.*

(2) (Data Link Control) *DLC* is the protocol used in IBM's Token Ring networks.

(3) (Digital Loop Carrier) See *loop carrier.*

DLL See *dynamic link library.*

DMA (Direct Memory Access) Specialized circuitry or a dedicated microprocessor that transfers data from memory to memory without using the main processor. Although DMA may periodically steal cycles from the processor, data is transferred much faster than using the processor for every byte of transfer.

DMPL (Digital Microprocessor Plotter Language) A vector graphics file format from Houston Instruments that was developed for plotters. Most plotters support the DMPL or HPGL standards.

do loop A high-level programming language structure that repeats a series of instructions a certain number of times by comparing a set of values. In a DO WHILE loop, the instructions within the loop are performed if the comparison is true. In a DO UNTIL loop, the instructions are bypassed if the comparison is true. The following DO WHILE loop prints 1 through 10 and stops.

```
COUNTER = 0
DO WHILE COUNTER   10
   COUNTER = COUNTER + 1
   ? COUNTER
ENDDO
```

do nothing instruction An instruction that just takes up space. Also called a *no op*, it is used for future insertion of a machine instruction.

document
(1) Any paper form that has been filled in.

(2) A word processing text file.

(3) In the Macintosh, any text, data or graphics file that is created in the computer. In this Glossary, document refers only to text files.

document handling A procedure for transporting and handling paper documents for data entry into scanning machines.

document mark In micrographics, a small optical blip on each frame on a roll of microfilm that is used to automatically count the frames.

document processing The processing of text documents, such as in word processing, but also includes indexing methods for text retrieval based on document content.

documentation The narrative and graphical description of a system. Documentation for an information system includes:

OPERATING PROCEDURES
(1) Instructions for turning the system on and getting the programs initiated (loaded).
(2) Instructions for obtaining source documents for data entry.
(3) Instructions for entering data at the terminal, which includes a picture of each screen layout the user will encounter.
(4) A description of error messages that can occur and the alternative methods for handling them.
(5) A description of the defaults taken in the programs and the instructions for changing them.

(6) Instructions for distributing the computer's output, which includes sample pages for each type of report.

SYSTEM DOCUMENTATION
(1) Data dictionary - Description of the files and databases.
(2) System flow chart - Description of the data as it flows from source document to report.
(3) Application program documentation - Description of the inputs, processing and outputs for each data entry, query, update and report program in the system.

TECHNICAL DOCUMENTATION
(1) File structures and access methods.
(2) Program flow charts.
(3) Program source code listings.
(4) Machine procedures (JCL).

docuterm A word or phrase in a text document that is used to identify the contents of the document.

domain

(1) In database management, all possible values contained in a particular field for every record in the file.

(2) In communications, all the resources that are under control of a computer system.

(3) In magnetic storage devices, a group of molecules that makes up one bit.

dominant carrier A telecommunications services provider that has control over a large segment of a particular market.

dongle Same as *hardware key*.

door

(1) In a bulletin board system (BBS), a portal, or interface that allows an online user to gain access to an application program stored in the system.

(2) See *drive door*.

dopant An element that is diffused into pure silicon in order to alter its electrical characteristics.

doping The altering of the electrical conductivity of a semiconductor material, such as silicon, by chemically combining it with foreign elements. Doping results in either an excess of electrons (N-type or N-channel) or a lack of electrons (P-type or P-channel) in the silicon.

DOS

(1) (Disk Operating System) Pronounced "doss." A generic term for operating system.

(2) (Disk Operating System) A single-user operating system for the PC, PS/1 and PS/2 series from IBM. Developed by Microsoft, DOS development is also shared by IBM from time to time. DOS is sometimes called PC-DOS to differentiate it from MS-DOS, the Microsoft version for non-IBM PCs. Both products are almost identical and both are referred to as DOS. See *PC (Operating Environment)*.

DOS box The DOS compatibility mode in OS/2.

DOS extender Software that allows a DOS application to run in memory beyond one megabyte on 286 and higher PCs. Some DOS extenders work with 286s and higher, while others require a 386 at minimum. The DOS extender routines are linked with the application to provide this capability.

The DOS extender runs the application in protected mode in order to gain access to extended memory (beyond 1MB). When the application requests input or output, the DOS extender resets the machine back into real mode, lets DOS service the request and then switches it back into protcted mode to use high memory. See *VCPI* and *DPMI*.

DOS prompt The symbol on screen that indicates that the operating system is ready to accept a command from the user. The DOS prompt for a hard disk in Microsoft's DOS or OS/2 operating systems is usually **C:** or **C:**.

DOS shell A user interface for Microsoft's DOS operating system that provides a menu-driven alternative to the DOS command line. The primary functions of the interface are to launch applications and manage files and directories. Shells may also provide file viewers and electronic mail capabilities.

DOS versions The following list highlights changes in each new release.

Version	Intro.	Major features and supported devices.
1.0	1981	SS, 8-sector, 160K floppy.
1.05		Bug fix.
1.1	1982	DS, 8-sector, 320K floppy.
2.0	1983	10M hard disk, 9-sector, 360K floppy, directories, more batch commands.
2.1	1983	PCjr cartridge support and bug fixes.
3.0	1984	20M hard disk, 1.2M floppy, VDISK RAM disk, new commands & PATH.
3.1	1985	Network support, bug fixes.
3.2	1986	720K microfloppy, new commands, such as XCOPY and improvements.
3.3	1987	1.44M microfloppy, improved commands, FDISK hard disk partitioning (32M).

| 4.0 | 1988 | Menu interface with mouse support, improved commands, EMS, hard disk partitions increased to 512M. |
| 4.01 | | Bug fix. |

DOS/VSE (Disk Operating System/Virtual Storage Extended) A
multiuser, multitasking, virtual memory operating system from IBM that typically runs on IBM's 43xx series of medium-scale mainframes.

dot A tiny round, rectangular or square spot that is one element in a matrix,
which is used to display or print a graphics or text image. See *dot matrix*.

dot addressable The ability to program each individual dot on a video
display, dot matrix printer or laser printer.

dot chart Same as *scatter diagram*.

dot matrix A pattern of tiny dots that form character and graphic images
on video screens and printers. Display screens use a matrix (set of rows and columns) of dots just like television sets. Serial printers use one or two columns of dot hammers that are moved across the paper. Laser printers "paint" dots of light a line at a time onto a light-sensitive photographic drum.

The more dots per square inch, the higher the resolution of the characters and graphics.

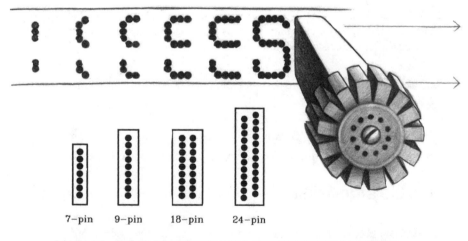

7–pin   9–pin   18–pin   24–pin

SERIAL DOT MATRIX PIN CONFIGURATIONS

dot matrix printer A printer that forms images out of dots. The
common desktop dot matrix printer uses one or two columns of dot hammers that are moved serially across the paper. The more dot hammers used, the higher the resolution of the printed image. 24-pin dot matrix printers produce typewriter-like output.

dot pitch The resolution of a dot matrix. For display screens, it is expressed as the width of an individual dot; for example, a .28 dot pitch refers to a dot that is 28/100ths of a millimeter in diameter. The smaller the number, the higher the resolution. For printers, it is expressed as the number of dots per linear inch; for example, a desktop laser printer prints at least 300 dpi. The larger the number, the higher the resolution.

double buffering A program technique that uses two buffers to speed up data retrieval in a computer that can overlap I/O functions and processing. For input, data in one buffer is being processed, while the second buffer is receiving the next set of data. For output, data is output from one buffer, while the next set of data is being prepared for output in the other buffer.

double click To press the mouse button twice in rapid succession.

double-dabble A method for converting binary numbers into decimal numbers by doubling the leftmost bit, adding the next lower bit, doubling the sum and repeating the process until the sum contains the lowest order bit.

double density disk A disk with twice the storage capacity of the previous model and less capacity than high density. For example, in PCs, the 360K 5.25" floppy is a double density disk; the 1.2M floppy is high density. The 720K 3.5" disk is double density; the 1.4M disk is high density.

double precision The use of two computer words instead of one to hold a number used for calculations, thus allowing twice as large a number for more arithmetic precision. Contrast with *single precision*.

double punch More than one punched hole within a column of a punched card.

double scan CGA A hardware method that doubles the effective resolution of the CGA display standard without requiring a change in software.

double sided disk A floppy disk that is recorded on both of its sides.

double strike In printing, to print each character twice in order to darken the image.

down Refers to a computer that fails to operate due to hardware or software failure. A communications line is down when it is unable to transfer data.

down link The communications channel from a satellite to an earth station.

download To transmit data from a central computer to a remote computer or from a file server to a workstation. It implies transmitting an entire file, rather than interacting back and forth in a conversational mode. Contrast with *upload*.

downtime The time during which a computer is not functioning due to hardware or system software failure. That's when you truly understand how important it is to have reliable hardware.

downward compatible Also called *backward compatible*. Refers to smaller or earlier models of a computer system that can run the same software as larger or newer models. Contrast with *updward compatible*.

DP See *data processing*.

dpi (Dots Per Inch) The number of dots that are printed or displayed within a linear inch.

DPMA (Data Processing Management Association) A membership organization, founded in 1951, with over 40,000 directors and managers of data processing installations, programmers, systems analysts and research specialists.

The DPMA is the founder of the Certificate in Data Processing (CDP) examination program, now administrated by an international organization. It also offers many professional educational programs and seminars, in addition to sponsoring student organizations around the country interested in data processing. For more information, contact DPMA, 505 Busse Highway, Park Ridge, IL 60068, (312) 825-8124.

DPPX (Distributed Processing Programming Executive) DPPX/SP is the operating system for the 8100 computer, now defunct. DPPX/370 is a 370 version that allows users to migrate to 9370 CPUs.

DPS A series of minicomputers from Bull HN.

DPSK (Differential Phase Shift Keying) The common form of phase modulation used in modems. It does not require complex demodulation circuitry, and it is not susceptible to random phase changes in the transmitted waveform. Contrast with *FSK*.

Drafix *Drafix 1 Plus* and *Drafix 3-D Modeler* are 2-D and 3-D computer-aided design packages respectively from Foresight Resources Corporation that run on PCs and the Atari ST. It features a unique user interface that provides constant on-screen information during drawing. Drafix combines professional-level features, such as curve fitting, multiple fonts and isometric slant.

drag To move an object on screen in which its complete movement is visible from its starting location to its destination. The movement may be activated with a stylus, mouse or keyboard keys.

drain The output side, or receiving side of the bridge, in a field effect transistor. When the *gate* is charged, current flows from the *source* to the drain. Same as *collector* in a bipolar transistor.

DRAM See *dynamic RAM*.

DRAW (Direct Read After Write) A method that reads the data right after it has been written to immediately check for errors in the recording process.

drawing program Graphics software that allows the user to design and illustrate products and objects. Drawing programs maintain an image in vector graphics format, which allows all the elements of the graphic object to be isolated and manipulated individually.

Drawing programs and CAD programs are similar; however, drawing programs usually provide a large number of special effects for fancy illustrations, while CAD programs provide precise dimensioning and positioning of each graphic element in order that the objects can be transferred to other systems for engineering analysis and manufacturing. Contrast with *paint program*.

DRDBMS (Distributed Relational DataBase Management System) A relational database management system that manages distributed databases. See *distributed database management system*.

drift A change in frequency or time synchronization of a signal that occurs slowly.

drive

(1) An electromechanical device that spins disks and tapes at a specified speed. Drive also refers to the entire peripheral unit such as *disk drive* or *tape drive*.

(2) To provide power and signals to a device. For example, "this control unit can drive up to 15 terminals."

drive door A panel, gate or lever used to lock a disk in a disk drive. In a 5.25" floppy drive, the drive door is the lever that is turned down over the slot after the disk is inserted.

driver

(1) Also called a *device driver,* a program routine that contains the instructions necessary to control the operation of a peripheral device. Drivers contain the detailed knowledge about the devices they manage, for example, the number of sectors per disk track or the number of lines of screen resolution. They contain

the precise machine language necessary to activate all the functions of each device.

The basic drivers come with the operating system, and additional drivers are added when new peripheral devices are installed. For example, if you add a mouse or CD ROM player to your personal computer, you have to install the appropriate driver so that the operating system knows how to handle it. Many word processing, desktop publishing and graphics programs also come with drivers for popular display screens and printers in order to provide complete control over the display and printing of a document. See *CONFIG.SYS*.

(2) A device that provides signals or electrical current to activate a transmission line or display screen. See *line driver*.

drop-down menu See *pull-down menu*.

drop in
The recognition of a 1 bit on a magnetic medium that was not intentionally recorded there. It may be due to a defect in the recording surface or to a malfunction in the transfer process.

drop out
(1) On magnetic media, a recorded bit that has lost its strength due to a defect in the recording surface or a malfunction of the recording process.

(2) In data transmission, a momentary loss of signal that is due to a malfunction in the system or excessive noise.

droupie
(data groupie) A person who likes to spend time in the company of programmers and data processing professionals.

drum See *magnetic drum*.

drum plotter
A graphics plotter that wraps the paper around a drum. It uses pens for plotting, and the drum turns to produce one direction of the plot. See *plotter*.

drum printer
A line printer that uses formed character images around a cylindrical drum as its printing

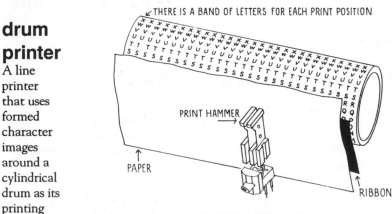

DRUM PRINTER

mechanism. There is a band of characters for each print position. When the desired character for the selected print position has rotated around to the hammer line, the hammer hits the paper from behind and pushes it into the ribbon and onto the character.

dry plasma etching A method for inscribing a pattern on a wafer by shooting hot ions through a mask to evaporate the silicon dioxide insulation layer. Dry plasma etching replaces the wet processing method that uses film and acid for developing the pattern.

drystone See *Dhrystone*.

DS/DD (Double Sided/Double Density) Refers to floppy disks, such as the 5.25" 360K PC format and 3.5" 720K PC and 800K Macintosh formats.

DS/HD (Double Sided/High Density) Refers to floppy disks, such as the 5.25" 1.2M PC format and 3.5" 1.4M PC and Macintosh formats.

DSA
(1) (Distributed Systems Architecture) Bull HN network architecture.

(2) (Directory Systems Agent) The X.500 routine that looks up the location of a message recipient. It accepts requests from the Directory User Agent counterpart in the workstation.

(3) (Digital Storage Architecture) A disk controller standard from Digital.

(4) (Digital Signal Analyzer) An oscilloscope from Tektronix, Inc., that samples high-frequency signals.

DSP See *digital signal processing*.

DSR (Data Set Ready) An RS-232 signal that is sent from the modem to the computer or terminal indicating that is able to accept data. Contrast with *DTR*.

DSS See *decision support system*.

DSTN (Double SuperTwisted Nematic) See *supertwist*.

DSU/CSU (Data Service Unit/Channel Service Unit) A communications device that connects an inhouse line to an external digital circuit (T1, DDS...). The DSU converts data into the required format, while the CSU terminates the line, provides signal regeneration and remote testing.

DTE (Data Terminating Equipment) A communications device that is the source or destination of signals on a network. It is typically a terminal or computer. Contrast with *DCE*.

DTP See *desktop publishing*.

DTR (Data Terminal Ready) An RS-232 signal that is sent from the computer or terminal to the modem indicating that is able to accept data. Contrast with *DSR*.

DTS

(1) (Digital Termination Service) Microwave-based, line-of-sight communications provided directly to the end user.

(2) (DeskTop Server) A Motorola 68000-based network server from Banyan.

(3) (Developer Technical Support) A tech-support group for developers at Apple Computer.

DUA (Directory User Agent) The X.500 routine that sends a request to the Directory Systems Agent to look up the location of a user on the network.

dual boot A computer that be started with either one of two different operating systems.

dual in-line package See *DIP*.

dumb terminal A display terminal without processing capability. It is entirely dependent on the main computer for processing. Contrast with *smart terminal* and *intelligent terminal*.

dump To print the contents of memory, disk or tape without any report formatting. See *memory dump*.

duplex channel A pathway that allows transmission in both directions at the same time. Same as *full-duplex*.

duplexed system Two systems that are functionally identical. They both may perform the same functions, or one may be standby, ready to take over if the other fails.

duplicate key A record that contains the same identification data as another record in the file. Duplicate keys may or may not be permitted in the database. For example, account numbers are often the primary key in a file and cannot be duplicated, since no two customers or employees should have the same account number. Dates may be a secondary key in a file and are often duplicated as there are many transactions for the same date.

DVI (Digital Video Interactive)   A technology from Intel for compressing and decompressing data, audio and full-motion video. On a CD ROM, it provides up to 72 minutes of full-screen video, 2 1/2 hours of half-screen video, 40,000 medium-resolution or 7,000 high-resolution images. It compresses full-motion video at ratios greater than 100 to 1 and still images at 10 to 1.

Split screen capabilities allow still and moving images side by side. For example, a training course could show an operation taking place along with pictures of the components being used.

DVI uses standard storage devices, but requires a DVI controller board in the personal computer. Developed by RCA's Sarnoff Research labs, Intel acquired it in 1988. See *CD*, *CD ROM*, *CD-I*.

Dvorak keyboard A typewriter keyboard with a special alphabet layout that was designed in the 1930s to speed up typing. Developed by August Dvorak, professor of Education at the University of Washington, and his brother-in-law, William Dealey, the Dvorak layout is set up so that 70% of all the words are typed on the home row, compared to 32% with the qwerty keyboard. In addition, more words are typed using both hands. In eight-hours, the fingers of a qwerty typist travel 16 miles, but only one for the Dvorak typist.

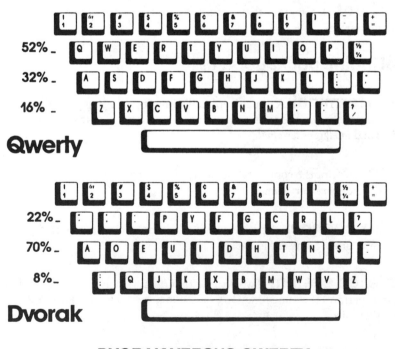

DVORAK VERSUS QWERTY

(Courtesy Dvorak International Federation)

In the Dvorak keyboard, 70% of the keystrokes are made on the home row compared to 32% with the qwerty keyboard.

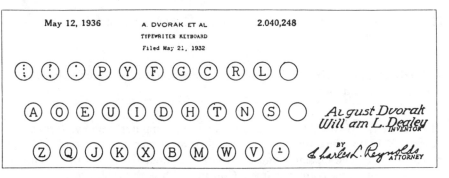

THE ORIGINAL DVORAK KEYBOARD
(Courtesy Dvorak International Federation)

DVST (Direct View Storage Tube) A graphics terminal that maintains the screen image without continuous refreshing. Any change to the image requires that the entire screen be erased and redrawn. This earlier design technique is no longer used.

DX (386DX) See 80386.

DXF A 2-D graphics file format developed by AutoDesk for the AutoCAD system. Many CAD systems import and export the DXF format for graphics interchange.

dyadic Meaning two; refers to operations in which two components are used or work together.

dye polymer recording A category of optical recording techniques that use dyed plastic layers as the recording medium. A single dye polymer layer is used in certain WORM devices. Erasable optical disks use a recording surface of two dyed plastic layers. The top layer is called the *retention layer* and the bottom layer is the *expansion layer*. A 1 bit is created (written) by shining a laser beam through the top retention layer and into the bottom expansion layer, which heats the area and causes it to expand into the retention layer to form a bump. The bumps in the retention layer are the actual bits that are read by the unit. In order to erase a bit, a laser with a different wavelength is used to strike the retention layer, and the bump subsides.

dynamic Refers to operations that are performed on the fly, while the program is running. In the expression, "the buffers are dynamically created," dynamic implies that the space is not fixed or reserved beforehand.

dynamic address translation In a virtual memory system, the ability to determine what the real address is at the time of execution.

dynamic link A connection that is established at run time from one program to another.

dynamic link library A set of program routines that are available to applications at run time.

dynamic RAM The most common type of computer memory. Dynamic RAM (DRAM) architecture usually uses one transistor and a capacitor to represent a bit. The capacitors must be energized hundreds of times per second in order to maintain the correct charges. Contrast with *static RAM*, which is usually faster and does not require refresh circuitry. Unlike firmware chips (ROMs, PROMs, etc.) both varieties of RAM lose their content when the power is turned off.

dynamic range The range of signals from the weakest to the strongest.

dynlink See *dynamic link*.

D4 A popular framing format for T1 transmission that places 12 T1 frames into a superframe. See *ESF*.

E

EAM (Electronic Accounting Machine) Another term for unit record equipment, the punched card tabulating machines that were the first data processing machines.

EAM ROOM (1952)
(Courtesy IBM)

early binding See *binding time*.

EAROM (Electrically Alterable Read Only Memory) Same as *EEPROM*.

earth station A transmitting and receiving station for satellite communications. Its antenna is shaped like a dish, which is used for microwave transmission to and from the satellite.

easy to learn and use Easy to learn refers to software that is logically designed and capable of being used right away. If you can make the program work right away, it's easy to learn.

Easy to learn implies easy to use right away, but it does not imply easy to use after you're thoroughly familiar with it. The very simple menus that coddled you in the beginning are the ones that become tiresome and time consuming when you use them day in and day out. Advanced programs have a macro recorder that lets you store the series of menu selections you make and play them back automatically.

EasyCAD 2 A CAD program for PCs from Evolution Computing. It's a full-featured program that is known for its ease of use. EasyCAD users can migrate to the more sophisticated FastCAD, which looks almost identical on screen, but provides multiple windows and is designed for high-speed operations.

EBCDIC (Extended Binary Coded Decimal Interchange Code) Pronounced "eb-suh-dick." A binary code for representing data developed by IBM for its 360 series in 1964. It is built into all IBM mainframes, most IBM minicomputers and other mainframes. It is an 8-bit code, allowing 256 possible character combinations, that stores one alphanumeric character or two decimal digits within a single byte.
   EBCDIC and ASCII are the two codes most widely used to represent data.

e-beam See *electron beam.*

ECF (Enhanced Connectivity Facilities) Software from IBM that allows DOS PCs to query and download data from mainframes as well as issue mainframe commands. It also allows printer output to be directed from the PC to the mainframe. ECF software resides in the PC (client) and mainframe (server) and uses the SRPI interface for interaction. Applications issue SRPI commands to request services.

echo cancellation A technique used in high-speed modems that isolates and filters out unwanted signals caused by echoes from the main transmitted signal. This permits full-duplex modems to send and receive on the same frequency. Telephone networks often use echo cancellers in addition to or in place of echo suppressors. Network-based echo cancellation can interfere with modems that do their own, such as V.32, so a method is provided for those modems to disable network echo cancellers.

echo check In communications, an error checking method that retransmits the data back to the sending device for comparison with the original.

echo suppressor A communications technique that turns off reverse transmission in a telephone line, thus effectively making the circuit one way. It is used to reduce the annoying effects of echoes in telephone connections, especially in satellite circuits.

echoplex A communications transmission technique in which the sending terminal does not display the data keyed in. Data is transmitted to the receiving station which then retransmits it back to the sending terminal for display.

ECL (Emitter-Coupled Logic) A type of microelectronic circuit design that is noted for its extremely fast switching speeds. ECL is a variety of bipolar transistor.

ECLIPSE A series of 32-bit minicomputers from Data General Corporation. The development of the initial 32-bit ECLIPSE MV/Family supermini, the MV/8000, was the subject of Tracy Kidders' best selling book, "Soul of a New Machine." The ECLIPSE line, running under the AOS/VS operating system, ranges from a single board processor up to dual-processor configurations that can handle over 500 terminals.

ECMA (European Computer Manufacturer's Association) The European counterpart of CBEMA, headquartered in Geneva, Switzerland.

edge connector A row of etched lines on the edge of a printed circuit board that is inserted into an expansion slot.

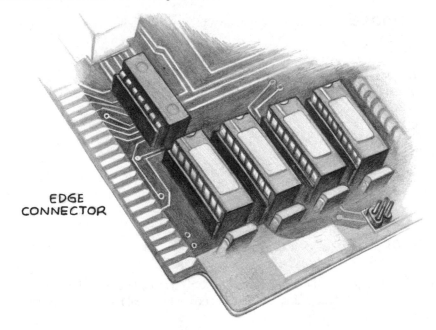

EDGE
CONNECTOR

EDI (Electronic Data Interchange) The electronic communication of transactions between organizations, such as orders, confirmations and invoices. Independent service organizations provide EDI services that enable users to interconnect with another organization's network regardless of type of equipment used. See X.12, Tradacoms and EDIFACT.

EDIFACT (Electronic Data Interchange For Administration Commerce and Transport) An ISO standard for EDI that is proposed to supersede both X.12 and Tradacoms standards to become the worldwide standard.

E-disk (Emulated-disk) Same as RAM disk.

edit To make a change to existing data. See update.

edit checking Same as *validity checking*.

edit instruction A computer instruction that formats a field for display or printing. Using an edit mask, it inserts decimal points, commas and dollar signs into the data.

edit key A key combination or function key that changes the program into edit mode when pressed.

edit mask A pattern of characters that represent formatting codes through which data is filtered for display or printing. See *picture*.

edit mode An operational state in a program that allows existing data to be changed.

edit program
(1) A data entry program that validates user input and stores the newly created records in the file.

(2) A program that allows users to change data that already exists in a file. See *update*.

edit routine A routine in a program that tests for valid data. See *validity checking*.

editor See *text editor* and *linkage editor*.

EDLIN The line editor in Microsoft's DOS and OS/2. EDLIN lets users create and modify batch files. In OS/2, it runs only in real mode, and OS/2's SSE, runs in protected mode.

EDP (Electronic Data Processing) The first acronym used to identify the computer field.

EDSAC (Electronic Delay Storage Automatic Calculator) One of the first stored program computers and one of the first to use binary numbers. Developed by Maurice Wilkes at Cambridge University in England and completed in 1949, it had 512 36-bit words of liquid mercury delay line memory. It used paper tape for input/output and was in use until 1958.

education The teaching of concepts that relate to a subject. Education about computers includes information about computer systems and information systems. Contrast with *training*, which provides detailed instruction about the use of a particular product.

EDSAC

(Coutesy Science Museum, London)

edutainment Educational materials that are also entertaining.

EE See *Extended Edition*.

EEMS (Enhanced Expanded Memory Specification) See *EMS*.

EEPROM (Electrically Erasable Programmable Read Only Memory) A memory chip that holds its content without power. It can be erased, either within the computer or externally, and usually requires more voltage for erasure than the common +5 volts used in logic circuits. It functions like non-volatile RAM, but writing to EEPROM is much slower than writing to RAM.

EEPROMs are used in devices that must keep data up-to-date without power. For example, a price list could be maintained in EEPROM chips in a point of sale terminal that is turned off at night. When prices change, the EEPROMs can be updated from a central computer during the day.

EFT (Electronic Funds Transfer) The electronic exchange of money. It refers to any transaction that originates at a terminal and transfers money from one account to another.

EGA (Enhanced Graphics Adapter) A video display standard from IBM that provides medium-resolution text and graphics. EGA supports previous display modes and requires a digital RGB Enhanced Color Display or equivalent monitor. EGA has been superseded by VGA. See *PC display modes*.

EIA (Electronic Industries Association) A membership organization, founded in 1924, that includes manufacturers of electronic parts and systems. With over 1,200 members, it sponsors shows and seminars and gives many awards for outstanding contributions to the electronics industry. The EIA sets electrical and electronic interface standards, such as the EIA RS-232-C interface. For more information, contact EIA, 2001 I Street, N.W., Washington, DC 20006.

EIS (Executive Information System) An information system for managers that consolidates and summarizes ongoing transactions within the organization. An EIS should be able to provide management with all the information it requires at all times from external as well as internal sources.

EISA (Extended Industry Standard Architecture) Pronounced "eesa." A bus standard for PCs that extends the AT bus architecture to 32 bits and allows more than one CPU to share the bus. EISA was announced in late 1988 as a counter to IBM's Micro Channel. Existing PC and AT boards, which cannot plug into the Micro Channel, can plug into an EISA slot. See *bus mastering*.

EL See *electroluminescent display*.

electricity The natural energy found in matter. The speed of electricity is the speed of light (approx. 186,000 miles per second). In a wire, it is slowed due to the resistance in the material.

The flow of electrons in a circuit is measured by its pressure, or force, in *volts* and by the size of current (thickness of the wire) in *amperes*, or *amps*. The total amount of energy is computed in *watts* by multiplying volts times amps.

Although we seem to know a lot about electricity and have been able to put it to a never-ending variety of uses, we only know how it works. We don't know, and maybe never will know, why.

electrode
A device that emits or controls the flow of electricity.

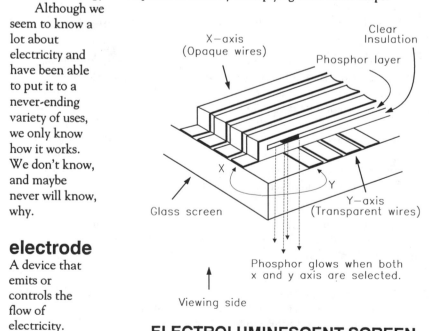

ELECTROLUMINESCENT SCREEN
(Courtesy Planar Systems, Inc.)

electroluminescent display A flat panel display technology that provides a sharp, clear image and wide viewing angle. It contains a powdered or thin film phosphor layer sandwiched between an x-axis and a y-axis panel. When an x-y coordinate is charged, the phosphor in that vicinity emits visible light. Phosphors are typically amber, but green is also used. In time, color electroluminescent displays will become available. See illustration on the previous page.

electromagnet A magnet that is energized by electricity. A coil of wire is wrapped around an iron core, and when current flows in the wire, the core generates an energy called magnetic *flux*.

electromagnetic radiation The energy transmitted through the air by a radio transmitter. By converting electrical energy into magnetic energy, we are able to control and direct it more accurately for wireless transmission.

All radiating energy in the universe is classified as electromagnetic radiation, which includes gamma rays, x-rays, ultraviolet light, visible light, infrared light and radar.

electromagnetic spectrum The range of electromagnetic radiation from the tiniest cosmic rays to radio waves and beyond. See chart on the following page.

electromechanical The use of electricity to run moving parts. Disk drives, printers and motors are examples. Electromechanical systems must be designed for the eventual deterioration of moving parts.

electromotive force The pressure in an electric circuit (measured in volts).

electron An elementary particle that circles the nucleus of an atom. Electrons are considered to be negatively charged.

electron beam A stream of electrons, or electricity, that is directed towards a receiving object.

electron gun A device which creates a fine beam of electrons that is focused on a phosphor screen in a cathode ray tube (CRT).

electron tube Same as *vacuum tube*.

electronic The use of electricity in intelligence-bearing devices, such as radios, TVs, instruments, computers and telecommunications. Electricity that is used as raw power for heating, lighting and motors, is considered electrical, not electronic. Although coined earlier, "Electronics" magazine (first published April 1930) brought the term to popularity. The subheading of the magazine read:

Electron Tubes - Their Radio, Audio, Visio and Industrial Applications. The term was derived from the electron tube, or vacuum tube, which was used as an amplifier of electronic signals.

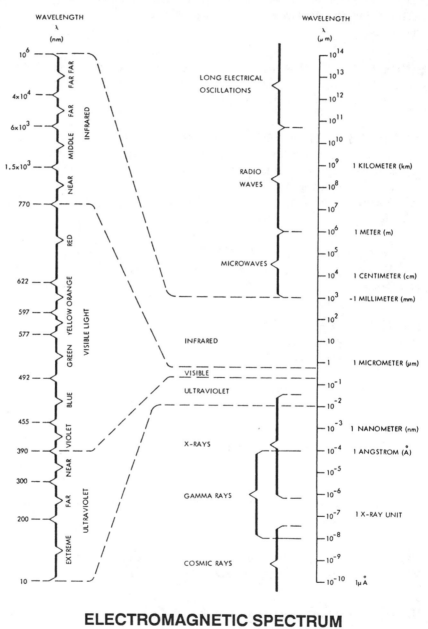

ELECTROMAGNETIC SPECTRUM

(Courtesy RCA)

electronic circuit An integrated series of electronic components that perform a function. It is a pathway through which electricity is directed in a prescribed pattern to accomplish a task. Electronic circuits used in digital computers deal with discrete on/off pulses (bits). Electronic circuits used in analog devices, such as radio and TV, deal with electrical vibrations (frequencies). See *digital circuit*.

electronic mail Also called *e-mail*. The transmission of memos and messages over a network. Electronic mail systems are implemented in mainframe, mini and personal computer LANs.

Users can send mail to a single recipient or broadcast it to multile users on the system. Sophisticated systems can prompt recipients for a reply if they haven't responded within a certain time frame. With multitasking workstations, mail can be delivered and announced while the user is working in an application. Otherwise, mail is sent to a simulated postal box in the network server or host computer, which must be interrogated by the recipient.

The most universal form of electronic mail today is the fax machine, which uses the dial-up network. See *X.400, X.500* and *EDI*.

Electronic Message Service See EMS *(2)*.

electronic messaging Same as *electronic mail*.

electronic printer A printer that uses electronics to control the printing mechanism. The term refers to a variety of printers, including laser printers and line printers.

electronic publishing The providing of information in electronic form to readers or subscribers of the service. See *information utility* and *videotex*.

electronic spreadsheet See *spreadsheet*.

electronic switch An on/off switch that is activated by electrical current and is used for local or remote operation. See *transistor*.

electronic typewriter See *memory typewriter* and *word processing*.

electrophotographic The printing technique used in laser printers and copy machines. A negative image made of dots of light is painted onto a photosensitive drum or belt that has been electrically charged. The light comes from a laser, a LEDs or liquid crystal shutters that function as gates.

Wherever light is applied, the drum becomes uncharged. A toner (dry ink) is applied and it adheres to the charged areas of the drum. The drum transfers the toner to the paper, and pressure and heat fuse the toner and paper permanently.

Some electrophotographic systems use a positive approach in which the toner is attracted to the laser-produced latent image. See illustration on next page.

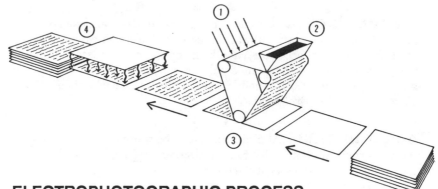

ELECTROPHOTOGRAPHIC PROCESS

(1) The belt (or drum) is charged.
(2) Dry ink (toner) is adhered to the charged areas.
(3) The toner is transferred onto the paper.
(4) The toner is fused to the paper.

electrosensitive printer A dot matrix printer that burns away dots on the outer silver coating of a special black paper.

electrostatic Stationary electrical charges in which no current flows.

electrostatic plotter A plotter that uses a special paper that is charged as it passes by a line of electrodes. Toner is then applied to the charged paper. These plotters can be either black and white or color. Some models are designed for paper up to six feet in width.

electrostatic printer Same as *electrostatic plotter*.

elegant program A program that is simple in design, uses the least amount of memory and runs fast.

elite A typeface that prints 12 cpi.

em In typography, a unit of measure equal to the width of the capital letter M in a particular font.

EMACS (Editor MACroS) A UNIX-based text editor developed at MIT that is used for writing programs. It provides a wide variety of editing features including multiple windows.

E-mail See *electronic mail*.

embedded command A code inserted within text that is used to command the printer to change fonts, print underline, boldface, etc. The embedded commands may be partially or totally invisible on screen and may be entirely revealed with a special command. At print time, embedded commands are converted into the machine codes needed to activate the printer.

Embedded commands are typically incompatible from one word processor to the other.

embedded system
A specialized computer that is used as a control function within the device it's controlling, for example, in avionics, rockets and space vehicles. It implies custom-programmed software that usually integrates system software and application software functions.

Emerald Bay
A network-ready database manager from Ratliff Software Productions, Inc. Introduced in 1988 and written by Wayne Ratliff, creator of dBASE II, it provides a binary field that can store any digitized information (text, graphics, voice). It is designed to interface with different languages.

EMI
(ElectroMagnetic Interference) The radiation released by an electronic device that may disrupt the operation of some other electronic system. Allowable limits are governed by the FCC.

emitter
The supply of current in a bipolar transistor. Same as source in a MOS transistor.

emitter-coupled logic
See ECL.

EMM
(Expanded Memory Manager) A software driver for PCs that manages expanded memory. In 8086 and 286 machines, expanded memory boards must be installed. In 386 and 486 machines, the hardware has built-in expanded memory capability and only requires the driver, or memory manager, to activate it. See EMS.

EMS
(1) (Expanded Memory Specification) A technique for expanding memory beyond one megabyte on PCs running under DOS. EMS Version 4.0 increases the amount of memory DOS applications can work with from one to 32MB by providing a bank switching capability that allows segments of conventional memory to point to EMS memory.

In 8086 and 286 machines, EMS is installed by plugging in an EMS memory board and adding an EMS driver to DOS. In 386 and higher machines, EMS is activated by adding a software driver called an EMM (expanded memory manager).

In order to use EMS, the application is either written to support it directly, or the application is run within a windows environment that supports it, such as DESQview .

In 1984, Lotus, Intel and Microsoft introduced EMS, which increased memory to 8MB. Later, AST, Quadram and Ashton-Tate introduced Enhanced EMS (EEMS), a superset of EMS. In 1987, Lotus, Intel and Microsoft introduced

Version 4.0, which increased memory to 32MB and incorporated both previous standards.

EMS (expanded memory) and extended memory are not the same. EMS can be installed in all PCs including 8086s, whereas extended memory is normal memory beyond one megabyte on 286 and higher machines. See *backfilling*.

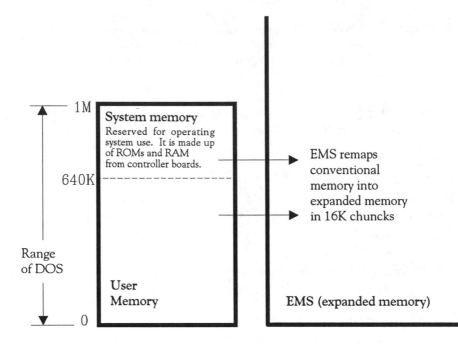

EXPANDED MEMORY

(2) (Electronic Message Service) A portion of the radio spectrum that has been assigned to electronic messaging over digital satellite circuits.

EMS emulator (Expanded Memory Specification emulator) In 8086 and 286 machines, and also called a *LIMulator*, it is a software driver that simulates expanded memory in extended memory and/or disk. EMS emulators are slower than EMS memory boards, because rather than performing high-speed bank switching, they copy data back and forth within memory or between memory and disk.

EMS memory manager See *EMM* and *EMS emulator*.

emulation mode The operational state of a computer when it is running a foreign program under emulation.

emulator A device that is built to work like another. A computer can be designed to emulate another computer and execute software that was written to run in the other machine. A terminal can be designed to emulate various communications protocols and hook into different networks. The emulator can be hardware, software or both.

en In typography, a unit of measure equal to one half the width of an em. An en is typically the width of one numeric digit.

enable To turn on. Contrast with *disable*.

Enable/OA An integrated software package for PCs from Enable Software, Inc. It provides relational database, word processing, spreadsheet, business graphics and communications capabilities. It is a very comprehensive package rivaling many stand-alone programs.

Encapsulated PostScript
The file format for the PostScript language. It contains PostScript code for the document as well as optional preview images in TIFF, Windows Metafile or Macintosh PICT formats. The PostScript code drives a PostScript printer directly, and the preview formats allow the image to be manipulated on screen. DOS and OS/2 files use an EPS extension.

encipher To encode data for security purposes. See *encryption*.

encode
(1) To assign a code to represent data, such as a parts code.

(2) Same as *encipher* or *encrypt*.

encryption The encoding of data for security purposes by converting the standard data code into a proprietary code. The encrypted data must be decoded in order to be used. Encryption is used to transmit documents over a network or to encode text so that it cannot be changed in a word processor. See *DES*.

end key A keyboard key that is used to move the cursor to the bottom of the screen or file or to the next word or end of line.

end points In vector graphics, the two ends of a line (vector). In 2-D graphics, each end point is typically made up of two numbers representing coordinates on x and y planes. In 3-D, each end point is made up of three numbers representing coordinates on x, y and z planes.

end user Same as *user*.

endless loop A series of instructions that are constantly repeated. An endless loop can be caused by an error in the program or it can be intentional, for example, a screen demo on continuous replay.

endnote See *footnote*.

engine
(1) A specialized processor, such as a graphics processor. Like any engine, the faster it runs, the quicker the job gets done.

(2) Software that performs a routine function; for example, a database engine or graphics engine.

(3) Slang for processor.

engineering drawing sizes
A - 8 1/2 x 11
B - 11 x 17
C - 17 x 22
D - 22 x 34
E - 34 x 44

Enhanced Keyboard A 101-key keyboard from IBM that supersedes the PC and AT keyboards. Function keys 11 and 12 were added, and all function keys, the escape key and control key were relocated. Additional control and alt keys were added, and the backspace key was restored to full size. It has a separate cursor key cluster located between the original numeric/cursor keypad and the letter keys.

ENHANCED KEYBOARD

enhancement Any improvement made to a software package or hardware device.

ENIAC (Electronic Numerical Integrator And Calculator) Completed in 1946, it was the first operational electronic digital computer. ENIAC was developed for the U.S. Army by John Eckert and John Mauchly at the Moore School of Electrical Engineering, University of Pennsylvania.

Taking up 1,800 square feet of space and made of 18,000 vacuum tubes, the decimal-based ENIAC performed 5,000 additions per second. It was the forerunner of all the machines that led to the creation of the UNIVAC I.

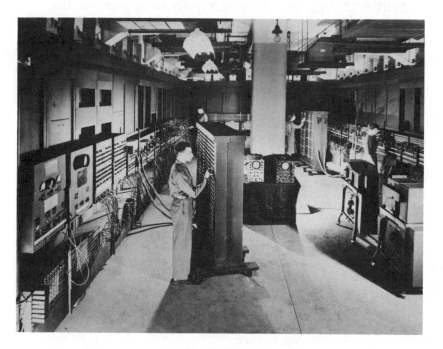

ENIAC

(Courtesy The Moore School of Electrical Engineering, University of Pennsylvania)

enquiry character In communications, a control character that requests a response from the receiving station.

enter key See *return key*.

Enterprise System Architecture See *ESA/370* and *MVS/ESA*.

entity In database management, a record.

entity type In database management, a particular kind of file, for example, a customer or product file.

entry The input of an item or set of items at a terminal. See *data entry*.

entry point In programming, the starting point of the instructions in a subroutine.

envelope
(1) A range of frequencies for a particular operation.

(2) A group of bits or items that is packaged and treated as a single unit.

environment A particular computer's configuration, which sets the standards for the application programs that run in it. It includes the CPU model and system software (operating system, data communications and database systems). It may also include the programming language used.

The term often refers only to the operating system; for example, "This program is running in a UNIX environment."

EOF (End Of File) The status of a file when its end has been reached or when an instruction or command has reset the file pointer to the end.

epitaxial layer In chip making, a semiconductor layer that is created on top of the silicon base rather than below it. See *molecular beam epitaxy*.

EPROM (Erasable Programmable Read Only Memory) A reusable PROM chip that holds its content until erased under ultraviolet light. See *PROM programmer*.

EPS See *Encapsulated PostScript*.

EQ (EQual to) See *relational operator*.

equalization In communications, techniques used to reduce distortion and compensate for signal loss (attenuation) over long distances.

equation An arithmetic expression that equates one set of conditions to another. For example, $A = B + C$ is an equation. In a programming language, assignment statements take the form of an equation. The above example would assign the sum of B and C to the variable A.

ERA (Electrically Reconfigurable Array) A programmable logic chip (PLD) technology from Plessey Semiconductor that allows the chip to be reprogrammed electrically.

erase See *delete*.

erase head In a magnetic tape drive, the device that erases the tape before a new block of data is recorded.

ergonomics The science of people-machine relationships. An ergonomically-designed product implies that the device blends smoothly with a person's body or actions.

Erlang A unit of traffic use that is used to specify the total capacity or average use of a telephone system. One Erlang is equivalent to the continuous usage of a telephone line. Traffic in Erlangs is the sum of the holding times of all lines divided by the period of measurement.

ERGONOMICS
(Courtesy Hewlett-Packard)

error checking
(1) The testing for accurate transmission of data over a communications network or internally within the computer system. See *parity checking* and CRC.

(2) Same as *validity checking.*

error detection & correction See *error checking* and *validity checking.*

error handling Routines in a program that respond to errors. The measurement of quality in error handling is based on how the system informs the user of such conditions and what alternatives it provides for dealing with them.

Poorly written programs may just hang up the computer when the wrong data is entered or a system error occurs, such as a disk error.

error rate The measurement of the effectiveness of a communications channel. It is the ratio of the number of erroneous units of data to the total number of units of data transmitted.

ESA/370 (Enterprise System Architecture/370) A mainframe upgrade from IBM that increases the performance of its 4381 and 3090 mainframes. Introduced in 1988, ESA/370 provides a number of performance enhancements, including a dramatic increase in virtual memory capability. See *MVS/ESA.*

ESC See *escape character* and *escape key.*

escape character A control character that is often used in conjunction with other codes to perform a function. For example, an escape character, followed by &l10, sets the HP LaserJet to landscape mode. In ASCII, escape has a numeric value of 27.

escape key A keyboard key that is used to exit a mode or routine, or cancel some function.

ESDI (Enhanced Small Device Interface) A hardware standard for connecting disk and tape drives to computers. ESDI devices can hold up to 1GB of data and can transfer data from one to three megabytes per second.

ESF

(1) (Extended SuperFrame) An enhanced T1 format that allows the line to be monitored during normal operation. It uses 24 frames grouped together (instead of the 12-frame D4 superframe) and provides room for CRC bits and other diagnostic commands.

(2) (External Source Format) A specification language for defining an application in IBM's CSP/AD application generator.

ESP

(1) (Enhanced-Service Provider) In telephone communications, an organization that adds value to the basic service by offering such features as call-forwarding, call-detailing and protocol conversion.

(2) (Executive Search and Placement) A recruiting software package for the Macintosh from Kevin J. Doyle Computer Systems.

(3) (Econometrics Software Package) An econometric time-series analysis program for PCs from Mikros, Inc.

(4) (Electronic System Processing) An electronic document interchange (EDI) program for PCs from Foretell Corporation.

(5) (E-tech Speedy Protocol) A proprietary protocol of E-Tech Research used in its modems.

(6) (Electronic Still Photography) The digitizing and transmission of images over a telephone line.

(7) (Emulex SCSI Processor) A proprietary chip used in Emulex's SCSI disk controller.

ESS

(1) (Electronic Switching System) A large scale computer system from AT&T that is used to switch telephone conversations in a central office.

(2) (Executive Support System) See EIS.

(3) (Electronic SpreadSheet) See *spreadsheet*.

Ethernet A local area network developed by Xerox, Digital and Intel that interconnects personal computers via coaxial cable. It uses the CSMA/CD access method and transmits at 10 megabits per second. Ethernet uses a bus topology that can connect up to 1,024 personal computers and workstations within each main branch. Ethernet has evolved into the IEEE 802.3 standard.

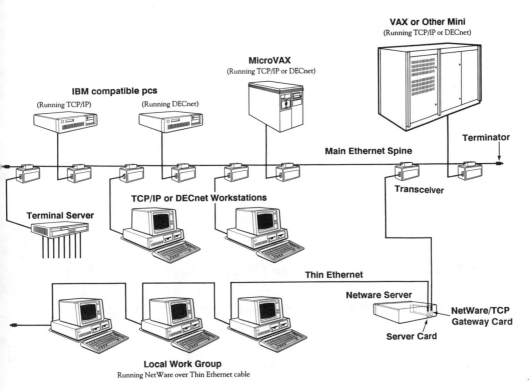

ETHERNET
(Courtesy Black Box Corporation)

This sample Ethernet installation uses TCP/IP, DECnet and NetWare Protocols)

EtherTalk Software for the Macintosh from Apple Computer that accompanies its Ethernet Interface NB Card and adapts the Macintosh to Ethernet networks.

E-time See *execution time*.

Eurocard A family of European-designed printed circuit boards that uses a 96-pin plug rather than edge connectors. The 3U is a 4x6" board with one plug; the 6U is a 6x12" board with two plugs; the 9U is a 14x18" board with three plugs.

even parity See *parity checking*.

Excel A spreadsheet from Microsoft for PCs and the Macintosh. It is a full-featured program that can link many spreadsheets together for consolidation. Excel provides a wide variety of business graphics and charts and takes full advantage of a laser printer for making presentation materials.

exception report A listing of abnormal items or items that fall outside of a specified range.

exclusive NOR See *NOR*.

exclusive OR See *OR*.

EXE file A DOS and OS/2 machine language program that can be loaded and executed in the computer. See *COM file*.

executable A program in machine language that is ready to run in a particular computer environment.

execute To follow instructions in a program. Same as *run*.

execution time The time in which a single instruction is executed. It makes up the last half of the instruction cycle.

executive Same as *operating system*.

exit
(1) To get out of the current mode or quit the program.

(2) In programming, to get out of the loop, routine or function that the computer is currently in.

expanded memory/manager See *EMS* and *EMM*.

expansion board
(1) A printed circuit board that plugs into an expansion slot.

(2) See *bus extender*.

expansion slot A receptacle inside a computer or other electronic system that printed circuit boards are plugged into. The number of slots determines future expansion. In personal computers, the expansion slots are directly connected to the bus.

ExperLogo A version of the Logo programming language from ExperTelligence, Inc., that runs on the Macintosh. It contains more functions similar to LISP than most versions of Logo.

expert system A artificial intelligence application that uses a knowledge base of human expertise to aid in solving problems. The degree of problem solving is based on the quality of the data and rules obtained from the human expert. Expert systems perform both well below and well above that of an individual expert.

The expert system derives its answers by running the knowledge base through an inference engine, a software program that interacts with the user and processes the results from the rules and data in the knowledge base.

Examples of expert systems are medical diagnosis, equipment repair, investment analysis, financial, estate and insurance planning, route scheduling for vehicles, contract bidding, counseling for self-service customers, production control and training.

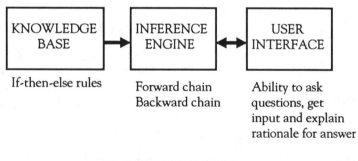

EXPERT SYSTEM

explode To break down an assembly into its component pieces. It may also refer to decompressing data back into its original form. Contrast with *implode*.

exponent A number written above the line and to the right of a number that indicates the power of a number, or how many zeros there are in it. For example 10 to the 3rd power indicates three zeros. The number 467,000 can be stated as 467 x 10 to the 3rd. On a display screen or printout, the same number is expressed as 467E3. In floating point arithmetic, the exponent raises the mantissa to a specified power.

exponential growth Extremely fast growth. On a chart, the line would curve up rather than be a straight line. Contrast with *linear*.

exponential smoothing A widely-used technique in forecasting trends, seasonality and level change. Works well with data that has a lot of randomness.

export To convert a data file in the current program into a foreign format for some other program.

expression In programming, a statement that describes data and processing. For example, `value = 2*cost` and `product="hat"` and `color="gray"`.

extended application A Microsoft DOS application that runs in extended memory under the control of a DOS extender.

extended ASCII The second half of the ASCII character set (characters 128 through 255). The symbols are defined by IBM for the PC and by other vendors for proprietary uses. It is non-standard ASCII.

Extended Edition A version of OS/2 from IBM that includes communications and database management. The Communications Manager has built-in protocols (LU 6.2 and X.25) that allow it to interconnect with IBM mainframes. The Database Manager is built around IBM's SQL database language and is designed to facilitate file transfers between PS/2s and mainframes and to coexist in a distributed database environment.

extended maintenance On-call service that is ordered for periods in addition to the primary period of maintenance.

extended memory In Intel 286 and higher computers, memory above one megabyte. It is often used for RAM disks and disk caching routines. Contrast with *EMS* (expanded memory), which is specialized to break the one megabyte barrier of DOS applications. Memory boards can usually be set up as extended or expanded memory or some mix of the two. See *EMS, XMS* and *DOS extender*.

extensible The capability of being expanded or customized. For example, with extensible programming languages, programmers can add new control structures, statements or data types.

extension A file category created under DOS and OS/2. All programs and most data files use extensions. However, many word processing files do not, and users can set up their own filing system by making up their own. File name and extension are separated with a dot, for example, ANSI.SYS, SALES.DBF, and GLOSS.EXE.

Commonly Used Extensions

Extension	Type of File	Created by these programs
ARC	Compressed file	PKARC
ASM	Source program	Intel Assembly language
BAK	Backup version	Common
BAS	Source program	BASIC
BAT	Batch	DOS and OS/2
C	Source program	C
CAP	Captions	Ventura Publisher
CDR	Graphics file	Corel Draw
CFG	Configuration	Common
CGM	Graphics	Common vector & raster format
CHP	Chapter	Ventura Publisher
CIF	Chapter information	Ventura Publisher
COB	Source program	COBOL
COM	Executable program	Compilers and assemblers
DB	Database	Paradox
DBF	Database	dBASE
DBT	Text	dBASE
DCA	Text	IBM
DOC	Document	MultiMate, Microsoft Word
DOX	Document	MultiMate Version 4.0
DRW	Graphics	Micrografx products
DXF	Graphics	AutoCAD common
DWG	Graphics	AutoCAD proprietary
EPS	Graphics/Text	Encapsulated Postscript
EXE	Executable program	Compilers and assemblers
FMT	Screen format	dBASE
FRM	Report layout	dBASE
GEM	Graphics	GEM draw format (vector)
GRF	Graph file	Micrografx products
HP	Graphics	Hewlett-Packard (vector)
IMG	Graphics	GEM paint format (raster)
LBL	Label description	dBASE
NDX	Index	dBASE
OBJ	Object module	Compilers and assemblers
OVL	Executable program	Compilers and assemblers
PCT	Graphics	Macintosh
PCX	Graphics	PC Paintbrush
PDF	Printer file	WordStar
PDV	Printer file	PC Paintbrush
PIC	Graphics	Lotus 1-2-3
PIC	Graphics	Micrografx products
PIF	Program information	Microsoft Windows
PM	Graphics/text	PageMaker
PM3	Graphics/text	PageMaker Version 3.0

PRD	Printer file	Microsoft Word
PRN	Printer file	XyWrite, DisplayWrite
PRS	Printer file	WordPerfect
PRG	Source program	dBASE
PS	Page description	PostScript
SC	Source program	Paradox
SCR	Screen layout	dBASE
SLD	Graphics	AutoCAD slide format
STY	Style sheet	Ventura Publisher
SYS	System	DOS and OS/2
TIF	Graphics	Common vector format
TMP	Temporary	Common
TXT	ASCII Text	Common
VGR	Chapter information	Ventura Publisher
VUE	Relational view	dBASE
WK1	Spreadsheet	Lotus 1-2-3 Version 2
WKS	Spreadsheet	Lotus 1-2-3 Version 1a
WMF	File transfer	Microsoft Windows
XLS	Spreadsheet	Excel
XLC	Chart	Excel
ZIP	Compressed file	PKZIP
$$$	Temporary	Common

extent A contiguous space on a disk reserved for a file or application.

external interrupt An interrupt caused by an external source such as the computer operator, external sensor or monitoring device, or another computer.

external reference In programming, a call to a program or function that resides in a separate, independent library.

external sort A sort that uses disk or tape as temporary workspace during the resequencing process.

external storage Peripheral storage that is outside of the CPU, such as disk and tape.

F connector A common plug and socket for coaxial cable that is typically used to connect antennas, TVs and VCRs. It is easily recognized: the small, inner wire is stripped bare and sticks out of the plug looking unfinished.

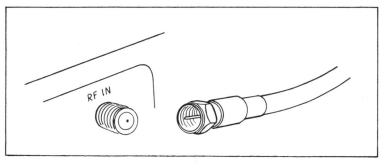

F CONNECTOR

F keys See *function keys*.

facilities management The management of an organization's own computer installation by an outside organization. All operations including systems, programming and the datacenter can be performed by the facilities management organization on the user's premises.

facsimile See *fax*.

factorial The total number of possible sequences that can exist with a set of items. For example, with three items, there are six arrangements: 1 2 3, 1 3 2, 2 3 1, 2 1 3, 3 1 2 and 3 2 1. The factorial is derived by continuously multiplying the number of items by the next lowest number until 1 is reached, for example, 3 x 2 x 1.

fail safe Failure proof operation. See *fault tolerant*.

fail soft The ability to fail with minimum destruction. Fail soft systems detect failures, and although they can't correct them, they provide for less destructive failure. For example, a disk drive can be built so that when power fails, the heads are automatically brought to the home position.

FAMOS (Floating gate Avalanche-injection Metal Oxide Semiconductor) Fabrication technology for making EPROM memory chips that hold their content until erased with ultraviolet light.

fan-fold paper Same as *continous forms*.

Farad A unit of electrical charge that is used to measure the storage capacity of a capacitor. In microelectronics, measurements are usually in microfarads or picofarads.

Fast An asynchronous communications protocol for personal computers that is used on high-quality lines to transmit files as quickly as possible. Error checking is done after the entire file has been transmitted.

Fast Fourier Transform A class of algorithms used in digital signal processing that break down complex signals into their elementary components.

FastCAD A family of computer-aided design programs for PCs with math coprocessors from Evolution Computing. FastCAD 2D is a full-featured CAD package that is known for its speed and well-designed user interface. Users with less sophisticated requirements can start out with EasyCAD 2, FastCAD's baby brother. FastCAD 3D includes the RenderMan interface for providing photo-realistic images. Multiple views of an image can be displayed on screen and all views can be plotted.

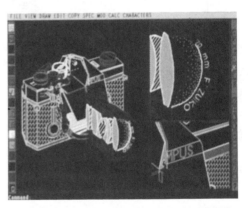

MULTIPLE FASTCAD VIEWS
(Courtesy Evolution Computing)

FAT (File Allocation Table) The part of the DOS and OS/2 file system that keeps track of where the data is stored on a disk. It is a table with an entry for each cluster on the disk, and the entire table is replicated twice. The directory, which contains file ID (name, extension, date of last update...) points to the FAT entries where the files start. If a file is larger than one cluster, that entry points to another entry and so on. If a cluster becomes damaged, its corresponding entry in the FAT is marked and not used again.

fatal error An error condition that prohibits continued processing. A disk or tape that cannot be read may cause a fatal error if the damaged part contains instructions or critical data. Fatal errors can also occur from anomalies (unexplainable situations due to inadequate programming).

FatBits The mode in Apple's MacPaint program that lets a user edit a pixel at a time. FatBits is an option in the Goodies menu.

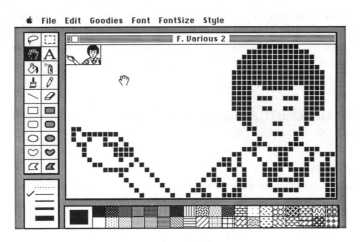

FAT BITS MODE
Note the picture in the upper left hand side of the screen.

father file See *grandfather, father, son*.

fault tolerant Continous operation in the event of failure. Fault tolerant computer systems can be created using two or more conventional computers that duplicate all processing, or having one system stand by if the other fails. They can also be built from the ground up, such as Tandem, Stratus and Sequoia computers, which offer commercially available redundant processors. Such systems have several processors, control units and peripheral units combined into a modular integrated system and are widely used in financial applications, such as stock market and online banking functions.

Total fault tolerant operation also requires backup power in the event of power failure. It may also imply duplication of systems in disparate locations in the event of natural catastrophe or vandalism.

fax (FACSimile) Originally called *telecopying*, it is the communication of a printed page between remote locations. Fax machines scan a paper form and convert its image into a code for transmission over the telephone system. The receiving machine reconverts the codes and prints a facsimile of the original. A fax machine is made up of a scanner, printer and fax modem.

Fax machines have evolved as follows:

Groups 1 and 2 transmit a single page in analog code at six and three minutes respectively and were used throughout the 1970s. Group 3 transmits one page in digital code up to 9,600 baud (with data compression) in less than one minute. Group 3 resolution is 203x98 dpi in standard mode and 203x196 dpi in fine mode.

The dramatic difference in speed between Group 3 and its predecessors led to the extraordinary increase in fax use in the late 1980s. Today, fax is the most universal form of electronic mail.

Higher-speed (Group 4) machines rely on all-digital networks which may not occur until the mid to late 1990s.

fax board
The modem part of a fax machine that plugs into a personal computer. The fax board generates signals directly from computer files or the screen and transmits a better image than a fax machine, which has to scan its image. In addition, with a laser printer, incoming faxes are printed sharper and on regular paper.

fax/data modem
A transmission device that provides Group 3 fax as well as data modem capabilities.

fax modem
(1) An external fax transmission device that connects to a port on a personal computer.

(2) Same as *fax board*.

FCC
(Federal Communications Commission) The regulatory body for all U.S. interstate telecommunications services as well as international service that originates in the U.S. It was created under the U.S. Communications Act of 1934, and its board of commissioners is appointed by the President.

FDDI
(Fiber optic Data Distribution Interface)   A set of ANSI standards for fiber optic local area networks. It deals with the bottom two layers of the OSI model (data link and physical) and transmits at 100 megabits per second. At this speed, high-resolution graphics can be quickly transmitted and digital video can be handled in realtime.

FDISK
A DOS utility that partitions the hard disk into several independent disks.

FDM
(Frequency Division Multiplexing) A communications transmission method that is widely used to transmit multiple signals over a single channel. Each signal transmitted (data, voice, etc.) is modulated onto a carrier of a different frequency. The multiple signals travel simultaneously over the channel. Contrast with *TDM* (time division multiplexing) in which digital signals are interleaved. See *carrier* and *broadband*.

FEA
(Finite Element Analysis) A mathematical technique for analyzing the stress on physical structures. The total structure is broken down into a series of

substructures, called *finite elements*. The finite elements and their interrelationships are converted into equation form and solved mathematically.

Graphics-based FEA software can display the model on screen as it is being built and, after analysis, display the object's reactions under load conditions. Models created in popular CAD packages, such as AutoCAD, can often be accepted by FEA software.

With the advent of high-performance workstations and personal computers, FEA is being performed on small and medium-size structures in desktop computers.

feasibility study An analysis of a problem to determine if it can be solved effectively. The operational (will it work?), economical (costs and benefits) and technical (can it be built?) aspects are part of the study. The results of a feasibility study provide data for a go/no-go decision to start the project.

FEC See *forward error correction*.

female connector A receptacle into which the male counterpart of the connector is plugged.

femtosecond One quadrillionth of a second. See *space/time*.

FEP See *front end processor*.

ferromagnetic The capability of a material, such as iron and nickel, to be highly magnetized.

FET (Field Effect Transistor) A type of transistor used in MOS integrated circuits.

fetch To locate the next instruction in memory for execution by the CPU.

FF See *form feed*.

FFT See *Fast Fourier Transform*.

fiber optic Communications systems that use optical fibers for transmission. See *optical fiber*.

Fibonacci numbers A series of integers (whole numbers) in which each number is the sum of the two preceding numbers. This series of numbers is implemented in various search and sort programs to speed up the processing.

fiche Same as *microfiche*.

field A physical unit of data that is one or more bytes in size. A collection of fields make up a record. A field also defines a unit of data on a source document, screen or report. Examples of fields are name, address, quantity and amount due.

The field is the common denominator between the user and the computer. When you interactively query and update your database using such programs as query languages, report writers and database management systems, you identify and reference your data by field name.

Technically, a field is the physical unit of storage, whereas a data element or data item refers to the data generically, or logically. For example, it is correct to say, "These data elements are stored in this field." The terms *field, data element, data item* and *variable* refer to the same unit of data and are often used interchangeably.

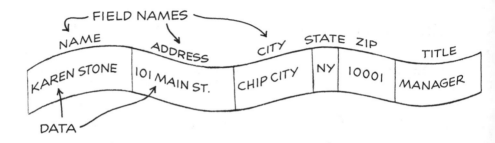

FIELDS IN A RECORD

field effect transistor See *FET*.

field engineer An individual who is responsible for hardware installation, maintentance and repair. Field engineers are service personnel who are trained in electromechanical engineering and digital electronics.

field separator A character that is used to mark the separation of fields in a record. See *comma delimited*.

field service representative Same as *field engineer*.

field squeeze In a mail merge, a function that eliminates extra blank spaces in a data field so that it prints correctly within the text of the letter. See *line squeeze*.

FIFO (First In-First Out) A storage method that retrieves the item stored for the longest time. Contrast with *LIFO*.

fifth-generation computer A computer that is designed for artificial intelligence applications. Appearing in the mid 1990s, these systems will represent the next quantum leap in computer technology.

file

(1) In data management, a collection of related records.

(2) In word processing, a single text document.

(3) In computer graphics, a set of image descriptors for one picture, either in TV-like format (raster graphics) or in line, or object, format (vector graphics).

(4) In programming, the source program and machine language program are stored as individual *files*.

(5) In computer operations, any collection of data that is treated as a single unit on a peripheral device, such as any of the examples in items 1 through 4 above.

file and record locking Techniques for managing data in a multiple user environment. File locking prevents users from gaining access to a data, text or image file. Record locking prohibits access to a single record within a data file.

File and record locking are initiated on a first-come, first-served basis. The first user to access the file or record prevents, or locks out, other users from accessing it. After the file or record is updated, it is unlocked so that others can access it.

file extension See *extension*.

file format The specification for the structure of a file. There are hundreds of proprietary formats for database, word processing and graphics files that have become standardized and used for data interchange. See *record layout*.

file layout Same as *record layout*.

file maintenance

(1) The periodic updating of master files. For example, adding and deleting employees and customers, making name and address changes and changing the prices in a product file. It does not pertain to an organization's daily transaction processing and batch processing (order processing, billing, etc.).

(2) The periodic reorganization of a computer system's disks. Data that has been continuously updated becomes physically fragmented over the disk space and requires regrouping. An optimizing program is run every cycle (daily, weekly, etc.) that organizes the data contiguously.

file manager

(1) A program that manages data files. Often erroneously called database managers, file managers provide the ability to create, enter, change, query and

produce reports on one file at a time. They have no relational capabilty and usually don't include a programming language.

(2) A program that is used to manage files on a disk. It provides functions to delete, copy, move, rename and view files as well as create and manage directories.

file name A name assigned by the user or programmer that is used to identify a file.

file protect ring A plastic ring inserted into a reel of magnetic tape for file protection.

file protection The prevention of accidental erasing of a disk or tape. Physical file protection is provided on the storage medium itself by turning a switch, moving a lever or covering a notch. In these cases, recording of new data is prohibited even if the software directs the computer to do so.

    To protect a floppy disk, do the following. On 3.5" disks, push the sliding lever on the bottom, back side of the disk toward the edge of the disk uncovering a hole through the disk. On 5.25" disks, cover the notch on the side of a disk with a stick-on label. On 8" disks, remove the stick-on label covering the notch on the side.

    On 1/2" tape reels, protection is provided by removing a plastic ring in the center of the reel (no ring-no write).

    Logical file protection is provided by the operating system, which can designate a single file as read only. This method allows both regular (read/write) and read only files to be stored on the same disk volume. In addition, files can often be designated as hidden files, which makes them invisible to most software programs.

file server A high-speed computer in a local area network that stores the programs and data files shared by the users on the network. Also called a *network server*, it acts like a remote disk drive. If the file server is dedicated to database operations, it is called a *database server*.

file sharing protocol A communications protocol that provides a structure for file requests (open, read, write, close...) between stations in a network. If file sharing is strictly between workstation and server, it is also called a *client/server protocol*. It refers to layer 7 of the OSI model.

file spec (file SPECification) The reference to the location of a file on a disk that includes the disk drive, directory name and file name. For example, in DOS and OS/2, `c:\words\books\chapter2` is a file spec for the file CHAPTER2 in the BOOKS subdirectory of the WORDS directory on drive C.

file system
(1) A method for cataloging files in a computer system. See *hierarchical file system*.

(2) A data processing application that manages individual files. Files are related by customized programming. Contrast with *relational database*.

file transfer protocol A communications protocol that can transmit files without loss of data. It implies that it can handle binary data as well as ASCII data.

file viewer A program that displays the contents of a file as it is normally displayed by the application that created it. For example, in Lotus' Magellan, the contents of a wide variety of spreadsheet, database and word processing files can be displayed one after the other as if each one were viewed by its original application.

FileMaker II A file manager for the Macintosh from Claris Corporation. It is a very popular program for general data management and provides a variety of statistical functions, fast search capabilities and extensive reporting features.

FileMan A public-domain MUMPS software package that provides a stand-alone interactive database management system as well as a set of utilities for the MUMPS programmer.

film recorder A device that takes a 35mm slide picture from a graphics file, which has been created in a CAD, paint or business graphics package. Film recorders generate much higher resolution than traditional display screens. Typical resolutions are 2,000 lines and go up to 4,000 lines.

The device usually works by recreating the image on a built-in CRT that shines through a color wheel onto the film in a standard 35mm camera. Some units provide optional Polaroid camera backs for instant previewing. Film recorders can be connected to personal computers by plugging in a controller board that is cabled to the recorder.

filter
(1) A pattern or mask through which only selected data is passed. For example, in dBASE, `set filter to file region4`, passes all data through the matching conditions specified in the query file REGION4.

(2) A process that changes data, such as a sort routine in an operating system.

financial planning language A language used to create data models and command a financial planning system.

financial planning system Software that aids the financial planner and manager in evaluating alternatives before making final decisions.

It allows for the creation of a data model, which is a series of data elements in equation form, for example, `gross profit = gross sales – cost of goods sold`. Different values can be plugged into the elements, and the impact of various options can be assessed (what if?).

Financial planning systems are a step above spreadsheets by providing additional analysis tools. For example, sensitivity analysis assigns a range of values to a data element, which causes that data to be highlighted if it ever exceeds that range.

Goal seeking is a feature that provides automatic calculation. For example, by entering `gross margin = 50%` as well as the minimums and maximums of the various inputs, the program will calculate an optimum mix of inputs to achieve the goal (output).

Finder The part of the Macintosh operating system that manages the desktop. It keeps track of the icons on the desktop and controls the Clipboard and Scrapbook. It allows for copying files from one disk to another. Finder manages one application at a time, whereas Multifinder allows two or more applications to be open at one time.

fingerprint reader A scanner that is used to identify an individual's fingerprint for security purposes. After a sample is taken, access to a computer or other restricted system is granted if the user's fingerprint matches the stored sample. A personal identification number (PIN) may also be used with the fingerprint sample.

FINGERPRINT READER
(Courtesy Identix Inc.)

finite element analysis See *FEA*.

firmware A category of memory chips that hold their content without electrical power and include ROM, PROM, EPROM and EEPROM technologies. Firmware becomes "hard software" when holding program code.

first-generation computer A computer that used vacuum tubes as switching elements, for example, the UNIVAC I.

fixed disk A non-removable hard disk such as is found in most personal computers. Programs and data are copied to and from the fixed disk.

fixed head disk A direct access storage device, such as a disk or drum, that has a read/write head for each track. Since there is no access arm movement, access times are significantly improved.

fixed length field A field that contains the exact same number of bytes in each record. For example, a 25-byte name field takes up 25 bytes no matter what size name is in it. Fixed length fields are easier to program, but waste disk space and restrict the design of the file.

Fixed length description and comment fields are always a dilemma. Short fields allow only abbreviated remarks, while long fields waste disk storage if lengthy comments are not required in every record. Contrast with *variable length field*.

fixed length record A data record that contains fixed length fields.

fixed point A method for storing and calculating numbers in which the decimal point is always in the same location. Contrast with *floating point*.

flag
(1) In communications, a code in the transmitted message which indicates that the following characters are a control code and not data.

(2) In programming, a status indicator that may be built into hardware or programmed in software. Flags are usually no more than a bit or a byte that store a yes or no.

flame Slang for communicating emotionally and/or excessively via electronic mail.

Flash-Up Windows A programming utility for PCs from Software Bottling Company. It creates popup menus and help screens that work with programming languages, such as BASIC and dBASE.

flat file A data file that does not physically interconnect with or point to other files. Any relationship between two flat files is logical, for example, matching account numbers. The term usually refers to file managers that have no relational capability.

flat panel display A thin display screen that uses any of a number of technologies, such as LCD, electroluminscent or plasma. Used today in laptops to reduce size and weight, they will eventually supersede CRTs.

flatbed plotter A graphics plotter that draws on sheets of paper that have been placed in a bed. The size of the bed determines the maximum size sheet that can be drawn.

flexible disk Same as *floppy disk* and *diskette*.

flicker A fluctuating image on a video screen.

flip-flop An electronic circuit that alternates between two states. When current is applied, it changes from its current state to the opposite (0 to 1, 1 to 0). Made of several transistors, a flip-flop is used in the design of static memories and hardware registers.

flippy-floppy A single-sided 5.25" floppy disk that is recorded on both sides. A second write protect notch is punched into the disk so that it can be flipped over and inserted upside down. This is not a recommended approach, because the disk's direction is different for each side.

floating point A method for storing and calculating numbers in which the decimal points don't line up as in fixed point numbers. The significant digits are stored as a unit called the *mantissa,* and the location of the radix point (decimal point in base 10) is stored in a separate unit called the *exponent.* Floating point methods are used for calculating a large range of numbers quickly.

Floating point operations can be implemented in hardware (math coprocessor), or they can be done in software. They can also be performed in a separate floating point processor that is connected to the main processor via a channel.

MANTISSA	EXPONENT		ACTUAL VALUE
6508	0	=	6508
6508	1	=	65080
6508	-1	=	650.8

FLOATING POINT

floating point processor An arithmetic unit that is designed to perform floating point operations. It may be a coprocessor chip in a personal computer, a CPU designed with built-in floating point capabilities or a separate machine, often called an *array processor,* which is connected to the main computer.

floppy disk A removable storage medium used with many computers. Also called a *diskette*, the medium itself is a single round disk of flexible, tape-like material that is housed in a square envelope or cartridge. The disk drive grabs the disk at its center and spins it inside its envelope.

Like magnetic tape, floppy disks can be recorded and erased hundreds of times. Some floppy disks are recorded on only one side (single sided or SS); however, most are recorded on both sides (double sided or DS).

The original floppy was developed by IBM and is housed in an 8" square envelope that holds from 100,000 to 500,000 bytes.

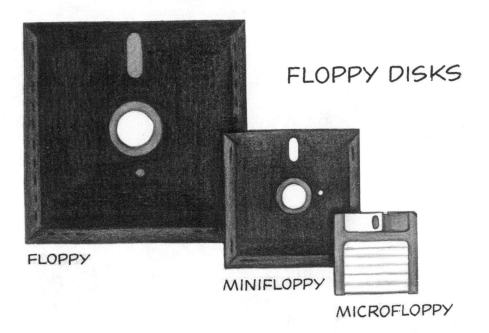

FLOPPY DISKS

FLOPPY

MINIFLOPPY

MICROFLOPPY

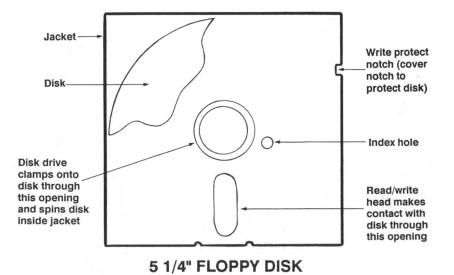

5 1/4" FLOPPY DISK

Shugart introduced the now-common minifloppy which resides in a 5.25" square envelope and holds from 100K to approximately 1.2 Mbytes.

Sony developed the 3.5" microfloppy, which is now the most popular, due to its compact and rigid case. Microfloppies hold from 400KB to 2MB and more.

A floppy disk, fresh out of the box, is blank. The disk drive it is used in determines its precise storage capacity. Most floppy disks are soft sectored disks, which requires that they be run first through a format program to record the sector identification on them. Although floppy disks may look the same, what's recorded on them determines their compatibility. An Apple II disk cannot be read or written in a PC without special hardware.

All floppies are vulnerable to extremes in temperature and magnetic influences; however, the older style (5.25" and 8") floppies are more susceptible to damage than the 3.5" disks.

FLOPPY DISK HANDLING AND STORAGE

(Courtesy Maxell Corporation)

FLOPS (FLOating point operations Per Second) The unit of measurement of floating point calculations. For example, 100 megaflops is 100 million floating point operations per second.

Floptical A floppy disk technology from Insite Peripherals, Inc. Data is written in the traditional magnetic method, but grooves in the disk are used to optically align the read/write head over the tracks. In 1989, Insite introduced a 20MB Floptical drive that can also read and write 1.44M and 720K disks.

flow chart A graphical representation of the sequence of operations in an information system or program. Information system flow charts show how data from source documents flows through the computer to final distribution to users. Program flow charts show the sequence of instructions in a single program or subroutine. Different symbols are used to draw each type of flow chart.

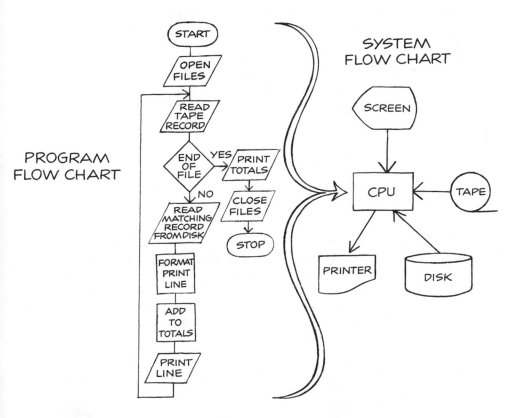

flow control The pacing of data in a transmission. It ensures that the receiving device can absorb the data that has been sent before sending more.

flush center

In typography, refers to centering text uniformly between the left and right margins as is this paragraph.

flush left In typography, the alignment of all text uniformly to the left margin. All text is typically set flush left with a ragged right margin as is this paragraph or as justified text with uniform margins.

flush right

In typography, the alignment of all text uniformly to the right margin while the left margin is set ragged left as is this paragraph.

flux The energy field generated by a magnet.

FM

(1) (Frequency Modulation) A communications transmission technique that modulates a data signal into a fixed carrier frequency by modifying the carrier frequency. Contrast with *amplitude modulation* (AM) and *phase modulation*; the two other major modulation categories.

(2) (Frequency Modulation) On magnetic media, a recording technique that places a clock bit onto the medium along with each data bit. FM is a low-density method for recording data and has been superseded by MFM (modified frequency modulation) and RLL (run length limited) techniques, which eliminate more of the clock bits.

Fn key (FuNction key) A key that works like a shift key to activate a second function on a keyboard key and is typically found on laptop computers to reduce keyboard size. The Fn key is separate and distinct from the set of function keys labelled F1, F2, etc.

FOCUS A database management system from Information Builders, Inc., that runs on PCs, IBM mainframes, VAXs, and Wang VSs. FOCUS provides relational, hierarchical and network data structures and can access a variety of databases, including standard IBM mainframe files, DB2, IMS, IDMS and others. It includes a fourth-generation language and a variety of decision support facilities, including financial planning and statistical analyses capabilities.

folder In the Macintosh, a simulated file folder that holds documents (text, data or graphics), applications and other folders. A folder is analogous to a DOS directory, while a folder within a folder is analogous to a DOS subdirectory.

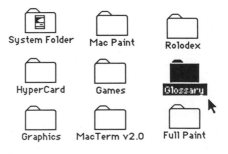

MACINTOSH FOLDERS

In the Macintosh desktop, folders are represented by tiny pictures (icons) with captions. The Glossary folder is currently selected.

folio In typography, a printed page number in contrast with the physical page. For example, folio 3 could be the 27th physical page in a book.

font A set of type characters of a particular design and size. In daisy wheel printers, fonts are changed by changing the daisy wheel. In dot matrix printers, the fonts are built in and can be selected by software or a control panel switch. In laser printers, some fonts are built in and others can be plugged in with a cartridge or downloaded from a computer.

There are several characteristics that make up a font. For example, the code sent to an HP LaserJet to select a font contains the following components:

Code	Characteristic
Typeface	Type design (Courier, Times Roman...)
Orientation	Portrait or landscape
Symbol set	Country or special characters
Spacing	Proportional or fixed spacing (width)
Pitch	Characters per inch (if fixed spacing)
Point size	Height of characters
Style	Upright or italic
Stroke weight	Light, medium or bold appearance

Font Structures

In a laser printer, characters are printed as patterns of dots, or bit maps, and these bit maps can be derived from several sources.

BIT-MAPPED FONTS

Laser printers have some number of built in fonts in a limited number of point sizes that are always available. Additional fonts are available as plug-in cartridges that contain from a couple to a dozen or more different typefaces in some fixed number of point sizes. They usually include the bold, italic and bold italic variations of the typeface, but each variation is considered a font. Thus, 12 fonts may be only three typefaces.

Fonts can also be purchased like software, copied into and stored in the computer and downloaded into the printer before printing. These "soft" fonts are available by typeface in a fixed number of point sizes.

If you need an ever changing supply of point sizes, you can use a font generation system, such as Bitstream's Fontware, which comes with a set of font outlines that can be scaled into any point size (within a range) that you want. Like any bit-mapped set of images, all the different point sizes take up room on the hard disk.

SCALABLE ON THE FLY

Scalable fonts, such as Adobe's PostScript, are outline fonts that are generated into the required bit maps as needed within the printer itself, or within a controller board inside the personal computer or workstation. They usually take longer to print, because the fonts are created with every print session, but there is no wasted hard disk space for fonts that are used only occasionally.

Like bit-mapped fonts, scalable outline fonts come built-in (some PostScript printers have 35 fonts; eight actual typefaces), as plug-in cartridges or as soft fonts that are downloaded into the printer for scaling.

font cartridge

A set of bit-mapped or outline fonts for one or more typefaces contained in a module that plugs into a slot in the printer. The fonts are stored in a ROM chip within the cartridge. Contrast with *soft font* and *internal font*.

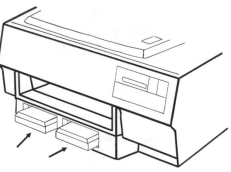

FONT CARTRIDGE

font compiler
Same as *font generator*.

font editor
A software program that allows fonts to be designed and modified.

font generator
A program that converts an outline font into the precise patterns of dots required for a particular size of font.

font utility
A software program that provides functions for managing fonts, including the ability to download, install, design and modify fonts.

Fontware
A font generation system for PCs from Bitstream Inc. It includes a library of outline fonts and a font generator that converts them into bit-mapped fonts from 6 to 99 points. Each typeface package includes four weights of the selected typeface: normal, italic, bold and bold italic. The user selects the weights and point sizes and the program scales the outlines into the required fonts that are stored on disk for future use.

footer
In a document or report, common text that appears at the bottom of every page. The footer may also contain the page number.

footnote
Text that appears at the bottom of a document page which adds explanation to the text within the page. For example, footnotes are often used to give credit to the source of a particular statement. When footnotes are accumulated and printed at the end of a chapter, they are called *endnotes*.

footprint
The amount of geographic space an object uses. A computer footprint is the amount of desk or floor surface it occupies. A satellite's footprint is the geographic area on earth that is covered by its downlink transmission.

for statement A high-level programming language structure that repeats a series of instructions a specified number of times. It creates a loop that includes its own control information. The following examples print "Hello" 10 times:

In BASIC	In C

```
FOR X = 1 to 10      FOR (X = 0;  X  10;  X++)
   PRINT "Hello"     PRINTF ("Hello");
NEXT X
```

Force A dBASE compiler from Sophco, Inc., that combines C and dBASE structures. It is known for its ability to generate very small executable programs.

foreground/background The priority assigned to programs running in a multitasking environment. Foreground programs have highest priority, and background programs have lowest priority. Online users are given the foreground, and batch processing activities, such as long sorts and updates, are given the background. If batch processing activities are given a higher priority, terminal response times may slow down considerably.

In a personal computer, the foreground program is the one the user is currently working with, and the background program might be a print spooler or communications program.

Forest & Trees A data analysis program for PCs from Channel Computing, Inc., that integrates data from a variety of applications. It provides a control room interface that lets users monitor important business information.

form
(1) Any paper used in a printer whether plain or imprinted, single sheet or continuous.

(2) A screen display that has been designed for a user's particular application.

form factor The physical size of a device.

form feed The advancing of a form in the printer to the top of the next page. It is accomplished manually by pressing the form feed or FF button on the printer, or it is a code sent to the printer from the computer. In ASCII, the form feed character has a numeric value of 12.

form view A screen display showing one item or record arranged in any required order like a preprinted form. Contrast with *table view*, which shows several items in rows and columns.

format

(1) The physical structure of an item.

(2) A *screen format* is the layout of fields on the screen.

(3) A *report format* is the layout of the printed page including print columns, page headers and footers. See *layout setting*.

(4) A *record format* is the layout of fields within the record.

(5) A *file* or *database format* is the layout of fields and records within a data file, layout codes within a word processing document or display lists (vector) or bit maps (raster) within a graphics file. It also includes the structure of header data, or identification data, that is typically affixed to the beginning of the file.

(6) See *disk format* and *low-level format*.

format program Software that initializes a blank disk by recording
sector identification on every storage sector that the disk can hold. See *low level format*.

formula

(1) An arithmetic expression that solves a problem. For example, `(fahrenheit-32)*5/9` is the formula for converting fahrenheit to centigrade.

(2) In spreadsheets, an algorithm that identifies how the data in a specific number of cells is to be calculated. For example, `+C3*D8` means that the contents of cell C3 are to be multipled by the contents of cell D8 and the results are to be placed where the formula is located.

FORTH (FOuRTH-generation language) A high-level programming
language created by Charles Moore in the late 1960s as a way of providing direct control of the computer. Its syntax resembles LISP, it uses reverse polish notation for calculations and is noted for its extensibility.

FORTH is both compiler and interpreter. The source program is compiled first and then executed by its operating system/interpreter. It is used extensively in process control applications in which tight control is necessary. Data acquired from instruments and sensors must be handled quickly in these realtime environments. It is also used in arcade game programming as well as robotics and other AI applications. The following polyFORTH examples convert fahrenheit to centigrade. FORTH handles only integers, and the first example would not allow decimal places. The second example adds two decimal places.

```
: CONV ( n) 32 - 5 9 * / . ." Centigrade
: USER_INPUT  ." Enter fahrenheit " CONV ;


: CONV ( n) 32 - 100 180 * / . ." Centigrade
: USER_INPUT  ." Enter fahrenheit " CONV ;
```

FORTRAN (FORmula TRANslator) The first high-level programming language and compiler, developed in 1954 by IBM. It was originally designed to express mathematical formulas, and although it is used occasionally for business applications, it is still the most widely used language for scientific, engineering and mathematical problems.

The following example converts fahrenheit to centigrade:

```
WRITE(6,*) 'Enter fahrenheit '
READ(5,*) XFAHR
XCENT = (XFAHR - 32) * 5 / 9
WRITE(6,*) 'Centigrade is ',XCENT
STOP
END
```

Fortune 500 The following computer and electronics companies represent over 300 billion dollars in sales for 1989. The figures are from the April 23, 1990 issue of Fortune Magazine and are reprinted with permission of Time Inc. Magazines. The rank is within all U.S. industrial corporations.

COMPUTERS (1989) Rank	Company	Sales (000,000)	Profit	Employees (000)
4	IBM	63,438	3,758	383
27	Digital Equipment	12,866	1,073	126
33	Hewlett-Packard	1,899	829	95
43	Unisys	10,097	(639)	82
78	NCR	5,956	412	56
96	Apple Computer	5,284	454	12
147	Wang Laboratories	3,078	(424)	28
152	Pitney Bowes	2,959	253	31
153	Control Data	2,952	(680)	18
157	Compaq Computer	2,876	333	10
201	Amdahl	2,154	153	8
232	Sun Microsystems	1,769	61	10
246	Tandem Computers	1,644	118	10
259	Prime Computer	1,518	(230)	—
281	Seagate Technology	1,382	0	29
290	Data General	1,324	(120)	14
342	Storage Technology	1,014	48	9
351	SCI Systems	990	21	9
365	Intergraph	874	80	8
374	AM International	855	31	8
391	Cray Research	785	89	5
417	Conner Peripherals	709	41	5
	TOTAL	136,424	5,660	955

ELECTRONICS (1989) Rank Company	Sales (000,000)	Profit	Employees (000)
5 General Electric	55,264	3,939	292
28 Westinghouse Elec.	12,844	922	122
48 Motorola	9,620	498	104
52 Raytheon	8,796	529	78
62 TRW	7,408	263	74
65 Honeywell	7,242	604	65
67 Emerson Electric	7,071	588	73
71 Texas Instruments	6,592	292	74
73 Whirlpool	6,289	187	39
74 N. American Philips	6,203	(178)	57
100 Litton Industries	5,130	178	51
101 Cooper Industries	5,129	268	58
109 Teledyne	4,664	259	43
137 Intel	3,281	391	22
146 Maytag	3,089	131	26
160 AMP	2,821	281	24
169 Zenith Electronics	2,611	(68)	32
180 Harris	2,477	21	35
187 Nat'l. Semiconductor	2,400	(23)	32
219 General Signal	1,925	78	19
234 Square D	1,723	102	19
248 E-Systems	1,633	83	18
255 Nat'l. Service Ind.	1,540	95	21
260 Loral	1,500	88	10
263 General Instrument	1,481	86	16
275 Reliance Electric	1,411	49	13
287 Varian Associates	1,345	32	12
300 Duracell Holdings	1,254	(106)	9
325 Advanced Micro Dev.	1,105	46	13
349 Western Digital	994	34	6
355 Magnetek	962	18	14
358 Allegheny Int'l.	950	(55)	12
375 Pittway	854	33	9
388 Valmont Industries	790	21	4
409 Mark IV Industries	742	23	13
411 Exide	752	(17)	6
430 Hubbell	684	79	5
431 LPL Technologies	680	28	7
447 SSMC	635	—	—
475 Ametek	588	38	6
484 Molex	576	58	6
493 Thomas & Betts	562	54	5
497 Scientific-Atlanta	552	36	3
499 LSI Logic	547	(25)	4
TOTAL	184,686	9,960	1,552

forward chaining In AI, a form of reasoning that starts with what is known and works toward a solution. Known as bottom-up approach. Contrast with *backward chaining*.

forward compatible Same as *upward compatible*.

forward error correction A communications technique that can correct bad data on the receiving end. Before transmission, the data is processed through an algorithm that adds extra bits for error correction. If the transmitted message is received in error, the correction bits are used to repair it.

fourth-generation computer A computer that is made up almost entirely of chips with limited amounts of discrete components. We are currently in the fourth generation.

fourth-generation language A computer language that is more advanced than traditional high-level programming languages. For example, in dBASE, the command LIST displays all the records in a data file. In second- and third-generation languages, instructions would have to be written to read each record, test for end of file, place each item of data on screen and go back and repeat the operation until there are no more records to process.

First-generation languages are machine languages; second-generation are machine dependent assembly languages; and third-generation languages are high-level programming languages, such as FORTRAN, COBOL, BASIC, Pascal, and C. Although many languages, such as dBASE, are called *fourth-generation languages*, they are actually a mix of third and fourth. The dBASE LIST command is a fourth-generation command, but applications programmed in dBASE are third-generation.

Query language and report writers are also fourth-generation languages. Any computer language with English-like commands that doesn't require traditional input-process-output logic falls into this category.

FoxBASE+ A dBASE III PLUS compatible database management system for PCs from Fox Software, Inc. It provides both interpreter and compiler versions of the language and is known for its speed and dBASE programming language enhancements.

FoxBase+/Mac is the Macintosh version which allows for the development of dBASE applications on the Mac and provides a vehicle for converting and running existing PC/dBASE applications.

FoxPro Introduced in 1989, the successor to FoxBASE+. It provides more than 200 language enhancements and features including a text-based windowing environment. FoxPro/Mac, the Macintosh version, is scheduled for a 1990 release.

FPGA (Field Programmable Gate Array) A programmable logic chip with a high density of gates.

FPS (Frames Per Second) See *frame*.

FPU (Floating Point Unit) The circuit within a computer that handles floating point operations.

fractals In computer graphics, the use of fractional mathematics to describe an image. It allow images of natural objects, such as trees, clouds and rivers, to be highly compressed for computer storage and transmission. Instead of turning an image into bit maps (raster graphics) or lines (vector graphics) as is done routinely in computer graphics, fractals turns an image into a set of data and an algorithm for expanding the data into the real object when required.

Fractals come from the science of chaos, which, contrary to its name, reveals an orderly pattern in the universe.

fragmentation The uneven distribution of data on a disk. As files are updated, they become less contiguous on the disk. When data is added, the operating system stores it in the available free space. As a result, parts of the file wind up in disparate areas of the disk, causing additional arm movement when the file is sequentially read. A disk maintenance, or optimizer, program is used to reorder the files in a contiguous manner.

FRAM (Ferromagnetic RAM) A memory technology that records microscopic bits on a magnetic surface. The advantage of FRAM memory is that, like disk and tape, the bits are non-volatile and remain permanent until intentionally changed.

frame

(1) In computer graphics, one screenful of data or its equivalent storage space.

(2) In communications, a group of bits that make up an elementary block of data for transmission by certain protocols.

(3) In artificial intelligence, a data structure that holds a general description of an object. The description is derived from basic concepts and experience.

frame buffer In computer graphics, a separate memory component that holds a graphic image. Frame buffers may have one plane of memory for each bit in the pixel. For example, if eight bits are used to represent one pixel, there are eight separate memory planes.

frame grabber In computer graphics, a device that converts video images into the computer. The frame grabber accepts standard TV signals and digitizes the current video frame into a computer graphics image.

Framework An integrated software package for PCs from Ashton-Tate Corporation. It provides database management, word processing, spreadsheet, communications and business graphics capability and its own programming language called Fred. Framework was one of the first integrated programs, and it continues to be refined and well liked by its users.

Fred The programming language used in Framework.

free-form database A database system that allows entry of text without regard to length or order. Although it accepts data as does a word processor, it differs by providing more elaborate methods for searching, retrieving and organizing the data after it has been entered.

free-form language A programming or command language in which statements can reside anywhere on a line or even cross over lines. It does not imply a looseness of structure or syntax, just more freedom in placement of the statements. For example, any number of blank spaces are allowed between symbols. Today, most high-level programming languages are free-form.

FreeHand A drawing program from Aldus Corporation that runs on the Macintosh. It is a powerful graphics program that combines a wide range of drawing tools with special effects.

freeware Software that is provided at no cost.

Freeway Advanced A communications program for PCs from Kortek, Inc. It is a menu-driven program with an optional command line for entering Crosstalk XVI commands.

frequency The number of oscillations, or vibrations, that are in an alternating current within one second. See *carrier*.

frequency division multiplexing See *FDM*.

frequency modulation See *FM*.

frequency shift See *FSK*.

frob From frobnicate. Slang for manipulating and adjusting dials and buttons for fun.

front end processor A communications computer. It connects to the communications channels on one end and the main computer on the other. Software in the front end processor directs the transmitting and receiving of messages according to the protocol used in the network. It detects and corrects transmission errors and assembles and disassembles messages.

A front end processor is sometimes synonymous with a communications control unit, although the latter is usually not as flexible as a front end processor.

In local area networks, intelligent network interface cards (NICs) perform the same functions as a front end processor.

FSK (Frequency Shift Keying) A simple communications modulation technique that merges binary data into a carrier frequency. It usually creates only two changes in the frequency, one for the 0 bit and another for the 1 bit.

FTAM (File Transfer Access and Management) A communications protocol for the transfer of files between systems of different vendors.

FTP (File Transfer Protocol) A TCP/IP protocol that is used to log onto the network, list directories and copy files. It can also translate between ASCII and EBCDIC. See *TFTP*.

FTS 2000 (Federal Telecommunications System 2000) A digital fiber-optic network providing voice, video, electronic mail and high-speed data communications for the U.S. government. AT&T and Sprint are the major providers of equipment.

FUD factor (Fear Uncertainty Doubt factor) A marketing strategy that instills caution in the minds of the buyer regarding the use of a competitive product. The organization that can employ the FUD factor is the one in control or in a privileged situation and it is usually accomplished by not revealing future plans.

full-duplex Transmitting and receiving simultaneously. In pure digital networks, this is achieved with two pairs of wires. In analog networks or in digital networks using carriers, it is achieved by dividing the bandwidth of the line into two frequencies, one for sending, one for receiving.

full-featured Hardware or software that provides capabilities and functions comparable to the most advanced models or programs in the same category.

full project life cycle A project from inception to completion.

full-screen A programming capability that allows data to be displayed in any row or column on the screen. Contrast with *teletype* mode.

fully populated Refers to a printed circuit board which contains the maximum number of chips that can be plugged into it.

function In programming, a routine that does a particular task. When the program passes control to a function, it performs the task and returns control to the instruction following the calling instruction.

The function may perform a stand-alone task, such as printing a message, or it may accept values (arguments) from the calling instruction, process them and pass the results back. Programming languages generally provide a set of standard functions and allow programmers to define their own. C is built entirely around functions. Contrast with *command*, which is a fundamental instruction within the language.

In programming, the term is specific. Outside of programming, it is used to describe any entity or component, such as the data entry function.

function keys A set of keyboard keys that are used to command the computer and are generally labelled F1, F2, etc. F1 is usually the help key. Function keys are also used with the control, alt and shift keys, allowing 40 functions to be performed with 10 keys. Software packages that make extensive use of function keys come with plastic templates that fit around the keys for visual identification.

IBM's PC and AT keyboards have 10 function keys (F1-F10) in a cluster on the left side of the keyboard. Keys F11 and F12 were added on its subsequent Enhanced keyboard, and all keys were relocated across the top of the keyboard.

SPECIAL-PURPOSE FUNCTION KEYS

GENERAL-PURPOSE FUNCTION KEYS

function library A collection of program routines. See *function*.

functional specification The blueprint for the design of an information system. It provides documentation for the database, human and machine procedures, and all the input, processing and output detail for each data entry, query, update and report program in the system.

fuse

(1) A protective device that is designed to melt, or blow, when a specified amount of current is passed through it. Programmable read only memory (PROM) chips are created as a series of fuses that are selectively blown in order to create the binary patterns in the chip.

(2) To bond together.

Futurebus+ A proposed IEEE standard for an advanced industrial 64-bit bus architecture that has 32- 128- and 256-bit variations. Futurebus+ is supported by Intel and Motorola, makers of the widely-used MULTIBUS and VMEbus architectures.

fuzzy computer A specially designed computer that employs fuzzy logic. Using such architectural components as analog circuits and parallel processing, fuzzy computers are designed for artificial intelligence applications.

fuzzy logic A mathematical technique for dealing with imprecise data and problems that have many solutions rather than one. Fuzzy logic can deal with values between 0 and 1 and is more analogous to human logic than the traditional binary logic of digital computers.

fuzzy search An inexact search for data that finds answers that come close to the desired data. Fuzzy searches can get results when the exact spelling is not known, and they can help users obtain information that is loosely related to a topic.

F1, F2.. See *function keys*.

G (Giga or Gigabyte) See *space/time*.

gain The amount of increase that an amplifier provides on the output side of the circuit.

GAL (Generic Array Logic) A programmable logic chip (PLD) technology from Lattice Semiconductor.

gallium arsenide An alloy of gallium and arsenic compound (GaAs) that is used as the base material for chips. It is several times faster than silicon.

gang punch To punch an identical set of holes into a deck of punched cards.

gap
(1) The space between blocks of data on a magnetic tape.

(2) The space in a read/write head over which magnetic flux (energy) flows causing the underlying magnetic tape or disk surface to become magnetized in the corresponding direction.

gapless Magnetic tape that is recorded in a continuous stream without interblock gaps.

garbage collection A routine that searches memory for program segments or data that are no longer active in order to reclaim that space for new instructions or data.

garbage in, garbage out Refers to the fact that invalid input produces invalid output. The data entry process is a critical one, and all possible tests should be made on data entered into a computer. More fitting perhaps is "garbage in, gospel out," since many people put a lot of faith in the accuracy of computer printouts.

gas discharge display See *plasma display*.

gas plasma See *plasma display*.

gate
(1) One of the AND, OR and NOT Boolean logic gates that ties transistors together. See *Boolean logic* and *gate array*.

(2) The line that triggers the switch in a MOS transistor.

gate array A chip that contains unconnected logic elements. The finished, customized chip is obtained by adhering the top metal layer of pathways between the elements. This final masking stage is less costly than designing the chip from scratch.

Gate array chips usually contain only two-input NAND gates, which can be used singularly or connected with other NAND gates to provide all the Boolean operations required for digital logic.

gateway A computer that connects two different types of communications networks together. It performs the protocol conversion from one network to the other. For example, a gateway could connect a personal computer LAN to a centralized mainframe network. Contrast with *bridge*, which connects similar networks together.

gather write A capability that allows data to be output from two or more noncontiguous memory locations with one write operation. See *scatter read*.

GatorBox A gateway from Cayman Systems, Inc., that interconnects LocalTalk and Ethernet networks and supports TCP/IP and NFS protocols. It also functions as a router to connect AppleTalk-based computers on a LAN with remote AppleTalk devices.

gauss A unit of measurement of magnetic energy.

Gaussian distribution A random distribution of events that is often graphed as a bell-shaped curve. It is used to represent a normal or statistically probable outcome.

Gaussian noise In communications, a random interference generated by the movement of electricity in the line. Also called *white noise*.

GB (GigaByte) See *space/time*.

GCOS An operating system used in Honeywell minicomputers and mainframes.

GDDM (Graphical Data Display Manager) Software that generates graphics images in the IBM mainframe environment. It contains routines to generate graphics on terminals, printers and plotters as well as accepting input from scanners. Programmers use GDDM for creating graphics, but users can employ the Interactive Chart Utility (ICU) within GDDM to create business graphics without programming.

GDDM/graPHIGS is a programming environment that combines graphics capability with a user interface similar to the Presentation Manager in OS/2.

GDI (Graphics Device Interface) The graphics language used in Microsoft Windows.

GDM See CGM.

GE (Greater than or Equal to) See *relational operators*.

GEM (Graphics Environment Manager) A graphical user interface PCs from Digital Research Inc. Many application programs come with a run time version of GEM, the most notable of which is Ventura Publisher.

gender changer A coupling unit that reverses the gender of one of the connectors in order that two wires with male connectors or two wires with female connectors can be joined together.

general-purpose computer A computer that follows a set of instructions. It refers to most computers from micro to mainframe. Computers in toys, games and other hand held devices may be general purpose, even though they follow only one program permanently placed into ROM. In contrast, computer chips and computer systems can also be designed from scratch for special purposes. See *ASIC*.

general-purpose controller A peripheral control unit that can service more than one type of peripheral device, for example, a printer and a communications line.

general-purpose interface bus See *GPIB*.

general-purpose language A programming language that can be used to solve a wide variety of problems. FORTRAN, COBOL and BASIC are examples of general purpose languages. Contrast with *special-purpose language*.

generalized program Software that serves a changing environment. By allowing variable data to be introduced, the program can solve the same problem for different users or situations. For example, the electronic versions of this Glossary can be programmed to read in a different title and thus be used for any type of dictionary.

generator
(1) A program that creates a program. See *application generator* and *macro generator*.

(2) A device that creates electrical power or synchonization signals.

Generic CADD A full-featured computer-aided design and drafting package for PCs from Generic Software, Inc. It offers three levels of implementation to fit the user's requirements. Level 1 is for the beginner, Level 2 for the intermediate user and Level 3 is aimed at the advanced CADD user. Level 1 is also available for the Macintosh.

GEnie (General Electric Network for Information Exchange) An information utility from General Electric Information Services that provides business information, news and access to special interest groups.

Genifer An dBASE application generator from Bytel Corporation. An application is built by creating the menu, data entry and update screens that the final application uses. Genifer generates traditional dBASE III source code that can be modified by a programmer if necessary.

genlock (generator lock) The circuitry that synchronizes video signals for mixing. In a personal computer, a genlock display adapter converts screen output into a standard NTSC video signal, which it then synchronizes with an external video source.

geostationary Same as *geosynchronous*.

geosynchronous Meaning earth aligned. Typically refers to communications satellites that are placed 22,300 miles above the equator and travel at the same speed as the earth's rotation, thus appearing to be stationary.

get In programming, a request for the next record in an input file. Contrast with *put*.

ghost

(1) A faint second image that appears close to the primary image on a display or printout. In transmission, a ghost is a result of secondary signals that arrive ahead of or later than the primary signal. On a printout, a ghost is caused by bouncing print elements as the paper passes by.

(2) To display a menu option in a dimmed, fuzzy typeface in order to indicate that the option is not currently available. Pull-down menus typically ghost unavailable options.

GHz (GigaHertZ) One billion cycles per second.

giga Billion. Abbreviated "G." For example, 10 Gbytes is 10 billion bytes; 12 GHz is 12 billion cycles per second. See *space/time*.

gigaflops (giga FLoating point OPerations per Second) One billion floating point operations per second.

GIGO (Garbage In Garbage Out or Garbage In Gospel Out!) What you get when you don't design a high level of data entry validation into your application!

GIS

(1) (Geographic Information System) A digital mapping system that is used for such purposes as exploration, demographics, dispatching and tracking.

(2) (Generalized Information System) A query and data manipulation language from IBM that runs on IBM mainframes.

GKS (Graphical Kernel System) A graphics system and language for creating 2-D, 3-D and raster graphics images. It is a device independent system that allows application programs to create and manipulate graphics on many varieties of display devices.

GKS allows applications to be developed on one system and easily moved to another with minimal or no change. GKS is the first true standard for graphics applications programmers and has been adopted by both ANSI and ISO.

glare filter A fine mesh screen that is placed over a CRT screen to reduce glare from overhead and ambient light.

glitch Any temporary or random malfunction in hardware. Contrast with *bug*, which is a permanent error. Sometimes a bug in a program may cause the hardware to appear as if it had a glitch in it (and vice versa). At times it can be extremely difficult to determine whether a problem lies within the hardware or the software.

global Pertains to an entire file, database, volume, program or system.

global variable In programming, a variable that is used by all modules in a program.

Glossary In Microsoft Word, a collection of shorthand entries for long words or phrases. For example, typing TCG could cause The Computer Glossary to be substituted in its place.

glue chip A chip that adds functionality to a microprocessor, for example, an I/O processor or extra memory.

gooey See *GUI*.

GOSIP (Government Open Systems Interconnection Profile) U.S. government mandate that as of August 15, 1990, all network procurements must comply with OSI. Testing is performed at the NIST, which maintains a database of OSI-compliant commercial products.

GOTO
(1) In a high-level programming language, a statement that directs the computer to go to some other part of the program. The equivalent in a low-level language is a *branch* or *jump* instruction.

(2) In dBASE, a command that directs the user to a specific record in the database file.

(3) In word processing, a command that directs the user to a specific page number.

GOTO-less programming The writing of a program without the use of GOTO instructions; an important rule in structured programming. A GOTO instruction points to a different part of the program without a guarantee of returning. Instead of using GOTOs, structures called *subroutines* or *functions* are used, which automatically return to the next instruction after the calling instruction when completed.

GPI (Graphical Programming Interface) The graphics language used in OS/2 Presentation Manager. It is a derivative of the GDDM mainframe interface and includes Bezier curves.

GPIB (General Purpose Interface Bus) The IEEE 488 standard interface that connects peripheral devices to a computer and is often used for attaching sensors and programmable instruments. GPIB is a parallel interface that uses a special 24 pin connector. Hewlett-Packard's version of the GPIB is the HPIB.

GPSS (General Purpose Simulation System) A programming language for discrete event simulation, which is used to build models of operations such as manufacturing environments, communications systems and traffic patterns. Originally developed by IBM and used on mainframes, PC versions are now available, such as GPSS/PC by Minuteman Software and GPSS/H by Wolverine Software.

graceful degradation A system that, after a failure of one of its components, can continue to perform at some reduced level of performance.

graceful exit The ability to get out of a problem situation in a program without having to turn the computer off.

grade The transmission capacity of a line. It refers to a range or class of frequencies that it can handle, for example, telegraph grade, voice grade and broadband.

grammar checker A program that checks the grammar of a sentence. It can check for and highlight incomplete sentences, awkward phrases, wordiness and poor grammar.

grandfather, father, son A method for storing previous generations of master file data that is continuously updated. The son is the current file, the father is a copy of the file from the previous cycle, and the grandfather is a copy of the file from the cycle before that one.

granularity The degree of modularity of a system. The more granularity (grains or granules), the more customizable or flexible the system.

graph A pictorial representation of information. See *business graphics*.

graphic character A printable symbol that includes digits and letters.

graphical interface See *GUI*.

graphics With regard to the computer, the creation and management of pictures. Pictures can be entered into the computer using input devices such as graphics tablets, mice or light pens, and existing pictures on paper can be scanned into the computer using scanners or cameras.

Once stored, pictures can be manipulated and copied in many ways. Colors can be changed, objects can be increased and decreased in size, slanted, squeezed and squashed. Frames of video recordings can be combined with drawn objects.

Text descriptions can be added to produce charts, reports, brochures and other kinds of presentation materials. Pictures can be printed on graphics printers and plotters, high-resolution COM (computer output microfilm) machines, or photographed with traditional cameras directly from the video display screen.

Business graphics software can generate graphic images, such as bar charts, scatter diagrams and pie charts directly from the data without human drawing efforts. These charts can be enhanced by using graphics tools, such as paint programs.

A graphics computer system requires a graphics display screen, a graphics input device (tablet, mouse, scanner, camera...), a graphics output device (dot matrix printer, laser printer, plotter...) and a graphics software package; for example, a CAD, draw or paint program.

The higher the resolution of the graphics output device, the better the printed image will look. The higher the resolution of the display screen, the more realistic the images will appear on it.

Computer Graphics versus TV Realism

Although a personal computer costs significantly more than a color TV, it can't produce animated pictures with the same quality as a TV, nor can it produce a still picture with the same visual quality. The reason is that a TV doesn't store the signal it receives from the broadcasting station; it simply transfers it directly to the screen.

Images created in computers are generated and held in memory and then copied to the screen. Personal computer memories haven't been large enough to represent all the dots in a single frame of TV, let alone been able to generate 30 full frames per second to provide realistic animation.

Today, realistic (TV-like and better) graphics require high-powered CAD workstations or expensive add-ons to a personal computer. Animation of realistic images requires extremely powerful workstations, and animation that can depict the intricate shading of human skin in a totally realistic fashion requires a high-end unit costing $100,000 or more.

As chip technologies advance, memories and high-resolution graphics will become cheaper, and the personal computer of the 1990s will resemble the specialized workstations of the 1980s.

Vector Graphics and Raster Graphics

Two methods are used for storing and maintaining pictures in a computer. The first method, called *vector graphics* (also known as object-oriented graphics), maintains the image as a series of points, lines, arcs and other geometric shapes.

The second method, called *raster graphics*, resembles television, where the picture image is made up of dots.

Understanding these two methods and how they intertwine in today's graphics systems is essential for mastering computer graphics. When you create a picture on a video display screen, it may not be immediately obvious which method is used. When you try to manipulate the image, it will become clear which method has been used.

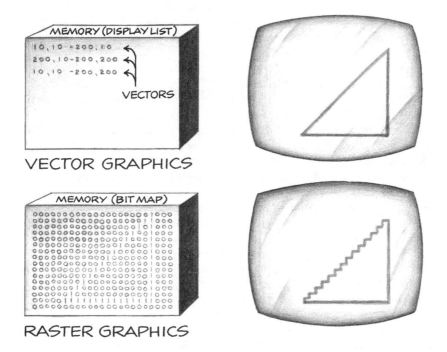

Vector Graphics for CAD and Drawing

Vector graphics is the method employed by CAD (computer-aided design) and drawing packages. As you draw, each line of the image is stored as a vector (two end points on an x-y matrix). For example, a square becomes four vectors, one for each side. A circle is turned into dozens or hundreds of tiny straight lines, the number of which is determined by the resolution of the drawing. The entire image is commonly stored in the computer as a list of vectors, called a *display list*.

If the display screen used is a vector graphics screen, as is found in some older CAD systems, the image is also "drawn" on screen. If it's a raster graphics screen (made up of dots), as is the case with personal computers and most graphics systems today, the vectors are converted into dots in order to display the image on screen. This is called the *rasterization of vectors*.

Vector graphics is used when it is essential to have geometric knowledge about the object created. In a vector graphics system, geometric shapes keep their integrity: a line can always be picked, extended or erased; for example, it never turns into just a string of dots in the database.

Vector graphics can be transmitted directly to x-y plotters that "draw" the images from the list of vectors.

Raster Graphics for Painting

Raster graphics is the TV-like method that uses dots to display an image on screen. Raster graphics images are created by scanners and cameras and are also generated by paint packages. A picture frame is divided into hundreds of horizontal rows, with each row containing hundreds of dots, called *pixels*.

Unlike TV, which uses a single standard (NTSC) for the entire country, there are dozens of raster graphics standards with new ones coming all the time. Also unlike TV, which records and displays the dots as infinitely variable shades and colors (analog), computer graphics have a finite number of shades and colors (digital) based on how large a number is used to represent each pixel.

When you scan an image or paint an object into the computer, the image is created in a reserved area of memory called a *bit map*, with some number of bits corresponding to each dot (pixel). In the simplest monochrome systems, one bit can represent a dot, either on or off. For gray scale (monochrome shades), several bits are required to hold the shade number for each dot. For color, more bits are required to hold a number for each intensity of red, green and blue in the dot.

The image in the bit map is continuously transmitted to the video screen, dot for dot, a line at a time, over and over again. Any changes made to the bit map are instantly reflected on the screen.

Since colors are designated with numbers, changing red to green is simply searching for the red number and replacing it with the green number, just as all occurrences of a word can be changed in word processing. Animation is accomplished by continuously copying new sequences from other areas in memory into the bit map, one after the other.

Raster graphics images may take up more space on disk than their vector graphics counterpart, because storage for each pixel is required even if it's part of the background. A small object in vector graphics format will take up only a few vectors in the display list file.

Screens vs Printers

Desktop laser printers and graphics plotters connected to personal computers have higher resolutions than the standard graphics screens that are used to display the images. The resolution of contemporary desktop laser printers is 300 dots per inch, or 90,000 pixels per square inch, whereas common display resolutions are less than 10,000 pixels per square inch. That means the jagged lines on a display screen can print more uniformly on a laser printer.

graphics accelerator Same as *graphics engine*.

graphics based The display of text and pictures as graphics images; typically bit-mapped images. Contrast with *text based*.

graphics engine Specialized hardware that performs graphics processing independently of the main CPU. It can perform any of a variety of functions, such as generating graphic geometry (display list processing), converting vectors to rasters (rasterization of vectors), compression, matrix multiplication (for fast rotation) as well as providing faster data transfer from memory to the display. Graphics engines are programmed in a graphics language.

graphics interface See *GUI*.

graphics language A set of instructions that let a programmer express a graphics image in a high-level language. The language is translated into graphics images by software or specialized hardware. See *graphics engine*.

graphics primitive An elementary graphics building block, such as a point, line or arc. In a solid modeling system, a cylinder, cube and sphere are examples of primitives.

graphics processor Same as *graphics engine*.

graphics tablet See *digitizer tablet*.

graphics terminal
(1) An input/output device that is capable of displaying pictures. Images are received via communications or entered with a device, such as a mouse or light pen. The keyboard may have specialized function keys, wheels or dials. Graphics terminals employ raster graphics, vector graphics or combination raster and vector technologies.

(2) A terminal or personal computer that displays graphics.

graPHIGS See *GDDM*.

gray scale In computer graphics, a series of shades from white to black. The more levels of gray scale, the more realistically an image can be displayed, especially a scanned photograph. Scanners differentiate typically from 16 to 256 levels of gray scale.

However, the amount of gray scale that can be created or entered into the computer depends on the memory and disk space that can be reserved. At the common desktop laser printer resolution of 300 dpi, each square inch is made up of 90,000 pixels. At 256 levels of gray scale (one byte per pixel), it takes 90,000 bytes for one square inch of image. Although compression techiques help reduce the size of graphics files, high-resolution gray scale requires huge amounts of storage.

greek To display text in a representative form in which the actual letters are not discernible. For example, when previewing a finished document in desktop publishing, if the display screen is not large enough to handle the resolution, the text is greeked.

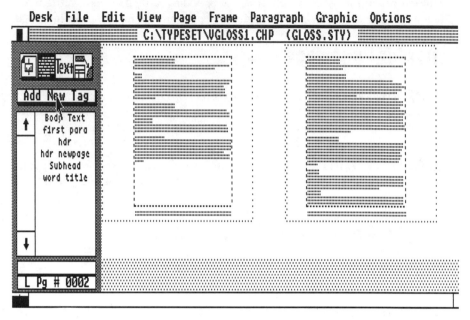

GREEKING

This Ventura Publisher example shows two facing pages of this book on a low-resolution screen, which cannot display the full characters.

groupware Software that is designed for use in a network and serve a group of users that work on a related project.

GT (Greater Than) See *relational operator*.

guard band A frequency that insulates one signal from another. In an analog telephone line, the low band is 0-300; the high band is 3300-4000Hz.

GUI (Graphical User Interface) A graphics-based user interface that incorporates icons, pull-down menus and a mouse, such as found in Macintosh, Windows, OS/2 Presentation Manager and GEM environments. Contrast with user interfaces that are character- or text-based, such as DOS, which displays data in the standard 25 line, 80 column text mode. Contrast with *CUI*.

gulp An unspecified number of bytes!

gutter In typography, the space between two columns.

h (Hexadecimal) A symbol that refers to a hex number. For example, 09h has a numeric value of 9, whereas 0Ah has a value of 10. See *hex chart*.

H&J (Hyphenation and Justification) The alignment of the right margin alignment in a document. Hyphenation breaks up words that exceed the margin, and justification aligns text uniformly at the right margin while spacing text evenly between both margins.

hacker A programmer who writes programs in assembly language or in system-level languages, such as C. Although it may refer to any programmer, it implies very tedious "hacking away" at the bits and bytes. It sometimes refers to a person who breaks a code and gains illegal entrance into a system.

half-adder An elementary electronic circuit in the ALU that adds one bit to another, deriving a result bit and a carry bit.

half-duplex The transmission of data in both directions, but only one direction at a time. Two-way radio was the first to use half-duplex, for example, while one party spoke, the other party listened. Contrast with *full-duplex*.

half height drive A 5.25" disk drive that takes up half the vertical space of first-generation drives. It is 1 5/8" high by 5.75" wide.

halftone In printing, the simulation of a continuous-tone image (shaded drawing, photograph) with groups of dots. All printing processes, except for Cycolor, print dots. The smaller the dots and the wider they're spaced apart, the lighter the image. The denser the dots, the darker the image.

If you look at a newspaper or magazine photograph through a magnifying glass, you'll see how different dot densities simulate continuous shades. See *dithering*.

hammer In a printer, the mechanism that pushes the typeface onto the ribbon and paper or pushes the paper into the ribbon and typeface.

Hamming code In communications, an error correction code that is interspersed with the bits of each character. At the receiving station, the code is checked in order to detect missing bits, and one-bit errors can be corrected automatically.

handle In computer graphics, a tiny square which is attached to a graphic image that is used for moving or reshaping the image. The handle is selected by moving the cursor onto it and pressing a key or mouse button.

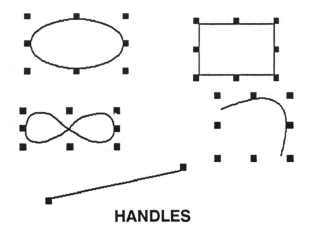

HANDLES

handler A software routine that performs a particular task. For example, upon detection of an error, an error handler is called upon to recover from the error condition.

handset The part of the telephone that contains the speaker and the microphone.

handshaking The signals transmitted back and forth over a communications network that establish a valid connection between two parties.

hanging paragraph In typography, a paragraph of text in which the first line starts at the left margin, but the second and subsequent lines are indented as is this paragraph.

hard coded Software that performs a fixed number of tasks or works with only a fixed number of devices. For example, a program could be written to work with only two types of printers and not allow any other types to be introduced. Hard coded solutions to problems are usually the fastest, but do not allow for future flexibility.

hard copy Printed output. Contrast with *soft copy*, which is spoken or displayed on screen.

hard disk A magnetic disk made of metal and covered with a magnetic recording surface. Hard disks come in removable and fixed varieties that hold from 10 to hundreds of megabytes. Contrast with *floppy disk*.

hard error

(1) A permanent, unrecoverable error such as a disk read error. Contrast with *soft error*.

(2) A group of errors that requires user intervention and includes disk read errors (retry, abort), disk not ready (no disk in drive) and printer not ready (out of paper).

hard return A control code that is entered into a text document by pressing the return key. The common hard return in DOS and OS/2 text files is a carriage return (CR) followed by a line feed (LF), but this is not standard. For example, WordPerfect uses only a line feed. In the Macintosh, a carriage return is consistently used as a hard return.

   Hard returns may be visible on screen such as the less than sign (<) in WordStar, or they may be invisible until revealed in a special expanded mode on screen. Contrast with *soft return*.

hard sectored An organization technique that identifies the sectors on a disk by some physical mark. For example, hard sectored floppy disks have a hole in the disk that marks the beginning of each sector. Contrast with *soft sectored*.

Hardcard A family of hard disks for PCs from Plus Development Corporation that houses the disk and controller on the same printed circuit board. It can be the first hard disk in a floppy system or additional storage in a hard disk system. Early BIOSs that make no provision for hard disks must be upgraded. The Hardcard is noted for its high reliability and allows for the inclusion of hard disks when all disk bays are currently filled.

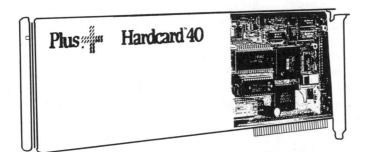

hardware All machinery and equipment. Contrast with *software*, which is a set of instructions that tell the computer what to do. Also contrast with *data*, which are the facts and figures that are stored in the hardware and controlled by software.

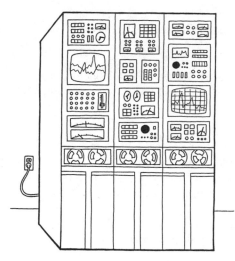

if you bump into it, it's hardware

Hardware vs Software

In operation, a computer is both hardware and software. One is useless without the other, and each rules the other. The hardware design specifies what instructions it can follow, and the instructions then tell it what to do.

As inseparable as hardware and software are in operation, they are quite different when they are being evaluated. Hardware is the world of storage and transmission. Software is the world of logic and language.

The more memory and disk storage a computer system has, the more work it can do. The faster the memory and disks transmit data and instructions between them and the CPU, the faster the work gets done. A user's problem can be translated into a hardware requirement based on the size of the files and databases that will be created and the number of concurrent users at terminals.

Software, on the other hand, is harder to specify. The programs must process the organization's business transactions properly, and even the smallest company can have complicated transactions.

Hardware always deals with the data processing problem the same way. How much? How fast? But software deals with the tedious details of an ever-changing business. It's much harder to analyze, design and develop the software solution than it is to specify the hardware.

hardware failure A malfunction within the electronic circuits or electromechanical components (disks, tapes) of a computer system. Contrast with *software failure*.

hardware interrupt An interrupt that is caused by some action of a hardware device, such as the depression of a key on a keyboard. See *interrupt*.

hardware key A copy protection device supplied with software that plugs into one of the computer's ports. The software interrogates the key's serial number during execution to verify its presence. The hardware key acts as a pass-through, but tests for a special code that reads the serial number.

hardware monitor A device that is connected to the circuits of a computer in order to analyze its performance.

hardwired
(1) Electronic circuitry that is designed to perform a specific task. See *hard coded*.

(2) Devices that are closely or tightly coupled. For example, a hardwired terminal is directly connected to a computer without going through a switched network.

harmonic distortion In communications, frequencies that are generated as multiples of the original frequency due to irregularities in the transmission line.

Harvard Graphics A business graphics program for PCs from Software Publishing Corporation. It is a highly-praised program that turns existing data into graphs and charts for presentations in a wide variety of styles and formats. It also provides the ability to create columnar and free form text charts.

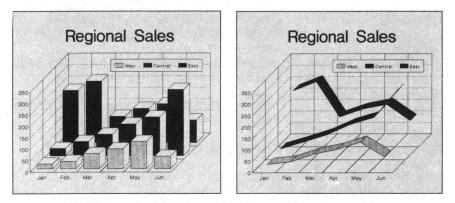

SAMPLE HARVARD GRAPHICS CHARTS
(Courtesy Software Publishing Corp.)

hash total A method for ensuring the accuracy of processed data. It is a total of several fields of data in a file, including fields not normally used in calculations, such as account number. At various stages in the processing, the hash total is recalculated and compared with the original. If any data has been lost or changed, the mismatch will signal an error.

Hayes compatible A modem that accepts the same command language as modems made by Hayes Microcomputer Products, Inc.

Hayes Smartmodem A family of intelligent modems for personal computers from Hayes Microcomputer Products, Inc. Hayes developed the intelligent modem for first-generation personal computers in 1978, and its command language (Hayes Standard AT Command Set) for modem control has become an industry-standard.

The Hayes Intelligent Modem

An intelligent modem has a command state and an online state. In the command state, it accepts instructions. In the online state, it dials, answers, transmits and receives.

Once connected, it performs the handshaking with the remote modem, which is similar to the opening exchange of a telephone call. The called party says "hello," the calling party says "hello, this is..." After this, the real conversation begins. If the modem's speaker is on, you can hear the whistles and tones used in the handshake.

Once the handshake is completed, you are online with the other computer, and data can be transmitted back and forth.

An important part of the Hayes standard is the escape sequence, which tells the modem to switch from online to the command state. It usually consists of three plus signs in sequence (+ + +) with a Hayes-patented, one-second guard time interval before and after it, which prevents the modem from mistaking a random occurrence of the escape sequence. The escape sequence and guard time interval can be programmed in the modem's Status registers.

To issue an escape sequence, hold down the shift key and press + + +. Pause one second before and after the sequence. The modem will return the OK result code, indicating it is ready to accept commands.

Hayes V-series A family of modems from Hayes Microcomputer Products, Inc., with built-in error correction, data compression, speed buffering and automatic negotiation of connections at the highest common feature set and transmission speed. All V-series products use the Hayes Standard AT Command Set. See AT *command set*.

HDLC (High-level Data Link Control) International communications protocol defined by ISO and used in X.25 packet switching networks. HDLC provides error correction at the data link layer. SDLC, LAP and LAPB are subsets of HDLC.

HDTV (High Definition TV) TV with double the resolution of the current 525-line NTSC standard. The problem is developing a technique that will transmit both signals at the same time.

head See *read/write head*.

head crash The physical destruction of a hard disk. Due to head misalignment or contamination with dust and dirt, the read/write head collides with the disk's recording surface. The data is destroyed, and both the disk platter and read/write head usually have to be replaced.

The read/write head touches the surface of a floppy disk, but on a hard disk, it hovers above its surface at a distance that is less than the diameter of a human hair. It has been said that the read/write head flying over the disk surface is like trying to fly a jet plane six inches above the earth's surface.

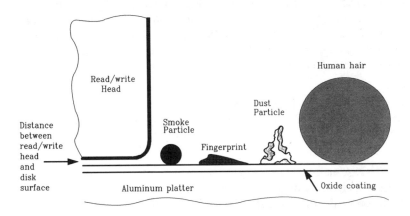

head-per-track disk A disk drive that has a read/write head positioned over each track, thus eliminating the access arm movement from track to track.

header
(1) In data processing, the first record in a file that identifies the file. The name of the file, date of last update and various other status data are stored in the header.

(2) In a document or report, common text that is printed at the top of every page.

(3) In communications, the first part of the message that contains controlling data, such as originating and destination stations, message type and priority level.

(4) Any caption or description used as a headline.

header label A record used for file identification that is placed at the beginning of the file.

heap In programming, the free memory currently available to load and run programs.

heat sink A material that absorbs heat.

helical scan The diagonal tracking used on videotape and digital audio tape (DAT), which increases storage capacity over parallel methods.

help On-screen instruction regarding the use of a program. On PCs, pressing F1 is the defacto standard for getting help. With graphics-based interfaces, such as the Mac, GEM and others, clicking a "?" or HELP button gets help. See *context sensitive help*.

Hercules Graphics A video display standard for PCs from Hercules Computer Technology Inc., that provides monochrome graphics and text with a resolution of 720x348 pixels. IBM's first PC monochrome display did not provide graphics, and Hercules introduced its display adapter to fill the void in 1982. It quickly became a de facto standard.

Hertz The frequency of electrical vibrations (cycles) per second. Abbreviated "Hz," one Hz is equal to one cycle per second. In 1883, Heinrich Hertz detected electromagnetic waves.

heuristic A method of problem solving using exploration and trial and error methods. Heuristic program design provides a framework for solving the problem in contrast with a fixed set of rules (algorithmic) that cannot vary.

Hewlett-Packard See *HP*.

hexadecimal (hex) Meaning sixteen; a base 16 numbering system used as a shorthand for representing all the possible values in a byte. Each half byte (four bits) is assigned a hex digit.

Hex is used for representing bytes because of its uniformity on a printout or display. Two hex digits always make up a byte, whereas the decimal values of a byte can be a number from one to three digits in length (0 through 255).

Dec	Hex	Binary	Dec	Hex	Binary
0	0	0000	8	8	1000
1	1	0001	9	9	1001
2	2	0010	10	A	1010
3	3	0011	11	B	1011
4	4	0100	12	C	1100
5	5	0101	13	D	1101
6	6	0110	14	E	1110
7	7	0111	15	F	1111

STANDARD ASCII

The first 32 characters (0-31) are control codes

00	NUL	Null	21	!	51	Q
01	SOH	Start of heading	22	"	52	R
02	STX	Start of text	23	#	53	S
03	ETX	End of text	24	$	54	T
04	EOT	End of transmit	25	%	55	U
05	ENQ	Enquiry	26	&	56	V
06	ACK	Acknowledge	27	'	57	W
07	BEL	Audible bell	28	(	58	X
08	BS	Backspace	29	)	59	Y
09	HT	Horizontal tab	2A	*	5A	Z
0A	LF	Line feed	2B	+	5B	[
0B	VT	Vertical tab	2C	,	5C	\
0C	FF	Form feed	2D	-	5D	]
0D	CR	Carriage return	2E	.	5E	^
0E	SO	Shift out	2F	/	5F	_
0F	SI	Shift in	30	0	60	`
10	DLE	Data link escape	31	1	61	a
11	DC1	Device control 1	32	2	62	b
12	DC2	Device control 2	33	3	63	c
13	DC3	Device control 3	34	4	64	d
14	DC4	Device control 4	35	5	65	e
15	NAK	Neg. acknowledge	36	6	66	f
16	SYN	Synchronous idle	37	7	67	g
17	ETB	End trans. block	38	8	68	h
18	CAN	Cancel	39	9	69	i
19	EM	End of medium	3A	:	6A	j
1A	SUB	Substitution	3B	;	6B	k
1B	ESC	Escape	3C	<	6C	l
1C	FS	Figures shift	3D	=	6D	m
1D	GS	Group separator	3E	>	6E	n
1E	RS	Record separator	3F	?	6F	o
1F	US	Unit separator	40	@	70	p
			41	A	71	q
20	SP	Blank space	42	B	72	r
		(Space bar)	43	C	73	s
			44	D	74	t
			45	E	75	u
			46	F	76	v
			47	G	77	w
			48	H	78	x
			49	I	79	y
			4A	J	7A	z
			4B	K	7B	{
			4C	L	7C	|
			4D	M	7D	}
			4E	N	7E	~
			4F	O	7F	▓
			50	P		

EXTENDED ASCII

(IBM and compatible pcs)

80	Ç	AE	«	DC	▄
81	ü	AF	»	DD	▌
82	é	B0	░	DE	▐
83	â	B1	▒	DF	▀
84	ä	B2	▓	E0	α
85	à	B3	│	E1	β
86	å	B4	┤	E2	Γ
87	ç	B5	╡	E3	π
88	ê	B6	╢	E4	Σ
89	ë	B7	╖	E5	σ
8A	è	B8	╕	E6	µ
8B	ï	B9	╣	E7	τ
8C	î	BA	║	E8	Φ
8D	ì	BB	╗	E9	Θ
8E	Ä	BC	╝	EA	Ω
8F	Å	BD	╜	EB	δ
90	É	BE	╛	EC	∞
91	æ	BF	┐	ED	φ
92	Æ	C0	└	EE	ε
93	ô	C1	┴	EF	∩
94	ö	C2	┬	F0	≡
95	ò	C3	├	F1	±
96	û	C4	─	F2	≥
97	ù	C5	┼	F3	≤
98	ÿ	C6	╞	F4	⌠
99	Ö	C7	╟	F5	⌡
9A	Ü	C8	╚	F6	÷
9B	¢	C9	╔	F7	≈
9C	£	CA	╩	F8	°
9D	¥	CB	╦	F9	•
9E	₧	CC	╠	FA	·
9F	ƒ	CD	═	FB	√
A0	á	CE	╬	FC	η
A1	í	CF	╧	FD	²
A2	ó	D0	╨	FE	■
A3	ú	D1	╤	FF	
A4	ñ	D2	╥		
A5	Ñ	D3	╙		
A6	ª	D4	╘		
A7	º	D5	╒		
A8	¿	D6	╓		
A9	⌐	D7	╫		
AA	¬	D8	╪		
AB	½	D9	┘		
AC	¼	DA	┌		
AD	¡	DB	█		

ASCII CODE IN HEXADECIMAL NOTATION

HFS (Hierarchical File System) The file system used in the Macintosh that allows files to be placed into folders, and folders to be placed within other folders.

HGC See *Hercules Graphics*.

hi-res Same as *high resolution*.

hidden file A disk file that has been given a status which prevents it from being viewed, changed or deleted. Hidden files are usually program files that are part of the system software; however, users can also hide files on disk to prevent unauthorized access.

hierarchical A structure made up of different levels like a company organization chart. The higher levels have control or precedence over the lower levels. Hierarchical structures are a one to many relationship; each item having one or more items below it.

In communications, a hierarchical network refers to a single computer that has control over all the nodes connected to it.

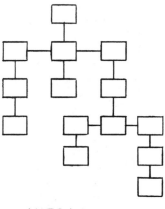

HIERARCHICAL

hierarchical file system A file organization method that stores data in a top-to-bottom organization structure. All access to the data starts at the top and proceeds throughout the levels of the hierarchy.

In DOS and OS/2, the root directory is the starting point. Files can be stored in the root directory, or directories can be created off the root that hold files and subdirectories.

In the Macintosh, the disk window is the starting point. Files can be stored in the disk window, or folders can be created that can hold files and additional folders.

high definition TV See *HDTV*.

high-level language A machine-independent programming language, such as FORTRAN, COBOL, BASIC, Pascal and C. High-level languages let the programmer concentrate on the logic of the problem to be solved rather than the intricacies of the machine architecture, such as is required with low-level assembly languages.

high resolution A high-quality image on a display screen or printed form. The more dots used per square inch, the higher the quality. To display totally realistic images including the shades of human skin requires about

1,000x1,000 pixels on a 12" diagonal screen. Desktop laser printers print respectable text and graphics at 300 dpi, but typesetting machines print 1,200 and 2,400 dpi.

highlight To identify an area on screen in order to select, move, delete or change it in some manner.

highlight bar A line in an on-screen menu that is displayed in reverse video or in a different color to signal the current selection.

HiJaak A graphics utility for PCs from Inset Systems Inc. It can capture a screen and convert it into any of a variety of graphics formats including PostScript output for Linotronic and Compugraphic typesetters. It can also redirect laser printer output to a fax board.

HIMEM.SYS An XMS driver from Microsoft that allows programs to cooperatively use extended memory in 286 and higher machines. It also manages the HMA (high memory area), the 64K block of memory just above 1MB.

hints Special additions to PostScript fonts that instruct the imaging device to alter space and other font features based on type size, especially for small font sizes.

HIPO (Hierarchy plus Input-Process-Output) Pronounced "hy-po." An IBM flow-charting technique that provides a graphical method for designing and documenting programs.

HLLAPI (High Level Language Application Program Interface) A programming interface from IBM that allows a PC application to communicate with a mainframe application. The hardware hookup is handled via normal micro to mainframe 3270 emulation. HLLAPI allows the personal computer or workstation program to interact with the mainframe application rather than the user at the keyboard.

HMA (High Memory Area) In PCs, a 64K region of extended memory above one megabyte (1024-1088K) that can be accessed by DOS. This capability was discovered after 286 machines became available. Microsoft's HIMEM.SYS driver uses this memory.

hog A program that uses an excessive amount of computer resources, such as memory or disk, or takes a long time to execute.

Hold Everything A set of library functions for PC languages from South Mountain Software. It allows C, BASIC, Clipper, Turbo Pascal and dBASE programs to be loaded into occupied memory by saving and restoring active programs to disk or EMS.

Hollerith tabulating machine The first automatic data processing system. It was used to count the 1890 U.S. census. Developed by Herman Hollerith, a statistician who had worked for the Census Bureau, the system used a hand punch to record the data in a dollar-bill-sized punched card and a tabulating machine to count them.

It was estimated that, with manual methods, the 1890 census wouldn't be completed until after 1900. With Hollerith's machines, it took two years and saved five million dollars.

Hollerith formed the Tabulating Machine Company and sold his machines throughout the world for a variety of accounting functions. In 1911, his company was merged into the company that was later renamed IBM.

HERMAN HOLLERITH
(Courtesy Library of Congress)

HOLLERITH TABULATING MACHINE
(Courtesy Smithsonian Institution)
These are replicas of the tabulating machine and sort box used in the 1890 census.

This November 11, 1891 issue of The Electrical Engineer extols the virtues of using electricity as a means of counting.

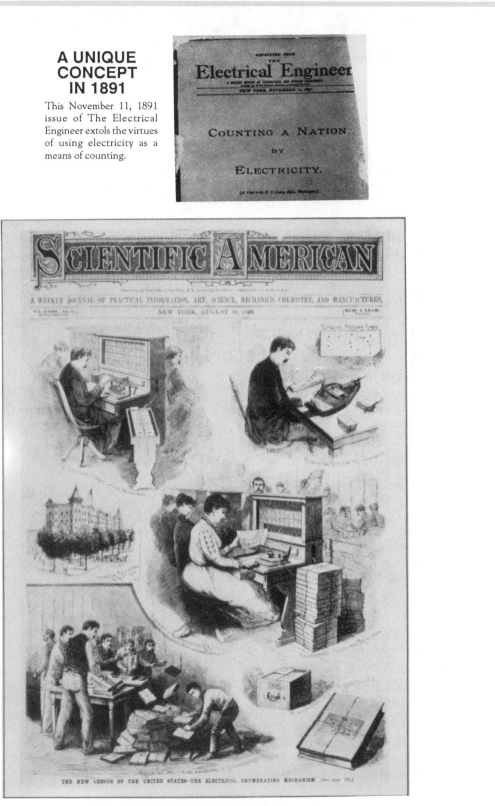

THE 1890 CENSUS

(Courtesy Scientific American)

home brew Products that are developed at home by hobbyists.

home button An icon that represents the beginning of a file or a set of operations.

home computer A low-priced personal computer that can do almost everything more-expensive computers can, but usually has a lot of entertainment and educational software available. The Apple II, Commodore 64 and 128, Tandy Color Computer and Atari ST are examples.

home key A keyboard key that is used to move the cursor to the top of the screen or file or to the previous word or beginning of line. See *home button*.

Honeywell See *Bull HN*.

hook In programming, instructions that provide logical breakpoints for future expansion. Hooks may be changed to call some outside routine or function or may be places where additional processing is added.

hopper A tray, or chute, that accepts input to a mechanical device, such as a disk duplicator.

HOS (Higher Order Software) A design and documentation technique that is used to break down an information system into a set of functions that are mathematically correct and error free. HOS uses a rigid set of rules for the decomposition of the total system into its elementary components. The resulting specifications are complete enough to have machine language programs generated directly from them.

host The central computer or controlling computer in a timesharing or distributed processing environment.

host based A communications system that is controlled by a large, central computer system.

hot link A predefined connection between programs so that when information in one database or file is changed, related information in other databases and files are also updated.

hotkey A selected key or key combination that causes some function to occur in the computer, no matter what else is currently running. Hotkeys are commonly used to activate a memory resident (TSR) program.

housekeeping A set of instructions that are executed at the beginning of a program. Housekeeping sets all counters and flags to their starting values and generally readies the program for execution.

HP (Hewlett-Packard Company) A major manufacturer of computers and electronics, commonly known as HP. It was founded in 1939 by William Hewlett and David Packard in a garage behind the Packard's California home. Its first product, an audio oscillator for measuring sound, was the beginning of a line of electronics that made HP an international supplier of electronic test and measurement instruments. Walt Disney Studios, HP's first big customer, purchased eight oscillators to develop and test a new sound system for the movie "Fantasia."

HP entered the computer field in 1966 with the 2116A, the first of the HP 1000 series designed to gather and analyze the data produced by HP instruments. HP 1000 computers are used for CIM applications, such as process monitoring and control, alarm management and machine monitoring.

In 1972, HP branched into business computing with the 3000 series, a multiuser system that became well known for its extremely high reliability, especially for that time. The successful 3000 family has continued to be HP's major computer series and has evolved into a full family of computers from micro to mainframe. Also in 1972, HP introduced the first

HP'S FIRST PRODUCT
(Courtesy Hewlett-Packard)

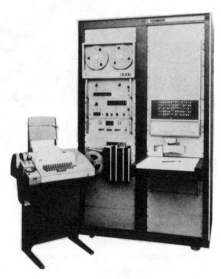

2116A
(Courtesy Hewlett-Packard)

scientific handheld calculator, the HP-35, obsoleting the slide rule and ushering in a new age of pocket-sized calculators. In 1982, the first HP 9000 workstation was introduced.

HP's first personal computer was the Touchscreen 150, an MS-DOS personal computer that gained only modest acceptance. In 1985, it introduced the Vectra, a 286-based machine that was the first of a complete line of IBM compatible PCs.

In 1984, HP revolutionized the printer market with its desktop LaserJet printer, which has set the standard for the industry.

In 1986, it introduced a new internal design for its 3000 and 9000 families that will carry the company into the 1990s. The new HP Precision Architecture provides a significant increase in performance.

In 1989, HP acquired Apollo Computer, which combined with its own line, made HP the market leader in workstations.

Hewlett-Packard sells over 10,000 different products in the electronics and computer field, and it has gained a worldwide reputation for its rugged and reliable engineering.

HEWLETT & PACKARD

(Courtesy Hewlett-Packard)

This photo of William R. Hewlett and David Packard was taken in 1964.

HP 1000 A family of minicomputers from Hewlett-Packard that are used in computer-integrated manufacturing (CIM) applications such as factory floor management. Introduced in 1966, HP 1000 machines are sensor-based computers that are used extensively in laboratory and manufacturing environments for collecting and analyzing data.

HP 3000 A family of business-oriented computers from Hewlett-Packard. Introduced in 1972, the HP 3000 minicomputers set a standard for reliability and rugged engineering and have been HP's major computer line ever since. The HP 3000 has evolved into a complete line from micro versions to medium-scale mainframes. New models of the 3000 incorporate the HP Precision Architecture and also provide compatibility with the original 3000 machines.

HP 9000 A family of high-performance UNIX workstations from Hewlett-Packard. Introduced in 1982, HP 9000 workstations are used extensively in computer-aided design (CAD) and engineering applications. The 9000 family is migrating to the HP Precision Architecture.

HP Precision Architecture An internal architecture and machine language from Hewlett-Packard that is being incorporated into new models of its 3000 and 9000 families of computers and workstations. Introduced in 1986, it is an HP proprietary architecture based on RISC design.

HP-UX Hewlett-Packard's version of UNIX that runs on its 9000 family of workstations. It is based on the System V Interface Definition (SVID) and incorporates features from Berkeley 4.2 BSD (Berkeley Software Distribution) as well as several HP innovations.

HPFS (High Performance File System) A file system, introduced with OS/2 Version 1.2, that handles larger disks (2TB volumes; 2GB files), long file names (256 bytes) and can launch the program by referencing the data as in the Macintosh. It coexists with the existing FAT system.

HPGL (Hewlett-Packard Graphics Language) A vector graphics file format from HP that was developed as a standard plotter language. Most plotters support the HPGL and DMPL standards.

HPIB (Hewlett-Packard Interface Bus) Hewlett-Packard's version of the IEEE 488 standard General Purpose Interface Bus (GPIB).

hue In computer graphics, a particular shade or tint of a given color.

hybrid circuit See *hybrid microcircuit*.

hybrid computer A digital computer that processes analog signals which have been converted into digital form. It is used in process control and robotics.

hybrid microcircuit An electronic circuit composed of different types of integrated circuits and discrete components, mounted on a ceramic base. Used in military and communications applications, hybrid microcircuits are especially suitable for building customized analog circuits, including A/D and D/A converters, amplifiers, modulators and integrators.

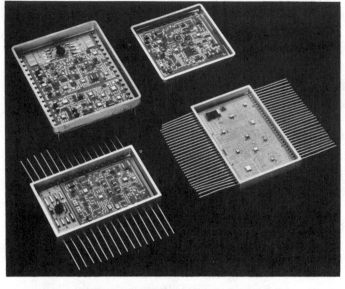

HYBRID MICROCIRCUITS
(Courtesy Circuit Technology Inc.)

hybrid network In communications, a network made up of equipment from multiple vendors.

Hyperaccess A communications program for PCs from Hilgraeve, Inc. It provides data compression for transfers to other Hyperaccess systems, has its own script language and supports a variety of terminals and protocols.

HyperCard An application development system for the Macintosh from Apple Computer that provides an array of advanced and integrated features. As a database system, it lets users build files in the form of a stack of cards that can hold data, text and graphics. As a control system, it is used as a main menu to launch applications. It can control multimedia devices, such as CD ROM and videodisc, and supports the building of interactive educational applications.

A HyperCard card is like an on-screen Rolodex card that can be designed with fixed fields, scrolling fields and graphics. It is also designed with button icons that, when clicked, activate processes. For example, a button can be set up to run a script in the HyperTalk programming language, or it can link the user to another associated card.

HyperCard comes with every Macintosh, and it has created an industry of HyperCard stacks and scripts; for example, *The Computer Glossary* is available as a HyperCard stack. The HyperCard approach has been brought to the PC world with software such as Brightbill-Robert's HyperPad and Asymetrix's ToolBook.

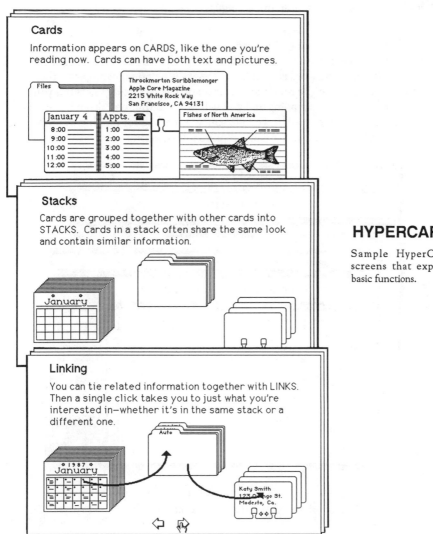

Cards

Information appears on CARDS, like the one you're reading now. Cards can have both text and pictures.

Files

Throckmorton Scribblemonger
Apple Core Magazine
2215 White Rock Way
San Francisco, CA 94131

January 4	Appts. ☎
8:00	1:00
9:00	2:00
10:00	3:00
11:00	4:00
12:00	5:00

Fishes of North America

Stacks

Cards are grouped together with other cards into STACKS. Cards in a stack often share the same look and contain similar information.

January

Linking

You can tie related information together with LINKS. Then a single click takes you to just what you're interested in—whether it's in the same stack or a different one.

Auto

◆ 1987 ◆
January

Katy Smith
123 Orange St.
Modesto, Ca.

HYPERCARD

Sample HyperCard screens that explain basic functions.

hypercube A parallel processing architecture made up of binary multiples of computers (4, 8, 16, etc.). The computers are interconnected so that data travel is kept to a minimum. For example, in two eight-node cubes, each node in one cube would be connected to the counterpart node in the other.

hypermedia The use of data, text, graphics, video and voice as elements in a hypertext system. All the various forms of information are linked together so that a user can easily move from one to another.

HyperPAD An application development system for PCs from Brightbill-Roberts & Company, Ltd. It is a HyperCard-like program that works in text mode and is used for launching applications, creating tutorials and prototyping new applications. It includes its own PADtalk scripting language.

HyperTalk The programming language used in HyperCard.

hypertext The linking of related information. For example, by selecting a word in a sentence, information about that word is retrieved if it exists, or the next occurrence of the word is found. A glossary is a perfect example of the value of hypertext . In the Mactinosh version of *The Computer Glossary*, you can click on any word you're reading and you will jump to that definition if it exists.

The concept was coined by Ted Nelson as a method for making the computer respond to the way humans think and require information.

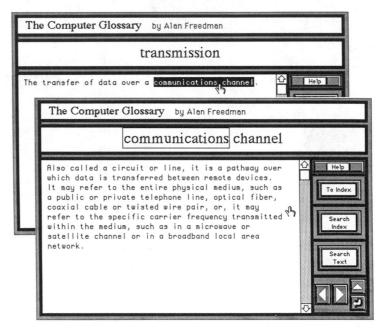

HYPERTEXT

Highlighting a term switches you to that definition.

hyphenation The breaking of words that extend beyond the right margin. In word processing and desktop publishing programs, hyphenation is determined by matching words against a hyphenation dictionary (file of words with predefined dashes) or by using a built-in set of rules, or both. Users can typically add their own words to the hyphenation dictionary, placing the hyphens where they want them. See *discretionary hyphen*.

hyphenation zone The distance from the right margin within which a word may be hyphenated.

hysteresis The lag between making a change, such as increasing or decreasing power, and the response or effect of that change.

Hz (HertZ) See *Hertz*.

IAC (InterApplication Communications) An extension of the Clipboard in Macintosh System 7.0 that allows independent applications to share and exchange information.

IBM (International Business Machines Corporation) The world's largest computer company. It started in New York City in 1911 when the Computing-Tabulating-Recording Co. (CTR) was created by a merger of The Tabulating Machine Co. (Hollerith's punched card company in Washington), International Time Recording Co. (time clock maker in NY state), Computing Scale Co. (maker of scales and food slicers in Dayton, Ohio), and Bundy Manufacturing (time clock maker in Poughkeepsie, NY). CTR started out with 1,200 employees and a capital value of $17.5 million.

THOMAS J. WATSON, SR.
(Courtesy IBM)

This photo of Watson, taken in 1920, was before his company was renamed IBM.

In 1914, Thomas J. Watson, Sr., became general manager. During the next 10 years, he dispensed with its non-tabulating business and turned it into an international enterprise renamed IBM in 1924. Watson was responsible for instilling a very strict professional demeanor in his employees that set IBMers apart from the rest of the crowd.

IBM achieved spectacular success by manufacturing tabulating machines and the punched cards that were fed into them. From the 1920s through the 1960s, it developed a huge customer base that was ideal for conversion to computers.

IBM launched its computer business in 1953 with the 701 and introduced the 650 a year later. By the end of the 1950s, the 650 was the most widely used computer in the world with 1,800 systems installed. The 1401, announced in 1959, was its second computer winner, and by the mid 1960s, an estimated 18,000 were in use.

In April 1964, it announced the System/360, the first family of compatible computers ever developed. The 360s were enormously successful and set a standard for all IBM mainframes to this day.

Although IBM achieved its greatest success with compatibility, it made a variety of incompatible minicomputers throughout the 1970s, including the System/3, System/34, System/38, Series 1 and 8100.

IBM 701

(Courtesy Charles Babbage Institute, University of Minnesota)

Ronald Reagan and Herbert Grosch at a customer installation in 1957.

In 1981, it introduced the PC. The chaotic personal computer field needed stability, and the PC quickly became the industry standard.

Throughout the 1990s, IBM's goal is to integrate its different product lines through a master plan called Systems Application Architecture. SAA is intended to provide common interfaces so that users will interact with and easily exchange information between all IBM machines from micro to mainframe.

IBM OFFICE, LONDON (1935)

(Courtesy IBM)

IBM-compatible PC A personal computer that is compatible with the IBM PC and PS/2 standards.

IBM PC A series of personal computers from IBM introduced in 1981. See PC and *personal computer*.

IBM PS/2 A series of personal computers from IBM introduced in 1987, which superseded the IBM PC line. See *PS/2* and *PC*.

IC See *integrated circuit* and *information center*.

icon A small, pictorial representation of an object, such as an application, file or disk drive, that is used in graphical user interfaces (GUIs). The user selects an object by pointing to its icon and clicking the mouse button. Icons can be moved around on the screen. To delete a file in the Macintosh for example, its icon can be "dragged" into the wastebasket icon.

UserPrep   General   Startup Device DA Handler Easy Access

ImageWriter Key Layout MultiFinder Keyboard   Mouse

ICONS

These are examples of icons used in the Macintosh.

iconic interface A user interface that uses icons.

IDE

(1) (Integrated Drive Electronics) A disk drive that contains its own controller electronics and eliminates using an expansion slot in the computer.

(2) (Integrated Devlopment Environment) A set of development tools that is run from a single user interface. For example, programming languages often include a text editor, compiler and debugger, which are all activated and function from a common screen and set of menus.

IDMS (Integrated Data Management System) A full-featured database management system from Computer Associates that runs on mainframes and minicomputers. Before DB2, IDMS gained wide acceptance due to the restrictions in IBM's IMS hierarchical database product.

IDMS was developed at GE in the 1960s and marketed by Cullinane, later renamed Cullinet. In 1989, Cullinet was acquired by Computer Associates and the IDMS/R relational version of IDMS was renamed CA-IDMS/DB.

I/E time See *instruction cycle*.

IEC (International Electrotechnical Commission) An organization that sets international electrical and electronics standards, founded in 1906 and headquartered in Geneva. It is made up of national committees from over 40 countries. For more information, contact ANSI, U.S. National Committee of the IEC, 1430 Broadway, New York, NY 10018.

IEEE (Institute of Electrical and Electronic Engineers) A membership organization that includes engineers, scientists and students in electronics and allied fields. Founded in 1963, it has over 290,000 members and is involved with setting standards for computers and communications.

The Computer Society of the IEEE has over 90,000 members and holds numerous meetings and technical conferences on computers and local meetings cover current topics of interest. For more information, contact The Computer Society of the IEEE, 10662 Los Vaqueros Circle, Los Alamitos, CA 90720.

IEEE 488 See *GPIB*.

IEEE 802.1 An IEEE standard for local area networks.
802.1 - Covers network management and other aspects related to LANS.
802.2 - Specifies the data link layer for the following access methods:
    802.3 - Specifies CSMA/CD, popularized by Ethernet.
    802.4 - Specifies a token passing bus.
    802.5 - Specifies a token passing ring, popularized by IBM's Token Ring.

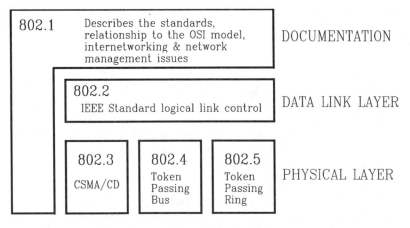

IEEE 802 LOCAL AREA NETWORK STANDARDS

if-then-else A high-level programming language statement that compares two or more sets of data and tests the results. If the results are true, the THEN instructions are taken; if not, the ELSE instructions are taken. The following is a BASIC example:

```
10  IF ANSWER = "Y"  THEN PRINT "Yes"
20 ELSE PRINT "No"
```

In certain structured programming languages, the THEN is implied. All statements between the IF and the ELSE are carried out if the condition is true. All instructions between the ELSE and the ENDIF are carried out if the condition is not true. The following dBASE example tests the same condition:

```
IF ANSWER = "Y"
 ? "The Answer is Yes"
ELSE
 ? "The Answer is No"
ENDIF
```

IFS (Installable File System) An OS/2 feature that supports multiple file systems. Different systems can be installed (UNIX, CD ROM, etc.) just like drivers are installed for new peripherals.

IGES (Initial Graphics Exchange Specification) An ANSI standard graphics file format. It is designed to be independent of all CAD and CAM systems and is also intended for human interpretation.

IGES Organization (Initial Graphics Exchange Specification Organization) An organization involved with the IGES standard for graphics images and the PDES format for describing a complete product model. It evolved out of the Air Force's Integrated Computer Automated Manufacturing (ICAM) program in 1979, which developed a method for data exchange that became known as IGES. For more information, contact IGES Coordinator, National Institute of Standards & Technology, Building 220, Room A-353, Gaithersburg, MD 20899, (301) 921-3691.

illustration program Same as *drawing program*.

Illustrator 88 A professional drawing program for the Macintosh from Adobe Systems, Inc., that enhanced the original Illustrator program in 1988. It provides sophisticated tracing and text manipulation capabilities, as well as colors and color separations.

image processing
(1) The analysis of a picture using techniques that can identify shades, colors and relationships that cannot be perceived by the human eye. It is used to solve

identification problems, such as in forensic medicine or in creating weather maps from satellite pictures and deals with images in raster graphics format that have been scanned in or captured with digital cameras.

(2) Image improvement, such as refining a picture in a paint program, which has been scanned or entered from a video source.

imagesetter A typesetting machine that can handle text and graphics.

imaging The recording of pictures into a machine format, for example, microfilm, videotape or computer.

immediate access Same as *direct access*.

immediate address A machine instruction that contains a value to be used in the execution of the instruction. Most instructions contain only addresses that point to memory locations or peripheral devices where the data is actually stored.

IMOS The operating system used on NCR's I-9000 series of computers.

impact printer A printer that uses a printing mechanism that bangs the character image into the ribbon and onto the paper. Line printers, dot matrix printers and daisy wheel printers are examples. See *printer*.

impedance The resistance to the flow of alternating current in a circuit.

implementation
(1) Computer system *implementation* is the installation of new hardware and system software.

(2) Information system *implementation* is the installation of new databases and application programs and the adoption of new manual procedures.

implode To link component pieces to a major assembly. It may also refer to compressing data using a particular technique. Contrast with *explode*.

import To convert a file in a foreign format to the format of the program being used.

IMS (Information Management System) A hierarchical database management system from IBM that is used on large IBM mainframes. IMS is a first-generation system that was widely used throughout the 1970s. Like CICS, IMS provides transaction processing capabilities and automatically handles the details of communications and SNA networking.

in hardware Refers to logic that has been placed into the electronic circuits of the computer.

in software Refers to logic in a program. For example, "that routine is done in software."

incident light In computer graphics, light that strikes an object. The color of the object is based on how the light is absorbed or reflected by the object.

increment To add a number to another number. Incrementing a counter means to add 1 or some other number to its current value.

IND$FILE An IBM mainframe program that transfers files between the mainframe and a PC functioning as a 3270 terminal.

indent To align text some number of spaces to the right of the left margin. See *hanging paragraph*.

index

(1) In data management, a directory that contains the location of records and files on a disk. Indexing is the most common method used for keeping track of data on a direct access storage device. An index of files contains an entry for each file name and its location. An index of records has an entry for each key field (account no., etc.) and its location. Indexes are maintained by the operating system or database management system.

(2) In programming, a method for keeping track of data in a table. See *indexed addressing*.

KEY	LOCATION
BETTY	TRACK 12 SECTOR 5
CHARLES	TRACK 26 SECTOR 3
DON	TRACK 15 SECTOR 12
EDMUND	TRACK 33 SECTOR 6
FRAN	TRACK 19 SECTOR 4

DISK INDEX

TABLE

SUN	MON	TUE	WED	THU	FRI	SAT

0 0 0 0 5

INDEX REGISTER

PROGRAM INDEX

index hole A hole punched into a hard sectored floppy disk that serves to mark the start of the sectors on each track.

index mark A physical hole or notch, or a recorded code or mark, that is used to identify a starting point for each track on a disk.

index register A high-speed memory circuit that is used to hold the current, relative position of an item in a table (array). At execution time, the index register value is added to the instructions that reference it.

indexed addressing A technique for referencing memory that automatically increments the address with the value stored in an index register. See *subscript (2)*.

indexed sequential See *ISAM*.

indexing
(1) The creating of indexes based on key data fields or key words.

(2) The creating of timing signals based on detecting a mark, slot or hole in a moving medium.

indirect addressing A technique for addressing a relative location. The instruction references a location that contains the address of the data rather than the data itself.

inductance The opposition to the changing flow of current in a circuit. Inductance is measured in units called *Henrys*.

induction The process of generating an electric current in a circuit from the magnetic influence of an adjacent circuit.

inference program The processing program in an expert system. It derives a conclusion from the facts and rules contained in the knowledge base using various artificial intelligence techniques.

infix notation The common way arithmetic operators are used to reference numeric values. For example, **A+B/C** is infix notation. Contrast with *Polish notation* and *reverse Polish notation*.

infopreneur An individual that is in business to gather and disseminate electronic information.

informate To dispense information, as coined by Professor Shoshana Zuboff of Harvard Business School.

information The summarization of data. Technically, data are raw facts and figures that are processed into information, such as summaries and totals. But since information can also be raw data for the next job or person, the two terms cannot be precisely defined. Both terms are used synonymously and interchangeably.

As office automation and data processing merge, it may be more helpful to view information the way data is defined and used, namely: data, text, spreadsheets, pictures, voice and video. Data are discretely defined fields. Text is a collection of words. Spreadsheets are data in matrix (row and column) form. Pictures are lists of vectors or frames of bits. Voice is a continuous stream of sound waves. Video is a sequence of frames.

In the future, information processing will have to integrate all these forms of information into common databases.

information center A section within an organization's IS department that provides personal computer tools, assistance and training to users. IC personnel provide assistance with such software packages as query languages, report writers, spreadsheets and financial planning systems. They are also available to provide ways of downloading data from the production databases in the company's datacenter.

information management A discipline that analyzes information as an organizational resource. It covers the definitions, uses, value and distribution of all data and information within an organization whether it is processed by the computer or not. Information management evaluates the kinds of data/information an organization requires in order to function and progress effectively.

Information is complex because the nature of business transactions is complex. It must be analyzed and understood before effective computer solutions can be developed. See *data administration*.

information processing Same as *data processing*.

information resource management See *information management*.

information science Same as *information management*.

Information Services Same as *Information Systems*.

information system A business application of the computer. It is made up of the database, application programs, manual and machine procedures and encompasses the computer systems that do the processing.

The database stores the subjects of the business (master files) and its activities (transaction files). The application programs provide the data entry, updating, query and report processing. The manual procedures document how data is obtained for input and how the system's output is distributed. Machine procedures instruct the computer how to perform the batch processing activities, in which the output of one program is automaticaly fed into another program.

The daily processing is the interactive, realtime processing of the transactions. At the end of the day or other period, the batch processing programs update the master files that have not been updated since the last cycle. Reports are printed for the cycle's activities.

The periodic processing of an information system is the updating of the master files, which adds, deletes and changes the information about customers, employees, vendors and products.

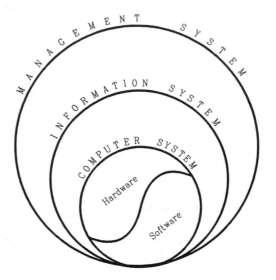

HOW SYSTEMS RELATE

Each system encompasses the systems below it:

STRUCTURE (is)   FUNCTION (does)

Management system
1. PEOPLE & MACHINES   Makes the decisions. Sets organization's goals and objectives, strategies and tactics, plans, schedules and controls.

Information system
1. DATABASE   Defines data structures.
2. APPLICATION   Data entry, updating, queries and reporting.
   PROGRAMS
3. PROCEDURES   Defines data flow.

Computer system
1. CPU   Processes (The 3 C's).
2. PERIPHERALS   Store and retrieve.
3. OPERATING SYSTEM   Manages computer system.

Information Systems The formal title for a data processing, MIS, or IS department within an organization. Other titles are Data Processing, Information Processing, Information Services, Management Information Systems and Management Information Services.

information utility An information service bureau that maintains up-to-date databases for public access.

INFORMIX A family of database products from Informix Software, Inc., which includes an SQL-based relational database management system, fourth-generation language and toolkits for embedding SQL in application programs.

infoware Electronic information packaged for sale, which may include the necessary software to make it accessible on the computer. The electronic versions of this Glossary are examples.

InfoWindow

(1) An IBM PC that includes a touch screen display and videodisc. Introduced in 1986, it is designed for multimedia education and training. The display is called the InfoWindow Touch Screen Display to differentiate it from the general line of InfoWindow displays.

(2) A line of monochrome and color video terminals from IBM, introduced in 1989, for its mini and mainframe computers.

infrared Invisible light at the high end of the light spectrum. Contrast with *ultraviolet*; light at the low end.

INGRES (INteractive Graphics and REtrieval System) A relational database management system from Ingres Corporation that runs on VAXs and UNIX workstations. It includes a fourth generation language, query by example and a forms management system that lets users create, edit and view the database as a series of forms.

Introduced in 1989, its Object Management extension allows user-defined data types, and its Knowledge Management extension allows an unlimited number of rules to be programmed into the database.

Ingres Corporation was formerly Relational Technology, a company founded in 1980 to market a commercial version of INGRES, which was developed at the University of California at Berkeley in the early 1970s.

inheritance In object-oriented programming, the ability of one class of objects to inherit properties from a higher class.

inhouse Any operation that takes place on the user's premises.

INIT (INITiate) A routine in the Macintosh that is run when the computer is started or restarted. It is used to load and activate drivers and system routines.

initial program load See *IPL*.

ink jet A printer mechanism that sprays one or more colors of ink onto paper and produces high-quality printing like that of a laser printer.

The continuous stream method produces droplets that are aimed onto the paper by electric field deflectors.

The drop-on-demand method uses a set of independently controlled injection chambers, the newest of which use solid ink developed by Exxon in 1983. Solid ink liquefies quickly when heated and solidifies instantly when it reaches the paper.

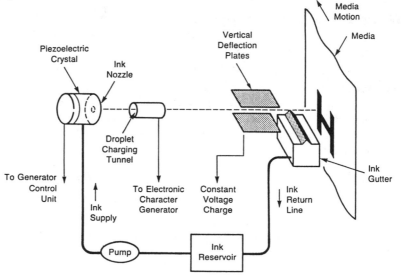

SINGLE NOZZLE INK JET PRINTING PROCESS
(Courtesy Dataquest)

INMARSAT (INternational MARitime SATellite Organization) An international organization that is involved in providing satellite communications to and from ships and offshore rigs. It is represented in the U.S. and partially owned by COMSAT.

input

(1) Any data ready for entry into the computer.

(2) To enter data into the computer.

input area A reserved segment of memory that is used to accept data or text from a peripheral device such as a keyboard, disk or tape. Same as *buffer*.

input device A peripheral device that generates input for the computer such as a keyboard, scanner, mouse or digitizer tablet.

input/output See I/O.

input program Same as *data entry program*.

input queue A reserved segment of disk or memory that holds messages that have been received or job control statements describing work to be done.

input stream A collection of job control statements, which describe the work to be done, that have been entered into the computer system.

inquiry program Same as *query program*.

Ins key (INSert key) A keyboard key that is used to switch between insert and overwrite mode or to insert an object at the current cursor location.

insert mode A data entry mode that causes new data typed on the keyboard to be inserted at the current cursor location on screen. Contrast with *overwrite mode*.

install program A program that prepares a software package to run in the computer. It copies the files from the distribution diskettes to the hard disk and also decompresses them, if necessary. If required, it asks the user to identify the types of peripheral devices that are attached in order to link in the appropriate drivers for a particular display, printer, scanner, etc. It may also request a serial number and name in order to customize the application's startup screen.

installation spec Documentation from an equipment manufacturer that describes how a product should be properly installed within a physical environment.

instance variable In object-oriented programming, the data in an object.

instantiate In object-oriented programming, to create an object of a specific class. Initializing the object's instance variables is commonly done at this time.

instruction

(1) A statement in a programming language.

(2) A machine instruction.

instruction cycle The time in which a single instruction is fetched from memory, decoded and executed. The first half of the cycle transfers the instruction from memory to the instruction register and decodes it. The second half executes the instruction.

instruction mix The ratio of the different types of instructions used in a program. It often refers to writing benchmarks, which requires that the instruction mix (amount of I/O, math, copying, etc.) accurately represents the kinds of programs that will be run.

instruction register A high-speed memory circuit that holds an instruction for decoding and execution.

instruction repertoire The set of operation statements that make up a programming language.

instruction set The entire group of machine language instructions that a computer can follow. Instruction sets are designed into the CPU and are one of the major components of its architecture. A set may contain from a handful (RISC) to several hundred instructions (CISC). Machine instructions are generally from one to four bytes long.

instruction time The time in which an instruction is fetched from memory and stored in the instruction register. It is the first half of the instruction cycle.

insulator A material that does not conduct electricity. Contrast with *conductor*.

integer A whole number. In programming for example, the integer function would yield 123 from 123.898.

Integer BASIC A version of BASIC for the Apple II series from Apple Computer that handles only fixed point numbers (non-floating point). Due to its speed, many games are written in Integer BASIC.

integrated A collection of distinct elements or components that have been built into one unit.

integrated circuit The formal name for chip.

integrated injection logic A type of bipolar transistor design known for its fast switching speeds.

integrated software package Software that combines several applications in one program, such as database management, word processing, spreadsheets, business graphics and communications. Programs such as Microsoft Works for the Macintosh, Apple Works for the Apple II and Framework for PCs are examples.

The advantage of an integrated package is that there's a common user interface and method of interacting with the computer. Integrated packages make it easier to copy and move data from one file structure to another, for example, from a spreadsheet to a word processing document.

The disadvantage is that no single integrated package provides all of the capabilities of stand-alone programs.

integrated voice/data PBX See *digital* PBX.

integrator In electronics, a device that combines an input with a variable, such as time, and provides an analog output. For example, a watt-hour meter provides a measurement of current over time.

integrity See *data integrity*.

Intel (Intel Corporation) A leading manufacturer of semiconductor devices that was founded in 1968 by Bob Noyce and Gorden Moore in Mountain View, California. A year later it introduced its first product, a 64-bit bipolar static RAM chip. By 1971, its very successful memory chips began to obsolete magnetic cores for memory storage.

Although it is best known for its 8086 family of microprocessors, Intel actually invented the microprocessor in 1971. In response to a calculator chip order from Japanese manufacturer Busicom, Intel engineer Marcian E. "Ted" Hoff decided it would make more sense to design a general-purpose machine. The resulting 4004 chip was the world's first microprocessor.

Throughout the years, Intel has developed a wide variety of chips and board-level products as well as its own MULTIBUS bus architecture that is used in numerous industrial applications. Intel started out with 12 people with first year revenues of $2672. In 20 years, it has grown into a three-billion dollar company with 20,000 employees.

Intellect A natural language query program from AI Corporation that runs on IBM mainframes and other computers. It understands many questions that can be stated in the English language, for example: "Tell me the number of employees in the personnel department."

Intellifont A scalable font technology from the Compugraphic division of the Agfa Corporation. It is included in HP's Series III LaserJet printer.

intelligence Processing capability. Every computer is intelligent!

intelligent cable Same as *smart cable*.

intelligent controller A peripheral control unit that uses a built-in microprocessor for controlling its operation.

intelligent database A database that contains knowledge about the content of its data. A set of validation criteria are stored with each field of data, such as the minimum and maximum values that can be entered or a list of all possible entries. See *database management system (Intelligent Databases)*.

intelligent form A data entry application that provides help screens and low levels of artificial intelligence in aiding the user to enter the correct data.

intelligent modem A modem that responds to commands and can accept new instructions during online transmission. It was originally developed by Hayes Microcomputer Products, Inc.

intelligent paper Same as *intelligent form*.

intelligent terminal A terminal with built-in processing capability, but no local disk or tape storage. It may use a general-purpose CPU or may have specialized circuitry as part of a distributed intelligence system. Contrast with *dumb terminal*.

INTELSAT (INternational TELecommunications SATellite Corporation) An international organization that is involved in launching and operating commercial satellites. It was created in 1964 with only 11 countries participating. Today, 114 nations have ownership. INTELSAT is represented in the U.S. and partially owned by COMSAT.

inter To cross over boundaries; for example, internetwork means from one network to another. Contrast with *intra*.

interactive A back-and-forth dialog between the user and a computer.

interactive cable TV A service in which viewers can take part in a TV program by voting on or reacting to issues. It implies full television viewing, in contrast with videotex or teletext services that provide limited animation. In time, all of these services may be provided over cable TV channels. A special decoder and keyboard are required.

interactive session A back-and-forth dialogue between the user and a computer. Contrast with *batch session*, in which there is no user interaction.

interactive video The use of a videodisc or CD ROM that is controlled by a computer for an interactive education or entertainment program. See *videodisc* and CD ROM.

interblock gap Same as *interrecord gap*.

interface A connection and interaction between hardware, software and the user. Hardware interfaces are the plugs, sockets and wires that carry electrical signals in a prescribed order. Software interfaces are the languages, codes and messages that programs use to communicate with each other, such as between an application program and the operating system. User interfaces are the keyboards, mice, dialogues, command languages and menus used for communication between the user and the computer.

Interfacing is a major part of what engineers, programmers and consultants do. Users "talk to" the software. The software "talks to" the hardware, as well as to other software. Hardware "talks to" other hardware. All this "talking to" is interfacing. It has to be designed, developed, tested and redesigned, and with each incarnation, a new specification is born that may become a de facto standard or a regulated standard.

FORMAT & FUNCTION

Every interface has structure and function. Electrical signals have a structure made up of voltage levels, frequencies and duration. The data message that is passed from one device or program to another has a particular format (header, body, trailer...).

At the hardware level, electronic signals activate functions; data is read, written, transmitted, received, analyzed for error, etc. At the software level, instructions activate the hardware (access methods, data link protocols...). At higher levels, the data transferred or transmitted may itself request functions to be performed (client/server, program to program...).

LANGUAGE & PROGRAMMING

An interface is activated by programming language commands. The complexity of the functions that can be performed and the design of the language determine how difficult it is to program the interface.

USER INTERFACE, PROTOCOL, API AND ABI

The specification of the interface between the user and the computer is called a *user interface*; between components in a network, a *protocol*; between two programs, an *API*, and between an application and a computer environment, an *ABI*. All of these interactions are interfaces.

interface adapter In communications, a device that connects the computer or terminal to a network.

interlaced A technique that refreshes a display screen by alternately displaying all the odd lines and then all the even lines. For example, TV uses an interlaced signal that generates 60 half frames per second, or the equivalent of 30 full frames per second.

Contrast with *non-interlaced*, which refreshes all the lines on the display sequentially from top to bottom. Interlaced methods require half as much signal information in the same time frame as non-interlaced methods.

interleaving See *sector interleave*.

interlock An *interlock* is a device that prohibits an action from taking place.

intermediate language Same as *pseudo language*.

intermittent error An error that occurs from time to time, but not consistently. Intermittent errors are extremely difficult to diagnose and repair.

internal font A set of characters for a particular typeface that is built into a printer. Contrast with *font cartridge* and *soft font*.

internal interrupt An interrupt that is caused by processing, for example, a request for input or output or an arithmetic overflow error. Contrast with *external interrupt*.

internal sort A sort that is accomplished entirely in main memory without using disks or tapes for temporary files.

internal storage Same as *memory*.

internet
(1) A large network made up of a number of smaller networks.

(2) Internet. A national research-oriented network comprised of over a thousand government and academic networks.

InterNet Router Software for the Macintosh from Apple Computer that allows internetworking of networks with different access methods, such as LocalTalk, EtherTalk and TokenTalk. It can reside in any Macintosh workstation or server in the network. Each InterNet Router can connect up to eight networks, with a maximum of 1,024 networks in the internet, addressing as many as 16 million nodes.

internetwork To go between one network and another.

interpolate To estimate values that lie between known values.

Interpress A page description language from Xerox Corporation that is used on the Xerox 2700 and 9700 page printers (medium to large-scale laser printers). Xerox's Ventura Publisher can provide output in Interpress.

interpret To run a program one line at a time. Each line of source language is translated into machine language and then executed.

interpreter A high-level programming language translator that translate and runs the program at the same time. It translates one program statement into machine language and executes it. It then proceeds to the next statement, and so on, until the program is finished.

Interpreted programs run more slowly than their compiler counterparts, because the compiler translates the entire program before it is run. However, it's convenient to write an interpreted program, since a single line of code can be tested interactively.

Interpreted programs must always be run with the interpreter. For example, in order to run a BASIC or dBASE program, the BASIC or dBASE interpreter must be in the computer.

If a language can be both interpreted and compiled, a program may be developed with the interpreter and compiled for the final version.

interpretive language A programming language that requires an interpreter in the computer in order to run it.

interprocess communication See IPC.

interrecord gap A space generated between blocks of data on magnetic tape, created by the starting and stopping of the reel of tape.

INTERRECORD (INTERBLOCK) GAPS

interrogate

(1) To search, sum or count records in a file.

(2) To test the condition or status of a terminal or computer system.

interrupt
A signal that gets the attention of the CPU and is usually generated when input or output is required. For example, hardware interrupts are generated when a key is pressed or when the mouse is moved. Software interrupts are generated by a program requiring disk input or output.

An internal timer may continually interrupt the computer several times per second to keep the time of day current or for timesharing purposes.

When an interrupt occurs, control is transferred to the operating system, which determines what action should be taken. All interrupts are prioritized; the higher the priority, the faster the interrupt will be serviced.

interrupt-driven
A computer or communications network that uses interrupts.

interrupt mask
An internal switch setting that controls whether an interrupt can be processed or not. The mask is a bit that is turned on and off by the program.

interrupt priorities
The sequence of importance assigned to the interrupts in a computer system. If two interrupts occur simultaneously, the interrupt with the highest priority is serviced first. In some systems, a higher-priority interrupt can gain control of the computer while it's processing a lower-priority interrupt.

interrupt vector
In the PC, one of 256 pointers that reside in the first 1,024 bytes of memory. Each vector points to an interrupt service routine, which is a BIOS routine, device driver or user-defined routine that provides detailed instructions for activating peripheral devices or performing some internal function.

intersect
In relational database, to match two files and produce a third file with records that are common in both. For example, intersecting an American file and a programmer file would yield American programmers.

intra
Within a boundary; for example, intraoffice refers to operations that take place within the office. Contrast with *inter*.

inverse video
Same as *reverse video*.

inverted file
In data management, a file that is indexed on many of the attributes of the data itself. For example, in an employee file, an index could be maintained for all secretaries, another for managers, and so on. It's faster to scan

the indexes than to search every record. Inverted file indexes use up a lot of disk space, and although searching is fast, updating is slow.

inverted list Same as *inverted file*.

inverter
(1) A logic gate that converts the input to the opposite state for output. If the input is true, the output is false, and vice versa. An inverter performs the Boolean logic NOT operation.

(2) An electrical circuit that converts DC current into AC current. Contrast with *rectifier*.

invoke To activate a program, routine, function or process.

I/O (Input/Output) A transfer of data between the CPU and a peripheral device. Every transfer is an output from one device and an input into another.

I/O area A reserved segment of computer memory that is used to accept data from an input device or to lay out data for transfer to an output device. They may be physically located within the application program, operating system or database management system. Same as *buffer*.

I/O bound Refers to an excessive amount of time getting data into and out of the computer in relation to the time it takes for processing within the computer. Faster I/O channels and disk drives will improve the performance of an I/O bound computer.

I/O channel A physical high-speed pathway between the computer and a peripheral device.

I/O interface In large computers, a channel between the CPU and a peripheral device. In small computers, it includes the controller and cable between the CPU and peripheral device.

I/O processor A hardware device or software program that is dedicated to handling only input and output operations. See *front end processor*.

I/O statement A programming language or command language statement that calls for data or stores data on a peripheral device.

IOCS (Input Output Control System) An early, rudimentary operating system for IBM computers in the 1950s. It was made up of a set of common I/O routines for tapes and disks. Its counterpart today in the PC is the ROM BIOS.

ion deposition A printing technology that is used in high-speed page printers. It is similar to laser printing, except that instead of using light to create a charged image on a drum, it uses a printhead that deposits ions onto the drum. After toner is attracted to the ions on the drum, the paper is pressed directly against the drum fusing the toner to the paper.

The quality of ion deposition is approaching that of a laser printer; however, the ink has not been embedded into the paper as deeply, and it can smear more easily.

IOS (Integrated Office System) See *office automation*.

IPC (InterProcess Communication) The exchange of data between one program and another either within the same computer or over a network. It implies a protocol that guarantees a response to a request. Examples are OS/2's Named Pipes, Windows' DDE, Novell's SPX and Macintosh's IAC.

Although IPCs are performed automatically by the programs, an analogous function is performed interactively when users cut and paste data from one file to another using the Macintosh or Windows Clipboard.

IPI (Intelligent Peripheral Interface) A high-performance interface that is used with large-capacity disks on minis and mainframes. It provides data transfer up to and exceeding 20MB per second.

IPL (Initial Program Load) Same as *boot*.

IPS (Inches Per Second) Measures the speed of tape passing by a read/write head or paper passing through a pen plotter.

IPX (Internet Packet EXchange) A Novell NetWare communications protocol that is used to route messages from one node to another. Application programs that manage their own client/server or peer-to-peer communications in a Novell network can access IPX, or NetWare's SPX protocol, directly. IPX does not guarantee delivery of a message as does SPX.

IR (Industry Remarketer) Same as *VAR* or *VAD*.

IRG (InterRecord Gap) See *interrecord gap*.

IRM See *information resource management*.

IRMAboard A micro to mainframe communications device for PCs from DCA, Inc. The IRMAboard emulates an IBM 3278 (mono) or 3279 (color) mainframe terminal. IRMA is not an acronym.

IRMALAN A family of gateway products from DCA, Inc., that allow PC users connected to NetBIOS-compatible LANs to access an SNA host. It includes gateways for IEEE 802.2, SDLC and DFT environments.

IRMALAN Standalone Workstation software provides connectivity to the host over a Token Ring LAN connected to an IBM communications controller.

iron oxide The material used to coat the surfaces of magnetic tapes and lower-capacity disks.

IRQ (Interrupt ReQuest) A hardware interrupt from a peripheral device that signals the processor for attention.

IRX The operating system used on large models of NCR's I-9000 series of mainframes.

IS (Information Systems or Information Services) A contemporary term for computer professionals and the computer department in an organization. See *Information Systems*.

ISA (Industry Standard Architecture) The 8-bit (PC, XT) and 16-bit (AT) buses in IBM's first personal computer series. EISA is a 32-bit extension of ISA. Contrast with *Micro Channel*.

ISAM (Indexed Sequential Access Method) A widely used disk access method that stores data sequentially, while also maintaining an index of key fields to all the records in the file for direct access capability. The sequential order of the file would be the one most commonly used for batch processing and printing, such as account number or name.

ISDN (Integrated Services Digital Network) An international telecommunications standard for transmitting voice, video and data over a digital communications line. It uses Out-Of-Band signalling, which provides a separate channel for control information. ISDN services come in two forms: (1) Basic Rate Interface (BRI) and (2) Primary Rate Interface (PRI).

BRI provides a 144 kilobits per second service, which includes two 64Kbps "B" channels for voice, data or video, and one 16Kbps "D" channel for control information.

PRI provides a 1.54 megabits per second service, which includes 23 64Kbps "B" channels and one 64Kbps "D" channel.

The Future of ISDN

ISDN's 64Kbps transmission rate provides a big boost for PCs communicating via modem, even at 9,600bps, but it doesn't provide an alternative for interconnecting LANs transmitting in the 10+ megabit per second range. However, Broadband ISDN (BISDN) should materialize around 1993, which utilizes broadband transmission and fiber optic cables to jump transmission speed to 150 megabits per second.

ISO (International Standards Organization) An organization that sets international standards, founded in 1946 and headquartered in Geneva. It deals with all fields except electrical and electronics, which comes under the jurisdiction of the older International Electrotechnical Commission (IEC), also in Geneva. With regard to information processing standards, ISO and IEC recently created JTC1, the Joint Technical Committee for information technology.

ISO carries out its work through more than 160 technical committees and 2,300 subcommittees and working groups and is made up of standards organizations from more than 75 countries, some of them serving as secretariats for these technical bodies. ANSI is the U.S. member body to ISO.

For more information, contact American National Standards Institute, 1430 Broadway, New York, NY 10018.

isometric view In computer graphics, a picture of a 3-D object that shows all three dimensions in equal proportions. Isometric views do not show true perspective.

Normal perspective   **Isometric view**

ISOMETRIC VIEW

(Courtesy Robo Systems Corporation)

isotropic Refers to identical properties in all directions; for example, an isotropic antenna transmits and receives in all directions.

ISR (Interrupt Service Routine) A software routine that is executed in response to an interrupt.

ISV (Independent Software Vendor) An individual or company that develops software.

item One unit or member of a group. See *data item*.

iteration One repetition of a sequence of instructions or events. For example, in a program loop, one iteration is once through the instructions in the loop.

iterative operation An operation that requires successive executions of instructions or processes.

I-time See *instruction time*.

IV See *interactive video*.

IVD (Interactive VideoDisc) See *interactive video*.

Iverson notation A special set of symbols developed by Kenneth Iverson for writing statements in the APL programming language.

IVR (Interactive Voice Response) See *voice response*.

IXC (IntereXchange Carrier) An organization that provides interstate communications services, such as AT&T, MCI and Sprint.

IZE A text management system for PCs from Persoft, Inc. It is noted for its flexible searching capability which uses key words for retrieval. Key words can be entered manually or can be created by IZE from a list or condition, such as the name between "Dear" and a comma.

I²L See *integrated injection logic*.

i486 See *80486*.

i860 See *80860*.

I-9000 A series of minicomputers from NCR.

J

jack A receptacle into which a plug is inserted.

Jacquard loom The automatic loom that transformed the textile industry in the 19th century and became the inspiration for future calculating and tabulating machine designs. Developed by the French silk-weaver, Joseph-Marie Jacquard (1752-1834), it used punched cards to control its operation. Although punched cards were used in earlier looms and music boxes, Jacquard's loom was a vast improvement and allowed complex patterns to be created swiftly.

JACQUARD LOOM
(Courtesy Smithsonian Institution)

jaggies The stairstepped appearance of diagonal lines on a low-resolution graphics screen.

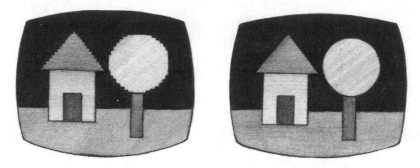

LOW RESOLUTION
GRAPHICS

HIGH RESOLUTION
GRAPHICS

Javelin Plus A spreadsheet for PCs from Javelin Software Corporation. Instead of row and column identifiers, it uses names to identify its cells and consolidate data into unique models.

Jazz An integrated software package for the Macintosh from Lotus. Modeled after its Symphony package, Jazz never caught on.

JCL (Job Control Language) A language that directs the operating system to run application programs. It specifies information such as priority, program size and running sequence, as well as the files and databases used. Originally an IBM term, it has become a generic term for a job management language.

JES (Job Entry Subsystem) Software that provides batch communications for IBM's MVS operating system. It accepts data from remote batch terminals, executes them on a priority basis and transmits the results back to the terminals. The JES counterpart in VM is called RSCS. Contrast with *TSO*, which provides interactive communications for MVS.

jitter A flickering transmission signal or display image.

job A unit of work running in the computer. A job may be a single program or a group of programs that are required to work together.

job class A descriptive category of a job that is based on the computer resources it requires when running.

job control language See *JCL*.

job managment See *JCL*.

job processing The handling and processing of jobs in the computer.

job queue A lineup of programs ready to be executed.

job stream A series of related programs that are run in a prescribed order. The output of one program is the input to the next program and so on.

join In relational database management, to match one file against another based on some condition creating a third file with data from the matching files. For example, a customer file can be joined with an order file creating a file of records for all customers who purchased a particular product.

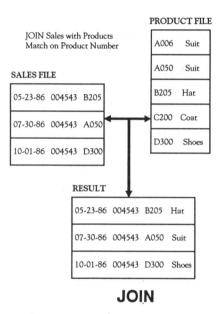

JOIN Sales with Products
Match on Product Number

PRODUCT FILE

A006	Suit
A050	Suit
B205	Hat
C200	Coat
D300	Shoes

SALES FILE

05-23-86	004543	B205
07-30-86	004543	A050
10-01-86	004543	D300

RESULT

05-23-86	004543	B205	Hat
07-30-86	004543	A050	Suit
10-01-86	004543	D300	Shoes

JOIN

Josephson junction An ultra-fast microelectronic circuit technology that employs superconductor materials, named after Brian Josephson, who developed the original theory. Josephson junction circuits are immersed in liquid helium to obtain near-absolute zero temperatures required for operation. A Josephson junction has been observed to switch in as little as 50 femtoseconds.

journal Same as *log*.

JOVIAL (Jules' Own Version of the International Algebraic Language) An ALGOL-like programming language developed by Systems Development Corporation in the early 1960s and widely used in military applications. The J in JOVIAL is for Jules Schwartz, one of its key architects.

joy stick An omnidirectional lever that is used to move the cursor on screen more rapidly than it can be

JOY STICK

moved with the directional arrow keys. It is used extensively in video games, but is also used as an input device in CAD systems.

JTC1
(Joint Technical Committee 1) See *ISO*.

Julian date The representation of a month and day by consecutively numbering the days starting with January 1. For example, February 1 is 32. Dates are converted into Julian dates for calculation.

jump Another term for a BRANCH or GOTO instruction, which directs the computer to some other place in the program.

jumper A metal bridge that is used to close a circuit. It can be a short length of wire or a plastic-covered metal block that is pushed onto two pins. Jumpers are often used in place of DIP switches on a printed circuit board.

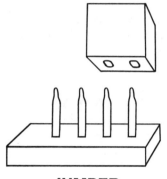

JUMPER

junction A point at which two elements make contact. In a transistor, a junction is the point where an N-type material makes contact with a P-type material.

justification In typography, the alignment of text evenly between left and right margins. Contrast with *ragged right*.

justify
(1) To shift the contents of a field or register to the right or left.

(2) To align text evenly between left and right margins.

K

K (Kilo) One thousand. K may stand for 1,000 or 1,024. Most computer specifications use binary numbers, which start with 1 and double: 1, 2, 4, 8, 16, 32, 64, 128, 256, 512, 1024. For example, 64K means 65,536 bytes when it refers to memory and storage devices (64x1024), but a 64K salary does mean $64,000.00.

According to the IEEE, upper case "K" stands for 1,024, and lower case "k" stands for 1,000.

KB, Kb (KiloByte, KiloBit) See *K* and *space/time*.

KBps, Kbps (KiloBytes Per Second, KiloBits Per Second) See *K* and *space/time*.

Kermit An asynchronous communications protocol for personal computers developed at Columbia University and used in several public-domain communications programs. It is a slow protocol but is noted for its transmission accuracy over noisy telephone lines, because it checks for errors in the commands it sends as well as the data. Kermit can also communicate effectively with IBM mainframes.

kernel The fundamental part of a program, such as an operating system, that resides in memory at all times.

kerning In typography, the spacing of certain letter combinations, such as WA, MW and TA, where each character overlaps into some of the space of the other character for improved appearance.

Fixed
Spacing

Proportional
Spacing

Kerned
Letters

KERNING

key

(1) A button on the keyboard.

(2) An item of data that identifies a record. For example, account number, product code and customer name are typical keys, or key fields, used to identify a record in a file or database. As an identifier, each key value must be unique for each record. See *sort key*.

(3) A numeric code that is used by an algorithm to create a code for encrypting data for security purposes.

key cap The visible part of a keyboard key that is pressed. In order to display references to commonly used codes, key caps can be replaced with new ones.

key click The audible feedback provided when a key is pressed. It is often adjustable by the user.

key-driven Any device that is activated by pressing keys.

key entry Data entry using a keyboard.

key field See *key (2)*.

key in To enter data by typing on a keyboard.

key rollover See *n-key rollover*.

key-to-disk machine A stand-alone data entry machine that stores the input on magnetic disk for processing by a computer.

key-to-tape machine A stand-alone data entry machine that stores the input on magnetic tape for processing by a computer. It was introduced by Mohawk Data Sciences in the mid 1960s and was the first advancement in batch-oriented data entry since the keypunch machine.

The key-to-tape machine revolutionized data entry, and Mohawk's stock soared by a factor of 100 within a few years.

key word

(1) A word used in a text search.

(2) A word in a text document that is used in an index to best describe the contents of the document.

(3) A reserved word in a programming or command language.

keyboard A set of input keys. Keyboards on terminals and personal computers contain the standard typewriter keys in addition to a number of specialized keys and features outlined below.

ENTER/RETURN KEY
The enter key, also called the *return key*, works similar to the carriage return key on a typewriter. In text applications, it ends a paragraph or short line. In data applications, it signals the end of the input for that field or line.

CURSOR KEYS
The four arrow keys move the cursor in the corresponding direction on the screen. Cursor keys are used in conjunction with the shift, alt and control keys to move the cursor in bigger jumps; for example, CONTROL UP ARROW might scroll the keyboard. Earlier keyboards may not have cursor keys. in which case, control or alt is used with some letter key to move the cursor.

CONTROL, ALT, COMMAND AND OPTION KEYS
These keys are used to command the computer and are used like a shift key. They are held down while another key is pressed.

ESCAPE KEY
The escape key is commonly used to exit or cancel the current mode. It is often used to get out of a menu. It is also used to clear an area or to repeat a function, such as redrawing the screen.

NUMERIC LOCK
The numeric lock key locks a combination number/cursor keypad into numeric mode only.

HOME AND END KEYS
The home and end keys move the cursor to the top or bottom of the current screen or to the extreme left or right side of the current line. The keys are often used in conjunction with shift, control and alt for various cursor movements; for example, CONTROL HOME and CONTROL END often move the cursor to the beginning and end of a file.

PAGE UP AND PAGE DOWN KEYS
The page up and page down keys move the cursor up and down a page, screen or frame. They are often used in combination with shift, control and alt.

FUNCTION KEYS
Function keys (labeled f1, f2, etc.) are additional keys used to command the computer. They are used to call up a menu or perform a specific function within the program. They are often used with the shift, control and alt keys providing 40 separate functions with f1 through f10.

BACKSPACE KEY
The backspace key deletes the character to the left of the cursor and may be used with the shift, control and alt keys to erase segments of text. Backspace is used to erase typos and the normally extra-wide, typewriter-style key is much preferred.

DELETE KEY
The delete key erases the character at the current cursor location. Used in conjunction with the shift, control and alt keys, delete is used to erase any segment of text, such as a word, sentence or paragraph.

INSERT KEY
The insert key usually toggles back and forth between insert mode and overwrite mode. It is also used to "paste" a segment of text or graphics into the document at the current cursor location.

REPEATING KEYS
Most computer keyboard keys repeat when held down, a phenomenon first-time computer users must get used to. If you hold a key down that is used to command the computer, you'll be entering the command several times.

AUDIBLE FEEDBACK
Some keyboards cause a clicking or beeping sound to be heard from the computer when keys are pressed. This is done to acknowledge that the character has been entered. Audible feedback is often, and should be, adjustable for personal preference.

All Keyboards Are Not Equal

Keyboard quality is critical for experienced typists. The feel of the keyboard (the amount of tension and springiness) varies greatly from one keyboard to another.

Key placement and size is also important. Older keyboards especially may have awkward return and shift key placements, and new keyboards may not have the wide backspace key, which is preferable.

To test a keyboard for speed, press A, S, D and F without lifting any fingers from the keys until you're finished. All four letters should display on screen. If not, the keyboard is not suitable for fast typing.

keyboard enhancer Same as *macro processor*.

keyboard interrupt A signal that gets the attention of the CPU each time a key is pressed on the keyboard. See *interrupt*.

keyboard macro processor See *keyboard enhancer*.

keyboard processor
(1) The circuit in the keyboard that converts keystrokes into the appropriate character codes.

(2) See *macro processor*.

keyboard template A plastic card that fits over the function keys on the keyboard and is used to identify the use of these keys for a particular software program.

KeyNotes A line of memory-resident electronic books for PCs from Digital Learning Systems, Inc. It includes such reference works as the Associated Press Stylebook, the Complete Secretary's Handbook and the Writer's Handbook.

keypad A small set or supplementary set of keyboard keys, for example, the number keys on a calculator or the number/cursor cluster on a computer keyboard.

CALCULATOR KEYPAD

TELEPHONE KEYPAD

keypunch To punch holes in a punched card. It is sometimes used to refer to typing on a computer keyboard.

keypunch department Same as *data entry department*.

keypunch machine A punched-card data entry machine. A deck of blank cards is placed into a hopper, and, upon operator command, the machine feeds one card to a punch station. As characters are typed, a series of dies at the punch station punch the appropriate holes in the selected card column.

THE FIRST KEYPUNCH
(Courtesy IBM)

Punched cards were first used in the 1890 census. Each card was manually placed in the unit for punching.

Khornerstones A benchmark test provided by Workstation Laboratories that measures CPU, input/output and floating point performance.

kicks See *CICS*.

kilo *See K.*

Kinetics FastPath A gateway from the Kinetics division of Excelan, Inc., that connects LocalTalk and PhoneNet systems, as well as LaserWriter printers, to VAX and MicroVAX computers, UNIX-based computers, PCs and other Ethernet-based hosts. It supports AppleTalk, TCP/IP and DECnet protocols.

kludge Also spelled "kluge" and pronounced "klooj." A crude, inelegant system, component or software program. It may refer to a makeshift, temporary solution to a problem as well as to any product that is poorly designed.

knowledge base A database of rules about a subject that is used in artificial intelligence applications. See *expert system*.

knowledge based system An artificial intelligence application that uses a database of knowledge about a subject, such as in an expert system.

knowledge engineer An individual who translates the knowlege of an expert into the knowledge base of an expert system.

KSR terminal (Keyboard Send Receive terminal) A terminal that uses a keyboard for entering and transmitting data. Contrast with *RO terminal*, which does not have a keyboard.

label

(1) In data management, a made-up name that is assigned to a file, field or other data structure.

(2) In spreadsheets, descriptive text that is entered into a cell.

(3) In programming, a made-up name used to identify a variable or a subroutine.

(4) In computer operations, a self-sticking form attached to the outside of a disk or tape in order to identify it.

(5) In magnetic tape files, a record used for identification at the beginning or end of the file.

LAN

(1) (Local Area Network) A communications network that serves several users within a confined geographical area.

(2) (Local Area Network) A network of personal computers within a confined geographical area that is made up of servers and workstations. File servers, or network servers, are high-speed machines that hold programs and data shared by all users in the network, while workstations act as user terminals. The

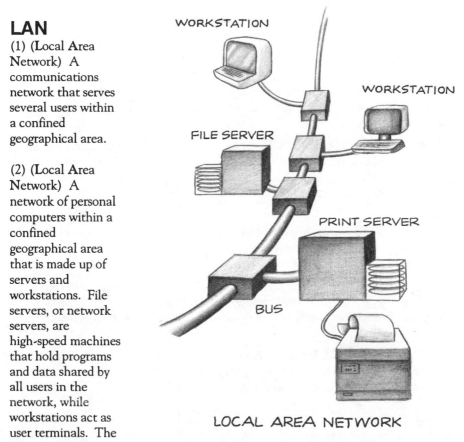

WORKSTATION

WORKSTATION

FILE SERVER

PRINT SERVER

BUS

LOCAL AREA NETWORK

workstation can be diskless, requiring all software and data be obtained from the server, or it can have local disk storage for applications that are not shared by others. Users may have their own printers or printers can be connected to servers and be shared.

Small LANs can allow one computer to be both server and workstation, but performance is improved when the server is an independent station in the network. Multiple servers can be installed for larger networks.

Bridges can connect like networks together and gateways can connect one type of network to another, allowing a personal computer network to interconnect with a mini or mainframe network, for example.

The controlling software in a LAN is the network operating system, such as Novell's NetWare, which resides in the server. A component part of the software resides in each workstation and allows the application to read and write data from the server as if it were on the local machine.

The physical transfer of data is performed by the media access method, such as Ethernet or Token Ring, which come in the form of network interface cards (NICs) that plug into each computer. The wiring type (twisted pair, coaxial cable or optical fiber) is based on the access method.

LAN Manager
A local area network operating system from Microsoft that runs as an application under OS/2 in a file server and supports both DOS and OS/2 workstations. It uses the Microsoft File Sharing protocol (SMB) for file sharing, the NetBIOS protocol for its transport mechanism and uses Named Pipes for interprocess communication (IPC).

LAN Requestor
The LAN Server software that resides in the workstation.

LAN Server
IBM's version of LAN Manager. Although these two versions have drifted apart, they may eventually be merged.

Landmark speed test
A performance test from Landmark Research International Corporation that measures CPU, video and math coprocessor speed of the PC. CPU speed is rated as the clock speed required in an AT-class machine that would provide the equivalent performance.

landscape
A printing orientation that prints data across the wider side of the form. Contrast with *portrait*.

language
A set of symbols and rules used to convey information. See *machine language, programming language, graphics language, page description language, fourth-generation language, standards & compatibility* and *user interface*.

language processor
Language translation software. Programming languages, command languages, query languages, natural languages and foreign languages are all translated by software.

LAP (Link Access Procedure) CCITT family of error correction protocols originally derived from the HDLC standard and used on X.25 packet networks.

LAP-B (LAP-Balanced) Used in current X-25 networks.

LAP-D (LAP-D channel) Used in the data channel of an ISDN transmission.

LAP-M (LAP-Modem) Defined in CCITT V.42, which uses some of the LAPD methods and adds additional ones.

LAP-X (LAP-Half-dupleX) Used for ship to shore transmission.

LapLink A file transfer program for PCs from Traveling Software, Inc., that is used to send data between laptop and desktop or between desktop computers. LapLink Mac transfers files between PCs and Macs.

laptop computer A portable computer that has a flat screen and usually weighs less than a dozen pounds. Laptops use AC power and/or batteries. Some units have connectors for an external video monitor and keyboard transforming them into full-size computers for the desktop. See *notebook computer* and *pocket computer*.

TOSHIBA T-1000 LAPTOP

laser (Light Amplification from the Stimulated Emission of Radiation) A device that generates a very uniform light that can be precisely focused. It is used in a wide variety of applications, such as communications, electrophotographic printing and optical disk storage. Lasers are used to transmit light pulses over optical fibers which, unlike electrical wires, are not affected by nearby electrical interferences.

The Laser Discovery

In 1957, the laser was conceived and named by Gordon Gould, a graduate student in physics at Columbia University. When Gould filed for patents in

1959, he found that Charles Townes, a Columbia professor, and Arthur Schawlow, who was working for Bell Labs, had already filed for them. The year before, AT&T had, in fact, demonstrated a working laser at Bell Labs. In 1977, after years of litigation, a court awarded Gould rights to the first of three patents and by the end of the 1980s, he owned the rights to all three. After almost 30 years of court battles, Gould finally reaped millions in royalties, but spent much of his life without the recognition he deserved.

DEVELOPING THE LASER
(Courtesy AT&T)

This photo of the development of the helium-neon laser was taken at AT&T's Bell Laboratories in 1964.

laser printer A printer that uses the electrophotographic method used in copy machines to print a page at a time. A laser is used to "paint" the dots of light onto a photographic drum or belt. The toner is applied to the drum or belt and then transferred onto the paper. Desktop laser printers use cut sheets of paper as in a copy machine, and large laser printers use either cut sheets or rolls of paper.

In 1975, IBM introduced the first laser printer, called the 3800, which was designed for high-speed printing. In 1978, Siemens introduced the ND 2 and Xerox introduced the 9700. These self-contained printing presses are either online to the mainframe or offline, accepting data in print image format on reels of tape or disk packs. Large-scale machines offer features such as printing on both sides of the page and collating. Since laser printers use dot matrix technology, an infinite variety of fonts can be printed, as well as graphics. In addition, the form can be printed along with the data. Special models are available that can print up to 36" widths.

In 1984, Hewlett-Packard announced the first desktop laser printer, called the LaserJet, which has revolutionized personal computer printing and has spawned desktop publishing. Laser printers now compete directly with high-end daisy wheel and dot matrix printers.

Although high-resolution color laser printers are also available, less expensive desktop versions are on the horizon and should become widely used throughout the 1990s.

Note: All medium to large-scale printers that print a page at a time do not use a laser. Some use ion deposition, which creates the image with electricity rather than light. See *electrophotographic*.

LaserJet A series of desktop laser printers from Hewlett-Packard. Introduced in 1984 at a retail price of $3,000, it set the standard for the desktop laser printer market. The LaserJets print up to 300 dpi, although third-party enhancements increase this resolution up to 800 dpi and more. The Series III includes its own resolution enhancement that approaches 600 dpi by creating smaller dots to even out the jaggies. The printer command language used to drive the LaserJets is HP's PCL.

The LaserJets accept bit-mapped fonts as plug-in cartridges or, except for the original LaserJet model, soft fonts downloaded from the computer. Adobe PostScript cartridges are available for the IID, IIP and III, and third-party add-ins provide PostScript for the II. With the Series III, scalable fonts have been added which include eight internal fonts and optional font cartridges. Drivers for PCL Version 5 are required to use the Series III scalable fonts. An upgrade kit provides scalable fonts (PCL 5) for the Series II.

MODEL	Date Intro	Speed (ppm)	Sheets In tray	Built-in Fonts	Font Cartridge Slots	RAM	Printer Engine
LaserJet	1984	8	100	2	1	28K-2M	Canon CX
LaserJet PLUS	1985	8	100	2	1	512K-2M	Canon CX
PLUS 500	1985	8	500	2	1		
Series II	1987	8	250	6	2	512K-4M	Canon SX
IID* **	1989	8	500	22	2	640K-4M	Canon SX
IIP*	1989	4	50	14	1	512K-4.5M	Canon LX
Series III*	1990	8	250	***	2	1-5M	Canon SX

LASERJET SPECIFICATIONS
* Adobe PostScript cartridge available
** Double sided printing
***14 bit-mapped fonts, 8 scalable fonts

LaserWriter A series of 300 dpi desktop laser printers from Apple Computer. All models handle bit-mapped fonts, and, except for the SC models, include PostScript, built-in AppleTalk connections, as well as RS-232 ports for connecting PCs via Diablo emulation. PCs can also use the LaserWriter through AppleTalk. Hard disks can be attached to the NTX's SCSI port for font storage.

MODEL	Date Intro	Speed (ppm)	Sheets In tray	Built-in Fonts	CPU	RAM	Printer Engine
LW	1985	8	250	11	68000	1.5M	Canon CX
LW Plus	1985	8	250	35	68000	1.5M	Canon CX
IISC*	1987	8	200	11	68000	1M	Canon SX
IINT	1987	8	200	35	68000	2M	Canon SX
IINTX	1987	8	200	35	68020	2-12M	Canon SX
Personal SC*	1990	4	250	11	68000	1M	Canon LX
Personal NT	1990	4	250	35	68000	2M	Canon LX

LASERWRITER SPECIFICATIONS
* Non-PostScript (uses QuickDraw) and not usable in networks

LATA (Local Access and Transport Area) A geographic region that has been set up to differentiate local and long distance telephone calls. Any telephone call between parties within a LATA is handled by the local telephone company.

latch An electronic circuit, such as a flip-flop, that maintains one of two states. It is set and then reset.

late binding The linking of routines at run time.

latency The time between initiating a request for data and the beginning of the actual data transfer. On a rotating medium, such as a disk, latency is the time it takes for the selected sector to come around and be positioned under the read/write head. Channel latency is the time it takes for a computer channel to become unoccupied in order to transfer data.

latent image An invisible image that is typically made up of electrical charges. For example, in a Xerographic copy machine process, a latent image of the page to be copied is created on a plate or drum as an electrical charge.

launch To cause a program to load and run.

layout setting A value that is used to format a printed page. Margins, tabs, indents, headers, footers and column widths are examples.

LCD (Liquid Crystal Display) A display technology that is commonly used in digital watches and laptop computers. Because they use less power, LCDs replaced LEDs (light emitting diodes) in digital watches years ago. Power is used only to move molecules rather than to energize a light-emitting substance.

Liquid crystals are rod-shaped molecules that flow like liquid, and are used to direct light between two polarizing filters. In their normal state, the crystals direct the light through the polarizers, allowing a natural light gray background color to show. When energized, they redirect the light to be absorbed in one of the polarizers, causing the dark appearance of crossed polarizers to show.

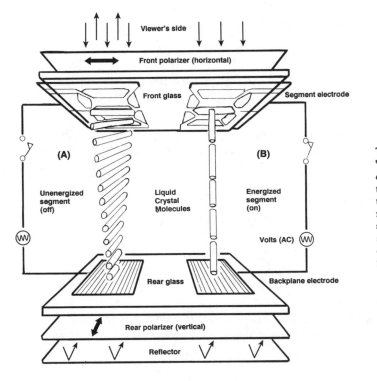

The two "figure-8" characters on the front glass of this example are made up of seven segments, allowing the digits 0 through 9 to be displayed.

TWISTED-NEMATIC LIQUID CRYSTAL DISPLAY

(Courtesy LXD Inc.)

Side A shows a light gray segment (background). The light source from the viewer's side shines through the front polarizer, through the front glass, down the liquid crystals, through the rear glass and through the rear polarizer. It bounces off the reflector, back through the rear polarizer and rear glass, back up the liquid crystals, back through the front glass and front polarizer to the viewer. In the normal state, the liquid crystals are induced to lay parallel with their polarizing plates.

Side B shows a dark segment (crossed polarizers). When the segment is energized, the liquid crystal molecules turn perpendicular to the polarizing plates. Light shines through the front polarizer and glass, down the molecules and through the rear glass. It is then absorbed in the rear polarizer.

The layer of liquid crystals (between the bottom of the front glass and the top of the rear glass) is only 3/10,000ths of an inch thick.

Backlit displays use a translucent reflector and shine a light source behind it. This "transflective" type of display helps make the background brighter, thus making the characters appear sharper.

LCD panel A data projector that accepts computer output and displays it on a see-through liquid crystal screen, which is placed on top of an overhead projector.

LE (Less than or Equal to) See *relational operator*.

leader
(1) The beginning length of unrecorded tape that is used to thread the tape onto the tape drive.

(2) The first record in a file that is used for identification purposes. See *header label*.

leaders Dots or dashes used to draw the eye across the printed page, such as in a table of contents.

leading In typography, the vertical spacing between lines of type (between baselines). The name comes from the early days of typesetting when the space was achieved with thin bars of lead.

leading edge
(1) The edge of a punched card or document that enters the reading station first.

(2) In digital electronics, a pulse as it changes from a 0 to a 1.

(3) In programming, a loop that tests a condition before the loop is entered.

leading zeros Zeros used to fill a field that do not increase the numerical value of the data. For example, all the zeros in 0000006588 are leading zeros.

leaf In database management, the last node of a tree.

leapfrog test A storage diagnostic routine that replicates itself throughout the storage medium.

leased line A private communications channel that is leased from a common carrier. Leased lines can be ordered in pairs, providing a four-wire channel for fast full-duplex transmission. The dial-up system provides only two-wire lines. Leased lines can also be conditioned, to improve line quality.

least significant bit The binary digit in the rightmost position of the byte, word or field.

least significant digit The digit in the rightmost position of the number.

LEC (Local Exchange Carrier) An organization that provides local telephone services.

LED (Light Emitting Diode) A display technology that uses a particular variety of semiconductor diode that emits light when charged with electricity. LEDs usually give off a red glow, although other colors can be generated as well. LEDs were the digit displays on the earliest digital watches.

Their higher power requirement caused them to give way to LCD, which is always visible and does not require the wearer to press a button to activate it. LEDs are used for the drive-in-use lights found on disk drives as well as in display panels for countless electronic products.

left justify Same as *flush left*.

Lempel Ziv A data compression algorithm that uses an adaptive compression technique.

LEN (Low Entry Networking) In SNA, peer-to-peer connectivity between adjacent Type 2.1 nodes, such as PCs, workstations and minicomputers. LU 6.2 sessions are supported across LEN connections.

letter quality The print quality of an electric typewriter. Laser printers, ink jet printers and daisy wheel printers provide letter quality printing. 24-pin dot matrix printers provide near letter quality (NLQ), but the characters are not as dark and crisp.

lexicographic sort A method for arranging items in alphabetic order without regard to case, such as in a dictionary and this Glossary. Computer codes group the cases separately, for example, in ASCII, "a" follows "Z" (see chart in *ASCII*), thus dictionary sequencing requires the additional steps performed in lexicographic sorting.

LF See *line feed*.

librarian An individual who works in the data library.

library
(1) A collection of programs or data files.

(2) A collection of pre-written functions, or subroutines. The functions are linked into the main program when it is compiled.

(3) See *data library*.

library routine A prewritten subroutine that is part of a macro or function library.

LIFO (Last In First Out) A queueing method in which the next item to be retrieved is the item most recently placed in the queue. Contrast with *FIFO*.

light bar Same as *highlight bar*.

light guide A transmission channel that contains a number of optical fibers packaged together.

light pen A light-sensitive stylus wired to a video terminal. The user brings the light pen to the desired point on the screen and presses a button, causing it to identify the current location. It is used to select options from a menu or to draw images.

The pixels on a display screen are constantly being refreshed. When the user presses the light pen button, allowing the pen to sense light, the pixel being illuminated at that moment identifies the screen location.

LIGHT PEN

lightwave Light in the infrared, visible and ultraviolet ranges, which falls between x-rays and microwaves. Wavelengths in this range are between 10 nanometers and one millimeter.

lightwave system An optical system that transmits light pulses over optical fibers; for example, the intercity trunks of the telephone companies are rapidly being converted to lightwave systems. Lightwave systems now in production can transmit over a billion light pulses per second.

LIGHTWAVE SYSTEM
(Courtesy Rockwell International)

Although this looks like a city of the future, it is actually a 10" square circuit board containing an advanced lightwave transmission system. This model LTS-21130, from Rockwell's Lightwave Systems Division, is capable of transmitting 1.13 billion bits per second. That means 16,000 digitized voice conversations can be transmitted simultaneously over one hair-thin optical fiber.

LIM EMS (Lotus/Intel/Microsoft Expanded Memory Specification) Same as *EMS*.

limited distance modem Same as *short-haul modem*.

limulator See *EMS emulator*.

Linda A set of functions added to languages, such as C and C++, that creates a parallel processing environment by allowing data to be created and transferred between processes.

line
(1) In text-based systems, a row of characters.

(2) In graphics-based systems, a row of pixels.

(3) A communications channel.

LINES

(Courtesy AT&T)

The exploding communications field in 1883. This photo was taken at Broadway and Courtlandt Streets in New York City.

line adapter In communications, a device similar to a modem, that converts a digital signal into a form suitable for transmission over a communications line and vice versa. It provides such functions as parallel to serial and serial to parallel conversion and modulation and demodulation.

line analyzer A device that monitors the transmission of a communications line.

line concentration See *concentrator*.

line conditioning See *conditioning*.

line dot matrix printer A line printer that uses the dot matrix printing method. See *printer*.

line drawing A graphic image outlined by solid lines. The mass of the drawing is imagined by the viewer. See *wire frame*.

line driver In communications, a hardware device that is used to extend the transmission distance between terminals and computers that are connected via private lines. It is used for digital transmission and is required at each end of the line.

line editor A simple editing program that allows text to be changed one line at a time, such as the EDLIN editor in DOS.

line feed

(1) A character code that advances the cursor on screen or the paper in the printer to the next line. The ASCII line feed (LF) character has a numeric value of 10. In DOS and OS/2 text files, the common end of line code is a return/line feed pair (ASCII 13 10).

(2) On a printer, a button that advances the paper one line.

line frequency The number of times each second that a wave or some repeatable set of signals is transmitted over a line. See *scan rate*.

line level In communications, the signal strength within a transmission channel, measured in decibels or nepers.

line load

(1) In communications, the percentage of time a communications channel is used.

(2) In electronics, the amount of current that is carried in a circuit.

line number

(1) A specific line of code in a programming language.

(2) On display screens, a specific row of text or row of dots.

(3) In communications, a specific communications channel.

line of code A statement in a programming language. In assembly language, it usually generates one machine instruction, but in a high-level language, it may generate a series of instructions.

Lines of code are used to measure the complexity of a program. However, comparisons are misleading if the programs are not in the same language or category. For example, eight lines of code in a report writer may be equivalent to 100 lines of code in a COBOL program.

line of sight An unobstructed view from the transmitter to the receiver.

line printer A printer that prints one line at a time. Line printers are usually connected to mainframes and minicomputers. See *printer*.

line segment In vector graphics, same as *vector*.

line speed See *data rate*.

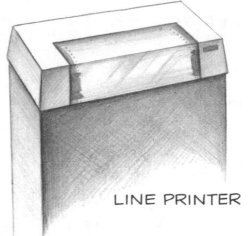

LINE PRINTER

line squeeze In a mail merge, the vertical adjustment of the body of text when a blank line is encountered in the name and address. In the following example, the company field is blank, and the name on the right is printed properly. See *field squeeze*.

Without line squeeze

```
Pat Smith

10 South Main
Bearcat, OR 80901
```

With line squeeze

```
Pat Smith
10 South Main
Bearcat, OR 80901
```

linear An arrangement along one line, one axis or one dimension. Linear operations imply uniformity, equality and regularity; for example, the outputs of a linear system are uniformly based on the inputs. An increase in the input provides an equal increase in output.

linear programming A mathematical technique that is used to obtain an optimum solution in resource allocation problems, such as production planning.

link
(1) In communications, a line, channel or circuit over which data is transmitted.

(2) In data management, a pointer embedded within a record that refers to data or the location of data in another record.

(3) In programming, a call to another program or subroutine.

link edit To use a linkage editor to prepare a program for running.

linkage editor A utility program which adapts a program that has been assembled or compiled into a particular computer environment. It formally links cross references between separate program modules, and it links the program to various libraries containing prewritten subroutines. Its output is a load module, a program ready to run in the computer.

linked list In data management, a group of items, each of which points to the next item. A linked list allows for the organization of a sequential set of data in noncontiguous storage locations.

linker See *linkage editor*.

Linpack A benchmark program for testing a computer's performance. Linpack is a FORTRAN program that executes 100 equations with 100 unknowns. The results of the test depend on the computer's floating point, CPU and memory speed as well as the compiler's efficiency.

LIPS (Logical Inferences Per Second) A unit of measurement of the thinking speed of an AI application. Humans can do about 2 LIPS. In the computer, one LIPS equals from 100 to 1,000 instructions.

liquid crystal shutters An alternative technique for controlling the image on a laser printer. Liquid crystal dots function as gates that open and close, allowing light to pass through to a photosensitive drum or belt.

Lisa Introduced in 1983 by Apple Computer, the first personal computer that offered integrated software. It was also the first computer to use a similar version of the desktop user interface introduced on the Xerox Star in 1981. The Lisa was ahead of its time, but never caught on due to its $10,000 price and slow performance. The Lisa, renamed Mac XL, lived out its remaining days as a Macintosh.

LISA

LISP (LISt Processing) A high-level programming language used extensively in non-numeric programming, in which objects, rather than numbers, are manipulated. Developed in 1960 by John McCarthy, it is very different in syntax and structure than languages like BASIC and COBOL. For example, in LISP there is no syntactic difference between data and instructions.

LISP is used extensively in AI applications, as well as in compiler creation, and is available in both interpreter and compiler versions. It automatically handles more program activities than conventional languages, such as dynamic memory management, and lets the programmer concentrate on manipulating the objects. The language itself can be modified and expanded.

Many varieties of LISP have been developed, including versions that perform calculations efficiently. The following Common LISP example converts fahrenheit to centigrade:

```
(defun convert ()
  (format t "Enter fahrenheit ")
  (let ((fahr (read)))
   (format t "Centigrade is ~D"
     (truncate (*(-fahr 32)
        (/ 5 9)))))))
```

list

(1) Any arranged set of data, but often in row and column format.

(2) In fourth-generation languages, a common command used to display or print a group of selected records. For example, in dBASE, the command **list name address** displays all names and addresses in the current file.

list processing
The processing of non-numeric data.

list processing language
A programming language used for processing non-numeric data, such as LISP, Prolog and Logo. It provides special commands that work with lists of data, such as names, words and objects. For example, a command might select the first or last object in the list, or next to first or next to last. Some languages have a command to reverse the order of all elements in a list.

Although these functions can be performed in a traditional programming language, list processing languages make it easier to do so. In addition, recursion is provided, which lets a subroutine call itself over again, thus allowing objects in a list to be repetitively analyzed.

listing
Any printed output generated from the computer.

literal
In programming, an unchanging item written into the program, such as a message that is displayed on screen. It is translated into machine language without conversion.

liveware A category of objects known as human beings.

lo-res See *low resolution*.

load

(1) To copy a program from disk or tape into memory for execution.

(2) To fill up a disk with data or programs.

(3) To insert a disk or tape into its drive.

(4) In programming, to store data in a register.

(5) In performance measurement, the current use of a system as a percentage of total capacity.

(6) In electronics, the flow of current through a circuit.

load module A program in machine language form ready to run in the computer. It is the output of a link editor.

loaded line In communications, a telephone line that uses loading coils to reduce distortion. The loading coils are used to restore high-end voice frequencies but can interfere with data transmission.

loader A program routine that copies program into memory for execution.

loader routine Same as *loader*.

loading coils See *loaded line*.

local area network See *LAN*.

local bypass An interconnection between two facilities without the use of the local telephone company.

local loop A communications line between a customer and the telephone company's central office. See *loop carrier*.

local variable In programming, a variable that is used only within the routine or function it is defined in.

LocalTalk A local area network access method from Apple Computer that uses twisted pair wires and transmits at 230,400 bps. It runs under AppleTalk and uses a daisy chain topology that can connect up to 32 devices within a

distance of 1,000 feet. Third party products allow LocalTalk to hook up with
bus, passive star and active star topologies.

   Apple's LocalTalk PC Card plugs into a PC, allowing it to gain access to an
AppleTalk network.

log A record of computer activity that is used for statistical purposes as well as
backup and recovery.

log-off To quit, or sign off, a computer system.

log-on To gain access, or sign in, to a computer system. If restricted, it
requires users to identify themselves by entering an ID number and/or password.
Service bureaus base their charges for the time between log-on and log-off.

logic A sequence of operations performed by hardware or software. Hardware
logic is the circuits and chips that perform the controlling operations of the
computer. Software logic, or program logic, is the sequence of instructions in a
program.

   Note: Logic is not the same as logical. Logical refers to the design of a system,
rather than its physical implementation. See *logical vs physical*.

logic analyzer
(1) A device that monitors the performance of a computer by timing various
segments of the running programs. The total running time and the time spent in
selected progam modules is analyzed and displayed in order to isolate the code
that is the least efficient.

(2) A device that is used to test and diagnose an electronic system, which
includes an oscilloscope for displaying various digital states.

logic array Same as *gate array* or PLA.

logic bomb A program routine that destroys data; for example, it may
reformat the hard disk or randomly insert garbage into data files. A logic bomb
may be brought into a personal computer by downloading a public-domain
program that has been tampered with. Once executed, it does its damage right
away, whereas a virus keeps on destroying.

logic chip A chip that performs processing functions. Contrast with
memory chip.

logic circuit A circuit that performs logic functions.

logic gate A collection of transistors and other electronic components that
make up a Boolean logical operation, such as AND, NAND, OR and NOR.

Transistors make up logic gates. Logic gates make up circuits. Circuits make up electronic systems.

logic operation
An operation that analyzes one or more inputs and generates a particular output based on a set of rules. See *AND, OR and NOT* and *Boolean logic*.

logic operator
One of the Boolean logical operation, such as AND, OR and NOT.

logic-seeking printer
A printer that analyzes the content of each line to be printed and skips over blank spaces at high speeds.

logical
(1) A reasonable solution to a problem.

(2) A higher level view of an object. For example, the user's view versus the computer's view. See *logical vs physical*.

logical field
A data field that contains a yes/no, true/false condition.

logical record
A reference to a data record that is independent of its physical location. It may be physically stored in two or more locations.

logical vs physical
A high-level view versus a low-level view. Logical implies a higher level than the physical as in the following examples.

Users relate to data logically by data element name; however, the actual fields of data are physically located in sectors on a disk. For example, if you want to know which customers ordered how many of a particular product this week, your logical view of this data is customer name and quantity. The physical organization of this data might have customer name in a customer file and quantity in an order file cross referenced by customer number. The physical sequence of the customer file could be indexed, while the sequence of the order file could be sequential.

A message transmitted from Phoenix to Boston is logically going between the two cities; however, the physical circuit could be Phoenix to Chicago to Philadelphia to Boston.

When you command your program to change the output from the video screen to the printer, that's a logical request. The program will perform the physical change of address from, say, device number 02 to device number 04.

Logo
A high-level programming language that is noted for its ease of use and graphics capabilities. Logo is a recursive language that contains many list processing functions that are in LISP, although Logo's syntax is more understandable for novices.

Logo's graphics language is called *turtle graphics*, which allows complex graphics images to be created with a minimum of coding. The turtle is a triangular-shaped cursor, which is moved on the screen with Logo commands that activate the turtle as if you were driving it, for example, go forward 100 units, turn right 45 degrees, turn left 20 degrees.

Stemming from a National Science Foundation project, Logo was created by Seymour Papert in the mid 1960s along with colleagues at MIT and members of Bolt Beranek & Newman. Originally developed on large computers, Logo has been adapted to most personal computers.

The following Object Logo example converts fahrenheit to centigrade:

```
convert
local [fahr]
print "|Enter fahrenheit |
make "fahr ReadWord
print "|Centigrade is |
print (:fahr - 32) * 5 / 9
end
```

long card In PCs, a full-length controller board that plugs into an expansion slot. Contrast with *short card*.

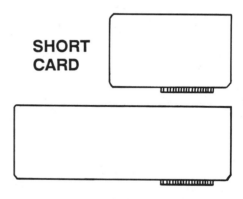

SHORT CARD

LONG CARD

long-haul In communications, modems or communications devices that are capable of transmitting over long distances.

long lines In communications, circuits that are capable of handling transmissions over long distances.

longitudinal redundancy check See LRC.

lookup A search for data within a table stored in memory or in a data file.

loop In programming, a repetition of a function in the program. Whenever any process must be repeated, a loop is set up to handle it. A program has a main loop and a series of minor loops, which are nested within the main loop. Learning how to set up loops is what programming technique is all about.

The following example prints an invoice. The main loop reads the order record and prints the invoice until there are no more orders to read. After printing date and name and addresses, the program prints a variable number of line items. The code that prints the line items is contained in a loop and repeated as many times as required.

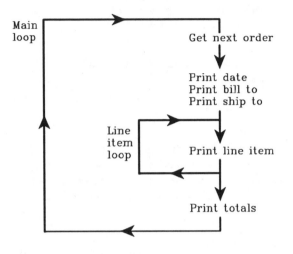

Loops are accomplished by various programming structures that have a beginning, body and end. The beginning generally tests the condition that keeps the loop going. The body comprises the repeating statements, and the end is a GOTO that points back to the beginning. In assembly language, the programmer writes the GOTO, as in the following example that counts to 10.

```
        MOVE        "0" TO COUNTER
LOOP    ADD         "1" TO COUNTER
        COMPARE     COUNTER TO "10"
        GOTO        LOOP IF UNEQUAL
        STOP
```

In high-level languages, the GOTO is generated by the interpreter or compiler; for example, the same routine as above using a WHILE loop.

```
    COUNTER = 0
    DO WHILE COUNTER <> 10
        COUNTER = COUNTER + 1
    ENDDO
    STOP
```

loop carrier In telephone communications, a system that concentrates a number of analog or digital lines from a remote termination station into the central office. It normally converts analog voice into digital at the remote station; however, it can be adapted to provide ISDN service to a customer.

loopback A diagnostic procedure in which a transmitted message or signal is sent back from its destination station for comparison with the original data. It may be implemented by a special circuit that causes the transmission from the sending side to go directly to the receiving side of the same unit without going over the line to a another device.

loosely coupled Stand-alone computers that are interconnected via a communications network. Loosely coupled computers process on their own and can exchange data on demand. Contrast with *tightly coupled*, which implies machines that are entirely dependent on each other.

lost cluster A set of disk records that have lost their identification with a file name. This happens when a file is not closed properly by the program, which can sometimes occur if the computer is turned off without formally quitting an application. In DOS, the CHKDSK /f command will turn lost clusters into files starting with the name FILE0000.CHK.

Lotus Add-in Toolkit A Pascal-like programming language from Lotus Development for Lotus 1-2-3, version 3.0, that works in both DOS and OS/2 environments and includes an editor, compiler and debugger. Users can create automated processes that can be executed while working in Lotus. The toolkit allows vendors of Lotus add-in products to convert them to version 3.0.

Lotus menu A simple, effective user interface designed into Lotus 1-2-3 that has become a de facto standard. It is made up of a row of menu options, which can be selected by highlighting the word and pressing Enter or by typing the first letter of the word. When the menu word is highlighted, a line of explanation is displayed either above or below it. Contrast with *pull-down menu*.

MITCHELL D. KAPOR
(Courtesy ON Technology, Inc.)

Mitch Kapor was co-programmer of Lotus 1-2-3 and founder of Lotus Development Corporation. He currently heads a new company called ON Technology.

Lotus 1-2-3 A spreadsheet for PCs, VAXs and IBM mainframes from Lotus Development Corporation. Introduced in 1982, it was the first, new and innovative spreadsheet developed for the PC.

Lotus 1-2-3 was the first to include graphics, file management and limited word processing along with traditional spreadsheet capabilities. Its ability to instantly convert numeric data into a graph was a dazzling new feature for its time. The program's user interface was also easy to learn and use (see *Lotus menu*).

Versions 2.0 and subsequent 2.01 introduced in 1986, have sold over four million copies. In 1989, Lotus introduced version 2.2 and 3.0. Version 2.2 needs 320K of memory and adds features, such as macro recording, an undo and a dynamic link from one spreadsheet to another.

Version 3.0 uses extended memory and runs on 286 and higher CPUs with at least 1MB of memory. It provides 3-D and dynamic linking capabilities as well as more sophisticated graphing. It also provides OS/2 compatibility and can access database files directly.

Spreadsheet file compatibility is maintained with version 2.2, but not with 3.0. Software add-ins designed for version 2.0 are not compatible with 3.0.

Additional versions of Lotus are as follows:
1-2-3/G - OS/2 Presentation Manager
1-2-3/M - IBM mainframes
1-2-3/U - Sun workstations
1-2-3/V - VAX computers

low frequency An electromagnetic wave that vibrates in the range from 30 to 300,000 Hertz (cycles per second).

low-level format The structure of the sectors on a disk. All disks have two levels of formatting. The low level initializes the disk and creates the physical layout of the sectors based on the hardware controller that drives it. The high level lays in place the components required by the operating system, such as the indexes and tables that reference the sectors.

low-level language A programming language that is very close to machine language. All assembly languages are low-level languages. Contrast with *high-level language*.

low resolution A low-grade image quality that is displayed or printed. It is due to a limited number of dots or lines per inch of image area.

LPM (Lines Per Minute) The number of lines a printer can print or a scanner can scan in a minute.

LPT1 The name assigned to parallel port #1 on a PC, which is usually connected to a printer. A second printer is assigned LPT2. Contrast with COM1.

LQ See *letter quality*.

LRC (Longitudinal Redundancy Check) An error checking method that generates a parity bit from a specified string of bits on a longitudinal track. In a row and column format, such as on magnetic tape, LRC is often used with VRC, which creates a parity bit for each character.

LSI (Large Scale Integration) Refers to the large numbers of electronic components built on a chip. LSI ranges approximately from 3,000 to 100,000 transistors on a chip.

LSI-11 A family of board-level computers from Digital that uses the micro version of the PDP-11 architecture. Introduced in 1974, it was the first implementation of Digital's Q-bus product line.

LT (Less Than) See *relational operator*.

LU (Logical Unit) In SNA, one end of a communications session.   The complete session, or LU-LU session, is defined by session type. Common sessions are between an application program in the host and a 3270 terminal (Type 2), or to a printer (Type 3). Type 6 is between two application programs.

LU 6.2 Also called APPC (Advanced-Program-to-Program Communications), it is an SNA session that provides peer-to-peer communications between systems, such as PCs, workstations, minicomputers and mainframes (not 3270 terminals). With LU 6.2, both sides have equal responsibility for initiating the session.

lumen A unit of measurement of the flow (rate of emission) of light. A wax candle generates 13 lumens while a 100 watt bulb generates 1,200 lumens. The intensity of light is measured in *candelas*. The wax candle generates one candela.

Lumena An advanced paint program for PCs from Time Arts, Inc., that is designed for artists and illustrators who require sophisticated special effects. It accepts video and scanned input and generates NTSC video output as well as hard copy. Lumena requires a video graphics board, such as the Targa board from TrueVision or the Vision 16 board from Everex.

luminance In computer graphics, the amount of brightness, measured in lumens, that is given off by a pixel or area on a screen.

M (Mega or Megabyte) See *space/time*.

Mac Common term for the Macintosh.

MAC driver (Media Access Control driver) A driver for a network interface card (NIC) that implements the Microsoft NDIS standard.

MacDFT Software that provides 3270 emulation for the Macintosh from Apple Computer. It accompanies Apple's TwinAx/Coax board and supports CUT and DFT modes and DFT multiple sessions under SNA.

MacDraw II A drawing program for the Macintosh from Claris Corporation that is an enhanced version of the original MacDraw from Apple. It is used for illustrations and elementary CAD work. MacDraw files are a subset of the Claris CAD file format.

machine Any electronic or electromechanical unit of equipment. A machine is always hardware; however, "engine" refers to hardware or software.

machine address Same as *absolute address*.

machine code Same as *machine language*.

machine cycle The shortest interval in which an elementary operation can take place within the processor. It is made up of some number of clock cycles.

machine-dependent Programs that run in only one kind of computer.

machine-independent Programs that run in a variety of computers.

machine instruction An instruction that the computer understands directly. It is made up of the operation code, or op code, and one or more operands. The op code specifies the type of instruction, such as INPUT or

COMPARE. The operands specify the references to data or peripheral devices. For example, the programming statement: `if a = b`, is converted into a COMPARE op code and operands that state the memory locations where A and B are stored.

There are machine instructions to INPUT and OUTPUT, to process data by CALCULATING, COMPARING and COPYING it, and to go to some other part of the program with a GOTO instruction.

In addition, there are machine instructions that test and control peripherals. For example, an instruction can check the printer to see if there is paper in it, or an instruction can cause the access arm to seek (go to) a specific track on a disk.

machine language
The computer's native language. In order for a program to run, it must be in the machine language of the computer that is executing it. Although programmers may modify machine language in order to fix a running program, they do not create it. It is created by programs called *assemblers, compilers* and *interpreters*, which convert programming language into machine language.

Machine language tells the computer what to do and where to do it. When a programmer writes: `total = total + subtotal`, that statement is converted into a machine instruction that tells the computer to add the contents of two areas of memory (where TOTAL and SUBTOTAL are stored).

A programmer deals with data logically, "add this, subtract that," but the computer must be told precisely where this and that are located.

Machine languages differ substantially. What may take one instruction in a mainframe, can take 15 instructions in a microcomputer. See *assembly language*.

machine readable
Data in a form that can be read by the computer, which includes disks, tapes and punched cards. Printed fonts that can be scanned and recognized by the computer are also machine readable.

Macintosh
A series of 32-bit personal computers from Apple Computer, introduced in 1984. It uses the Motorola 68000 family of processors and a proprietary operating system that simulates a user's desktop on screen. This standard user interface, combined with its built-in QuickDraw graphics language, has provided a measure of consistency and uniformity that is unique. See *Macintosh user interface*.

MACINTOSH

MAC AND MAC PLUS
In 1984 the Macintosh was introduced with a unique cabinet design; a semi-portable, boxlike, self-contained unit with a built in 9" black on white screen. It had 128K of memory, one floppy disk, two serial ports and a four-voice

sound generator. Memory was increased to 512K (Fat Mac) soon after, and in 1986, the Mac Plus added an external SCSI port for hard disks and other devices.

MAC SE

Introduced in 1987, the SE added more memory, an optional 20MB hard disk and one internal expansion slot. The SE 30 is much faster, has more memory and still uses the original Mac case.

MAC II FAMILY

The Mac II family, introduced in 1987, separated the display screen from the computer and offered full-size screens and color for the first time. Mac II models use faster CPUs, can handle large amounts of memory and much larger hard disks. The Mac II family is designed for expandability with three NuBus expansion slots in the IIcx and six in the II and IIx.

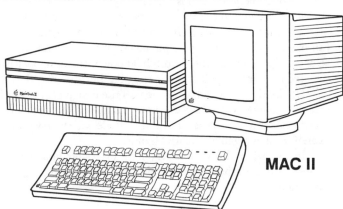

MAC II

MODEL	CPU # (32 bits)	CLOCK SPEED (MHz)	BUS SIZE	RAM (Bytes)	FLOPPY DISK (Bytes)	HARD DISK (Bytes)	SCREEN RESOLUTION
Mac	68000	7.8	16 bits	128-512K	3.5" 400K	20M	512x342 Black on white 9" diagonal
Mac Plus	68000	7.8	16 bits	1-4M	3.5" 400/800K		
Mac SE	68000	7.8	16 bits	1-4M	3.5" FDHD "SuperDrive" 400K, 800K & 1.4M Mac formats; Also MS-DOS, OS/2 & ProDOS disks		
Mac SE 30	68030	15.7	32 bits	1-8M*			
Mac II	68020	15.7	32 bits	1-8M*		20-160M	640x480, 12" 256 cols. or B/w; 640x870. 15" & 1152x870, 21" Black on white
Mac IIx	68030	15.7	32 bits	1-8M*			
Mac IIcx	68030	15.7	32 bits	1-8M*			
Mac IIci	68030	25.0	32 bits	1-8M*			
Mac IIfx	68030	40.0	32 bits	4-8M*			
Portable	68000	15.7	32 bits	1-2M*		40M	640x400 Active Matrix LCD

MACINTOSH SPECIFICATIONS
*Based on 1Mb chips. Memory increases by 4 times with 4Mb chips or by 16 times with 16Mb chips.

Macintosh user interface The method of operating a Macintosh, originally developed by Xerox and introduced on the Xerox Star in 1981. It uses a graphics screen that places familiar office objects on a two-dimensional desktop. Programs, files, folders and disks are represented by small pictures (icons) that look like the objects they represent. An object is selected by moving a mouse over the real desktop and correspondingly moving the pointer on the screen desktop. When the pointer touches an icon, the object is selected by clicking the mouse button.

A hierarchical file system is provided that lets a user "drag" a document icon into and out of a folder icon. Folders can also contain other folders and so on. To delete a document, its icon is literally dragged into a trash can icon. For people that are not computer enthusiasts, managing files on the Macintosh is a delight.

The Macintosh always displays a row of menu titles at the top of the screen. The full menu appears as if it were pulled down from the top of the screen when selected. With the mouse button held down, the option within the menu is selected by pointing to it and releasing the button.

Unlike the PC world, which leaves the design of the user interface up to the software vendor, Macintosh developers almost always conform to the Mac interface. As a result, users are comfortable with a new program from the start even if it takes a while to learn all of it.

In operation, the Macintosh operating system and application programs are almost indistinguishable, and Apple also keeps technical jargon down to a minimum.

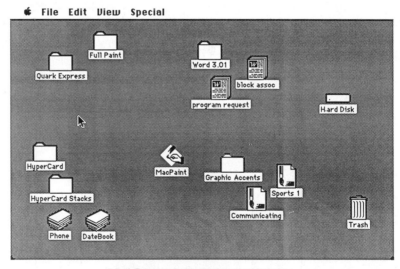

MACINTOSH DESKTOP

Although the Macintosh interface provides consistency; it does not guarantee that an application is well designed. Not only must the menus be clear and understandable, but the icon locations on screen must be considered. Since the mouse is the major selecting method, mouse movement must be kept to a minimum. In addition, for experienced typists, the mouse is a cumbersome substitute for well-designed keyboard commands.

The Mac interface style has been adapted to many non-Apple products. Windows, Presentation Manager, GEM, New Wave, X Window and countless other programs and operating environments incorporate some or many of the desktop features popularized on the Macintosh.

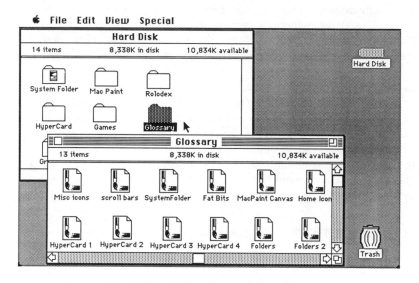

MACINTOSH FILE SYSTEM

The HARD DISK window at the top shows a series of folders with the GLOSSARY folder selected. The GLOSSARY window shows the series of documents contained within the folder.

MacIRMA
A micro to mainframe communications device for the Macintosh from DCA, Inc. The MacIRMA board emulates an IBM 3270 mainframe terminal.

MacLink Plus
A file transfer program for the Macintosh from DataViz Corporation that transfers data between Macs and PCs. Versions are also available for NeXt and Sun workstations. MacLink Plus Translators are also included, which provide document translation for over 45 different Mac and PC text, data and spreadsheet file formats.

MacLink Plus/Wang OIS provides file transfer between Macintosh and Wang OIS systems. MacLink Plus/Wang VS provides emulation of the Wang 2110 workstation as well as file transfer and document conversion between the Mac and VS computers. It also allows the Mac access Wang Office functions.

MacPaint II
A full-featured paint program for the Macintosh from Claris Corporation. Originally developed by Apple and bundled with every Mac up until the Mac Plus, it was then sold separately by Apple until Claris was formed in 1987. Claris enhanced MacPaint by adding color and many other features.

The MacPaint file format (PICT) is still used for printing screen dumps. By pressing command-shift-3 on the Mac, the current screen is stored in a PICT file for printing either in MacPaint or other program that accepts that format.

macro The term implies substitution, and refers to a number of different techniques.

(1) In application programs, a small routine, or script, that automates operations normally activated by selecting menus or entering commands one at a time. Macro languages may include common programming controls, such as IF THEN, GOTO and DO WHILE. For execution, the macro is assigned a key command. When pressed, the macro is substituted for the keystroke.

(2) In assembly language, a prewritten subroutine that is called upon at various places in the program. At assembly time, the macro calls are substituted with either the complete subroutine or a series of instructions that branch to the subroutine. The equivalent in a high-level language is called a *function*.

(3) In the dBASE programming language, a variable which references another variable that actually contains the data. At run time, the macro variable is substituted with the data variable.

macro assembler A assembler program that lets the programmer create and use macros.

macro call Same as *macro instruction*.

macro generator See *macro recorder*.

macro instruction An instruction in an assembly language program that refers to and is replaced with a series of instructions.

macro language
(1) The language used in a macro processor.

(2) An assembly language that uses macros.

macro processor
(1) Software that creates and executes macros from the keyboard. Same as *keyboard enhancer*.

(2) The part of an assembler that substitutes the macro subroutines for the macro calls.

macro recorder A function in a program that captures routine keystrokes and converts them into a macro. For example, a user turns on the recorder, calls up a menu and selects a variety of options, then turns the recorder off. The macro is assigned a key combination, which when pressed, reruns the series of selections as if they were entered at the keyboard.

MacTerminal Terminal emulation software for the Macintosh from Apple Computer that allows a Mac to function as an IBM 3278 Model 2 (when used with an AppleLine Protocol Converter) or Digital VT 52 or VT 100 terminal.

MacWrite II A full-featured word processing program for the Macintosh from Claris Corporation. Originally developed by Apple and packaged with every Mac 128 and 512, Claris has substantially upgraded the package with professional word processing features.

mag disk See *magnetic disk*.

mag tape See *magnetic tape*.

Magellan A disk management utility for PCs from Lotus Development Corporation that lets users view, find and manage files on their hard disks, floppies and removable disk cartridges.

File contents can be browsed as if they were being viewed by the programs that created them. For example, a Lotus spreadsheet looks like it does in Lotus; a dBASE file looks like it was displayed in dBASE. Magellan provides extensive search capabilities for finding file names and contents, and it allows for copying, renaming and deleting files and directories.

magnetic card
(1) See *magnetic stripe*.

(2) A plastic card with a magnetic recording surface that was used for data storage in early computer and word processing systems. See *CRAM, RACE* and *Data Cell*.

magnetic coercivity The amount of energy required to alter the state of a magnet. The higher the coercivity index of a magnetic disk, the more data it can store.

magnetic core See *core storage*.

magnetic disk Direct access storage devices that are the primary storage medium for computers. Disks are analogous to phonograph records and turntables. The flat sides of the disk platter are the recording surfaces, the tone arm is the access arm, and the stylus (needle) is the read/write head. The major difference is that phonograph records are permanently recorded; whereas magnetic disks can be recorded, erased and rerecorded just like tape.

TRACKS AND SECTORS
The disk surface is divided into several concentric tracks (circles within circles). The thinner the tracks, the more storage capacity of the disk. The data bits are recorded as tiny spots on these tracks. The tinier the spot, the more bits per inch

and the greater the storage
capacity. Most disks hold the
same number of bits on each
track, even though the outer
tracks are physically longer
than the inner ones. Some
disks pack the bits as tightly as
possible within each track.

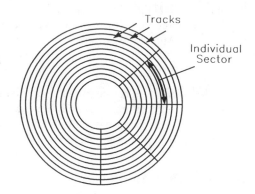

The circular tracks are further
divided into segments, called
sectors, which determine the
least amount of data that can
be read or written at one time.
In order to update the disk, a
sector is read into the
computer, changed and written

SECTORS ON A DISK

back to the disk. A sector can contain several records, or one record can span
several sectors. The access method, one of the primary components of an
operating system, figures out how to fit data into these fixed spaces.

HARD AND SOFT SECTORED DISKS
Hard sectored disks identify sectors with some mark or hole that is physically part
of the disk. Soft sectored disks contain sector identification within the recording
tracks, which is initially placed there with a format program.

HARD DISKS
Hard disks on personal computers
hold from ten to over 600MB of
data. Minicomputer and
mainframe hard disks hold from
several million to billions of bytes.
Fixed hard disks are permanently
sealed and cannot be removed
from the drive, whereas removable
hard disks are encased in modules
called *disk packs* or *disk cartridges*
and can be moved from one
computer to another.

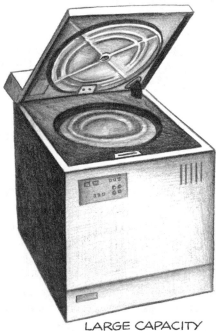

Hard disks provide fast retrieval
of data because they rotate from
2,400 to 3,600 rpm and are
constantly spinning, except in
laptops, which stop the spinning to
preserve battery life. Hard disks
are made up of one or more
aluminum platters of the same
size, from about two to 14 inches
in diameter, each side coated with
a ferromagnetic material.

Ultra-fast hard disks can be
designed with a separate
read/write head over each track.

**LARGE CAPACITY
REMOVABLE HARD DISK**

Since these fixed head disks have no access arm to move, the only delay is a couple of milliseconds of latency time, the time it takes the disk to spin around to the beginning of the requested sector.

FLOPPY DISKS

Floppy disks are a removable medium that hold approx. 150,000 to 2MB of data. They are slower than hard disks, since the disk does not spin until a data transfer is requested, and then it only reaches a rotation speed of about 300 rpm. It has a single plastic platter with magnetic coating on both sides and is encased in either a stiff, but bendable, plastic envelope (8" and 5.25" disks) or in a plastic shell (3.5").

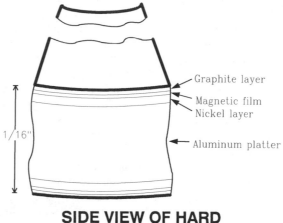

1/16"

Graphite layer
Magnetic film
Nickel layer

Aluminum platter

SIDE VIEW OF HARD DISK PLATTER

HARD DISK ←

FLOPPY DISK ←

MEASUREMENTS

Disk capacity is measured in bytes, and speed is measured in milliseconds. The average time it takes to go to a random track on the disk is called *access time*. Fast hard disks range from .12 to 28ms. A slow hard disk can take 85ms or more.

magnetic disk & tape The primary, reusable storage media for computers. Each disk or tape unit can hold from hundreds of thousands to hundreds of millions of bytes. When both media are available, the choice depends on the accessing requirements.

Tape is sequential; disk is direct access. Tape is a long string that must be moved across the read/write head. Locating a program or data on tape can take from several seconds to minutes.

Disks are rotating platters with a mechanical arm that moves the read/write head between the outer and inner edges. It can take as long as one second to find a location on a floppy disk to as short as 1/300th of a second on an ultra-fast hard disk.

Disks are almost always used for daily transaction processing, and tapes are used for backup and historical purposes. The larger the organization, the more economical tape becomes for archival storage. In addition, reels of tape are easier to transport than large disk packs.

For personal computers, disks are used for all interactive processing, and both floppy disks and tapes are used for backup. Since 1986, Bernoulli disks have provided a removable option for both processing and backup, and removable hard disk cartridges, which emerged in the late 1980s, are becoming popular alternatives in the 1990s.

In time, magnetic disks and tapes may become as obsolete as the punched card. Erasable optical disks are emerging that hold billions of bytes. If optical disks don't obsolete magnetic media, some day, some new, solid state storage device will. After all, we're still using electric motors to whirl disks and tapes around, a rather incongruous contrast to the magic of the chip.

magnetic drum A direct access storage device designed with a spinning cylinder like a roll of paper towels. Its outside surface is divided into band-like tracks that run around the circumference. There are no access arms; a separate read/write head is fixed over each track. Drums used to provide the fastest retrieval, but are no longer widely used.

magnetic field An invisible electrical energy field that is emitted by a magnet. Same as *flux*.

magnetic ink An ink containing magnetic particles that is detectable by sensors. It is used to print the MICR characters that encode account numbers on bank checks.

magnetic oxide An oxide (acid) that is capable of being magnetized, which is used to coat the recording surfaces of magnetic disks and tapes.

magnetic recording The technique used to record digital data on disks and tapes. Writing (recording) is accomplished by passing the recording surface on or near a read/write head that discharges an electric impulse onto the surface at the appropriate time.

Although various electromagnetic signalling techniques are used, the concept is simple. A tiny spot with either a positive or negative polarity, representing a 0 or 1 bit, is deposited on the disk or tape surface. When tapes are recorded, an erase head clears the surface first, since blocks of data are not fixed in size as they are with disks. Reading is accomplished by passing the surface by the read/write head and sensing the polarity of the bit or the changes of polarity.

Note that bubble memory is also a form of magnetic recording; however, unlike tapes and disks, the surface is not moved.

magnetic stripe A small length of magnetic tape that is adhered to ledger cards, badges and credit cards. Magnetic stripes are read by specialized readers that are sometimes incorporated into accounting machines and terminals. Due to heavy wear, the digital data recorded on the magnetic stripe is a low-density format that may be duplicated several times.

magnetic tape A sequential storage device that is used for data collection, backup and historical purposes. Just like audio or videotape, computer tape is made of flexible plastic with one side coated with a ferromagnetic material. Tapes come in reels, cartridges and cassettes of many sizes and shapes.

As with any tape mechanism, locating a specific item on it requires reading everything in front of it. There is no way to fast forward. In order to add and delete records on a tape, the current tape is input to the computer and a blank tape is used for output. If data on tape is only changed and the physical number of records is not altered, some tape drives can update in place by reading a block of data and writing back over the same place.

½" REEL-TO-REEL TAPE

Data bits are usually recorded on a number of parallel recording tracks that run the length of the tape. For example, 9-track tape holds one byte of data across the tape's width, 8 bits for each byte plus a parity bit. Data is recorded in blocks of contiguous bytes, separated by a space, called an *interrecord* or *interblock gap*, created during the start-up and stop-down of the tape mechanism.

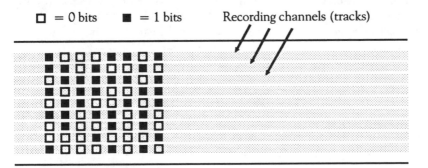

□ = 0 bits　■ = 1 bits　Recording channels (tracks)

RECORDED BITS ON MAGNETIC TAPE

Tape is often used as an interchange medium between mainframes and minicomputers, since 1/2" open-reel tape provides a common standard. Tape is also less expensive than disk packs and cartridges and provides economical storage for large amounts of historical data. When tapes are used for archival storage, they must be periodically recopied or the tightly coiled magnetic surfaces may contaminate each other.

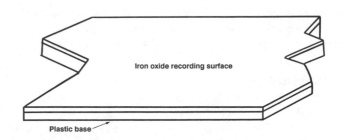

CROSS SECTION OF MAGNETIC TAPE

Storage capacity is measured in bits per inch (bpi); however, tape is laid out in parallel tracks, and bpi is thus equivalent to bytes per inch. Common 1/2" recording densities are 1650 and 6250bpi; early densities were 200, 556 and 800bpi. Tape drive speed is measured in inches per second (ips), and its transfer rate is determined by multiplying speed times recording density.

magneto-optic A recording method that combines laser and magnetic technologies to create high-density erasable storage disks. The recording surface is made of a magnetic recording material, such as a turbium iron alloy, that records magnetic spots (bits) in the typical positive and negative orientation as with regular magnetic disks and tapes. The difference is that the bits are much smaller, because a laser is used to pinpoint the bit. The laser heats the bit to approximately 300 degrees centigrade, at which temperature the bit is realigned when subjected to a magnetic field. In order to record new bits on the surface, the existing bits have to be reset, or prealigned, in one direction first. See *optical disk*.

magnetographic A non-impact page printer technology from Groupe Bull that prints up to 90 ppm. A magnetic image is created by a set of recording heads across a magnetic drum. Monocomponent toner is applied to the drum to develop the image, which is transferred to paper by light pressure and an electrostatic field. The toner is then fused by heat.

The print quality is not as good as a laser printer, but the machines require less maintenance. Original models used fan-fold paper, but newer models use cut sheets and can print on both sides.

mail box The computer storage assigned to a user for electronically transmitted mail.

mail merge The printing of a customized form letter that is usually an option in a word processing or database program. It is made up of a letter and a list of names and addresses. For example, in the letter, Dear A: Thank you for ordering B from our C store..., A, B and C are merge points into which data is inserted from the list. See *field squeeze* and *line squeeze*.

main line See *main loop*.

main loop In programming, the set of instructions that constitute the primary structure of the program. For example, in an invoice print program, the main loop reads the next order and prints the invoice. It repeats itself until there are no more orders to print. In a batch update program, the main loop reads the transaction, updates the master record and repeats itself until all the transactions have been processed. See *loop*.

main memory Same as *memory*.

main storage Same as *memory*.

mainframe A large computer. In the mid 1960s, the ancient days of computers, all computers were mainframes, since the term referred to the cabinet that held the CPU. Although, mainframe still means main housing, it usually refers to a large computer system and all the associated expertise that goes with it.

There are small, medium and large-scale mainframes, handling from a handful to several thousand online terminals. Large-scale mainframes can have hundreds of megabytes of main memory and hundreds of gigabytes of disk storage. Medium and large-scale mainframes use smaller computers as front end processors that connect directly to the communications networks.

The original mainframe vendors were Burroughs, Control Data, GE, Honeywell, IBM, NCR, RCA and Univac, otherwise known as IBM and the seven dwarfs. After GE and RCA's computer divisions were absorbed by Honeywell and Univac respectively, the mainframe vendors were known as IBM and the BUNCH.

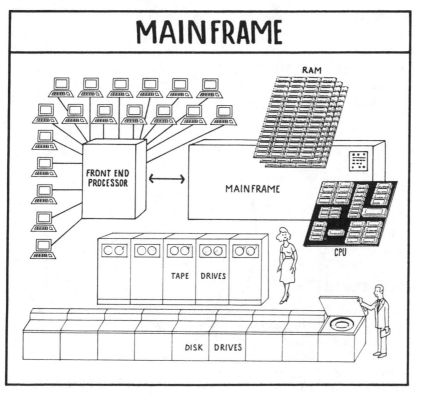

maintenance

(1) Hardware *maintenance* is the testing and cleaning of equipment in order to prevent future problems.

(2) Information system *maintenance* is the routine updating of master files, such as adding and deleting employees and customers and changing credit limits and product prices.

(3) Software or program *maintenance* is the updating of application programs in order to meet changing information requirements.

(4) Disk or file *maintenance* is the periodic reorganizing of online disk files that have undergone fragmentation due to continuous updating.

maintenance credits
Monetary credits that are issued to a customer by the vendor for qualified periods during which the vendor's products are not functioning properly.

maintenance service
The service that is provided in order to keep a product in good operating condition.

major key
The primary key used to identify a record, such as account number or name.

male connector
A plug that is designed to fit into a particular socket, which is the female counterpart.

management science
The study of statistical methods, such as linear programming and simulation, in order to analyze and solve organizational problems. Same as *operations research*.

management support systems
See *decision support system*.

management system
The leadership and control within an organization. It is made up of people interacting with other people and machines that, together, set the goals and

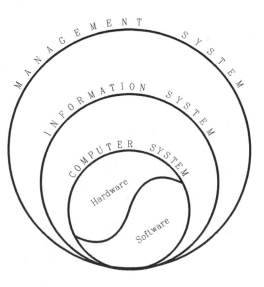

HOW SYSTEMS RELATE

objectives, outline the strategies and tactics, and develop the plans, schedules and necessary controls to run an organization. See *information system*.

Manchester coding See *phase encoding*.

MANTIS
An application development language from Cincom Systems, Inc., that runs on IBM mainframes, Digital's VAX series, Wang, Honeywell, NCR, ICL and Siemens computers. It provides both a procedural and non-procedural language for developing prototypes and applications. MANTIS creates its own internal file and database structures and it works with Cincom's SUPRA database, as well as DB2, IMS and other database managers.

mantissa
The numeric value in a floating point number. See *floating point*.

MAP
(Manufacturing Automation Protocol) A communications protocol introduced by General Motors in 1982. MAP's goal is to provide common standards for the interconnection of computers and programmable machine tools used in factory automation. At the lowest physical level, MAP uses the IEEE 802.3 token bus protocol. Although MAP has provided vitally needed consolidation of standards, it continues to be in a constant state of revision.

MAP is often used in conjunction with TOP, an office protocol developed by Boeing Computer Services. TOP is used in the front office and MAP is used on the factory floor.

map
(1) A set of data that has a corresponding relationship to another set of data.

(2) A list of data or objects as they are currently stored in memory or disk.

(3) To transfer a set of objects from one place to another. For example, program modules on disk are mapped into memory. A graphic image in memory is mapped onto the video screen.

(4) To relate one set of objects with another. For example, a logical database structure is mapped to the physical database. A vendor's protocol stack is mapped to the OSI model.

MAPPER
(MAintaining, Preparing and Processing Executive Reports) A fourth-generation language from Unisys that runs on Unisys mainframes. In 1980, it was introduced as a high-level report writer for use by non-technical personnel. It was later turned into a full-featured, programming system. MAPPER has been used very successfully by many users.

mapping See *map* and *digital mapping*.

marginal test
A system test that introduces values far above and far below the expected values.

mark

(1) A small blip printed on or notched into various storage media used for timing or counting purposes.

(2) To identify a block of text in order to perform some task on it such as deletion, copying and moving.

(3) To identify an item for future reference.

(4) In digital electronics, a 1 bit. Contrast with *space*.

(5) On magnetic disk, a recorded character used to identify the beginning of a track.

(6) In optical recognition and mark sensing, a pencil line in a preprinted box.

(7) On magnetic tape, a *tape mark* is a special character that is recorded after the last character of data.

Mark I An electromechanical calculating machine proposed by Harvard professor Howard Aiken. It was designed and built by IBM from 1939 to 1943 and installed at Harvard in 1944. It used 78 adding machines strung together to perform three calculations per second. It was 51 feet long, weighed five tons and had two card readers, a card punch and two typewriters, all standard IBM equipment of the era. Made of 765,000 parts and 3,300 relays, it sounded like a thousand pairs of knitting needles according to Admiral Grace Hopper, one of its original users. It provided IBM with the experience necessary to develop its own computers in the late 1940s.

MARK I

(Courtesy Smithsonian Institution)

MARK IV See *Crosstalk Mark IV* and *MARK IX*.

MARK IX An application generator from the Answer Systems Div. of Sterling Software that runs on IBM mainframes and personal computers. It stems from MARK IV, the first program generator that used fill-in-the-blanks forms for describing the problem instead of programming it. MARK V was a subsequent online version.

mark sensing The detection of pencil lines in predefined boxes on paper forms or punched cards. The form is designed with boundaries for each pencil stroke that represents a yes, no, single digit or letter, providing all possible answers to each question. A mark sense reader detects the presence or absence of the marks and converts them into the appropriate digital code, or in the case of punched cards, punches holes in the card for punched card entry into the computer.

mask

(1) A pattern that is used to transfer a design onto an object. See *photomask*.

(2) A pattern of bits that is used to accept or reject bit patterns in another set of data. For example, the Boolean AND operation can be used to match a mask of 0s and 1s with a string of data bits. When a 1 occurs in both the mask and the data, the resulting bit will contain a 1 in that position.

Hardware interrupts are often enabled and disabled in this manner with each interrupt assigned a bit position in a mask register.

mask bit A 1 bit in a mask used to control the corresponding bit found in data.

maskable interrupts Hardware interrupts that can be enabled and disabled by software.

masked The state of being disabled or cut off.

mass storage A high-capacity storage device, such as a disk or tape. The term is used to refer to external peripheral storage, in contrast with internal memory.

massage To process data.

massively parallel A parallel processing architecture that uses hundreds or thousands of processors.

master card A master record in punched card format.

master clock A clock that provides the primary source of internal timing for a processor or stand-alone control unit.

master console The primary terminal used by the computer operator or systems programmer to command the computer system.

master control program See *operating system*.

master file A collection of records pertaining to one of the main subjects of an information system, such as customers, employees, products and vendors. Master files contain descriptive data, such as name and address, as well as summary information, such as amount due and year-to-date gross sales. Contrast with *transaction file*.

master record A set of data for an individual subject, such as a customer, employee or vendor. See *master file*.

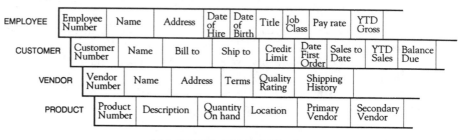

EMPLOYEE	Employee Number	Name	Address	Date of Hire	Date of Birth	Title	Job Class	Pay rate	YTD Gross	
CUSTOMER	Customer Number	Name	Bill to	Ship to		Credit Limit	Date First Order	Sales to Date	YTD Sales	Balance Due
VENDOR	Vendor Number	Name	Address	Terms		Quality Rating	Shipping History			
PRODUCT	Product Number	Description	Quantity On hand	Location			Primary Vendor	Secondary Vendor		

MASTER RECORDS
(Typical Subjects Within an Organization)

math coprocessor A mathematical circuit that performs high-speed floating point operations. It increases the performance of CAD and desktop publishing applications, but the programs must be written to activate its use. See *array processor* and *vector processor*.

mathematical expression A group of characters or symbols representing a quantity or an operation. See *arithmetic expression*.

mathematical function A rule for creating a set of new values from an existing set; for example, the function $f(x) = 2x$ creates a set of even numbers (if x is a whole number).

matrix An array of elements in row and column form. See *x-y matrix*.

matrix printer See *dot matrix* and *printer*.

MAU (Multi-station Access Unit) A central hub in a token ring local area network.

MB, Mb (MegaByte, MegaBit) See *space/time*.

MBps, Mbps (MegaBytes Per Second, MegaBits Per Second) See *space/time*.

MC68000 See *68000*.

MCA (Micro Channel Architecture) See *Micro Channel*.

MCGA (Multi Color Graphics Array) A video display standard built into low-end models of IBM's PS/2 series. Due to the limited number of models that use it, it is not well supported by software vendors. See *PC display modes*.

MCI decision The FCC decree in 1969 that granted MCI the right to compete with the Bell System by providing private, intercity telecommunications services.

MDA (Monochrome Display Adapter) The first PC video display standard for monochrome text from IBM. Due to its lack of graphics, MDA cards were often replaced with Hercules Graphics cards, which provided both text and graphics. MDA was superseded by VGA. See *PC display modes*.

mechanical mouse A mouse that uses a rubber ball that makes contact with several wheels inside the unit. Contrast with *optical mouse*.

media The material that stores or transmits data, for example, floppy disks, magnetic tape, coaxial cable and twisted wire pair.

media access method An access method used in a local area network, such as Token Ring, Ethernet and ARCNET.

media conversion The converting of data from one storage medium to another, such as from disk to tape or from one type of disk pack to another.

media failure The condition of not being able to read from or write to a storage device, such as a disk or tape, due to a defect in the magnetic recording surface.

medium frequency An electromagnetic wave that oscillates in the range from 300,000 to 3,000,000 Hz. See *electromagnetic spectrum*.

meg Same as *mega*.

mega
Million. Abreviated "M." For example, 10Mbytes is 10 million bytes. Mega may refer more precisely to the value 1,048,576 when the number is derived from binary notation. See *space/time*.

MEGA A personal computer series from Atari that is compatible with the Atari ST series. It uses a 68000 CPU and comes with its TOS operating system built into ROM. The GEM interface is included which provides a graphical interface for applications. A built-in floppy disk is standard, and hard drives and removable hard disk cartridges are available. Also included is a MIDI interface and a three-voice sound chip.

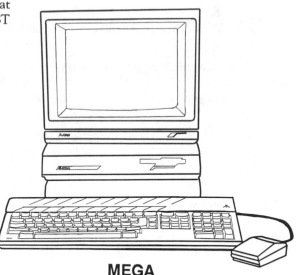

MEGA

megabit 1,000,000 or 1,048,576 bits. It is also written as Mb, Mbit and M-bit. See *space/time*.

megabyte 1,000,000 or 1,048,576 bytes or characters. It is also written as MB, Mbyte and M-byte. See *space/time*.

megaflops (mega FLoating point OPerations per Second) One million floating point operations per second.

megahertz One million cycles per second. See *MHz*.

megapel display In computer graphics, a display system that handles a million or more pixels. A resolution of 1,000 lines by 1,000 dots requires a million pixels for the full screen image.

membrane keyboard A flat keyboard used as an economical keyboard alternative or as a dust and dirtproof keyboard for hazardous environments. It is constructed of two thin plastic sheets (membranes) that contain flexible printed circuits made of electrically conductive ink. The circuits oppose each other in the middle. Covering the top membrane is a printed keyboard panel, and sandwiched between the two membranes is a spacer sheet with holes corresponding to the keys on the keyboard. When a user presses a simulated key, the top membrane is pushed through the hole in the spacer, making contact with the bottom membrane and completing the circuit.

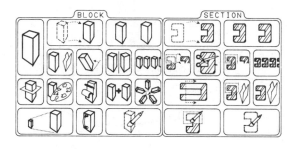

Typical overlay for restaurant management

Overlay for DesignCAD software package

MEMBRANE KEYBOARD

(Courtesy Polytel Computer Products Corp.)

This Polytel KEYPORT 300 membrane keyboard is used with an overlay for many different applications.

memo field A field in a database that holds a variable amount of text. The text in memo fields may be stored in a companion file, but it is treated as if it were part of the data record. For example, in the dBASE command: `list name, biography`, the name would come from the DBF data file and the biography would come from the DBT text (memo field) file.

memory The computer's working storage that is physically a collection of RAM chips. It is an important resource of the computer, since it determines the size and number of programs that can be run at the same time, as well as the amount of data that can be processed instantly.

All program execution and data processing takes place in memory. The program's instructions are copied into memory from a disk or tape and are then extracted from memory into an electronic circuit for analysis and execution. The

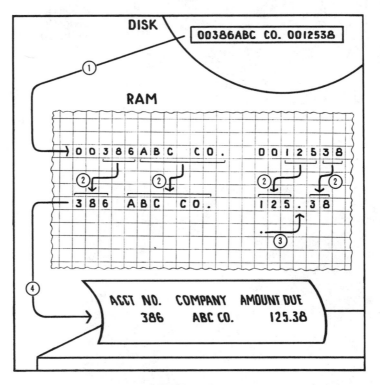

MEMORY

Memory allows data to be broken apart and rearranged in any prescribed manner.

(1) An entire data record is read from the disk and written into memory.

(2) The individual characters are copied from the input buffer to the output buffer. Numeric data is stripped of preceding zeros by a special format instructions that filters out the unwanted zeros.

(3) The decimal point also comes from a format instruction, which copies it into the specified location.

(4) The formatted line is read from memory and transmitted to the printer.

instructions direct the computer to input data into memory from a keyboard, disk, tape or communications channel.

As data is entered into memory, the previous contents of that memory space is lost. Once the data is in memory, it can be processed (calculated, compared and copied). Then the results can be output from memory to a screen, printer, disk, tape or communications channel.

Memory can be viewed as an electronic checkerboard with each square on the board holding one byte of data or instruction. Since each square has a separate address like a post office box, the individual character within the square can be manipulated independently from all the rest of the squares. Because of this, the computer can break apart programs into instructions and data records into fields, all of which are stored as large blocks on disks and tapes.

Memory Doesn't Usually Remember

Oddly enough, the computer's memory doesn't remember anything when the power is turned off. That's why you have to save your files before you quit your program. Although there are memory chips that do hold their content permanently (ROMs, PROMs, EPROMs, etc.), they're used for internal control purposes and not for the user's data.

The "remembering" memory in a computer system is its disks and tapes, and although they are also called *memory devices,* many prefer to call them storage devices in order to differentiate them from internal memory.

Other terms for memory are RAM, *main memory, main storage, primary storage, read/write memory, core* and *core storage*.

memory bank
(1) A physical section of computer memory. Computers can be designed with multiple memory banks that allow data transfers to take place within each of the memory banks at the same time.

(2) Refers generically to a computer system that holds data.

memory based Programs that hold all data in memory for processing. Almost all spreadsheets are memory based so that a change in data at one end of the spreadsheet can be instantly reflected at the other end.

memory cache See *cache memory*.

memory cell One bit of memory. In dynamic RAM memory, a cell is made up of one transistor and one capacitor. In static RAM memory, a cell is made up of about five transistors.

memory chip A chip that holds programs and data either temporarily or permanently. The major categories of memory chips are RAMs and ROMs.

memory cycle The series of operations that take place to read or write a byte of memory. For destructive memories, it includes the regeneration of the bits.

memory cycle time The time it takes to perform one memory cycle.

memory dump A display or printout of the contents of memory. When a program abends, a memory dump can be taken in order to examine the status of the program at the time of the crash. The programmer looks into the buffers to see which data items were being worked on when it failed. Counters, switches and flags in the program can also be inspected.

memory management The way a computer deals with its memory, which includes memory protection, virtual memory and bank switching techniques. See *virtual memory*, EMS and EMM.

memory protection A technique that prohibits one program from accidentally clobbering another active program. A protective boundary is created around the program, and instructions within the program are prohibited from referencing data outside of that boundary.

An example of a technique is the subdivision of all memory into small blocks of 2,048 bytes. An index to all the blocks is maintained in which each entry becomes a key to that block. When a program is brought into memory, it is assigned a number, and all the blocks it occupies are assigned the same number in the key index. Before the computer executes an instruction, it matches the memory block number with the program number, and if it doesn't match, it prohibits the operation by interrupting the computer.

memory sniffing A diagnostic routine that continually tests memory while the computer is processing data. The processor uses cycle stealing techniques that allow it to perform its memory test during unused machine cycles. An entire memory bank can be sniffed every few minutes. The term was coined by Data General Corporation.

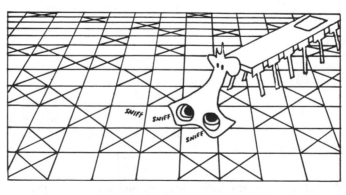

MEMORY SNIFFING

memory typewriter An enhanced typewriter that holds a limited number of pages of text in its memory, and, with a display screen of one or two lines, allow for text editing. It provides various word processing functions, such as headers, footers, page numbering, centering, underline, boldface and italics. A memory typewriter with disk storage is more like a word processor; however, the small displays make many operations more tedious and cumbersome than a full screen.

menu

A list of available options and commands displayed on screen in an interactive program. Selection of a menu option is accomplished by entering the number or letter assigned to it, by pressing the letter key of the first letter of the word or by highlighting the option and pressing the return key or the mouse button. See *Lotus menu* and *pull-down menu*.

Menu A software subsidiary of Black Box Corporation that offers the world's most complete listing of software information for local area networks and PC, Apple II, Macintosh and Commodore personal computers.

menu bar A row of on-screen menu options.

menu-driven A program that is commanded by selecting options from a list. Contrast with *command-driven*.

merge See *mail merge* and *concatenate*.

mesa A semiconductor process used in the 1960s for creating the sublayers in a transistor. The deep etching of the Mesa process gave way to the planar process that creates sublayers by implanting chemicals into the substrate.

mesh network

A net-like communications network in which there are at least two pathways to each node. The term network means net-like as well as communications network. Thus, the term mesh is used to avoid saying network communications network.

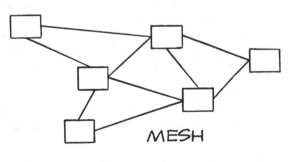

MESH

message In communications, a set of data that is transmitted over a communications line. Just as a program becomes a job when it's running in the computer, data becomes a message when it's transmitted over a network.

message handling

(1) In communications, a system of electronic mail that handles text (memos, letters) in document form.

(2) In communications, the lower level protocols that transfer data over a network, which assemble and disassemble the data into the appropriate codes for transmission.

message queue A storage space in memory or on disk that holds incoming transmissions until the computer can process them.

message switch A computer that is used to switch data from one point to another. Computers have always been ideal message switches due to their input/output and compare capabilities. When a computer acts as a message switch, it inputs the message, compares its destination with a set of stored destinations and then outputs it to a selected communications channel.

metafile Refers to various file formats used for data interchange, for example, CGM (computer graphics metafile) and Windows Metafile.

metalanguage A language that is used to describe another language.

meter The basic unit of the metric system (39.37 inches). A yard is about 9/10ths of a meter (0.9144 meter).

MFM (Modified Frequency Modulation) A recording technique commonly used for magnetic disks. MFM reduces the number of synchronization bits required on the disk from earlier FM recording methods.

MHS

(1) (Message Handling Service) An electronic mail system developed by Action Technologies, Inc., and licensed by Novell for its NetWare operating systems. It allows for the transfer and routing of messages between users and provides store and forward capabilities. MHS also provides gateways into IBM's PROFS, Digital's All-in-1 office automation system and X.400 message systems.

(2) (Message Handling System) An electronic mail system. MHS often refers to mail systems that conform to the OSI (open systems interconnect) model, which are based on CCITT's X.400 international message protocol.

MHz (MegaHertZ) One million cycles per second. It is often used with reference to a computer's clock rate, which is a raw measure of its internal processing speed. For example, a 12MHz 286 computer processes data internally (calculates, compares, etc.) twice as fast as a 6MHz 286. However, disk speed and caching play a major role in the computer's actual performance.

mickey A unit of mouse movement typically set at 1/200th of an inch.

MICR (Magnetic Ink Character Recognition) The special encoded characters on bank checks and deposit slips. MICR readers detect the encoded characters and convert them into digital data.

ꓱ 234 567890

ıꞁ ꞁıı ꞁꓽ ꞁ

MICR CHARACTERS

micro
(1) A microcomputer or personal computer.

(2) One millionth. See *space/time*.

(3) Microscopic, or tiny.

(4) In CDC assembly language programming, a macro call that is substituted with a single variable.

Micro Channel A 32-bit bus used in high-end models of IBM's PS/2 series, RS/6000 series and certain 9370 models. It is designed for multiprocessing, which allows two or more CPUs to work in parallel within the computer at the same time. Micro Channel boards are not interchangeable with PC bus boards.

Micro Channel boards are designed with built-in identification that is interrogated by the operating system, thus eliminating manual switch settings that are sometimes required and the conflicts that can arise with the original PC bus. It transfers data at 20MB per second and has special modes for increasing speeds to 40 and 80MB/sec. Future enhancements are planned to take it to 64 bits and 160MB/sec.

micro manager An individual who manages the personal computer operations within an organization. A micro manager is responsible for the analysis, selection, installation, training and maintenance of personal computer hardware and software. See *information center*.

Micro PDP-11 A microcomputer version of the PDP-11 minicomputer from Digital. Introduced in 1975, it uses the Q-bus architecture and serves as a stand-alone computer or is built into other equipment.

micro to mainframe The interconnection of personal computers to mainframes. A personal computer can be made to emulate a mainframe terminal with a plug-in board, such as an IRMAboard, and have an interactive session with the mainframe. Data can also be downloaded from the mainframe into the personal computer for analysis.

microchip Same as *chip*.

microcircuit A miniaturized, electronic circuit, such as is found on an integrated circuit. See *chip*.

microcode A permanent memory that holds the elementary circuit operations that the computer must perform for each machine instruction in its instruction set. It acts as a translation layer between the instruction and the electronic level of the computer and enables the computer architect to more easily add new types of machine instructions without having to design electronic circuits. See *microprogramming*.

Microcom Protocol See MNP.

microcomputer A computer that uses a microprocessor for its CPU. Synonymous with personal computer.

microelectronics The miniaturization of electronic circuits. See *chip*.

microfiche Pronounced "micro-feesh." A 4x6" sheet of film that holds several hundred miniaturized document pages. See *micrographics*.

microfilm A continuous film strip that holds several thousand miniaturized document pages. See *micrographics*.

microfloppy disk A 3.5" floppy disk encased in a rigid plastic shell. Developed by Sony, these disks have quickly become the medium of choice. They hold more data and are much easier to store, transport and handle than their 5.25" counterparts.

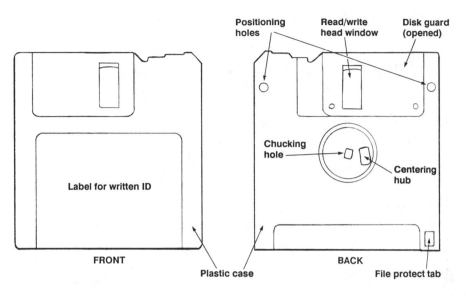

Positioning holes · Read/write head window · Disk guard (opened)

Chucking hole

Centering hub

Label for written ID

FRONT

BACK

Plastic case

File protect tab

MICROFLOPPY DISK

microform In micrographics, a medium that contains microminiaturized images such as microfiche and microfilm.

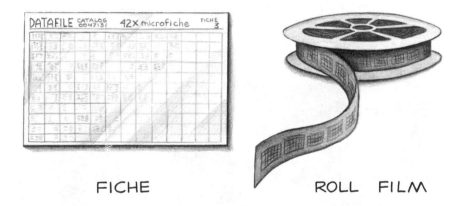

FICHE

ROLL FILM

micrographics The production, handling and use of microfilm and microfiche (microforms). Microforms are generated by devices that take pictures of paper documents, or by COM (computer output microfilm) units that accept output directly from the computer. The documents are magnified for human viewing by specialized readers, some of which can automatically locate a particular page using various indexing techniques.

Microfiche and microfilm have always been an economical alternative for high-volume data and picture storage. However, optical disks are beginning to compete with film-based systems and, in time, may become the preferred storage medium.

microimage In micrographics, a *microimage* is any photographic image of information that is too small to be read without magnification.

microinstruction An instruction in microcode. It is the most elementary computer operation that can take place, for example, moving a bit from one register to another. It takes several microinstructions to carry out one machine instruction. See *microprogramming*.

microjacket In micrographics, two sheets of transparent plastic that are bonded together to create channels into which strips of microfilm are inserted and stored.

micromainframe A personal computer with mainframe or near mainframe speed.

micromini A personal computer with minicomputer or near minicomputer speed.

micron One millionth of a meter. Approx. 1/25,000 of an inch. The tiny elements that make up a transistor on a chip are measured in microns. Measurements below the micron level are made in Angstroms, in which 10,000 Angstroms equals one micron.

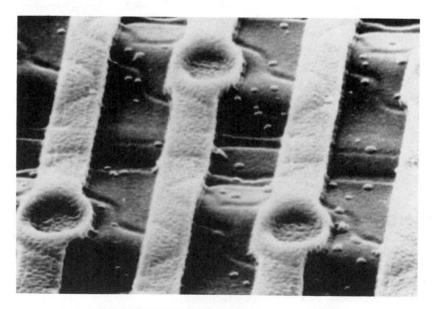

A MICROSCOPIC VIEW OF A CHIP

(Courtesy AT&T)

MicroPhone II A communications program for the Macintosh from Software Ventures, Inc. It supports a variety of terminals and protocols and includes a script language for automating communications tasks.

microprocessor A CPU on a single chip. In order to function as a computer, it requires a power supply, clock and memory. First-generation microprocessors were Intel's 8080, Zilog's Z80, Motorola's 6800 and Rockwell International's 6502. The first microprocessor was created by Intel. See *Intel*.

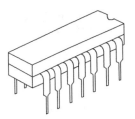

MICROPROCESSOR

microprogram Same as *microcode*.

microprogramming The programming of microcode, which is the translation layer between a machine instruction and the elementary operations (microinstructions) necessary to carry out the instruction.

micropublishing In micrographics, the issuing of new or reformatted information on microfilm for sale or distribution.

microrepublishing In micrographics, the issuing of microfilm that has been previously or is simultaneously published in hardcopy for sale or distribution.

microsecond One millionth of a second. See *space/time*.

Microsoft (Microsoft Corporation) A leading microcomputer software company founded in 1975 by Paul Allen and Bill Gates, two college students who wrote the first BASIC interpreter for the Intel 8080 microprocessor. They licensed it to Micro Instrumentation and Telemetry Systems to accompany its Altair 8800 microcomputer kit. By the end of 1976, more than 10,000 Altairs were sold with Microsoft's BASIC.

Versions of MBASIC were licensed to Radio Shack, Apple Computer and

WILLIAM H. GATES
(Courtesy Microsoft Corporation)

myriads of other hardware vendors. Eventually, a version called GW-BASIC (Gee Whiz BASIC) was developed for 16-bit personal computers. Although Microsoft quickly became a leader in microcomputer programming languages, its outstanding success is due to supplying IBM with its DOS operating system and the compatible companies with the MS-DOS version.

Paul Allen has since left and founded his own software company called Asymetrix Corporation.

Microsoft's position as the supplier of the major operating systems to the world's largest computer base gives it considerable influence over the future of this industry.

PAUL G. ALLEN
(Courtesy Asymetrix Corporation)

Microsoft Word
A full-featured word processing program for PCs and the Macintosh from Microsoft. The PC version provides both graphics-based and text-based interfaces for working with a document. Version 3.1 provides up to eight document windows.

Microsoft Works
An integrated software program for PCs and the Macintosh from Microsoft. It provides file management with relational-like capabilities, word processing, spreadsheet, business graphics and communications capabilities in one package.

MicroStation
A full-featured, computer-aided design and drafting system (CADD) for PCs from Intergraph Corporation. It is a major subset of and fully compatible with Interactive Graphics Design System (IGDS), the core software of all Intergraph VAX-based systems. Microstation provides 3-D capabilities, dual screens, a powerful user command language, an interface to dBASE III and many powerful drafting features.

MicroVAX
A series of entry-level VAX computers from Digital Equipment Corporation, introduced in 1983, which run under VMS or ULTRIX. Models I, II, 3300, 3400, 3800 and 3900 are Q-bus machines. Models 2000 and 3100 are non-Q-bus machines.

microwave
An electromagnetic wave that vibrates at 1GHz and above. Microwaves are the transmission frequencies used in communications satellites as well as in line-of-sight systems on earth.

MIDI (Musical Instrument Digital Interface) A standard protocol for the interchange of musical information between musical instruments, synthesizers and computers. It defines the codes for a musical event, which includes the start of a note, its pitch, length, volume and musical attributes, such as vibrato. It also defines codes for various button, dial and pedal adjustments used on synthesizers. MIDI is commonly used to synchronize notes produced on several synthesizers. Its control messages can orchestrate a series of synthesizers, each playing a part of the musical score.

A computer with a MIDI interface can be used to record a musical session, but instead of recording the analog sound waves as in a tape recorder, the computer stores the music as keystroke and control codes. The recording can be edited in an entirely different manner than with conventional recording, for example, the rhythm can be changed by editing the timing codes in the MIDI messages. In addition, the computer can easily transpose a performance from B major into D major.

The original objective of MIDI was to allow the keyboard of one synthesizer to play notes generated by another synthesizer. However, since Version 1.0 in August 1983, the standard has synthesized more than just music; it has brought the world of electronic control of music to virtually everybody and has benefitted musicians and teachers alike.

MIDI devices require a special plug and connector (port) that is built into the musical instruments and synthesizers. The MIDI port is standard on Atari ST personal computers and can be adapted to other personal computers. The Macintosh is also popular among MIDI enthusiasts, since its graphics-based screen produces a crisp image for musical notation.

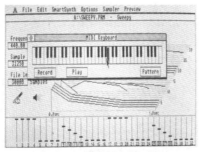

SOFTSYNTH™ Digidesign

Digidesign's Softsynth program, which runs on Atari and Macintosh computers, is an Additive Synthesis program that lets users create sounds and mix waveforms together. The keyboard on screen simulates a MIDI keyboard that is attached to the system and allows users to play the keyboard from the computer.

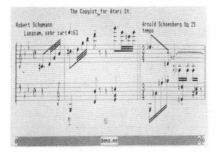

THE COPYIST™ Dr. T's™ Music Software

Dr. T's Music Software program, The Copyist, which runs on Ataris, Amigas and PCs, is a musical scoring program. It lets users create scores from scratch, or take MIDI recorded music and transcribe it into traditional musical notation.

MIDI SOFTWARE

(Courtesy Digidesign and Dr. T's Music Software)

midicomputer A computer that has a performance and capacity somewhere between a minicomputer and a mainframe.

mill A very old term for processor, in the context of number crunching.

millimeter One thousandth of a meter, or 1/25th of an inch.

million One thousand times one thousand. See *mega* and *microsecond*.

millisecond One thousandth of a second. See *space/time*.

MIMD (Multiple Instruction stream Multiple Data stream) A computer architecture that uses multiple processors, each processing its own set of instructions simultaneously and independently of the others. Contrast with *SIMD*.

mini See *minicomputer*.

mini-supercomputer A supercomputer that is 25% to 100% as fast as a supercomputer, but costs considerably less. Major vendors in this arena are Convex Computer, Alliant Computer Systems and Multiflow Computer.
   Note: A mini-supercomputer is not the same as a supermini.

minicomputer A small to medium-scale computer that functions as a single workstation, or as a multiuser system with up to several hundred terminals. A minicomputer system costs roughly from $20,000 to $250,000.

In 1959, Digital launched the minicomputer industry with its PDP-1. Soon after, Data General and Hewlett-Packard introduced minicomputers, and eventually Wang, Tandem, Datapoint and Prime joined the ranks. IBM has introduced several minicomputer series, including the System/34, System/36, System/38, Series/1, 8100 and AS/400. See *supermini*.

Since high-end microcomputers and low-end mainframes offer price and performance in the traditional minicomputer niche, the term is beginning to have less significance. Some companies are replacing this term with small, medium and large-scale designations.

minifloppy A 5.25" floppy disk, introduced by Shugart in 1978, that is used extensively in personal computers. It superseded IBM's 8" floppy, and it, too, is slowly being superseded by the 3.5" microfloppy developed by Sony.

minor key A secondary key used to identify a record. For example, if transactions are sorted by account number and date, account number is the major key and date is the minor key.

MIPS (Million Instructions Per Second) The execution speed of a computer. For example, .5 MIPS is 500,000 instructions per second. A large mainframe can perform 10 to 50 MIPS, whereas an inexpensive microprocessor might be in the .05 MIPS range.

MIPS rates are not uniform across all vendors' lines. Some rates are best-case mixes and some are averages. As a result, MIPS has been referred to as "MisInformation to Promote Sales."

MIPS rate, which is tied to the computer's clock speed, is only one factor in overall performance. Bus and channel speed and bandwidth (8-bit, 16-bit, 32-bit), disk and memory speed, memory management techniques and system software also determine total throughput of a computer system.

Mirror II A communications program for PCs from Softklone Distributing Corporation that supports a variety of terminals and protocols and provides a learn mode for recording commonly used sequences.

Mirrors A program conversion package from Micrografx, Inc., that allows DOS/Windows programs to be converted to run under OS/2's Presentation Manager with little or no modification. To create a PM application, a Window's application is recompiled and linked to Mirrors. Calls to the Windows library are redirected to calls to the PM library routines.

MIS

(1) (Management Information System) An information system that has integrated the data for all of the departments it serves. It implies a system that provides operations and management with the information they require.

MIS was the buzzword of the mid to late 1970s, when online systems were being implemented within all large organizations. See *decision support system*.

(2) (Management Information Systems or Management Information Services) A formal name for the information processing department within an organization.

mixed object Refers to the ability to handle some combination of text, graphics, voice and video within the same file or document. See *compound document*.

ML A symbolic programming language developed in the 1970s at the University of Edinburgh, Scotland. It is similar to LISP with commands and structures like Pascal.

MMU

(1) (Memory Management Unit) A circuit that translates logical addresses into physical addresses for virtual memory and other memory management functions.

(2) (Memory Management Unit) In PCs, may refer to a plug-in board that allows DOS applications to access unused memory in the 640 to 1024K area.

mnemonic Pronounced "nuh-monic" and means memory aid. A name assigned to a machine function. For example, in DOS, COM1 is the mnemonic assigned to serial port #1. Programming languages are almost entirely mnemonics.

MNP (Microcom Networking Protocol) A family of communications protocols from Microcom, Inc., that have become de facto standards for error correction and data compression.

Class 1	Half-duplex asynchronous transmission.
Class 2	Full-duplex asynchronous transmission.
Class 3	Full-duplex synchronous transmission using HDLC framing techniques using 64-byte blocks. Start/stop bits stripped.
Class 4	Increased throughput. Shorter headers, frames up to 256 bytes. Some vendors adjust frame size based on line quality.
Class 5	Compresses data up to two times.
Class 6	Starts at V.22bis modulation and switches to V.29 if possible. Uses pseudo-duplexing ping-pong method for faster turnaround of V.29 transmission.
Class 7	Compresses data up to three times.
Class 8	Not in use.

Class 9	Adds Piggy-back Acknowledgement* and selective retransmission for more efficient transport of data. Provides better performance over variety of links.
Class 10	Adds Adverse Channel Enhancements* for efficient operation on extremely noisy lines and is well suited for rural, cellular and international lines.

* Proprietary techniques of Microcom, Inc.

Mockingboard A sound synthesizer board for the Apple II from Sweet Micro Systems that generates stereo music, sound effects and synthetic speech. A text-to-speech program is also included.

MODCA (Mixed Object Document Content Architecure) An extension of IBM's DCA file format that includes text, graphics and scanned images. DCA provides for only text.

mode An operational state that a system has been switched to. It implies at least two possible conditions. There are countless modes for hardware and software. See *protected mode, burst mode, insert mode, supervisor state* and *program state*.

model
(1) A particular style or type of hardware device.

(2) A mathematical representation of a device or process that is used for analysis and planning. Models are sets of equations that represent a condition or set of operations in the real world. It differs from a list of descriptions, in that it also describes the interrelationships of the components. For example, a data model indicates how data is perceived by different departments and is used to forecast bottlenecks if users request certain kinds of information.

Marketing, distribution and manufacturing models are a series of equations into which variables can be plugged in order to test the impact of a variety of decisions.

Whereas a business model can be very simple, **net income = gross revenues - expenses**, scientific models require elaborate formulas to represent airplanes, rivers and planets. Scientific models are used to simulate the movement and change of real-world objects.

model-based expert system
An expert system that is based on fundamental knowledge of the design and function of an object. Such systems are used to diagnose equipment problems, for example. Contrast wtih *rule-based expert system*, which follows the path a human expert would take in diagnosing the situation.

modeling The simulation of a condition or activity by performing a set of equations on a set of data. See *model, financial planning system* and *spreadsheet*.

modem (MOdulator-DEModulator) A device that adapts a terminal or computer to a telephone line. It converts the computer's digital pulses into frequencies within the audio range of the telephone and converts them back into pulses at the receiving side.

Specialized modems are used to connect computers to a broadband local area network, which, similar to telephones, use electromagnetic waves for transmission signals.

The modem handles the dialing and answering of the call and controls the the transmission speed. Modems used on telephone lines transmit at speeds of 300, 1200, 2400, 4800, 9600 and 19200 bits per second. The effective data rate is about 10% of the bit rate; thus, 300bps is equivalent to 30 characters per second. It would take a full minute to fill up a video screen at 300bps; 15 seconds at 1200bps and about seven seconds at 2400bps.

Using a modem with a personal computer requires a free serial port to hook it up and a communications program.

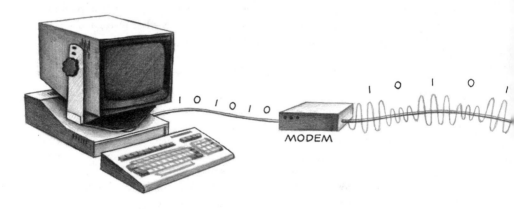

modem eliminator In communications, a device that allows two computers in close proximity to be hooked up without modems. In asynchronous systems, such as when the serial ports of two personal computers are connected together, a modem eliminator connects the send line on one end to the receive line on the other. In this case, a modem eliminator is the same as a *null modem cable*.

In synchronous systems, the modem eliminator provides active intelligence with regard to synchronizing the lines.

modify structure A command in a database language that allows the user to change the structure of the records in the file. For example, field lengths and field names can be changed, and fields can be added or deleted. It also usually converts the old data file into the new structure without the loss of data, unless, of course, fields have been truncated or deleted.

Modula-2 (MODUlar LAnguage-2) A high-level programming language developed by the Swiss professor Nicklaus Wirth, creator of Pascal. Modula-2 was introduced in 1979 and is an enhanced version of the Pascal language. Modula-2 supports separate compilation of modules, whereas Pascal does not.

The following example changes fahrenheit to centigrade in Modula-2:

```
    MODULE FahrToCent;
FROM InOut IMPORT ReadReal,WriteReal,
WriteString,WriteLn;
VAR Fahr:REAL;
BEGIN
WriteString("Enter fahrenheit ");
ReadReal(Fahr);
WriteLn;
WriteString("Centigrade is ");
WriteReal((Fahr - 32) * 5 / 9);
    END  FahrToCent
```

modular programming

A technique that breaks down the design of a problem into separate components or modules, each of which can be programmed as a single unit. It allows different programmers to develop parts of the program so that each part can be tested separately and then merged together. It imposes a structure onto the design of the program that aids in documenting and maintaining the program.

modulate

To mix a voice or data signal onto a carrier for transmission in a communications network. Data is modulated onto the carrier by various methods, including *amplitude modulation*, in which the height of the wave is changed; or *frequency modulation*, in which the frequency is changed; or *phase modulation*, in which the phase (polarity) of the wave is changed. Contrast with *demodulate*.

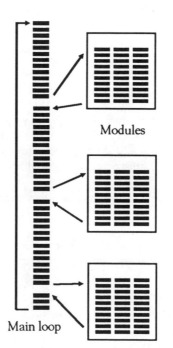

Modules

Main loop

module A self-contained hardware or software component that interacts with a larger system. Hardware modules are often made to plug into a main system. Program modules are designed to handle a specific task within a larger program.

modulo A mathematical operation in which the result is the remainder. For example, 20 modulo-3 generates a remainder of 2, 20 modulo-2 results in a 0.

moire Pronounced "mor-ray." An objectionable pattern that results from families of curves being superimposed on one another. For example, many halftones are made up of curved patterns that can cause moire patterns when scanned into the computer.

molecular beam epitaxy A technique that builds up the tiny layers of a chip at the atomic level. Layers as thin as two atoms can be deposited on the chip in extremely precise locations. It may replace the traditional chip-making process, which creates layers by implanting materials into an existing substrate.

monadic Meaning one; a single item or an operation that deals with one item or operand.

monitor
(1) A high-resolution screen that is used to display the output of a computer, camera, VCR or other video-generating device.

(2) A software program that provides various utility and control functions, such as setting bit rates for communications and other devices. The monitor, which usually resides in a ROM chip, may also contain the autostart routine, which performs diagnostics upon startup and loads the operating system.

(3) A software program that monitors the progress of activities within a computer system.

(4) A device that provides performance statistics of a running system. It is attached to various printed circuit boards within the processor cabinet.

monochrome The display of one foreground color and one background color; for example, black on white, white on black and blue on white.

monolithic integrated circuit An integrated circuit in which the base material, or substrate, not only holds the circuit, but contains active elements that take part in the operation of the circuit. This is the most common form of chip fabrication.

monospacing A set of characters that have uniform horizontal spacing, such as 10 characters per inch. Contrast with *proportional spacing*.

Monte Carlo method A set of techniques which provides approximate solutions to problems that can be expressed mathematically. Using random numbers and trial and error, the Monte Carlo method repeatedly calculates the equations to arrive at a solution.

MORE II A desktop presentation program and outline processor for the Macintosh from Symantec Corporation. It provides a variety of functions, including writing and spell checking, outlining, presentation-quality text and graphics and 35mm slide output.

morray See *moire*.

Morse code A data code represented by dots and dashes, developed by Samuel Morse in the mid-19th century. A dot can be a voltage, carrier wave or light beam of one duration, while a dash is a longer duration. It was used to send telegraph messages before the telephone and was used in World War II for line-of-sight signalling with a light beam.

MOS (Metal Oxide Semiconductor) Pronounced "moss." One of two major categories of designing and making logic and memory chips (the other is bipolar). MOS technology derives its name from its use of metal, oxide and semiconductor layers. There are several varieties of MOS technologies, including PMOS, NMOS and CMOS.

MOSFET (Metal Oxide Semiconductor Field Effect Transistor) A common type of transistor fabricated as a discrete component or into MOS integrated circuits.

most significant bit The leftmost 1 bit in a byte, word or field. It is the bit with the greatest value in the number or item.

most significant digit The digit, other than 0, that is in the leftmost position of the number. It is the digit with the greatest value in the number.

motherboard The main printed circuit board in an electronic device which contains sockets that accept additional boards. In a personal computer, the motherboard contains the bus, the microprocessor and all the chips used for controlling the peripherals that come with the system, such as the keyboard, text and graphics display, serial and parallel ports and joystick and mouse interfaces.

Motif See *OSF/Motif*.

Motorola (Motorola, Inc.) A leading manufacturer of semiconductor devices that was founded in 1928 by Paul V. Galvin in Chicago. Its first product allowed radios to operate from household current instead of batteries. In the

1930s, the company commercialized car radios under the Motorola brand suggesting "sound in motion," and in 1947, changed the company name.

By the 1960s, Motorola was a leader in communications and consumer electronics and had built its first semiconductor facility. It eventually began to move away from consumer electronics, selling off its color TV business by the mid-1970s.

Although Motorola is known within the computer industry for its 68000 family of microprocessors, it is a nine billion dollar company (1989) involved in semiconductors, radio and data communications systems and automotive and industrial products, among others.

mouse A puck-like object that is used as a pointing and drawing device. As it is rolled across the desktop in any direction, the cursor, or pointer, moves correspondingly on the screen.

MOUSE

A mouse is similar to the pen-like or puck-like device on a digitizer tablet, formally called the *tablet cursor*. However, the tablet cursor makes contact with the tablet with absolute reference. Placing it on the upper left part of the tablet moves the screen cursor to that same location on screen. With a mouse, the movement is relative. When the mouse is moved, the screen cursor moves from its existing location. The mouse could be moved across your arm, and the screen cursor would move as well. See *mechanical mouse, optical mouse, serial mouse* and *bus mouse*.

MOV (Metal Oxide Varister) An electronic component that prevents power surges from passing through a line.

move

(1) In programming, to copy data from one place in memory to another. At the end of the move, the source and destination data are identical.

(2) In word processing and graphics, to relocate text and images to another part of the document or drawing.

MPE (MultiProgramming Executive) A multitasking operating system that runs on the Hewlett-Packard 3000 series of minicomputers.

MPU (MicroProcessor Unit) Same as *microprocessor*.

ms (MilliSecond) See *space/time*.

MS-DOS (MicroSoft-Disk Operating System) A single user operating system for PCs from Microsoft. It is almost identical to IBM's version, which is named DOS, and both versions are called DOS generically. See *PC (Operating Environment)*.

MS-Net Microsoft's version of PC-Network introduced in 1985.

MS-Windows (MicroSoft Windows) See *Windows*.

MSI (Medium Scale Integration) Refers to a small number of electronic components built onto a single chip. MSI ranges approximately from 100 to 3,000 transistors on a chip.

MTBF (Mean Time Between Failure) The average time a component works without failure. It is the number of failures that occur divided into the total number of hours under observation.

MTS (Modular TV System) The stereo channel added to the NTSC television standard, which includes the SAP audio channel for special use.

MTTR (Mean Time To Repair) The average time it takes to repair a failed component.

MULTIBUS A bus architecture from Intel that is used in a variety of industrial, military and aerospace applications. It is considered an advanced bus because of features, such as message passing, auto configuration and software interrupts. MULTIBUS I is a 16-bit bus, and MULTIBUS II is a 32-bit architecture.

multicomputer Same as *parallel computer*.

MULTICS (MULTiplexed Information and Computing Service) An operating system that runs on Honeywell computers. Developed at MIT and Bell Labs in the mid 1960s, it introduced advanced concepts and was the first timesharing operating system. It was used on GE's mainframes, which were later absorbed into the Honeywell product line.

multidrop line See *multipoint line*.

MultiFinder See *Finder*.

multiline A cable, channel or bus that contains two or more transmission paths (wires or optical fibers).

multimastering See *bus mastering*.

MultiMate A word processing program for PCs from Ashton-Tate Corporation that was originally noted for its similarity to the Wang word processing systems of the 1970s. MultiMate Version 4.0, introduced in late 1989, has a large number of advanced features.

multimedia The communicating of information in more than one form and includes the use of text, audio, graphics, animated graphics and full-motion video.

MultiPlan A spreadsheet for CP/M machines and PCs from Microsoft. It was one of the first spreadsheets and came out soon after SuperCalc.

multiplexing The transmission of multiple signals over a single communications line or computer channel. The two common multiplexing techniques are FDM, which separates signals by modulating the data onto different carrier frequencies, and TDM, which separates signals by interleaving bits one after the other.

multiplexor In communications, a device that merges several low-speed transmissions into one high-speed transmission and reverses the operation at the other end. See multiplexing.

multiplexor channel A computer channel that interchanges signals between the CPU and several low-speed peripheral devices, such as terminals and printers. Some multiplexor channels have an optional burst mode that can provide a high-speed transfer of data to only one peripheral device at a time.

multipoint line In communications, a single line that interconnects three or more devices.

multiported memory A memory that provides more than one access path to its contents. It allows the same bank of memory to be read and written simultaneously, but not the exact same bit location.

multiprocessing The simultaneous processing with two or more processors in one computer, or two or more computers that are processing together. When two or more computers are used, they are tied together with a high-speed channel and share the general workload between them. In the event one fails to operate, the other takes over. In fault tolerant systems, two or more processors are built into the same cabinet.

Multiprocessing is also accomplished in special-purpose computers, such as array processors, which provide concurrent mathematical processing on sets of data.

Although computers are built with various overlapping features, such as executing instructions while inputting and outputting data, multiprocessing refers specifically to concurrent instruction executions. See *bus mastering*.

multiprogramming Same as *multitasking*.

multisync monitor

A display monitor that adjusts automatically to the synchronization frequency of the video signal it receives. It can adjust to a range of frequencies, but not all of them. The multisync monitor was popularized by NEC, and MultiSync is the NEC trade name.

NEC MULTISYNC MONITOR

multitasking The

running of two or more programs in one computer at the same time. Multitasking is controlled by the operating system, which loads the programs and manages them until finished. The number of programs that can be effectively multitasked depends on the amount of memory available, CPU speed, capacity and speeds of peripheral resources, as well as the efficiency of the operating system.

Multitasking is accomplished due to the differences in input/output and processing speed. While one program is waiting for input, instructions in another program can be executed. With interactive programs, the seconds of delay between keyboard entries are used to execute instructions in other programs. In batch processing systems, the milliseconds of delay getting data into and out of the computer are used to execute instructions in other programs.

Traditionally, multitasking meant running two or more tasks within the same program at the same time, and *multiprogramming* meant running two or more programs in the computer at the same time. Today, multitasking means multiprogramming, and *multithreading* means multitasking.

multithreading The concurrent processing of transactions. It implies that transactions, or messages, can be worked on in parallel, and that one transaction may not be completely processed before another is started. Multithreading is also required for creating synchronized audio and video applications, for example.

Multithreaded programs are often written in *reentrant code* so that one routine can serve multiple processes at the same time.

multiuser A computer that is shared by two or more users.

multivariate The use of multiple variables in a forecasting model.

MUMPS An advanced, high-level programming language and integrated database used to develop business applications. It has extensive string handling capabilities making it suitable for databases with vast amounts of free text. MUMPS has unique features including the ability to store both data and program statements in its database, a fundamental property of object-oriented programming. In addition, formulas written in a program can be permanently stored and used by other programs. Developed in 1966 at Massachusetts General Hospital where it derived its name (Mass. Utility MultiProgramming System), MUMPS has been used extensively in the health-care field.

The following MUMPS example converts fahrenheit to centigrade:

```
READ "Enter fahrenheit ",FAHR
SET CENT=(FAHR-32)*5/9
WRITE "Centigrade is", CENT
```

The MUMPS Users' Group supports the MUMPS community through training, meetings and distribution of publications and software. For more information, contact MUMPS Users' Group, 4321 Hartwick Road, Suite 100, College Park, MD 20740, (301) 779-6555.

MUX (MUltipleXor) See *multiplexor*.

MVS/ESA (Multiple Virtual Storage/Enterprise Systems Architecture) An operating system from IBM which runs on IBM mainframes that have been upgraded to the ESA/370 architecture. Introduced in 1988, MVS/ESA increases virtual memory capability to 16 terabytes (trillion bytes).

MVS/XA (Multiple Virtual Storage/eXtended Architecture) One of the two major operating systems (the other is VM) that runs on large IBM mainframes. MVS/XA is primarily a batch processing-oriented operating system that manages large amounts of memory and disk space. Online operations are provided with CICS, TSO and other system software.

The original MVS was introduced in 1974, and in 1981, the XA version increased its virtual memory capability to two gigabytes (billion bytes).

MYCIN An expert system for diagnoising blood infections developed at Stanford University in the early 1970s by Bruce Buchanan and Edward Shortliffe.

N

NACOMEX (NAtional COMputer EXchange) A commodity exchange through which the general public can buy and sell used computers. After a match, the buyer sends a check to NACOMEX and the seller shows the equipment to the buyer. If the buyer accepts it, the money is sent to the seller minus a 10% commission (minimum $50). There are no fees unless a sale is made. The NACOMEX price index is printed weekly in MIS Week. For more information, call (212) 614-0700 or fax (212) 777-1290.

NAK (Negative AcKnowledgement) In communications, a code which is used to indicate that a message was not received, or that a terminal does not wish to transmit.

Named Pipes The interprocess communications (IPC) facility in LAN Manager. It allows data to be exchanged from one application to another either over a network or running within the same computer.

The use of the term *pipes* for interprocess communication was coined in UNIX.

NAND (Not AND) A Boolean logic operation that is true if any single input is false. Two-input NAND gates are often used as the sole logic element on gate array chips, because all Boolean operations can be created from NAND gates.

Inputs		Output
0	0	1
0	1	1
1	0	1
1	1	0

nanometer One billionth of a meter.

nanosecond One billionth of a second. It is used to measure the speed of logic and memory chips. A nanosecond seems unbelievably fast, but it can be brought down to earth a bit by converting it to distance. In one nanosecond, electricity travels about a foot; thus, it can be visualized as a one-foot length of wire.

The advantage of the tiny chip is the decreased time electricity has to travel between circuits and logic elements. Electricity travels at the speed of light

(186,000 miles per second); yet, it's never fast enough for the hardware designer who will worry over an extra few inches of circuit path. The slightest delay is multiplied millions of times, since millions of pulses are sent through a wire in a single second. See *space/time*.

NAPLPS (North American Presentation-Level Protocol Syntax) An ANSI-standard transmission format developed for videotex and teletext systems. It compresses data for transmission over narrow-bandwidth lines and requires processing on the receiving end to decompress it.

narrowband In communications, a voice grade transmission of 2,400bps or less, or a sub-voice grade transmission from 50 to 150bps.

NAS (Network Application Support) Digital's network strategy for interconnecting PCs, Macintoshes and other non-DEC devices in a DECnet environment. Introduced in 1988, NAS includes the X.400 mail protocol, X Windows, PostScript language and SQL for database manipulation.

native language Same as *machine language*. See *native mode*.

native mode
(1) A computer that is running a program in its native machine language. Contrast with *emulation mode*.

(2) A computer that is running in its highest-performance state, such as the 386 running in 32-bit protected mode.

Natural A fourth-generation language from Software AG of North America that runs on a variety of computers from micro to mainframe.

natural language program Software that can understand a large vocabulary of English, Spanish, etc. By the turn of the century, you should be able to phrase your question any way you'd like to a large number of computers.

NAU
(1) (Network Access Unit) An interface card that adapts a computer to a local area network.

(2) (Network Addressable Unit) An SNA component that can be referenced by name and address, which includes the SSCP, LU and PU.

NB card (NuBus card) See *NuBus*.

NC See *numerical control*.

NCB (Network Control Block) The packet structure used by the NetBIOS transport protocol.

NCGA (National Computer Graphics Association) An organization of individuals and major corporations dedicated to developing and promoting the computer graphics industry and improving graphics applications in business, industry, government, science and the arts.

NCGA strives to encourage communication among computer graphics users, consultants, educators and vendors; increase general awareness of potential computer graphics applications; raise national productivity and encourage the effective use of existing resources; and maintain a clearinghouse for industry information. For more information, contact NCGA, 2722 Merrilee Drive, Suite 200, Fairfax, VA 22031, (800) 225-NCGA.

NCP

(1) (Network Control Program) A program that controls the traffic between multiple terminals and a mini or mainframe. It typically resides in a front end processor and performs such operations as polling the terminals.

(2) (NetWare Core Protocol) Proprietary language used in Novell's NetWare to communicate between the workstation and the server.

(3) (Not Copy Protected) A program that can be freely copied.

NCR (NCR Corporation) A major manufacturer of computers and financial terminals. In 1884, John Henry Patterson purchased the National Manufacturing Company of Dayton, Ohio, and renamed it National Cash Register. It became the leading cash register company in the country and, by 1911, had sold its one millionth cash register.

Throughout the 1930s and 1940s, NCR gained a reputation in the banking and retail industries as a maker of accounting machines that were used for posting customer accounts. NCR has specialized in both industries ever since.

In 1952, it acquired the Computer Research Corporation, a fledgling electronics firm, which, by 1955 had created and sold 30 CRC 102 scientific-oriented data processing systems. Turning its new acquisition towards the business world and bypassing the vacuum tube age, NCR introduced a transistorized computer in 1957, called the 304. It accepted data from its cash

JOHN H. PATTERSON
(Courtesy NCR)

registers and banking terminals via paper tape. Due to its high reliability, it was widely accepted in the retail and banking industries.

One of NCR's more novel devices was its CRAM (Card Random Access Memory) storage unit, introduced in 1961. It held removable cartridges containing strips of magnetic tape offering large amounts of peripheral storage for its time. CRAM units were more reliable than magnetic strip devices of competing vendors.

From its Century series of the 1960s, the Criterion series of the 1970s, to the 9300

EARLY CASH REGISTER
(Courtesy NCR)

mainframes of the 1980s, NCR has kept abreast of the times, providing a complete line of integrated point-of-sale and financial computer systems.

NCR paper (No Carbon Required paper) A multiple-part paper form that does not contain sheets of carbon paper between the forms. The ink for the second and subsequent sheets is adhered to the reverse side of the previous sheet.

NCSC (National Computer Security Center) An arm of the U.S. National Security Agency that defines criteria for trusted computer products. The security levels in its Orange Book (Trusted Computer Systems Evaluation Criteria, DOD Standard 5200.28) follow. Each level adds more features and requirements.

D Non-secure system.

Level C provides discretionary control. The owner of the data can determine who has access to it.

C1 Requires user log-on, but allows group ID.
C2 Requires individual user log-on with password and an audit mechanism.

Levels B and A provide mandatory control. Access is based on standard DOD clearances.

B1 DOD clearance levels.

B2 Guarantees path between user and the security system. Provides assurances that system can be tested and clearances cannot be downgraded.

B3 System is characterized by a mathematical model that must be viable.

A1 System is characterized by a mathematical model that can be proven. Highest security.

n-dimensional Some number of dimensions.

NDIS (Network Driver Interface Specification) A Microsoft specification for writing hardware-independent drivers at the data link (media access method) layer. When transport protocols communicate to the NDIS specification, network cards with NDIS-compliant MAC drivers can be freely interchanged.

NE (Not Equal to) See *relational operator*.

negative logic The use of a high voltage for a 0 bit and a low voltage for a 1 bit. Contrast with *positive logic*.

nematic The stage between a crystal and a liquid that has a threadlike nature, for example, a liquid crystal.

neper A unit of measurement that is based on Napierian logarithms and represents the ratio between two values, such as current or voltage.

nerd A person typically thought of as dull. Nerds often like technical work and are generally introspective and frequently antisocial. Contrast with *hacker*, a technical person that may or may not be a nerd.

nesting In programming, the positioning of a loop within a loop. The number of loops that can be nested may be limited by the programming language. See *loop*.

NetBEUI (NetBIOS Extended User Interface) Pronounced "net-booey." The implementation of the NetBIOS transport protocol within LAN Manager and LAN Server. It communicates to the network interface cards (NICs) via NDIS (Network Driver Interface Specification).

The term was originally used to define the NetBIOS protocol after it was upgraded to support the Token Ring Network.

NetBIOS A commonly used transport protocol for PC local area networks introduced with IBM's PC Network and implemented in Microsoft's MS-Net and LAN Manager. Application programs use NetBIOS for client/server or peer-to-peer communications.

There are two NetBIOS modes for communicating. The Datagram is the fastest method, but does not guarantee delivery of a message. It is a self-contained packet with sender and receiver name, usually limited to 512 bytes. If the recipient device is not listening for messages, the datagram is lost.

The Session mode establishes a connection until broken. It guarantees delivery of messages up to 64K bytes long.

NetBIOS-compliant protocols refer to layers 3, 4 and 5 on the OSI model.

Netview A group of network monitoring and control programs for SNA networks from IBM. It controls SNA as well as non-SNA and non-IBM devices and provides central control over the network. NetView/PC is a product that interconnects NetView with Token Ring local area networks, Rolm CBXs and non-IBM modems, while maintaining control in the host.

NetWare A family of network operating systems from Novell, Inc., that runs on 286 and higher PCs and supports DOS, OS/2 and Macintosh workstations. It also supports a large number of LAN access methods, including Token Ring, Ethernet, ARCNET and Starlan.

ELS NetWare (Entry Level System) Levels I and II run on 286 and higher CPUs and provide support for up to four and eight workstations respectively. ELS allows the server to function in the same machine as a workstation.

The most widely installed NetWare operating system is Advanced NetWare 286, which runs on a dedicated file server, 286 and higher, and provides support for up to 100 users. NetWare is the sole control program in the server and does not coexist with DOS.

SFT NetWare (System Fault Tolerant) runs on a 286 and higher PC and provides automatic recovery from network malfunctions.

NetWare 386 runs on 386 and higher file servers and provides increased functionality and performance. It supports up to 250 users with future potential for up to 4,000.

NetWare for VMS provides NetWare connectivity to VAX networks, and Portable NetWare provides fundamental NetWare services in source code for conversion and use on other hardware platforms.

network

(1) An arrangement of objects that are interconnected. See *local area network* and *network database*.

(2) In communications, the transmission channels and supporting hardware and software.

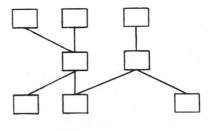

NETWORK

network adapter See *NIC*.

network administrator An individual who is responsible for the operation of a communications network. The network administrator installs applications on the servers, monitors network activity and is generally responsible for its efficient operation.

network architecture

(1) The design of a communications system, which includes the hardware, software, access methods and protocols used. It also defines the method of control, for example, whether computers can act independently or whether they are controlled by other computers that are constantly monitoring the network. Network architectures determine future flexibility and connectability to foreign networks.

(2) The access method in a local area network, such as Ethernet, Token Ring and LocalTalk.

network card See NIC.

network control program See NCP.

network database

(1) A database that resides in a network. It implies that the system was designed to be used as a database server with a client/server orientation.

(2) A database that holds addresses of other users in the network.

(3) A database organization method that allows for data relationships in a net-like form. A single data element can point to multiple data elements and can itself be pointed to by other data elements. Contrast with *relational database*.

network management The monitoring of an active network in
order to diagnose problems and gather statistics for network administration and fine tuning.

network modem A modem that is shared by all users in a network.
See ACS.

network operating system A control program that resides in a
file server within a local area network. It handles the requests for data from all the users (workstations) on the network.

network ready A program that is designed to run in a network. It
implies that multiple users can share the databases without conflict.

network server See *file server*.

neural network A modeling technique that is based on the observed
behavior of biological neurons and is used to mimic the performance of a system.

It consists of a set of elements that start out connected in a random pattern, and, based upon operational feedback, are molded into the pattern required to generate the required results. Neural networks are used in applications such as robotics, diagnosing, forecasting, image processing and pattern recognition.

NewWave An operating environment for PCs from Hewlett-Packard, which runs on top of Microsoft Windows (between DOS and Windows). It integrates data and activates tasks within the system. Its object-management facility allows data from different applications to be merged together to create a compound document. In addition, "hot connects" can be created that automatically update the document if data in one of the source files is updated.

NewWave allows for the creation of automatic procedures, called *agents*, which can be activated on a prescribed timetable or when other events occur in the computer. For example, at the end of the month, an agent can be set up to extract data out of the corporate mainframe and prepare a report using two or more application programs.

Programs must be modified to run under NewWave.

NeXT Computer Introduced in late 1988, a UNIX-based computer system from NeXT, Inc., that includes a 68030 CPU, high-resolution (1120x832) gray-scale graphics, hi-fi stereo output and a 256MB erasable optical disk. Also included is a variety of bundled applications and the NextStep object-oriented environment for building graphics-based UNIX applications.

NeXT was founded in 1985 by Steven Jobs, co-founder and former chairman of Apple Computer.

NEXT COMPUTER

NeXTStep An object-oriented software development environment from NeXT, Inc., that allows for the creation of graphics-based, windows applications under UNIX. IBM has licensed NextStep for its UNIX-based (AIX) workstations.

NFS (Network File System) A distributed file system from Sun Microsystems, Inc., that allows data to be shared with many users in a network. NFS allows users to share data regardless of processor type, operating system, network architecture or protocol.

nibble A *nibble* is one half a byte, or four bits.

NIC (Network Interface Card) A printed circuit board that plugs into a workstation or network server and controls the exchange of data over a network. The transmission medium (twisted pair, coax or fiber optic cable) physically interconnects all the NICs in the network. The NIC performs the electronic functions of the access method, or data link protocol, such as Ethernet, Token Ring and LocalTalk.

NIST (National Institute of Standards & Technology) The standards-defining agency of the U.S. government, formerly called the National Bureau of Standards.

N-key rollover A keyboard feature that allows a typist to press a series of keys in fast sequence. Each subsequent key can be pressed without having to raise the finger off the last key. To test for N-key rollover, press four adjacent keys in sequence without removing your fingers from any of the keys. If all four letters appear on screen, the keyboard has N-key rollover.

NLM (NetWare Loadable Module) A program that enhances or provides additional server functions in a NetWare 386 server. Support for different kinds of workstations, database engines, fax and print servers are examples. In NetWare 286, the NLM is called a Value Added Process (VAP).

NLQ (Near Letter Quality) Print quality that is almost as sharp as an electric typewriter. The slowest speed of a dot matrix printer often provides NLQ.

NMOS (N-Channel Metal Oxide Semiconductor) Pronounced "en-moss." A type of microelectronic circuit design that is used for logic and memory and chips. NMOS transistors are faster than their PMOS counterpart and more of them can be put on a single chip. NMOS transistors are also used in CMOS technology.

node
(1) In communications, a junction or connection point in a network (a terminal or a computer).

(2) In database management, an item of data that can be accessed by two or more routes.

(3) In computer graphics, an endpoint of a graphical element.

noise Any extraneous signal that invades an electrical transmission. It can come from strong electrical or magnetic signals in nearby lines, from poorly fitting electrical contacts, and from power line spikes.

NOMAD A relational database management system from Must Software International that runs on IBM mainframes, PCs and VAXs. It provides cooperative processing by offloading part of the processing from the mainframe to the PC. SQL NOMAD adds SQL functionality to the product. Introduced in the mid 1970s, it was one of the first database systems to provide a non-procedural language for data manipulation.

non-blocking The ability of a signal to reach its destination without interference or delay.

non-document mode A word processing mode that is used for creating batch files, source language programs or any text file that will be transferred to another program. It creates an ASCII file rather than a document with proprietary format codes. Word processors that create only ASCII files do not need this option.

non-impact printer A printer that prints without banging a ribbon onto paper, such as a thermal or ink jet printer. See *printer*.

non-interlaced See *interlaced*.

non-numeric programming Programming that deals with objects, such as words, board game pieces and people, rather than numbers. Same as *list processing*.

non-procedural language A computer language that does not require traditional programming logic to be stated. For example, a command, such as LIST, might display all the records in a file on screen, separating fields with a blank space. In a procedural language, such as COBOL, all the logic for inputting each record in the file, testing for end of file and separating the data on the screen has to be implicitly programmed.

Query languages, report writers, interactive database programs, spreadsheets and application generators provide non-procedural languages for user operation.

non-return-to-zero See *NRZ*.

non-trivial A favorite word among some programmers for any task that is difficult to do.

non-volatile memory A memory that holds its content without power. Firmware chips, such as ROMs, PROMs, EPROMs and EEPROMs are examples of non-volatile memory. Magnetic disks and tapes may also be classified as non-volatile memory, although they are usually considered storage devices.

nonlinear A system in which the output is not a uniform relationship to the input.

NonStop A family of fault tolerant computer systems from Tandem Computers. NonStop systems are used for online transaction processing applications that demand 100% availability, such as in the financial community.

NOR (Not OR) A Boolean logical operation that is true if all inputs are false, and false if any input is true. An exclusive NOR is true if both inputs are the same.

NOR			EXCLUSIVE NOR		
Inputs		Output	Inputs		Output
0	0	1	0	0	1
0	1	0	0	1	0
1	0	0	1	0	0
1	1	0	1	1	1

normal wear The deterioration due to natural forces that act upon a product while it is being operated within proper specifications and for the purpose for which it was intended.

normalize See *third normal form.*

Norton SI (Norton System Information) A Norton Utilities program that measures computer performance. It provides a computing index (CI) that measures CPU speed, a disk index (DI) for disk speed and a performance index (PI) that is a composite of the two.

The IBM PC XT is used as a base reference of 1.0. For example, the CI for the original 8 Mhz HP Vectra is 7.7, which means it is almost eight times as fast as the XT internally. The DI is 1.1, which means the Vectra disks are only slightly faster than the XT's. The PI is 5.5 indicating that the Vectra is five and one half times as powerful as the XT.

Norton Utilities A package of utility programs for PCs from Peter Norton Computing, Inc. The programs allow the user to restore deleted files on the disk, search and edit files no matter what format they are in and list and manage disk directories, among other things. Programs such as these provide an invaluable aid to both the novice and the advanced personal computer user. See *Norton SI.*

NOS (Network Operating System) The operating system that runs on Control Data's CYBER series of large mainframes.

NOS/VE (Network Operating System/Virtual Environment) A multitasking, virtual memory operating system from Control Data that runs on its medium to large-scale mainframes.

NOT A Boolean logic operation that reverses the input. If a 0 is input, a 1 is output, and vice versa. See *AND, OR & NOT*.

Input	Output
0	1
1	0

Nota Bene A word processing system for PCs from Dragonfly Software that uses the XyWrite word processor as its foundation. Nota Bene adds a number of features, including menus, a different keyboard layout and more sophisticated handling of foreign characters and laser printers. It also includes a text handling system that allows retrieval of correspondence from pages of unstructured notes.

notation The way a system of numbers, phrases, words or quantities is written or expressed. Positional notation is the location and value of digits in a numbering system, such as the decimal or binary system.

notebook computer A portable computer that usually weighs less than five pounds. A notebook computer is between a pocket computer and a laptop computer.

TI TRAVELMATE

Nova A series of minicomputers from Data General Corporation. When introduced in 1969, it was the first 16-bit minicomputer that used four accumulators in its CPU, an advanced technology for its time. Novas, running under its RDOS operating system, were used extensively in the OEM marketplace; for example, as controllers for cat scanners.

Novell network A local area network that is controlled by one of Novell's NetWare operating systems. See *NetWare*.

NRZ (Non-Return-To-Zero) A signalling method used both in magnetic recording and communications that does not automatically return to a neutral state after each bit is transmitted.

ns (NanoSecond) See *nanosecond*.

NSTL (National Software Testing Laboratory) An independent organization headquartered in Philadelphia that evaluates computer hardware and software. It adheres to controlled testing methods in order to ensure accurate and objective results and publishes its results in Software Digest Ratings Report and PC Digest.

NTSC (National Television Standards Committee) Refers to the TV standard for the U.S., created by the NTSC and administered by the FCC. NTSC is 525 lines of resolution transmitted at 60 half frames (interlaced) per second. The signal is generated as a composite of red, green and blue signals for color and includes an FM frequency for audio and an MTS signal for stereo.

NuBus A 32-bit bus architecture originally developed at MIT and defined as a Eurocard (9U). Rights to the bus were purchased by Western Digital and TI. Apple Computer licenses it from TI and has changed its electrical and physical specs for its Mac II family.

null character A character that has all bits set to 0. It is the first character in the ASCII character set and has a numeric value of zero. In hex, a null prints as 00. In decimal, a null prints as a blank.

Nulls are naturally found in binary numbers when a byte contains no 1 bits. They are also used for special purposes, such as to pad fields and to serve as delimiters. In C, for example, a null is used to specify the end of a character string.

null modem cable An RS-232-C cable that is used to interconnect two personal computers that are in close proximity. The cable connects to the serial ports and crosses connections so that the sending wire on one end becomes the receiving wire on the other end.

number crunching Refers to computers running mathematical, scientific or CAD applications in which large amounts of calculations are required.

numbers In a computer, numbers can be stored in several forms. Although they are all coded as binary digits (bits), BCD and packed decimal numbers retain the decimal relationship of a number, whereas fixed and floating point do not.

BINARY CODED DECIMAL (BCD)
The BCD method encodes each decimal digit in a single byte. The number 6508 would take four bytes. A variation of BCD, called *packed decimal*, encodes two

decimal digits in one byte. The number 6508 would take two bytes.

BINARY FIXED POINT
With this method, the entire number is converted into a binary number and stored in a fixed unit of storage. The number 6508 would require at least two bytes. Binary numbers can be calculated faster than decimal (BCD) numbers.

Bytes	Bits	Values
1	8	0 to 255
2	16	0 to 65,535
4	32	0 to 4,294,967,295

BINARY FLOATING POINT
With floating point numbers, very small fractions and very large numbers can be represented and calculated quickly. Both the mantissa (significant digits of the number) and the exponent (power to which the number is raised) are converted into binary numbers. See *floating point*.

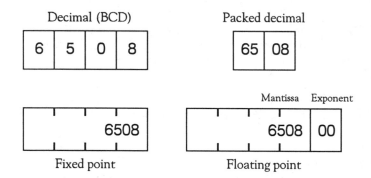

numeric data Refers to quantities and money amounts that are used in calculations. Contrast with *string* or *character data*.

numeric field A data field that holds only numbers and allows the numbers to be calculated. Contrast with *character field*.

numerical control A category of automated machine tools, such as drills and lathes, that operate from instructions in a program. Numerical control (NC) machines are used in manufacturing tasks, such as milling, turning, punching and drilling.

First-generation machines were either hardwired to perform a specific set of tasks or programmed in a very low-level machine language. Today, they are controlled by their own microcomputers and are programmed in high-level languages, such as APT and COMPACT II, which automatically generate the tool path, the physical motions of the machine required to perform the operation.

The term was coined in the 1950s when the instructions to the machine tool were numeric codes. Just like the computer industry, symbolic languages were soon developed, but the original term remained.

O

OA See *office automation*.

object code Same as *machine language*.

object computer The computer a program runs in. The term is used to distinguish between the computer the program is intended for and the computer it is created on. See *cross assembler/compiler*.

object language Same as *object program*.

object module The direct output of an assembler or compiler. Object modules cannot execute in the computer until they have been link edited, which ties the cross references between modules together and creates an executable format.

object-oriented database A database that supports abstract data types. See *object-oriented programming*.

object-oriented graphics Same as *vector graphics*.

object-oriented interface A graphical interface that uses icons and a mouse, such as the Macintosh, Windows and GEM environments.

object-oriented programming A programming technology that is generally more flexible and adaptable than standard programming. With this method, the nouns carry the thrust of the program, rather than the verbs. Its important features are *abstract data types, inheritance* and *polymorphism*.

Abstract data types are self-sufficient modules that contain the data and the processing: the data structure and the functions needed to manipulate that data. These user-defined data types are called *classes*. One instance of a class is called an *object*.

Classes are created in hierarchies, and **inheritance** allows the knowledge in one class to be passed down the hierarchy or inherited. New and powerful objects can be created quickly by inheriting characteristics from existing classes. For example, the object MACINTOSH could be one instance of the class PERSONAL COMPUTER, which could inherit properties from the class

COMPUTER SYSTEMS. Adding a new computer requires entering only what makes it different from other computers, while all the general characteristics of personal computers can be inherited.

Object-oriented programming lets you create procedures about objects whose exact type is not known until run time. For example, a screen cursor may change its shape from an arrow to a line depending on the program mode. The routine to move the cursor on screen in response to mouse movement would be written for "cursor," and **polymorphism** would allow that cursor to be whatever shape is required at run time. It would also allow a new shape to be easily integrated into the program.

Xerox's Smalltalk was the first object-oriented language and was used to create the graphical user interface whose derivations and imitations are so popular today. C++ is an object-oriented programming language that is gaining a lot of popularity, because it combines traditional C programming with object-oriented features.

object program A machine language program ready to run in a particular operating environment. It has been assembled, or compiled, and link edited. Contrast with *object module*, which cannot execute because it has not been link edited.

Objective-C An object-oriented C programming language from The Stepstone Corporation that runs on PCs and popular workstations. It was the first commercial object-oriented extension of the C language. It includes packages sets of classes, called ICpaks for both general-purpose data structure manipulation and iconic user interface construction.

occam A programming language for parallel processing machines, specifically, the INMOS Transputer, which executes occam almost directly. The language is designed to handle concurrent operations. In the following statements, two items of data are read and incremented at the same time. PAR specifies that following statements are to be executed concurrently, and SEQ indicates that the following statements are executed sequentially.

```
PAR
  SEQ
    chan1 ? item1
    item1 := item1 + 1
  SEQ
    chan2 ? item2
    item2 := item2 + 1
```

OCO (Object Code Only) A policy announced by IBM in 1983 that withholds source code and provides only object code to its customers. Large mainframe customers often want to get into the source code in order to customize the programs for their own use. Without the source code, they cannot make modifications without inordinate difficulty.

It is customary for all vendors to provide only object code of their proprietary software packages.

OCR (Optical Character Recognition) The machine recognition of printed characters. OCR systems can recognize many different kinds of special OCR fonts, as well as typewriter and computer-printed characters. Advanced OCR systems can recognize hand printing.

OCR-A (FULL ALPHA)

NUMERIC   0123456789

ALPHA   ABCDEFGHIJKLMNOPQRSTUVWXYZ

SYMBOLS   >$/-+-#"

OCR-A (NRMA/EURO BANKING)

NUMERIC   0123456789

ALPHA   ACDMNPRUXY

SYMBOLS   >$/+#"♪Ұн

OCR-B(SUBSET 1, ECMA 11 and ANSI X3.49-1975)

NUMERIC   00123456789

ALPHA   ACENPSTVX

SYMBOLS   <+>-¥

OCR MULTIFONT

OCR-B	¥00123456789><++#
12L/12F	¥0123456789 +#
1403-OCR	00123456789><+#
407-1	0123456789

SAMPLE OCR FONTS

(Courtesy Recognition Equipment Corporation)

octal A numbering system that uses eight digits. It is used as a shorthand method for representing binary numbers that use six-bit characters. Each three bits (half a character) is converted into a single octal digit.   Okta is Greek for 8.

Decimal	Binary	Octal
0	000	0
1	001	1
2	010	2
3	011	3
4	100	4
5	101	5
6	110	6
7	111	7

odd parity See *parity checking*.

OEM (Original Equipment Manufacturer) A manufacturer that sells equipment to a reseller. The term is also used to refer to the reseller, as well. OEM customers typically purchase hardware from a manufacturer and resell it under their own brand names. They may combine units from several vendors as well as add software. The terms OEM and VAR are often used synonymously.

off-hook The state of a telephone line that allows dialing and transmission but prohibits incoming calls from being answered. The term goes back to the days when a telephone handset was lifted off of a hook. Contrast with *on-hook*.

off-the-shelf Refers to products that are packaged and available for sale.

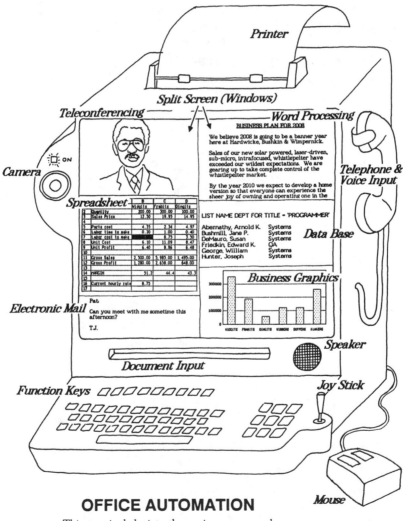

OFFICE AUTOMATION

This terminal depicts the various paper and electronic functions of an integrated office system.

office automation The integration of all information functions in the office, which include word processing, data processing, electronic mail, graphics and desktop publishing.

The backbone of office automation is a local area network, which serves as a pathway between all users and computers. Users can create, store and retrieve any form of information (message, mail, data, voice, etc.) and transmit it to any other user within the organization.

All traditional office functions, such as dictation, typing, filing, copying, TWX and Telex operation, microfilm and records management and telephone and telephone switchboard operations, are candidates for integration into an office automation system.

Office automation often refers to the word processing operation, and although word processing is often the first approach taken, office automation implies many new ways of looking at work in the office. While it is viewed as a solution to bottlenecks and backlogs in office operations, its implementation will eventually change the way people perform their jobs.

The irony of the so-called Office of the Future is that once we have all the technology to implement it properly, we probably won't need the office. If people can access all the information required to do a job from a terminal, and through video conferencing can interact with whomever they're talking to as if they were in the same room, then, in time, the concept of the central office as a workplace will undergo dramatic change.

Office Vision A series of integrated office automation applications from IBM that runs across all of its major computer families. It represents the first significant implementation of IBM's SAA and incorporates the OS/2 Presentation Manager interface across OS/2 networks, AS/400 minicomputers and 370 mainframes.

Introduced in 1989, Office Vision is designed to glue IBM hardware lines together by offering electronic mail, scheduling, document creation and distribution as well as decision support and graphics capabilities among all users. Although DOS-based personal computers can run in an Office Vision environment, they cannot provide the concurrent operations of OS/2-based machines.

OS/2 users can transmit and receive mail or exchange data from other databases in the network while working with applications on screen.

offline Not connected to or not installed in the computer. Even if a terminal, printer or other device is physically connected to the computer, it is still offline if it is not turned on, or not in ready mode. Disks and tapes that have been demounted and stored in the data library are considered offline. Contrast with *online*, which means connected and ready to go.

offline storage Disks and tapes that are kept in a data library.

offload To remove work from one computer and do it on another. See *cooperative processing*.

offset A value that is added to a base value in order to derive the actual value. For example, a relative address is the offset added to each instruction when the program is executing. In word processing, an offset is the amount of space the document will be printed from the left margin.

OLTP (OnLine Transaction Processing) See *transaction processing*.

omnidirectional Meaning in all directions. For example, an omnidirectional antenna can pick up signals in all directions.

OmniPage Page recognition software for PCs and the Macintosh from Caere Corporation. It was the first personal computer software that could distinguish text from graphics and convert a wide variety of fonts into ASCII text.

on-hook The state of a telephone line that can receive an incoming call. Contrast with *off-hook*.

ONA (Open Network Architecture) An FCC plan that allows users and competing enhanced service providers (ESPs) equal access to unbundled, basic telephone services. The Open Network Provision (ONP) is the European counterpart.

one-chip computer See *computer on a chip*.

onion diagram A graphical representation of a system that is made up of concentric circles. The innermost circle is the core, and all outer layers are dependent on the core.

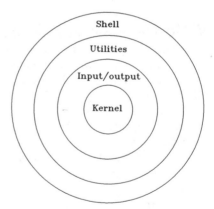

ONION DIAGRAM OF AN OPERATING SYSTEM

online
(1) A peripheral device, such as a terminal or printer, that is ready to operate. A printer can be attached and turned on, yet still not online, if the ONLINE or SEL light is out. Pressing the ONLINE button will usually turn it back online.

(2) An online computer system refers to a system with terminals, but does not imply how the system operates. For example, a data collection system is an online system that accepts and stores data from several terminals, but does not update any master files.
 An interactive system is an online system that implies data entry and updating.

A transaction processing system is an online system that updates the necessary files as the work comes in, such as in an order processing system.

A realtime system is an online system that provides an immediate response to a question.

Although complete overkill, it is not incorrect to say that one has an "online, realtime, interactive, transaction processing system," especially if you're trying to impress someone. Hopefully, not an experienced systems analyst!

on-line means happiness!

OODB (Object Oriented DataBase) A database that holds object oriented data. See *object-oriented programming*.

OODMS (Object Oriented Database Management System) A database management system that is designed to manage object oriented data. See *object-oriented programming*.

OOPS (Object Oriented Programming System) See *object-oriented programming*.

op amp (Operational Amplifier) A device that amplifies analog signals. It uses two inputs; one for power and one for data. Op amps are used in myriads of applications from communications to stereo.

op code See *operation code*.

open architecture A system in which the specifications are made public in order to encourage third-party vendors to develop add-on products for it. For example, much of Apple Computer's early success was due to its open architecture of the Apple II. IBM followed Apple's lead in making the PC open architecture as well.

Open Look An X Window-based graphical user interface (GUI) for the UNIX operating system that was developed by Sun Microsystems and is defined and distributed by AT&T's UNIX Software Operation (USO). It conforms to POSIX, ANSI C and X/Open's XPG3 standards.

open shop A computing environment that allows users to program and run their own programs. Contrast with *closed shop*.

open system A vendor-independent system that is designed to interconnect with a variety of products that are commonly available. It implies that standards for such a system are determined from a consensus of interested parties rather than one or two vendors. Contrast with *closed system*. See *OSI* and *X/Open*.

operand The part of a machine instruction that references data or a peripheral device. In the instruction, `add a to b`, A and B are the operands (nouns), and ADD is the operation code (verb). In the instruction `read track 9, sector 32`, track and sector are the operands.

operating system A master control program that runs the computer and acts as a scheduler and traffic cop. It is the first program loaded (copied) into the computer's memory after the computer is turned on, and the central core, or kernel, of the operating system must reside in memory at all times. The operating system may be developed by the vendor of the hardware it's running in or by an independent software house.

The operating system is an important component of the computer system, because it sets the standards for the application programs that run in it. All programs must be written to "talk to" the operating system.

Also called an *executive* or *supervisor*, the operating system performs the following functions.

JOB MANAGEMENT
In small computers, the operating system responds to commands from the user and loads the requested application program into memory for execution. In large computers, the operating system carries out its job control instructions (JCL), which can describe the mix of programs that must be run for an entire shift.

TASK MANAGEMENT
In single tasking computers, the operating system has virtually no task management to do, but in multitasking computers, it is responsible for the concurrent operation of one or more programs (jobs). Advanced operating systems have the ability to prioritize programs so that one job gets done before the other.

In order to provide users at terminals with the fastest response time, batch programs can be put on lowest priority and interactive programs can be given highest priority. Advanced operating systems have more fine-tuning capabilities so that a specific job can be speeded up or slowed down by commands from the computer operator.

Multitasking is accomplished by designing the computer to allow instructions to be executed during the same time data is coming into or going out of the computer. In the seconds it takes one user to type in data, millions of instructions can be executed for dozens, or even hundreds, of other users. In the milliseconds it takes for data to come in from or go out to the disk, thousands of instructions can be performed for some other task.

DATA MANAGEMENT
One of the major functions of an operating system is to keep track of data on the disk; hence the term DOS, or disk operating system. The application program

does not know where the data is actually stored or how to get it. That knowledge is contained in the operating system's access method, or device driver, routines. When a program is ready to accept data, it signals the operating system with a coded message. The operating system finds the data and delivers it to the program. Conversely, when the program is ready to output, the operating system transfers the data from the program onto the available space on disk.

DEVICE MANAGEMENT

In theory, the operating system is supposed to manage all devices, not just disk drives. It is supposed to handle the input and output to the display screen as well as the printer. By keeping the details of the peripheral device within the operating system, a device can be replaced with a newer model, and only the routine in the operating system that deals with that device needs to be replaced.

In the PC world, device management is left up to the vendor of the application, because vendors write their programs to directly access the screen and the printer. They bypass the operating system, because DOS either doesn't support

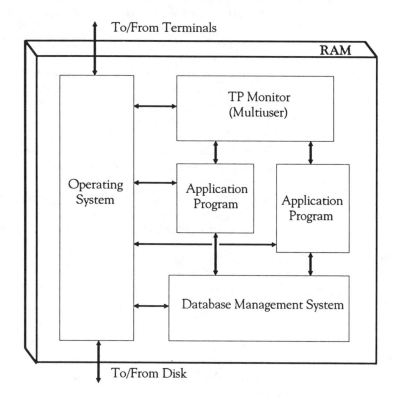

OPERATING SYSTEM

This chart depicts the interaction of the operating system with other system and application programs within the computer. The actual storage and retrieval of data on disk and transmission and receipt of data at the terminals is provided by program routines, called *access methods*, which are components of the operating sytem.

the device or adds too much performance overhead. As a result, software vendors have become responsible for providing drivers (routines) for all the popular display and printer standards, adding an enormous burden to their development efforts.

SECURITY

Multiuser operating systems maintain a list of authorized users and provide password protection to unauthorized users who may try to gain access to the system. Large operating systems also maintain activity logs and accounting of the user's time for billing purposes. They also provide backup and recovery routines to start over again in the event of a system failure.

HISTORY

The earliest operating systems were developed in the late 1950s to manage tape and disk storage, but programmers often felt more comfortable writing and using their own I/O routines. In the mid 1960s, operating systems became essential to manage the complexity of timesharing and multitasking. Today, all multi-purpose computers from micro to mainframe use an operating system. Special-purpose devices, such as appliances, games and toys, do not. They usually employ a single program that performs all the required input, output and processing tasks.

In the past, when a vendor introduced a new operating system, users had little understanding of the time and effort required by computer professionals to convert to it. This is no longer a behind-the-glass-enclosed-datacenter phenomenon, but squarely in the hands of the users. Switching from DOS to OS/2 or UNIX is not a trivial issue. We will no doubt soon find desktop computers running operating systems, such as IBM's VM, which are capable of running multiple operating systems, each controlling their own applications. History has an uncanny way of repeating itself.

Perhaps the Japanese have the right idea with their TRON operating system, which is ultimately intended to be a common interface across all applications from a microwave oven to the largest supercomputer!

COMMON OPERATING SYSTEMS

PCs use DOS, OS/2, SCO XENIX and AIX. Apple II's use DOS (from Apple) and ProDOS. Macintoshes use the System along with Finder and Multifinder, as well as A/UX. Digital uses VMS and Ultrix. IBM mainframes use MVS, VM or DOS/VSE.

operation code The part of a machine instruction that tells the computer what to do, such as input, add or branch. The operation code is the verb, and the operands are the nouns.

operations See *datacenter*.

operations research See *management science*.

operator An individual who operates the computer and performs such activities as commanding the operating system, mounting disks and tapes and placing paper in the printer. Operators may also write the job control language (JCL), which schedules the daily work for the computer.

optical disk A disk that is written and read by light. CDs, CD ROMs and videodiscs are optical disks that are recorded at the time of manufacture and cannot be erased. WORM (write once read many) disks are optical disks that are recorded in the user's environment, but cannot be erased.

Erasable optical disks function like magnetic disks and can be rewritten over and over again. In the late 1980s, a variety of erasable optical disks were introduced that use magneto-optic, dye polymer and phase change recording technologies.

Throughout the 1990s, erasable optical disks may become a viable alternative to magnetic disk. Optical disk storage capacities are considerably greater than their magnetic disk counterparts, and optical technology could eventually replace all magnetic tape and disk media. In addition, lasers can be moved electronically and could be built into a whole new breed of storage device that doesn't spin and move mechanical arms, which would have a dramatic impact on future computer systems.

ERASABLE OPTICAL DISKS
(Courtesy Maxtor Corporation)

The small 3 1/2" Fiji I drive holds 160-megabyte removable cartridges and has an average seek time of 100 milliseconds. The large 5 1/4" Tahiti I drive holds one-gigabyte removable cartridges and has seek times of less than 30 milliseconds.

optical fiber A very thin glass wire designed for the transmission of light. Optical fibers have enormous transmission capacities capable of carrying billions of bits per second. In addition, unlike electrical pulses, light pulses are not affected by interference caused by random radiation in the environment.

When the telephone companies eventually replace the copper wire from their central stations into everyone's home with optical fiber, all varieties of information services will be interactively available to the consumer, including high definition TV.

optical mouse
A mouse that uses light to get its bearings. It is rolled over a small desktop pad that contains a reflective grid. The mouse emits a light and senses its reflection as it is moved. Contrast with *mechanical mouse*.

OPTICAL FIBERS
(Courtesy AT&T)

Each of these hair-thin optical fibers can carry thousands of digitized voice conversations at the same time.

optical reader
An input device that recognizes typewritten or printed characters and bar codes and converts them into their corresponding digital codes.

optical recognition
See *OCR*.

optical scanner
An input device that reads characters and images into the computer that are printed or painted on a paper form. The scanner does not recognize the data it's reading. Page recognition and image processing software do the actual recognition. See *OCR*, *bar code* and *scanner*.

optimizer
Hardware or software that improves performance. See *disk management*.

optoelectronics
The merging of light and electronics technologies, such as in optical fiber communications systems.

OR
A Boolean logic operation that is true if any of the inputs is true. An exclusive OR is true if only one of the inputs is true, but not both.

OR			EXCLUSIVE OR		
Inputs		Output	Inputs		Output
0	0	0	0	0	0
0	1	1	0	1	1
1	0	1	1	0	1
1	1	1	1	1	0

ORACLE A relational database management system from Oracle Corporation that runs on a wide variety of microcomputers, minicomputers and mainframes. It was the first DBMS to incorporate the SQL language.

Oracle A European broadcast television text-message service.

ordinal number A number that identifies the sequence of an item, for example, record #34. Contrast with *cardinal number*.

orphan See *widow & orphan*.

OS

(1) (Operating System) Any operating system.

(2) May refer to OS/2.

OS 1100 An operating system from Unisys that runs on its 1100 Series of mainframes.

OS/2 A single user, multitasking operating system for PCs with Intel 286 and higher CPUs jointly developed by Microsoft and IBM. OS/2 is more advanced than DOS and is designed to run multiple programs concurrently; however, it requires a fast CPU and three to four megabytes of memory for maximum efficiency. It can address all available memory (16MB of RAM and 1GB of virtual memory) and isn't restricted to DOS's infamous 1MB limit. Although new commands have been added, many OS/2 commands are the same as in DOS.

OS/2's Presentation Manager, which is also part of IBM's SAA, provides a user interface similar to Windows 3.0 under DOS.

IBM's Extended Edition is an OS/2 version that provides built-in communications and database management.

OS/2 16-bit
The first versions of OS/2 (1.0, 1.1, etc.) are written for the 16-bit architecture of the 286. Only one DOS application (up to approximately 500K) can be run in compatibility mode.

OS/2 32-bit
The 32-bit version of OS/2, Version 2.0 (expected early 1991), is written for the 32-bit architecture of the 386 and higher CPUs. It also takes advantage of the virtual 86 mode, allowing multitasking of up to 16 DOS applications with over 600K of RAM for each.

OS/3 An operating system from Unisys that runs on the System 80 family of IBM 370 compatible mainframes.

OS/8 A single user, multitasking operating system from Digital that runs on its PDP-8 series of minicomputers. Variants of OS/8 run on Digital's DECstation and DECmate systems.

oscillate To swing back and forth between the minimum and maximum values of a range. An oscillation is one cycle, typically one complete wave in an alternating frequency.

oscillator An electronic circuit that is used to generate high-frequency pulses. See *clock*.

oscilloscope A test instrument that displays electronic signals (waves and pulses) on a screen. It creates its own time base against which the signals can be measured, and the display frames can be frozen for visual inspection.

OSCILLOSCOPE

OSF (Open Software Foundation) A non-profit research and development organization dedicated to develop and deliver an open operating environment based on standards. Formed in 1988, it solicits technologies from the industry at large and invites member participation to set technical direction for its development efforts. For more information, contact Open Software Foundation, 11 Cambridge Center, Cambridge, MA 02142.

OSF/Motif (Open Software Foundation/Motif) A graphical user interface (GUI), developed by OSF, that offers a PC-style behavior and appearance for applications running on any system that supports X Window, Version 11. It conforms to POSIX, ANSI C and X/Open's XPG3 standards.

OSI (Open System Interconnection) A reference model that has been defined by ISO (International Standards Organization) as a standard for worldwide communications. It defines a framework for implementing protocols in seven layers.

Control is passed from one layer to the next, starting at the application layer in one station, proceeding to the bottom layer, over the channel to the next station and back up the hierarchy.

Similar functionality exists in all communications networks; however, existing non-OSI systems often incorporate two or three layers of functionality into one.

Most vendors have agreed to support the OSI model in one form or another.

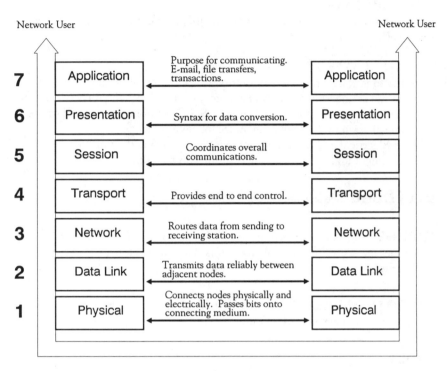

Network User   Network User

7	Application	Purpose for communicating. E-mail, file transfers, transactions.	Application
6	Presentation	Syntax for data conversion.	Presentation
5	Session	Coordinates overall communications.	Session
4	Transport	Provides end to end control.	Transport
3	Network	Routes data from sending to receiving station.	Network
2	Data Link	Transmits data reliably between adjacent nodes.	Data Link
1	Physical	Connects nodes physically and electrically. Passes bits onto connecting medium.	Physical

OSI LAYERS

APPLICATION - LAYER 7
Defines the rules for gaining entrance into the communications system. Programs communicate with other programs through this layer.

PRESENTATION - LAYER 6
Negotiates and manages the way data is represented and encoded. Provides a common denominator for transferring data from different systems, ASCII, EBCDIC, binary, etc.

SESSION - LAYER 5
Provides coordination of the communications in an orderly manner. For example, it marks significant parts of the transmitted data to ensure that the entire message is received properly.

TRANSPORT - LAYER 4
Responsible for end to end validity and integrity of the transmission. OSI transport services include layers 1 through 4, which are collectively responsible for getting the bits from the sending station to the receiving station.

NETWORK - LAYER 3
Establishes the route between the sending and receiving stations. For example, this layer is the switching function of the dial-up telephone system.

DATA LINK - LAYER 2
Responsible for node to node validity and integrity of the transmission. See *data link protocol*.

PHYSICAL - LAYER 1
Defines the functional characteristics for passing data bits onto and receiving them from the connecting medium. For example, it includes the RTS (request to send) and CTS (clear to send) signals in an RS-232 environment, as well as the TDM (time division multiplexing) in an ISDN environment.

Note: Electrical and mechanical characteristics define the interface between the OSI environment and the connecting transmission medium.

out of band See *signaling out of band*.

outline font A font that is made up of basic outlines for each character. The outlines are scaled into actual characters (bit maps) before printing. See *scalable fonts*.

outline processor Software that allows the user to type in thoughts and organize them into an outline form.

output
(1) Any computer-generated information displayed on screen, printed on paper or in machine readable form, such as disk and tape.

(2) To transfer or transmit from the computer to a peripheral device or communications line.

output area A reserved segment of memory that is used to lay out data or text in order to be transferred to an output device such as a disk or tape. Same as *buffer*.

output bound A computer that is slowed down by its output functions, typically to slow-speed communications lines or printers. See *print buffer*.

output device Any peripheral device that receives output from the computer, such as a video screen, printer, card punch or COM unit. Although disk and tape drives receive output from the computer, they are considered storage devices.

overflow error A error that occurs when calculated data cannot fit within the designated field. The result field is usually left blank or is filled with some special character in order to flag the error condition.

overhead

(1) The amount of processing time used by system software, such as the operating system, TP monitor or database manager.

(2) In communications, the additional codes transmitted for control and error checking purposes.

overlay

(1) A preprinted, precut form that is placed over a screen, key or tablet for indentification purposes. See *keyboard template*.

(2) A program segment that is called into memory when required. When a program is larger than the memory capacity of the machine it's running in, parts of the program that are not continuously used can be set up as overlays. When an overlay is called in, the instructions and associated user functions in the previous overlay are lost. The delays from calling in overlays are very noticeable on a floppy disk computer.

   The overlay process is inherent and automatic in a computer that has virtual memory.

overstrike

(1) To type over an existing character.

(2) A character with a line through it.

overwrite mode A data entry mode that writes over existing characters on screen when new characters are typed in. Contrast with *insert mode*.

P

PABX (Private Automatic Branch eXchange) Same as *PBX*.

pack
(1) To compress data in order to save space. Unpack refers to decompressing data. See *data compression*.

(2) An instruction that converts a decimal number into a packed decimal format. Unpack converts a packed decimal number into decimal.

(3) In database programs, a command that removes records that have been marked for deletion.

package See *software package*.

packaged software See *software package*.

packed decimal A storage mode that places two decimal digits into one byte, each digit occupying four bits of the byte. The sign occupies four bits in the least significant byte.

packet switching A technique for handling high-volume traffic in a network by breaking apart messages into fixed length packets that are transmitted to their destination through the most expedient route. All packets in a single message may not travel the same route (dynamic routing). The destination computer reassembles the packets into their proper sequence.

This method is used to efficiently handle messages of different lengths and priorities in large networks, such as Telenet, Tymnet and AT&T's Accunet. X.25 is the international standard for such a network.

Packet switching networks also provide value added services, such as protocol conversion and electronic mail.

packetized voice The transmission of realtime voice in a packet switching network.

packing density The number of bits or tracks per inch of recording surface. It also refers to the number of memory bits or other electronic components on a chip.

pad

(1) To fill a data structure with padding characters.

(2) PAD (Packet Assembler Dissassembler) A communications device that formats outgoing data into packets of the required length for transmission in a packet switching network. It also strips the data out of incoming packets.

padding Characters that are used to fill up the unused portion of a data structure, such as a field or communications message. A field might be padded with blanks, zeros or nulls.

paddle An input device that controls the cursor on screen in a back-and-forth motion. It has a dial and one or more buttons and is typically used in video games to hit balls and steer objects. Objects that move in all directions are controlled with a joy stick rather than a paddle.

page

(1) In virtual memory systems, a segment of the program that is transferred into memory.

(2) In videotex systems, a transmitted frame.

(3) In word processing, a printed page.

page break In printing, a code that marks the end of a page. A hard page break is inserted by the user, and the page will always break at that location. A soft page break is created by a word processing or report program based on current settings. Soft page breaks change as data is added or when the page length is changed.

page description language A high-level language for defining printer output. If an application generates output in a page description language (PDL), the output can be printed on any printer that supports it.

With a PDL, much of the character and graphics shaping is done within the printer rather than in the user's computer. Instead of downloading an entire font from the computer to the printer, which includes the design of each character, a command to build a particular font with a specific point size is sent, and the printer creates the characters of the font from basic design elements (outlines) of the font. Likewise, a command to draw a circle is sent to the printer rather than sending the actual bits of the circle image.

page header Common text that is printed at the top of every page. It generally includes the page number and headings above each column.

page makeup The setting up, or formatting, of a printed page, which includes the layout of headers, footers, columns, page numbers, graphics, rules and borders.

page printer A printer that prints a page at a time. See *laser printer* and *ion deposition*.

page recognition Software that recognizes the content of a printed page which has been scanned into the computer. It uses optical character recognition to convert the printed words into computer text, but it implies that the text can be automatically differentiated from other elements on the page, such as pictures and captions.

PageMaker A desktop publishing program for the PC and Macintosh from Aldus Corporation. Originally introduced for the Mac in 1985, it set the standard for desktop publishing. In fact, Paul Brainerd, president of Aldus, coined the term desktop publishing. The PC version was introduced in 1987, which has also been widely accepted.

pagination
(1) The numbering of pages.

(2) The laying out of printed pages, which includes the setting up and printing of columns, rules and borders. Although pagination is used synonymously with *page makeup*, the term often refers to the printing of long manuscripts rather than ads and brochures.

paging In virtual memory, the transfer of program segments (pages) into and out of memory.

paint
(1) In computer graphics, to literally "paint" the screen using a tablet stylus or mouse to simulate a paintbrush.

(2) To transfer a dot matrix image as in the phrase "the laser printer paints the image onto a photosensitive drum."

(3) To create a screen form by typing anywhere on screen. To "paint" the screen with text.

paint program A graphics program that allows the user to simulate painting on the screen with the use of a graphics tablet or mouse. Paint programs create raster graphics images.

PAL
(1) (Paradox Application Language) The programming language in Paradox.

(2) (Programmable Array Logic) A programmable logic chip (PLD) technology from Advanced Micro Devices.

(3) The European TV standard that uses 625 lines of resolution, 100 more lines than the NTSC standard.

palette
(1) In computer graphics, the total range of colors that can be used for display, although typically only a subset of them can be used at one time.

(2) A set of functions or modes.

pan
(1) In computer graphics, to move (while viewing) to a different part of an image without changing magnification.

(2) To move (while viewing) horizontally across a text record.

paper tape
(1) A sequential access storage medium that holds data as patterns of punched holes. It is a slow, low-capacity medium that, although extremely popular in the first half of the century, is in limited use today.

(2) A roll of paper that is printed by a calculator or cash register.

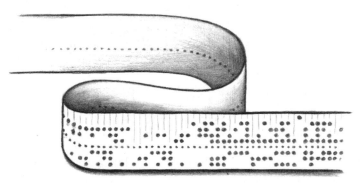

PAPER TAPE

paperless office An office in which all information is stored in electronic form. Long predicted since the beginning of computers, the paperless office is still somewhat of a myth. Although paper usage has been reduced in many organizations, it has also increased in others. Today's personal computers make it easy to spit out any number of copies of a document.

In time, laptop computers with immense amounts of storage and high-resolution screens will serve to replace paper when a person is travelling. Optical fiber networks will allow anyone at home or in the office to send data, text, pictures, voice and video anywhere in the world electronically.

As color laser printers become commonplace, it will be easy to reproduce any document, no matter how complex. People will eventually get used to the idea that a paper document is no better proof of a transaction than its electronic form. When this occurs, the paperless office will arrive.

paradigm Pronounced "para-dime." A model, example or pattern.

Paradox A network-ready relational database management system for PCs from Borland International. It has a unique programming language, called PAL, for application development. Many PAL statements are interactive Paradox commands, so that a Paradox user can adjust to programming more easily. Paradox is known for its ease of use and query by example, which allows users to easily ask complicated questions.

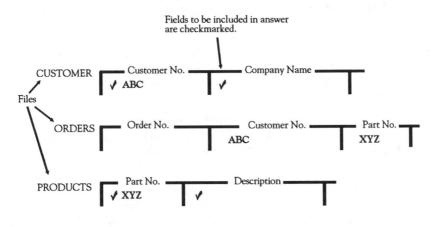

A RELATIONAL QUERY IN PARADOX

This example links three files together for a query. The ABC links the customer file with the orders file by customer number. The XYZ links the orders file with the products file by part number. The ABC and XYZ are arbitrary examples. The user can type in any words or letters to be used as matching examples as long as they are the same in both records.

Paradox engine The database part of Paradox that can be accessed by C programs, allowing C applications to create and manage Paradox data.

parallel computer A computer architecture made up of multiple processors. See *array processor* and *hypercube*.

parallel interface A multi-line channel that transfers one or more bytes simultaneously. For example, personal computers often connect printers via a Centronics 36-wire parallel interface, which transfers one byte at a time over eight wires, the remaining wires used for control signals.

Large computer parallel interfaces transfer more than one byte at a time. Contrast with *serial interface*. See *Centronics interface*.

parallel port An external connector on a computer that is used to hook up a printer or other parallel device. On PCs, the parallel port uses a DB-25 connector at the computer side and a Centronics 36-pin connector at the printer side.

parallel processing

(1) An architecture within a single computer that performs more than one operation at the same time. See *pipeline processing* and *vector processor*.

(2) A multiprocessing architecture made up of multiple processors or multiple computers. In a SIMD architecture, such as an array processor, one operation is performed on many sets of data. In a MIMD architecture, multiple computers work on different parts of a job simultaneously. See *hypercube* and *multiprocessing*.

parallelizing To generate instructions for a parallel processing computer.

parameter A value that customizes a program for a particular purpose. Parameters include such information as file names, coordinates and ranges of values. If parameters are optional, then default settings are used.

parameter-driven A program that requires parameters for its use. It implies that the program solves a problem that has to be entirely or partially described with values (parameters) that are given to it.

PARC (Palo Alto Research Center) Xerox Corporation's research and development center where the Smalltalk programming language and icon-oriented interface (GUI) were developed. Established in 1970, it is located in the Stanford University Industrial Park in Palo Alto.

parent-child In database management, a relationship between two files. The parent file contains required data about a subject, such as employees and customers. The child is the offspring of the parent, for example, the child of a customer file may be the order file.

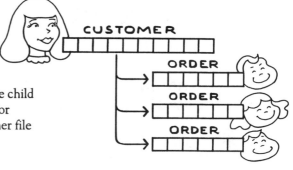

PARENT-CHILD

parity bit An extra bit attached to the byte, character or word used to detect errors in transmission.

parity checking An error detection technique that checks for the accurate transmission of digital data either within the computer system or over a network. Parity checking uses an extra bit (ninth bit) that holds a 0 or 1 depending on the data content of the byte.

For even parity systems, the parity bit is made a 1 when there are an even number of bits in the byte. In odd parity, the parity bit is a 1 when the byte contains an odd number of bits. In order to detect a transmission error, the parity bit is tested each time a byte is transmitted.

parity error An error condition that occurs when the parity bit of a character is found to be incorrect.

park To retract the read/write head on a hard disk to its home location before the unit is physically moved, in order to prevent damage.

parse To analyze a sentence or language statement. Parsing breaks down words into functional units that can be converted into machine language. For example, to parse the dBASE expression, `sum salary for title = "MANAGER"`, SUM must be identified as the primary command, FOR as a conditional search, TITLE as a field name and MANAGER as the data to be searched.

Parsing breaks down a natural language request, such as "What's the total of all the managers' salaries" into the commands required by a high-level language, such as in the example above.

parser The routine that performs parsing operations on a computer or natural language.

partition A reserved part of disk or memory that is set aside for some purpose.

Pascal A high-level programming language developed by Niklaus Wirth (Swiss) in the early 1970s and named after the French mathematician, Blaise Pascal. It is noted for its structured programming, which caused it to achieve popularity initially in academic circles.

Pascal is available in both interpreter and compiler form and has unique ways of defining variables. For example, a range of values or set of unique values can be stated and applied to any variable. If any other type of data is stored in the variable, the program will generate an error at run time. This automatic error trapping is helpful in program development. Another feature, called a *set*, is an array-like structure that can hold a varying number of predefined values. Sets can be matched and manipulated providing powerful non-numeric programming capabilities.

Pascal has had strong influence on subsequent languages, such as Ada, dBASE and PAL, although most of them have not implemented all its features. The following Turbo Pascal example converts fahrenheit to centigrade:

```
program convert;
var
fahr, cent : integer;
begin
  write('Enter fahrenheit ');
  readln(fahr);
  cent := (fahr - 32) * 5 / 9;
  writeln('Centigrade is ',cent)
end.
```

THE PASCALINE

(Courtesy The Computer Museum, Boston)

Pascaline A calculating machine developed in 1642 by Blaise Pascal, a French mathematician and philosopher. It could only add and subtract and was not the most advanced machine of its time. However, it got a lot of attention because 50 of them were placed in prominent locations throughout Europe. Accountants of the era expressed great concern that they might be replaced by this technological advancement!

passive star A network topology that joins wires from several nodes without providing any additional processing. Contrast with *active star*.

password A word or code used to identify an authorized user and is normally provided by the operating system or DBMS. Passwords serve as a security measure against unauthorized access to data; however, the computer can only verify the legitimacy of the password and not the legitimacy of the user.

paste See *cut & paste*.

patch A temporary or quick fix to a program. Too many patches in a program make it difficult to maintain. Patch may also refer to changing the actual machine code when it is inconvenient to recompile the source program.

path

(1) In communications, the route between any two nodes. Same as line, channel, link or circuit.

(2) In database management, the route from one set of data to another, for example, from customers to orders.

(3) In programming, a set route taken by the program to process a set of data.

(4) The route to a file on a disk. For example, in DOS and OS/2, if a file named MYLIFE is located in subdirectory STORIES within directory JOE on drive C,

the path to retrieve the file is: C:\JOE\STORIES\MYLIFE. In the Macintosh, the equivalent path (using the name "hard disk" for drive C) would look like: HARD DISK:JOE:STORIES:MYLIFE.

PAX

(1) (Private Automatic Exchange) An inhouse intercom system.

(2) (Parallel Architecture Extended) A parallel processing environment standard based on Intel's i860 RISC chip, UNIX System V and Alliant Computer's parallel and 3-D graphics technologies.

PAX-1
Software from VXM Technologies that allows a network of computers to function as a single parallel processing system. It runs in an Ethernet network with the TCP/IP protocol and supports personal computers, minis and mainframes.

PBX
(Private Branch eXchange) An inhouse telephone switching system that electronically interconnects one telephone extension to another, as well as to the outside telephone network.

A PBX can perform various telephone management functions, such as least cost routing for outside calls, call forwarding, conference calling and call accounting. Modern PBXs use all-digital methods for switching and can often handle digital terminals and telephones as well as the common analog telephone.

PBX

(Courtesy AT&T)

This PBX was installed in Bangor, Maine in 1883.

PC

(1) (Personal Computer) All machines that conform to the IBM PC and PS/2 standards.

(2) (Personal Computer) The original PC models (PC, XT, AT), in contrast with PS/2 models.

(3) (Personal Computer) Any personal computer.

(4) (Printed Circuit) See *printed circuit board*.

(5) *The Computer Glossary* uses definition #1 above and refers to all personal computers that conform to the IBM PC and PS/2 standards, which, collectively, are the largest installed base of computers worldwide.

PCs are used as stand-alone personal computers or as workstations and file servers in a local area network. They are predominantly used as single-user systems under DOS; however, they are also used as a central computer in a multiuser environment under UNIX and other multiuser operating systems, such as PC-MOS from The Software Link, Inc., and Concurrent DOS from Digital Research Inc.

IBM's first PCs used acronyms and names: XT, AT, Convertible, etc. Its current PS/2 series use numbers: Model 30, 55, 80, etc. Compatibles often use names that reference the CPU model; for example, "The 386 Turbo."

CPU # (Size)	CLOCK SPEED (MHz)	BUS SIZE	RAM (Bytes)	FLOPPY DISK (Bytes)	HARD DISK (Bytes)	OS
8088 (16 bits)	4.8-10	8 bits	1M*	5.25" 360K 3.5" 720K 3.5" 1.44M	10-40M	DOS
8086 (16 bits)	6-12	16 bits	1M*		20-60M	
80286 (16 bits)	6-20	16 bits	1-8M*	5.25" 360K 5.25" 1.2M 3.5" 720K	20-300M	DOS OS/2 UNIX
80386 (32 bits)	16-33	32 bits	1-16M**	3.5" 1.44M	40-600M	
80386SX (32 bits)	16-33	16 bits	1-16M**		40-300M	
80486 (32 bits)	25-50	32 bits	2-64M**		150-2000M	

PC SPECIFICATIONS
*Under DOS, RAM is increased beyond 1MB with EMS memory boards
**Under DOS, EMS can be activated in extended memory with an EMM (expanded memory manager) driver

Performance

Although there are hundreds of computers to choose from, they are all based on one of the following Intel microprocessors and the standards that go with them:

8086/88 COMPUTERS

In 1981, the Intel 8088 chip was launched in the original PC. Both it and the 8086 (faster version) are good for word processing and low-volume applications. To increase memory beyond one megabyte, EMS memory boards are used.

286 COMPUTERS

The Intel 80286, first used in the IBM AT in 1984, provides users with a more responsive machine than 8088-based models. Additional memory beyond one megabyte can be added and configured as either extended memory or EMS memory, depending on the programs and operating environment used in it (see Operating Environment below).

386 AND 386SX COMPUTERS

The Intel 80386, first used in the Compaq 386, is a high-performance computer with a much more advanced and flexible architecture than the 286. It has a special virtual 86 mode that can run multiple DOS applications concurrently and can ease the transition from DOS to OS/2 when necessary.

The 386SX is a slower speed version of the 386 with the same flexibility.

486 COMPUTERS

With initial models introduced in late 1989, the Intel 80486 is a higher-speed version of the 386 and has a built-in math coprocessor. The 486 is approximately 50% to 300% faster than the 386, depending on application, and is suited for graphics workstations, network file servers and multiuser computers.

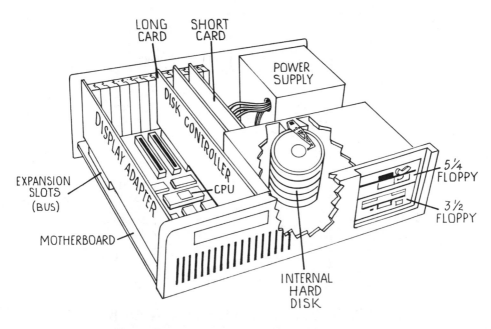

INTERNAL LAYOUT OF AN IBM PC

Operating Environment

Almost all PCs use Microsoft's DOS operating system that was designed for the Intel 8088 chip, which can address one megabyte of memory and leaves only 640K for user applications. Subsequent chips, starting with the 286, can address memory beyond 1MB called *extended memory.*

This original memory limitation is a major problem. It gave rise to a number of operating environments that often conflict with each other. As users get more comfortable with computers, they want more applications open and active at the same time.

In 1984, Borland introduced Sidekick, which popularized the TSR, or popup, program. It swapped itself in and out of view by pressing a hotkey. Users got a taste of switching back and forth quickly to a handy notepad or calendar, and vendors have been writing this popular brand of popup program ever since. However, keeping many TSRs in memory can quickly use up memory, and older ones don't always work with newer ones.

From 1984 through 1987, a new EMS memory standard was formulated to break the memory barrier. The additional memory is used directly by applications that

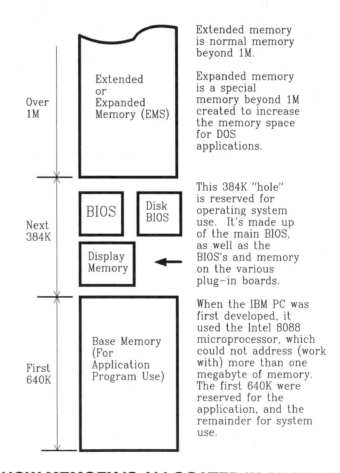

Extended memory is normal memory beyond 1M.

Expanded memory is a special memory beyond 1M created to increase the memory space for DOS applications.

This 384K "hole" is reserved for operating system use. It's made up of the main BIOS, as well as the BIOS's and memory on the various plug-in boards.

When the IBM PC was first developed, it used the Intel 8088 microprocessor, which could not address (work with) more than one megabyte of memory. The first 640K were reserved for the application, and the remainder for system use.

HOW MEMORY IS ALLOCATED IN AN IBM PC

are EMS aware or by operating environments, such as DESQview and Microsoft Windows.

Microsoft Windows creates a Macintosh-like windowing environment with a program in each window. In addition, data can be exchanged between programs, but applications must be written for Windows in order to take advantage of it. Windows 3.0 is a significant improvement over previous versions and allows users to run and switch between multiple standard DOS applications. In addition, with Windows 3.0 in 386 Enhanced Mode, most standard DOS applications can be run in a window and data can be exchanged between them.

Another technique is the use of a DOS extender for 286 and higher machines, which allows the application to run in extended memory without constraint. For example, Lotus 1-2-3 Version 3.0 was one of the first major programs to use one. Windows 3.0 uses a DOS extender and thus manages up to 16MB of memory. It also introduced the DPMI standard for DOS extenders, which is incompatible with the first DOS extenders using the de facto VCPI standard.

Although Microsoft's OS/2 operating system solves the memory problem, there are millions of existing DOS users with thousands coming on board daily. OS/2 computers need more memory and disk space, and the original 16-bit versions of OS/2 can't run large DOS applications in compatibility mode. OS/2 will eventually flourish on 386 and 486 machines using the 32-bit version of OS/2 (Version 2.0).

The transition from DOS to OS/2 will take years, just like it did to convert from the old mainframe DOS to OS in the 1960s and 1970s. In the meantime, EMS, TSRs, windowing environments and DOS extenders all compete to make the machine more flexible and usable under DOS.

Compatibility

The first attempts at cloning the IBM PC were only partially successful. There were a lot of "almost compatible" computers. However, as soon as the difficult ROM BIOS was successfully cloned and made commercially available, true compatibles appeared in abundance. Most compatibles are very compatible today, but there are exceptions.

In addition, vendors never cease to develop some proprietary technique to improve performance, and a conflict can arise at any time. The only way of guaranteeing that something works is to try it.

This has been true since day one in the computer business, however.

Video Display

Since 1981, IBM has introduced several display standards that are implemented by plugging in a board, called a *display adapter,* and connecting the appropriate monitor to it. Each new standard incorporates the previous ones for compatibility, however, vendors have to modify their programs to handle the higher resolution graphics each time.

Monochrome monitors dominated the business world for the first half of the 1980s, because IBM's first color display (CGA) was too coarse for text. With the advent of EGA, and now VGA, color monitors are becoming popular in the corporate world.

Unlike the Macintosh, which is entirely graphics based, PCs operate in two modes. Data processing applications are usually text based, while paint and design programs, as well as Microsoft Windows, are graphics based. The program switches the computer into the appropriate video mode. The computer is more responsive in text mode than in graphics mode, and this has been one of the appealing attributes of the PC world.

For desktop publishing and design requirements, there are many high-resolution graphics systems from third parties. To activate these displays, the hardware vendor provides a driver that works with popular software packages, such as Windows or Ventura, etc. However, once a display becomes widely used, it is often supported by the software vendors. See PC *display modes*.

PC & PS/2 DISPLAY STANDARDS

MDA	720x350 text - monochrome
Hercules	720x348 text and graphics - mono (non-IBM)
CGA	320x200 text and graphics (4 colors)*
EGA	640x350 text and graphics (16 colors)*
MCGA	640x400 text, 320x200 graphics (256 cols)
VGA	720x400 text, 640x480 graphics (16 cols)*
8514	1,024x768 text and graphics (256 colors)

* More colors available from 3rd-party vendors.

Printers

There are hundreds printers that work with PCs from dot matrix to laser printers. Support for these printers is provided by the vendor of the application software.

Word processing, desktop publishing, CAD and drawing programs, or any other package that offers full-featured printing, must provide drivers for the popular printers. These drivers are selected by the user when installing the program.

Keyboards

The original PC keyboard used an awkward return and left shift key placement. Finally corrected on the AT keyboard, the backspace key was shortened making it awkward to reach. Then came the Enhanced keyboard with a host of relocated keys, making it impossible to use the function keys intelligently. What was easy to reach on one is hard to reach on the other. There are only a few keyboards that dare to be different and incorporate the best features of both, such as Northgate's OmniKey/102.

Floppy Disks

The most common floppy is the 360KB, 5.25" disk introduced soon after the first IBM PC. Later, the AT model introduced the 1.2 megabyte floppy, and, although used for backup, it is not used much for distributing software. The

1.2MB drives can read and write the 360KB disks, but earlier models of the drive cannot be used to format 360KB disks.

IBM introduced the 720KB, 3.5" microfloppy on its Convertible laptop, then doubled the capacity to 1.4MB with the PS/2 line. Due to their greater capacity and convenience, the 3.5" floppies have been retrofitted to many machines. The 1.4MB drives can read, write and format 720KB disks.

FLOPPY DISK FORMATS

360KB Minifloppy disk (double density 5.25")
1.2MB Minifloppy disk (high density 5.25")
720KB Microfloppy disk (double density 3.5")
1.4MB Microfloppy disk (high density 3.5")

Hard Disks

Non-removable, hard disks for PCs are available with storage capacities from 20 to 600MB, with multiple drive capabilities reaching the gigabyte level. If a hard disk is added that is not compatible with the existing disk controller, a new controller board must be plugged in. However, one disk's internal standard does not conflict with another, since all programs and data must be copied onto it.

Removable disk cartridges that hold 20 to 40 and more megabytes are also becoming popular.

As the storage capacity grows, so does performance. Disk access times run from 15 milliseconds (fast) to 100 ms (slow). The larger ESDI and SCSI drives also transfer data faster. Hard disks, 100 megabytes and over, are generally very fast and are the type required for use as a network server.

Data Bus

When a peripheral device, such as a graphics display or scanner, is installed in the computer, the appropriate controller board must be plugged into the data bus. The peripheral is then plugged into the controller board.

In 8088-based PCs, the bus transfers 8-bits simultaneously. With the 286-based AT model, the bus was extended to 16-bits, and AT-class machines come with a mix of 8-bit and 16-bit slots. 386s have both slots as well as proprietary slots for 32-bit memory. New 386s are being built with either the Micro Channel or EISA bus.

The Micro Channel is a 32-bit bus introduced with the PS/2, and it is the first architectural change in the IBM personal computer line. PC and AT (8-bit and 16-bit) boards can't be used with it.

To counter the higher-speed Micro Channel and extend the life of the original bus, EISA was conceived by the compatible vendors in late 1988. EISA accepts new 32-bit EISA boards as well as the original 8-bit and 16-bit boards.

IBM PERSONAL COMPUTER MODELS

PC Series

Model	Date of Intro.	CPU	Significance
PC	(8/81)	8088	No. 1 (floppy disk)
XT	(3/83)	8088	Slow-speed hard disk
XT 286	(9/86)	286	Slow-speed hard disk
XT/370	(10/83)	8088	IBM 370 emulation
AT	(8/84)	286	Medium-speed hard disk
3270 PC	(10/83)	8088	3270 emulation
PCjr	(11/83)	8088	Floppy-based home use
PC Portable	(2/84)	8088	Floppy-based portable
Convertible	(4/86)	8088	Microfloppy laptop

PS/1 Series

Model	Date of Intro.	CPU	Significance
MO1	(6/90)	286	PC bus, single 3.5" floppy
M34	(6/90)	286	PC bus, hard disk
CO1	(6/90)	286	PC bus, color monitor
C34	(6/90)	286	PC bus, color, hard disk

PS/2 Series

Model	Date of Intro.	CPU	Significance
25	(8/87)	8086	PC bus (limited expansion)
30	(4/87)	8086	PC bus
30-286	(9/88)	286	PC bus
50	(4/87)	286	Micro Channel
50Z	(6/88)	286	Improved performance
55SX	(5/89)	386SX	Micro Channel
60	(4/87)	286	Micro Channel
65	(3/90)	386SX	Micro Channel
70	(6/88)	386	Micro Channel
70-486	(12/89)	486	Micro Channel
P70	(5/89)	386	Micro Channel portable
80	(4/87)	386	Micro Channel tower style
90	(9/90)	486	Micro Channel desktop
95	(9/90)	486	Micro Channel tower style

PC board See *printed circuit board.*

PC bus The bus architecture used in first-generation IBM PCs. PC bus refers to two versions: the original 8-bit bus and the 16-bit extension introduced with the AT. 8-bit boards will fit into 8-bit and 16-bit slots, but 16-bit boards fit only in the 16-bit slot. None of the PC bus boards plug into the Micro Channel of the PS/2.

PC display modes The following table contains the video display standards of the IBM PC and PS/2 series.

Mode		Colors	Chars	Pixels	Display adapters			
0	Text	16 gray	40x25	320x200	CGA	EGA	MCGA	VGA
0	Text	16 gray	40x25	320x350		EGA		VGA
0	Text	16 gray	40x25	320x400			MCGA	
0	Text	16 gray	40x25	360x400				VGA
1	Text	16	40x25	320x200	CGA	EGA	MCGA	VGA
1	Text	16	40x25	320x350		EGA		VGA
1	Text	16	40x25	320x400			MCGA	
1	Text	16	40x25	360x400				VGA
2	Text	16 gray	80x25	640x200	CGA	EGA	MCGA	VGA
2	Text	16 gray	80x25	640x350		EGA		VGA
2	Text	16 gray	80x25	640x400			MCGA	
2	Text	16 gray	80x25	720x400				VGA
3	Text	16	80x25	640x200	CGA	EGA	MCGA	VGA
3	Text	16	80x25	640x350		EGA		VGA
3	Text	16	80x25	640x400			MCGA	
3	Text	16	80x25	720x400				VGA
4	Graphics 4			320x200	CGA	EGA	MCGA	VGA
5	Graphics 4 gray			320x200	CGA	EGA	MCGA	VGA
6	Graphics 2			640x200	CGA	EGA	MCGA	VGA
7	Text	2 B&W	80x25	720x350	MDA	EGA		VGA
7	Text	2 B&W	80x25	720x400				VGA
13	Graphics 16			320x200		EGA		VGA
14	Graphics 16			640x200		EGA		VGA
15	Graphics 2 B&W			640x350		EGA		VGA
16	Graphics 4			640x350		EGA		
16	Graphics 16			640x350		EGA		VGA
17	Graphics 2 B&W			640x480			MCGA	VGA
18	Graphics 16			640x480				VGA
19	Graphics 256			320x200			MCGA	VGA

Modes 8-10 (PCjr), 11-12 used by EGA internally.

PC-DOS The DOS operating system supplied by IBM for its personal computers in contrast with MS-DOS for compatible machines. Currently, both versions are almost identical, and both are simply called DOS.

PC keyboard The keyboard introduced with the IBM PC in 1981, which was severely criticized for its non-standard return and left shift key placements. It provides a dual-function keypad for numeric entry and cursor movement. Regardless of key placement, the feel of IBM keyboards is highly praised.

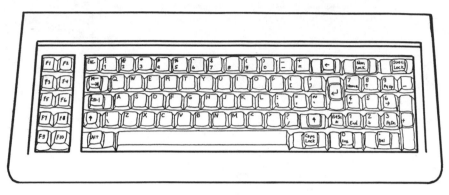

PC KEYBOARD

PC-MOS/386 A multiuser operating system for PCs from The Software Link, Inc. It runs almost all standard DOS applications as well as applications written for the 386's 32-bit protected mode.

PC Network The first PC local area network from IBM introduced in 1984. It uses the CSMA/CD access method and introduced the NetBIOS interface, which is now widely used in many types of PC networks. Token Ring Network support was later added. Microsoft's version is called MS-Net.

PC Paintbrush A paint program for PCs from ZSoft Corporation that is widely used. Its PCX raster graphics format is accepted by many graphics, word processing and desktop publishing programs.

PC Probe A diagnostic package for the PC from Landmark Research International that analyzes all hardware components and includes utilities for fixing common problems. Also included is the popular Landmark speed test.

PC Tools Deluxe A comprehensive package of utilities for the PC from Central Point Software that includes a DOS shell as well as file management, communications, disk caching, backup and data compression utilities.

PCB See *printed circuit board*.

PCjr (PC junior) IBM's first home computer, introduced in 1983. It was initially offered with a keyboard that was not suitable for typing, but adequate keyboards were later included. The PCjr was not widely accepted and was discontinued in 1985.

PCL (Printer Control Language) The printer language from Hewlett-Packard that activates the LaserJet printers. PCL has become an industry standard that is used with many different brands of laser printers and typesetters. If a machine supports the PCL language, it accepts the same printer files that are sent to LaserJet printers.

PCL Level 5, introduced with the LaserJet Series III in 1990, also supports Compugraphic's Intellifont scalable fonts.

PCM

(1) (Pulse Code Modulation) A technique for digitizing speech by sampling the sound waves and converting each sample into a binary number. PCM uses waveform coding which samples a 4KHz bandwidth 8,000 times a second. Each sample is an 8 bit number, resulting in 64K bits of data per second. See ADPCM.

(2) (Plug Compatible Manufacturer) An organization that makes a computer or electronic device that is compatible with an existing machine.

p-code See *pseudo language* and *UCSD P-system*.

PDES (Product Data Exchange Specification) A standard format for the exchange of data between advanced computer-aided design (CAD) and computer-aided manufacturing (CAM) programs. It describes a complete product, including the geometric aspects of the images as well as manufacturing features, tolerance specifications, material properties and finish specifications. See *IGES Organization*.

PDL See *page description language*.

PDP

(Programmed Data Processor) A family of minicomputers from Digital Equipment Corporation. The first PDP was the PDP-1, an 18-bit computer introduced in late 1959. Its $120,000 price was

PDP-8

(Courtesy Charles Babbage Institute, University of Minnesota)

considerably less than the million dollar machines of the time, and 50 of them were built. In 1962, the PDP-4 cost half as much as the PDP-1 and 65 were built. The PDP-7, 9 and 15 were 18-bit successors to the PDP-1, and were introduced throughout the 1960s and early 1970s. In 1963, came the 12-bit PDP-5.

In 1965, Digital introduced the PDP-8 at a price starting around $20,000, and it quickly legitimized the minicomputer industry. By the late 1970s, with its processor on a single chip, the PDP-8 was available for under $3,000 and found its way into DECmate workstations used for word processing.

In 1963, Digital introduced its largest PDP model, the 36-bit PDP-6. It was followed by various PDP-10 models during the 1970s, and eventually this series evolved into the DECsystem 10 and DECsystem 20.

In 1970, Digital introduced the 16-bit PDP-11, which became the most widely used minicomputer in the world with over 50,000 systems sold.

The PDP series was followed by the VAX series in 1977; however, PDP-11s are still in production.

peek-a-boo To check for the same character code in the same column of two or more punched cards by placing them on top of each other and looking through them.

peek/poke Instructions that view and alter a byte of memory by referencing its specific memory address. Peek displays the contents, and poke changes it.

peer In communications, a functional unit that is on the same protocol layer as another.

peer-to-peer communications The communicating from one user to another user on a network. It implies the ability to initiate the session at the user's discretion.

peer-to-peer network A local area network that allows all users access to data on all workstations. A dedicated file server is not required, but may be used.

pel Same as *pixel*.

pen plotter See *plotter*.

PEPPER board A family of graphics display boards for PCs from Number Nine Computer Corporation. PEPPER boards provide the extremely high-resolution images that are required in CAD, high-end graphics and certain desktop publishing applications.

peripheral Any hardware device connected to a computer, such as a monitor, keyboard, printer, plotter, disk or tape drive, graphics tablet, scanner, joy stick, paddle and mouse.

peripheral controller An electronic circuit that controls the operation of a peripheral device. See *control unit (2)*.

permanent memory Same as *non-volatile memory*.

permutation One possible combination of items out of a larger group of items. For example, with the group of numbers 1, 2 and 3, there are six possible permutations: **12, 21, 13, 31, 23** and **32**.

perpendicular recording See *vertical recording*.

persistence In a CRT, the length of time a phosphor dot remains illuminated after it has been energized. Long-persistence phosphors reduce flicker, but generate ghost-like images that linger on screen for a fraction of a second.

personal computer Synonymous with microcomputer, a computer that is functionally similar to larger computers, but serves only one user. It is used at home and in the office for almost all applications traditionally performed on larger computers.

   With the addition of a modem, a personal computer becomes a terminal to the outside world, capable of retrieving information from other computers and information utilities.

   There are a wide variety of personal computers on the market, priced from $300 to over $10,000. The size of the computer is based on its memory and disk capacity. Its speed is based on the CPU that runs it, and its visual quality is based on the resolution of its display screen and printer.

   Most personal computers run one program at a time, but multitasking machines, which run more than one program concurrently, will become more common in the 1990s.

Major Suppliers of Personal Computers

The personal computer world is overwhelmingly dominated by IBM PCs and IBM-compatible PCs. There are dozens of vendors and hundreds of models to choose from, although all available models fall into a handful of categories (see PC).

   The next largest supplier is Apple Computer, which provides the Apple II and Macintosh families. The Apple II series is the most widely used computer in elementary and high schools as well as at home. The Macintoshes are popular with small businesses and are increasingly being purchased by large corporations.

Both Atari and Commodore continue to carve out a niche and are popular as home and small business computers. Each of them has support from software vendors providing a rounded supply of applications.

The History of Personal Computers

The personal computer industry began in 1977, when Apple, Radio Shack and Commodore introduced the first off-the-shelf computers as consumer products.

The first machines used an 8-bit microprocessor with a maximum of 64K of memory and floppy disks for storage. The Apple II, Atari 500, and Commodore 64 became popular home computers, and Apple was successful in the business market after the VisiCalc spreadsheet was introduced. However, the business world was soon dominated by the Z80 processor and CP/M operating system. It was used by countless vendors in the early 1980s, such as Vector Graphic, NorthStar, Osborne and Kaypro. By 1983, hard disks began to show up on these machines, but CP/M was soon to be history.

In 1981, IBM introduced the PC, an Intel 8088-based machine, slightly faster than the genre, but with 10 times the memory. It was floppy-based, and its DOS operating system from Microsoft was also available (MS-DOS) for clone makers. The 8088 was cleverly chosen so that CP/M software vendors could convert to it easily. They did!

dBASE II was introduced in 1981 bringing mainframe database functions to the personal computer level and launching an entire industry of compatible products and add-ons.

THE FIRST PERSONAL COMPUTER
(Courtesy Xerox Corporation)

In the mid 1970s, Xerox developed the Alto computer, which was the forerunner of its Star workstation and the inspiration for Apple's Lisa and Macintosh computers.

Lotus 1-2-3 was introduced in 1982, and its refined interface and combined graphics helped spur sales of the new IBM standard.

The IBM PC was successfully cloned by Compaq and unsuccessfully cloned by others. However, by the time IBM announced the AT in 1984, vendors were effectively cloning the PC and, as a group, eventually succeeded in grabbing the majority of the personal computer market.

In 1983, Apple introduced the Lisa, a graphics-based machine that simulated the user's desktop. The Lisa was way ahead of its time, but Apple all but abandoned it for the Macintosh in 1984. The graphics-based desktop evironment caught on big with the Mac, especially in desktop publishing, and the graphical interface, or "gooey," (GUI) worked its way to the PC world with Microsoft Windows, and, eventually Ventura Publisher with its GEM interface.

In 1986, the Compaq 386 ushered in the first Intel 80386-based machine, a more advanced computer than its predecessors that can manage huge amounts of memory and disk.

In 1987, IBM introduced the PS/2, its next generation of personal computers, which added improved graphics, 3.5" floppy disks and an incompatible bus to help fend off the cloners. OS/2, jointly developed by IBM and Microsoft, was also introduced to effectively handle the new, larger machines, but it has been slow to catch on.

In the same year, more powerful Macintoshes were introduced, including the Mac SE and Mac II. The Mac II family has opened up new doors for Apple and has become a very competitive machine.

In 1989, IBM and compatible vendors introduced 80486-based computers, and faster Macintoshes were also introduced.

Inspired by Radio Shack's Model 100 in 1984 and ignited by Toshiba and Zenith, the laptop market provides one of the most fascinating growth areas in personal computing. More and more power is being stuffed into less and less space, providing computing power on the go that few would have imagined back in 1977.

The Future

The personal computer industry sprang up without any cohesive planning. All of a sudden, it was there, and individual machines were bought to solve individual problems, such as automating a budget, typing a letter or searching a file.

However, in large organizations, the real data exists in the mainframe, and it doesn't serve the organization to have an employee retype the mainframe reports into the micro in order to analyze and manipulate it.

The personal computer, originally out of the control of IS professionals, is now back in their hands. Personal computers can serve as invaluable tools for the user when they are designed into the fabric of the organization. The major issue of the 1990s will be to tie them together in local area networks and to interconnect them with the organization's minis and mainframes.

The new, fast personal computers (Intel 386, 486, Motorola 68020, 68030, etc.) are changing the marketplace forever. Not only do they begin to compete with minicomputer workstations, but, as we enter the 1990s, networks of these machines will be installed for applications that were previously relegated to minis and mainframes.

These high-powered desktop computers will encourage the development of more artificial intelligence applications that are the backbone of the next generation of computing. By the turn of the century, you should be able to talk to your computer as easily as typing on it.

As stand-alone machines, personal computers have placed creative capacity into the hands of an individual that would have cost millions of dollars less than 20 years ago. Its use is slowly but surely shifting the balance of power from the large company to the small company, from the elite to the masses, from the wealthy to individuals of modest means. In little more than a decade, the personal computer has revolutionized the computer industry and the world.

Personal System/1, Personal System/2 See *PS/1, PS/2* and *PC*.

PET computer (Personal Electronic Transaction computer) A CP/M and floppy disk-based personal computer introduced in 1977 by Commodore Business Machines, Inc. It was one of the three first personal computers.

PFS:First Choice An integrated software package for PCs from Software Publishing Corporation. It provides word processing, database, spreadsheet, graphics and communications capabilities.

PFS:Professional Write A word processing program for PCs from Software Publishing Corporation. It is very easy to learn and use and meets the needs of many people who write uncomplicated letters and memos. Software Publishing provides an entire series of PFS programs for database, spreadsheets and other applications.

PGA
(1) (Professional Graphics Adapter) An IBM PC display standard from IBM that provides 640x480 pixels, 256 colors, and a separate 3-D video coprocessor. PGA has had minimal support.

(2) (Pin Grid Array) A chip housing that contains a high density of pins. For example, a 1.5" square PGA can have nearly 200 pins. PGAs are used for large amounts of input and output.

(3) (Programmable Gate Array) A special type of gate array that is programmed on site rather than in a manufacturing process.

phase change recording An optical recording technique that uses a laser to alter the crystalline structure of a metallic surface. The crystal structure is altered to create a bit that reflects or absorbs light when the bits are read. See *optical disk*.

phase encoding A magnetic recording technique used for high-speed devices that records a 0 bit as a split negative-positive sequence and a 1 bit as a positive-negative sequence.

phase locked A technique for maintaining synchronization in an electronic circuit. The circuit receives its timing from input signals, but also provides a feedback circuit for synchronization.

phase modulation In communications, a transmission technique that modulates (merges) a data signal into a fixed carrier frequency by modifying the phase of the carrier wave. Contrast with AM and FM, the two other major techniques for modulating a carrier.

phase modulation recording Same as *phase encoding.*

PHIGS (Programmer's Hierarchical Interactive Graphics Standard) A graphics system and language that is used to create 2-D and 3-D graphics images. Like the GKS standard, PHIGS is a device independent interface between the application program and the graphics subsystem.

 PHIGS manages graphics objects in a hierarchical manner so that a complete assembly can be specified with all of its subassemblies. It is a very comprehensive standard requiring high-performance workstations and host processing.

phone connector A plug and socket for a two or three-wire coaxial cable that is commonly used to plug microphones and other audio equipment into amplifiers. See *phono connector.*

phone hawk
Slang for a person who calls up a computer via modem and either copies or destroys data.

phoneme An utterance of speech, such as "k," "ch," and "sh," that is used in synthetic speech systems to compose words for audio output.

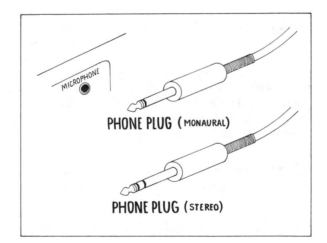

PhoneNET A series of products from Farallon Computing, Inc., that extends the reach of LocalTalk from 1,000 feet to 3,000 feet and allows unshielded twisted phone lines to be used instead of shielded twisted pair. Configurations include daisy chain and passive star topologies, as well as an active star topology with Farallon's star controller that extends distances even farther. Optional Traffic Watch software provides network management and administration capabilities.

With EtherTalk boards intalled, a PhoneNet active star controller is also available for Ethernet on twisted pair.

phono connector Also called an *RCA connector,* it is a plug and socket for a two-wire coaxial cable that is used for audio and video signals. It is commonly used to interconnect high fidelity components as well as the composite video output from a computer to a television, such as found on the Apple II. See *phone connector.*

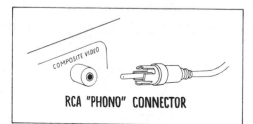

RCA "PHONO" CONNECTOR

phosphor A rare earth material that is used to coat the inside face of a CRT. When struck by an electron beam, the phosphor emits a visible light for a few milliseconds. In color displays, red, green and blue phosphor dots are grouped as a cluster.

photocomposition The composition of a printed page using electrophotographic machines, such as phototypesetters and laser printers. See *page makeup* and *pagination.*

photolithography A technique that uses a photomask to imprint a design onto an object. For example, the design of the circuit paths and electronic elements on a chip are transferred onto a wafer's surface using this method.

A photomask is created with the design for each layer of the chip. The wafer is coated with a light-sensitive film and is exposed to light shining through the photomask. The light reaching the wafer hardens the film, and when the wafer is exposed to an acid bath (wet processing) or hot ions (dry processing), the unhardened areas are etched away.

photomask An opaque image on a transluscent plate that is used as a light filter to transfer an image from one device to another. See *chip.*

photomicrography The photographing of microscopic images.

photon An elementary particle of light. A photon is much smaller than its electron counterpart and can thus allow even greater miniaturization within photonic circuits.

photonics The science of building machine circuits that use light instead of electricity.

photooptic memory A storage device that uses a laser beam to record data onto a photosensitive film.

photorealistic image synthesis In computer graphics, a format for describing a picture that depicts the realism of the actual image. It includes such attributes as surface texture, light sources, motion blur and reflectivity.

photoresist The light-sensitive film used in photolithography that temporarily holds the pattern to be etched away.

photosensor A light-sensitive device that is used in optical scanning machinery.

phototypesetter A device that creates professional-quality text. Input to the phototypesetter comes from the keyboard, over a communications channel or via disk or tape. The output is a paper-like or transparent film that is processed into a camera-ready master for printing. Advanced industrial machines generate the actual printing plates.

Phototypesetters employ various light technologies for the creation of the characters. Older machines use a spinning film strip that is used as a photomask for a particular font. Light passing through the film strip is enlarged by lenses to the appropriate type size, exposing the film. Other machines create images on CRTs that are used to expose the film, and the latest units use lasers to generate the image directly onto the film like a laser printer.

The phototypesetter has been used to print books, magazines and all commercially printed materials, and was originally the only machine that could handle multiple fonts and text composition capabilities, such as kerning.

Today, desktop laser printers are being used to typeset text, and although they can't produce the ultra-fine lines of the high-resolution (1,200 to 2,400 dots per inch) phototypesetters, they can produce excellent printed matter.

physical Devices at the electronic, or machine, level. Contrast with *logical*. See *logical vs physical*.

physical address The actual, or machine, address of an item or device.

physical link
(1) The electronic connection between two devices.

(2) In data management, a pointer in an index or record that refers to the physical location of data in another file.

pica
(1) In word processing, a font that prints at 10 characters per linear inch.

(2) In typography, approximately 1/6th of an inch.

Pick System An operating environment from Pick Systems, Inc., that runs in a variety of computers. It includes an advanced virtual memory operating system and relational database.

It was originally developed by Richard Pick, who created a system for the U.S. Army while working at TRW Corporation. He later transformed it into the Reality operating system for Microdata. Later, Pick obtained the right to license the system to other vendors.

The Pick environment is highly praised for its ease of use and flexibility and is used in a variety of multiuser computer systems.

picosecond One trillionth of a second. Pronounced "pee-co-second."

PICT (PICTure) A graphics file format for the Macintosh that stores images in the QuickDraw vector format.

picture In programming, a pattern that describes the type of data allowed in a field or how it will print. The pattern is made up of a character code for each character in the field; for example, 9999 is a picture for four numeric digits. A picture for a telephone number could be (999) 999-9999. XXX999 represents three alphanumerics followed by three numerics. Picture codes are similar but not identical in all programming languages.

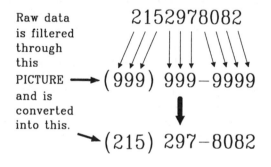

Raw data is filtered through this PICTURE and is converted into this.

PICTURE FIELD

picture element See *pixel.*

Picturephone A proposed video/telephone from AT&T that lets users see who they are talking to. Although many thought it was going to be a reality by the end of the 1980s, it may not occur until after the turn of the century.

PicturePower A picture database management system for PCs from PictureWare, Inc., that accepts scanned images and provides facilities for editing them. It lets the user build screen forms that incorporate images and text. It can also be used to add graphics to dBASE applications allowing images to be displayed from within dBASE. PicturePower-HC is a high-compression version that includes an add-in board for compressing images as much as 20 to 1.

PICTUREPOWER

(Courtesy PictureWare, Inc.)

pie chart A graphical representation of information in which each unit of data is represented as a pie-shaped piece of a circle. See *business graphics*.

piezoelectric The generation of electricity from a crystal that is subjected to pressure. Certain crystal oscillators and microphones are piezoelectric devices.

PIF file A program description file that is used in Microsoft Windows. It is created with the PIF Editor program, and it holds information that Windows needs to know about the program, such as how much memory it uses and if it bypasses the operating system and writes directly to the screen or takes over the keyboard.

piggyback board A small printed circuit board that plugs into another printed circuit board in order to enhance its capabilities. It does not plug into the motherboard, but would plug into the boards that plug into the motherboard.

PILOT (Programmed Inquiry Learning Or Teaching) A high-level programming language used to generate CAI (computer assisted instruction) programs. It generates question-and-answer types of courseware. A version of PILOT that incorporates turtle graphics runs on Atari personal computers.

PIM (Personal Information Manager) A combination word processor, database and desktop accessory program that organizes a variety of information. It allows the user to tie together more loosely structured information than traditional programs.

PIMs vary widely, but all of them attempt to provide methods for managing information the way people think about their jobs and functions. Apple's HyperCard is used as a PIM.

pin One of the male leads on a multiple line plug, such as an RS-232 connector. Each pin is connected with its female counterpart to close a circuit. A pin is also one of the footlike leads on a chip that plugs into a socket on the printed circuit board.

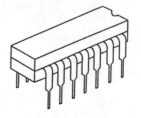
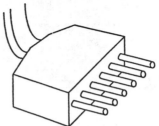

PIN (Personal Identification Number) A number chosen by the user as a personal password for identification purposes.

pin feed A paper movement method that contains a set of pins on a platen or tractor. The pins engage the paper through perforated holes in its left and right borders.

PINS

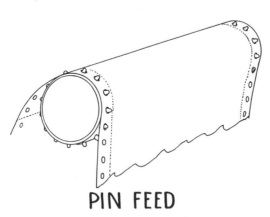

PIN FEED

pinch roller A small, freely-turning wheel that pushes the magnetic tape against a motor-driven wheel in order to move the tape in a tape drive.

ping pong
(1) Same as *half-duplex*.

(2) Various techniques that perform an operation in one direction and then in the other.

ping-pong buffer See *double buffering*.

pinouts The description and purpose of each pin in a multiline connector.

PIP (Peripheral Interchange Program) A CP/M utility program used to copy and transfer files.

pipe A shared space that accepts the output of one program for input into another. In DOS and OS/2, the pipe command is a vertical line (|). The statement, `dir | sort newlist`, directs the output of the directory listing to be sorted and then stored in a file called NEWLIST.

pipeline processing A category of techniques that provide simultaneous, or parallel, processing within the computer It refers to overlapping operations by moving data or instructions into a conceptual pipe with all stages of the pipe processing simultaneously. For example, while one instruction is being executed, the computer is decoding the next instruction. In vector processors, several steps in a floating point operation can be processed simultaneously.

piracy The illegal copying of software either for personal or commerical use.

pitch The number of printed characters per inch. With proportionally spaced characters, the pitch is variable and must be measured as an average. See *dot pitch*.

pixel (PIX [picture] ELement) The smallest element on a video display screen. A screen is broken up into thousands of tiny dots, and a pixel is one or more dots that are treated as a unit. A pixel can be one dot on a monochrome screen, three dots (red, green and blue) on color screens, or clusters of these dots.

For monochrome screens, the pixel, normally dark, is energized to different light intensities, creating a range from dark to light. For color, each red, green and blue dot is energized to different intensities, creating a range of colors perceived as the mixture of these dots. Black is all three dots off, white is all three dots on, and grays are even intensities of each color.

The number of bits assigned to each pixel in its associated digital memory determines the number of shades and colors that can be represented. The most economical system is monochrome in which one bit is used per pixel, either on or off. In the most elaborate color displays, which use up to four full bytes for each of the red, green and blue dots, each pixel can display billions of different shades. Considering that a high-resolution screen may use a million pixels, many megabytes of memory would have to be reserved to hold such an image.

pixel graphics Same as *raster graphics*.

PixelPaint A drawing program for the Macintosh from SuperMac Technologies that is known for its extensive paint palette and color mixing schemes.

PKARC, PKZIP Shareware programs from PKware Inc., that are used to compress and decompress PC files for storage or distribution. PKZIP is the more recent version of the product and provides greater compression. For example, version 1.01 of PKZIP reduced the text of this Glossary 61%. The PK stands for Phil Katz, the company's founder.

PLA (Programmable Logic Array) A programmable logic chip (PLD) technology from Philips/Signetics.

planar A technique developed by Fairchild Instrument that is used to create the sublayers of a transistor in a chip by forcing chemicals under pressure into the exposed areas. The planar process was a major step in the creation of the microchip. Contrast with the earlier *mesa* process, which created more deeply etched channels in the semiconductor material.

planar area In computer graphics, an object that has boundaries, such as a square, circle or polygon.

planning system See *spreadsheet* and *financial planning system*.

plasma display A flat-screen technology that contains an inert ionized gas sandwiched between an x-axis panel and a y-axis panel. An individual dot (pixel) is selectable by charging an x-wire on one panel and a y-wire on the other panel. When the x-y coordinate is charged, the gas in that vicinity glows a bright orange color. A plasma display is also called a *gas discharge display*.

platen The long, thin cylinder in a typewriter or printer that guides the paper through it and serves as a backstop for the printing mechanism to bang into.

platform The hardware architecture of a particular model or family of computers. The platform is the standard to which software developers write their programs. The term sometimes refers to the operating system included with the hardware. See *environment*.

PLATO (Programmed Logic for Automatic Teaching Operations) An advanced CBT system developed by Donald Bitzer and marketed by Control Data Corporation and W. R. Roach & Associates. PLATO was the first to combine graphics and touch-sensitive screens for interactive training.

platter One of the disks in a disk pack or hard disk drive. Resembling a phonograph record covered with magnetic tape, each platter provides a top and bottom recording surface. There are usually from two to eight platters in a hard disk and up to a couple of dozen in large disk packs. Diameters vary from two to five inches for small drives, and up to about 15" for large drives.

PLD (Programmable Logic Device) A logic chip that is programmed at the customer's site. There are a wide variety of PLD techniques; however, most PLDs are compatible with the PAL method from Advanced Micro Devices. The PLD is not a storage chip like a PROM or EPROM, although fuse-blowing techniques are used. PLDs contain different configurations of AND, OR and NOR gates that are "blown" together. Contrast with *gate array*, which requires a manufacturing process to complete the programming.

PL/I (Programming Language 1) A high-level programming language from IBM that was introduced in 1964 with its System/360 family of computers. It was designed to combine features of and eventually supplant COBOL and FORTRAN, which, of course, never happened.

A PL/I program is made up of modules called *procedures* that can be compiled independently. There is always a main procedure and zero or more additional procedures. Functions, which pass arguments back and forth, are also provided.

PL/M (Programming Language for Microprocessors) A dialect of PL/I developed by Intel as a high-level language for their microprocessors. PL/M+ is an extended version of PL/M, developed by National Semiconductor for its microprocessors.

plot To create an image by drawing a series of lines. In programming, a plot statement creates a single vector (line) or a complete circle or box that is made up of several vectors.

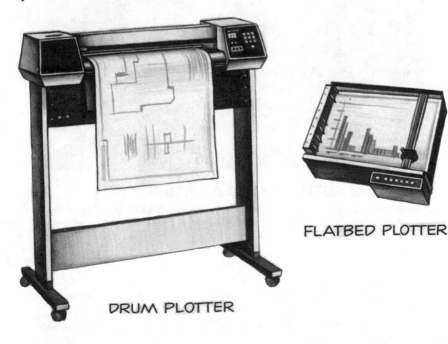

FLATBED PLOTTER

DRUM PLOTTER

plotter A graphics printer that draws images with ink pens. Plotters require data in vector graphics format, which makes up an image as a series of point-to-point lines. See *flatbed plotter* and *drum plotter*.

PLP (Presentation Level Protocol) The North American standard protocol for videotex transmission.

plug compatible A hardware device that is designed to perform exactly like another vendor's product. For example, a plug compatible CPU is a computer that runs the exact same software as the machine it's compatible with. A plug compatible peripheral can be connected to the computer and work the same as the device it's replacing.

plugboard A board with holes (sockets) that is used to program a machine. One end of a wire is inserted into an output socket, and the other end into an input socket, closing a circuit and activating a function. Plugboards were used to program punched card tabulating machines, and complicated programs looked like "mounds of spaghetti."

THE AUTHOR HARD AT WORK (1962)

In those days, "Tabulating Technicians" were the lucky ones. Instead of standing all day at their sorters and tabulators, they were allowed to sit down in order to wire their plugboards.

plugs & sockets The physical connectors that are used to link together all variety of electronic devices. The following three pages show common computer and communications plugs and sockets. Also see *F connector*, *phono connector* and *phone connector*.

If your equipment has this connector type	For this interface
DB25 (4-, 12- or 24-pin)	RS-232 (V.24), IBM® Parallel, RS-530
DB37	RS-449, 442, 423; Bernoulli®
DB50	Dataproducts® Datapoint®, UNIVAC® and others
DB15	Texas Instruments®, NCR® POS; Ethernet
DB9	449 Secondary, ATARI®, DAA and Video interfaces
5-Pin Din	IBM PC Keyboard
36-pin	Parallel printers: Centronics®, EPSON®, Gemini®
Mate-N-Lok®	Current Loop, Telephone
IEEE-488	GPIB, HPIB
M/34	V.35
M/50	Dataproducts, UNIVAC, DEC™ and others
BNC	Coaxial
BNC and TNC	WANG®, Dual Coaxial
Twinaxial	IBM Systems 34, 36, 38, 5520 and others
Telco	Telephone
RJ-11	Voice Telephone
RJ-45	Data Telephone
Barrier Block	Utility current loop, and other 2- or 4-wires

DB-25

DB-37

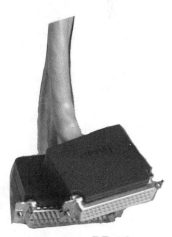

DB-50

PLUGS & SOCKETS

(Chart and photos courtesy Black Box Corporation)

DB-15 **DB-9** **DIN (5-Pin)**

Mate-N-Lok

Centronics 36-pin

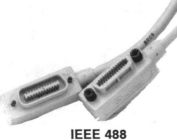

IEEE 488 **M/34**

PLUGS & SOCKETS
(All photos courtesy Black Box Corporation)

M/50

BNC

Twinaxial

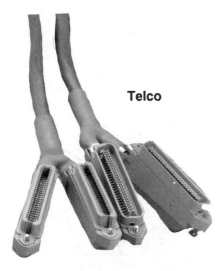

Telco

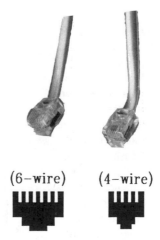

(6-wire)   (4-wire)

RJ-11

RJ-45

PLUGS & SOCKETS

(All photos courtesy Black Box Corporation)

PM See *preventive maintenance, Presentation Manager* and *phase modulation.*

PMOS (Positive channel Metal Oxide Semiconductor) Pronounced "P-moss." A type of microelectronic circuit design in which the substrate, or base material, is positively charged. PMOS transistors were used in the first microprocessors and are still used in CMOS fabrication. They are also used in low-cost products, such as calculators and digital watches.

pocket computer A hand-held calculator-sized computer that runs on batteries. Pocket computers can be plugged into a personal computer for data transfer.

point
(1) To moving the cursor onto a line or image on screen by rolling a mouse across the desk or by pressing the arrow keys.

(2) In typography, equal to 1/72nd of an inch and is used to measure the vertical height of a printed character.

point and shoot To select a menu option or activate a function by moving the cursor onto a line or object and pressing the return key or mouse button.

point of sale
The capture of data at the time and place of sale. Point of sale systems use personal computers or specialized terminals that are combined with cash registers, optical scanners for reading product tags, and/or magnetic stripe readers for reading credit cards.

BAR CODE

POINT OF SALE

Point of sale systems may be online to a central computer for credit checking and inventory updating, or they may be stand-alone machines that store the daily transactions until they can be delivered or transmitted to the main computer for processing.

pointer

(1) In database management, an address embedded within the data that specifies the location of data in another record or file.

(2) In programming, a variable that is used as a reference to the current item in a table (array) or to some other object, such as the current row or column the cursor is on.

(3) A device, such as a mouse, tablet cursor or stylus, that moves the cursor on the screen.

(4) A value in a register that points to an instruction or data.

(5) The screen cursor in the Macintosh.

pointing device
A input device, such as a mouse or graphics tablet, that is used to move the cursor on the screen or to draw an image.

Poisson distribution
A statistical method developed by the 18th century French mathematician S. D. Poisson, which is used for predicting the probable distribution of a series of events. For example, when the average transaction volume in a communications system can be estimated, Poisson distribution is used to determine the probable minimum and maximum number of transactions that can occur within a given time period.

poke
See *peek/poke*.

polarity

(1) The direction of charged particles, which determines the binary status of a bit.

(2) In micrographics, the change in the light to dark relationship of an image when copies are made. Positive polarity is dark characters on a light background; negative polarity is light characters on a dark background.

polarized
The one-way direction of a signal or the molecules within a material pointing in one direction.

Polish notation
A method for expressing a sequence of calculations that does not require parentheses. It was developed by the Polish logician Jan Lukasiewicz in 1929. For example, A(B+C) would be expressed as * A + B C. In reverse Polish notation, it would be A B C + *.

polling
A communications technique that determines when a terminal is ready to send data. The computer continually interrogates all of its attached terminals in a round robin sequence. If a terminal has data to send, it sends back an acknowledgement and the transmission begins. Contrast with *interrupt-driven*, in which the terminal generates a signal when it has data to send.

polling cycle One round in which each and every terminal connected to the computer or controller has been polled once.

polygon In computer graphics, a multi-sided object that can be filled with color or moved around as a single entity.

polyline In computer graphics, a single entity that is made up of a series of connected lines.

polymorphic tweening An animation technique that, based on information about its starting and ending shapes, creates the necessary "in-between" steps to change one object into into another.

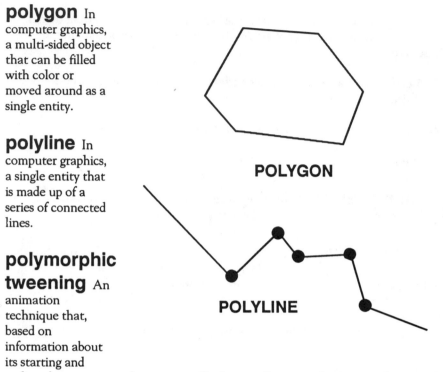

POLYGON

POLYLINE

polymorphism Meaning many shapes; in object-oriented programming, refers to creating procedures about objects whose exact type is not known until run time. See *object-oriented programming*.

pop See *push/pop*.

pop-down menu See *pull-down menu*.

populate To plug in chips or components into a printed circuit board. A fully populated board is one that contains all the devices it can hold.

popup
(1) A menu that is called for and displayed on top of the existing screen text or images. When the item is selected, the menu disappears and the screen is restored.

(2) A memory-resident program (TSR) that is called for by pressing a hotkey. The program is displayed either as a small window on top of the existing screen

text or images, or it takes up the full screen. When the program is exited, the previous screen contents are restored.

port

(1) An external connector on a computer that is used to hook up a modem, printer or other device. On a front end processor, a port connects to a communications line or modem.

The ports specified on a personal computer, such as two serial and one parallel port, refer only to external connectors; however, the computer has several internal expansion slots that accept control units for devices, such as disks, display screens and scanners.

(2) To convert software to run in a different computer environment.

port expander A device that connects several lines to one port in the computer. A line is given access to the port either by a hardware switch or through software selection.

portable computer A personal computer that can be easily transported. Compared to desktop models, it has limited expansion slots and disk capacity.

The first portable was the Osborne I, a CP/M machine that was soon followed by many others, such as the Kaypro and Otrona's Attache. In late 1982, Compaq introduced the first MS-DOS portable. See *laptop computer, notebook computer* and *pocket computer*.

porting See *port*.

portrait An orientation in which the data is printed across the narrow side of the form.

POS See *point of sale*.

positive logic The use of a low voltage for a 0 bit and a high voltage for a 1 bit. Contrast with *negative logic*.

POSIX (Portable Operating System Interface for UNIX) An IEEE standard that defines the language interface between application programs and the UNIX operating system. Adherence to the standard ensures compatibility when programs are moved from one UNIX computer to another.

postfix notation See *reverse Polish notation*.

postprocessor Software that provides some final processing to data, such as formatting it for display or printing.

PostScript A page description language from Adobe Systems, Inc., that is used in a wide variety of printers. Software that provides PostScript output is able to print text and graphics on any PostScript printer or imagesetter.

PostScript printers have a built-in interpreter that translates PostScript instructions into the printer's machine language, which generates the required dot patterns. Fonts are scaled to size by the interpreter, thus eliminating the need to store a variety of font sizes on the disk.

Type 1 PostScript fonts are encrypted and can be deciphered only by an Adobe interpreter. They also use hints, which improve the appearance of text, especially for smaller font sizes at desktop laser printer resolutions (300 dpi). Type 3 fonts do not use encryption or hints and are created by many third-party PostScript font designers.

pot See *potentiometer*.

potentiometer A device that controls the amount of current that flows through a circuit, such as a volume switch on a radio.

POTS (Plain Old Telephone Service) The traditional analog telephone network.

power See *computer power*.

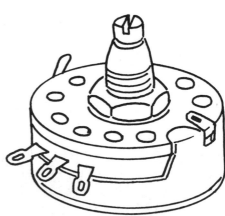

POTENTIOMETER

power down To turn off the computer in an orderly manner by making sure all applications have been closed normally and then shutting the power.

Power Platform A replacement processor board for PS/2 models from IBM that contains an 80486 CPU.

power supply An electrical system that converts AC current from the wall outlet into the DC currents required by the computer circuitry.

power up To turn the computer on in an orderly manner.

power user An individual that is very proficient with personal computers feels very comfortable them. It implies knowledge of a variety of software packages.

PowerPoint A desktop presentation program for the Macintosh from Microsoft. It was the first desktop presentation program for the Mac and provides the ability to create output for overheads, handouts, speaker notes and film recorder. The color palettes for Genigraphics slide product accompany the product.

PPM (Pages Per Minute) Used to measure the speed of a page printer, such as a laser printer.

PR/SM (Processor Resources/Systems Manager) A hardware upgrade from IBM that turns a large-scale 3090 mainframe into as many as four logical processors, each capable of running a different operating system and set of application programs.

PRAM (Parameter RAM) Pronounced "P-RAM." A battery-backed part of the Macintosh's memory that holds Control Panel settings and the specifications for the hidden desktop file. If the command and option keys are held down at startup, the desktop specifications are cleared and a dialog to rebuild the desktop is initiated.

precedence The order in which an expression is processed. Mathematical precedence is normally:
- (1) unary + and - signs
- (2) exponentiation
- (3) multiplication and division
- (4) addition and subtraction.

The formula to convert fahrenheit to centigrade is (1) subtract 32 from the fahrenheit temperature, (2) multiply the result by five, and (3) divide that result by nine. In the following two mathematical expressions:

```
(1)  fahrenheit-32*5/9
(2)  (fahrenheit-32)*5/9
```

the first one is incorrect, because multiplication is evaluated before addition.

Logical precedence is normally:
  (1) NOT
  (2) AND
  (3) OR.

In the dBASE query:

```
list for item = "TIE" .and. color = "GRAY"
         .or. color = "RED"
```

all gray ties and anything red will be selected, since ANDs are evaluated before ORs. Grouping the colors in parentheses: (color = "GRAY" .or. color = "RED") yields only gray and red ties.

precision The number of digits used to express the fractional part of a number. The more digits, the more precision. See *single precision* and *double precision*.

predicate In programming, a statement that evaluates an expression and provides a true or false answer based on the condition of the data.

prefix notation See *Polish notation*.

prepress In typography and printing, the preparation of camera-ready materials up to the actual printing stage, which includes typesetting and page makeup.

preprocessor Software that performs some preliminary processing on the input before it is processed by the main program.

presentation graphics Business graphics, such as bar charts and graphs, that are used as presentation material in meetings and lectures. It implies a highly designed set of business graphics that employs artistic type fonts and stylized graphics, such as 3-D charts.

Presentation Manager A windows environment and graphical user interface (GUI) from Microsoft that runs under OS/2. Similar to Windows for DOS, PM allows users to keep applications open as multiple windows on screen and to command the computer with icons and a mouse.

Prestel A commercial videotex service of British Telecom (formerly part of the British Post Office).

preventive maintenance The routine checking of hardware that is performed by a field engineer on a regularly scheduled basis. See *remedial maintenance*.

primary index The index that controls the current processing order of a file. See *secondary index*.

primary storage The computer's internal memory (RAM). Contrast with *secondary storage*.

Prime (Prime Computer, Inc.) A computer manufacturer founded in 1972 by seven engineers from Honeywell and one venture capitalist with the goal of creating a faster minicomputer. By the end of its first year, Prime introduced its 200 system, the first to use MOS memory.

With the introduction of innovative technology throughout the 1970s, Prime's revenues quickly accelerated. In 1980, its stock climbed 273%, the greatest appreciation of any stock on the New York exchange at that time.

Prime has been a successful computer vendor in the scientific and engineering community as well as in commercial data processing. It has also done well in foreign markets.

primitive

(1) In computer graphics, a graphics element that is used as a building block for creating images, such as a point, line, arc, cone or sphere.

(2) In programming, a fundamental instruction, statement or operation.

(3) In microprogramming, a microinstruction, or elementary machine operation.

print buffer See *printer buffer*.

print column A column of data on a printed report that may or may not be subtotalled or totalled. Print columns are the heart of a report description for a report writer.

print image format A document that has been prepared for the printer. The layout codes for a particular printer have been embedded into the text at the appropriate places.

print queue Disk space that holds output designated for the printer until the printer can receive it.

print server A computer in a network that controls one or more printers. It stores the print image output from the users of the system and feeds it to the printer a job at a time. The print server function can be added to a network server that provides other file sharing.

print spooler A program that allows printing to take place in the background while other tasks are being performed in the foreground. When a word processor or desktop publishing program is told to print, it generally creates a temporary file that contains the text along with special codes for the printer. This step takes a lot of processing time, but sending the resulting file to the printer doesn't. Thus, this second step can often be overlapped with an interactive application without appreciably slowing it down.

print to disk To redirect output to the disk that is normally sent to a printer. The print image file that is created contains the text and all the required layout, or format, codes embedded within it. The file can be printed at a later date or at a remote location by transmitting it to the printer without requiring the word processor or desktop publishing program that created it.

printed circuit board A flat board that holds chips and other electronic components. The back side of the board is "printed" with electrically conductive pathways between the components. The printed circuit board of the 1960s connected discrete (elementary) components together. The printed circuit board of the 1990s connects chips together, each chip containing hundreds of thousands of elementary components.

PRINTED CIRCUIT BOARD
(Courtesy Rockwell International)

This printed circuit board is a 9,600 bps modem.

printer A device that converts computer output into printed images. The following is an overview of printer types.

SERIAL PRINTERS
Serial printers print a character at a time from approximately 10 to 400 characters per second (CPS), which is equivalent to about 6 to 240 lines per minute (LPM). Serial printers use dot matrix and character printer technologies. Serial printers are referred to as character printers regardless of the printing technology employed.

LINE PRINTERS
Line printers print a line at a time from approximately 100 to 5,000 LPM and are the standard impact printers found in the datacenter. Line printers use drum, chain, train, band, dot matrix and dot band technologies.

PAGE PRINTERS
Page printers, also called *laser printers*, print a page at time from approximately 4 to 215 pages per minute (400 to 14,000 LPM), and primarily employ the electrophotographic technique used in copy machines. High-speed page printers are widely used in large datacenters, and desktop laser printers are becoming commonplace for personal computers.

GRAPHICS PRINTERS
Graphics printers use impact serial dot matrix, impact line dot matrix, impact line dot band and all non-impact technologies.

COLOR PRINTERS
Color printers use impact dot matrix with multiple color ribbons, electrophotographic with multiple color toners, electrostatic plotters with multiple color toners, printers using the Cycolor technology, ink jet with multiple color inks and thermal-transfer with multiple colors.

Impact Printers

BAND, CHAIN & TRAIN
A continuous loop of several character sets connected together spins horizontally around a set of hammers. When the desired character is in front of the selected print location, that particular hammer hits the paper forcing the shaped character image on the band, chain, or train into the ribbon and onto the paper.

Since the chain, band, or train moves so fast, it appears to print a line at a time. A band is a solid loop, while the chain is individual character images (type slugs) chained together. The train is individual character images (type slugs) revolving in a track, one pushing the other. See *band printer* and *chain printer*.

DRUM
A rotating drum (cylinder) contains the character set carved around it for each print location, like an odometer. When the desired character for the selected print location has rotated around to the hammer line, the appropriate hammer hits the paper from behind, forcing it against the ribbon that is between the paper and the drum. Since the drum rotates so fast, it appears to print a line at a time. See *drum printer*.

CHARACTER
Character printers are similar to Selectric typewriters, printing one character at a time. A daisy wheel or similar mechanism is moved serially across the paper. At the selected print location, a hammer hits the shaped character image on the wheel into the ribbon and onto the paper.

SERIAL DOT MATRIX
A vertical set of printing wires moves serially across the paper, formulating characters by impacting a ribbon and transferring dots of ink onto the paper. The clarity of the character is determined by how close the dots print together.

LINE DOT MATRIX

A stationary or oscillating line of printing wires generates images by impacting a ribbon and transferring dots of ink onto the paper a line at a time.

DOT BAND MATRIX

A combination band and dot matrix configuration. A steel band is etched to create fingers (petals). At the tip of each finger is an anvil with a steel dot attached. Print hammers impact the anvils, which are larger than the dots, allowing the dots to be printed in areas between the hammer faces. Different size dots may be used on different bands to change the speed of printing and the print resolution.

Non-Impact Printers

ELECTROPHOTOGRAPHIC

A drum is charged with a high voltage and an image source paints a negative light copy of the image to be printed onto the drum. Where the light falls onto the drum, the drum is discharged. A toner (ink) is allowed to adhere to the charged portion of the drum. The drum then fuses the image onto the paper by pressure and heat. See *electrophotographic*.

ELECTROSENSITIVE

Dots are charged onto specially coated silver-colored paper, usually in a serial fashion. The charge removes the alumnimum coating, leaving a black image.

ELECTROSTATIC

Dots are charged onto specially coated paper, usually a line at a time. An ink adheres to the charges that become embedded into the paper by pressure or by heat.

INK JET

Continuous streams of ink are sprayed onto paper, or droplets of ink generate a dot matrix image, usually in a serial fashion. Another technique uses ink in a solid form, which is melted just before it is ejected.

IONOGRAPHIC

A technology that uses ion deposition and is similar to direct electrostatic, except that in this type of indirect electrostatic, the image is formed on a dielectric surface and then transferred to plain paper.

MAGNETOGRAPHIC

A magnetic image is created by a set of recording heads across a magnetic drum. Monocomponent toner is applied to the drum to develop the image. It is transferred to paper by light pressure and an electrostatic field. The toner is then fused by heat.

THERMAL

Dots are burned onto specially coated paper that turns black or blue when heat is applied to it. A line of heat elements forms a dot matrix image as the paper is passed across it, or a serial head with heating elements is passed across the paper.

THERMAL WAX TRANSFER
Dots of ink are transferred from a mylar ribbon onto paper by passing the ribbon and the paper across a line of heat elements, or by passing a serial head with heating element across the paper. See *thermal wax transfer*.

printer buffer A memory device that accepts printer output from one or more computers and transmits it to the printer. It lets the computer rid itself of its printer output at high speed and be used for another task while the printer is printing. Printer buffers with automatic switching are connected to two or more computers and accept their output on a first-come, first-served basis.

printer cable A wire that connects a printer to a computer.

printer driver A software routine that converts an application program's printing request into the language the printer understands.

printer engine The part of a printer that does the actual printing.

printer file
(1) A file that contains the printer language for a specific printer that is required by a printer driver. It includes all the codes that activate functions in the printer, for example, to turn on boldface and underline, to switch fonts and colors. Width tables that contain the horizontal spacing for every character in each represented font are also included.

(2) A document in print image format ready to be printed. Printer files are created by a PRINT TO DISK option in a program.

printer font A font that is in the required format for downloading to a printer. Contrast with *screen font*. See *font*.

printout (PRINTer OUTput) Same as *hardcopy*.

privacy The authorized distribution of information (who has a right to know?). Contrast with *security*, which deals with unauthorized access to data.

private line
(1) A dedicated line leased from a common carrier.

(2) A line owned and installed by the user.

problem-oriented language A computer language designed to handle a particular class of problems. For example, COBOL was designed for business applications. FORTRAN, ALGOL and APL were designed for scientific and mathematical problems. GPSS and SIMSCRIPT were designed for simulation problems. Query languages are designed for phrasing questions (interrogation problems).

procedural language
A programming language that requires programming discipline, such as COBOL, FORTRAN, BASIC, C, Pascal and dBASE. Programmers writing in such languages must develop a proper order of actions in order to solve the problem, based on a knowledge of data processing and programming. Contrast with *non-procedural language*.

The following dBASE example shows procedural and non-procedural language to list a file.

```
        Procedural                      Non-procedural (interactive)
    USE FILEX                       USE FILEX
    DO WHILE .NOT. EOF              LIST NAME, AMOUNTDUE
      ? NAME, AMOUNTDUE
      SKIP
    ENDDO
```

procedure
(1) A manual *procedure* is a series of human tasks.

(2) A machine *procedure* is a list of routines or programs to be executed, such as described by the job control language (JCL) in a minicomputer or mainframe, or the batch processing language in a personal computer.

(3) In programming, another term for a subroutine or function.

process
To manipulate data in the computer. The computer is said to be processing no matter what action is taken upon the data. It may be updated or simply displayed on screen.

In order to evaluate a computer system's performance, the time it takes to process data internally is analyzed separately from the time it takes to get it in and out of the computer. Input/output is usually more time consuming than processing. See *computer (The 3 C's)*.

process bound
An excessive amount of processing causing an imbalance between I/O and processing. Process-bound applications may slow down other users in a multiuser system.

A personal computer is process bound when it is recalculating a spreadsheet, for example.

process control
The automated control of a process, such as a manufacturing process or assembly line. It is used extensively in industrial operations, such as oil refining, chemical processing and electrical generation.

Process control uses analog devices to monitor real-world signals and digital computers to do the analysis and controlling. It makes extensive use of analog to digital and digital to analog conversion.

processing The manipulation of data within the computer. However, the term is used to define a variety of computer functions and methods. See *centralized processing, distributed processing, batch processing, transaction processing, multiprocessing* and *computer (The 3 C's)*.

processor
(1) Same as *CPU*.

(2) May refer to software. See *language processor* and *word processor*.

processor unit Same as *computer*.

Procomm A shareware communications program for PCs from Datastorm Technologies, Inc., that supports a wide number of protocols and terminals and is available on many bulletin boards for downloading.

PRODIGY An information utility that provides a variety of services to personal computer users, such as weather and stock market reports, airline scheduling and at-home shopping. PRODIGY is a partnership of IBM and Sears and is provided for a fixed monthly fee rather than a usage charge.

Customers receive a special communications program that must be installed in their personal computer. The PRODIGY software provides full-screen displays and simplifies the log-on.

production database A central database containing an organization's master files and daily transaction files.

production system A computer system that is used to process an organization's daily work. Contrast with a computer system that is used only for development and testing or for ad hoc inquiries and analysis.

Professional 300 A desktop PDP-11 from Digital Equipment Corporation that was introduced with the DECmate II and Rainbow 100 in 1982.

Professional YAM (Professional Yet Another Modem) A communications program for PCs from Omen Technology. It is a powerful, flexible, full-featured program for the serious communications user. It supports a wide variety of terminals and protocols.

PROFS (PRofessional OFfice System) An office automation program from IBM that runs in a VM mainframe environment. It provides an electronic mail facility for text and graphics, a library service for centrally storing text, electronic calendars and appointment scheduling, and it allows document interchange with DISOSS users.

program A collection of instructions that tell the computer what to do. A program is called *software*; hence, program, software and instructions are synonymous. A program is written in a programming language and is converted into the computer's machine language by software called *assemblers* and *compilers*.

A program is made up of (1) instructions, (2) buffers and (3) constants. Instructions are the directions that the computer will follow, and a particular sequence of instructions is called the program's *logic*. Buffers are reserved spaces in the program that will accept and hold the data while it's being processed. Constants are fixed values within the program that are used for comparing.

The program calls for data in an input-process-output sequence. After data has been input into one of the program's buffers from a peripheral device, such as a keyboard or disk, it is processed. The results are then output to a peripheral device such as a display screen or printer. If data has been updated, it is output back onto the disk.

The application program, the program that does the organization's data processing, does not instruct the computer to do everything. When the program needs input or is ready to output data, it sends a request to the operating system, which contains the actual instructions to perform those activities. The operating system performs the task and turns control back to the application program.

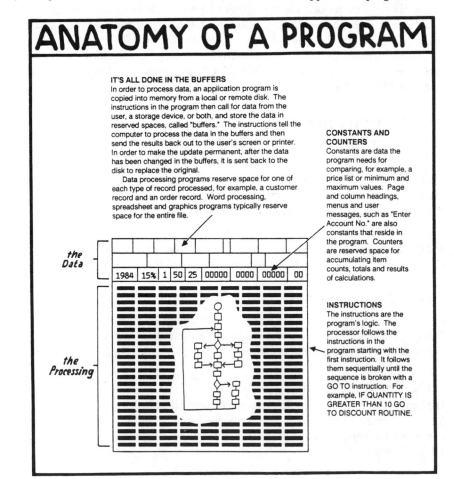

ANATOMY OF A PROGRAM

IT'S ALL DONE IN THE BUFFERS
In order to process data, an application program is copied into memory from a local or remote disk. The instructions in the program then call for data from the user, a storage device, or both, and store the data in reserved spaces, called "buffers." The instructions tell the computer to process the data in the buffers and then send the results back out to the user's screen or printer. In order to make the update permanent, after the data has been changed in the buffers, it is sent back to the disk to replace the original.

Data processing programs reserve space for one of each type of record processed, for example, a customer record and an order record. Word processing, spreadsheet and graphics programs typically reserve space for the entire file.

CONSTANTS AND COUNTERS
Constants are data the program needs for comparing, for example, a price list or minimum and maximum values. Page and column headings, menus and user messages, such as "Enter Account No." are also constants that reside in the program. Counters are reserved space for accumulating item counts, totals and results of calculations.

the Data

| 1984 | 15% | 1 | 50 | 25 | 00000 | 0000 | 00000 | 00 |

INSTRUCTIONS
The instructions are the program's logic. The processor follows the instructions in the program starting with the first instruction. It follows them sequentially until the sequence is broken with a GO TO instruction. For example, IF QUANTITY IS GREATER THAN 10 GO TO DISCOUNT ROUTINE.

the Processing

program generator See *application generator*.

program logic The order of instructions in a program. There are many logical solutions to the same problem. If you give a specification to ten programmers, each one may create program logic that is slightly different than all the rest, but the results can be the same. The solution that runs the fastest is usually the most desired, however.

Program logic is written using three classes of instructions: (1) sequential processing, (2) selection, and (3) iteration.

(1) Sequential processing is the series of steps that do the actual data processing. Input, output, calculate and move (copy) instructions are used in sequential processing.

(2) Selection is the decision making within the program and is performed by comparing two sets of data and branching to a different part of the program based on the results. In assembly languages, the compare and branch instructions are used. In high-level languages, IF THEN ELSE and CASE statements are used.

(3) Iteration is the repetition of a series of steps and is accomplished with DO LOOPS and FOR LOOPS in high-level languages and GOTOs in assembly languages. See *loop*.

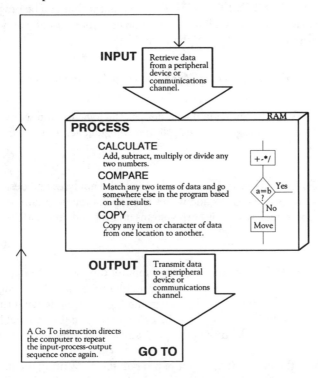

PROGRAM LOGIC

INPUT, PROCESS, OUTPUT and GO TO operations are the primary instructions built into every computer. Although program logic becomes quite complicated in actual practice, it is all based on inputting data into the computer, processing it and outputting the results. The main loop of many data processing programs performs this sequence over and over again.

program maintenance The updating of programs to reflect changes in the organization's business or to adapt to new operating environments.

program state An operating mode of the computer that executes instructions in the application program. Contrast with *supervisor state*.

program statement A phrase in a high-level programming language. One program statement may result in several machine instructions when the program is compiled.

program step An elementary instruction, such as a machine language instruction or an assembly language instruction. Contrast with *program statement*, which is an instructional in a high-level language.

programmable Capable of following instructions. What sets the computer apart from all other electronic devices is its programmability.

programmable calculator A calculator that can be programmed. A programmable calculator is a limited-function computer, usually only capable of working with numbers and not alphanumeric data.

programmatic interface Same as *application program interface*.

programmer An individual who designs the logic for and writes the lines of codes of a computer program. See *application programmer* and *systems programmer*.

programmer analyst An individual who analyzes and designs information systems and designs and writes the application programs for the system. A programmer analyst is both systems analyst and applications programmer.

programming The creation of a computer program. The steps are (1) developing the program logic to solve the particular problem, (2) writing the program logic in the form of a specific programming language (coding the program), (3) assembling or compiling the program to turn it into machine language, (4) testing and debugging the program, and (5) preparing the necessary documentation.

The logic is the most difficult part of programming. Writing the language statements is comparatively easy once the solution has been developed. However, regardless of how difficult the design of the program may be, documenting it is considered the most annoying activity by most programmers.

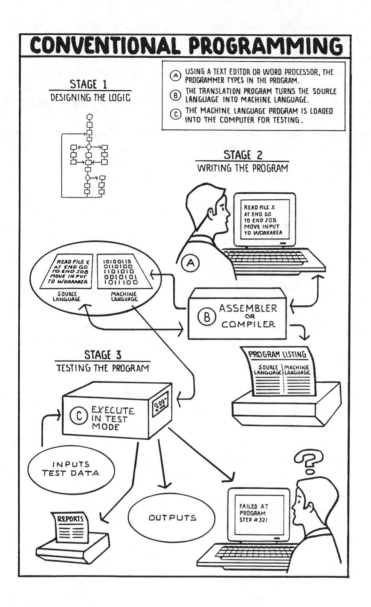

CONVENTIONAL PROGRAMMING

STAGE 1
DESIGNING THE LOGIC

(A) USING A TEXT EDITOR OR WORD PROCESSOR, THE PROGRAMMER TYPES IN THE PROGRAM.

(B) THE TRANSLATION PROGRAM TURNS THE SOURCE LANGUAGE INTO MACHINE LANGUAGE.

(C) THE MACHINE LANGUAGE PROGRAM IS LOADED INTO THE COMPUTER FOR TESTING.

STAGE 2
WRITING THE PROGRAM

READ FILE X
AT END GO
TO END JOB
MOVE INPUT
TO WORKAREA

READ FILE X
AT END GO
TO END JOB
MOVE IN PUT
TO WORKAREA

SOURCE LANGUAGE

MACHINE LANGUAGE

(A)

(B) ASSEMBLER OR COMPILER

STAGE 3
TESTING THE PROGRAM

PROGRAM LISTING
SOURCE LANGUAGE | MACHINE LANGUAGE

(C) EXECUTE IN TEST MODE

INPUTS
TEST DATA

REPORTS

OUTPUTS

FAILED AT PROGRAM STEP #321

programming language A language used to write instructions for the computer. It lets the programmer express data processing in a symbolic manner without regard to machine-specific details. The statements that are written by the programmer are called *source language*, and they are translated into the computer's *machine language* by programs called *assemblers*, *compilers* and *interpreters*. For example, when a programmer writes:

```
multiply hours times rate
```

the MULTIPLY must be turned into a code that means multiply, and HOURS and RATE must be turned into memory locations where those items of data are actually located.

Like human languages, each programming language has its own grammar and syntax. There are many dialects of the same language, and each dialect requires its own translating system. Standards have been set by ANSI (American National Standards Institute) for many programming languages, and any language said to conform to ANSI, is therefore a dialect-free language. However, it can take years for new features to be included in ANSI standards, and new dialects will always spring up as a result.

Programming languages fall into two major categories: low-level assembly languages and high-level languages. Assembly languages are available for every CPU family, and they translate one line of code into one machine instruction. High-level languages translate programming statements into several machine instructions.

Today's popular high-level languages for business are BASIC, COBOL, dBASE and Pascal. FORTRAN and APL are used in scientific areas, and C is used extensively for commercial software. LISP and Prolog are used in AI applications, FORTH is used in process control, and Ada is used by the Department of Defense. The newest wave is object-oriented programming, and C++ is gaining popularity.

Prokey A keyboard macro processor for PCs from RoseSoft, Inc. It allows users to eliminate repetitive typing by setting up an occurrence of text or a series of commands as a macro.

Prolog (PROgramming in LOGic) A programming language used in the development of AI applications, such as natural language, expert systems and abstract problem solving. Developed in France in 1973, it is used throughout Europe and Japan and is gaining popularity in the U.S. Very similar to LISP, it is designed to deal with symbolic representations of objects. The following example, written in Univ. of Edinburgh Prolog, converts fahrenheit to centigrade:

```
convert:- write('Enter fahrenheit'),
 read(Fahr),
 write('Centigrade is '),
 Cent is (5 * (Fahr - 32)) / 9,
 write(Cent),nl.
```

PROM (Programmable Read Only Memory) A permanent memory chip that is programmed, or filled, by the customer rather than by the chip manufacturer. Contrast with ROM, which is programmed at the time of manufacture. See PROM *programmer*.

PROM blower Same as PROM *programmer*.

PROM programmer A device that writes instructions and/or data into PROM chips. The bits in a new PROM are all 1s (continuous lines). The PROM programmer only creates 0s, by "blowing" the middle out of the 1s.

PROM programmers are available for programming only PROMs, only EPROMs or both. The bits in EPROMs, which are not permanently altered, can be erased under ultraviolet light and reprogrammed.

PROM PROGRAMMER

prompt A message from the software that requests some action by the user, for example, "Type ? for Help" or "Enter employee name." It can also be a very cryptic symbol that indicates it is ready to accept a command, for example, in dBASE the prompt is simply a period.

property list In a list programming language, an object that is assigned a descriptive attribute (property) and a value. For example, in Logo, `putprop "Karen "language "Paradox` assigns the value PARADOX to the property LANGUAGE for the person named KAREN. To find out what language Karen speaks, the Logo statement `print getprop "Karen "language` will generate PARADOX as the answer.

proportional spacing Character spacing based on the width of each character. For example, an I takes up less space than an M. In monospacing (fixed-spacing), the I and M each take up the same space. See *kerning*.

Proportional spacing

Now is the

Fixed spacing (Monospacing)

Now is the

PROPORTIONAL SPACING

protected mode In Intel 286 and higher machines, an operational state that allows the computer to address all of its memory. See *real mode, virtual 86 mode* and *memory protection*.

protocol In communications, a set of rules and regulations that govern the transmitting and receiving of data. See *OSI*.

protocol stack The hierarchy of protocols used in a communication network. See *OSI*.

protocol suite Same as *protocol stack*.

prototyping The creation of a system on a trial basis for testing and approval. With regard to information systems development, prototyping has become essential for clarifying information requirements. In the traditional approach, the functional specs, which are the blueprint and design of the information system, must be finalized and frozen before the system can be built. While the analytically-oriented person may have a clear picture of information requirements, others may not.

Using the fourth-generation capabilities of a database management system as a prototyping tool, systems analysts and users can develop the new system together. Databases can be created and manipulated at a mainframe terminal or on a personal computer while the user monitors the progress.

Once users see tangible output on a display screen or printed report, they can figure out what's missing or what the next question might be if this were a production system. If prototyping is carefully done, the end result can be a working system.

Even if the final system must be reprogrammed in other languages for standardization or machine efficiency, the prototyping has served to provide specifications for a working system rather than a theoretical one.

PS (Personal Services) A series of office automation programs that run on IBM personal computers, minis and mainframes, which includes word processing, electronic mail and library services.

PS/1 A series of home computers from IBM introduced in June 1990. They feature an integrated monitor and easy-to-open case. Models first introduced use the 286 CPU and traditional PC bus. See *PC*.

PS/2 A series of personal computers from IBM, introduced in April 1987, that superseded its original PC line. The PS/2 introduced three advances: 3.5" microfloppy disk, VGA graphics and the Micro Channel bus. The disks and graphics have been integrated into almost all PCs, and the Micro Channel is offered by selected compatibles makers. Smaller PS/2 models still use the original PC bus. See *PC*.

PS/2 bus Same as *Micro Channel*.

PS/370 See *VM/SP Technical Workstation*.

pseudo compiler A compiler that generates a pseudo language, or intermediate language, which must be further compiled or interpreted for execution.

pseudo-duplexing A communications technique that simulates full-duplex transmission in a half-duplex line by turning the line around very quickly.

pseudo language An intermediate language that is generated from source language, but is not yet executable. The pseudo language has to be interpreted or compiled into machine language for execution.

Since a large amount of the translation has already been done in the pseudo language, it is faster to create an interpreter or compiler to translate the pseudo language into a new CPU architecture than to create a compiler that translates source language into the new architecture.

PSK See *DPSK*.

PSTN (Public Switched Telephone Network) The worldwide voice telephone network.

p-System See *UCSD P-System*.

PTT (Postal, Telegraph & Telephone) The national governmental agency responsible for combined postal, telegraph and telephone services in many European countries.

PU (Physical Unit) In SNA, software that is responsible for managing the resources of a node, such as data links. A PU supports a connection to the host (SSCP) for gathering network management statistics.

PU 2.1 (Physical Unit 2.1) In SNA, the original term for Node Type 2.1, which is software that provides peer-to-peer communications between intelligent devices, such as PCs, workstations and mincomputers. Only LU 6.2 sessions are supported between Type 2.1 nodes (PU 2.1).

public domain software Software that is freely distributed to anyone who desires to use it.

puck The puck-like tablet cursor used on a digitzer tablet.

pull-down menu Also called a *pop-down menu*, it is a screen menu that is displayed from the top of the screen downward when its title is selected. The menu remains displayed while the mouse button is depressed. To select a menu option, the highlight bar is moved (with the mouse) to the appropriate line and the mouse button is let go.

A variation of this is called a *drop-down menu*, which keeps the menu open after its title is selected. To select a menu option, the highlight bar is moved to the

line and the mouse button is clicked. Key commands may also activate
drop-down menus.

pulse code modulation See PCM.

punch block Also called a *quick-connect block,* it is a device that
interconnects telephone lines from remote points. The wires are pushed, or
punched, down into metal teeth that strip the insulation and make a tight
connection.

punched card A storage medium made of card stock that holds data as
patterns of punched holes. A card has 80 or 96 columns, each capable of storing
one character. The holes are punched into the card by a keypunch machine or
card punch connected to a computer. Cards are read into the computer by a card
reader.

Although punched cards are still used as turnaround documents, they have long
since seen their heyday. From 1890 until the early 1960s, punched cards were
synonymous with data processing. In those days, concepts were simple: the
database was the file cabinet, and a record was a punched card. Each processing
activity was performed on a separate machine, the collective group of which was
called *unit record equipment, tabulating equipment* or EAM *machines.*

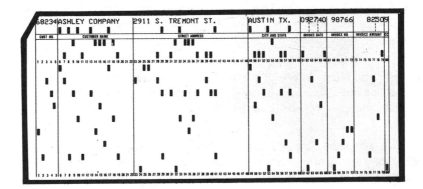

80-COLUMN PUNCHED CARD

(Courtesy IBM)

This is the common 80-column "IBM" card that evolved from Hollerith's original punched card.
Throughout the greater part of the 19th century, billions of thesecards were put through sorters,
collators, reproducers and tabulators, in which each machine performed one data processing function.

push/pop Instructions that store and retrieve an item on a stack. Push
enters an item on the stack, and pop retrieves an item, moving the rest of the
items in the stack up one level. See *stack.*

put In programming, a request to store the current record in an output file.
Contrast with *get.*

The Computer Glossary

Q&A An integrated file manager and word processor for PCs from Symantec Corporation. It includes a mail merge capability as well as a programming language for customizing data entry forms and reports. Its Intelligent Assistant feature provides a query language that can learn new words from the user. Although Q&A works with only single files and has no relational capability, it is powerful and easy-to-use for the beginner.

QAM

(1) (Quadrature Amplitude Modulation) A modulation technique that generates four bits out of one baud. For example, a 600 baud line (600 shifts in the signal per second) can effectively transmit 2,400 bits per second using this method. Both phase and amplitude are shaped with each baud, resulting in four possible patterns.

(2) (Quality Assessment Measurement) A system used to measure and analyze voice transmission.

QBE (Query By Example) A method for describing a query that was originally developed by IBM for its mainframe systems. A replica of an empty record is displayed and the search conditions are typed in under their respective columns. The following query selects all Pennsylvania records that have a balance due of $5000 or more.

CUSTOMER FILE

NAME	ADDRESS	CITY	STATE	ZIP	BALANCE
			PA		>=5000

"Select all Pennsylvania customers with balances of $5000 or more"

QUERY BY EXAMPLE

Q-bus A bus architecture that is used in PDP-11 minicomputers as well as in MicroVAX versions of the VAX series.

QEMM-386 (Quarterdeck Expanded Memory Manager-386) An expanded memory manager from Quarterdeck Office Systems for 386 and higher machines. QEMM-386 is a stand-alone product for 386 machines, but is a companion product to Quarterdeck's DESQview windowing and multitasking program. See EMS.

QEMM-50/60 (Quarterdeck Expanded Memory Manager-50/60) An expanded memory manager for PS/2 Model 50 and 60 personal computers from Quarterdeck Office Systems. Memory boards for these machines have built-in translation features that allow EMS memory to be activated.

QMF (Query Management Facility) A fourth-generation language from IBM intended for end-user interaction with IBM's DB2 database system.

quantize To break into discrete values for sampling purposes.

Quark Xpress A desktop publishing program for the Macintosh from Quark, Inc. It integrates full-featured word processing so that text can be created, edited and published within the same program. It is noted for its precise typographic control and sophisticated graphics capabilities. For example, users can create their own frame designs that are used to box in text and graphics, and the custom designs are then automatically displayed in the frame menu. The example below shows the frame editor. The left side of the screen zooms in on the selected portion of the frame, which, in this case, is the upper left hand side. The pattern is created or modified a pixel at a time.

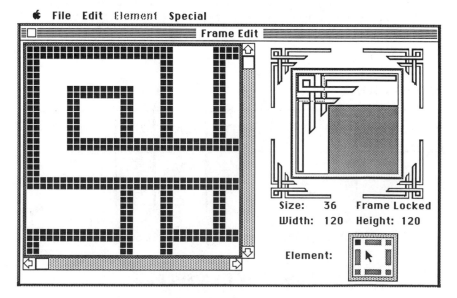

QUARK EXPRESS

quartz crystal A thin slice of quartz that has been cut and ground to a prescribed thickness, which vibrates at a specific and steady frequency when stimulated by electricity. The tiny crystal, about 1/20th by 1/5th of an inch, creates the computer's heartbeat.

Quattro

(1) A spreadsheet for PCs from Borland International that provides an optional interface that is keystroke, macro and file compatible with Lotus 1-2-3. Quattro Pro, introduced in 1989, provides advanced graphics and presentation capabilities.

(2) A family of multiprocessing computers from Nixdorf Computer Ltd.

query An interrogation of a database that allows users to count, sum and list selected records contained in it. Contrast with *report*, which is usually a more elaborate printout with headings and page numbers. The report may also be a selective list of items; hence, the two terms may refer to programs that produce the same results.

query by example See *QBE*.

query language A generalized language that allows a user to select records from a database. Query languages provide either a command language, a menu-driven method or a query by example (QBE) format for expressing the matching condition.

Query languages are usually provided in database managment systems, and stand-alone packages are available for interrogating files that are part of non-DBMS applications. See *query program*.

query program Software that counts, sums and retrieves selected records from a database. It may be part of a large application and be limited to one or two kinds of retrieval, such as pulling up a customer on screen by account number, or it may refer to a query language that allows any condition to be searched and selected.

queue Pronounced "Q." A temporary holding place for data in memory or on disk. See *message queue* and *print queue*.

QuickBASIC A BASIC compiler from Microsoft that provides an advanced number of features to the BASIC language and is quite popular.

QuickC A C compiler from Microsoft that is compatible with its larger C compiler and is used by the beginner or occasional programmer.

Quickdraw A graphics display system built into the Macintosh. It accepts commands from the application and draws the corresponding objects on the screen. Quickdraw provides a consistent interface that software developers can work with.

QuickPascal A Pascal compiler from Microsoft that is compatible with Turbo Pascal and provides object oriented capabilities.

Quicksilver A dBASE compiler from WordTech Systems, Inc., that adds scrolling text windows to the dBASE language. Quicksilver/UNIX is a version of the compiler that translates dBASE source code into the UNIX environment, and Oracle Quicksilver allows dBASE commands to manage an Oracle database.

quit To exit the current program. It's a good habit to quit a program before turning the computer off. Some programs don't close all files properly until the quit is activated.

qwerty keyboard The standard English language typewriter keyboard. Q, w, e, r, t and y are the first letters starting at the top left, alphabetic row. It was originally designed to slow down the typist to prevent the keys from jamming.

STANDARD TYPEWRITER KEYBOARD

R

RACE (Randon Access Card Equipment) An early mass storage device from RCA that used magnetic cards. The cards were released from their cartridge and made to pass down a raceway after which they were wrapped around a read/write head. The cards often jammed, damaging all the data contained on them.

rack A frame or cabinet into which components are mounted.

rack mounted Components that are built to fit in a metal frame. Electronic devices, such as testing equipment and tape drives, are often rack mounted units.

RAD (Rapid Application Development) An approach to systems development that incorporates a variety of automated design tools (CASE). Developed by industry guru, James Martin, it focuses on human management and user involvement as much as on technology.

radio The transmission of electromagnetic energy (radiation) over the air or through a hollow tube called a *waveguide.* Although radio is often thought of as only AM or FM, all airborne transmission, including satellite and line-of-sight microwave, is radio.

radio frequency See *RF.*

radix The base value in a numbering system. For example, in the decimal numbering system, the radix is 10.

radix point The location in a number that separates the integral part from the fractional part. For example, in the decimal system, the radix point is the decimal point.

ragged right In typography, non-uniform text at the right margin, such as the text you're reading.

RAM (Random Access Memory) Same as *memory.*

RAM cram Insufficient memory to run applications, especially in PCs under DOS with its 1MB memory limit.

RAM disk A disk drive that is simulated in memory. To use a RAM disk, program and data files are copied from the disk into the RAM disk first. Then inputs and outputs that normally go to the disk are diverted to the RAM disk. Processing is speeded up, because there's no mechanical disk action, only memory transfers. However, if the power fails, all the updated data in the RAM disk will be lost. Same as *E-disk* and *virtual disk*.

RAM refresh The recharging of dynamic RAM chips many times per second in order to keep the bit patterns valid.

RAM resident program A program that remains in memory and is instantly available to the user or to work with another program. See *TSR*.

RAMAC (Random Access Method of Accounting and Control) The first computer with a disk drive. Introduced by IBM in 1956, each of it's 24" diameter platters (see photo above) held 100K of data. All 50 platters held a "whopping"

RAMAC 305 COMPUTER
(Courtesy IBM)

Although IBM had a direct access disk system in the 1950s, it wasn't until the late-1960s that online disks started to become widely used.

five million characters. It was half computer, half tabulating machine, and had a drum memory for program storage, but required plugboard wiring for its input and output.

RAMIS II A database management and decision support system from On-Line Software International, Inc., that runs on IBM mainframes. The earlier version of RAMIS II was one of the first database packages with a non-procedural language.

random access Same as *direct access*.

random noise Same as *Gaussian noise*.

random number generator A program routine that produces a random number upon request. Random numbers can be created very easily in a computer, since there are many random events that take place, for example, the duration between depressions of keys on the keyboard. Only a few milliseconds' difference is enough to seed a random number generation routine with a different number each time. Once started, an algorithm can be used to compute different numbers throughout the session.

range
(1) In data entry validation, a group of values from a minimum to a maximum.

(2) In spreadsheets, a series of cells that are worked on as a group. The range may refer to a row, column or rectangular block defined by one corner and its diagonally opposite corner.

raster display A display terminal that generates dots line by line on the screen. Contrast with *vector display*.

raster graphics In computer graphics, a technique for representing a picture image as a matrix of dots. It is the digital counterpart of the analog method used in television. However, unlike TV, which uses one standard, there are many raster graphics standards. See *graphics*. Contrast with *vector graphics*.

raster image processor See *RIP*.

raster scan The line by line displaying or recording of a video image.

rasterization of vectors The conversion of graphic objects made up of vectors, or line segments, into dots for output to raster graphics screens, dot matrix and laser printers. Unless vector graphics terminals and plotters are used, all object-oriented graphics must be converted to raster images for display and printing.

raw data Data that has not been processed.

ray tracing In computer graphics, the creation of reflections, refractions and shadows on a graphics image. It follows a series of rays from a specific light source and computes each pixel in the image to determine the effect of the light. Ray tracing is a very process-intensive operation.

RAY TRACING
(Courtesy Computer Sciences Department, University of Utah)

R:BASE A relational database management system for PCs from Microrim, Inc., that provides interactive data processing, a complete programming language and an application generator. R:BASE was the first database system to compete with dBASE II back in the early 1980s.

RBOC (Regional Bell Operating Company) One of seven regional telephone companies created by divestiture: Nynex, Bell Atlantic, BellSouth, Southwestern Bell, US West, Pacific Telesis and Ameritech.

RCA connector Same as *phono connector*.

RCS
(1) (Remote Computer Service) A remote timesharing service.

(2) (Revision Control System) A UNIX utility that provides version control.

Rdb (Relational DataBase/VMS) A relational database management system from Digital Equipment Corporation that runs on its VAX computers.

RDBMS (Relational DataBase Management System) See *relational database*.

read To input into the computer from a peripheral device, such as a disk or tape. Like reading a book or playing an audio tape, reading does not destroy what is read. A read is both an input and an output (I/O), since data is being output from the peripheral device and input into the computer. Memory is also said to be read when it is accessed to transfer data out to a peripheral device or to somewhere else in memory. Every peripheral or internal transfer of data is a read from somewhere and a write to somewhere else.

read error A failure to read the data on a storage or memory device. If a magnetic or optical recording surface becomes contaminated with dust or dirt, or is physically damaged, the bits may become indecipherable. If there is a malfunction of one of the electronic components in a memory chip, the contents may be unretrievable.

When a read error occurs, the program will allow you to bypass it and move on to the next set of data, or it will end, depending on the operating system. However, if the damaged part of a disk contains control information, the rest of the file may be unreadable. In such cases, a special recovery program must be used to retrieve the remaining data if there is no backup.

read only Refers to any storage media that permanently holds its content, such as a ROM, PROM, CD ROM, compact disc, videodisc or phonograph record.

reader A machine that captures data for the computer, such as an optical character reader, magnetic card reader and punched card reader. A microfiche or microfilm reader is a self-contained machine that reads film and displays its contents.

readme file A text file copied onto software distribution disks that contains last-minute updates or errata that have not been printed in the documentation manual.

read/write channel Same as *I/O channel*.

read/write head A device that reads (senses) and writes (records) data on a magnetic disk or tape. For writing, the surface of the disk or tape is moved past the read/write head. By discharging electrical impulses at the appropriate times, bits are recorded as tiny, magnetized spots of positive or negative polarity.

For reading, the surface is moved past the read/write head, and the bits that are present induce an electrical current across the gap.

See illustration on the following page.

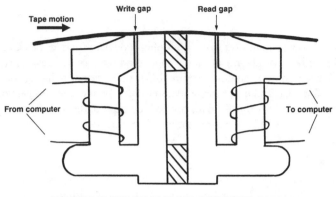

TAPE DRIVE READ/WRITE HEAD

read/write memory Same as *RAM*.

real address Same as *absolute address*.

real mode In Intel 286 and higher machines, an operational state in which the computer functions as if it were an 8086 or 8088. It is limited one megabyte of memory. See *protected mode* and *virtual 86 mode*.

real storage Real physical memory in a virtual memory system.

realtime

(1) Immediate response. The term may refer to fast transaction processing systems for business applications; however, it is always used to refer to process control applications. For example, in airplane instrumentation (avionics) and space flight, realtime computers must respond instantly to the signals that are sent to them.

(2) An electronic operation that is performed in the same timeframe as its real-world counterpart. For example, it takes a fast computer to simulate complex, solid models moving on screen at the same rate they move in the real world. Realtime video transmission produces a live broadcast.

realtime clock A electronic circuit that maintains the time of day. It may also provide timing signals for timesharing operations.

realtime image In computer graphics, a graphics image that can be animated on screen in the same time frame as in real life.

realtime information system A computer system that can respond to transactions by immediately updating the appropriate master files

and/or generating a response in a time frame fast enough to keep an operation moving at its required speed. See *transaction processing*.

realtime operating system A master control program that can provide immediate response to input signals and transactions.

realtime system A computer system that can respond to input signals fast enough to keep an operation moving at its required speed.

reasonable test A test of a value to determine if it falls within a range considered normal or logical. It can be made on electronic signals to detect extraneous noise as well as on data to determine possible input errors.

reboot To reload the operating system and restart the computer. See *boot*.

receiver A device that accepts signals. Contrast with *receiver*.

record

(1) A group of related fields that are used to store data about a subject (master record) or activity (transaction record). A collection of records make up a file.

Master records contain permanent data, such as account number, and variable data, such as balance due. Transaction records contain only permanent data, such as quantity and product code.

(2) In a data organization method, a block of data that is read and written at one time, which has no relationship to records in a data processing system.

record format Same as *record layout*.

record head A device that records a signal on a disk or tape. In computer devices, the record head is called the *read/write head*.

record layout The format of a data record, which includes the name, type and size of each field in the record.

NAME	ADDRESS	CITY	STATE	ZIP	
Conrad, James R.	809 Garibaldi Lane	Benton Falls	TN	37255-0265	

RECORD LAYOUT

record locking See *file and record locking*.

record mark A symbol used to identify the end of a record.

record number A sequential number assigned to each physical record in a file. Record numbers will vary when the file is sorted or records are added and deleted.

records management The creation, retention and scheduled destruction of an organization's paper and film documents. Computer-generated reports and documents fall into the records management domain, but traditional data processing files do not.

rectifier An electrical circuit that converts AC into DC current with the use of diodes that act as one-way valves. Contrast with *inverter*.

recursion In programming, the ability of a subroutine or program module to call itself. Recursion is helpful for writing routines that solve problems by repeatedly processing the output of the same process.

redirector The software component within LAN Manager and LAN Server that is used to control requests between workstations and servers. The redirector module resides within each workstation and server.

redundancy check In communications, a method for detecting transmission errors by appending a calculated number onto the end of each segment of data. See CRC.

reentrant code A programming technique that allows the program to be used by multiple users simultaneously. When a program is written in reentrant style, only one copy of the machine code is loaded into memory, and the code is shared among any number of users on the system.

Reentrant code is written without keeping track of the progress of the processing it's performing. The progress, in the form of counters, flags and other indicators, is maintained within the calling program in order to keep the reentrant program from being modified.

Reentrant processing is analogous to several people each baking their own cake from a single recipe on the wall. Everyone keeps track of their own progress on the master recipe by jotting down the step they're at on their own sheets of paper.

Reentrant code is used in system software, such as operating systems and TP monitors. It also lends itself to multithreading operations, where concurrent events are taking place within the computer.

referential integrity In relational database management, a built-in safeguard that ensures every foreign key matches a primary key. For example, in an order processing system, the customer numbers in the customer file are the primary keys, and the customer numbers in the order file are the foreign keys. If a customer record is allowed to be deleted without question, the order records are left without a primary key match and thus no referential integrity.

If a database system doesn't provide referential integrity, it has to be programmed into the individual application programs.

reflective spot A metallic foil that is placed on each end of a magnetic tape. Light is shined onto the tape, and when it is reflected back to a photosensor, the end of tape is signalled.

reformat
(1) To change the record layout of a file or database.

(2) To initialize a disk over again.

refraction The bending of a ray of light, heat or sound as it passes through different materials.

refresh To continuously charge a device that cannot hold its content. For example, CRTs must be constantly refreshed, because the color phosphors hold their glow for only a few milliseconds. Dynamic memory chips (DRAMs) require constant refreshing to maintain their charged bit patterns.

refresh rate In computer graphics, the time it takes to redraw or redisplay an image on screen.

regenerator
(1) In communications, the same as a *repeater*.

(2) In electronics, a circuit that repeatedly supplies current to a memory or display device that continuously loses its charges or content.

ReGIS (REmote Graphics InStruction) A graphics language from Digital Equipment Corporation used on graphics terminals and first introduced on its PDP-11 machines.

register A small, high-speed circuit that holds addresses and values of internal operations. For example, registers keep track of the address of the instruction being executed and the data being processed. When a program is debugged, the contents of the registers may be displayed to determine the status of the computer at the moment of failure.

In microcomputer assembly language programming, programmers reference registers for routine functions, such as calculating and moving data within memory. Assembly languages in larger computers are often at a higher level.

register level compatibility A hardware component that is 100% compatible with another device. It implies that the same type, size and names of registers are used.

related files Two or more data files that can be matched on some common condition, such as account number or name.

relational capability Implies that two or more data files can be linked together for viewing, editing or the creation of reports. For example, a customer file and an order file can be treated as one file in order to ask a question that relates to information in both files, such as the names of the customers that purchased a particular product. Many routine business queries involve more than one data file.

relational database A method for organizing files in a database that prohibits linking files together. In non-relational systems (hierarchical, network), records in one file point to the locations of records in another, such as customers to orders and vendors to purchases. These links are set up ahead of time in order to provide very fast daily processing.

In a relational database, relationships between files are created by comparing data, such as account numbers and names. A relational system can take any two or more files and generate a new file from the records that meet the matching criteria.

In practice, a pure relational query can be very slow. In order to speed up the process, indexes are built and maintained on the key fields used for matching. Sometimes, indexes are created "on the fly" when the data is requested.

Although relational database became a popular buzzword in the mid 1980s, the term was coined in 1970 by Edgar Codd, whose objective was to easily accomodate a user's ad hoc (special) request for selected data.

Relational terms	Common terms
table or relation	file
tuple	record
attribute	field

relational operator A symbol that specifies a comparison between two values.

Relational Operator	Symbol
EQ Equal to	=
NE Not equal to	< > or # or !=
GT Greater than	>
GE Greater than or equal to	>=
LT Less than	<
LE Less than or equal to	<=

relational spreadsheet See *spreadsheet*.

relative address An address that is relative to the first location of the program rather than a fixed location of memory. The relative address is added to the base address in order to derive the absolute address, the actual current location of the data. See *relocatable code* and *base/displacement*.

relative vector In computer graphics, a vector with end points designated in relative coordinates. Contrast with *absolute vector*.

relay An electrical switch that is used to allow a small current to control a larger one. The small current energizes the relay, which then closes a gate, allowing the large current to flow through.

Relay Gold A communications program for PCs from Microcom, Inc., that provides standard asynchronous transmission as well as mainframe file transfer and local area network support.

Relay Silver A communications program for PCs from Microcom, Inc., that supports a variety of terminals and protocols and can be controlled by programming languages, such as BASIC, Pascal and 8086 assembly language.

relocatable code A machine architecture that allows programs to reside anywhere in memory. It also allows more than one program to reside in memory at the same time. It is accomplished with a relative addressing scheme in which the hardware increments the addresses of the machine instructions at run time. The increment is based on where the program was loaded.

REM statement (REMarks statement) A statement in a programming language that is used to document the program and contains no executable code.

remedial maintenance A repair service that is required due to a malfunction of the product. Contrast with *preventive maintenance*.

remote batch Same as *RJE*.

remote communications A technique that allows one computer to control or duplicate the operation of another computer in a remote location. Software resides in both computers and allows a user to be an interactive participant in the remote computer. Support personnel can use this to oversee users actually running their applications.

remote job entry See *RJE*.

removable disk A disk that is inserted into its respective disk drive for reading and writing and removed when not required. Floppy disks and disk cartridges are removable disk media.

rendering In computer graphics, a 3-D image that incorporates the simulation of lighting effects, such as shadows and reflection.

RenderMan interface A graphics format from Pixar Corporation that includes the photorealistic image synthesis methods for capturing the description of a real image.

repeater In communications, a device that amplifies or regenerates the data signal in order to extend the distance of the transmission. It is available for both analog and digital signals. Repeaters are used extensively in long distance transmission systems to keep the signals from losing their strength. They are used in local area networks to extend normal distance limitations.

report A printed or microfilmed collection of facts and figures with page numbers and page headings. In a database program, the report option is typically used to prepare any kind of printed output, including mailing labels. See *query*.

report file A file that contains the information about the design of a printed report.

report format The layout of a report with page and column headers, page numbers and totals.

report generator Same as *report writer*.

report writer A program that prints a report based on a description of the printed layout and can be a stand-alone program or part of a database management system. It can be used to print only selected records from a file and to sort them into a new sequence before printing.

   The report is customized by entering text for the page header, identifying the print columns (data fields) and indicating which columns are totalled or subtotalled. Once a report is designed, it is stored in a report file for future use.

   Developed in the early 1970s, report writers, or *report generators* as they were originally called, were the precursor to today's query languages and were the first programs to generate computer output without having to be programmed.

reproducer A tabulating machine that makes a duplicate deck of punched cards.

reprographics The duplicating of printed materials using various kinds of printing presses and high-speed copiers.

reserved word A word in a programming or command language that describes some action or function. Reserved words usually cannot be used to name user-defined objects, such as fields and files.

reset button A button, or special key, on a computer that restarts (reboots) the computer. All current screen activities are cleared, and any data in memory is erased. The reset button on a printer clears the printer's memory and readies it to accept new data from the computer.

Resident C A library of C routines for PCs from South Mountain Software Inc., that allow a C program to terminate and stay resident (TSR). The PC version of this Glossary uses Resident C to provide its popup capability.

resident module The part of a program that must remain in memory at all times. Instructions and data that stay in memory can be accessed instantly.

resistor An electronic component that resists the flow of current in an electronic circuit.

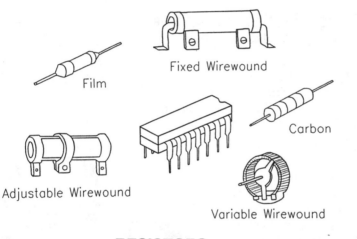

RESISTORS

resolution The degree of sharpness of a displayed or printed character or image. On screen, resolution is expressed as the number of dots per line by the number of lines. A 680x400 resolution means 680 dots across each of 400 lines. The same resolution looks sharper on a small screen than it does on a large screen.

For printers, resolution is expressed as the number of dots per linear inch. A desktop laser printer prints at 300 dpi (300 across, 300 down) or 90,000 dots per square inch.

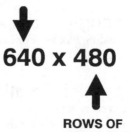

COLUMNS OF RESOLUTION

640 x 480

ROWS OF RESOLUTION

resolve To change, transform or solve a problem. In the phrase "external references are resolved," it refers to determining the addresses that link modules together; that is, solving the unknown links.

resource fork In the Macintosh, a file that contains executable code, menus, windows, dialog boxes, buttons, fonts and icons for a particular application. Contrast with *data fork*, which stores raw data (text, graphics and scripts).

response time The time it takes for the computer to comply with a user's request, such as looking up a customer record.

restart To resume computer opertion after a planned or unplanned termination. See *boot*, *warm boot* and *checkpoint/restart*.

restricted function A computer or operating system function that cannot be used by an application program.

retrieve To call up data that has been stored in a computer system. When a user interrogates (queries) a database, the data is retrieved into the computer first and then transmitted to the terminal screen.

return key Also called *enter key*. The large key on the right side of the keyboard. In data entry operations, pressing return ends the line of input and signals the computer to process it. In word processing, pressing return ends the line or paragraph and actually inserts a return code into the document.

The return key does not function entirely like a typewriter carriage return. It is not used to end lines in the middle of a paragraph; the computer wraps the words to the next line automatically. See CR.

reverse engineer To analyze a completed system in order to isolate its individual building blocks. For example, when a chip is reverse engineered, all the separate circuits that make up the chip are isolated and identified.

reverse polish notation A method for expressing mathematical expressions in certain programming languages, such as FORTH. In reverse Polish notation, the numbers precede the operation. For example, 2 + 2 would be expressed as 2 2 +, and 10 - 3 * 4 would be 10 3 4 * -.

reverse video A display mode that is used for highlighting characters on the screen. For example, if the normal display mode is black on white, the reverse video would be white on black.

revision level See *version number*.

REXX (REstructured EXtended eXecutor) A general-purpose, structured programming language that runs in IBM mainframes under VM/CMS and MVS/TSO-E, Version 2. An OS/2 version, called Personal REXX, is available from the Mansfield Software Group. The following REXX example converts fahrenheit to centigrade:

```
Say "Enter fahrenheit "
Pull FAHR
Say "Centigrade is " (FAHR - 32) * (5 / 9)
```

RF (Radio Frequency) The range of electromagnetic frequencies above the audio range and below visible light. All broadcast transmission, from AM radio to satellites, falls into this range, which is between 30KHz and 300GHz.

RF modulation Refers to the transmitting of a signal through a carrier frequency. For example, some home computers and all VCRs provide RF modulation of a TV channel, such as Channel 3 or 4, to hook up directly to a TV.

RF shielding A material that prohibits electromagnetic radiation from penetrating it. Personal computers and electronic devices used in the home must meet U.S. government standards for electromagnetic interference.

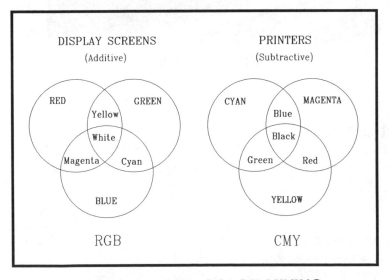

RGB AND CMY COLOR MIXING

RGB (Red Green Blue) The method of recording and generating colors in a video system. On a television or color monitor, colors are displayed as varying intensities of red, green and blue dots. When red, green and blue are all turned on high, white is produced. As the intensities are equally lowered, shades of gray are produced. When all dots are turned off, the base color of the screen appears.

Color printing uses the CMY, or cyan, magenta, yellow system for mixing colors. In RGB, colors are added to create white. In CMY, colors are subtracted to create white. See *colors*, and see illustration on previous page.

RGB monitor A video display screen that requires separate red, green and blue signals from the computer. It generates a higher-quality image than composite signals, in which all three colors are transmitted together (standard TV). RGB monitors come in both analog and digital varieties.

ribbon cable A thin, flat, multiconductor cable that is widely used in electronic systems, for example, to interconnect peripheral devices to the computer internally and externally.

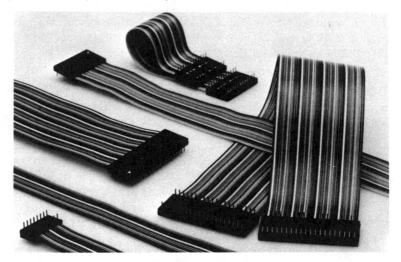

RIBBON CABLES
(Courtesy 3M Company)

right justify Same as *flush right*.

rigid disk Same as *hard disk*.

ring network A communications network that connects terminals and computers in a circular fashion.

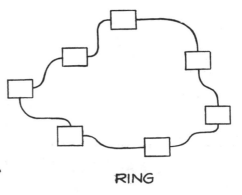

RING

RIP (Raster Image Processor) In computer graphics, the component (hardware, software or both) that prepares data for a raster output device, which is typically a printer. RIPs are designed for a specific type of input, such as vectors, PostScript as well as different raster data.

RISC (Reduced Instruction Set Computer) A computer architecture that performs a limited number of instructions. The concept is that most programs generally use only a few instructions, and if those basic instructions are made to execute faster, performance is increased.

RISC eliminates a layer of overhead called *microcode*, which is commonly used to make it easier to add new and complex instructions to a computer. RISC computers have a small number of instructions built into the lowest level circuits that work at maximum speed.

Although RISC machines are only 15% to 50% faster than their CISC (complex instruction set computer) counterparts, RISC chips are less expensive to produce. Thus, the dollars per MIPS is decidedly in favor of RISC.

There's controversy over RISC. Its proponents claim its speed and lower cost is an extreme advantage. Its opponents claim its improvements are not worth proliferating the world with new machine languages and that far greater performance improvements will be coming anyway. In addition, because many instructions are eliminated, the software (assemblers, compilers) has to generate more code to do what used to be done in hardware.

In the early days, there were no multiply and divide instructions. It was done by software with repetitive additions and subtractions. Later, multiply and divide were built into the hardware. Eventually, instructions that performed an entire table lookup were built in. With RISC, we're back to where we started.

Once the ties get wider and the hemlines get higher, the only choice is to make the ties thinner and the hemlines lower.

RJE (Remote Job Entry) The transmission of batches of transactions from a remote terminal or computer. The receiving computer processes the data and may transmit the results back to the RJE site for printing. RJE hardware at remote sites can employ teleprinters with disk or tape storage, or complete micro or minicomputer systems.

RLL (Run Length Limited) A technique used for encoding data on a magnetic disk that packs more bits into the same space than the common MFM method. It is used in ESDI and SCSI disks.

RMS

(1) (Record Management Services) The file management system used in Digital's VAX series.

(2) (Root Mean Square) A method used to measure electrical output in volts and watts.

RO terminal (Receive Only terminal) Teleprinters, or printing terminals, without keyboards. Constrast with *KSR terminal*, which uses a keyboard.

RoboCAD A computer-aided design program for PCs from Robo Systems Corporation. It provides up to 256 colors and layers, has two drawing pages and a scratch pad, and can transfer data to RoboSOLID, a solids modeling program. In addition to standard drawing capabilities, it includes a wide variety of features and text functions.

robot A stand-alone hybrid computer system that performs physical and computational activities. Robots can be designed similar to human form, although most industrial robots don't resemble people at all. They have one or more arms and joints designed for specific activities. The advantage of a robot is that it is a multiple-motion device, capable of performing many different tasks like a person can.

Robots are used extensively in manufacturing, performing such functions as welding, riveting, scraping and painting. Office and consumer applications are also being developed. Robots are being designed with artificial intelligence so they can respond more effectively to unstructured situations. For example, specialized robots can identify objects in a pile, select the objects in the appropriate sequence and assemble them into a unit.

Robots use analog sensors for recognizing objects in the real world and digital computers for their direction. Analog to digital converters convert temperature, motion, pressure, sound and images into binary code for the robot's computer. The outputs of the computers direct the physical actions of the arms and joints by pulsing their motors.

robotics The art and science of the creation and use of robots.

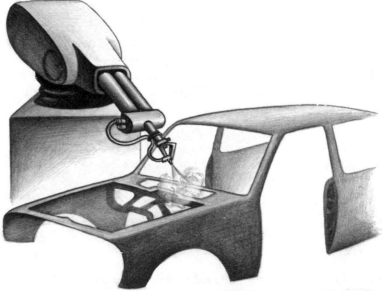

INDUSTRIAL ROBOT

robust Refers to a solid program that works properly under all normal and most abnormal conditions.

roll in/roll out A swapping technique for freeing up memory temporarily in order to perform another task. The current program or program segment is stored (rolled out) on disk, and another program is brought in (rolled in) that memory space.

rollover See *n-key rollover*.

ROM (Read Only Memory) A memory chip that permanently stores instructions and data. Its contents are placed into the ROM at the time of manufacture and cannot be altered. It is used extensively to hold codes and programs that are permanent.

ROMs are used in the cartridges that plug into calculators, game computers and laser printers. They are used in laptop computers to hold operating systems and application programs; however, if there is an update to any of the programs, the ROM chip has to be replaced with a new one. See *PROM*.

ROM BIOS (Read Only Memory Basic Input Output System) A set of routines stored in a ROM chip in a PC. The BIOS contains the drivers, or access methods, that activate the peripheral devices directly. See *driver*.

root directory In hierarchical file systems, the starting point in the hierarchy. When the system is first started, the root directory is the current directory.

Access to directories in the hierarchy requires naming the directories that are in its path. In DOS and OS/2, going down the hierarchy requires naming the directories in the path from the current directory to the destination directory, but going back up or sideways requires naming the entire path starting from the root directory.

rotational delay The amount of time it takes for the disk to rotate until the required location on the disk reaches the read/write head.

round robin A continuously repeating sequence, such as the polling of a series of terminals, one after the other, over and over again.

router In communications, a device that selects an appropriate travel path and routes a message accordingly. Routers are used in complex networks where there are many pathways between users in the network. The router examines the destination address of the message and determine the most effective route. See *bridge, gateway* and *brouter*.

routine A set of instructions that perform a task. Same as *subroutine, module, procedure* and *function*.

row A horizontal set of data or components. In a graph, it is called the *x-axis*. Contrast with *column*.

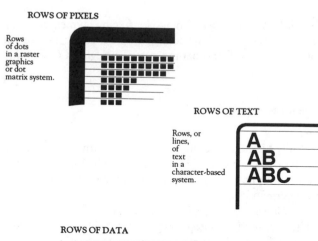

ROWS OF PIXELS

Rows
of dots
in a raster
graphics
or dot
matrix system.

ROWS OF TEXT

Rows, or
lines,
of
text
in a
character-based
system.

A
AB
ABC

ROWS OF DATA

Rows, lines
or records
in a
spreadsheet,
text
or database
file.

NAME	STREET	BALANCE
Jones, Jennifer A.	10 West Main Ave.	0000208.49
Russo, George C.	23 East Benton St.	0000107.49
Morrison, Emil T.	1240 Parkway East	0001005.77
Fernandez, Joseph R.	39 Gate Drive	0003484.49

ROWS

RPC (Remote Procedure Call) An interface that allows one program to call another in a remote location. A standard RPC allows an application to be used in a variety of networks without change.

RPG (Report Program Generator) One of the first program generators designed for business reports, introduced in 1964 by IBM. RPG II, introduced in 1970, was an advanced version that has been widely used as a programming language for business applications on small computers. RPG statements are written on preprinted forms with fixed columns for each part of the statement.

RPM (Revolutions Per Minute) Used to measure the speed of a disk drive. Floppy disks rotate at 300 rpm, while hard disks rotate at 2,400 to 3,600 rpm.

RPN See *reverse polish notation*.

RPQ (Request for Price Quotation) A document that requests a price for hardware, software or services to solve a specific problem. It is created by the customer and delivered to the vendor.

RS-170 The standard for NTSC composite video signals.

RS-232-C A 25-wire electrical interface between a computer and a peripheral device, such as a modem, mouse, drawing tablet or printer. It is an EIA standard for serial transmission that uses a 25-pin DB-25 or 9-pin DB-9 connector. Its normal cable limitation of 50 feet can be extended to several hundred feet with high-quality cable.

RS-232 defines the purposes, electrical characteristics and timing of the signals in the cable. However, all 25 wires in the cable are not used all the time; many applications use less than a dozen.

Note: The same DB-25 connector used in RS-232 serial cables is also used as a connector for parallel printer cables.

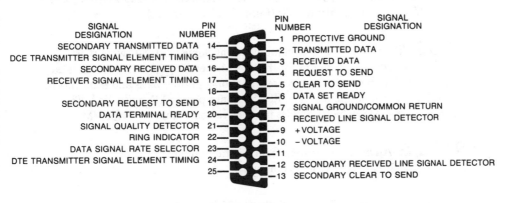

RS-232 INTERFACE

(Courtesy Black Box Corporation)

RS-422, RS-423, RS-449 EIA standards for serial transmission that extend the distances and speeds beyond the RS-232 standard. Both interfaces typically use a DB-37 connector, but may be implemented with a variety of other connectors. RS-422 is a balanced system requiring more wire pairs than RS-423 and is intended for use in multidrop, or multipoint, lines.

RS-449 specifies the pin definitions for RS-422 and 423. RS-422 and 423 are subsets of RS-449, each specifying the electrical and timing characteristics of the lines.

SIGNAL DESIGNATION	PIN NUMBER		PIN NUMBER	SIGNAL DESIGNATION
			1	SHIELD
RECEIVE COMMON	20		2	SIGNALING RATE INDICATOR
	21		3	
SEND DATA	22		4	SEND DATA
SEND TIMING	23		5	SEND TIMING
RECEIVE DATA	24		6	RECEIVE DATA
REQUEST TO SEND	25		7	REQUEST TO SEND
RECEIVE TIMING	26		8	RECEIVE TIMING
CLEAR TO SEND	27		9	CLEAR TO SEND
TERMINAL IN SERVICE	28		10	LOCAL LOOPBACK
DATA MODE	29		11	DATA MODE
TERMINAL READY	30		12	TERMINAL READY
RECEIVER READY	31		13	RECEIVER READY
SELECT STANDBY	32		14	REMOTE LOOPBACK
SIGNAL QUALITY	33		15	INCOMING CALL
NEW SIGNAL	34		16	SELECT FREQUENCY
TERMINAL TIMING	35		17	TERMINAL TIMING
STANDBY/INDICATOR	36		18	TEST MODE
SEND COMMON	37		19	SIGNAL GROUND

RS-449 INTERFACE

(Courtesy Black Box Corporation)

RS-485 EIA standard for multidrop, or multipoint, communications lines. It can be implemented with as little as a wire block with four screws or with DB-9 or DB-37 connectors. By using lower impedance drivers and receivers, RS-485 allows more nodes on a multidrop line than RS-422.

RS/6000 (RISC System/6000) A family of RISC-based workstations from IBM introduced in 1990. It comes in workstation (POWERstation) and server (POWERserver) models and uses the Micro Channel bus architecture. It introduced Version 3 of AIX (IBM's version of UNIX) and two graphical user interfaces: AIXwindows Environment/6000 (enhanced X Window system) and AIX NeXTStep Environment/6000 (from NeXT Computer).

RSCS (Remote Spooling Communications Subsystem) Software that provides batch communications for IBM's VM operating system. It accepts data from remote batch terminals, executes them on a priority basis and transmits the results back to the terminals. The RSCS counterpart in MVS is called JES. Contrast with CMS, which provides interactive communications for VM.

RSTS/E An operating system from Digital Equipment Corporation that is used on its PDP-11 series of minicomputers.

RSX-11 (Resource Sharing eXtension-PDP 11) A multiuser, multitasking operating system from Digital Equipment Corporation that runs on its PDP-11 series of minicomputers.

RT A RISC-based workstation from IBM introduced in 1986. Its proprietary microprocessor is not compatible with IBM's PC or PS/2 line.

RT-11 A single user, multitasking operating system from Digital that runs on its PDP-11 series.

RTF (Rich Text Format) A Microsoft format that uses ASCII characters to encode layout settings. For example, \ul is the code for underline.

RTS (Request To Send) An RS-232 signal sent from the transmitting station to the receiving station requesting permission to transmit. Contrast with CTS.

rtVAX 300 A board-level computer system for realtime applications from Digital Equipment Corporation, which includes VAX and Ethernet processors and a floating-point coprocessor on a 3x5" card. It runs under the VAXELN operating system.

rubber banding In computer graphics, the moving of a line or object where one end stays fixed in position.

rubout key The key on a terminal keyboard deletes the last character that was entered.

rule-based expert system An expert system based on a set of rules that a human expert would follow in diagnosing a problem. Contrast with *model-based expert system.*

ruler line A graphic representation of a ruler on screen that is used for laying out text and graphics.

rules
(1) A set of conditions or standards which have been agreed upon.

(2) In printing, horizontal and vertical lines between columns or at the top and bottom of a page in order to enhance the appearance of the page.

run
(1) To execute a program.

(2) A single program that is to be executed, or a group of programs that are to be executed sequentially.

run around In desktop publishing, the flowing of text around a graphic image.

run length limited See *RLL.*

run time Refers to the actual execution of a program.

run time version Software that allows another program to run or that enables a program to run with some enhanced capability.

For example, a run time version of a windowing environment, such as Windows or GEM, provides a graphical interface for the accompanying application, but cannot be used with any other program.

Database management systems often provide an interpreted programming language requiring the full DBMS to reside in the computer in order to execute the programs developed in it. A run time version of such a package would run the programs and allow them to be distributed to users that don't have the DBMS.

SAA (System Application Architecture) Introduced in 1987, a set of IBM standards that provide consistent interfaces among all IBM computers from micro to mainframe. It is made up of user interfaces, programming interfaces and communications protocols, as follows:

(1) Common User Access (CUA) - Interfaces based on the graphics-based Presentation Manager of OS/2 and the character-oriented interfaces of 3270 terminals.

(2) Common Programming Interface (CPI) - A common set of application programming interfaces (APIs) that would, for example, allow a program developed on the PC to be easily moved to a mainframe. The standard database language is SQL.

(3) Common Communications Support (CCS) - A common set of protocols, including LU 6.2 (APPC) and HLLAPI.

sabermetrician Slang for a statistician who uses computers to predict future performance of sports teams and players.

SAM

(1) (Symantec AntiVirus for Macintosh) The leading antivirus program for the Macintosh from Symantec Corporation. It scans hard disks and floppies for viruses, provides specific identification of virus types and contains a disk clinic routine for eradicating the virus.

(2) See *sequential access method*.

Samna A word processing program for PCs and UNIX workstations from Samna Corporation. Introduced in 1983, it was one of the first full-featured word processors for personal computers. In 1986, Samna integrated desktop publishing features into its Word IV and Plus IV programs. Word IV was the first word processor approved by the American Bar Association.

sampling

(1) In statistics, the analysis of a group by determining the characteristics of a significant percentage of its members chosen at random.

(2) In digitizing operations, the conversion of real-world signals or movements at regular intervals into digital code.

sampling rate In digitizing operations, the frequency with which samples are taken and converted. The higher the sample rate, the closer real-world objects are represented in digital form.

sans-serif A typeface style without the serifs, which are the short horizontal lines added at the tops and bottoms of the vertical member of the letter. Helvetica is a common sans-serif font.

SANS-SERIF   SERIF

SAP (Secondary Audio Program) An NTSC audio channel that is used for auxiliary transmission, such as foreign language broadcasting or teletext transmission.

SAS (Statistical Analysis System) An integrated data management, analysis and presentation system from the SAS Institute Inc., that runs on a wide variety of computers, including IBM mainframes and VAXs. It includes data management, spreadsheets, CBT, presentation graphics, project management, operations research, scheduling, linear programming, statistical quality control, econometric and time series analysis, mathematical, engineering and statistical applications as well as full application development.

satellite See *communications satellite*

satellite channel A particular carrier frequency for the radio transmission of data.

satellite computer A computer in a separate location that is available to communicate with the host computer or is under the control of the host. It can function as a slave to the master computer or perform off-line auxiliary tasks.

satellite link A signal that travels from the earth to a communications satellite and back down again. Contrast with *terrestrial link*.

saturation
(1) On magnetic media, occurs when the magnetizable particles are completely aligned and a more powerful writing signal will not improve the reading back.

(2) In a bipolar transistor, occurs when the current on the gate (the trigger) is equal to or greater than what is necessary to close the switch.

(3) In a diode, occurs when the diode is fully conducting.

save To write the contents of memory to disk or tape. Some applications save data automatically, others do not. Memory-based word processors, and most all spreadsheets require that the user saves the data before exiting the program.

SBS (Satellite Business Systems) An organization that was developed to offer satellite communications services to business. It is currently part of MCI.

scalable font A font that is created in the required point size at the time a document is printed. The actual dot patterns used for printing are generated from a set of outline fonts, or base fonts, which contain a mathematical representation of the typeface. Scalable fonts provide more flexibility than bit-mapped fonts by eliminating the need to store a variety of different font sizes in the computer. Contrast with *bit-mapped fonts*.

scalar A single item or value. Contrast with *vector* and *array*, which are made up of multiple values.

scalar processor A computer that performs arithmetic computations on one number at a time. Contrast with *vector processor*.

scalar variable In programming, a variable that contains only one value.

scale
(1) In computer graphics and printing, to resize an object, making it smaller or larger.

(2) To change the representation of a quantity in order to bring it into prescribed limits of another range. For example, values such as 1249, 876, 523, -101 and -234 might need to be scaled into a range from -5 to +5.

(3) To designate the position of the decimal point in a fixed or floating point number.

scan
(1) In optical technologies, to view a printed form a line at a time in order to convert images into bit-mapped representations, or to convert characters into ASCII text or some other data code.

(2) In video, to move across a picture frame a line at a time, either to detect the image in an analog or digital camera, or to refresh a CRT-based video screen.

(3) To sequentially search a file.

scan head An optical sensing device in an optical scanner or facsimile machine that is moved across the image to be scanned.

scan line One of many horizontal lines in a graphics frame.

scan rate
(1) The total number of lines that are illuminated on a video display screen in one second. For example, a resolution of 400 lines that is refreshed 60 times per second requires a scan rate of 24KHz (24,000 cyles per second). Scan rate is called *horizontal synchronization frequency* in the television industry.

(2) The number of times per second a scanning device samples its field of vision.

scanner A device that reads text, images and bar codes. Text and bar code scanners recognize printed fonts and bar codes and convert them into a digital code, such as ASCII. Graphics scanners convert a printed image into a video image (raster graphics) without recognizing the actual content of the text or pictures.

scatter diagram A graph that is plotted with dots or some other symbol at each data point. A scatter diagram is also called a *scatter plot* or *dot chart*.

scatter plot Same as *scatter diagram*.

scatter read A capability that allows data to be input into two or more noncontiguous locations of memory with one read operation. See *gather write*.

SCERT (Systems and Computers Evaluation and Review Technique) Pronounced "skirt." A program that measures the performance of a system by modeling the computer environment and application programs.

scheduler A part of the operating system that initiates and terminates jobs (programs) in the computer. Also called a *dispatcher*, the scheduler maintains a list of jobs to be run and allocates appropriate computer resources as required.

scheduling algorithm The method used to schedule jobs for execution. Priority, length of time in the job queue and available resources are examples of criteria used in a scheduling algorithm.

schema The definition of an entire database. See *subschema*.

Scheme A dialect of LISP developed at MIT and the University of Indiana. TI has a personal computer version of Scheme called PC Scheme.

Schottky A category of bipolar transistors that is known for its fast switching speeds in the three-nanosecond range. Schottky II devices have switching speeds in the range of a single nanosecond.

scientific applications Applications that simulate real-world activities using mathematics. Real-world objects are turned into mathematical models and their actions are simulated by manipulating the models using mathematical formulas.

For example, an airplane can be described mathematically, and some of its flight characteristics can be simulated in the computer. Rivers, lakes and mountains can also be simulated. Virtually any objects with known characteristics can be modeled and simulated.

Scientific applications require enormous calculations and often require supercomputers to perform the simulations. As personal computers become more powerful, more laboratory experiments will be converted into computer models that can then be interactively examined by students without the risk and cost of the actual experiments.

scientific computer A computer that is specialized for high-speed mathematic processing. See *array processor* and *floating point processor*.

scientific language A programming language that is designed for mathematical formulas and matrices, such as ALGOL, FORTRAN and APL. Although all programming languages allow for this kind of processing, statements in a scientific language make it easier to express these actions.

scientific notation The display of a number in floating point form. The number (mantissa) is always equal to or greater than one and less than 10, and the base is 10. For example, 2.345E6 is equivalent to 2,345,000. The number following E (exponent) represents the power to which the mantissa should be raised (the number of zeros following the decimal point).

scissoring In computer graphics, the deleting of any parts of an image which fall outside of a window that has been sized and laid over the original image. Also called *clipping*.

SCO UNIX An AT&T-licensed implementation of UNIX System V/386 3.2 for 386 and higher PCs from The Santa Cruz Operation. It is a multiuser, multitasking environment that runs both XENIX and UNIX applications. It has more security and networking features and more standards conformance than SCO XENIX. When used with SCO VP/ix or SCO's Open Desktop, it can also run DOS applications.

SCO VP/ix A system program for 386 and higher PCs from The Santa Cruz Operation that allows DOS applications to run concurrently with SCO UNIX or SCO XENIX in a virtual memory environment. Each application runs in its own secure virtual address space.

SCO XENIX An AT&T-licensed, SVID-conforming implementation of UNIX System V for 286 and higher PCs from The Santa Cruz Operation. Originally developed by Microsoft, it has become the standard for personal computers running UNIX. It is faster and smaller than SCO UNIX and added features include improved documentation and easier installation.

scope

(1) A CRT type of screen, such as used on an oscilloscope or common display terminal.

(2) In programming, the visibility of variables within a program; for example, whether one function can use a variable created in another function.

(3) In dBASE, a range of records, such as the "next 50" or "current record to end of file."

scrambler A device or software program that encodes data for encryption.

scrambling The encoding data to make it indecipherable. See *encryption* and *DES*.

Scrapbook In the Macintosh, a disk file that holds frequently-used text and graphics objects, such as a company letterhead. Contrast with *Clipboard*, which holds data only for the current sesssion.

scratch tape A magnetic tape that contains data that is no longer needed and can be erased and reused.

scratchpad A special register or a reserved section of memory or disk that is used for temporary storage.

screen The display area of a video terminal or monitor. It is either a CRT or one of the flat panel technologies.

screen capture The transfer of the image on the current display screen into a graphics file.

screen dump A printout of the contents of the current display screen. In PCs, pressing Shift-PrtSc prints the screen if the screen contents are in text mode. For a graphics dump, a screen capture program must be preloaded and activated with a hotkey.
  In the Macintosh, pressing Apple-Shift-3 creates a MacPaint file of the current screen.

screen font A font that is used for on-screen display. For true WYSIWYG systems, screen fonts must be matched as close as possible to the printer fonts.

screen overlay

(1) A clear, fine-mesh screen that reduces the glare on a video screen.

(2) A clear touch panel that allows the user to command the computer by touching displayed buttons on screen.

(3) A window of data displayed on screen temporarily. The part of the screen that was overlaid is saved and restored when the screen overlay is removed.

screen saver A utility program that blanks the screen after a specified number of minutes without keyboard activity. Pressing any key usually restores the screen.

script

(1) A typeface that looks like handwriting or calligraphy.

(2) A program or macro.

scroll To continuously move forward, backward or sideways through the images on screen or within a window. Scrolling implies continuous and smooth movement, a line, character or pixel at a time, as if the data were on a paper scroll being rolled behind the screen.

VERTICAL SCROLLING

scroll arrow An icon that points up, down, left or right and is clicked in order to scroll the screen in the corresponding direction. The screen moves one line, or increment, with each click of the mouse.

scroll bar A horizontal or vertical bar that contains a box that looks like an elevator in a shaft. The bar is clicked to scroll the screen in the corresponding direction, or the box is clicked and then dragged to the desired direction.

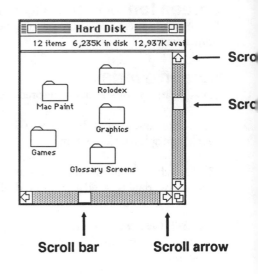

Scroll bar   Scroll arrow

scrollable field A short line on screen that can be scrolled to allow entry of larger amounts of data into a small entry space. Scrollable fields allow narrow columns to be displayed, and the excess data is revealed by scrolling.

SCSI (Small Computer System Interface) Pronounced "scuzzy." A peripheral interface for up to seven devices. It is standard on the Macintosh since the Mac Plus and is available on PCs by plugging in a SCSI controller board. SCSI provides a high-speed, parallel data transfer of up to 4MBytes/sec and has the advantage of connecting multiple peripherals while taking up only one slot in the computer.

scuzzy See *SCSI*.

SDF (Standard Data Format) A simple file format that uses fixed length fields and is commonly used to transfer data between different programs.

SDF

```
Robin Smith    5 E. 12 St.    Rye          NY
J. Jones       2168 Main St.  Palo Alto    CA
```

Comma delimited

```
"Robin Smith","5 E. 12 St.","Rye","NY"
"J. Jones","2168 Main St.","Palo Alto","CA"
```

SDK (Software Developer's Kit) See *developer's toolkit*.

SDLC (Synchronous Data Link Control) The primary data link protocol used in IBM's SNA networks. It is a bit-oriented synchronous protocol that is a subset of the HDLC protocol.

SE See *systems engineer* and *Macintosh*.

seamless integration The addition of a new program or routine that works smoothly with the existing system. It implies that the new feature can be activated and used without problems. Contrast with *transparent*, which implies that there is no discernible change after installation.

search and replace To look for an occurrence of data or text and replace it with another set of data or text.

search key The data being looked up in a search routine.

second-generation computer A computer that is made of discrete transistors and electronic components. In the early 1960s, the IBM 1401 and Honeywell 400 were examples.

second source An alternative supplier of an identical product. A second source manufacturer is one that holds a license to produce an original product from another manufacturer.

secondary channel In communications, a subchannel that is derived from the main channel. It is used for diagnostic or supervisory purposes, but does not carry data messages.

secondary index An index that is maintained for a data file, but does not control the current processing order of the file. See *primary index*.

secondary storage External storage, such as disk and tape.

sector The smallest unit of storage read or written by a disk. Sectors are fixed in length, and the same number of sectors usually reside in one track. However, the hardware may vary the disk speed to fit more sectors into tracks located on the outer edges of the disk platter. The sector is the physical unit called for by an instruction, for example, READ TRACK 17 SECTOR 23.

sector interleave The way sectors are numbered on a hard disk. The interleave can be sequential: 0,1,2,3 or staggered: 0,3,6,1,4,7,2,5,8. In sequential numbering, if data in sector 1 is read, by the time the access to 2 is given, the beginning of sector 2 has passed the head and must rotate around to come under the head again. The staggering of sectors optimizes sequential reads and writes to a disk. Also called *sector map*.

sector map See *sector interleave*.

security The protection of data against unauthorized access. Programs and data can be secured by issuing identification numbers and passwords to authorized users of a computer. However, systems programmers, or other technically competent individuals, will ultimately have access to these codes.

Passwords can be checked by the operating system to prevent users from logging onto the system in the first place, or they can be checked in software, such as database management systems, where each user can be assigned an individual view (subschema) of the database. Any application program running in the computer can also be designed to check for passwords.

Data transmitted over communications networks can be secured by encryption to prevent eavesdropping.

Although precautions can be taken to detect an unauthorized user, it is extremely difficult to determine if a valid user is performing unauthorized tasks. Effective security measures are a balance of technology and personnel management. See *NCSC*.

security kernel The part of the operating system that grants access to users of the computer system.

SEED (Self-Electro-optic-Effect Device) An optical transistor developed by David Miller at Bell Labs in 1986.

seed A starting value used by a random number generation routine to create random numbers.

seek
(1) To move the access arm to the requested track on a disk.

(2) An instruction in a low-level assembly language that activates a seek operation on the disk.

(3) A command in a high-level programming language that is used to select a record by key field.

seek time The time it takes to move the read/write head to a particular track on a disk after the instruction has been executed. The majority of a disk's access time is made up of seek time.

segment
(1) Any partition, reserved area, partial component or piece of a larger structure.

(2) One of the bars that make up a single character in an LED or LCD display.

selection sort A search for specific data, starting at the beginning of a file or list. It copies each matching item to a new file so that the selected items are in the same sequence as the original data.

selective calling In communications, the ability of the transmitting station to indicate which station in the network is to receive the message.

selector channel A high-speed computer channel that connects a peripheral device, such as a disk or tape, to the computer's memory.

selector pen Same as *light pen*.

Selectric typewriter Introduced in 1961 by IBM, the first typewriter to use a golf-ball-like print head that moved across the paper, rather than moving the paper carriage across the print mechanism. It rapidly became one of the world's most popular typewriters. IBM has always excelled in electromechanical devices.

self-checking digit See *check digit*.

self-clocking The recording of digital data on a magnetic medium such that the clock pulses are intrinsically part of the recorded signal, and a separate timer clock is not required. Phase encoding is a commonly-used self-clocking recording technique.

self-documenting code Programming statements that can be easily understood later either by the original programmer or another programmer. COBOL provides more self-documenting code than does C, for example.

semantic gap The amount of difference between a data or language structure and the real world. For example, in an order processing system that uses a hierarchical database, a company cannot be both customer and supplier within the database. Since there is no way to model this real-world possibility, the semantic gap is said to be large. A network database could handle this condition, resulting in a smaller semantic gap. See *object-oriented database*.

semantics The study of the meanings of words. As applied to computer languages, semantics governs the basic rules of the language. For example, a reserved word, such as DISPLAY or LIST, should not be used as the name of a data file or field so that you don't wind up with LIST LIST. Contrast with *syntax*, which deals with the correct order or symbols used in combining words in a phrase.

semaphore
(1) A hardware or software flag that is used to indicate the status of some activity.

(2) A shared space for interprocess communications (IPC) that is controlled by "wake up" and "sleep" commands. The source process fills a queue and goes to sleep until the destination process uses the data and tells the source process to wake up.

semiconductor A solid state substance that can be electrically altered. Certain elements in nature, such as silicon, perform like semiconductors when they are chemically combined with other elements. A semiconductor is halfway between a conductor, a material that conducts electricity, and an insulator, a material that resists electricity. When charged with electricity or light, semiconductors change their state from nonconductive to conductive or vice versa. The most significant semiconductor is the transistor, which simply acts like an on/off switch, allowing current to pass or not to pass through it.

semiconductor device An elementary component, such as a transistor, or a larger unit of electronic equipment comprised of chips.

sensor A device that measures or detects a real world condition, such as motion, heat or light and converts the condition into an analog or digital representation of it. An optical sensor detects the intensity or brightness of light, or the intensity of red, green and blue for color systems.

sequel See *SQL*.

sequence check The testing of a list of items or file of records for correct ascending or descending sequence based on the item or key fields in the records.

sequential access method The organization of data in a prescribed ascending or descending sequence. Data stored in this fashion must be searched for by reading and comparing each record, starting from the beginning or end of the file.

serial One after the other. Sequential also implies one after the other, but in a consecutive order, such as by account number or name.

serial and parallel port One serial and one parallel connector for connecting peripheral devices to a personal computer. Although more than one of each may be necessary for a particular requirement, the serial port allows you to hook up a modem, mouse or printer, and the parallel port lets you hook up to a printer.

For minicomputers and mainframes, there are myriads of connectors that are referenced by many designations.

serial computer A single-processor computer that executes one instruction after the other. Contrast with *parallel computer*.

serial interface A data channel that transfers digital data in a serial fashion: one bit after the other. Communications lines are generally serial interfaces, and many peripheral devices connect to a computer using a serial interface. Serial interfaces may have multiple lines, or wires, but only one line is used for data. Contrast with *parallel interface*.

serial mouse A mouse that connects to a computer's serial port. See *bus mouse*.

serial number A unique number that is assigned by the vendor to each unit of hardware or software. See *signature*.

serial port An external connector on a computer that is used to connect a modem or other serial device. The typical serial port uses a DB-25 or DB-9 connector. Contrast with *parallel port*.

serial printer A printer that prints one character at a time, in contrast to a line or page at a time. The term serial in this context has no relationship to a serial or parallel interface that is used to attach the printer to the computer. See *printer*.

serial transmission The transmission of data one bit at a time, one bit following the next. Contrast with *parallel interface*, which transmits one or more bytes (8, 16 bits, etc.) at the same time.

serialize To convert a parallel signal that is made up of one or more bytes into a serial signal that transmits one bit after the other.

Series/1 A series of minicomputers from IBM, introduced in 1976, used in general business computing, as communications processors and as data collection and analysis systems in process control.

serif The short horizontal lines that are added to the tops and bottoms of traditional typefaces, such as Times Roman. Contrast with *sans-serif*.

server A computer in a network that is shared by multiple users. See *file server* and *print server*.

service Another term for functionality derived from a particular software program. For example, network services may refer to programs that transmit data or provide conversion of data in a network. Database services provides for the storage and retrieval of data in a database.

service bureau An organization that provides data processing and timesharing services to its customers. It offers a wide variety of software packages, as well as customized programming. Customers pay for storage of data on the system and processing time used.

Connection is made to a service bureau through dial-up terminals, private lines, or other networks, such as Telenet or Tymnet.

In addition, service bureaus can offer or specialize in batch processing services, such as data entry or COM (computer output microfilm) processing.

servo An electromechanical device that uses feedback to provide precise starts and stops for such functions as the motors on a tape drive or the moving of an access arm on a disk.

session

(1) In communications, the active connection between a user and a computer or between two computers.

(2) The time between starting up and ending an application program.

set theory A branch of mathematics or logic that is concerned with sets of objects and rules for their manipulation. UNION, INTERSECT and COMPLEMENT are its three primary operations and they are used in relational database as follows. Given a file of Americans and a file of Barbers, UNION would create a file of all Americans and Barbers. INTERSECT would create a file of American Barbers, and COMPLEMENT would create a file of Barbers who are not Americans, or of Americans who are not Barbers.

setup program A program that configures a system for a particular environment. In personal computers, it is used to inform the operating system of a major device change, such as a new disk drive or video display. See *install program*.

setup string A group of commands that initialize a device, such as a printer. See *escape character*.

seven dwarfs IBM's early competitors in the mainframe business: Burroughs, CDC, GE, Honeywell, NCR, RCA and Univac.

seven-segment display A

common display found on digital watches and readouts that looks like a series of 8s. Each digit or alphabetic letter is formed by the selective illumination of up to seven separately addressable bars.

shadow batch A data collection system that simulates a transaction processing environment. Instead of updating master files, such as customer and inventory files, when orders or shipments are initiated, the transactions are only stored in the computer system for reference.

When a user makes a query, the master record from the previous update cycle is retrieved; but before it's displayed, it's updated in memory with any transactions that may affect it. The up-to-date master record is then displayed for the user. At the end of the day or period, the transactions are then actually batch processed against the master file.

shadow RAM In a PC, a copy of the operating system's BIOS routines in RAM to improve performance. RAM chips are faster than ROM chips.

shared DASD (shared Direct Access Storage Device) A disk that is accessed by two or more computers within a single datacenter. Disks shared in personal computer networks are called *file servers* or *database servers*.

shared logic The use of a single computer that provides processing for two or more terminals. Contrast with *shared resource*.

shared resource A peripheral device, such as a disk or printer, that is shared by multiple users. For example, a file server and laser printer in a local area network are shared resources. Contrast with *shared logic*.

shareware Software that is distributed free of charge to users. Shareware programs ask you to pay a nominal charge for the program if you use it and like it. In that way, you'll be registered with the company and be able to receive additional support and notifications of updates. Shareware is usually available on electronic bulletin boards that let you dial up and download the program directly into your computer.

sheet feeder A mechanical device that feeds stacks of standard cut forms, such as letterheads and legal paper, into a printer.

shelfware Products that remain unsold on a dealer's shelf.

shell An outer layer of a program that provides the user interface, or way of commanding the computer. Shells are typically add-on programs created for command-driven operating systems, such as UNIX and DOS. The shell provides a menu-driven or graphical icon-oriented interface to the system in order to make it easier to use.

shell out Refers to an option in an application that lets a user temporarily leave the program, switch back to the operating system, perform some function and return.

shift register A high-speed circuit that holds some number of bits for the purpose of shifting them left or right. It is used internally within the processor for multiplication and division, serial/parallel conversion and various timing considerations.

short card In a PC, a plug-in printed circuit board that is half the length of a full-size board. See *long card*.

short-haul modem In communications, a device that transmits signals up to about a mile. Similar to a line driver that can transmit up to several miles.

SI See *Norton SI*.

sideband In communications, the upper or lower half of a carrier wave. Since both sidebands are normally mirror images of each other, one of the halves can be used for a second channel to increase the data-carrying capacity of the line or for diagnostic or control purposes.

Sidekick A desktop accessory program for PCs from Borland International. Introduced in 1984, it was the first popup program for the PC. It includes a calculator, WordStar-compatible notepad, appointment calendar, phone dialer and ASCII conversion table by pressing a hotkey.

Sidekick Plus, introduced in 1988, adds more notepad commands, calendar alarms, scientific and programming calculators, limited file management and an outliner.

Sieve of Eratosthenes A benchmark program that is used to test the pure mathematical speed of a computer. The program calculates prime numbers based on Eratosthenes's algorithm.

SIG (Special Interest Group) A group that meets and shares information about a particular topic of interest. It is usally a part of a larger group or association.

SIGGRAPH A special interest group on computer graphics that is part of the ACM.

sign A symbol that identifies a positive or negative number. In digital code, it is either a separate character or part of the byte. In ASCII, the sign is kept in a separate character typically transmitted in front of the number it represents (+ and - is 2B and 2D in hex).

In EBCDIC, the minus sign can be stored as a separate byte (60 in hex), or, more commonly, as half a byte (+ and - is C and D in hex), which is stored in the high-order bits of the least significant byte. For packed decimal, it is in the low-order bits of the least significant byte.

sign on/sign off Same as *log-on/log-off*.

signal The physical form of transmitted data, such as electrical pulses and frequencies, or light pulses and frequencies.

signal converter A device that changes the electrical or light characteristics of a signal.

signal processing See *digital signal processing*.

signal to noise ratio The ratio of the amplitude (power, volume) of a data signal to the amount of noise (interference) in the line. Usually measured in decibels, the signal to noise ratio measures the clarity or quality of a transmission channel or electronic device.

signaling in band In communications, to send control signals within the same frequency range as the data signal.

signaling out of band In communications, to send control signals outside of the frequency range of the data signal.

signature A unique number that is built into hardware or software for identification purposes.

significant digits The digits in a number that add value to the number. For example, in the number 00006508, 6508 are the significant digits.

silica Same as *silicon dioxide*.

silica gel A highly absorbent form of silicon dioxide that is often wrapped in small bags and packed in with equipment to absorb moisture during shipping and storage.

silicon (Si) The base material for making chips. Next to oxygen, silicon is the most abundant element in nature and is found in a natural state in the majority of rocks and sand on earth. The silicon used in chips is mined from rocks and then purified.

Its atomic structure and abundance make it an ideal semiconductor material. Pure silicon is obtained by putting it through a chemical process at high temperatures. In its molten state, the silicon is mixed (doped) with other chemicals to alter its electrical nature. See *semiconductor* and *chip*.

silicon compiler A program that translates the electronic design of a chip into the actual layout of the components.

silicon dioxide (SiO^2) A hard, glassy mineral found in such materials as rock, quartz, sand and opal. In MOS chip fabrication, silicon dioxide is used to create the insulation layer between the metal gates of the top layer and the silicon elements below it.

silicon disk A disk drive that is simulated in memory. Typically used in laptops for weight reduction, a silicon disk requires constant power from a battery or other source in order to maintain its contents.

silicon foundry A company that makes chips for other companies that have only design, but not manufacturing facilities. It is typically a large chip maker that uses its excess manufacturing capacity in this manner.

silicon nitride (Si^3N^4) A silicon compound that is capable of holding a static electric charge and is used as a gate element on some MOS transistors.

Silicon Valley An area around Palo Alto and Sunnyvale in the Santa Clara Valley of California, (south of San Francisco) that is noted for its large number of high-technology companies.

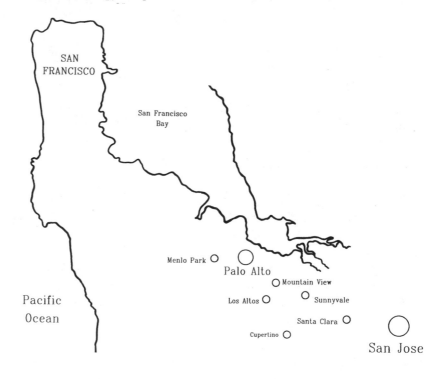

SIM (Society for Information Management) Founded originally as the Society for Management Information Systems in 1968, it is an organization of MIS professionals. SIM members can use the society as an exchange or marketplace for technical information. It offers educational and research programs, competitions and awards to its members. For more information, contact Society for Information Management, 111 East Wacker Drive, Suite 600, Chicago, IL 60601.

SIMD (Single Instruction stream Multiple Data stream)   A computer architecture that performs one operation on multiple sets of data, for example, an array processor. One computer or processor is used for the control logic and the remaining processors are used as slaves, each executing the same instruction. Contrast with *MIMD*.

SIMM (Single In-line Memory Module) A narrow printed circuit board about three inches long that holds eight or nine memory chips. SIMMs plug into special sockets.

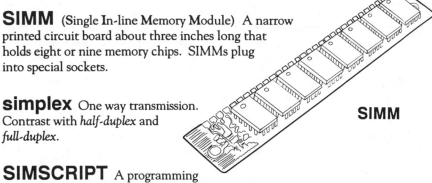

SIMM

simplex One way transmission. Contrast with *half-duplex* and *full-duplex*.

SIMSCRIPT A programming language that is used for discrete simulations.

simulation

(1) The mathematical representation of the interaction of real-world objects. See *scientific applications*.

(2) The execution of a machine language program designed to run in a foreign computer.

sine wave A uniform wave that is generated by a single frequency.

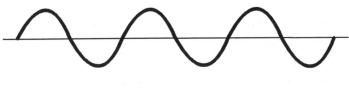

SINE WAVE

single board computer A computer that contains the processor and memory on a single printed circuit board.

single density disk A first-generation floppy disk.

single precision The use of one computer word to hold a numeric value for calculation. Contrast with *double precision*.

single sided disk A floppy disk that stores data on only one side.

single threading The processing of one transaction to completion before processing another transaction.

sink A device or place that accepts something. For example, a heat sink accepts heat in an electronic circuit in order to dissipate it. A message or data sink stores messages or data temporarily, such as in a communications system.

SIP (Single In-line Package) A type of chip module that looks like a SIMM, but uses pins rather than edge connectors.

SISD (Single Instruction stream Single Data stream) The architecture of a serial computer. Contrast with *SIMD* and *MIMD*.

site license A license to use software within a single facility. It provides authorization to make copies and distribute them freely within the jurisdiction.

SIXEL A graphics language from Digital Equipment Corporation that supersedes ReGIS. ReGIS to SIXEL conversion programs are available.

skew
(1) The misalignment of a document or punched card in the feed tray or hopper that prohibits it from being scanned or read properly.

(2) In facsimile, the difference in rectangularity between the received and transmitted page.

(3) In communications, a change of timing or phases in a transmission signal.

sky wave A radio signal that is transmitted into the sky and is reflected back down to earth from the ionosphere.

slave A computer or peripheral device that is controlled by another computer. For example, a terminal or printer in a remote location that only receives data is a slave. When two personal computers are hooked up via their serial or parallel ports for transmission, the file transfer program may make one computer the master and the other the slave.

slave tube A a display monitor connected to another monitor in order to provide an additional viewing station.

sleep
(1) In programming, an inactive state due to an endless loop or programmed delay. A sleep statement creates a delay for some specified amount of time.

(2) The inactive status of a terminal, device or program that is awakened by sending a code to it.

slot

(1) A receptacle for additional printed circuit boards.

(2) A receptacle for the insertion and removal of a disk or tape cartridge.

(3) In communications, a narrow band of frequencies.

(4) A time *slot* is a continuously repeating interval of time or a time period in which two devices are able to interconnect.

(5) May refer to any reserved space for the temporary or permanent storage of instructions, data or codes.

slow scan TV The transmission of individual video frames over ordinary telephone lines. It is not realtime transmission; it takes several seconds to transmit one frame. Also called *electronic still photography* (ESP).

SLSI (Super Large Scale Integration) Refers to ultra-high-density chips that contain 10 million or more transistors and electronic components. SLSI chips should materialize by the mid-1990s.

slug A metal bar containing the carved image of a letter or digit that is used in a printing mechanism.

Smalltalk An operating system and object-oriented programming language that was developed at Xerox Corporation's Palo Alto Research Center. As an integrated environment, it eliminates the distinction between programming language and operating system. It also allows the programmer to customize the user interface and behavior of the system.

Smalltalk was the first object-oriented programming language, and it was used on Xerox's Alto computer, which was designed for it. It was originally used to create prototypes of simpler programming languages and the graphical interfaces that are so popular today.

Smalltalk V A version of Smalltalk for PCs from Digitalk, Inc. Smalltalk V/PM provides a complete OS/2 Presentation Manager development environment.

smart cable A connecting cable between two devices that has a built-in microprocessor. It analyzes incoming signals and converts them from one protocol to another.

smart card A credit card with a built-in microprocessor and memory that can be used as an ID or financial transaction card. When inserted into a reader, it transfers data to and from a central computer. It is more secure than a magnetic stripe card and can be programmed to self-destruct if the wrong password is entered too many times. As a financial transaction card, it can store transactions and maintain a bank balance.

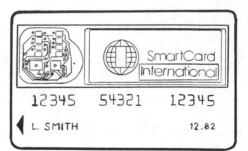

SMART CARD

smart terminal A
video terminal with various display characteristics, such as blinking characters, reverse imaging (dark on light), underlines and boldface. Smart terminals may also contain built-in communications protocols to connect to minicomputers and mainframes. Sometimes smart terminal is used to refer to intelligent terminal. See *intelligent terminal* and *dumb terminal*.

Smartcom III
A communications program for PCs from Hayes Microcomputer Products, Inc. It will work with any modem, but is naturally suited for Hayes modems and has a special protocol for error checking modems, such as the Hayes V-series. It supports a number of terminals and protocols and can run two communications sessions concurrently if two modems are attached to the computer. It has its own SCOPE script language that lets users automate communications activities and a learn mode that will automate routine log-on operations.

SmartKey
A keyboard macro processor for PCs from Software Research Technologies. SmartKey was one of the first macro processors allowing users to eliminate repetitive typing by setting up an occurrence of text or a series of commands as a macro. SmartKey can be programmed to initiate actions based on time, date and keyboard input.

SmartWare
An integrated software package for PCs and various UNIX-based systems from Informix Software, Inc. It combines database, word processing, spreadsheet, business graphics and communications with a programming language that works with all of the modules.

SMB
(Server Message Block) The message format used in the Microsoft/3Com file sharing protocol for PC Network, MS-Net and LAN Manager. It is used to transfer file requests between workstations and servers as well as within the server for internal operations. When transferred across the network, SMBs are carried within the NetBIOS network control block (NCB) packet.

SMD
(Storage Module Device) A peripheral interface that is used with large-capacity disk drives. It transfers data in the 2-4MB per second range.

smoke test A test of new or repaired equipment by turning it on. If there's smoke, it doesn't work.

smoothed data Statistical data that has been averaged or otherwise manipulated so that the curves on its graph are smooth and free of irregularities.

smoothing circuit A electronic filtering circuit in a DC power supply that removes the ripples that come from the AC power lines.

SMT
(1) (Surface Mount Technology) A board packaging technique that mounts chips directly on the board rather than into receptacles that have been previously soldered onto the board. Boards can be smaller and built faster with this technique.

(2) (Station ManagemenT) The network management protocol of the FDDI fiber optic interface. It provides direct management, requiring only one node to have the network management software.

SMTP (Simple Mail Transfer Protocol) An electronic mail protocol used in TCP/IP networks.

SNA (Systems Network Architecture) IBM's primary networking strategy, introduced in 1974. SNA is made up of a variety of hardware and software products that all interact together. Following are some of SNA's basic concepts and components.

Nodes and Data Links

In SNA, nodes are end points or junctions and data links are the pathways between them. Nodes are made up of hosts (Type 5), communications controllers (Type 4) and peripheral devices, such as terminals, PCs and minicomputers (Type 2). Type 2.0 nodes can communicate only with the host, and Type 2.1 nodes can communicate with other 2.1 nodes (peer-to-peer communications) without going to the host. Data links include high-speed local channels, the SDLC data link protocol and Token Ring.

SSCPs, PUs and LUs

The heart of an SNA network is the SSCP (System Services Control Point) software that resides in the host. It manages the entire network.

Within all nodes of an SNA network, including the host, there is PU (Physical Unit) software that manages node resources, such as data links, and controls the transmission of network management information.

In order to communicate user data, a session path is created between two end points, or LUs (Logical Units). When a session takes place, an LU-LU session is established between an LU in the host (CICS, TSO, user application...) and an LU in the terminal controller or PC.

An LU 6.2 session provides peer-to-peer communication and lets either side initiate the session.

VTAM and NCP

VTAM (Virtual Telecommunications Access Method) resides in the host and contains the SSCP, the PU for the host and establishes the LU sessions within the host.

NCP (Network Control Program) resides in the communications controller (front end processor) and manages the routing and data link protocols, such as SDLC and Token Ring.

SNA Layers

SNA is implemented in functional layers with each layer passing control to the next layer. This layering is called a *protocol stack*.

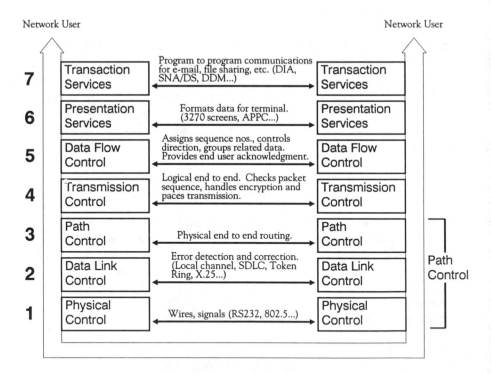

SNA LAYERS

SNADS (SNA Distribution Services) An electronic mail system for SNA networks from IBM. It also provides store and forward capabilities if a user's machine is unavailable to receive a transmission.

snapshot The storing of the entire contents of memory including all hardware registers and status indicators. It is periodically taken in order to restore the system in the event of a failure.

snapshot dump A memory dump of selection portions of memory.

snapshot program A trace program that provides selected dumps of memory when specific instructions are executed or when certain conditions are met.

sneaker net The human alternative to a local area network. It is made up of people who carry floppy disks from one machine to another.

SNMP (Simple Network Management Protocol) A protocol used to gather activity information on a TCP/IP networks for monitoring and statistical purposes. See *CMIP*.

SNOBOL (StriNg Oriented symBOlic Language) One of the first list processing languages. Developed at Bell Labs in the early 1960s, it was used for text processing and for developing compilers. SNOBOL4 was a later version used for general-purpose programming.

snow Flickering snow-like spots on a video screen caused by display electronics that are too slow to respond to changing data.

soft Flexible and changeable. Software can be reprogrammed for different results. The computer's soft nature is its greatest virtue; however, the reason it takes so long to get new systems developed has little to do with this concept. It is based on how systems are developed (file systems vs database management), the programming languages used (assembly vs high-level), combined with the skill level of the technical staff, compounded by the organization's bureaucracy.

soft copy Refers to data displayed on a video screen. Contrast with *hard copy*.

soft error A recoverable error, such as a garbled message that can be retransmitted. Contrast with *hard error*.

soft font A set of characters for a particular typeface that is stored in the computer and downloaded to the printer before printing. Contrast with *internal font* and *font cartridge*.

soft hyphen See *discretionary hyphen*.

soft key A keyboard key simulated by an icon on screen.

soft patch A quick fix to the machine language currently in memory that lasts only as long as the program is running.

soft return A control code inserted into a text document to mark the end of the line. When the document is formatted for printing, it is converted into the return code required by the printer. Soft returns are determined by the right margin and are changed when the right margin is changed.

In graphics-based environments, such as in the Macintosh, soft returns are not used as the text must be free to change within movable windows.

With PCs, soft return codes differ, for example, WordPerfect uses a return (ASCII 13), while WordStar uses a line feed (ASCII 10), and XyWrite doesn't use them at all.

Contrast with *hard return*, which is the code inserted when the user presses the return key.

soft sectored The common method of identifying sectors on a disk by initially recording sector information on every track with a format program. Contrast with *hard sectored*.

Softstrip An optical scanning system from Cauzin Systems, Inc., for PCs, Apple IIs and the Macintosh that uses a special encoded pattern that holds from 50 to 600 bytes of data per inch, depending on the printer. It is scanned into the computer by a Softstrip reader connected to the serial port.

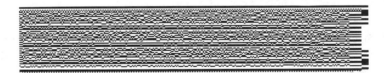

SOFTSTRIP
(Courtesy Cauzin Systems, Inc.)

SoftSwitch A family of conversion programs from SoftSwitch, Inc., that allows electronic mail to be transmitted between IBM mainframes and a variety of other vendor's electronic mail systems.

software Instructions for the computer. A series of instructions that performs a particular task is called a *program* or *software program*. The two major categories of software are *system software* and *application software*. System software is made up of control programs, including the operating system, communications software and database manager. Application software is any program that processes data for the user. For example, inventory and payroll programs as well as spreadsheets and word processors fall into the application software category.

Software Carousel A switching program for PCs from SoftLogic Solutions, Inc., that allows the user to have up to a dozen applications open at the same time and switch back and forth between them.

Software Distribution Kit An install and compression program for PCs from Clarion Software Corporation. It allows users and developers to create a customized install program for software distribution.

software engineering The design, documentation and development of software.

software failure The inability of a program to continue processing due to erroneous logic. Same as *crash, bomb* and *abend*.

software house An organization that develops customized software for a customer. Contrast with *software publisher*, which develops and markets software packages.

Software-IC An object-oriented programming class that has been packaged for sale from The Stepstone Corporation. It is based on Stepstone's Objective-C programming language.

software interface Same as *API*.

software interrupt An interrupt that is caused by an instruction in the program. See *interrupt*.

software package An application program that has been developed for sale to the general public. Although a set of programs developed and written for only one organization may be called a *package*, package usually refers to an off-the-shelf program.

software programmer Same as *systems programmer*.

software protection See *copy protection*.

software publisher An organization that develops and markets software. Software publishers do market research, development, production and distribution of software. They may develop their own software, contract for outside development or obtain software that has already been written.

TOP 50 INDEPENDENT SOFTWARE VENDORS

The fiscal 1989 figures are reprinted from the June "extra" 1990 issue of Software Magazine with permission of Sentry Publishing Co. Inc., Westborough, MA.

The figures below (in millions) are software revenues only, and total revenues may exceed these amounts. Fiscal 1989 figures show worldwide as well as U.S. only software revenues. Fiscal 1988 figure is worldwide revenues only.

Company	Date Founded	1989 World (U.S.)	1988 World	Number Employees
Computer Associates Int'l. Inc. Garden City, NY	1976	1,300 (765)	925	6,500
Microsoft Corporation Redmond, WA	1975	691 (285)	625	4,000
Lotus Development Corporation Cambridge, MA	1981	556 (355)	469	2,800
Dun & Bradstreet Corporation (Includes MSA and McCormack & Dodge) New York, NY	1841	450	200	70,000
Oracle Corporation Redwood Shores, CA	1977	418 (251)	280	4,148
Software AG of North America* Reston, VA	1969	294 (71)	221	2,800
Novell, Inc. Provo, UT	1983	282	200	--
WordPerfect Corporation* Orem, UT	1979	281 (229)	179	2,150
Ashton-Tate Corporation Torrance, CA	1980	265 (265)	307	1,430
Pansophic Systems, Inc. Lisle, IL	1969	232 (146)	182	1,900
SAS Institute Inc.* Cary, NC	1976	206 (122)	170	1,950
Ask Computer Systems Mountain View, CA	1972	190 (166)	155	920
Autodesk, Inc. Sausalito, CA	1982	179 (81)	117	--
Cincom Systems, Inc.* Cincinnati, OH	1968	171 (58)	167	1,600
Information Builders, Inc.* New York, NY	1975	143 (89)	130	1,150
Informix Software, Inc. Menlo Park, CA	1980	142 (72)	89	1,200
Legent Corporation Vienna, VA	1989	140 (95)	103	800
Ingres Corporation Alameda, CA	1980	131 (78)	91	1,200
Candle Corporation Los Angeles, CA	1977	128 (81)	100	850
Software Publishing Corporation Mountain View, CA	1980	110 (88)	82	566
McDonnell Douglas St. Louis, MO	1960	110 (98)	88	2,000
Sterling Software Inc. Dallas, TX	1983	101 (83)	99	1,800
American Management Systems Arlington, VA	1970	99 (99)	78	2,700

Company	Date Founded	1989 World (U.S.)	1988 World	Number Employees
Bolt, Baranek and Newman Inc. Cambridge, MA	1948	97 (87)	90	2,850
Borland International Inc. Scotts Valley, CA	1983	97 (82)	94	550
Aldus Corporation Seattle, WA	1984	88 (45)	79	590
Metier Management Systems Houston, TX	1977	85 (26)	90	700
The Santa Cruz Operation Santa Cruz, CA	1979	85 est.	57	1,000
Compuware Corporation* Farmington Hills, MI	1973	82 (48)	68	1,179
BMC Software Corporation Sugar Land, TX	1980	82 (51)	54	378
Cognos, Inc. Ottawa, Ontario	1969	81 (40)	70	1,038
Boole & Babbage, Inc. Sunnyvale, CA	1967	79 (49)	61	520
Comshare, Inc. Ann Arbor, MI	1966	77 (39)	58	897
System Software Associates, Inc. Chicago, IL	1981	72 (67)	53	400
Goal Systems International Inc. Columbus, OH	1975	69 (48)	52	600
On-Line Software International Fort Lee, NJ	1969	69 (51)	65	662
Systems Center, Inc. Reston, VA	1981	66 (47)	52	483
Interleaf, Inc. Cambridge, MA	1981	60 (48)	49	750
Micro Focus, Inc. Palo Alto, CA	1976	57 (31)	35	441
Software Engineering of America* Lake Success, NY	1982	51 (36)	40	200
Attachmate Corporation* Bellevue, WA	1982	50 (38)	25	230
American Software, Inc. Atlanta, GA	1971	50 (42)	46	663
CompuServe Inc. Columbus, OH	1969	47 (32)	41	1,485
Symantec Corporation Cupertino, CA	1982	47 (39)	35	309
Softlab, Inc.* San Francisco, CA	1971	42 (.8)	37	518
Knowledgeware, Inc. Atlanta, GA	1979	42 (31)	17	325
WordStar International, Inc. Novato, CA	1978	42 (22)	42	300
Cadre Technologies* Beaverton, OR	--	41 (32)	15	330
Information Resources Inc. Waltham, MA	1979	38 (23)	32	--
Digital Research, Inc.* Monterey, CA	1976	37	34	--

*Privately held.

software stack A stack that is implemented in memory. See *stack*.

software tools Programs that aid in the development of other software programs. Software tools may assist the programmer in the design, coding, compiling, link editing or debugging phases.

solder mask An insulating pattern applied to a printed circuit board that exposes only the areas to be soldered.

solenoid A magnetic switch that closes a circuit and is very often used as a relay.

solid logic Same as *solid state*.

solid modeling A mathematical technique for representing solid objects. It is the least abstract form of computer-aided design. Unlike wireframe and surface modeling, solid modeling systems ensure that all surfaces meet properly and that the object is geometrically correct. A solid model can also be sectioned (cut open) to reveal its internal features. Solids allow interference checking, which tests to see if two or more objects occupy the same space.

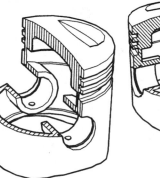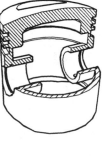

SOLID MODELING
(Courtesy Robo Systems Corporation)

solid state An electronic component or circuit that is made of solid materials, such as transistors, chips and bubble memories. There is no mechanical action in a solid state device; however, there is an unbelievable amount of electromagnetic action inside semiconductor and thin film materials.

For data storage, solid state devices are much faster and more reliable than mechanical disks and tapes, but they are more expensive. Although solid state costs continually drop, disks, tapes and optical disks also continue to improve their cost/performance ratio. It appears that there will always be a hierarchy of storage environments, ranging from slower mass storage devices to the highest speed solid state devices.

The first solid state device was the "cat's whisker" of the 1930s, in which a whisker-like wire was moved around on a solid crystal in order to detect a radio signal.

solid state memory Any transistorized, semiconductor or thin film memory that contains no mechanical parts. Disks, tapes and vacuum tube memories are not in this category.

solid state relay A relay that contains no mechanical parts, and all switching mechanisms are semiconductor or thin film components.

SONET (Synchronous Optical Network) An international standard for broadband transmission through fiber optic cables in the 50 megabit to 13 gigabit per second range. It is included in the Broadband ISDN (BISDN) specification.

sort To reorder data into a new sequence. Sorting capabilities are provided within the operating system and many application programs, such as word processing and database management programs.

In word processing programs, sorting allows for all the text in the document or a marked block of text to be resequenced into either an ascending (normal) or descending sequence.

In database programs, sorting resequences all the records in the file by one or more fields and often generates an entirely new copy of the file.

The operating system typically has a sort capability that allows file names to be put into a particular order.

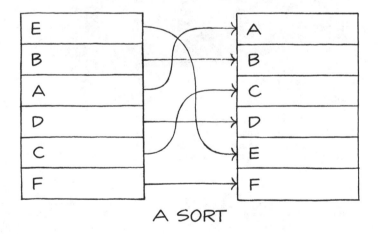

A SORT

sort algorithm The formula used to reorder data into a new sequence. Like all complicated problems, there are many solutions that can achieve the same results. One sort algorithm can resequence data faster than another. In the early 1960s, when tape was "the" storage medium, the sale of a computer system may have hinged on the sort algorithm, since without direct access capability, every transaction had to be sorted into the sequence of the master file.

sort field
Same as *sort key*.

sort key
The field or fields in a record that dictate the sequence of the file. For example, sort keys STATE and NAME arrange the file alphabetically by name within an alphabetical order of states. STATE is the major sort key and NAME is the minor sort key.

sorter
(1) A sort program.

(2) An individual who manually puts data into a specific sequence.

(3) A punched card machine that distributes punched cards into separate stackers based on the contents of a card column. The complete operation requires passing the cards through the machine once for each column being sorted.

SORTER
(Courtesy IBM)

This Model 083 Sorter could read 1,000 punched cards per minute and distribute them into their respective stackers. These kinds of machines were used extensively throughout the 1950s and 1960s.

SOS
(1) (Silicon On Sapphire) A MOS chip-fabrication method that places a thin layer of silicon over a sapphire substrate (base).

(2) (Sophisticated Operating System) The operating system that was used in the Apple III computer.

sound bandwidth The range of frequencies of sound. The human ear can perceive approximately from 20 to 20,000Hz, but human voice is confined to within 3,000Hz.

source
(1) The source of current in a MOS transistor. Same as *emitter* in a bipolar transistor.

(2) The Source was an information utility in McLean, Virginia, launched in 1979 and purchased by CompuServe in 1989.

source code A program in its original form as written by the programmer. Source code is not executable by the computer directly. It must be converted into machine language by compilers, assemblers and interpreters.

In some cases, source code may be automatically converted into another dialect or different language by a conversion program.

source computer The computer in which a program is being assembled or compiled. Contrast with *object computer*.

source data Original data that is handwritten or printed on a source document or typed into the computer system from a keyboard or terminal.

source data acquisition Same as *source data capture*.

source data capture The capturing of data electronically when a transaction occurs, for example, at the time of sale.

source disk A disk from which data is obtained. Contrast with *target disk*.

source document A paper form onto which data is written. Order forms and employment applications are examples of source documents.

source language Same as *source code*.

source program A program in its original form, as written by the programmer.

source statement An instructional phrase in a programming language (source language).

space In digital electronics, a 0 bit. Contrast with *mark*.

space/time

Kilo (K)	Thousand	1,000 or 1,024
Mega (M)	Million	1,000,000
Giga (G)	Billion	1,000,000,000
Tera (T)	Trillion	1,000,000,000,000

Millisecond (ms)	Thousandth	1/1,000
Microsecond (μs)	Millionth	1/1,000,000
Nanosecond (ns)	Billionth	1/1,000,000,000
Picosecond (ps)	Trillionth	1/1,000,000,000,000
Femtosecond (fs)	Quadrillionth	1/100,000,000,000,000

Storage capacities are measured in:

Disk, tape, memory	Bytes
CPU and memory chips	Bits

Data transmission and transfer is measured in:

Disk access time	Milliseconds
Memory access time	Nanoseconds
Machine cycle	Microseconds/Nanoseconds
Instruction execution	Microseconds/Nanoseconds
Transistor switching	Nanoseconds, Picoseconds & Femtoseconds

spaghetti code A

program that is written without a coherent structure. It often implies an excessive use of the GOTO instructions. Each decision point in a program (if this, do that) directs the computer to branch to some other part of the program. A GOTO instruction directs the computer elsewhere in the program with no assurance of returning. If, after branching to another routine, another GOTO instruction branches somewhere else, the logic in the program is hard to follow.

However, if a branch is made to a function or subroutine that, after accomplishing its task,

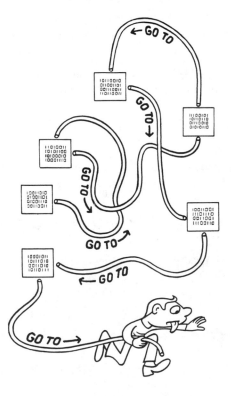

SPAGHETTI CODE

automatically returns to the place in the program that called it, the logic in the program can be followed. See *structured programming*.

SPARC (Scalable Performance ARChitecture) A 32-bit RISC computer from Sun Microsystems, Inc.

spatial data Data represented as 2-D or 3-D images.

spec See *specification*.

special character A character other than a 0 to 9 or A to Z. For example, @, #, $, %, &, * and + are special characters.

special-purpose computer A computer designed from scratch to perform a specific function. Contrast with the *general-purpose computer*.

special-purpose language A programming language that is designed to solve a specific problem or class of problems. For example, LISP and Prolog are designed to solve non-numeric problems and are used extensively in AI applications. Even more specialized are languages, such as COGO (Coordinate Geometry), for solving civil engineering problems, and APT (Automatic Programmed Tools), for directing machine tools.

specification A definition of a data structure or processing routine in a program. Functional specifications for an information system include the database structure and the detailed processing for each data entry, update, query and report function in the system.

spectral color In computer graphics, the color of a single wavelength of light, starting with violet at the low end and proceeding through indigo, blue, green, yellow and orange and ending with red.

spectral response The variable output of a light-sensitive device that is based on the color of the light it perceives.

spectrum A range of electromagnetic frequencies.

speech recognition Same as *voice recognition*.

speech synthesis The generation of machine voice by arranging phonemes (speech utterances, such as "k," "ch," and "sh") into words. It is used in text to speech applications, which turns text input into spoken words for the deaf or handicapped. Although spoken words can be digitized and stored in the computer, it would require a much larger database of words compared to speech synthesis methods.

speed buffering A technique that compensates for speed differences between input and output. Data is accepted into the buffer at high speed and transferred out at low speed, or vice versa.

speed of electricity/light Approximately 186,000 miles per second. Electricity and light travel around the equator over seven times in one second. This inherent speed of Mother Nature is why computers are so fast. Within the tiny chip, electricity has to flow only a couple of millimeters, and, within an entire computer, only a few feet.

Yet, as fast as that is, it's never fast enough. There is resistance in the lines, and it does take time to cause an electronic switch to open and close. Even though switching speeds are in the billionths and trillionths of a second, the application of computers, especially in the areas of graphics, CAD, image processing and scientific exploration, is always exhausting the fastest computers.

spelling checker A separate program or function within a word processor that tests for the correctly spelled words. It can test the spelling of an entire document, group of documents or just a marked block within a document. Advanced systems can check for spelling as the user types and correct common typos and misspellings on the fly.

Spelling checkers simply compare words to a dictionary of words and the wrong use of a correctly-spelled word cannot be detected. See *grammar checker*.

spherization In computer graphics, turning an image into a sphere.

spike Also called a *transient*. A burst of extra voltage in a power line that lasts only a fraction of a second. See *surge*.

spindle The rotating shaft in a disk drive. In a fixed disk, the platters are attached to the spindle. In a removable disk, the spindle remains in the drive.

SpinRite A special formatting program for PCs from Gibson Research Corporation that reformats the hard disk without erasing the existing data. It rewrites only the sector identification data on the disk in order to reestablish the alignment, which may have drifted over time.

SPL
(1) (Systems Programming Language) An assembly language from Hewlett-Packard that runs on the HP 3000 series of minicomputers. See *assembly language* for an SPL program example.

(2) (Structured Programming Language) See *structured programming*.

spline In computer graphics, a smooth curve that runs through a series of given points. The term is often used to refer to any curve. See *Bezier* and *B-spline*.

split screen The display of two or more sets of data on screen at the same time. It implies that one set of data can be manipulated independently of the other. Split screens, or windows, are usually created by the operating system or application software, rather than the hardware.

spooling (Simultaneous Peripheral Operations OnLine) The overlapping of low-speed operations with normal processing. It originated with mainframes in order to optimize slow operations such as reading cards and printing. Card input was read onto disk and printer output was stored on disk. In that way, the actual business data processing was done at high speed, since all I/O was on disk. Today, spooling is used to buffer data for the printer as well as remote batch terminals. See *print spooler*.

spreadsheet Software that simulates a paper spreadsheet, or worksheet, in which columns of numbers are summed for budgets and plans. It appears on screen as a matrix of rows and columns, the intersections of which are identified as cells. Spreadsheets can have thousands of cells and can be scrolled horizontally and vertically in order to view them.

The cells are filled with:
     (1) labels
     (2) numeric values
     (3) formulas.

The labels, can be any descriptive text, for example, RENT, PHONE or GROSS SALES. The values are the actual numeric data used in the budget or plan, and the formulas command the spreadsheet to do the calculations, for example, SUM CELLS A5 TO A10. Formulas are easy to create, since spreadsheets allow the user to point to each cell and type in the arithmetic operation that affects it. Roughly speaking, a formula is created by saying "this cell PLUS that cell TIMES that cell."

The formulas are the spreadsheet's magic. After numbers are added or changed, the formulas will recalculate the data either automatically or with the press of a key. Since the contents of any cell can be calculated with or copied to any other cell, a total of one column can be used as a detail item in another column. For example, the total from a column of detailed expense items can be carried over to a summary column showing all expenses. If data in the detail column changes, its column total changes, which is then copied to the summary column, and the total in the summary column changes as a result.

If this were done manually, each change of data would require

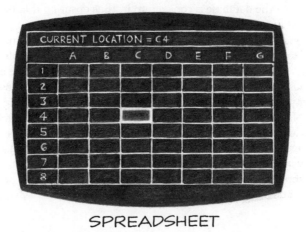

SPREADSHEET

recalculating, erasing and changing the totals of each column. This automatic ripple effect allows users to create a plan, plug in different assumptions and immediately see the impact on the bottom line. This "what if?" capability makes the spreadsheet an indispensable tool for budgets, planning, financial statements and many other equation-based tasks.

The spreadsheet originated with VisiCalc in 1978 for the Apple II, and was followed by SuperCalc, Multiplan, Lotus 1-2-3 and a host of others.

Classes of Spreadsheets

STANDARD
Every spreadsheet creates a two-dimensional matrix of rows and columns. In order to summarize data, totals from various parts of the spreadsheet can be summed to another part of the spreadsheet.

DYNAMIC LINKING
Dynamic linking allows data in one spreadsheet to automatically update another spreadsheet. Although often referred to as 3-D spreadsheets, dynamic linking creates the effect of a third dimension in a separate file. For example, several detail files can be summarized into one summary file. Excessive linking is difficult to manage, since the relationships span several physical files.

3-DIMENSIONAL
3-D spreadsheets make summarizing data easy, because each cell in the spreadsheet has an X, Y and Z reference. For example, a spreadsheet of expense items by month uses two dimensions, but expense items by month by department requires three dimensions.

While the 3-D method is superior for consolidating data, it lacks some of the flexibility inherent in the dynamic linking approach, since all pages must have essentially the same structure. In addition, all data must reside in one file as with a standard 2-D spreadsheet.

RELATIONAL
Relational spreadsheets provide an optional method for storing the data separate and apart from the formulas. The data is stored in a central database and the formulas are stored in the spreadsheet. When the spreadsheet is called up, the data from the database is copied into it, thus ensuring that everyone's spreadsheet always contains the most current data.

Relational spreadsheets reference data by name rather than by row and column number. With name references, data can be used in multiple spreadsheets with greater accuracy, and new spreadsheets can be created more easily. A spreadsheet that analyzes the budget for one department can analyze the budget for any department simply by changing the department name and recalculating.

Name references make it possible to analyze data from multiple perspectives. Since data isn't tied to cell references as with 3-D spreadsheets, more than three dimensions can be created. For example, in a corporate budget, numbers are kept for every combination of accounts, time periods and departments in both forecast and actual versions. A view of accounts by department by period can be automatically switched to a view of accounts by period by version. Instead of requiring inordinately complicated spreadsheet programming by the user, the relational spreadsheet prepares the views and consolidations automatically.

spreadsheet compiler A program that translates spreadsheets into stand-alone programs that run without the spreadsheet package that created them.

sprocket feed Same as *pin feed*.

SPS (Standby Power System) A UPS system that switches to battery backup upon detection of power failure.

SPS Association A nonprofit organization dedicated to an open PostScript standard. For more information, contact SPS Association, 7 Stuart Road, Chelmsford, MA 01824.

SPSS A statistical package from SPSS, Inc., that runs on over 40 mainframes and minicomputers, as well as PCs. It provides over 50 statistical processes, including regression analysis, correlation and analysis of variance, and is used extensively in the marketing research field. SPSS, originally named Statistical Package for the Social Sciences, was written in 1968 by Norman Nie, a professor at Stanford University. In 1976, Nie formed SPSS, Inc.

SPX (Sequenced Packet EXchange) A Novell NetWare communications protocol that is used for interprocess communications (IPC). It guarantees that an entire message arrives intact and uses the NetWare IPX protocol as its delivery mechanism.

SQL (Structured Query Language) Pronounced "SQL" or "see qwill." A language used to interrogate and process data in a relational database. Originally developed by IBM for its mainframes, there have been many implementations created for mini and micro database applications. SQL commands can be used to interactively work with a database or can be embedded within a programming language to interface to a database.

SQL engine A program that accepts SQL commands and accesses the database to obtain the requested data. Users' requests in a query language or database language must be translated into an SQL request before the SQL engine can process it.

SQL Server A relational database management system from Sybase, Inc., that runs on OS/2-based PCs, VAXs and a variety of UNIX workstations. It is designed for network use and can be accessed by applications using the SQL interface, or via Sybase's own query by example and decision support utilities. For OS/2 systems, the product is available from Microsoft under the name Microsoft SQL Server.

square wave A graphic image of a digital pulse as visualized on an oscilloscope. It appears square because it rises quickly to a particular amplitude, stays constant for the duration of the pulse and drops fast at the end of it.

SQUARE WAVE

SQUID (Superconducting Quantum Interference Device) An electronic detection system that uses Josephson junctions circuits. A SQUID is an extremely sensitive device that is capable of detecting the most minute signals.

SRAM See *static RAM*.

SRPI (Server Requester Programming Interface) The programming interface from IBM that allows a personal computer to interact with a mainframe. See ECF.

SS/DD (Single Sided/Double Density) Refers to earlier floppy disk formats that store data on only one side of the disk.

SSCP (System Services Control Point) The controlling program in an SNA network. It resides in the host and is a component within the VTAM software. See *SNA*.

SSD (Solid State Disk) An auxiliary memory bank that is used as interim storage between disk and high-speed memory. It is usually constructed of slow-speed memory chips, which are still considerably faster than disk accesses.

SSE A protected mode, full-screen editor in Microsoft's OS/2 operating system.

SSI (Small Scale Integration) Refers to a very small number of electronic components that are built onto a single chip. SSI ranges from two to approx. 100 components (transistors, etc.).

SSP (System Support Program) A multiuser, multitasking operating system from IBM that is the primary control program for System/34 and System/36.

ST A personal computer series from Atari Corporation that is used in homes and small businesses. It uses a Motorola 68000 CPU and comes with its TOS operating system built into ROM. The GEM operating environment is also included which provides a Mac-like interface for applications.

The 520ST comes with 512K of RAM, and the 1040ST comes with 1MB. Display resolution is 640x200 with 16 colors on a 12" screen. A built-in 720K microfloppy disk is standard, and a 20MB hard drive is optional for the 1040ST. Also included is a MIDI interface and a three-voice sound chip with a range from 30 to 20,000Hz.

ATARI ST

ST506 A hard disk controller for PCs that uses MFM encoding and transfers data at 500Kbps. Almost all drives 40MB and under use this controller.

ST506 RLL (ST506 Run-Length Limited) A hard disk controller for PCs. It handles higher capacity disks than the ST506 and transfers data at 750Kbps.

stack

(1) A set of hardware registers or a reserved amount of main memory that is used for arithmetic calculations or for keeping track of internal operations. Stacks are used to keep track of the sequence of routines that are called in a program. For example, one routine calls another, which calls another and so on. As each routine is completed, the computer must return control to the calling routine all the way back to the first routine that started the sequence. Stacks usually work on a last-in-first-out basis; the last item, or address, placed (pushed) onto the stack is the first item removed (popped) from the stack.

(2) A file in HyperCard.

stack pointer The address that identifies the location of the most recent item placed on the stack.

stacker An output bin in a document feeding or punched card machine. Contrast with *hopper*.

stackware A HyperCard application that is made up of a HyperCard stack (data) and HyperTalk programming.

STAIRS (STorage And Information Retrieval System) A text document management system from IBM that runs on IBM mainframes. It allows users to search for documents based on key words or word combinations.

standard cell The finished design of an electronic function ready for chip fabrication. It can be as small as a clock circuit or as large as a microprocessor. Standard cells are used to make custom-designed chips.

standard deviation In statistics, the average amount a number varies from the average number in a series of numbers.

standards & compatibilty The most important issue in the computer field. As an unregulated industry, we have wound up with thousands of data formats and languages, but very few standards that are universally used. This subject is as heated as politics and religion to hardware and software vendors and industry planners.

No matter how much the industry talks about compatibility, new formats and languages appear routinely. The standards makers are always trying to cast a standard in concrete, while the innovators are trying to create a new one. Even when standards are created, they are violated as soon as a new feature is added by the vendor.

If a format or language is used extensively and others copy it, it becomes a de facto standard and may become as widely used as official standards from such organizations as the American National Standards Institute (ANSI) or the Institute of Electrical and Electronic Engineers (IEEE). When de facto standards are sanctioned by these organizations, they become stable, at least, for a while.

In order to truly understand this industry, it is essential to understand the categories for which standards are created.

Machine Languages

Machine language is the fundamental standard for hardware compatibility. Vendors often have several families of computers, each with different machine languages. For example, although all IBM mainframes use the same machine language, IBM's AS/400, Series/1, RT and PC series are each different.

After a program is written, it must be translated (assembled, compiled or interpreted) into the machine language that the computer understands. In order to run in a different machine, the program must be reassembled or recompiled into a different machine language, providing there are appropriate translators.

Since the late 1960s, companies seeking a chunk of the IBM market have designed computers that run the same machine language as the IBM computers. RCA's Spectra 70 was the first IBM-compatible mainframe, and companies, such as Amdahl, Itel, National Advanced Systems, Hitachi and Fujitsu have introduced IBM-compatible mainframes at one time or another.

IBM PC machine language compatibility is achieved by using a processor from Intel's 8086 family of microprocessors.

Machine language compatibility can also be achieved by simulation or emulation. A simulator is a software program that translates and executes a program in a foreign machine language. An emulator is hardware that executes the machine language of another computer and is used to encourage customers to buy a new series of computers. For example, in the 1960s, IBM provided an optional emulator in its System/360 series that executed most of the customer's existing 1401 programs.

Data Codes

The data code is built into the computer and determines how each character (letter, digit or special character) is represented in binary code. Fortunately, there are only two major data codes in wide use today, EBCDIC and ASCII. That means data stored in one code can easily be converted to the other. IBM mainframes and minicomputers use EBCDIC, and so do other mainframes. ASCII is used by all personal computers, most minicomputers and some mainframes.

Other codes are used in various different machines, but all data codes can be converted from one to another with one possible exception. If numbers are stored in floating point and the new machine can't handle as many digits as the old machine, a loss of precision may occur.

When data is moved to a different computer, data code conversion is often only one small part of the conversion process. Data, text and graphics file formats must also be converted if different programs are going to process them.

The following is a small sample of the ASCII and EBCDIC data codes:

Character	ASCII	EBCDIC
space	01000000	00100000
period	01001011	00101110
< sign	01001100	00111100
+ sign	01001110	00101011
$ sign	01011011	00100100
A	11000001	01000001
B	11000010	01000010
C	11000011	01000011

Hardware Interfaces

The hardware interface specifies the plugs, sockets, cables and electrical signals that pass through each line between the CPU and a peripheral device or communications network.

Common hardware interfaces for personal computers are the Centronics parallel interface, typically used for printers, and the RS-232-C interface, typically used for modems, graphics tablets, mice and printers. In addition, the SCSI (Small Computer System Interface) is used for high-speed peripherals, such as disks and tapes, and the GPIB (General Purpose Interface Bus)

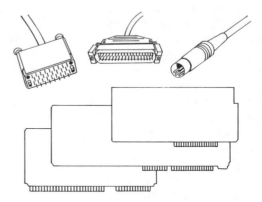

IEEE 488 standard is used to connect instruments in process control applications.

The bus in a computer's motherboard, into which additional printed circuit boards are inserted, is a hardware interface. For example, the Micro Channel in IBM's PS/2 series accepts a physically different board than the original PC bus.

Local area networks (LANs), such as ARCNET and Ethernet, also dictate the hardware interface as part of their specifications.

Storage Media

There are many varieties of disk packs, disk cartridges, floppy disks, reel-to-reel tapes, tape cartridges and tape cassettes. Each one has its own unique shape and size and can be used only in drives designed to accommodate them.

With removable media, the physical standard is half the compatibility issue. The other half is the recording patterns, which are invisible to the human eye.

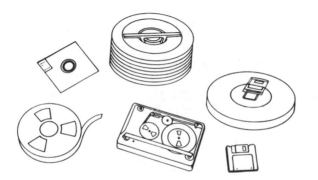

Magnetic tapes and disks fresh out of the box are blank recording surfaces. The actual recording tracks are placed onto the surface by the read/write head of the storage drive. Thus, the same floppy disk that stores 720,000 bytes in one disk drive, can hold 800,000 bytes if formatted for another. If the computer reads an incompatible tape or reads and writes and incompatible disk, it will signal a read/write error.

For minicomputers and mainframes, the half-inch magnetic tape reel is a common interchangeable storage medium. For personal computers, the 5.25" minifloppy and the 3.5" microfloppy disks are commonly used.

Operating Systems

An operating system is a master control program that manages the running of the computer system. In all environments, except for specialized scientific and process control applications, the operating system interacts with the application programs. The application programs must "talk" to the operating system.

If application programs are moved to a different computing environment, they have to be converted to interface with a different operating system. If a new operating system is installed that is not compatible with the old one, the application programs have to be converted to the new operating system.

Communications

Transmitting between two personal computers or between a personal computer and a timesharing or information service is relatively simple. All that's required

is a modem for each computer, a telephone line and a communications program in each computer that uses the same error checking protocol to ensure that data has not been lost. Most communications programs support several protocols. If data is not critical, an ASCII protocol without error checking can be used, which is found in every communications program.

Transmitting in a network is another story. Traditional minicomputer and mainframe networks allow multiple users to have access to central databases via terminals. The control is typically in the main, or host, computer. Personal computer local area networks have evolved to share information within a small work group. The major problem most large organizations have is to tie independent networks together so that each user's workstation can communicate with any other user's workstation within the company.

Since each type of network uses different protocols, conversion from one protocol to another is required. In today's multivendor environment, protocol conversion can be performed by black boxes, gateways, digital PABXs or via interconnection to value added communication services.

The OSI (Open Systems Interconnection) is a seven-layer reference model for worldwide communications that has been defined by ISO (International Standards Organization). Although most vendors have committed to support OSI in one form or another, it will take a long time before universal communications is achieved.

Computers were originally developed for computations, not communications. In the early days, nobody realized the implications or computer communications might have been standardized as was the telephone industry.

Programming Languages

Every software program is written in a programming language, and there is at least one programming language for every major CPU series. There is typically an assembly language and a number of high-level languages for each series or family. Assembly languages are machine specific, and the machine language they generate runs on only one CPU family. Unless the machine languages are very similar, it is very difficult to translate an assembly language program from one CPU series into another.

The high-level programming language was created to eliminate this machine dependency. Programming languages, such as COBOL, FORTRAN and BASIC are supposed to be able to run on many different computers. However, due to many dialects of each language, compatibility is still an issue. Each compiler vendor keeps adding new features to its language thereby making it incompatible with previous or other versions. By the time a new feature becomes a standard, a dozen new features have been already implemented. For example, dBASE has

become a de facto standard business programming language. Since 1981, dBASE has spawned competitive products, such as Clipper, QuickSilver, Force III, dbXL and Foxbase, all of which are incomplete versions of dBASE. None of them provides every command in dBASE, and many of them provide features not found in dBASE.

There's no rule of thumb for translating one dialect of a programming language into another. The job may be very difficult or very easy. At times, software is written to translate one dialect into another, as well as one programming language into another. If the translation program cannot translate the program entirely, then manual tailoring is necessary. In these cases, it is often easier to rewrite the program from scratch.

Compatibility can be achieved when a programming language conforms to the ANSI (American National Standards Institute) standard for that language. If the same version of an ANSI COBOL compiler is available for two different CPUs, a program written in ANSI COBOL will run on both machines.

File Management Systems

In its simplest form, a data file uses fields of the same length for each item of data, for example, a plain EBCDIC or ASCII file would look like:

Chris Smith	34 Main St.	Bangor	ME 18567
Pat Jones	10 W. 45 St.	New York	NY 10002

A common format created by BASIC programming languages is an ASCII comma delimited file; for example, the data above would look as follows:

"Chris Smith","34 Main St.","Bangor","ME","18567"
"Pat Jones","10 W. 45 St.","New York","NY","10002"

Both file formats above are simple, contain only data (except for quotes and commas) and can be easily manipulated by a word processor. However, data files may also contain special codes that identify the way the data is structured within the file. For example, variable length records require a code in each field that indicates the size of the field.

Whether fixed length or variable length fields, the data in non-DBMS systems is linked directly to the processing. The program must know the sequential order of fields in each record that it processes, and it cannot accept records in a different format. If a program is to process a different file format, either it must be changed or the file format must be changed. Incompatible file formats can exist within the same organization as a result of systems being developed for different purposes at different times.

NAME	ADDRESS	CITY	ST	ZIP

NAME	ADDRESS	CITY	ST	ZIP

RECORD FORMATS

These two fixed length record layouts are incompatible even though they contain the same kinds of data. The same program can't process them unless it's designed to input both record formats. In order to process a different file, the program has to be changed or the file structure (record layout) has to be changed.

Database Management Systems

Database management systems typically have their own proprietary formats for storing data. For example, a header record with a unique format that contains identification data is typically placed at the beginning of each file. Codes may also be embedded in each record. Many database programs have an importing and exporting capability that automatically converts common database formats into their proprietary format. If not, the program usually can import and export a plain EBCDIC or ASCII file, which is stripped of all proprietary codes and can be used as a common denominator between both systems. If conversion facilities cannot be found, a custom program can be written to convert one database format into another providing documentation describing the old format is available.

The application program interface (API), or language used by the application program to "talk" to the database, is typically a proprietary language in every DBMS. SQL (Structured Query Language) has recently become popular as a standard language and has been implemented in many DBMSs. That means any application program requesting data in the SQL language would work with any database management system that supports SQL.

Text Systems

Although the basic structure of an English-language text file is standard throughout the world: word, sentence, paragraph, page; every word processing, desktop publishing and typesetting program uses its own codes to set up the layout within a document. For example, the code that turns on boldface in WordPerfect Version 5.0 is **[BOLD]**; in WordStar, it's ^**PB**.

The codes that define a header, footer, footnote, page number, margin, tab setting, indent and font change are unique to the word processing program in which the document was created or the desktop publishing program into which the text file is converted. Even the codes to end a line or paragraph are not the same.

Document conversion is accomplished with special conversion programs or black boxes. Although every word processing program has a search and replace capability, it may not be effective for converting embedded layout codes from one format to another. In some programs, the search & replace simply does not handle layout codes. In addition, while some systems use one code to turn a function on and another code to turn it off, other systems use the same code for on and off, requiring manual verification and tailoring when using the search & replace function.

Graphics Systems

There are many formats for storing a picture in a computer; but, unlike text and data files, which are primarily made up of alphanumeric characters, graphics formats are much more complex.

To begin with, there are the two major categories of graphics: vector graphics (objects made up of lines) and raster graphics (television-like dots). Images stored in vector format can be moved to another vector system typically without loss of resolution. There are 2-D vector formats as well as 3-D vector formats.

In transferring raster images among different devices, resolution is a major concern. Such transfers can occur without loss of resolution as long as the new format has the same or higher resolution as the older one.

Standard graphics formats allow graphics data to be moved from machine to machine, while standard graphics languages let graphics programs be moved from machine to machine. For example, GKS and PHIGS are major graphics languages that have been adopted by many high-performance workstation and CAD vendors. Apple's consistent use of its QuickDraw language has helped the Macintosh become very popular in graphics-oriented applications.

High-resolution graphics has typically been expensive to implement due to its large storage and fast processing requirements. However, as personal computers become more powerful, graphics will become more widely used in business applications. The ability to see a person's face or a product's appearance on screen will eventually become as commonplace as text and data. In the meantime, it will be important for business consultants and database designers to begin to familiarize themselves with graphics standards.

Standards Organizations

The following organizations set standards for computers, communications and related products throughout the world.

UNITED STATES
ANSI   American National Standards Institute
EIA   Electronic Industries Association
IEEE   Institute of Electrical and Electronics Engineers
NIST   National Institute of Standards & Technology
          (formerly National Bureau of Standards)

INTERNATIONAL
CCITT Consultative Committee for International Telephony & Telegraphy
ISO   International Standards Organization
IEC   International Electrotechnial Commission

DE FACTO STANDARDS
When a vendor's product is widely used, it becomes a de facto standard. Apple, Ashton-Tate, Digital, HP, IBM, Intel, Lotus, Microsoft, Motorola and many other hardware and software vendors have set de facto standards.

The Future

The problem of standards and compatibility is a never ending dilemma. However, the fact is that standards could be created that would embrace the future and allow for expandability far more than they currently do. Ironically, in a field that is on the very forefront of the future, this industry has a very myopic view of it.

Some day, a standard for defining the standard will have to be implemented in order that one program can ask another what language it speaks. A program could also interrogate a data file and determine its format as well. If the program can't understand the other program's language or the file's format, the interfacing problem would still exist as it does today. However, as programs become more multi-lingual, a standard identification protocol would go a long way to establishing an artificial intelligence link between all computers in the future.

Star A workstation from Xerox Corporation that formally introduced the desktop user interface in 1981. Although the Star was not successful, it was the inspiration for Xerox's subsequent computer systems and for Apple's Lisa and Macintosh. See *Alto*.

star network

A communications network in which all terminals are connected to a central computer or central hub. PBXs are prime examples as well as IBM's Token Ring and AT&T's Starlan local area networks.

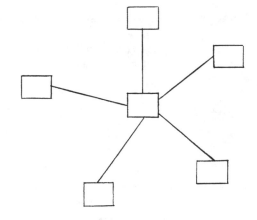

Starlan
A local area network from AT&T that uses twisted wire and the CSMA/CD access method transmitting at 1Mbit per second. It uses both a star topology in which all computers connect to a central hub, as well as a bus topology in which up to 10 computers can be daisy chained.

In 1988, Starlan was renamed Starlan 1, and Starlan 10 was introduced, a 10Mbit Ethernet version that uses twisted wire or optical fibers.

start bit
In asynchronous communications, the bit transmitted before each character.

start/stop transmission
Same as *asynchronous transmission*.

startup routine
A routine that is executed when the computer is booted or when an application is loaded. It is used to customize the environment for its associated software.

STARTUP.CMD
(startup CoMmanD) An OS/2 file that is executed immediately when the computer is started (booted). It contains instructions that can initialize operating system settings and/or automatically call in a specific application program.

The equivalent file in DOS is the *AUTOEXEC.BAT* file; however, in OS/2, the AUTOEXEC.BAT file is also executed when the computer is switched to DOS mode (real mode).

stat mux
(STATistical MUltipleXor) See *statistical multiplexor*.

state-of-the-art
The most current technique or method applied to designing and developing hardware and software.

statement In a high-level programming language, a descriptive phrase that generates one or more machine language instructions in the computer. In a low-level assembly language, programmers write instructions rather than statements, since each source language instruction is translated into one machine language instruction.

static electricity A stationary electrical charge that is the result of intentional charging or of friction in low-humidity environments.

static RAM (static Random Access Memory) Memory chips that require power to hold their content. A static RAM bit is made up of a pretzel-like flip-flop circuit that lets current flow through one side or the other based on which one of two transistors is activated. Static RAM chips have access times in the 10 to 30-nanosecond range, whereas dynamic RAMs are usually above 30, and Bipolar and ECL memories are under 10.

statistical multiplexor In communications, a device that combines several low-speed channels into a single high-speed channel and vice versa. A standard multiplexor is set to a fixed interleaving pattern, but the statistical multiplexor can analyze the traffic load and dynamically switch to different channel patterns to speed up transmission.

status line An information line displayed on screen that shows current activity.

STD bus An 8-bit bus architecture used extensively in medical and industrial equipment due to its small size and rugged design. Recent extensions to the STD bus allow it to be used with MS-DOS and have increased the data path to 16 and 32 bits.

stepper motor A motor that rotates in small, fixed increments and is used to control the movement of the access arm on a disk drive. Contrast with *voice coil*.

stick model A model made of lines, or vectors. For example, in biomedical applications, the limbs of a person or animal are converted into lines so that the motion can be visually observed and graphically plotted and analyzed.

STN (SuperTwist Nematic) See *supertwist*.

stop bit In asynchronous communications, a bit transmitted after each character.

storage device A hardware unit that holds data. In this Glossary, it refers only to external peripheral equipment, such as disk and tape, in contrast with memory (RAM).

storage hierarchy The range of memory and storage devices within the computer system. The following list runs from lowest to highest speed.

Low	Punched cards
Speed	Punched paper tape
	Removable cartridge mass storage devices (non-disk)
	Magnetic tape
	Floppy disks
	CD ROM and optical disks
	Magnetic disks (movable heads)
	Magnetic disks (fixed heads)
	Bubble memory
	Low-speed bulk memory
	Main memory
	Cache memory
High	Microcode
Speed	Registers

storage media Refers to disks, tapes and bubble memory cartridges.

store and forward In communications, the temporary storage of a message for transmission to its destination at a later time. Store and forward techniques allow for routing over networks that are not accessible at all times; for example, messages headed for different time zones can be stored and forwarded when daytime arrives at the destination location. Messages can be stored and forwarded at night in order to obtain off-peak rates.

stored program concept The basic architecture of a computer in which it acts upon internally-stored instructions. See *von Neumann architecture*.

Strand88 A programming langauge for parallel processing developed by AI Ltd., England.

stream-oriented file A file, such as a text document or digital voice file, that is more openly structured than a data file. Text and voice are continuous streams of characters, whereas database records are repeating structures with a fixed or reasonably uniform format.

streaming tape A high-speed magnetic tape drive that is frequently used to make a backup copy of an entire hard disk.

Streamline A tracing program for the Macintosh from Adobe Systems Inc., that automatically converts scanned or MacPaint images into PostScript files, which can be modified in Illustrator 88.

STREAMS An architecture in the UNIX System V operating system used for creating layered communications protocols. Each layer is comprised of a STREAMS module, which passes messages to other modules. AT&T's TLI transport protocol, for example, is a STREAMS module. See *OSI*.

STRETCH The code name for IBM's first "supercomputer," the 7030, which was started in 1955 and completed in 1961. The first of eight units was delivered to Los Alamos Scientific Lab and used for 10 years. It was IBM's first transistorized computer that would "stretch" performance.

STRETCH was very sophisticated, but IBM lost an estimated $40 million in developing it. That experience was applied to subsequent and very profitable computers.

STRETCH

(Courtesy Charles Babbage Institute, University of Minnesota)

string

(1) In programming, a contiguous set of alphanumeric characters that does not contain numbers used for calculations, for example, names, addresses, words and sentences. Contrast with *numeric* data.

(2) Any connected set of structures, such as a string of bits, fields or records.

Stringy Floppy A continuous loop cartridge of 1/16" wide magnetic tape from Exatron, Inc., that was offered in the early days of personal computers.

stroke

(1) In printing, the weight, or thickness, of a character. For example, in the HP LaserJet, one of the specifications of the font description is the stroke weight from -3 to +3.

(2) In computer graphics, a pen or brush stroke or to a vector in a vector graphics image.

stroke writer Same as *vector display*.

structured programming A variety of techniques that impose a logical structure on the writing of a program. Large routines are broken down into smaller, modular routines. The use of the GOTO statement is discouraged, which prevents the programmer from branching to a routine that does not guarantee a return to the place in the program that called it.

For documentation, certain programming statements are indented, so that beginnings and endings of loops are easily identified. In addition, structured walkthroughs, which invite criticism from peer programmers, are part of structured programming.

Structured languages, such as Pascal, Ada and dBASE, force the programmer to write a structured program. However, unstructured languages such as FORTRAN, COBOL and BASIC require discipline on the part of the programmer. See *spaghetti code* and CASE.

Stuffit A shareware program for the Macintosh from Aladdin Systems that compresses files and allows them to be split onto multiple floppies. A commerical verison is also available that adds a scripting language, provides file viewing and supports multiple compression techniques. Stuffit was developed by Raymound Lau at age 16.

style sheet In word processing and desktop publishing, a file that contains layout settings for a particular category of document. Style sheets include such settings as margins, tabs, headers and footers, columns and fonts.

stylus A pen-shaped instrument that is used to "draw" images or point to menus. See *light pen* and *digitzer tablet*.

subarea node In an SNA network, a system that contains network controlling functions. It refers to a host computer or a communications controller and its associated terminals.

submarining The temporary visual loss of the moving cursor on a slow display screen such as found on a laptop computer. See *active matrix LCD*.

subroutine A group of instructions that perform a specific function, such as a function or macro. A large subroutine is usually called a *module* or *procedure*, but all terms are used interchangeably.

subschema In database management, a individual user's partial view of the database. The schema is the entire database.

subscript

(1) In word processing and mathematical notation, a digit or symbol that appears below the line. Contrast with *superscript*.

(2) In programming, a method for referencing data in a table. For example, in the table PRICETABLE, the statement to reference a specific price in the table might be `pricetable (item)`, ITEM being the subscript variable. In a two-dimensional table that includes price and discount, the statement `pricetable (item, discount)` could reference a discounted price. The relative locations of the current ITEM and DISCOUNT are kept in two index registers.

substrate A base supporting material upon which integrated circuits are built. Silicon is the most widely used substrate for the manufacturing of chips.

substring A specific subset of an alphanumeric field or variable. A substring function in a programming language or application program, such as a spreadsheet or database management system, extracts the subset out of an alphanumeric field or variable. For example, `substr(prodcode,4,3)` extracts characters 4, 5 and 6 out of a product code field.

subtract In relational database, an operation that generates a third file from all the records in one file that are not in a second file.

SUM II (Symantec Utilities for Macintosh) A set of utilities for the Macintosh from Symantec Corporation that provides hard disk optimization, disk analysis and repair, as well as a disk security system that splits the hard disk into password-protected partitions.

Sun Microsystems (Sun Microsystems, Inc.) A manufacturer of network-based, high-performance workstations founded in 1982. The Sun-3, Sun-4 and Sun386i product lines include stand-alone and networked systems, diskless workstations and file servers. The Sun-4 family is based on the SPARC microprocessor, and the Sun 386i is based on the Intel 386 CPU.

Sun supports an open systems model of computing throughout its product line which allows it to interact in networks of computer systems from other vendors. Its Open Network Computing software is supported by over 100 vendors, including Apple, Digital and HP. Sun's Network File System (NFS) software, which allows data sharing across the network, has become an industry standard.

Super VGA See VGA.

SuperCalc A spreadsheet for PCs from Computer Associates. It was one of the first spreadsheets following in VisiCalc's footsteps in the early 1980s. SuperCalc5, introduced in 1988, provides 3-D capability, enhanced graphics and the ability to link up to 256 spreadsheets. It can display three spreadsheets on screen at one time.

supercomputer The fastest computer available. It is typically used for simulations in petroleum exploration and production, structural analysis, computational fluid dynamics, physics and chemistry, electronic design, nuclear energy research and meteorology. It is also used for realtime animated graphics.

superconductor A material that has little resistance to the flow of electricity. Traditional superconductors operate at -459 Fahrenheit (absolute zero).

Thus far, the major use for superconductors, made of alloys of niobium, is for high-powered magnets in medical imaging machines that use magnetic fields instead of x-rays.

Using experimental materials, such as copper oxides, barium, lanthanum and yttrium, IBM's Zurich research lab in 1986 and the University of Houston in 1987 raised the temperature of superconductivity to -59 degrees Fahrenheit. If superconductors can work at reasonable temperatures, they will have a dramatic impact on the future. See *Josephson junction*.

Superdrive A Macintosh floppy disk drive that is compatible with a variety of disk formats. It stores 1.4MB of data in its highest density format; however, it also reads and writes earlier Mac 400 and 800K disks, as well as Apple II, DOS and OS/2 formats.

superframe T1 transmission formats made up of 12 T1 frames (superframe) and 24 frames (extended superframe). See *D4* and *D12*.

SuperKey A keyboard macro processor for PCs from Borland International that lets users create keyboard macros, partially or completely rearrange the keyboard and also encrypt data and programs.

supermini A large-scale minicomputer that overlaps in processing capability with a small-scale mainframe. The difference in terminology is point of view. If you're a mini maker, your largest machine is "super." If you're a mainframe maker, your smallest machine isn't worth talking about.

Note: Supermini is not the same as mini-supercomputer.

superscript Any letter, digit or symbol that appears above the line. Contrast with *subscript*.

supertwist A technology that provides larger size, wider viewing angle and improved contrast on LCD screens. By twisting the liquid crystals beyond the standard 90 degrees to 180 degrees and more, the light is better controlled.

supervisor Same as *operating system*.

supervisor call The instruction in an application program that interrupts the computer and changes it to the supervisory state. The operating system then analyzes the call and directs the appropriate routine to handle it.

supervisor control program The part of the operation system that always resides in memory. Same as *kernel*.

supervisor state An operating mode of the computer that executes instructions in the operating system. In this mode, the computer can execute privileged instructions that are not available to the application program, such as input/output instructions. Contrast with *program state*, which is the operating mode for executing the application program. These terms are normally associated with large computers; however, all computers differentiate between these two states.

support
(1) The assistance provided by a hardware or software vendor in installing and maintaining its product in the customer's environment.

(2) Software or hardware that is designed to work with some other software or hardware product. For example, if a word processor supports a particular printer, it is written to utilize the special features of that printer.

SUPRA A relational database management system from Cincom Systems, Inc., that runs on IBM mainframes and VAXs. It includes a query language and a program that automates the database design process.

surface
(1) In CAD, the external geometry of an object. Surfaces are generally required for NC (numerical control) modeling rather than wireframe or solids.

(2) A language that interfaces to a database engine, coined by Wayne Ratliff.

surface modeling In CAD, a mathematical technique for representing solid-appearing objects. Surface modeling is a more complex method for representing objects than wireframe modeling, but not as sophisticated as solid modeling.
    Although surface and solid models can appear the same on screen, they are quite different. Surface models cannot be sliced open as can solid models. In addition, in surface modeling, the object can be geometrically incorrect; whereas, in solid modeling, it must be correct.

surge An oversupply of voltage from the power company that can last up to several seconds. See *spike*.

surge protector A device that protects a computer from excessive voltage (spikes and surges) in the power line. See *voltage regulator* and *UPS*.

surge suppressor Same as *surge protector*.

SV (Scientific Visualization) See *visualization*.

SVID (System V Interface Definition) The specification from AT&T for the UNIX System V operating system. SVID Release 3 specifies the interface for UNIX System V Release 4.

swapping The replacing of one segment of a program in memory with another and restoring it back to the original when required. In virtual memory systems, swapping is called *paging*.

switch

(1) A mechanical or electronic device that directs the flow of electrical or optical signals. See *data switch* and *transistor*.

(2) In programming, any bit or byte used to keep track of some function. Switch sometimes refers to a branch in a program.

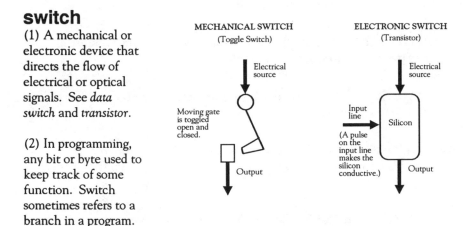

MECHANICAL SWITCH
(Toggle Switch)

ELECTRONIC SWITCH
(Transistor)

(3) A parameter that modifies a command. In the following DOS example, the /S switch is used with the format command to copy the operating system to the newly formatted disk: **format a: /s**

switched line In communications, a link that was established in a switched network.

switched network

(1) The international dial-up telephone system.

(2) A network in which a temporary connection is established from one point to another for each transmission session.

SX (386SX) See *80386SX*.

SYLK file (SYmbolic LinK file) A spreadsheet file format originating with Multiplan that is used by a number of spreadsheet programs.

symbol set In printing, a group of symbols that are extensions to standard characters for use in a particular country or specific application. Symbol sets provide codes for the non-standard upper half of the ASCII character set.

symbolic language

(1) A programming language that uses symbols, or mnemonics, for expressing operations and operands. All modern programming languages are symbolic languages.

(2) A language that manipulates symbols rather than numbers. See *list processing*.

Symphony
An integrated software package for PCs from Lotus Development Corporation. It combines word processing, database management, speadsheet, business graphics and communications into one software package and contains its own macro language.

sync character
In synchronous communications systems, a special character transmitted to synchronize timing.

sync generator
A device that supplies synchronization signals to a series of cameras to keep them all in phase.

synchronous protocol
A communications protocol that controls a synchronous transmission, such as bisync, SDLC and HDLC. Contrast with *asynchronous protocol*.

synchronous transmission
The transmission of data in which both stations are synchronized. Codes are sent from the transmitting station to the receiving station to establish the synchronization, and data is then transmitted in continuous streams. Modems that transmit at 1200bps and higher often convert the asynchronous signals from a computer's serial port into synchronous transmission between the other modem. Contrast with *asynchronous transmission*.

syntax
The rules governing the structure of a language statement. It specifies how words and symbols are put together to form a phrase.

syntax error
An error that occurs when a program cannot understand the command that has been entered. See *parse*.

sysgen
(SYStem GENeration) The installation of a new or revised operating system. It includes selecting the appropriate utility programs and identifying the peripheral devices and storage capacities of the system the operating system will be controlling.

sysop
(SYStem OPerator) Pronounced "siss-op." An individual who runs an online communications system or bulletin board. The sysop may also act as mediator for system conferences.

SysReq key (SYStem REQuest key) A key on a terminal keyboard that is pressed to get the attention of the central computer. The key exists on PC keyboards, but is rarely used by applications.

system

(1) A group of related components that interact to perform a task.

(2) A *computer system* is made up of the CPU, operating system and peripheral devices.

(3) An *information system* is made up of the database, all the data entry, update, query and report programs and manual and machine procedures.

(4) "The system" often refers to the operating system.

system development cycle The sequence of events in the

development of an information system (application), which requires mutual effort on the part of user and technical staff. See illustration on the following page.

I. SYSTEMS ANALYSIS & DESIGN
feasibility study
general design
prototyping
detail design
functional specifications

II. USER SIGN OFF

III. PROGRAMMING
design
coding
testing

IV. IMPLEMENTATION
training
conversion
installation

V. USER ACCEPTANCE

system development methodology The formal

documentation for the phases of the system development cycle. It defines the precise objectives for each phase and the results required from a phase before the next one can commence. It may provide specialized forms for the preparation of the documentation throughout each phase.

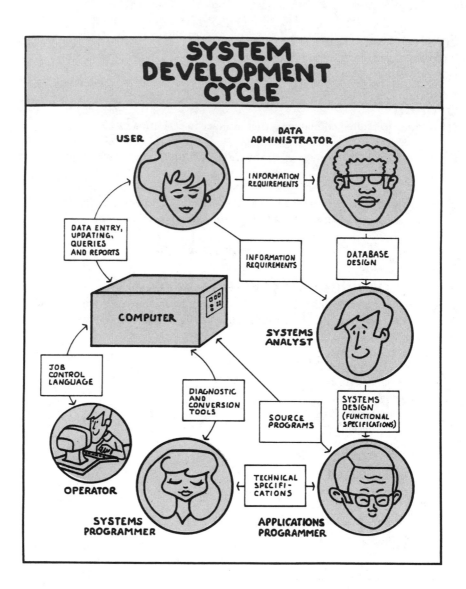

SYSTEM DEVELOPMENT CYCLE

USER

DATA ADMINISTRATOR

INFORMATION REQUIREMENTS

DATA ENTRY, UPDATING, QUERIES AND REPORTS

INFORMATION REQUIREMENTS

DATABASE DESIGN

COMPUTER

SYSTEMS ANALYST

JOB CONTROL LANGUAGE

DIAGNOSTIC AND CONVERSION TOOLS

SOURCE PROGRAMS

SYSTEMS DESIGN (FUNCTIONAL SPECIFICATIONS)

OPERATOR

TECHNICAL SPECIFI- CATIONS

SYSTEMS PROGRAMMER

APPLICATIONS PROGRAMMER

system disk A disk that contains part or all of the operating system or other control program.

system failure A hardware or software malfunction. System failure often refers specifically to a problem within the operating system.

system file A machine language file that is part of the operating system or other control program. It may also refer to a configuration file used by such programs.

system folder The operating system folder in the Macintosh that contains the System, Finder and MultiFinder, printer drivers, fonts, desk accessories, INITs and cdevs.

system level An operation that is performed by the operating system or some other control program.

system life cycle The useful life of an information system. The length of the life cycle depends on the nature and volatility of the business, as well as the software development tools used to generate the databases and application programs. Eventually, an information system that is patched over and over no longer is structurally sound enough to be expanded.

Tools like database management systems allow for changes more readily, but increased transaction volumes can negate the effectiveness of the original selection and design later on.

system memory Memory used by the operating system or other control program.

system program Software that is part of the operating system or other control program.

system prompt The symbol or message displayed by the operating system that indicates it is able to accept a command from the operator.

system software A category of programs that are used to control the computer and run an organizations application programs. It includes operating systems, TP monitors, network control programs, network operating systems and database managers. Contrast with *application program*.

system test The running of a complete system for testing purposes.

System/3 A batch-oriented minicomputer from IBM. Introduced in 1969, it introduced a new punched card about half the size of previous ones. With the addition of the Communications Control Program (CCP), it could handle interactive terminals.

System/7 A sensor-based minicomputer from IBM that was introduced in 1970 and used in process control applications. It was superseded by the Series/1.

System/32 A batch-oriented minicomputer from IBM. Introduced in 1975, it provided a single terminal for operator use. It was superseded by the System/34, which could run System/32 applications in a special mode.

System/34 A multiuser, multitasking minicomputer from IBM, introduced in 1977. The typical system had from a handful to a dozen terminals and could run System/32 programs in a special mode. Most large System/34 users migrated to the System/38, while small users migrated to the System/36.

System/36 A multiuser, multitasking minicomputer from IBM that was introduced in 1983. It superseded the System/34 and is almost entirely compatible with it. System/34 programs run in the System/36 after recompilation. The typical System/36 supports from a handful to a couple of dozen terminals. The System/36 has been superseded by the AS/400.

System/38 A minicomputer from IBM that includes an operating system with an integrated relational database management system. Introduced in 1978, the System/38 was an advanced departure from previous System/3x minicomputers. The typical System/38 handles from a dozen to several dozen terminals. The System/38 has been superseded by the AS/400.

System/360, System/370 See *360, 370 series.*

System 2000

(1) A hierarchical, network and relational database management system from the SAS Institute that runs on IBM, CDC and Unisys computers. It has been integrated into the SAS System.

(2) See *FTS 2000.*

Systemantics An unusual and insightful book about the systems process by John Gall, published in 1977. The following summation is copied with permission from Random House.

A Concise Summary of the Field of General Systemantics
Systems are seductive. They promise to do a hard job faster, better, and more easily than you could to it by yourself. But if you set up a system, you are likely to find your time and effort now being consumed in the care and feeding of the system itself. New problems are created by its very presence. Once set up, it won't go away, it grows and encroaches. It begins to do strange and wonderful things. Breaks down in ways you never thought possible. It kicks back, gets in the way, and opposes its own proper function. Your own perspective becomes distorted by being in the system. You become anxious and push on it to make it work. Eventually you come to believe that the misbegotten product it so grudgingly delivers is what you really wanted all the time. At that point encroachment has become complete...
you have become absorbed...
you are now a systems person!

systems A general term for the department, the people or the work involved in systems analysis & design activities.

systems analysis & design The examination of a problem and the creation of a solution. Systems analysis is effective when all sides of the problem can be reviewed. Systems design is most effective when more than one solution can be proposed, for example, a manual alternative, or a second automated alternative.

Systems are solutions to problems, but in and of themselves, they create other problems. They have a life of their own, and the plans for the care and feeding of any new system are as important as the problems they solve. When systems are considered as solutions only and not problems themselves, there is a good chance that they will not perform as expected. See *Systemantics*.

systems analyst
An individual who is responsible for the development of an information system. They design and modify systems by turning user requirements into a set of functional specifications, which are the blueprint of the system. They design the database or help design it if data administrators are available. They develop the manual and machine procedures and the detailed processing specs for each data entry, update, query and report program in the system.

Systems analysts are the architects, as well as the project leaders, of an information system. It is their job to develop solutions to user's problems, determine the technical and operational feasibility of their solutions, as well as estimate the costs to develop and implement them.

In today's environment, systems analysts develop prototypes of the system along with the users, so that the final specifications are examples of screens and reports that have been carefully reviewed by the users. Experienced systems analysts should leave no doubt in users' minds as to the kind of system that's being developed for them, and they should insist that all responsible users review and sign off on every detail.

Systems analysts require a balanced mix of business and technical knowledge, interviewing and analytical skills, as well as a good understanding of human behavior. See *Systemantics*.

systems disk
A disk pack or disk drive reserved only for system software, which includes the operating system, assemblers, compilers and other utility and control programs.

systems engineer
A professional title often used by hardware vendors for individuals who perform systems related tasks, such as analysis, design and programming. Systems engineers are often involved in pre-sales activities.

systems house
An organization that develops customized software and/or turnkey systems for customers. Contrast with *software house*, which develops software packages for sale to the general public. Systems house and software house are often used synonymously.

systems integrator
Same as *OEM* or *VAR*.

systems program
See *system software*.

systems programmer
(1) In the data processing department of a large organization, a technical expert on some or all of the computer's system software, such as the operating system, network control program and database management system. Systems

programmers are responsible for the efficient performance of the computer systems.

Systems programmers usually don't write programs, but perform a lot of technical tasks that integrate vendors' software. They also act as technical advisors to systems analysts, application programmers and operations personnel. For example, they would know the capacity of the computer and whether additional tasks can be added. They would recommend conversion to a new operating system or database system in order to optimize performance.

In mainframe environments, there is one systems programmer for approximately 10 or more application programmers. In smaller environments, users rely on vendors or consultants for systems programming assistance.

(2) In a computer hardware or software organization, an individual that designs and writes system software.

SYZYGY Pronounced "SIZE-uh-gee." Workgroup software for PCs from Information Research Corporation. SYZYGY is an integrated system for coordinating schedules, resources and budgets for group projects. It includes a calendar with to-do and activity lists as well as electronic mail.

S-100 bus The IEEE 696 standard for a bus architecture primarily used in personal computers. It was used extensively in first-generation personal computers using CP/M.

S/360 (System/360) See *360, 370 series*.

S/370 (System/370) See *360, 370 series*.

T (Tera or Terabyte) See *space/time*.

tab character A special character that is inserted into a word processing or text document to indicate one tab movement. The ASCII horizontal tab character has a numeric value of 9; the vertical tab is 11.

tab delimited A text file format that uses tab characters as separators between the fields. Unlike comma delimited files, alphanumeric data is not surrounded by quotes. In ASCII, the horizontal tab character has a numeric value of 9.

tab key A key on the keyboard that moves the cursor to the next tab stop.

tabbing The moving of a cursor on a video display screen or the print head on a printer to a specified column.

table
(1) In programming, a collection of adjacent fields. Also called an *array*, a table contains data that is either constant within the program or is called in when the program is run. See *decision table*.

(2) In relational database management, the same as a database file; a collection of records.

table lookup The act of searching for data in a table. Table lookups are commonly used in data entry validation to check for valid codes.

table view A screen display of several items or records in rows and columns. Contrast with *form view*.

tablet See *digitizer tablet*.

tabular form Same as *table view* with respect to printed output.

tabulate

(1) To arrange data into a columnar format.

(2) To sum and print totals.

tabulating equipment Punched card data processing machines, including keypunches, sorters, collators, interpreters, reproducers, calculators and tabulators.

TABULATING EQUIPMENT

(Courtesy IBM)

The photo of this early sorter was taken in 1918. The cards were placed in the hopper at the top and distributed into the stackers below. Apparently, gravity must have helped.

tabulator A punched card accounting machine that prints and calculates totals.

tag

(1) A set of bits or characters that identifies various conditions about data in a file and is often found in the header records of such files.

(2) A name (label, mnemonic) assigned to a data structure, such as a field, file, paragraph or other object.

(3) A key field in a record.

(4) A brass pin on a terminal block that is connected to a wire by soldering or wire wrapping.

tag sort A sorting procedure in which the key fields are sorted first to create the correct order, and then the actual data records are placed into that order.

Tandem (Tandem Computers Inc.) A manufacturer of fault tolerant computers. It was founded in 1974 to address the online transaction processing (OLTP) market that was becoming dependent on computers for inventory, reservations and financial transfers.

In 1976, Tandem introduced the first commercial computer based on a multiprocessor, fault tolerant architecture.

Tandem's NonStop series is built around multiple parallel processors rather than redundant processors. All the processors are used to process data, but if one fails, the system is capable of distributing the workload to the remaining processors. Its architecture allows for expansion even when the computer is running. Most systems can be expanded to 16 processors, or to as many as 224 processors using a fiber optic link. With its network software, up to 4,080 processors can be tied together.

James G. Treybig is the principal founder of Tandem and has been president of the company since its formation.

JAMES G. TREYBIG
(Courtesy Tandem Computer Inc.)

tandem processors Two processors hooked together in a multiprocessor environment.

Tandy (Tandy Corporation) A leading manufacturer of personal computers and electronics. Tandy grew out of a family leather business that traces its roots back to 1919. In 1963, it acquired the Radio Shack chain which was made up of nine electronics stores in the Boston area. Radio Shack originally started in 1921 when the amazing electronic marvel of the times was the radio. After acquiring Radio Shack, Tandy began to devote itself to the consumer electronics business and eventually spun off all unrelated products.

In 1977, Tandy introduced one of the first personal computers, the TRS-80 Model I. Since then, it has introduced a variety of models to meet the needs of home computer enthusiasts and small businesses. Tandy's Model 100 and 200 lap-size portables have been very popular and were an inspiration to the laptop generation. Initially, Tandy's personal computers adhered to their own standards, but starting with the Model 1000 in 1984, Tandy changed its policy and built in a high degree of IBM PC compatibility.

During the past dozen whirlwind years in which countless computer manufacturers and dealers have come and gone, Tandy's stable Radio Shack distrubution channel has obviously accounted for its success in personal computers. Today, Tandy has over 7,000 company-owned stores and dealer franchises.

tap In communications, a connection onto the main transmission medium of a local area network. See *transceiver*.

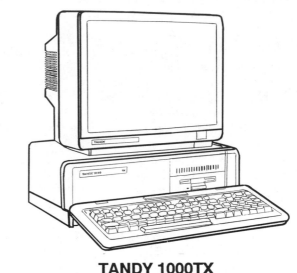

TANDY 1000TX

tape See *magnetic tape & disk*.

tape backup The use of magnetic tape for storing duplicate copies of hard disk files. 1/4" tape cassettes are the common tape backup on personal computers, but digital audio tape (DAT) that uses 4mm cassettes holding over 1GB are quickly emerging.

tape drive The physical unit that holds, reads and writes the magnetic tape. See *magnetic tape & disk*.

tape dump A printout of tape contents without any report formatting.

tape mark A special character code used to indicate the end of a tape file.

tape transport The mechanical part of a tape drive.

Targa board A video graphics board from Truevision that is used in high-resolution graphics applications.

target computer Same as *object computer*.

target disk A disk onto which data is recorded. Contrast with *source disk*.

target language Same as *object language*.

tariff A schedule of rates for common carrier services.

task A program that is run as an independent unit. See *multitasking*.

task management The part of the operating system that controls the running of one or more programs (tasks) within the computer at the same time.

task switching To switch from one program to another either under direction of the operating system in a multitasking environment or by the user. See *context switching*.

TB (Terabyte) See *space/time*.

TBps, Tbps (TeraBytes Per Second, TeraBits Per Second) See *space/time*.

TCAM (TeleCommunications Access Method) A communications program that is widely used to transfer data between IBM mainframes and 3270 terminals. See *access method*.

T-carrier A digital transmission service from a common carrier or telephone company. Introduced by AT&T in 1983 as a voice transmission service, its use for data transmission has grown steadily.

    T-carrier service requires multiplexors at both ends that merge the various signals together for transmission and split them at the destination. Multiplexors can analyze the traffic load and vary the speeds of the channels for optimum transmission.

    T1 is a 1.544 megabit T-carrier channel that can handle 24 voice or data channels at 64 kilobits per second. The standard T1 frame is 193 bits long, which holds 24 8-bit voice samples and one synchronization bit. 8,000 frames are transmitted per second. See *D4* and *ESF*.

    T2 is a 6.312 megabit T-carrier channel that can handle 96 voice or data channels at 64 kilobits per second.

    T3 is a 44.736 megabit T-carrier channel that can handle 672 voice or data channels at 64 kilobits per second. T3 requires optical fiber cable.

TCM (Trellis-Coded Modulation/Viterbi Decoding) A technique that adds forward error correction to a modulation scheme by adding an additional bit to each baud. TCM is used with QAM modulation, for example.

TCP/IP (Transmission Control Protocol/Internet Protocol) A set of communications protocols developed for the Defense Advanced Research Projects Agency (DARPA) to internetwork dissimilar systems. It runs on a large number of VAXs and UNIX-based computers and is supported by many hardware vendors from personal computers to mainframes. It is used by many corporations and almost all American universities and federal organizations.

    The File Transfer Protocol (FTP) and Simple Mail Transfer Protocol (SMTP) provide file transfer and e-mail capability. The TELNET protocol provides a terminal emulation capability that allows a user to interact with any other type of computer in the network. The TCP protocol controls the transfer of the data, and the IP protocol provides the routing mechanism.

The TCP/IP layers are mapped with the DOD and OSI model in the following chart.

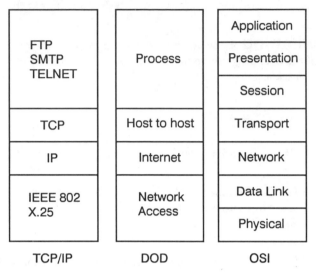

TCP/IP	DOD	OSI
FTP SMTP TELNET	Process	Application
		Presentation
		Session
TCP	Host to host	Transport
IP	Internet	Network
IEEE 802 X.25	Network Access	Data Link
		Physical

TCU (Transmission Control Unit) A communications control unit that is controlled by the computer and does not execute internally stored programs. Contrast with *front end processor*, which executes its own instructions.

TDM (Time Division Multiplexing) A technique that mixes several low-speed signals into one high-speed transmission. For example, if A, B & C are three digital signals of 1,000bps each, they can be interwoven into one 3,000bps as follows: AABBCCAABBCCAABBCC. At the receiving end, the different signals are divided out and merged back into single streams.

tear-off menu A screen menu that can be moved off of its primary position, relocated to any part of the screen and kept active.

tech writer An individual who is responsible for writing documentation for a hardware or software product.

telco (TELephone COmpany) A company that provides telephone services.

tele
(1) Operations that are performed remotely.

(2) Operations that are performed by telephone.

telecom Same as *telecommunications*.

telecommunications The communication of all forms of information, including voice and video. See *communications*.

telecommunity A society in which information can be transmitted or received freely between all members without technical incompatibilities.

telecommuting Working at home and communicating with the office.

teleconferencing

(1) Video *teleconferencing* is a video conference among several users that is provided by video cameras and monitors set up in the customer's premises or in a public conferencing center. Video teleconferencing requires its own communications network that uses coaxial cable, optical fibers, microwave or satellite transmission, since conventional computer networks can't handle video.

Video conferencing is very slowly being integrated into data networks. In time, all data networks will provide this capability.

(2) Audio *teleconferencing* is a telephone conference among several users that is provided internally by an organization's PBX and externally by the telephone companies.

(3) Computer *teleconferencing* is a keyboard conference among several users at their terminals or personal computers that is provided by specialized software in a host computer or bulletin board system.

telecopying (long distance copying) The formal term for fax.

telegraph A low-speed communications device that transmits up to approximately 150 bps. Telegraph grade lines, stemming from the days of the telegraph key and Morse code, can't transmit a voice conversation.

THE FIRST "DIGITAL" COMMUNICATIONS
Telegraph keys and receivers like these were used to tap out morse code.

telemanagement The management of an organization's telephone systems.

telemarketing Selling over the telephone.

Telematics The convergence of telecommunications and information processing.

telemetry The transmitting of data sensed by instrumentation and measuring devices to a remote station where it is recorded and analyzed. For example, data from a weather satellite is telemetered to the earth.

Telenet A value-added, packet switching network that enables many varieties of terminals and computers to exchange data. It is a subsidiary of US Sprint.

telephony The science of converting sound into electrical signals that can be transmitted within cables or via radio and be reconverted back into sound.

teleprinter
A terminal that includes a keyboard for input and a printer for output. Teleprinters provide hard copy, display terminals provide soft copy. Contrast with *video terminal*.

TELEPRINTER

teleprocessing (long distance processing) An early IBM term for data communications.

teleprocessing monitor See *TP monitor*.

Teletex See *Telex*.

teletext A broadcasting service that transmits information to a subscriber's television set. It uses the unused part of the TV signal (vertical blanking interval), the black line between frames when the vertical hold is not properly adjusted. Only about a hundred frames can be transmitted this way; however, thousands of frames can be provided when dedicated channels are used. A special decoder and keypad adapts the teletext signal to the TV. See *videotex*.

Teletype A trade name of the Teletype Corporation and refers to a variety of teleprinter devices used for communications. The Teletype machine was one of the first communications terminals in the U.S.

teletype interface Same as *teletype mode*.

teletype mode Refers to producing output a line at a time as if typed on a typewriter. It implies that data is displayed or printed serially, one line following the other.

teletypewriter A low-speed teleprinter, often abbreviated TTY.

televaulting The continuous transmitting of data to vaults for backup purposes. The term was coined by TeleVault Technology Inc.

Telex An international dial-up communications service that uses teleprinters for terminals and transmits Baudot code at 50 bits per second, or 66 words per minute. In the U.S., it is administered by Western Union, which in 1971 purchased the Bell System's TWX service and connected it to the Telex network.

In the early 1980s, a new service called Teletex was initiated that provides higher speeds and upper and lowercase text transmission to subscribers using intelligent terminals and personal computers.

template

(1) A plastic or stiff paper form that is placed over the function keys on a keyboard to identify their use.

(2) The programmatic and descriptive part of a programmable application; for example, a spreadsheet that contains only descriptions and formulas or a HyperCard stack that contains only programming scripts and backgrounds. When the template is filled with data, it becomes a working application.

ter The third version.

tera Trillion. Abbreviated "T." For example, 10 Tbytes is 10 trillion bytes. See *space/time*.

terabit One trillion bits. See *space/time*.

terabyte One trillion bytes. See *space/time*.

terminal

(1) An input/output device for a computer that usually has a keyboard for input and a video screen or printer for output.

(2) An input device, such as a scanner, video camera or punched card reader.

(3) An output device in a network, such as a monitor, printer or card punch.

(4) A connector used to attach a wire.

terminal emulation The use of a personal computer to simulate a mainframe or minicomputer terminal.

terminal session The time in which a user is working at a terminal.

terminal strip An insulated bar that contains a set of screws to which wires are attached.

terminate and stay resident See TSR.

terminator

(1) A character that ends a string of alphanumeric characters.

(2) A hardware component that is connected to the last peripheral device in a series or the last node in a network.

terrestrial link A communications line that travels on, near or below ground. Contrast with *satellite link*.

test data A set of data created for testing new or revised programs. It should be developed by the user as well as the programmer and must contain a sample of every category of valid data as well as many invalid conditions.

testing The running of new or revised programs to determine if they process all data properly. See *test data*.

TeX A typesetting language that is used in a variety of computers and typesetting environments. It uses embedded codes within the text of the document to initiate changes in layout including the ability to describe elaborate scientific formulas.

text Words, sentences and paragraphs. Contrast with *data*, which are defined units, such as name and amount due. Text may also refer to alphanumeric data, such as name and address, to distinguish it from numeric data, such as quantity and dollar amounts. A page of text takes about 2,000 to 4,000 bytes. See *text field*.

text based Also called *character based*. The display of text and graphics as a fixed set of predefined characters. For example, 25 rows of 80 columns. Contrast with *graphics based*.

text editing The ability to change text by adding, deleting and rearranging letters, words, sentences and paragraphs.

text editor Software used to create and manage text files, such as source language programs and name and address lists. Unlike word processors, text editors do not have elaborate formatting and printing features, such as word wrap, underline and boldface. Text editors designed for programming have special features such as automatic indention and multiple windows.

text field A data structure that holds alphanumeric data, such as name and address. If a text field holds large, or unlimited, amounts of text, it may be called a *memo field*. Contrast with *numeric field*.

text handling See *text management*.

text management Refers to the creation, storage and retrieval of long, or unlimited, lengths of text. It implies flexible retrieval capabilities that can search for text based on a variety of criteria. Although a word processor manages text, it usually has limited retrieval capabilities.

text mode
(1) A screen display mode that displays only text and not graphics.

(2) A program mode that allows text to be entered and edited.

text to speech The converting of text into voice output using speech synthesis techniques.

texture mapping In computer graphics, the creation of a special surface on a graphics image. Through the use of algorithms, all varieties of textures can be produced, for example, the rough skin of an orange, the metallic surface of a can and the irregularity of a brick.

TFT (Thin Film Transistor) See *thin film*.

TFT LCD (Thin Film Transistor LCD) See *active matrix LCD*.

TFTP (Trivial File Transfer Protocol) A version of the TCP/IP FTP protocol that has no directory or password capability.

thermal printer A non-impact printer that uses a print head of electrically heated pins and special heat-sensitive paper. The pins are pushed against the paper, and, when selectively heated, the paper darkens upon contact. Thermal printers are quiet, low-cost devices that provide a low to medium-resolution print image.

thermal wax transfer A printing process that transfers a waxlike ink onto paper. For example, in a color printer, a mylar ribbon is used that contains several hundred repeating sets of full pages of black, cyan, magenta and yellow ink. A sheet of paper is pressed against each color and passed by a line of heating elements that transfers the dots, or pixels, of ink onto the paper.

thick film A layer of magnetic, semiconductor or metallic material that is thicker than the microscopic layers of the transistors on a chip. For example, metallic thick films are silk screened onto the ceramic base of hybrid microcircuits. Contrast with *thin film*.

thimble printer A letter quality printer similar to a daisy wheel printer. Instead of a wheel, characters are formed facing out and around the rim of a thimble-shaped cup. For example, the NEC Spinwriters are thimble printers.

thin Ethernet A widely used Ethernet technology that uses a smaller diameter and more economical coaxial cable than standard Ethernet.

thin film A microscopically thin layer of semiconductor or magnetic material that is deposited onto a metal, ceramic or semiconductor base. For example, the layers that make up a chip and the surface coating on high-density magnetic disks are called *thin films*.

thin film head A read/write head for high-density disks that is made from thin layers of a conducting film deposited onto a nickel-iron core.

third-generation computer A computer that uses integrated circuits, disk storage and online terminals. The third generation started roughly in 1964 with the advent of the IBM System/360.

third normal form In database management, the final result of a process which breaks down data into record groups that are more efficiently processed in a relational database. Data stored in third normal form relates only to the key field in the record. For example, data in order records relate only to the order number (key field) in the record. Data in customer records relate only to the customer number (key field).

THOR (Tandy High-intensity Optical Recorder) An erasable CD recorder from Tandy Corporation that is scheduled for introduction in the early 1990s. It records audio on a special disc that can be erased and reused and also played on a standard CD player. Models for recording data are also projected.

thrashing Excessive paging in a virtual memory computer. If programs are not written to run in a virtual memory environment, the operating system may spend excessive amounts of time swapping program pages in and out of the disk.

three-state logic element An electronic component that provides three possible outputs: off, low voltage and high voltage.

throughput The speed with which a computer can process data. A computer's throughput is a combination of its peripheral input and output speeds, its internal processing speed, and the efficiency of its operating system and other system software all working together.

THz (TeraHertZ) One trillion cycles per second.

TI (Texas Instruments, Inc.) A leading semiconductor manufacturer, commonly known as TI, that was founded in 1930 as Geophysical Service, Inc., to provide services to the petroleum industry. During the war, GSI manufactured electronic equipment for the U.S. Navy, and in 1946, formally added electronics to its product line.

In 1951, the company was renamed Texas Instruments and soon after entered the semiconductor business. TI was the first to commercialize the silicon transistor, pocket radio, integrated circuit, hand-held calculator, single-chip computer and the LISP chip.

In the early 1980s, TI introduced and sold a large number of its low-priced 99/4a home computers. It later introduced a high-quality MS-DOS computer, but eventually pulled out of the personal computing business.

With 1988 revenues of over six billion, TI's strength is integrated circuits, but, it also creates computer systems for AI applications, composite metals, electrical control products and consumer electronics, including its well-known line of calculators and educational math and reading machines.

TIFF (Tagged Image File Format) A popular file format used to capture graphic images. TIFF stores images in a bit-mapped (raster graphics) format.

tightly coupled Refers to two or more computers linked together and dependent on each other. One computer may control the other, or both computers may monitor each other. For example, a database machine is tightly coupled to the main processor. Two computers tied together for multiprocessing are tightly coupled. Contrast with *loosely coupled*, such as personal computers in a local area network.

tiled The display of objects side by side; for example, tiled windows cannot be overlapped on top of each other.

time base generator An electronic clock that creates its own timing signals for synchronization and measurement purposes.

time-division multiplexing See TDM.

time slice A fixed interval of time that is allotted to each user or program in a multitasking or timesharing system.

timer interrupt An interrupt that is generated by an internal clock. See *interrupt*.

timesharing A computer environment that allows several authorized users to gain access to selected programs and databases. It implies that users can initiate the required sessions as needed.

   If a computer system serves multiple users who all interact with the same program, such as in a data collection system (entering transactions), that is not considered timesharing.

   In today's multitasking computers and local area networks, the ability to initiate a program is implicit. The term is now more often used to refer to large computers in service bureaus.

timing clock See *clock*.

timing signals Electrical pulses that are generated in the processor or in external devices in order to synchronize computer operations. The main timing signals come from the computer's clock, which provides a frequency that can be divided into many slower cycles. Other internal timing signals may come from a timesharing or realtime clock.

   In disk drives, timing signals for reading and writing are generated by holes or marks on one of the platters, or by the way the digital data is actually recorded.

Tiny BASIC A subset of BASIC that has been used in first generation personal computers with limited memory.

TLI (Transport Level Interface) An AT&T product part of UNIX System V.library of routines for user programs that are used to communicate with a documented OSI (level-4) transport interface inside the UNIX system kernel. TLI is implemented as a STREAMS module.

TM/1 (Tables Manager/1) A relational spreadsheet for PCs from Sinper Corporation. TM/1 uses the common matrix layout of a spreadsheet, but stores the data in a separate database and links it to the spreadsheet by names, such as JAN, FEB and GROSS SALES, instead of cell references (row x, col. y). When the database is updated, all the spreadsheet models are automatically updated.

   In addition, the database itself can be viewed in up to eight dimensions. For example, a table of products by period can be instantly switched to products by location, categories by location and categories by period.

A Spreadsheet Connector option allows Lotus users to access a TM/1 database directly from a Lotus 1-2-3 spreadsheet.

```
          A              B                C                D
1       YEARS           LOCS           EXPENSES          MONTHS
2        1988        NEW ENGLAND        *LIN*            *COL*
3       1986         CONNECTICUT     OFFICERS SALARIES   JAN
4       1987         MAINE           OFFICE SALARIES     FEB
5       1988         MASSACHUSETTS   ADVERTISING         MAR
6       1988 FORECAST NEW HAMPSHIRE  AUTOMOBILE EXPENSE  1ST-QTR
7       1988 VARIANCE RHODE ISLAND   BAD DEBT EXPENSE    APR
8                    VERMONT         BANK SERVICE CHARGE MAY
9                    NEW JERSEY      CLEANING            JUN
10                   NEW YORK        COLLECTION EXPENSE  2ND-QTR
11                   PENNSYLVANIA    COMMISSIONS         JUL
12
13
          A              C              D            E            F
1                      1987           1988      1988 FORECAS 1988 VARIANC
2   OFFICERS SALARIES    7,227,235     7,551,668    8,044,544  ( 492,876)
3   OFFICE SALARIES     10,080,505    11,146,052   11,687,114  ( 541,062)
4   ADVERTISING          1,032,194     1,088,082    1,145,724  ( 57,642)
5   AUTOMOBILE EXPENSE     516,319       562,698      589,021  ( 26,323)
6   BAD DEBT EXPENSE       104,402       115,026      115,431  (    405)
7   BANK SERVICE CHARGE    105,506       111,421      121,065  (  9,644)
8   CLEANING               214,029       224,177      231,724  (  7,547)
9   COLLECTION EXPENSE     311,353       347,897      342,771     5,126
10  COMMISSIONS          1,540,364     1,665,071    1,744,908  ( 79,837)
11  CONTRIBUTIONS           53,946        59,509       60,675  (  1,166)
12  DELIVERY EXPENSE        53,021        60,764       61,173  (    409)
13  DEPRECIATION         1,561,434     1,682,673    1,762,323  ( 79,650)
14  DUES & SUBSCRIPTIONS    308,235       327,300      347,703  ( 20,403)
15  EMPLOYEE BENEFITS    1,516,213     1,699,308    1,695,326     3,982
16  ENTERTAINMENT          207,399       223,045      234,888  ( 11,843)
17  FREIGHT                405,362       444,283      464,805  ( 20,522)
18  HEAT POWER & LIGHT   1,035,314     1,119,713    1,173,805  ( 54,092)
19  INSURANCE            1,726,455     1,910,275    1,952,562  ( 42,287)
20  INSURANCE OFFICER LIFE  54,255        58,336       62,103  (  3,767)
21  INTEREST               928,142     1,015,396    1,058,734  ( 43,338)
    YEARS LOCS          EXPENSES MONTHS
    *COL* NEW ENGLAND *LIN*   YEAR    TABLE: BUDGET             371/1765k
    1        2in/out 3modify 4disply 5graph  6jmp w  7recalc 8goto   9edit   0help
```

TM/1 STRUCTURES

(Courtesy Sinper Corporation)

This slice of year-end totals across years for each expense (bottom screen) was derived from the four-dimensional structure (top screen) with just a few keystrokes.

TN (Twisted Nematic) An LCD technology that twists the liquid crystal molecules 90 degrees between polarizers. See *supertwist*.

TOF (Top Of Form) The beginning of a physical paper form. In order to position paper in some printers, the printer is turned off-line, the forms are aligned properly and the TOF button is pressed.

toggle To alternate back and forth between two states.

token passing A communications network access method that uses a continuously repeating frame (the token) that is transmitted onto the network by the controlling computer. When a terminal or computer wants to send a message, it waits for an empty token. When it finds one, it fills it with the address of the destination station and some or all of its message.

Every computer and terminal on the network constantly monitors the passing tokens to determine if it is a recipient of a message, in which case it "grabs" the message and resets the token status to empty. Token passing uses bus and ring topologies.

token ring network

A communications network that uses the token passing technology in a sequential manner. Each station in the network passes the token on to the station next to it.

Token Ring Network
A local area network from IBM that uses a special twisted wire cable and the token passing access method transmitting at four or 16Mbits per second.

It uses a star topology in which all computers connect to a central wiring hub, but passes tokens to each of up to 255 stations in a sequential, ring-like sequence. Token Ring conforms to the IEEE 802.5 standard.

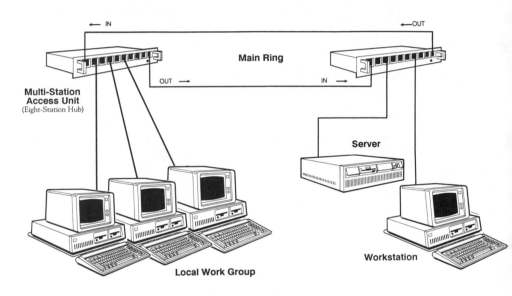

TOKEN RING NETWORK
(Courtesy Black Box Corporation)

TokenTalk
Software for the Macintosh from Apple Computer that accompanies its TokenTalk NB board and adapts the Macintosh to 4 megabit/second Token Ring Networks.

toner
An electrically charged ink that is used in copy machines and laser printers. The toner adheres to an invisible image that has been charged with the opposite polarity onto a plate or drum or onto the paper itself.

tool

(1) An on-screen function in an interactive program; for example, a line draw, circle draw or paintbrush option in a graphics program.

(2) A program used for software development or system maintenance. Utility programs, editors, debuggers and graphics routines are examples. A program that helps a user customize, adapt or work with a computer may be called a tool.

tool palette A collection of on-screen functions, typically graphics related, that are grouped in a menu structure for interactive selection.

ToolBook An application development system for PCs running under Windows 3.0 from Asymetrix Corporation. It uses a "page and book" metaphor as its data structure that is analogous to HyperCard's "card and stack" from Apple Computer, and its OpenScript language is similar to the HyperTalk scripting language.

toolbox, toolkit A set of software routines that allow a program to be written for and work in a particular environment. The routines are called by the application program to perform various functions, for example, to display a menu or draw a graphic element.

TOP (Technical Office Protocol) A communications protocol for office systems from Boeing Computer Services. It uses the Ethernet access method and is often used in conjunction with MAP, the factory automation protocol developed by General Motors. TOP is used in the front office, and MAP is used on the factory floor.

top of file Beginning of a file. In word processing, it is the first character in the document. In a data file, it is either the first record in the file or the first record in the index. For example, in an indexed dBASE file, `goto top` could go to physical record #608 if record #608 is AARDVARK.

topdown design A design technique that starts with the highest level of an idea and works its way down to the lowest level of detail.

topdown programming A programming design and documentation technique that imposes a hierarchical structure on the design of the program. See *structured programming*.

topology

(1) In a communications network, the pattern of interconnection between nodes; for example, a bus, ring or star configuration.

(2) In a parallel processing architecture, the interconnection between processors; for example, a bus, grid, hypercube or Butterfly Switch configuration.

TOPS

(1) A multiuser, multitasking, timesharing, virtual memory operating system from Digital Equipment Corporation that runs on its PDP-6, DECsystem 10 and DECsystem 20 minicomputers.

(2) (Transparent OPerating System) A local area network from TOPS Corporation that uses the LocalTalk access method and connects Apple computers, PCs and Sun workstations. TOPS' Flashcard plugs LocalTalk capability into PCs.

TOPS does not require a dedicated file server. It provides peer-to-peer communications in which each user on the network can gain access to authorized files from any workstation in the network.

TOPVIEW A PC windowing environment from IBM that enabled users to view more than one program at a time. As a first-generation program, it never caught on.

TOTAL A network database management system from Cincom Systems that runs on a wide variety of mainframes and minicomputers.

total bypass The bypassing of both local and long distance telephone lines by using satellite communications.

touch screen A clear panel that covers a display screen. The panel is a matrix of cells, each cell about a half inch square to accommodate the end of a person's finger. The program displays options on screen in the form of graphic buttons, and the user touches one of the buttons.

tower configuration A

floor-standing cabinet that is taller than it is wide. Desktop computers can be made into towers by turning them on their side and inserting them into a floor-mounted base.

TP monitor (TeleProcessing monitor) A communications control program that manages the transfer of data between multiple local and remote terminals and the application programs that serve them. The TP monitor may also include programs that format the terminal screens and validate the data entered. CICS is an example of a TP monitor in the IBM mainframe environment.

TPI (Tracks Per Inch) Used to measure the density of tracks recorded on a disk or drum.

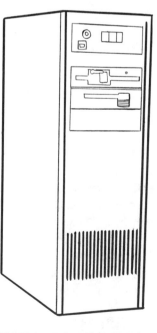

TOWER CONFIGURATION

TPS

(1) (Transactions Per Second) The number of transactions that can be processed within one second in a transaction processing system.

(2) (Transaction Processing System) Originally used as an acronym for such a system. The acronym now refers to the measurement of the system as in definition #1 above.

track A storage channel on a disk or tape. On disks, tracks are concentric circles (data storage) or spirals (CDs and videodiscs). On tapes, they are parallel lines. Their format is determined by the specific drive they are used in. On magnetic devices, data bits are recorded as reversals of polarity in the magnetic surface. On CDs, data bits are recorded as physical pits underneath a clear, protective layer.

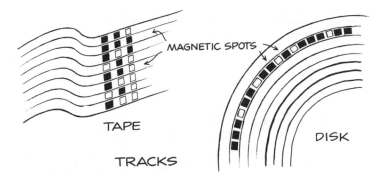

trackball An input device that is used in video games, graphics applications and as a mouse alternative. It is a stationary unit that contains a movable ball that is rotated with the fingers or palm of the hand and, correspondingly, moves the cursor on the screen.

tractor feed A mechanism that provides high speed movement of paper forms through the printer. It contains pins on tractors that engage the paper through perforated holes in its left and right borders. Contrast with *sheet feeder*.

Tradacoms A European standard for electronic data interchange (EDI) developed by the Article Numbering Association (ANA). The American counterpart is ANSI's X.12 standard, and OSI's EDIFACT proposes to supersede both of them.

trailer

(1) In data processing, the last record in a file, which usually contains the number of records in the file and hash totals.

(2) In communications, a code or set of codes that make up the last part of a transmitted message.

trailer label The last record in a file and contains identification data about the file.

train printer A line printer that uses type slugs that ride around in a track as its printing mechanism. It is similar to a chain printer, but the type slugs are not connected together; they are pushed around the track by engaging with a drive gear at one end of the mechanism. The slugs and track are usually assembled as a cartridge and can be replaced with new cartridges when the type faces wear out or fonts need to be changed. See *chain printer*.

training

(1) The teaching of the details of a particular subject. With regard to software, training provides instruction for each command used in an application. Contrast with *education*.

(2) In communications, the process by which two modems determine the correct protocols and transmission speeds to use.

(3) In voice recognition systems, the recording of the user's voice in order to provide samples and patterns for recognizing that voice.

transaction An activity or request. Orders, purchases, changes, additions and deletions are examples of transactions that are recorded in a business information environment. Queries and other requests are also transactions to the computer, but are usually just acted upon and not recorded in the system. Transaction volume is a major factor in determining the size and speed of a computer system.

transaction file A collection of records that record the activity of an organization. The data in transaction files is used to update the data in master files, which contain the subjects of the organization. Transaction files also serve as audit trails and are usually transferred from active disk files to the data library after some period of time.

As optical disks become more economical, transaction files will remain online in the computer so that an organization's history will be immediately available for ad hoc queries. See *information system*.

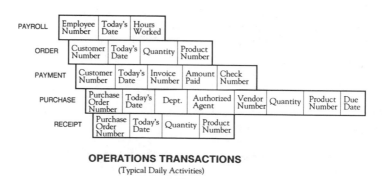

OPERATIONS TRANSACTIONS
(Typical Daily Activities)

PAY RAISE	Employee Number	Today's Date	Transaction Type	New rate	Management Authorization
CREDIT LIMIT CHANGE	Customer Number	Today's Date	New limit	Management Authorization	
PRODUCT DESCRIPTION CHANGE	Product Number	Today's Date	New Description	Management Authorization	

MAINTENANCE TRANSACTIONS
(Typical Periodic Activities)

transaction processing
The processing of transactions as they are received by the system. Transaction processing systems, also called *online* or *realtime* systems, update master files as soon as they are entered at terminals or arrive over communications lines. Contrast with *batch processing*, which stores transactions and updates the necessary files at a later date.

If you save receipts in a shoebox and add them up at the end of the year for tax purposes, that's batch processing. However, if you buy something and immediately add the amount to the running total, that's transaction processing!

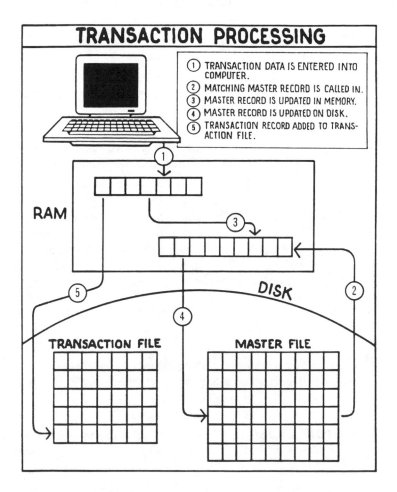

TRANSACTION PROCESSING

1. TRANSACTION DATA IS ENTERED INTO COMPUTER.
2. MATCHING MASTER RECORD IS CALLED IN.
3. MASTER RECORD IS UPDATED IN MEMORY.
4. MASTER RECORD IS UPDATED ON DISK.
5. TRANSACTION RECORD ADDED TO TRANSACTION FILE.

RAM

DISK

TRANSACTION FILE   MASTER FILE

transceiver A transmitter and receiver of analog or digital signals that comes in many forms, for example, a transponder on a communications satellite or the NIC (network interface card) that adapts a computer to a local area network.

transcribe To copy data from one medium to another, for example, from one source document to another, or from a source document to the computer. Transcribe often implies a change of format or codes, as well.

transducer A device that converts one energy into another; for example, a read/write head converts magnetic energy into electrical energy and vice versa. In process control applications, a transducer is used to convert pressure into an electrical reading.

transfer The transmission of data between remote stations in a network, between memory and peripheral devices in a computer system, or from one place in memory to another. Transfers within the computer are actually copies, since the data is in both locations at the end of the transfer. Input, output and move instructions activate data transfers in the computer.

transfer protocol See *file transfer protocol*.

transfer rate Also called *data rate*. The transmission speed of a communications or computer channel. Transfer rates are measured in bits or bytes per second.

transfer time The time it takes to transmit or move data from one place to another. It is the time interval between starting the transfer and the completion of the transfer.

transformer An electromagnetic device that changes the voltage of alternating current (AC). It is made up of a number of steel laminations that are wrapped with two coils of wire; the primary coil on the input side and the secondary coil on the output side. The voltage change is derived from the number of windings in each coil. For example, if the input is 120 volts, the primary coil has 1,000 windings, and the secondary coil has 100 windings, the output voltage will be 12 volts. In order to create direct current (DC), the output of the secondary coil is passed through a rectifier.

transient A malfunction that occurs at random intervals, for example, a rapid fluctuation of voltage in a power line or a memory cell that intermittently fails.

transient area An area in memory used to hold programs while they are processing data. The bulk of a computer's main memory is used as a transient area.

transient state The exact point at which a device changes modes, for example, from transmit to receive or 0 to 1.

transistor A semiconductor device that is used to amplify a signal or open and close a circuit. In digital computers, it functions as an electronic switch. When activated, it bridges the gap between two wires and allows current to flow. The gap is a material that normally resists electricity, but can change its state. When activated (a voltage on the gate), it becomes conductive and allows current to flow (from source to drain).

THE FIRST TRANSISTOR (1947)

(Courtesy AT&T)

Transistors, resistors, capacitors and diodes, make up logic gates. Logic gates make up circuits, and circuits make up electronic systems.

MOSFET TRANSISTOR

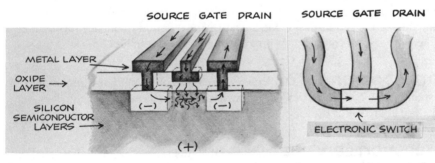

A PULSE ON THE GATE TEMPORARILY ALLOWS
CURRENT TO FLOW FROM ONE SIDE TO THE OTHER

translate
(1) To change one language into another; for example, assemblers, compilers and interpreters translate source language into machine language.

(2) In computer graphics, to move an image on screen without rotating it.

(3) In telecommunictions, to change the frequencies of a band of signals.

TransLISP PLUS A version of LISP for PCs from Solution Systems, Inc. It provides an interface to Microsoft C that allows the programmer to write a C routine and add it to the LISP library as a function.

transmission The transfer of data over a communications channel.

transmission channel A path between two nodes in a network. It may refer to the physical cable, the signal transmitted within the cable or to a subchannel within a carrier frequency. In radio and TV, it refers to the assigned carrier frequency.

transmission control unit See TCU.

transmit To send data over a communications line. The term is normally used with communications systems; however, the routine operation of a computer is to generate and transmit digital signals between the computer's internal circuits and between the computer and its peripheral devices.

transmitter A device that generates signals. Contrast with *receiver*.

transparent Refers to a change in hardware or software that, after installation, causes no noticeable change in the operation of the computer.

transponder A receiver and transmitter in a communications satellite. The transponder receives a transmitted microwave signal from earth (uplink), amplifies it and retransmits it back to earth at a different frequency (down link). There are several transponders on a communications satellite.

transport protocol A communications protocol that is responsible for establishing a connection and ensuring that all data has arrived safely. It is defined in layer 4 of the OSI model.

transport services The collective functions of layers 1 through 4 of the OSI model.

transputer (TRANSistor comPUTER) A computer that contains a processor, memory and communications capability on a single chip. Transputers are strung together in hypercube or grid-like patterns to create large parallel processing machines. It is used for scientific, realtime control and artificial intelligence applications.

trap To test for a particular condition in a running program. Error traps test for error conditions and provide routines for recovery. Debugging traps test for the execution of a particular instruction. Traps can test for specific hardware interrupts to cause a special routine to be activated.

trapdoor An alternate way of gaining access to an interactive program. It implies a special entrance or exit that can be used if necessary.

trash can An icon on the Macintosh desktop used for deleting files, folders and applications.

trashware Software that is so poorly designed that it winds up in the garbage can.

tree structure A hierarchical structure with many branches.

trichromatic In computer graphics, the use of red, green and blue to create all the colors in the spectrum.

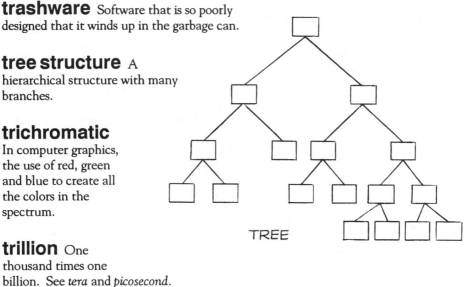

TREE

trillion One thousand times one billion. See *tera* and *picosecond*.

Trilogy A company founded in 1979 by Gene Amdahl to commercialize wafer scale integration and built supercomputers. It raised over a quarter of a billion dollars, the largest funding for a startup in history. Trilogy came close to success, but never quite made it. By 1984, it dropped the supercomputer project and soon after, the entire "superchip" project. In October 1985, Trilogy acquired Elxsi Corporation, a manufacturer of VAX-compatible multiprocessor systems. Eventually Trilogy merged itself into Elxsi.

THE TRILOGY SUPERCHIP

(Courtesy Elxsi Corporation)

This is the actual size of the chip Trilogy had tried to develop using wafer scale integration.

triple precision The use of three computer words to hold a number used for calculation, providing an enormous amount of arithmetic precision.

Trojan horse A program routine that invades a computer system by being secretly attached to a valid program that will be downloaded into the computer. It may be used to locate password information, or it may alter an existing program to make it easier to gain access to it. A virus is a Trojan horse that continues to infect programs over and over.

TRON (The Realtime Operating System Nucleus) An advanced realtime computer architecture and operating system under development by Japanese universities and corporations. Its ultimate goal is a common architecture and user interface from the smallest consumer appliance to the largest supercomputer. TRON-based intelligent cars are also under research and development.

C-TRON is the OSI-compliant communications system; B-TRON is for business applications and I-TRON is the version for industrial applications.

There's considerable controversy over TRON, as its adoption may exclude foreign vendors from competing in the Japanese market.

TRS (Text Retrieval System) Text processing software from Software AG that adds text handling features to its ADABAS database management system.

TRS-80 (Tandy Radio Shack-80) The first family of personal computers from Tandy Corporation introduced in 1977.

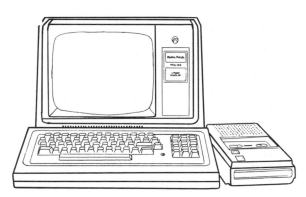

TRS-80

True Image An enhanced PostScript interpreter from Microsoft that supports Apple's True Type scalable fonts. It is also licensed by Apple Computer.

True Type A scalable font technology from Apple Computer that is also licensed by Microsoft. Each font contains its own algorithm for generating the final bit maps. True Type is supported in the Macintosh (System 7), as well as Microsoft Windows and OS/2.

truncate To cut off leading or trailing digits or characters from an item of data without regard to the accuracy of the remaining characters. Truncation occurs when data is converted into a new record with smaller field lengths than the original.

trunk A communications channel between two points. The term is typically used with telephone systems and often refers to large bandwidth channels between major switching centers, which are capable of transmitting many simultaneous voice conversations or data signals.

truth table A chart that defines the inputs and outputs of a logical operation. The following example is a truth table for the Boolean AND operation.

Inputs		Output
0	0	0
0	1	0
1	0	0
1	1	1

TSO (Time Sharing Option) Software that provides interactive communications for IBM's MVS operating system. It allows a user or programmer to launch an application from a terminal and interactively work with it. The TSO counterpart in VM is called CMS. Contrast with JES, which provides batch communications for MVS.

TSR (Terminate and Stay Resident) Programs that remain in memory at all times so that they can be instantly activated. On PCs running under DOS, TSR programs have become popular in order to have instant access to a calculator, calendar or dictionary, while working with a word processor or other application.

There have been many conflicts with TSRs running together, and older TSRs may conflict with newer ones. However, it is possible to keep many TSRs in memory at the same time if they have been written properly.

Operating and switching environments for DOS, such as DESQview and Software Carousel, provide the ability to switch back and forth between multiple applications, thus making all programs function as a TSR.

TTL (Transistor Transistor Logic) A digital circuit in which the output is derived from two transistors. Although TTL technology is a specific design method, the term often refers generically to digital connections in constrast with analog connections. For example, a TTL input on a monitor requires digital output from the display board rather than analog output.

TTY (TeleTYpewriter) See *teletypewriter*.

TTY protocol A low-speed asynchronous communications protocol with limited or no error checking.

tube See CRT and *vacuum tube*.

tuner The electronic part of a radio or television that locks on to a selected carrier frequency (station, channel) and filters out the audio and video signals for amplification and display.

tuple In relational database management, a record, or row. See *relational database*.

turbo A trade name for hardware and software that implies high speed. It often refers to faster clock rates in personal computers. Borland has popularized its use in its language products, such as Turbo C and Turbo Pascal.

Turbo C A C compiler from Borland International that is used to create a wide variety of commercial products. It is known for its exceptionally well-designed debugger. The PC version of this Glossary was written in Turbo C.

Turbo Mouse A mouse alternative for the Macintosh from Kensington Microware, Ltd., that uses a trackball. If the ball is moved slowly, the cursor moves slowly, but if the ball is moved quickly, the same spatial movement moves the cursor a greater distance on the screen. Its counterpart for the PC is called the Expert Mouse.

TURBO MOUSE
(Courtesy Kensington Microware)

Turbo Pascal A Pascal compiler from Borland International that is used in a wide variety of applications from accounting to extremely complex commercial products. With Turbo Pascal, Borland is responsible for moving the Pascal language from the academic halls to the commercial world.

turnaround document
A paper document or punched card that is prepared for re-entry into the computer system. Paper documents are printed with special fonts for optical scanning, and punched cards are punched with appropriate codes. Invoices and inventory stock cards are examples.

turnaround time
(1) In batch processing, the time it takes to receive finished reports after submission of documents or files for processing. In an online environment, turnaround time is the same as *response time*.

(2) In half-duplex transmission, the time it takes to change from transmit to receive and vice versa.

turnkey system
A complete system of hardware and software delivered to the customer in a ready-to-run condition. Turnkey systems typically have all software installed and ready to go.

turnpike effect
In communications, a lock up due to increased traffic conditions and bottlenecks in the system.

turtle graphics
A method for creating graphic images in Logo. The turtle is an imaginary pen that is given drawing commands, such as go forward and turn right. On screen, the turtle is shaped like a triangle.

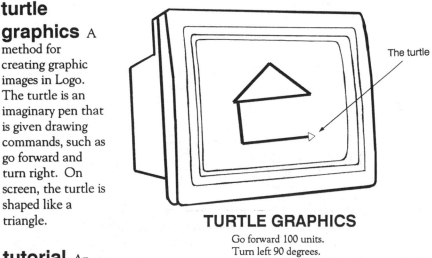

The turtle

TURTLE GRAPHICS

Go forward 100 units.
Turn left 90 degrees.

tutorial
An instructional book or program that takes the user through a prescribed sequence of steps in order to learn a product. Contrast with *documentation*, which, although instructional, tends to group features and functions by category.

tweak
To make minor adjustments in an electronic system or in a software program in order to improve performance.

TwinAxcess
An IBM midrange terminal emulation system for the Macintosh from Andrew/KMW. It includes a controller card and software that

emulates the IBM 5250 terminal used on System/3x and AS/400 computers. It allows the user to have seven concurrent sessions, and the sessions may be broadcast over LocalTalk, EtherTalk or TokenTalk networks.

twinaxial A cable that is similar to coaxial cable, but with two inner conductors instead of one. Twinaxial cables are used in IBM System 34, 36 and 38 communications environments.

twisted pair A pair of small insulated wires that are commonly used in telephone cables. The wires are twisted around each other to minimize interference from other wires in the cable. Cables containing from one to several hundred twisted pairs are used in myriads of electronic and telephone interconnections. Twisted pair wires have limited bandwidths compared to coaxial cable or optical fiber.

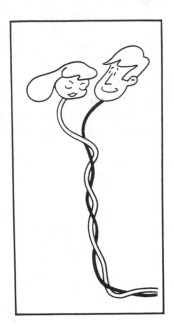

TWISTED PAIR

two-out-of-five code A numeric code that stores one decimal digit in five binary digits in which two of the bits are always 0 or 1 and the other three are always in the opposite state.

two-wire lines A transmission channel made up of only two wires, such as used in the common dial-up telephone network.

TWX (TeletypeWriter eXchange Service) A dial-up communications service within the U.S. and Canada, which uses teleprinters for terminals and can transmit 5-bit Murray code or 7-bit ASCII code at up to 150 bps. Originally part of the Bell Telephone System, TWX was sold to Western Union in 1971 and was interconnected with its Telex network.

Tymnet A domestic communications service from Tymshare Corporation. It is a value-added, packet switching network that enables many varieties of terminals and computers to exchange information.

type
(1) In data or text entry, to press the keys on the keyboard.

(2) In programming, a category of variable that is determined by the kind of data stored in it. For example, integer, floating point, string, logical, date and binary are common data types.

(3) In DOS and OS/2, a command that displays the contents of a text file.

type ball A golf ball-sized element used in typewriters and low-speed teleprinters that contains all the print characters on its outside surface. It was introduced with IBM's Selectric typewriter.

type font A set of print characters of a particular design (typeface), size (point size) and weight (light, medium, heavy). See *font*.

typeface The design of a set of printed characters, such as Courier, Helvetica and Times Roman. For example, the typeface you're reading is Goudy Old Style. The bold titles for the terms are Helvetica. The following chart shows common typeface measurements.

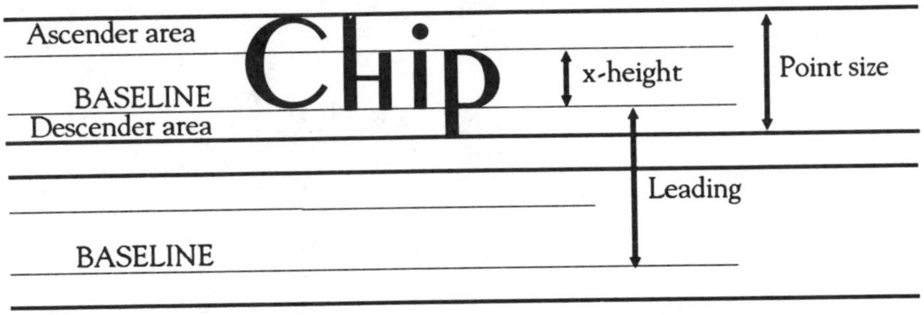

Ascender area

BASELINE

Descender area

Chip

x-height

Point size

Leading

BASELINE

TYPEFACE MEASUREMENTS

typeface family A group of typefaces that include the normal, bold, italic and bold-italic variations of the same design.

typeover mode In word processing and data entry, a state in which each character typed on the keyboard replaces the character at the current cursor location. Contrast with *insert mode*.

UART (Universal Asynchronous Receiver Transmitter) An electronic circuit that transmits and receives data on the serial port. It converts bytes into serial bits for transmission, and vice versa, and generates and strips the start and stop bits appended to each character.

UCSD p-System (University of California at San Diego p-System) A software development system designed for portability. Programs are written in languages, such as BASIC and Pascal, and p-System compilers translate them into an interim p-code, which is executed by an interpreter in the target machine.

UHF (Ultra High Frequency) A range of electromagnetic frequencies from 300MHz to 3GHz.

UI See *UNIX International.*

UIMX (User Interface Management System for X Window) Software from Visual Edge Software that allows a user to design and modify a user interface while the application is running. UIMX provides this capability for AT&T's Open Look interface and eventually OSF/Motif.

ultimate wafer A semiconductor wafer that contains an integrated set of circuits throughout its entire surface. See *wafer scale integration.*

ultrafiche Pronounced "ultra feesh." A microfiche that holds up to 1,000 document pages per 4x6" sheet of film. Normal microfiche stores around 270 pages.

ultraviolet A band of invisible radiation within the light spectrum, but just before visible light. It takes about 10 minutes of ultraviolet light to erase an EPROM chip.

Ultrix A version of the UNIX operating system from Digital Equipment Corporation that runs on its VAX and PDP-11 line of computers.

unary Meaning one; a single entity or operation, or an expression that requires only one operand.

unbundled Separate prices for each component in a system. Contrast with *bundled*.

unconditional branch In programming, a GOTO, BRANCH or JUMP instruction that passes control to a different part of the program. Constrast with *conditional branch*.

undelete To restore the last delete operation that has taken place. In word processing, there may be more than one level of undelete, allowing several or all previous deletions to be restored.

In order to undelete a file that has been deleted in Microsoft's DOS operating system, a separate utility program is required, and it must be used before any additional data has been recorded on the disk.

underflow

(1) An error condition that occurs when the result of a computation is smaller than the smallest quantity the computer can store.

(2) An error condition that occurs when an item is called from an empty stack.

undo To restore the last editing operation that has taken place. For example, if a segment of text has been deleted or changed, performing an undo will restore the original text. Programs may have several levels of undo, including being able to reconstruct the original data for all edits performed in the current session.

Unibus A bus architecture from Digital that was introduced in 1970 along with its PDP-11 computers. Unibus peripherals can be connected to a VAX computer through Unibus attachments on the VAXs.

unidirectional The transfer or transmission of data in a channel in one direction only.

Unisys (Unisys Corporation) A computer company formed in 1986 as a merger of the Burroughs and Sperry corporations. This was the largest merger in the computer field and one of the largest industrial mergers in history.

Sperry started in 1933 in the navigational guidance and control equipment business. In 1955, it merged with Remington Rand to form Sperry Rand. Five years earlier, Remington Rand had acquired the Eckert-Mauchly Computer Corporation, founded by J. Presper Eckert and Dr. John W. Mauchly, who guided the development of the ENIAC. In 1951, Remington Rand introduced the UNIVAC I, which became the first commercially successful general-purpose computer.

Throughout the 1960s and 1970s, Sperry became known for its large-scale mainframes in commercial and government installations, providing communications and realtime systems for the military and NASA. In 1971, it absorbed RCA's Spectra 70 computer line and provided support and maintenance for the products until they phased into obsolescence.

Burroughs started out as a maker of calculating machines and cash registers in 1886. It was first involved with computers by supplying memory for the ENIAC in 1952. A decade later, it introduced the B5000 computer system, which quickly became known for its advanced timesharing and virtual memory operating systems. Burroughs' B series computers became firmly entrenched in the banking and financial industries in the 1960s and 1970s.

BURROUGHS ADDING MACHINE (CIRCA 1895)
(Courtesy Smithsonian Institution)

Unisys continues to emphasize both product lines in their respective niches. Large Burroughs mainframes were renamed the A Series while the smaller ones were renamed the V Series. Sperry product lines were renamed the 1100 and System 80 series. In 1987, the 2200 series replaced the 1100 series.

Unisys offers the 5000, 6000 and 7000 series of minicomputers as well as a complete line of PC-based products. It also supports the UNIX operating system from micro to mainframe.

In 1988, it acquired Convergent Technologies, a prominent workstation vendor, and Timeplex, the leader in T1 networking equipment.

Since the merger, Unisys has concentrated on providing integrated solutions to vertical markets, such as financial, airlines and communications. Its commercial base accounts for about 78% of revenues, and the rest is derived from defense contracts.

unit record equipment Same as *tabulating equipment*.

UNIVAC I (UNIVersal Automatic Computer) The first commercially-successful computer, introduced in 1951 by Remington Rand. Over 40 systems were sold. Its memory was made of mercury-filled acoustic delay lines that held 1,000 12-digit numbers. It used magnetic tapes that stored 1MB of data at a density of 128cpi.

In 1952, it predicted Eisenhower's victory over Stevenson, and UNIVAC became synonymous with computer, at least, for a while. See photograph on the following page.

UNIVAC I
(Courtesy Unisys)

UNIX A multiuser, multitasking operating system from AT&T that runs on a wide variety of computer systems from micro to mainframe. UNIX is written in C (also developed at AT&T), which is a language designed for system-level programming. It is C's inherent transportability that allows UNIX to run on so many different computers.

UNIX is made up of the kernel, the heart of the operating system, the file system, a hierarchical directory method for organizing files on the disk and the shell, the user interface which provides the way the user commands the system. Normal UNIX commands are very cryptic but they can be replaced with shells that are easier to use, including graphical user interfaces (GUIs), such as X Window, Open Look and OSF/Motif. The following list shows typical UNIX commands with their Microsoft DOS counterparts:

Command	UNIX	DOS
List directory	ls	dir
Copy a file	cp	copy
Delete a file	rm	del
Rename a file	mv	rename
Display contents	cat	type
Print a file	lpr	print
Check disk space	df	chkdsk

The History of UNIX

UNIX was developed in 1969 by Ken Thompson for the PDP-7. Additional work was done by Dennis Ritchie, and, by 1974, UNIX had matured into a state-of-the-art operating system primarily running on PDP computers. UNIX became very popular in scientific and academic environments.

Considerable enhancements were made to UNIX at the University of California at Berkeley, and versions of UNIX include the Berkeley extensions, which became widely used on Digital's VAX systems. By the late 1970s, commercial versions of UNIX, such as IS/1 and XENIX, became available.

In the early 1980s, AT&T began to consolidate the many versions of UNIX into standards which evolved into System III and eventually System V. Before divestiture (1984), AT&T licensed UNIX to universities and other organizations, but was prohibited from outright marketing of the product. After divestiture, it began to market UNIX aggressively.

In January 1989, the UNIX Software Operation was formed as a separate division devoted exclusively to the product. In November 1989, it introduced the most significant release of UNIX: System V Release 4.0, which incorporates XENIX, Sun OS, Berkeley 4.3BSD and System V into one standard. AT&T's SVID (System V Interface Definition) specifies the requirements for UNIX compatibility. In June 1990, UNIX Software Operation was turned into UNIX System Laboratories, Inc., a subsidiary of AT&T.

The name UNIX was coined for a single-user (un) version of MULTICS, as it was intended to be a scaled-down version of that very elaborate operating system. Ironically today, UNIX's multiuser capabilities are one of its most important features. See *UNIX International, X/Open, OSF* and *POSIX.*

UNIX International
An independent, international, non-profit industry association funded by its members to promote and provide future direction of the UNIX System V operating system. It has over 130 members and works closely with X/Open. For more information, contact UNIX International, 20 Waterview Blvd., Parsippany, NJ 07054, (201) 263-8400.

unload
To remove a program from memory or take a tape or disk out of its drive.

unmark
(1) In word processing, to deselect a block of text, which usually removes its highlight.

(2) To deselect an item that has been tagged for a particular purpose.

unpack
See *pack.*

UPC
(Universal Product Code) The standard bar code that is printed on retail merchandise. It contains the vendor's identification number and the product number, which is read by passing the bar code over a scanner.

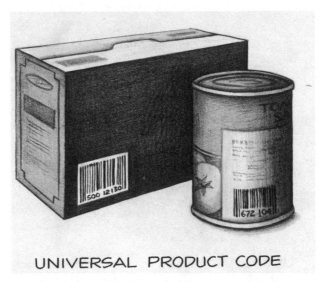

UNIVERSAL PRODUCT CODE

update To change data in a file or database. Update and edit are often used synonymously; however edit implies changing existing data, while update also implies adding and deleting records.

upload To transmit data from a personal computer or workstation to a central computer or file server. Upload implies transmitting a block of data rather than an interactive session. Contrast with *download*.

UPS (Uninterruptible Power Supply) Backup power for a computer system when the electrical power fails or drops to an unacceptable voltage level. Small UPS systems provide battery power for only a few minutes; enough to power down the computer in an orderly manner. Sophisticated systems are tied to electrical generators and can provide power for days.

A UPS system can be interconnected with a file server in a local area network so that, in the event of a problem, all users in the network can be alerted to save files and shut down immediately.

An online UPS provides a constant source of electrical power from the battery, while the batteries are being recharged from AC power. An offline UPS, also known as a standby power system (SPS), switches to battery within a few milliseconds after detecting a power failure.

A surge protector filters out surges and spikes, and a voltage regulator maintains uniform voltage during a brownout, but a UPS keeps a computer running when there is no electrical power. UPS systems typically provide surge suppression and may also provide voltage regulation.

uptime The time during which a system is working without failure. Contrast with *downtime*.

upward compatible Also called *forward compatible*. Refers to larger or newer models of a computer that can run the same software as smaller or earlier models. Contrast with *downward compatible*.

user Any individual who interacts with the computer at an application level. Programmers, operators and other technical personnel are not considered users when working in a professional capacity on the computer.

user area A reserved part of a disk or memory for user data.

user defined Any format, layout, structure or language that is developed by the user.

user friendly A system that is easy to learn and easy to use. This term has been so abused that many vendors are reluctant to use it.

user group An organization of users of a particular hardware or software product. Members share experiences and ideas to improve their understanding and use of a particular product. User groups are often responsible for influencing vendors to change or enhance their products.

user interface A combination of menus, screen design, keyboard commands, command language and help screens, which together create the way a user interacts with a computer. Hardware, such as a mouse and touch screen, are also included.

A well-designed user interface is vital to the success of a software package. In time, interactive video, voice recognition and natural language understanding will dramatically change current-day user interfaces. See *Macintosh user interface* and *Lotus menu*.

USL (UNIX System Laboratories, Inc.) A subsidiary of AT&T, formed in June 1990, that develops, produces, licenses and distributes operating systems technology, including the UNIX System V operating system.

USO (UNIX Software Operation) The name of AT&T's UNIX division before it was turned into the UNIX System Laboratories subsidiary in June 1990.

USRT (Universal Synchronous Receiver Transmitter) An electronic circuit that transmits and receives data on the serial port. It converts bytes into serial bits for transmission, and vice versa, and generates the necessary signals for synchronous transmission.

utility program A program that supports the operation of the computer. Utility programs, or simply utilities, provide file management capabilities, such as sorting, copying, comparing, listing and searching, as well as diagnostic and measurement routines that check the health and performance of the computer system.

UVC A set of video capture/display boards from UVC Corporation designed for videoconferencing and other types of video transmission. The boards fit into an AT-class machine and provide extensive compression/decompression in realtime. A complete VP-2000 workstation is also available. Compressed files can be decompressed on VGA-equipped AT-class machines using software only.

V Series

(1) A line of small to medium-scale mainframes from Unisys. It is a new name for the B2500 and B3500 product lines from Burroughs that were originally introduced in 1966.

(2) See *Hayes V-series*.

VAC (Volts Alternating Current) See *volt* and AC.

vacuum tube An electronic device that controls the flow of electrons in a vacuum and is used as a switch, amplifier or display screen. Used as on/off switches, they allowed the first computers to perform digital computations. Today, it is primarily used as the CRT in monitors and TVs.

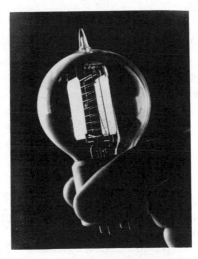

VACUUM TUBE (1915)
(Courtesy AT&T)

CRT   AMPLIFIER OR SWITCH

VACUUM TUBES

VAD (Value Added Dealer) Same as VAR *(value added reseller)*.

Valdocs (VALuable DOCumentS) An earlier word processor from Epson America, Inc., that ran on its QX-10 computer and provided text, calculation, drawing and calendar functions. It was introduced in 1982 with the HASCI keyboard, which provided dedicated keys for common tasks.

validity checking A set of routines in a data entry program that tests the input for correct and reasonable conditions, such as numbers falling within a range and correct spelling, if possible. See *check digit*.

value

(1) The content of a field or variable. It can refer to alphabetic as well as numeric data. For example, in the expression, `state = "PA"`, PA is a value.

(2) In spreadsheets, the numeric data within the cell.

value-added network A communications network that provides services beyond normal transmission, such as automatic error detection and correction, protocol conversion and message storing and forwarding. Telenet and Tymnet are examples of value-added networks.

VAN See *value-added network*.

VAP (Value Added Process) A program that enhances or provides additional server functions in a NetWare 286 server. Support for different kinds of workstations, database engines, fax and print servers are examples. In NetWare 386, the VAP is called a NetWare Loadable Module (NLM).

vaporware Software that has been advertised but not delivered.

VAR (Value Added Reseller) An organization that adds value to a system and resells it. For example, a VAR could purchase a computer and peripherals from different vendors and a graphics software package from another vendor and package it all together as a specialized CAD system. See *OEM*.

variable In programming, a structure that holds data and is uniquely named by the programmer. It holds the data assigned to it until a new value is assigned to it or until the program is finished.

Variables are used to hold control values. For example, in the C statement: `for (x=0; x<5; x++)`, x is a variable that is set to zero (x=0), incremented (x++) and tested five times (x<5) to perform an operation. Variables are also used to hold items of data temporarily while they're being processed.

Variables are usually assigned with an equal sign; for example, `counter = 1`, places a 1 in the variable COUNTER. Unquoted data is used for numeric data: `counter = 1`, while character data requires quotes: `product = "A4326"`.

In some languages, the type of data must be declared before it is assigned, for example, in C, the statement, `int counter;` creates a numeric variable that will only hold whole numbers.

A local variable is one that can be referenced only within the subprogram, function or procedure it was defined in. A global variable can be used by the entire program.

variable length field

A record structure that holds fields of varying lengths. For example, PAT SMITH would take up nine bytes and GEORGINA WILSON BARTHOLOMEW would take up 27 bytes of storage. A couple of bytes of control information would also be added. If fixed length fields were used in this example, 27 or more bytes would have to be reserved for every name.

There's more programming with variable length fields, because every record has to be separated into fixed length fields after it is brought into memory. Conversely, each record has to be coded into the variable length format before it is written to disk.

The same storage savings can be achieved by compressing data on its way to the disk, and decompressing it when it comes back. All the blank spaces in fixed length fields will be filtered out; however, unless this method is integrated into the operating system, it may provide unacceptable performance.

Each data field is preceded by an identification field that indicates its length.

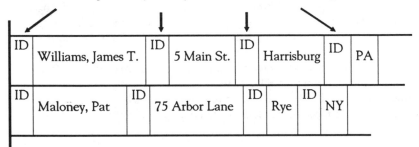

ID	Williams, James T.	ID	5 Main St.	ID	Harrisburg	ID	PA
ID	Maloney, Pat	ID	75 Arbor Lane	ID	Rye	ID	NY

VARIABLE LENGTH FIELDS/RECORDS

variable length record

A record that contains one or more variable length fields.

VAX

(Virtual Address eXtension) A family of 32-bit computers from Digital Equipment Corporation introduced in 1977 with the VAX-11/780 model. VAX machines range from desktop personal computers to large-scale mainframes. Large VAX computers can be clustered together to provide a multiprocessing environment serving thousands of online users.

All VAXs use the same VMS operating system, and programs running on one VAX can run on any other. VAX systems also provide a compatibility mode for running PDP software. Due to its compatible architecture, the VAX family achieved outstanding success throughout the 1980s.

VAXcluster A group of VAX computers that are coupled together in a multiprocessing environment.

VAXELN A realtime operating environment for VAX computers from Digital Equipment Corporation. It runs on a VAX under VMS and provides application development in Pascal and other languages. The resulting programs are downloaded into the target systems.

VAXmate A partially IBM-compatible PC from Digital Equipment Corporation introduced in 1986, which has been superseded by the DECstation 200 and 300 series in 1989.

VAXstation A single-user VAX computer that runs under VMS introduced in 1988.

VCPI (Virtual Control Program Interface) A DOS-extender specification that allows multiple real mode programs and multiple DOS-extended programs to run at the same time in 386 and higher machines. See *DPMI*.

VCR (Video Cassette Recorder) A videotape recording and playback machine that comes in several formats. One inch tape is used for mastering video recordings. Sony Umatic 3/4" tape is widely used for commercial training. VHS 1/2" tape, first used in the home, is now widely used in industry. Sony's 1/2" Beta tape, the first home VCR, is now defunct, although many units are in use.

Although VCRs are analog recording machines, they are used to back up computer files and can store digital data with a special adapter.

Honeywell's Very Large Archive Server is a VCR juke box that is used for data storage. It uses VHS tapes that hold 5.3GB of data per cassette.

VDI (Virtual Device Interface) An ANSI standard format for creating device drivers. For example, if a vendor sells a screen display and adapter board with a proprietary resolution, and also includes a driver written in the VDI format, software packages that support VDI will be able to use the new monitor.

The VDI standard has been incorporated into the CGI standard. When CGI is officially endorsed by ANSI, it may supersede VDI.

VDISK (Virtual disk) A RAM disk that was released with IBM's version 3.0 of DOS. As the first program to use extended memory, VDISK did not provide a method for sharing extended memory with other programs.

VDM See CGM.

VDT (Video Display Terminal) A terminal with a keyboard and a video display screen.

VDU (Video Display Unit) Same as *VDU*.

vector
(1) In computer graphics, a line designated by its end points (x-y or x-y-z coordinates). When a circle is drawn, it is made up of many small vectors.

(2) In matrix algebra, a one-row matrix.

vector display A display terminal that draws vectors on the screen. Contrast with *raster display*.

vector graphics In computer graphics, a technique for representing a picture as points, lines and other geometric entities. See *graphics*. Contrast with *raster graphics*.

vector processor A computer with built-in instructions that perform multiple calculations on vectors (one-dimensional arrays) simultaneously. It is used to solve the same or similar problems as an array processor; however, a vector processor passes a vector to a functional unit, whereas an array processor passes each element of a vector to a different arithmetic unit. See *pipeline processing* and *array processor*.

Vectra Hewlett-Packard's trade name for its line of PCs. The Vectras are noted for their ruggedness and reliability.

Venn diagram A graphic technique for visualizing set theory concepts using overlapping circles and shading to indicate intersection, union and complement.

Ventura Publisher A desktop publishing program for PCs from Ventura Software, Inc. (a Xerox company), that provides full-scale pagination for large documents. It is designed to import data created in other graphics and word processing programs, although it does have its own rudimentary text and graphics creation capabilities. Ventura comes with a run time version of the GEM environment.
      Version 2.0 introduced a Professional Extension option that provides table and equation creation, vertical justification, more extensive cross-referencing and an expanded hyphenation dictionary. The Network Server option allows users to edit and browse chapters simultaneously.
      The Ventura Publisher Gold Series includes the above options and provides versions for Windows and OS/2 PM, as well as GEM.

verify In data entry operations, to compare the keystrokes of a second operator with the files created by the first operator.

VersaCAD A family of CAD systems for PCs and the Macintosh from VersaCAD Corporation. It is a fully-integrated system that features 2-D geometric and construction drafting and 3-D modeling with 16 viewports. It has an extensive number of features including complete programmability and universal CAD communications. The Macintosh version includes CAD-oriented HyperCard stacks, including bill of materials.

version control The management of the source code of a large software project. Version-control software provides a database that keeps track of the revisions made to a program by all the programmers involved in it.

version number The identification of a release of a software package. The difference between version 2.2 and 2.3 can be night and day, since new releases not only add new features, but more often than not correct annoying bugs. That means the problem that's been driving you crazy may have been fixed.

Version number 1.0 drives terror into the hearts of experienced users, since it means that the program has just been released, and bugs are still to be uncovered after extensive customer use.

Version numbers, such as 3.1a or 3.11, indicate a follow-up release only to fix a bug in the previous version, whereas 3.1 and 3.2 usually indicate routine enhancements in the product.

vertical recording A magnetic recording method that records the bits vertically instead of horizontally, taking up less space and providing greater storage capacity. The vertical recording method uses a specialized material for the construction of the disk.

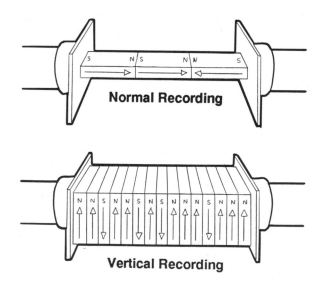

Normal Recording

Vertical Recording

vertical refresh The number of times an entire display screen is refreshed in one second. The typical frequency for a computer screen is around 70Hz (70 times per second). A TV is refreshed 60 half-frames per second (interlaced) resulting in 30 full frames per second. Contrast with *scan rate*.

vesicular film A film that is used to make copies of microfilm or microfiche. It contains its own developer and creates a pink negative or positive copy when exposed to a negative master through ultraviolet light.

VGA (Video Graphics Array) A video display standard from IBM that is built into high-end models of IBM's PS/2 series and provides medium to high resolution text and graphics. VGA has become the preferred video standard, and boards are commonly available for all PC and AT-bus machines.

VGA supports previous display standards and requires an analog RGB monitor. It has 16 colors in its highest graphics mode (640x480), but vendors have boosted the colors to 256 and have added a higher-resolution "Super VGA" 800x600 mode.

The Video Electronics Standards Association (VESA) has set a standard for Super VGA; an important step, as many independent versions have been developed. See *PC display modes*.

VHD (Very High Density) Floppy disk technologies that place 20MB and more of data on a 3.5" disk. See *Floptical*.

VHF (Very High Frequency) A range of electromagnetic frequencies from 30 million to 300 million Hz.

VHSIC (Very High Speed Integrated Circuit) Pronounced "vizik." Ultra-high-speed chips employing LSI and VLSI technologies.

video The audio/visual playback and recording technology used in the TV industry. It also refers to computer screens and terminals. However, there is only one TV/video standard in the U.S., but there are dozens of computer/video display standards.

video adapter Same as *video display board*.

video board Same as *video display board*.

video camera A camera that takes continuous pictures and generates a signal for display or recording. It captures images by breaking down the image into a series of lines. Each line is scanned one at a time, and the continuously varying intensities of red, green and blue light across the line are filtered out and converted into a variable

FIRST TV STAR
(Courtesy RCA)
One of the first video images ever seen.

signal. The standard signal of 525 scan lines used in the U.S. and Canada is governed by the NTSC.

Most video cameras are analog, but digital video cameras are also available. See *digital camera.*

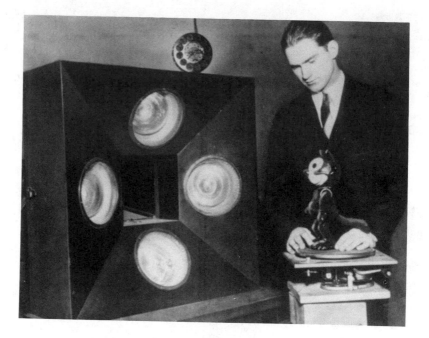

VIDEO CAMERA
(Courtesy RCA)
In the late 1920s, Felix the Cat was one of the first video recording stars.

video card Same as *video display board.*

video codec A circuit that converts NTSC video into digital code and vice versa. It incorporates a compression technique to reduce the data and may or may not provide full-motion video.

video digitizer Same as *frame grabber.*

video display board A printed circuit board that plugs into a personal computer and generates the text and graphics images on a monitor's display screen. Also called a *display adapter* or *graphics adapter*, it is responsible for the resolution quality and number of colors that can appear on screen.

It converts the characters or graphic patterns (bit map) within a reserved segment of the computer's memory into signals that are used to refresh the display screen. In digital display systems, the video display board generates digital signals for the monitor. The monitor then does the conversion from digital to analog. In analog systems, the video display board does the digital to analog conversion and sends analog signals to the monitor.

The monitor must be capable of handling the frequency range of the display board (number of lines per second). Multisync monitors can accept a range of frequencies and work with more than one type of display standard. Following are the major categories of video output that can be generated:

Monochrome Display Systems

Digital
Analog

Color Display Systems

Digital RGB
Analog composite
Analog RGB
Analog RGB with NTSC video input and output (see *video graphics board*)

video display card Same as *video display board*.

video display terminal/unit Same as *video terminal*.

video editor A dedicated computer that controls two or more videotape machines for editing purposes. It keeps track of frame numbers in its own database and switches the recording machine from playback to record. The video editor does accept video signals; only SMPTE time codes that are provided on professional tape formats.

video graphics board A video display board that generates text and graphics and accepts video from a camera or VCR. Truevision's Targa board and Vision Technologies Vision board are examples.

The terms video graphics board and video display board sound alike, but video display boards (display adapters) do not handle NTSC video.

Video Overlay Card A video graphics board for Apple IIe and IIGS computers from Apple Computer. It includes Video Mix software that allows text, graphics and animation to be overlaid onto NTSC video images through the use of color keying.

video RAM A specially designed memory that is used to hold and transfer an image onto the video screen. The video RAM contains a certain amount of processing logic that converts the pixel data onto the screen in the required format.

video teleconferencing See *teleconferencing*.

video terminal A data entry device that uses a keyboard for input and a display screen for output. Although the display screen resembles a TV, it usually does not accept TV/video signals.

videodisc A read-only optical disc that holds up to two hours of video data. Like a phonograph record and CD player, most videodisc players provide direct access to any location on the disc.

Various videodisc systems were introduced during the 1970s, but only the LaserVision optical disc technology has survived. As of 1990, videodiscs have barely made a dent in the home market, where VCRs are commonplace. It appears that videotapes will continue to be the major video recording and playback medium until such time as an erasable optical system can be economically mass produced. Videodiscs are used for interactive instructional training courses, however.

Videodiscs used for movies use a constant linear velocity (CLV) format that records the signal on a continuous, spiraling track, as does a phonograph record. In addition, the signal density is uniform, and the player increases or decreases the speed of rotation depending on which part of the disc is being played.

Videodiscs used for interactive purposes use a constant angular velocity (CAV) format like that of a magnetic disk, in which the tracks are concentric circles, each one containing one frame of video. Each side of a CAV videodisc holds 54,000 frames, which is 30 minutes of continuous video at 30 frames per second.

Videodiscs are recorded in an analog format like videotape.

videotex An interactive information technology that includes shopping, banking, news, weather and electronic mail services. It can also provide a gateway to other timesharing and information services.

It is delivered over a telephone line to a decoder, which contains a keyboard attached to the subscriber's TV. Videotex information is stored in the decoder and is displayed as predefined screens, or frames, which can be retrieved by number or by menu selection. Due to the low bandwidth of telephone lines, videotex delivers simple graphics and limited animation.

Although videotex experiments have been tried in various parts of the U.S., it has yet to catch on.

view
(1) To display and look at data on screen.

(2) In relational database management, a special display of data that is created as needed. A view temporarily ties two or more files together so that the combined files can be displayed, printed or queried. For example, customers and orders or vendors and purchases can be linked. All the fields to be included are specified by the user. The original files are not permanently linked or altered; however, if the system allows the viewed data to be directly edited, the data in the original files will be changed.

Viewdata British term for videotex.

---

viewer See *file viewer*.

VINES (VIrtual NEtworking System) A UNIX System V-based network operating system from Banyan Systems Inc., that runs on DOS and OS/2-based servers. It provides internetworking of PCs, minis, mainframes and other computer resources providing information sharing across organizations of unlimited size.

Incorporating mainframe-like security with a global directory service, VINES lets users access all other users and resources on the network regardless of location. Options include printer sharing, e-mail, remote PC dial-in access, bridges and gateways.

virtual A simulated or conceptual environment, which, as a result, may refer to virtually anything.

virtual 86 An operational mode in Intel 386 and higher CPUs that allows it to perform as multiple 8086 CPUs. Each virtual machine runs an application under its own copy of DOS or other operating system, and all virtual machines are multitasked together.

virtual circuit The resulting pathway that is created between two devices communicating with each other in a packet switching system. A message from NY to LA may actually start in New York and go through Atlanta, St. Louis, Denver and Phoenix before it winds up in Los Angeles.

virtual device Same as *virtual peripheral*.

virtual disk A disk that is simulated in memory. See *RAM disk*.

virtual image In graphics, the complete graphic image stored in memory, not just the part of it that is displayed at the current time.

virtual machine
(1) A computer that runs multiple operating systems with each operating system running its own programs; for example, an IBM mainframe running under VM or a 386-based personal computer running multiple DOS applications in its virtual mode.

(2) One operating system and its associated application programs running within a virtual machine environment.

(3) A computer that uses virtual memory in contrast with one that does not.

virtual memory A technique that simulates more memory than actually exists and allows the computer to run several programs concurrently regardless of their size.

The virtual memory system breaks up a program into segments, called *pages*. Instead of bringing the entire program into memory, it brings as many pages into memory as it can fit based on the current mix of programs, and leaves the remaining pages on disk. When instructions are called for that are not in memory, the appropriate disk page is called in, overlaying the page in memory.

If a memory page contains variables or other data that are altered by the running of the program, then the page is temporarily stored on disk when room is needed for new pages. The input and output of program pages is called *paging* or *swapping*.

In order to take total advantage of virtual memory techniques, programs should not contain a lot of spaghetti code, in which the logic of the program points back and forth to opposite ends of the program. If they do, *thrashing* will result, which is an excessive amount of disk accesses to bring in program segments. Disk access should be reserved for calling in the next set of data, not the same instructions over and over again.

Although virtual memory can be implemented in software, for efficient operation, virtual memory requires specialized hardware features.

Application programs sometimes claim virtual memory capability, but only use some sort of swapping technique to run large programs, not true virtual memory.

virtual networking As defined by Banyan Systems, the ability for users to transparently communicate locally and remotely across similar and dissimilar networks through a simple and consistent user interface.

virtual peripheral A peripheral device that is simulated by the operating system. For example, if a program is ready to output to the printer, but a printer is not available, the operating system will transfer the printer output to disk and keep it there until a printer becomes available.

virtual processing A parallel processing technique that simulates a processor for applications that require a processor for each data element. It creates virtual processors for data elements above and beyond the number of processors available.

virtual processor A simulated processor in a virtual processing system.

virtual reality A computer-simulated reality that can interact with all the senses. See *cyberspace*.

virtual route Same as *virtual circuit*.

virtual storage Same as *virtual memory*.

virus A program that is used to infect a computer. After the virus code is written, it is buried within an existing program. Once that program is executed, the virus code is also activated and it attaches copies of itself to other programs in the system. Whenever an infected program is run, the virus copies itself to other programs.

The purpose of the virus can range from a simple prank that pops up a message on the screen out of the blue, to the actual destruction of programs and data that may occur at any time in the future.

A virus cannot be attached to data. It must be attached to a runnable program that is downloaded into or installed in the computer. The virus-attached program must be executed in order to activate the virus. See *worm*.

VIS (Voice Information Service) A variety of voice processing service applications.

VisiCalc The first electronic spreadsheet. It was introduced in 1978 for the Apple II. Conceived by Dan Bricklin, a Harvard student,

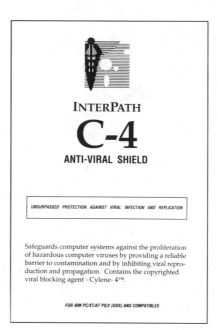

VIRUS PROTECTION

(Courtesy InterPath)

Users are very happy to install a software package such as this one in order to protect themselves from "disease."

and programmed by a friend, Bob Frankston, it became a major success. VisiCalc launched an industry and was almost entirely responsible for the Apple II being used in business. Thousands of $3,000 Apples were bought just to run the $150 VisiCalc program.

VisiCalc was a command-driven program that was soon followed by SuperCalc, MultiPlan and a host of others, each one improving the user interface. Eventually Lotus 1-2-3 dominated the spreadsheet market for PCs, and Microsoft Excel for the Macintosh. Spreadsheets have also been implemented on minis and mainframes, and it all started with VisiCalc.

visualization In computer graphics, the converting of numeric data into picture form to allow humans to recognize patterns that are difficult to identify in numeric form. It is used especially in research situations, both theoretical and practical.

VLSI

(1) (Very Large Scale Integration) Refers to the very large number of electronic transistors and other components that are built onto a single chip. VLSI is in the range of approximately 100,000 to 1,000,000 components per chip.

(2) *VLSI Technology, Inc.*, is a designer and manufacturer of customized computer chips.

VM See VM/SP.

VM/386 (Virtual Machine/386) A multitasking operating environment for 386 machines from IGC Corporation. It uses the 386's virtual 86 mode which allows multiple copies of DOS to run in the machine, each running its own application.

VM/386 MultiUser Starter creates a three-user system from one 386 with the addition of two terminals or PCs connected to the 386 via serial ports. Each user runs in a virtual machine within the 386.

VM/SP (Virtual Machine System Product) An operating system that runs on IBM mainframes. Originally developed by IBM customers, VM/SP has been adopted by IBM as a major system product. VM/SP has the ability of running multiple operating systems within the computer at the same time, each operating system running its own programs.

VM/SP Technical Workstation
An IBM PS/2 computer with extended 370 programming capability. It runs the VM/SP operating system that is downloaded from the mainframe in conjunction with normal PS/2 operations.

VMEbus (VersaModule Eurocard bus) A 32-bit bus developed by Motorola, Signetics, Mostek and Thompson CSF. It is widely used in industrial, commercial and military applications with over 300 manufacturers of VMEbus products worldwide.

VMS
(1) (Virtual Memory System) VMS is a multiuser, multitasking, virtual memory operating system from Digital Equipment Corporation which runs on its VAX line of computers. Any application program running under VMS will run on any VAX computer from the smallest MicroVAX to the largest VAX model.

(2) (Voice Messaging System) See *voice mail*.

voice channel A transmission channel or subchannel that carries human voice.

voice coil A type of motor that is used to move the access arm of a disk drive in very small increments. Like the voice coil of a speaker, the amount of current determines the amount of movement. Contrast with *stepper motor*, which works in fixed increments.

voice grade Refers to the bandwidth required to transmit human voice, which is usually about 4,000 Hz.

voice mail A computerized voice store and forward system (like a telephone answering system) that digitizes incoming voice messages and stores them on disk. Voice mail usually provides auto attendant capability, which uses prerecorded messages to route the caller to the appropriate person, department or mail box.

voice messaging The use of voice mail as an alternative to electronic mail, in which voice messages are intentionally recorded, not because the recipient was not available.

voice processing The computerized handling of voice, which includes voice store and forward, voice response, voice recognition and text to speech technologies.

voice recognition The conversion of spoken words into computer text. Speech is first digitized and then matched against a dictionary of coded waveforms. The matches are converted into text as if the words were typed on the keyboard.

Speaker-dependent systems must be trained before using, by taking samples of actual words from the person who will use it. Speaker-independent systems can recognize limited vocabularies such as numeric digits and a handful of words. In the telephone companies, these systems will begin to replace the human operator for services, such as collect and credit card calls, for example.

In the future, voice recognition systems will be able to understand large vocabularies from just about anybody; however, it could be well past the turn of the century before voice recognition is part of every computer system.

voice response The generation of voice output by computer. It provides pre-recorded information either with or without selection by the caller. Interactive voice response allows interactive manipulation of a database. See *audiotex*.

voice store and forward The technology behind voice mail and messaging systems. Human voice is digitized, stored in the computer, possibly forwarded to another mail box, and retrieved by the called party.

volatile memory Memory that does not hold its contents without power. A computer's main memory, made up of dynamic RAM or static RAM chips, loses its content immediately upon loss of power.

volt A unit of measurement of force, or pressure, in an electrical circuit. The common voltage of an AC power line is 120 volts of alternating current (alternating directions). Common voltages within a computer are from 5 to 12 volts of direct current (one direction only).

volt-amps The measurement of electrical usage that is computed by multiplying volts times amps. See *watts*.

voltage regulator A device that is used to maintain a level amount of voltage in the electrical line. Contrast with *surge suppressor*, which filters out excessive amounts of current, and contrast with *UPS*, which provides backup power in the event of a power failure.

volume

(1) A physical storage unit, such as a hard disk, floppy disk, disk cartridge or reel of tape.

(2) A logical storage unit that spans some number of physical drives.

von Neumann architecture
A computer that stores its own instructions and acts upon them sequentially; the stored program concept. Hungarian-born John von Neumann (1903-1957), an internationally renowned mathematician, promoted this concept in the 1940s.

The term is often used to refer to the sequential nature of current-day computers. An instruction is analyzed; data is processed. The next instruction is analyzed, and so on.

VP/ix
See *SCO VP/ix.*

VP-Planner Plus
A relational spreadsheet and data analysis program for PCs from Paperback Software. It is keystroke, file and macro compatible with all versions of Lotus 1-2-3, while providing additional features, such as background recalculation, the ability to manipulate a variety of disk-based database files, and a built-in word processor and report generator. It includes a multi-dimensional database that stores categories of data in up to five dimensions. The spreadsheet program is used as an interface to both enter and retrieve data from the multi-dimensional file.

VP ratio
(Virtual Processor ratio) The number of virtual processors that a physical processor is simulating.

VPS
(Vectors Per Second) Used to measure the speed of a vector or array processor.

VRAM
See *video RAM.*

VRC
(Vertical Redundancy Check) An error checking method that generates and tests a parity bit for each byte of data that is moved or transmitted.

VROOMM
(Virtual Realtime Object Oriented Memory Manager) A compiler technology from Borland that allows programs to be broken up into very small routines which are brought into memory as needed.

VRX
The operating system used on NCR's V8500 and V8600 mainframes.

VS

(1) (Virtual Storage) Same as *virtual memory.*

(2) (Virtual Storage) A family of minicomputers from Wang Laboratories, Inc., introduced in 1977, which use virtual storage techniques.

VSAM (Virtual Storage Access Method) An IBM access method for storing data, which is widely used in IBM mainframes. It uses the B+tree method for organizing data.

VSAT (Very Small Aperture satellite Terminal) Small earth stations for satellite transmission that handle up to 56,000 bits of digital transmission per second. VSATs that can handle the T1 data rate of up to 1.544mbps are called TSATs.

VSX (Verification Suite for X/Open) A testing procedure from X/Open that verifies complance with their endorsed standards. VSX3 has over 5,500 tests for compliance with XPG3.

VT 100, 200... (Video Terminal) A series of asynchronous display terminals from Digital that are used on its PDP and VAX computers. They are available in text and graphics models in both monochrome and color.

VTAM (Virtual Telecommunications Access Method) Also called ACF/VTAM (Advanced Communications Function/VTAM). Software that controls communications in an IBM SNA environment. It usually resides in the mainframe under MVS or VM, but may be offloaded into a front end processor that is tightly coupled to the mainframe. It supports a wide variety of network protocols, including SDLC and Token Ring. VTAM can be thought of as the network operating system of SNA.

VTR (Video Tape Recorder) A video recording and playback machine that uses reels of magnetic tape. Contrast with VCR, which uses tape cassettes.

Vulcan A dBASE-like programming language from Ratliff Software Productions, Inc., that runs under the Emerald Bay database engine. It was first introduced in 1988 by Migent, Inc., under the name Eagle. Vulcan was the original name of dBASE II.

The following example converts fahrenheit to centigrade:

```
ACCEPT "Enter fahrenheit " TO FAHR
? "Centigrade is", (FAHR-32) * 5 / 9
```

VUP (VAX Unit of Performance) A unit of measurement equal to the performance of the VAX 11/780, the first VAX machine.

V.21 CCITT standard (1964) for asynchronous 0-300 bps full-duplex modems for use on dial-up lines. It uses FSK modulation.

V.22 CCITT standard (1980) for asynchronous and synchronous 600 and 1,200 bps full-duplex modems for use on dial-up lines. It uses DPSK modulation.

V.22bis CCITT standard (1984) for asynchronous and synchronous 2,400 bps full-duplex modems for use on dial-up lines and two-wire leased lines, with fallback to V.22 1,200 bps operation. It uses QAM modulation.

V.23 CCITT standard (1964) for asynchronous and synchronous 0-600 and 0-1,200 bps half-duplex modems for use on dial-up lines. It has an optional split-speed transmission method with a reverse channel of 0-75 bps (1,200/75, 75/1,200 bps). It uses FSK modulation.

V.24 CCITT standard (1964) that defines the functions of all circuits for the RS-232 interface. It does not describe the connectors or pin assignments; those are defined in ISO 2110. In the U.S., EIA-232 incorporates the control signal definition of V.24, the electrical characteristics of V.28 and the connector and pin assignments defined in ISO 2110.

V.25 CCITT standard (1968) for automatic calling and/or answering equipment on dial-up lines. It uses parallel circuits and is similar in function to RS-366 and Bell 801 autodialers used in the U.S. The answer tone defined in V.25 is the first thing heard when calling a modem. It serves a dual function of identifying the answering equipment as being a modem and also disabling the echo suppression and echo cancellation equipment in the network so that a full-duplex modem will operate properly.

V.25bis CCITT standard (1968) for automatic calling and/or answering equipment on dial-up lines. It has three modes: asynchronous (rarely used), character-oriented synchronous (bisync) and bit-oriented synchronous (HDLC/SDLC). Both synchronous versions are used in IBM AS/400 and other small-to-medium sized computers that do automatic dialing for remote job entry. Due to the popularity of the Hayes Standard AT Command Set, V.25bis is not used as widely in North America. It does not perform any modem configuration functions and is limited to dialing and answering calls.

V.26 CCITT standard (1968) for synchronous 2,400 bps full-duplex modems for use on four-wire leased lines. It uses DPSK modulation and includes an optional 75 bps back channel.

V.26bis CCITT standard (1972) for synchronous 1,200 and 2,400 bps full-duplex modems for use on dial-up lines. It uses DPSK modulation and includes an optional 75 pbs back channel.

V.26ter CCITT standard (1984) for asynchronous and synchronous 2,400 bps full-duplex modems using DPSK modulation over dial-up and two-wire leased lines. It includes a 1,200 bps fallback speed and uses echo cancellation, permitting a full-duplex modem to send and receive on the same frequency.

V.27 CCITT standard (1972) for synchronous 4,800 bps full-duplex modems for use on four-wire leased lines. It uses DPSK modulation.

V.27bis CCITT standard (1976) for synchronous 2,400 and 4,800 bps full-duplex modems using DPSK modulation for use on four-wire leased lines. The primary difference between V.27 and V.27bis is the addition of an automatic adaptive equalizer.

V.27ter CCITT standard (1976) for synchronous 2,400 and 4,800 bps half-duplex modems using DPSK modulation on dial-up lines. It includes an optional 75 bps back channel. V.27ter is used in Group 3 fax transmission without the back channel.

V.28 CCITT standard (1972) that defines the functions of all circuits for the RS-232 interface. In the U.S., EIA-232 incorporates the electrical signal definitions of V.28, the control signals of V.25 and the connector and pin assignments defined in ISO 2110.

V.29 CCITT standard (1976) for synchronous 4,800, 7,200 and 9,600 bps full-duplex modems using QAM modulation on four-wire leased lines. It has been adapted for Group 3 fax transmission over dial-up lines at 9,600 and 7,200 bps.

V.32 CCITT standard (1984) for asynchronous and synchronous 4,800 and 9,600 bps full-duplex modems using QAM modulation over dial-up or two-wire leased lines. TCM encoding may be optionally added. V.32 uses echo cancellation to achieve full-duplex transmission. V.32bis is a proposed 1990 standard that extends V.32 to 7,200, 12,000 and 14,400 bps and adds additional features.

V.33 CCITT standard (1988) for synchronous 12,000 and 14,400 bps full-duplex modems for use on four-wire leased lines using QAM modulation. It includes an optional time-division multiplexor for sharing the transmission line among multiple terminals.

V.35 CCITT standard (1968) for group band modems that combine the bandwidth of several telephone circuits to achieve high data rates. V.35 has become known as a high-speed RS-232 interface rather than a type of modem. The large, rectangular V.35 connector was never specified in V.35, but has become a de facto standard for a high-speed interface.

V.42 CCITT standard (1989) for modem error correction that uses LAPM as the primary protocol and provides MNP Classes 2 through 4 as an alternative protocol for compatibility.

V.42bis CCITT standard (1989) for modem error correction and data compression. It uses V.42 error correction with a compression technique (British Telecom Lempel Ziv) that increases transmission speed up to four times the bps rating.

V.54 CCITT standard (1976) for various loopback tests that can be incorporated into modems for testing the telephone circuit and isolating transmission problems. Operating modes include local and remote digital loopback and local and remote analog loopback.

V.56 CCITT standard (1972) for a method of testing modems to compare their performance. Newer procedures are under currently under study.

V.110 CCITT standard (1984) that specifies how data terminal equipment (DTE) with asynchronous or synchronous serial interfaces can be supported on an ISDN network. It uses rate adaption, which involves a bit-by-bit alignment between the DTE and the ISDN B channel.

V.120 CCITT standard (1988) that specifies how DTEs with asynchronous or synchronous serial interfaces can be supported on an ISDN network using a protocol (similar to LAP-D) to encapsulate the data to be transmitted. It includes the capability of using statistical multiplexing to share a B channel connection between multiple DTEs.

V8500, V8600 The V8500 and V8600 are series of mainframes manufactured by NCR.

wafer

(1) The base material in chip making. It is a slice, approx. 1/30" thick, from a salami-like silicon crystal from 3 to 6" in diameter. The wafer goes through a series of photomasking, etching and implantation steps. See *chip*.

(2) A small, continuous-loop magnetic tape cartridge that is used for the storage of data.

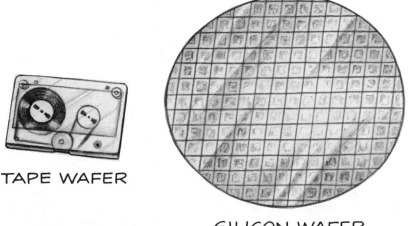

TAPE WAFER

SILICON WAFER

wafer scale integration
The next evolution in semiconductor technology. It builds a gigantic circuit on an entire wafer. Just as the integrated circuit eliminated cutting out thousands of transistors from the wafer only to wire them back again on printed circuit boards, wafer scale integration will eliminate cutting out chips from the wafer only to connect them back again.

However, this next step is a difficult one. Trilogy, formed in 1980 by the famous computer designer Gene Amdahl, was funded with the largest amount of venture capital in the history of the world, yet it failed to achieve wafer scale integration. Trilogy's "superchip" was 2 1/2" square.

Perhaps, we'll have to take more modest steps by creating chips that are 3/4" or 1" square before we can achieve wafer scale integration.

wait state An amount of time spent waiting for some operation to take place. It can refer to a variable length of time a program has to wait before it can be processed, or it may refer to a specific duration of time, such as a machine cycle.

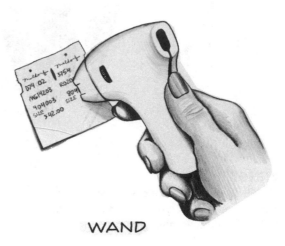

WAND

wand A hand-held optical reader that is used to read typewritten fonts, printed fonts, OCR fonts and bar codes. The wand is waved over each line of characters or codes in a single pass.

Wang (Wang Laboratories, Inc.) A major manufacturer of computers and applications for financial, legal and professional services, manufacturing and government. Founded in 1951 by Dr. An Wang, the company initially produced specialized electronic devices. In the 1960s, it introduced an electronic desk calculator, which became an industry standard by the end of that decade.

In the 1970s, Wang introduced its first word processing systems and computers, which later evolved into the WPS and VS families. By 1978, it was the largest supplier of small business computers in North America and the largest worldwide supplier of CRT-based word processors.

Throughout the 1980s, Wang enhanced its commitment to office automation with the introduction of integrated voice and data networks. In 1987, it introduced its integrated image system, which enable paper documents to be stored, viewed and transmitted on a computer.

For the 1990s, Wang is making its products available on industry-standard hardware platforms while continuing to focus on imaging as a leading technology.

DR. AN WANG
(Courtesy Wang Laboratories)

An Wang came from China to the U.S. in 1945 to study applied physics at Harvard. Six years later, he started the company he guided for almost 40 years. In March 1988, two years before he died, Dr. Wang was inducted into the National Inventors Hall of Fame for his 1948 invention of a pulse transfer device that enabled magnetic core memories to be used in computers. The Hall of Fame has recognized the achievements of an elite group of inventors, which includes Thomas Edison, Louis Pasteur and Alexander Graham Bell.

Wangnet A broadband local area network from Wang Labs that handles data, voice and video.

warm boot A bootstrap operation that is performed after the system has been running.

WANG CALCULATOR (1965)

(Courtesy Wang Laboratories)

Warnier-Orr diagram A graphic charting technique used in software engineering for system analysis and design.

watts A measurement of electrical usage that is obtained by multiplying volts, amps and the power factor (VOLTS x AMPS x POWER FACTOR). The power factor is a number between 0 and 1, which represents 0 to 100% of the useful energy. In electric heaters or incandescent light bulbs, the power factor is 1, or 100%. Because of the switching nature of the power supplies used, computers have a power factor of approximately 60 to 70%, or .6 to .7. Thus, watt ratings for personal computers are less than the traditional computation for watts, which is VOLTS x AMPS.

wave The shape of radiated energy. All radio signals, light rays, x-rays, and cosmic rays radiate an energy that looks likes rippling waves. Try to visualize the wave. Take a piece of paper and start drawing an up and down line very fast while pulling the paper slowly in a direction perpendicular to the line. You should wind up with waves on the paper.

waveform The pattern of a particular sound wave or other electronic signal in analog form.

waveguide A rectangular, circular or elliptical tube through which radio waves are transmitted.

weak typing Programming languages that allow different types of data to be moved freely among data structures, as is found in Smalltalk and other earlier object-oriented languages.

Weitek coprocessor A math coprocessor for micro and minicomputers from Weitek Corporation. Since 1981, the company has been making coprocessors that run on high-performance CAD and graphics workstations. Weitek coprocessors for Intel-based machines run faster than Intel's 80287 and 80387 coprocessors. In order to use the Weitek coprocessor, the software must be written to activate it.

well behaved, well mannered Refers to programs that do not deviate from a standard.

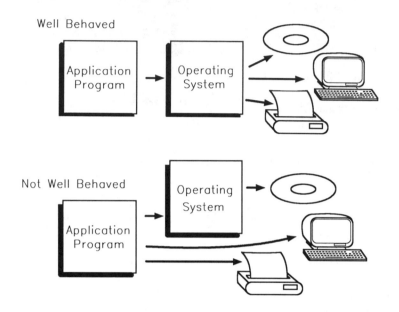

Well Behaved

Application Program → Operating System

Not Well Behaved

Operating System

Application Program

what if? The fundamental concept behind the use of a spreadsheet as a planning tool. When new data is entered into the spreadsheet, results are calculated based upon the formulas in the spreadsheet. Assumptions can be plugged in that ripple through to the bottom line. For example, "what if the hourly labor rate is increased by $2, how much does it affect this product's profit?"

Whetstones A benchmark program that tests floating point operations. The results of the program are expressed in Whetstones per second. Whetstone I tests 32-bit, and Whetstone II tests 64-bit floating point operations. Contrast with *Dhrystones*, which tests a general mix of instructions.

WHIRLWIND The first digital computer with realtime capability and the first to use core memory. Developed at MIT throughout the 1940s, it became operational in the early 1950s. The machine was continually enhanced, eventually using over 12,000 vacuum tubes and 20,000 diodes and occupying two floors. It wound up with 2K of 16-bit core memory and used a magnetic drum and magnetic tape for storage.

WHIRLWIND made many contributions towards future computers, including circuit design, the use of CRTs and realtime communications. Project members later worked on IBM's 700 series, and one in particular named Kenneth Olson, founded Digital.

WHIRLWIND I
(Courtesy The MIT Museum)

white noise Same as *Gaussian noise*.

wide area network In communications, a network that interconnects geographical boundaries such as cities and states.

widow & orphan A *widow* is the last line of a paragraph that appears alone at the top of the next page, and an *orphan* is the first line of a paragraph that appears alone at the bottom of a page. Widow and orphan settings in word processing and desktop publishing programs are usually set for a minimum of two lines, but can be changed by the user.

wild cards Symbols used to represent any value when naming files. For example, in DOS and OS/2, the * stands for any name of up to eight characters, and the ? stands for any single character. The description *.WK1 references all files with a WK1 extension. The description CR*.* references all files that start with CR no matter what their extension.

wimp interface (Windows, Icons, Menus and a Pointing device) Same as *GUI*.

Winchester disk A sealed disk technology that was developed by IBM, which incorporates the access arm, read/write heads and disk platters into a sealed unit. By aligning the read/write heads to their own set of disks, greater capacities and speeds are obtainable than with removable disk cartridges.

The Winchester was originally designed as a dual 30MB configuration, and its 30-30 specification, the same as a Winchester rifle, gave rise to its name. Although originally a self-contained, removable module, the term is used today to refer to any fixed hard disk.

window

(1) A separate viewing area on a
display screen as provided by the
software. Operating systems
can provide multiple windows
on screen, allowing the user to
keep several application
programs active and visible
at the same time.

WINDOWS

Individual application
programs can provide
multiple windows as well,
providing a viewing capability
into more than one document,
spreadsheet or data file.

(2) A reserved area of main memory.

(3) A period of time in which an event can or must occur.

windowing software Same as *windows program*.

Windows A graphics-based operating environment from Microsoft that
runs under DOS. With Windows, two or more applications can be open at the
same time and users can switch back and forth between them.

Windows provides a desktop environment that is similar to the Macintosh.
Different applications, or multiple copies of the same application, are kept active
in windows that can be resized and relocated on screen. The windows can be
converted into icons and placed on the desktop when not required. Windows
provides a point and shoot method for working with DOS directories, however, it
does not simulate file folders like the Mac.

Standard DOS applications can run under Windows in full-screen mode as they
normally do, but under Windows/386 or Windows 3.0 in 386 Enhanced Mode,
standard DOS applications can be run in a window and data can be exchanged
between them.

WINDOWS/286

As of version 2.1, Windows was renamed Windows/286, and although it still runs
on 8086/88 machines, it requires a 286 for tolerable performance. It uses
expanded memory as well as the 64K block of extended memory located from
1024K to 1086K (HMA). Windows/286 multitasks Windows applications, but
not standard DOS applications.

WINDOWS/386

Windows/386 runs on 386 and higher CPUs and multitasks Windows and
standard DOS applications in the 386's virtual mode. It comes with its own EMS
4.0 expanded memory manager and will not run with any other memory
manager. Windows/386 is the foundation for Windows 3.0's 386 mode.

WINDOWS 3.0

A major upgrade that provides its own DOS extender, thus allowing Windows 3.0 applications to run in up to 16MB of memory. Its user interface is significantly improved and looks more like OS/2's Presentation Manager. Windows 3.0 operates in the following modes:

Real Mode - For computers with less than 1MB of memory. Provides most compatibility with previous versions of Windows applications and uses EMS (expanded) memory if available. This mode does not use extended memory.

Standard Mode - Normal operating mode. Provides access to extended memory and allows users to switch between standard DOS applications, which appear in full-screen mode as they normally do. Uses EMS (expanded) memory if available.

386 Enhanced Mode - Allows multitasking of standard DOS applications. Most standard DOS applications can run in a window (character-based programs are actually converted to bit-mapped graphics), and data can be exchanged between them. EMS memory is activated with the use of the EMM386.SYS memory manager that comes with Windows 3.0.

windows environment

Any operating system, operating system extension or application program that provides multiple windows on screen. DESQview, Microsoft Windows, Presentation Manager, Finder, MultiFinder and X Window are examples.

Windows Metafile

A text and graphics file format for Microsoft Windows. It allows parts of the screen to be highlighted, saved and transferred to other Windows applications, for example.

windows program

(1) Software that adds a windows capability to an existing operating system.

(2) An application program that is written to run under Microsoft Windows.

WINGZ

A presentation-oriented spreadsheet for the Macintosh from Informix Software. Text, graphs and charts, scanned images, freehand illustration and worksheet data can be displayed and printed in any combination on any page. If spreadsheet data is updated, related graphics and numerical references within the text will be changed.

wire wrap

A technique for making wired connections between electronic devices. A special tool strips the end of the wire and coils it. The coil is then pressed onto a metal prong (pin). It used to be a common form of connection between computer components.

wireframe modeling

In CAD, a technique for representing 3-D objects, in which all surfaces are visibly outlined in lines, including the opposite sides and all internal components that are normally hidden from view. Compared to surface and solid modeling, wireframe modeling is the least complex method for representing 3-D images.

WIREFRAME
(Courtesy CADKEY, INC.)

wireless

Same as *radio*.

wiring closet

A central distribution or servicing point for cables in a network.

wizzy wig

See *WYSIWYG*.

WK1 file

A worksheet file created in Lotus 1-2-3, version 2.0.

WKS file

A worksheet file created in Lotus 1-2-3, version 1A.

word

(1) The computer's internal storage unit and refers to the amount of data it can hold in its registers and process at one time. For example, a 16-bit computer processes two bytes in the same time it takes an 8-bit computer to process one byte, providing the timing clocks are of equal speed.

(2) The primary text element, which is identified by a word separator (blank space, comma...) before and after a group of contiguous characters.

(3) See *Microsoft Word*.

word addressable

A computer that can address memory only on word boundaries. Contrast with *byte addressable*.

word processing

The creation and management of text documents, which replaces operations associated with a typewriter. The word processing advantage is that documents are permanently stored in the computer and can be called back for editing and reprinting at any time.

Electronic documents can be searched faster than paper documents, and, the ability to easily rearrange words on screen, has helped writers immensely.

After a document is created, it can be printed with an infinite variety of type fonts if the program supports a laser printer or ink jet printer. Advanced word processors function as elementary desktop publishing systems.

Word processing machines are computers that are specialized for word processing only. However, full-featured word processing can be performed on any general purpose computer, from micro to mainframe.

Word processing is often the first step towards office automation; however, it has not obsoleted the typewriter for occasional labels and envelopes or for straight typing from dictation.

Functions of a
Full-featured Word Processor

WORD WRAP AND CENTERING
Words that extend beyond the right margin are wrapped around to the next line. Text can be centered between left and right margins.

TEXT EDITING
Text can be changed by deleting it, typing over it or by inserting additional text within it.

SEARCH & REPLACE, MOVE & COPY
Any occurrence of text can be replaced with another block of text. You can mark a block of text and move it elsewhere in the document or copy it throughout the document.

LAYOUT SETTINGS
Margins, tabs, line spacing, indents, font changes, underlining, boldface and italics can be set and reset anywhere within the document.

HEADERS, FOOTERS AND PAGE NUMBERING
Headers and footers are common text that is printed on the top and bottom of every page. Headers, footers and page numbering can be set and reset anywhere within the doucment. Page numbering in optional Roman numerals or alphabetic letters is very common.

STYLE SHEETS
After designing a document, its format can be used again. Layout codes, such as margins, tabs, fonts, headers and footers, are selected and stored in a separate file known as a style sheet. An overall format is assigned to a new document by choosing one of the previously-defined style sheets.

MAIL MERGE
Mail merge creates customized letters from a form letter and a list of names and addresses. The list can be created as a document or can be imported from popular database formats.

MATH AND SORTING
Math capability adds columns of numbers and computes arithmetic expressions within the document. Sorting reorders lines of text in the document into ascending (a to z) or descending (z to a) sequence.

PREVIEW, PRINT AND GROUP PRINT
A document can be previewed before it is printed to show any layout change that is not normally shown on screen, such as page breaks, headers, footers and footnotes. Documents can be printed individually or as groups of documents with page numbers consecutively numbered from the first to the last document.

FOOTNOTES
Footnote entries can be made at any place in the document, and the footnotes printed at the end of a page or document.

SPELLING CHECKER AND THESAURUS
Spelling for an individual word, marked block of text or an entire document can be checked. When words are in doubt, possible corrections are suggested. Advanced systems can correct the misspellings automatically the next time. A thesaurus displays synonyms for the word at the current cursor location.

FILE MANAGEMENT
Documents can be copied, renamed and deleted, and directories, or folders, can be created and deleted from within the program. Advanced systems set up a purge list of names or glimpses of document contents in order to allow a user to easily rid the disk of unwanted files.

Advanced Functions

WINDOWS
Windows allows two or more documents to be worked on at the same time. Text can be moved or copied from one document to the other.

COLUMNS
Columns can be created in all word processors by tabbing to a tab stop. However, true columns wrap the words within each column. Although often considered an advanced feature, columns are required for common documents, such as writing a resume with employer information on the left and work history on the right. Script writing also requires column capability.

Magazine-style columns are another variety of columns that wrap words from the bottom of one column to the top of the next column.

TABLES OF CONTENTS AND INDEXES
Tables of contents and indexes can be generated from entries typed throughout the document.

DESKTOP PUBLISHING
Graphics can be merged into the text and either displayed on screen with the text or in a preview mode before printing. A graphic object can be resized (scaled),

rotated and anchored so that it remains with a particular segment of text. Rules and borders can also be created within the text.

Graphics Based versus Text Based

Graphics-based word processing programs, such as Microsoft Word on PCs or all the Macintosh word processing programs, show you a reasonable facsimile on screen of the typeface that will be printed. Text-based programs always show the same type size on screen.

Graphics-based systems are far superior for preparing newsletters and brochures that contain a variety of font sizes. Text-based screens are fine for office typing or for documents that require only a few fonts. Text-based systems are very responsive and very good for creative writing.

Format Standards

Almost every word processing program generates its own proprietary codes for layout settings. For example, in WordStar, ^PB turns on and off boldface. In Version 5.0 of WordPerfect, [BOLD] turns boldface on, and [bold] turns it off.

Conversion programs are used to translate documents from one format to another. If a conversion program doesn't exist for the two formats in question, multiple search & replace commands can be performed on the original document. However, if the same code turns a mode on as well as off, as in the WordStar example above, then each search & replace has to be verified manually to ensure that the correct code is being changed.

The User Interface

The design of a word processing program runs from the ridiculous to the sublime. Some of the most awkward programs have sold well due to clever marketing. As a novice, it's difficult to tell a good user interface from a bad one. It takes time to explore all the nuances. In addition, what's acceptable for the occasional user might be horrendous for the experienced touch typist.

Functions that are done repetitively, such as centering, changing display attributes (boldface, italics, etc.) should be accomplished with a couple of keystrokes at most. Changing margins, tabs, indents and fonts should also be easy.

The two most important components in a word processing system are its keyboard and display screen. The feel of a keyboard is personal, but proper key placement is critical. Display screens should have the highest resolution possible, and color screens are better than monochrome as long as the program allows the user to change colors. Color preference is personal, too.

word processing machine A computer that is specialized for only word processing functions.

word processor
(1) Software that provides word processing functions on a computer.

(2) A computer that has been specialized for word processing functions. Until the late 1970s, word processors were always dedicated machines. Today, personal computers are rapidly replacing the dedicated word processor.

word publishing Word processing programs that provide a certain number of desktop publishing features such as merging, displaying and printing graphics with text.

word separator Any character that separates a word, such as a blank space, comma, period, dash, question mark and explanation point.

word wrap A feature of all word processing and other text handling systems that aligns text automatically within the preset margins. Unlike a typewriter which requires the carriage return key to be pressed in order to move to the beginning of the next line, word wrap keeps track of the characters being typed and performs the operation automatically. In some word processing programs, word wrap is a feature that can be switched off for writing programming source code.

WordPerfect A word processing program from WordPerfect Corporation, introduced in 1980. It runs on IBM, Apple II, Macintosh, Amiga and Atari personal computers. It is a full-featured program that is extremely popular.

Version 5.0, introduced in 1988, is a significantly improved program that includes many desktop publishing features and enhancements for using a laser printer. Graphics can be merged into the document and then resized and rotated, and a WYSIWIG preview mode allows users to see the finished document before printing.

WordStar A word processing program for PCs from WordStar International. Introduced in 1978 for CP/M machines, it was the first full-featured word processing program for microcomputers. Although often criticized for its elaborate and arcane keyboard commands, it gave sophisticated word processing capabilities to personal computer users at significantly less cost than the dedicated word processing machines of the time. Ironically, many users still prefer the instant-action key commands over the variety of menus that have been added on later versions.

The program was formally renamed WordStar Professional to distinguish it from WordStar 2000, a more elaborate version introduced in 1984. WordStar Professional has also been enhanced many times and both versions are still offered.

WordStar commands have become an industry standard and are used in many text editors and notepads that are integrated into larger systems.

work group Two or more individuals who share files and databases. Local area networks are designed around work groups to provide for the electronic sharing of the required data.

worksheet Same as *spreadsheet*.

worksheet compiler Same as *spreadsheet compiler*.

workstation

(1) A high-performance, single user micro or minicomputer that has been specialized for graphics, computer-aided design, computer-aided engineering or scientific applications.

(2) In a local area network, a personal computer that serves a single user in contrast with a file server that serves all the users in the network.

(3) Any terminal or personal computer.

worm

(1) A destructive program that replicates itself throughout disk and memory, using up the computers resources and eventually putting the system down. See *virus* and *logic bomb*.

(2) A program that moves throughout a network and deposits information at each node for diagnostic purposes, or causes idle computers to share some of the processing workload.

(3) WORM (Write Once Read Many) A storage device that uses an optical medium that can be recorded only once. Updating requires destroying the existing data (all 0s made 1s), and writing the revised data to an unused part of the disk.

WP See *word processing*.

write To record data into or onto a memory or storage device, such as disk, tape, memory and firmware. Read and write is analogous to play and record on an audio tape recorder.

computers write funny!

write error The inability to record data into or onto a memory or storage device. Dust, dirt, or damaged portions of the magnetic recording surface on disk or tape, or malfunctioning electronic components in memory devices will cause the storage locations to be unusable. The operating system may be able to flag the damaged portions of the storage device and keep processing.

write only code Jokingly refers to programming code that is extremely difficult to read.

write protect Prohibits the erasing or changing of a disk file. See *file protection*.

write protect notch A small, square cutout on the side of a floppy disk that is used to prevent it from being written over and erased. On 5.25" floppy disks, the notch must be covered for protection. On older 8" floppies, the notch must be left uncovered for protection.

WXmodem (Window Xmodem) A faster version of the Xmodem communications protocol that allows the sending system to transmit data without waiting for the receiving system to acknowledge the transfer.

WYSIWYG (What You See Is What You Get) Pronounced "wizzy-wig." Refers to displaying text and graphics on screen the same way it will be printed. Although a 24-point font will show up on screen in a proper ratio to a 10-point font, if the screen and printer fonts are not matched, there will be either slight or obvious differences between the screen characters and the printed characters. In addition, a desktop laser printer, at 300 dots per inch, has a much higher resolution than almost any display screen; therefore, the screen and printout cannot be 100% identical.

WYSIWYG

WYSIWYG-MOL (What You See Is What You Get-More Or Less) Quite often what you get, when what you want is WYSIWYG!

x-axis See *x-y matrix*.

XCMD (eXternal CoMmanD) A a user-developed HyperCard command that is written in C, Pascal or other language. See *XFNC*.

xcopy A utility program that accompanies DOS and OS/2. It allows all subdirectories within a directory to be copied at one time. The following example copies all files and subdirectories in the current directory to the XYZ directory. New subdirectories will be created in the XYZ directory if they do not already exist. The /S copies subdirectories, and the /E copies them even if they're empty.

```
xcopy *.* \xyz /s /e
```

XDOS A program from Hunter Systems, Inc., that takes executable code for Intel-based processors and converts it into executable Motorola 68020 code ready to run under UNIX. A PC program can be translated into a running program on a UNIX-based 68020 computer.

XENIX See *SCO XENIX*.

XFCN (eXternal FunCtioN) A user-developed HyperCard function that is written in C, Pascal or other language. XFCNs usually return a value. See *XCMD*.

X/GEM A multitasking, protected mode version of the GEM graphical user interface from Digital Research Inc., that is designed to run under its FlexOS operating system.

x-height In typography, the height of the letter x in lower case. Point size includes the x-height, the height of the ascender and the height of the descender. See *typeface* for an illustration.

XLISP A microcomputer version of the LISP programming language that has been in the public domain for a number of years.

XMI A high-speed bus from Digital Equipment Corporation used in high-end models of its VAX series.

Xmodem A simple asynchronous communications protocol for personal computers that can detect most transmission errors, but not all. Xmodem was originally developed by Ward Christensen to transfer data between first-generation personal computers using CP/M.

Xmodem-CRC An advanced Xmodem protocol that uses a cyclic redundancy check (CRC) to detect all transmission errors.

XMS (eXtended Memory Specification) An interface that allows DOS programs to use extended memory in 286 and higher machines. In July 1988, Lotus, Intel, AST and Microsoft finalized XMS Version 2.0, which provides a set of functions for reserving, releasing and transferring data to and from extended memory.

DOS programs that are XMS aware can allocate extended memory without conflict. Contrast with *DOS extender*, which actually runs programs in extended memory.

XMT In communications, an abbreviation for transmit.

XNS/ITP (Xerox Network Systems/Internet TransPort) The main protocol used in early Ethernet networks. Although widely used, it is often replaced with TCP/IP.

xon-xoff In communications, a simple asynchronous protocol that keeps the receiving device in synchronization with the sending device. When the buffer in the receiving device is full, it sends an *x-off* signal (transmit off) to the sending device, telling it to stop transmitting. When the receiving device is ready to accept more, it sends the sending device an *x-on* signal (transmit on) to start again.

X/Open A consortium of international computer vendors, founded in 1984, to resolve standards issues. Incorporated in 1987 and headquartered in London, current members include AT&T, Bull, DEC, Ericsson, HP, International Computers, Nixdorf, Olivetti, Philips, Siemens and Unisys. X/Open's North American offices are in San Francisco.

X/Open's purpose is to integrate evolving de facto and international standards in order to achieve a user-driven and open environment, or Common Application Environment. X/Open's XPG defines the specification, and VSX defines the testing and verification procedure.

X.PC A communications protocol developed by McDonnell Douglas for connecting a PC to its Tymnet packet-switched public data network.

XPG (X/Open Portability Guide) Standards that specify compliance with X/Open's Common Application Environment (CAE). XPG3 (Release 3), introduced in early 1989, specifies standards for UNIX System V Release 4.0.

XT (EXtended Technology) The first IBM PC with a hard disk, introduced in 1983. See PC.

XTRA PC A host to PC data transfer program from Cone Software that works without additional mainframe software. It requires a terminal emulation board, such as an IRMAboard, and transfers the data from the PC screens to a format usable in spreadsheets, databases and graphics applications.

XTree A disk management program and DOS shell for PCs from the XTree division of Executive Systems, Inc. Introduced in 1985, it was the first program to help users manage hard disks by providing a hierarchical display of directories.

In 1987, XTreePro added such features as a built-in text editor and the ability to manage multiple drives concurrently.

In 1989, XTreeMac was introduced for the Macintosh and XTreePro Gold added features to the PC line, such as an application menu for single-key launching of applications, split windows and file viewers for popular formats.

XVT (EXtensible Virtual Toolkit) A set of C routines from Graphic Software Systems that allows programs to be built with a GUI interface that can be ported to Windows, OS/2 Presentation Manager, the Macintosh and OSF/Motif environments.

X Window A windowing environment for graphics workstations that was developed at MIT with participation from Digital and IBM. It is designed to allow graphics generated in one computer system to be displayed on another workstation in the network. X Window is designed to run under any operating system and is supported by all major workstation vendors.

x-y matrix A group of rows and columns. The x-axis is the horizontal row, and the y-axis is the vertical column. An x-y matrix is the reference framework for two-dimensional structures, such as mathematical tables, display screens, digitizer tablets, dot matrix printers and 2-D graphics images.

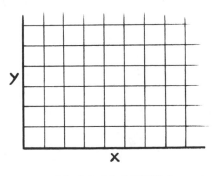

X-Y MATRIX

x-y monitor In graphics, the display screen of a vector display terminal. The entire vector display comprises the monitor and vector graphics controller.

x-y plotter Same as *plotter*.

x-y-z matrix A three-dimensional structure. The x and y axes represent the first two dimensions; the z axis, the third dimension. In a graphic image, the x and y denote width and height; the z denotes depth.

XyWrite III Plus Pronounced "zy-write." A word processing program for PCs from XyQuest, Inc., that is used extensively in the editing rooms of major newspapers and magazines. It is noted for its flexibility and typesetting orientation, as well as its speedy performance on slow computers. It is a command-driven program, but its user interface can be completely customized by the user. It provides up to nine windows for documents and includes a programming language for programmer-oriented users. In 1988, menus were added to assist first-time users.

X.3 CCITT standard (1977) for a PAD (packet assembler/disassembler), which divides a data message into packets for transmission over a packet-switched network and reassembles them at the receiving side.

X.12 An ANSI standard protocol for electronic data interchange (EDI). See *Tradacoms* and *EDIFACT*.

X.21 CCITT standard protocol for a circuit switching network.

X.25 CCITT standard (1976) for the protocols and message formats that define the interface between a terminal and a packet switching network.

X.28 CCITT standard (1977) for exchange of information between a DTE and a PAD; commonly known as PAD commands.

X.29 CCITT standard (1977) for exchange of information between a local PAD and a remote PAD; procedures for interworking between PADs.

X.32 CCITT standard (1984) for connecting to an X.25 network by dial up. It defines how the network identifies the terminal for billing and security purposes and how default parameters are negotiated for the connection.

X.75 CCITT standard for connecting X.25 networks.

X.400 CCITT standard mail and messaging protocol that is OSI compliant.

X.500 CCITT standard mail and messaging protocol that includes the capability of maintaining directories of users. X.500 is OSI compliant.

y-axis See *x-y matrix*.

Ymodem An asynchronous communications protocol for personal computers that is identical to the Xmodem-CRC protocol, with the addition of batch file transfer.

z-axis The third dimension in a graphics image. The width is the x-axis and the height is the y-axis.

zap A command that typically deletes the data within a file but leaves the file structure intact so that new data can be entered.

ZBR (Zone Bit Recording) A technique that records more bits on a disk. The tracks on a disk become longer the farther they are from the center. However, on regular disks, the clock rate that records the bits doesn't change, which results in the outer tracks being less densely packed than the inner tracks. With ZBR, the clock rate is changed based on which track is being written, and each track is filled to capacity.

zenix See *SCO XENIX*.

zero wait state Refers to a high-speed memory that transfers its data immediately upon being accessed without waiting one or more machine cycles to respond.

Zmodem An asynchronous communications protocol for personal computers that can handle larger transfers of data without error than its Xmodem-CRC predecessor. Zmodem is especially effective in satellite transmission, where end-to-end delays can be several seconds long.

Z80 An 8-bit microprocessor from Zilog Corporation that was the successor to the Intel 8080. The Z80 was widely used in first-generation personal computers that used the CP/M operating system.

Z8000 A 16-bit microprocessor from Zilog Corporation that is the successor to the Z80.

1.2M May refer to the 1.2M high-density 5.25" floppy disk used on IBM AT and compatible machines.

1-2-3 See *Lotus 1-2-3*.

1.4M May refer to the 1.4M high-density 3.5" disk used on PCs and Macintoshes.

10BaseT IEEE standard for 10 Mbps 802.3 (Ethernet) local area networks running over unshielded twisted pair rather than coaxial cable.

16-bit See *bit specifications*.

1401 A second-generation IBM computer system that was introduced in 1959 and used until the late 1960s. It provided a maximum of 16K of core memory, six tape drives and used punched cards for input. The 1401 was an outstanding success due to its reliability and compactness. An estimated 18,000 units were installed. To ease migration, 1401 emulators were built into IBM's 360 series.

IBM 1401
(Courtesy IBM)

286 See 80286.

2780, 3780 Standard communications protocols for transmitting batch data. The numbers originated with early IBM remote job entry (RJE) terminals that included a card reader and a printer.

3Com 3+ A network operating system from 3Com Corporation that is based on MS-Net and supports PC and Macintosh workstations.

3Com 3+ Open LAN Manager is a network operating system that runs on an OS/2 file server and supports DOS, OS/2 and Mac workstations.

3Com Corporation provides a wide variety of hardware and software for local area networks.

32-bit See *bit specifications*.

360, 370 series The System/360 series, announced by IBM in 1964, was the first family of compatible computer systems ever introduced. The fundamental architecture of the 360s has been carried into all the models that followed it; however, there have been considerable enhancements over the years.

In 1970, IBM upgraded to the System/370. Later series in order of introduction include the 303x, 43xx, 308x and 309x. In 1983, IBM introduced the PC XT/370, a personal computer that runs 370 programs. In 1987, the 9370 was introduced, the first small-scale computer with 370 architecture. In 1989, 370 processing was again brought down to the PC level with the VM/SP Technical Workstation.

IBM 360 "SOLID LOGIC"
(Courtesy IBM)

The three transistors on this module used in the 360 series were a sign of advanced technology of the day.

360K May refer to the 360K 5.25" minifloppy disk used with PCs.

370 architecture Refers to a computer that will run programs written for the IBM System/370 mainframe series. See *360, 370 series*.

370 Workstation See *VM/SP Technical Workstation*.

386^{Max} A memory management program for 386-based PCs from Qualitas. It activates EMS memory and moves memory-resident (TSR) programs into unused portions of memory above 640K.

386SX See *80386SX*.

303x A series of medium to large-scale IBM mainframes introduced in 1977, which includes the 3031, 3032 and 3033. See *360, 370 series*.

308x A series of large-scale IBM mainframes introduced in 1980, which includes the 3081, 3081 Model Group K and 3084. See *360, 370 series*.

309x A series of large-scale IBM mainframes introduced in 1986. This is IBM's largest mainframe series in use today. See *360, 370 series*.

3270 The communications protocol for interactive terminals connected to IBM mainframes, which includes the 3278 monochrome and 3279 color terminals. In order to communicate with IBM mainframes, 3270 emulators are plugged into micro and minicomputers. The mainframe thinks it's interacting with a regular user terminal, but it could be communicating with a VAX or a Macintosh.

37xx Refers to communications controllers from IBM that includes the 3704, 3705, 3720, 3725 and 3745 models. The 3704 and 3705 are early units, and the 3745 models are newer and more versatile. The 3745 includes a cluster controller that can connect up to 512 terminals and printers, eight token ring networks and 16 T1 communications lines.

3770 A standard communications protocol for batch transmission in an IBM SNA environment.

3780 See *2780, 3780*.

386 See *80386*.

4GL See *fourth-generation language*.

486 See *80486*.

4004 The first microprocessor. Designed by Marcian E. "Ted" Hoff at Intel, it was a 4-bit, general-purpose CPU that was initially developed for the Japanese Busicom calculator.

43xx A series of medium-scale IBM mainframes initially introduced in 1979, which include the 4300, 4321, 4331, 4341, 4361 and 4381. See 360, *370 series*.

5100 The first desktop computer from IBM. Introduced in 1974, it came with up to 64K of RAM, a built-in tape drive and either APL or BASIC. Eight inch floppy disks became available in 1976.

64-bit See *bit specifications*.

650 IBM's first major computer success. Introduced in 1954, it used a magnetic drum for memory, magnetic tape for storage and punched cards for input. By the end of the 1950s, there were an estimated 1,800 units installed, making it the most widely used computer in the world.

IBM 650
(Courtesy IBM)

6502 An 8-bit microprocessor from Rockwell International Corporation that is used in the Apple II series and earlier models of Atari and Commodore computers.

6800 An 8-bit microprocessor from Motorola, Inc. The 6801 is a computer-on-a-chip version of the Motorola 6800.

68000 A line of 32-bit microprocessors from Motorola, Inc., that are the CPUs in Macintoshes and a wide variety of workstations.

68000	Addresses up to 16MB of memory and uses a 16-bit data bus.
68020	Addresses up to 4GB of memory and uses a 32-bit data bus.
68030	Addresses up to 4GB of memory and uses a 32-bit data bus. It runs at higher clock speeds than the 68020 and has built-in cache memory.
68040	Redesigned version of the 68030 that can run up to three times as fast.

7-track Refers to older magnetic tape formats that record 6-bit characters plus parity, or seven tracks.

720K May refer to the 720K microfloppy disk used in PCs.

7437 See *VM/SP Technical Workstation*.

8-bit See *bit specifications*.

802.1, 802.2, etc. See *IEEE 802.1*.

8080 An 8-bit microprocessor from Intel Corporation that was introduced in 1974. It was the successor to the 8008, the first commercial 8-bit microprocessor and the precursor to the 8086 family.

8086 A 16-bit microprocessor from Intel Corporation that can address 1MB of memory and uses a 16-bit data bus. Introduced in 1978, the 8086 defines the architecture of the 8086 family, which includes the 8088, 80286, 80386 and 80486. DOS applications can run in all models of the 8086 family, but software written specifically for the 80286 or 80386/80486 can only run in the required machines. OS/2 applications run in 80286 and higher CPUs. The math coprocessor for the 8086 is the 8087.

8088 A 16-bit microprocessor from Intel Corporation that can address 1MB of memory and uses an 8-bit data bus. This slower speed version of the 8086 was chosen for the original IBM PC in order to ease software migration from existing Z80-based CP/M applications. The math coprocessor for the 8088 is the 8087.

8100 A minicomputer from IBM that was introduced in 1978. It was designed for departmental computing and uses the DPPX/SP operating system.

8514 A monitor from IBM that is used with its 8514/A display adapter.

8514/A A high-resolution display adapter from IBM that provides an interlaced display of 1024x768 pixels with up to 256 colors or 64 shades of gray. The 8514/A can coexist with VGA for dual monitor capability.

The 8514/A includes a video coprocessor that performs 2-D graphics functions, thus relieving the CPU of graphics tasks and improving performance. The 8514/A is faster than VGA and requires about a tenth of the CPU's time for graphics functions.

The 8514/A was introduced for the Micro Channel, but 8514/A boards for the AT bus are available from third-party vendors. Also available are non-interlaced versions of the 8514/A, which reduce flicker.

80286 Commonly known as the 286, a 16-bit multitasking microprocessor from Intel Corporation that can address 16MB of memory and uses a 16-bit data bus. Its operation modes are Real mode, which performs as an 8086 CPU (limited to 1MB memory), and Protected mode, which addresses all memory. The math coprocessor for the 80286 is the 80287.

80386 Commonly known as the 386 (or 386DX), a 32-bit multitasking microprocessor from Intel Corporation that can address 4GB of physical memory, 64TB of virtual memory and uses a 32-bit data bus. It has four operation modes:
  (1) Real mode - performs as an 8086 CPU.
  (2) 16-bit Protected mode - can address all of memory, but uses 16-bit registers.
  (3) 32-bit Protected mode - can address all of memory and uses 32 bit registers.
  (4) Virtual 86 mode - runs 8086 applications as virtual machines.

The 80386 is far more flexible than the 80286, and its advanced modes are only starting to be utilized as we enter the 1990s. The math coprocessor for the 80386 is the 80387.

80386SX Commonly known as the 386SX, a version of the 80386 that is somewhat slower, uses less power and dissipates less heat. It uses a 16-bit bus instead of 32 bits and is suitable for ultra light laptops. The math coprocessor for the 80386SX is the 80387SX.

80486 Commonly known as the i486 or 486, a 32-bit multitasking microprocessor from Intel Corporation that contains a built-in math coprocessor. It contains 1.2 million transistors and runs at higher speeds than the 80386.

80860 Commonly known as the i860 or 860, a 64-bit RISC-based microprocessor from Intel Corporation that uses a 64-bit data bus, has built-in floating point and 3-D graphics capability and contains over one million transistors. It can be used as a standalone CPU or to accelerate performance in existing systems.

88000 A family of 32-bit RISC microprocessors from Motorola, Inc. The 88100 is the first processor in the 88000 family. Introduced in 1988, it incorporates four built-in execution units that allow up to five operations to be performed in parallel.

9-track Refers to magnetic tape that records 8-bit bytes plus parity, or nine parallel tracks. This is the common format for 1/2" tape reels.

9370 A series of entry-level mainframes from IBM, introduced in 1986, that uses the 370 architecture. In 1990, the Enterprise System models (ES/9370) were introduced, which use the Micro Channel bus and a 386 for I/O processing. The ES/9370 Model 14 biprocessor system adds a second 386 that can run DOS and OS/2 applications. An optional Data Exchange Adapter provides a high-speed link between the 386 and 370 processors.

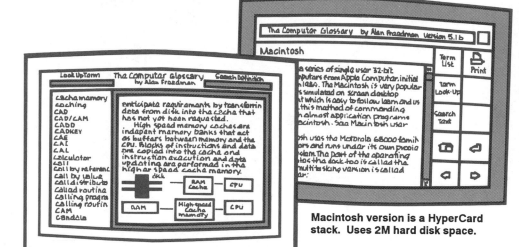